# THE STORY OF POTTERY IN CANAAN-ISRAEL-PALESTINE

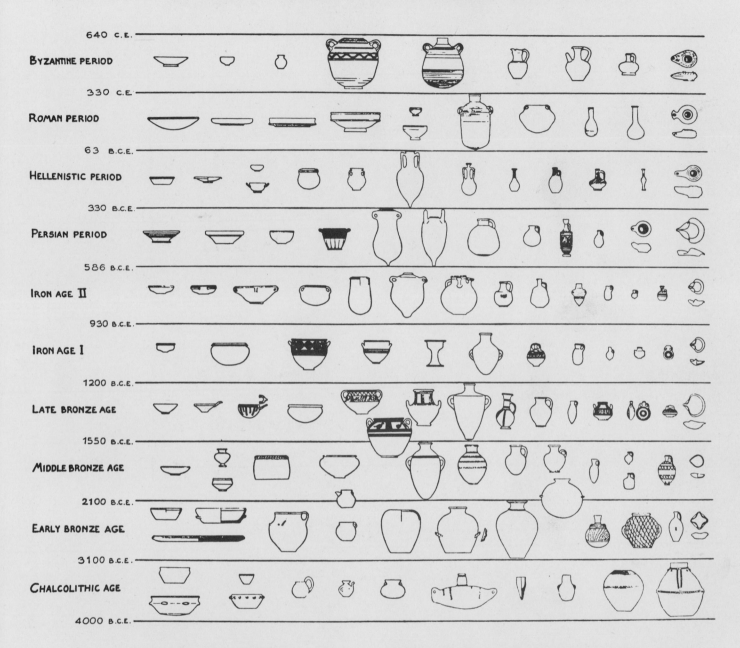

| Period | (date range) |
|---|---|
| **BYZANTINE PERIOD** | 640 C.E. – 330 C.E. |
| **ROMAN PERIOD** | 330 C.E. – 63 B.C.E. |
| **HELLENISTIC PERIOD** | 63 B.C.E. – 330 B.C.E. |
| **PERSIAN PERIOD** | 330 B.C.E. – 586 B.C.E. |
| **IRON AGE II** | 586 B.C.E. – 930 B.C.E. |
| **IRON AGE I** | 930 B.C.E. – 1200 B.C.E. |
| **LATE BRONZE AGE** | 1200 B.C.E. – 1550 B.C.E. |
| **MIDDLE BRONZE AGE** | 1550 B.C.E. – 2100 B.C.E. |
| **EARLY BRONZE AGE** | 2100 B.C.E. – 3100 B.C.E. |
| **CHALCOLITHIC AGE** | 3100 B.C.E. – 4000 B.C.E. |

## CHART OF POTTERY

From a wall-chart prepared by the Israel Department of Antiquities in 1949, chiefly under the supervision of Dr. Immanuel Ben-Dor. The chart was reproduced on p. 188 of Ruth Amiran's article, "The Story of Pottery in Palestine" (in *The Holy Land: Antiquity and Survival* [The Hague and Jerusalem], II, 2-3 [1957]). As noted in the article (p. 187), "Far from pretending to be a complete Corpus of Palestinian Pottery, this wall-chart is intended to serve only as an elementary introduction to the study of that pottery, and therefore many types and a great many variants will naturally be found lacking in every period. No scale is given, and only approximate proportions between the various vessels have been taken into account." The standard work on the subject is now Ruth Amiran, *Ancient Pottery of the Holy Land*

(Rutgers, 1970), where complete, accurate, and up-to-date data—including the chronological—are systematically and attractively presented.

The importance of pottery in archaeological investigation derives from the fact that pottery exhibits as no other material or object (except an intelligible text that can be dated) the changes and influences in the material, historical, political, economic, and artistic character of the society of ancient Canaan-Israel-Palestine. Pottery has those important qualities precisely because it is very plentiful all over the country wherever and whenever it was occupied, is imperishable, is worthless economically—who would bother (except the modern archaeologist and museum) to put together pieces of broken pottery and who would engage in buying or selling potsherds?—and reflects immediately the everyday needs of the population.

# UNDERSTANDING THE
# BIBLE
## THROUGH HISTORY
## AND ARCHAEOLOGY

HARRY M. ORLINSKY

*Hebrew Union College—Jewish Institute of Religion*
*New York City*

KTAV PUBLISHING HOUSE, INC.
New York

SBN87068-096-X

MANUFACTURED IN THE UNITED STATES OF AMERICA
LIBRARY OF CONGRESS CATALOG CARD NUMBER: 78-75014

TO MY WIFE
and
OUR CHILDREN and GRANDCHILDREN

# TABLE OF CONTENTS

# LIST OF MAPS

## Acknowledgments for Maps

Maps on pp. 28, 50, 58, 78, 90, 102, 108, 156, 170, and 224 adapted with permission of The Macmillan Company from *The Macmillan Bible Atlas* by Yohanan Aharoni and Michael Avi-Yonah. Copyright © 1968 by Carta, Jerusalem. □ Map on p. 138 adapted from *The Rise and Fall of Arabia Felix* by Gus W. van Beek. Copyright © 1969, Scientific American Inc. All Rights Reserved. □ Map on p. 70 adapted from a United Nations map. □ Map on p. 74 from THE LAND OF THE BIBLE, by Yohanan Aharoni, translated by A. F. Rainey. © Yohanan Aharoni, 1962, 1967. Published in the United States by The Westminster Press, 1967. Used by permission.

# FOREWORD

THIS essay, *Ancient Israel,* by Mr. Harry M. Orlinsky, was originally written as one of a series in "The Development of Western Civilization," published by Cornell University Press for use in college survey courses. However, this particular essay, organizing for the first time in terms accessible to the general reader the results of the recent spectacular archaeological discoveries in Israel and the Near East, promised to arouse interest outside the college library. It was decided, therefore, to issue it simultaneously within the series and in this independent edition.

It was the purpose of the author to provide a brief narrative account of the history of the people who created the Hebrew Bible and, at the same time, to outline the integral relationship between the development of their society and the growth of the Biblical tradition. The importance of this subject can hardly be overstated. Not only do we draw our earliest and deepest social and moral—not to mention religious — concepts from the experiences of ancient Israel, but throughout its entire history western European civilization has maintained the Bible as the central document of its cultural inheritance. Therefore, any heir of the western European tradition who would understand the development of his society must at once look for its earliest roots in Biblical society and study not only the content, but the expression, of its principal moral precepts in the Biblical writings. It is hoped that this essay will provide an introduction to both aspects of the subject and, while indicating the significance of the historical origins of our tradition, will lead the reader to return to a new reading and new understanding of the Bible itself.

Needless to say, the organization of such a vast range of new materials within such a difficult field has called for frequent consultation with other scholars in the field. Both author and editor wish to express their gratitude to Dr. Solomon Grayzel, Dr. Benajmin Maisler (Mazar), Dr. Ellis Rivkin, Dr. G. Ernest Wright, and Dr. Kenneth E. Stein. Miss Linda Altman, with the aid of Dr. Israel Renov, is responsible for the maps.

EDWARD WHITING FOX

*Ithaca, New York*
*January, 1954*

# BY WAY OF A PREFACE

THE credit for the idea of producing this novel approach to the study of Biblical Israel — combining as it does pertinent Hebrew texts, their translation in modern English, the use of illustrations, charts, maps, extra-Biblical texts, all in conjunction with and pertinent to the narrative text of my *Ancient Israel*—belongs to the Scharfsteins, Solomon and Bernard, of KTAV Publishing House.

I must confess to reacting with some misgivings when it was first suggested that I cite the Biblical evidence — through direct reproduction of the Hebrew texts proper and their translation into modern, literate English—for the statements made in my narrative text. Since when is a scholar expected to let facts stand in the way of his theories? Or to put it differently: How would scholars be able to function if they had to cite Biblical Hebrew passages in context—not merely content themselves (and often burden their readers, even the more scholarly among them, to the point of frustration) with the bare reference to the chapter and verse numbers of the Biblical Book involved — to substantiate their statements and theories?

There was also the matter of illustrations, maps, charts, and extra-Biblical documentation. One would think that this would offer few difficulties; after all, there are dozens of books readily available on Biblical Archaeology that contain thousands of pictures of objects that excavators have unearthed, and there are numerous volumes that offer the reader ancient Near Eastern documents that relate to the Bible. And by the same token there is almost an embarrassment of riches in the number of books that are devoted exclusively to or that contain an abundance of maps and charts pertaining to the World of the Bible.

All this was true until actual work was begun on my *Ancient Israel*—with the kind permission and blessings of Cornell University Press and Prof. Edward W. Fox, Editor of the series in which my book appeared, *The Development of Western Civilization: Narrative Essays in the History of our Tradition from Its Origins in Ancient Israel and Greece to the Present*-to turn it into *Understanding the Bible through History and Archaeology*. What Biblical passages ought to be selected as "proof texts?" What objects, events, structures, peoples, gods, persons, and the like, ought to be shown? What prehistoric, Sumerian, Egyptian, Babylonian, Assyrian, Hurrian, Hittite Canaanite-Phoenician, Aramean-Syrian, etc., inscriptions should be utilized? What events and battles and travels and commercial routes should be illustrated and clarified by maps? What chronological charts, Near Eastern as well as Israelite, should be offered for the reigns, careers, events, etc., involving rulers, prophets, tribes, and kingdoms?

I am not sure that I would have undertaken this task without the aid of a younger scholar whose knowledge of the ancient Near East and Biblical Israel was intimate and current; so that it was a stroke of good fortune that Mr. Samuel M. Paley, then on the last lap of his doctoral dissertation in the Department of Middle East Languages and Cultures at Columbia University, was able and willing to join us in this project. Singly and/or together, Mr. Paley, Mr. S. Scharfstein, and I selected passages from the Hebrew Bible (Mrs. Yael Paley, student in the Graduate Division of the Teachers Institute of Jewish Theological Seminary, sometimes assisted her husband in selecting the passages) and illustrations from the ancient Near East, wrote captions for them, decided on what kind of maps to work up, and so on; the task was incredibly time- and energy-consuming. Ultimately, grateful as I am for the major contributions of my colleagues, especially Mr. Paley, the responsibility for this is mine; and all criticism of the work, including of course constructive suggestions for its improvement, should be directed to me.

A word about the translations of the Biblical Hebrew passages. The Torah selections were reproduced—virtually without change—from *The Torah. The Five Books of Moses: A New Translation of the Holy Scriptures according to the Masoretic Text* (1962; second edition), with the kind permission of the Jewish Publication Society of America; I have added the *caveat* "virtually without change" in order to defend, e.g., my rendering of the Third Commandment (p. 101; Exodus 20.7//Deuteronomy 5.11) as "You shall not utter the name of the Lord your God improperly . . ." as against "You shall not swear falsely by the name of the Lord your God . . ." (on which see pp. 175-6 of my edition of *Notes on the New Translation of the Torah;* 1969). The translations of the passages from the Prophets and the Writings are mine; naturally, I made use not only of the same materials that went into making of the New Jewish Version of *The Torah* (and add now the new Jewish Publication Society translation of *The Five Megilloth and Jonah,* 1969) but also of such newer translations as the British Catholic *Jerusalem Bible* (1966; something of a variation on the theme of the Jerusalem Catholic *La Sainte Bible,* 1956), the British Protestant *New English Bible* (1970), and the American Catholic *New American Bible* (1972; known previously as the *Confraternity Bible*).

The reader will note that occasionally one and the same Hebrew passage is translated one way in my narrative text and somewhat differently on the page opposite (see, e.g., Micah 1.6 on pp. 188-9); this is sometimes due to my inability to decide between two possible renderings and so offering both, letting the reader make his own decision.

As for the Hebrew text, it was decided not to reproduce both the Kethib and the Qere forms of a word; there is no reason to burden the reader with, e.g., the form וּמְבַלְּהִים (Ezra 4.4; see p. 227) in the text and the unvocalized phrase ומבהלים קרי in the margin, when וּמְבַהֲלִים is what the masoretes and tradition decided upon. It will be further noted that I have used throughout the term "the Hebrew text" rather than "the masoretic text;" the reason for this is that it is becoming increasingly the scholarly consensus that "there never was any such thing as *'the* masoretic text' in existence" (pp. XVIII-XXXII of my Prolegomenon, "The Masoretic Text: A Critical Evaluation," to the KTAV reissue of C. D. Ginsburg's *Introduction to the Massoretico-Critical Edition of the Hebrew Bible;* 1966).

Half of the more than fifty aids interspersed among the Biblical passages offer bibliographical references, of current vintage. But due to the publisher's deadline, it was not possible to work up anew a single updated bibliography for this edition; this will be made available in a forthcoming printing. In the meantime, so as not to leave the reader without any bibliography, two additional bibliographies have been reproduced in the present work: (1) most of the updated (1960) bibliography of the hardcover edition of my *Ancient Israel* (pp. 174-184), in two parts, "Suggestions for Further Reading" and "Selected Bibliography for Teachers and Advanced Readers" (pp. 277-279); and (2) on pp. 279-282 my convenient descriptive listing of "Books on Biblical History and Archeology :1960-1966" in the *Jewish Book Annual,* 25 (5728/1967-68), pp. 176-183. Numerous additional works are cited in my chapter on "Old Testament Studies" (pp. 51-109) in *Religion,* ed. P. Ramsey (1965; in *The Princeton Studies: Humanistic Scholarship in America*).

In this connection the reader may be interested to know that the Commission on Adult Jewish Education of B'nai B'rith, under the directorship of Lily Edelman, published in 1965 *Bible Backgrounds: A Discussion Guide based on Ancient Israel* by Rabbi Leon M. Kahane (33 pages); and the Department of Continuing Education of the Union of American Hebrew Congregations (in cooperation with the National Federation of Temple Sisterhoods), under the directorship of Abraham Segal, published in 1971 *A Course Syllabus on Ancient Jewish History* by Dr. Dorothy G. Axelroth, based on my *Ancient Israel* (22 pages).

Finally, and most pleasantly, the task of working up this volume in its various aspects having proved much more arduous than anticipated, I appreciate more than usual the fact that the time of sending forth this aid to the understanding of the Bible coincides with *zeman heruthénu,* "the time of our liberation."

Harry M. Orlinsky

Erev Pesach 5732/March 29, 1972

# INTRODUCTION

THE tribes of Israel, though small in numbers and relatively late to arrive, were destined to remain unique among the many peoples who appeared in western Asia at the dawn of history. Out of their way of life grew three great religions, the Jewish, the Christian, and the Moslem.

The history and religious experiences of the Israelites are interwoven in a collection of writings called the Bible. No other single book, or collection of books, has played so important and prolonged a role in the development of western civilization; cf. the opening statement in P. Marion Simms, *The Bible in America: Versions That Have Played Their Part in the Making of the Republic* (New York, 1936), Introduction, p. 1: "The Bible as a book stands alone. The vast majority of all the books that have ever been published has been Bibles." Indeed, the simple use of the word Bible, which derives from Greek *ta biblia* "the books," with no more identification than the capital "B," points to its significance as "the Book" *par excellence.*

*Τò βίβλια*

## Influence of the Bible

No other description is needed because the Bible has constituted the supreme religious and moral fount and authority for the numerous nations who have professed the Hebrew, Christian, and Moslem faiths. The moral codes of western Europe have drawn heavily on the ethical teachings of the Bible, particularly on the concepts of social justice which the prophets so forthrightly and dramatically expressed. Indeed, it is generally accepted that the spirit and the democratic ideals of the Constitution of the United States derive in some measure from this Biblical inheritance. ✱

As literature, too, and as a factor in the development of the literature of western culture, the Bible has no equal. There is scarcely a book in the Bible which has not been described at some time as a literary masterpiece. The Book of Job was described by Carlyle as "the grandest book ever written with pen." The Book of Ruth has frequently been cited as a model of short-story writing. Such books as Psalms and the Song of Songs have probably never been matched. If, as has been said,

✱ and certainy the Bible's influence on the framers of the constitution— even religious liberals like Jefferson (a Unitarian)

5

great literature is the expression of arresting thoughts in brilliant diction, then the writings of Amos, Isaiah, Jeremiah, and other prophets are supreme examples of their kind.

In the matter of influence, it is generally recognized that English literature cannot be understood apart from the Bible. In its classical English form, the King James Version, the Bible has constituted from the beginning a standard of prose style. No other single work, be it Latin, Greek, or English, has so deeply affected the style and thinking of English writers.

## What Is the Bible?

The Bible is a collection of various kinds of writings composed in different periods which came in time to be regarded as divinely inspired scripture. These writings deal with the career of Israel from its beginning shortly after the twentieth century B.C.E. until the successful Maccabean war of independence of the Jews against Hellenistic Syria in 165 B.C.E. To the Jews, the Bible consists of twenty-four books. During the first four centuries C.E. the Christian Church compiled an additional twenty-seven books, and named them the New Testament, to distinguish them from the Old Testament, the term which it came to use for the Hebrew Bible. In addition, the Roman Catholic Church recognized several other books, which it introduced into the Old Testament. The Protestant Church, however, followed the Jewish tradition in rejecting these additional books, which are now generally known as the Apocrypha. In this book, the term Bible will be used for the twenty-four books of the Hebrew Bible.

## The Threefold Division of the Bible

The first, and most authoritative, division of the Hebrew Bible is the Law, or the Five Books of Moses, also called the Pentateuch (Greek for "Five Books"). These five books include Genesis, Exodus, Leviticus, Numbers, and Deuteronomy. This section contains two kinds of material: historical and legal, both terms being taken in their widest sense. The historical data relate the story of mankind, as understood by the Biblical writers, from the Creation until the days of Abraham (Genesis 1–11), proceeding from there to the career of the Hebrews in Canaan, Egypt, and the wilderness of Sinai, up to the death of Moses on the eve of the invasion of Canaan in the thirteenth century B.C.E. The legal part details the essential constitution of Israel.

The second great division of the Bible, the Prophets, consists of eight books and covers a period lasting about 750 years. In this epoch, Canaan was conquered, Israel's united and divided kingdoms rose and fell, and the state of Judah and the Temple of Solomon were restored, in part, after the Babylonian Exile, at the end of the sixth century B.C.E.

During this phase, the role of the prophetic movement was dominant. First of all, its adherents took the royal archives and other source material and wove them together carefully and vividly into a social and political history of Israel, carving out for themselves, in the process, a reputation as the world's first systematic historians. The books of Joshua, Judges, Samuel, and Kings—these books are sometimes called the Former Prophets—constitute this great achievement. Secondly, in intervening in the political and social life of their fellow Israelites, the prophets expressed their ideas so forthrightly and in such beautiful and powerful prose and poetry that they placed themselves forever among the greatest social moralists of all time. The books of Isaiah, Jeremiah, Ezekiel (the so-called Major Prophets) and the twelve so-called Minor Prophets—among whom Hosea, Amos, and Micah stand out—

6

are the repository of this unsurpassed material.

The third and final division of the Bible is called the Writings, or the Hagiographa. This section consists of eleven books which run a considerable gamut in variety of style and content, and nearly every one of which is a classic in its own right. Devotional literature is well represented by the familiar Book of Psalms. Wisdom literature, the speculation of what constitutes the good life and the practical means of achieving it, is exhibited in such books as Proverbs, Job, and Ecclesiastes. The Song of Songs is a lyrical poem of love, tender and passionate; in later times the lover and his beloved became identified with God and His beloved people Israel. The Book of Daniel, in its final form a product of the second century B.C.E., tells a dramatic story of the purported career of a Judean youth living in the Babylonian Exile in the days of Nebuchadnezzar (early sixth century B.C.E.), a time which to this day symbolizes for the Jews the pit of despair. Daniel's dreams and visions, which among other things supposedly foretold Maccabean victory over Syria about 165 B.C.E., became the forerunner and model of the apocalypses or supernatural revelations which appeared first in Jewish and then in Christian literature. The memoirs of Ezra and Nehemiah constitute both interesting autobiography and important source material for the restoration of Judea after the Babylonian Exile. These postexilic memoirs appear to have been edited by the person who wrote the Book of Chronicles, which provides a survey of Biblical history from Adam to Nehemiah (about 400 B.C.E.). Chronicles is the last of the twenty-four books of the Hebrew Bible.

## The Bible as History

The Bible is the major source for our knowledge of the history of Israel in ancient times; yet its value for the historian has not always been appreciated sufficiently.

Until the eighteenth century the Bible was universally accepted as a trustworthy history book of antiquity. Indeed, the Book was regarded as being literally true, the Creation, the Flood, Noah's Ark, the walls of Jericho, and all. But as the Age of Reason dawned and in turn gave way to nineteenth-century philosophies of evolution and scientific materialism, the Bible, in common with the New Testament and all records of antiquity, Greek, Roman, and the rest, came to be very considerably discounted as a reliable basis for the reconstruction of history.

The heroic doings of the patriarchs, Abraham, Isaac, and Jacob, as described in the Book of Genesis, were discounted as mere myth. The very existence of Moses was doubted. Joshua was believed to have had little or nothing to do with the Israelite conquest of Canaan. David and Solomon were considered greatly overrated. Extensive parts of the prophetic books were attributed not to the prophets themselves but to redactors and disciples who lived several centuries later in different circumstances. The story of the Babylonian Exile was relegated by some to the realm of fiction. And so on.

This negative attitude to the Bible was reflected in more recent times, for example, in the writings of the well-known social philosopher Bertrand Russell, and the historiographer R. G. Collingwood. In his popular *History of Western Philosophy* (1944) Lord Russell wrote:

The early history of the Israelites cannot be confirmed from any source outside the Old Testament, and it is impossible to know at what point it ceases to be purely legendary. David and Solomon may be accepted as kings who probably had a real existence, but at the earliest point at which we come to something certainly historical there are already two kingdoms of Israel and Judah [ninth century B.C.E.]

A year later, in his posthumous book on *The Idea of History* (1945), Collingwood dismissed—in less than one page—the entire Biblical material as but "theocratic history and myth," that is, as stories and legends revolving about a single mighty god (in contrast, for example, to the ancient Greeks, whose stories and legends revolved about numerous mighty, and not-so-mighty, gods and goddesses and their offspring).

It is unfortunate that these scholars had not kept up with the current discoveries and analyses of the ancient Near East. For today, in considerable degree, the pendulum has swung the other way. Modern historians do not, to be sure, accept every part of the Bible equally as literal fact. Yet they have come to accept much of the Biblical data as constituting unusually reliable historical documents of antiquity, documents which take on new meaning and pertinence when they are analyzed in the light of the newly discovered extra-Biblical sources.

## Archaeology and the Bible

This radical re-evaluation of the significance of the Bible has been necessitated by the archaeological discoveries of the past several decades. The civilizations which flourished in the Fertile Crescent of old are better known today than anyone before World War I thought possible. The material, social, and religious configurations of the Sumerian, Egyptian, Babylonian, Hurrian, Assyrian, Canaanite, Hittite, and Aramean societies can be delineated to an increasingly satisfactory degree. It is now possible to see the entire ancient Near East from a thoroughly new perspective, and so it has become necessary to re-examine the Biblical record in the light of our broadened understanding.

The older view, that the Biblical data were suspect and even likely to be false, unless cor-roborated by extra-Biblical facts, has had to give way more and more to the view that, by and large, the Biblical accounts are more likely to be true than false, unless clear-cut evidence from sources outside the Bible demonstrate the reverse.

## The Bible as Sacred History and Its Interpretation

From the foregoing it would seem that it is possible, at long last, to write a thoroughly acceptable history of ancient Israel, one which will conform to the highest standards of modern, scientific historiography; yet the fact is that the time has not yet come, and well may never come, for such a work to be achieved.

The major problems that confront the modern historian in handling the sources of the Biblical period are twofold. First, the historian cannot fulfill his task when his sources are inadequate and of uncertain authorship and date. The sources for Biblical history are even now neither sufficient nor chronologically secure. It is only occasionally that a Biblical book, or its component parts, can be ascribed to a definite time, place, author, and purpose; and, furthermore, extensive as the extra-Biblical material has become, it generally suffices only for the broadest sort of understanding. Secondly, in the handling of the Biblical material there is the major problem of discovering the fundamental economic, social, and political forces from documents couched almost exclusively in religious terminology and given to interpret all historical experiences as manifestations of divine intervention.

Those who were responsible for the composition of the Hebrew Bible believed that what they uttered and wrote derived from the God who entered into a mutual Covenant with Israel. According to the terms of the

Covenant, God loved and protected Israel and no other people, and Israel worshipped no other god but Him. The modern historian, however, cannot accept such an interpretation, but must seek—behind the religious terminology—the same kind of documented human story, with an examination of its underlying dynamics, that would be his proper objective in any other field. Otherwise he would achieve no more than a compilation of myths, chronicles, annals, oracles, autobiographies, court histories, personal apologia.

The historian cannot regard any human activity or statement, be it religious or secular, sacred or profane, as beyond his domain. His competence is limited only by the nature and adequacy of his sources. The limitations inherent in the Biblical sources thus militate against an historical reconstruction which will be clear in every respect; in spite of these inherent difficulties, scholarly researches have been supplying flashes of light where none existed before. So the work of interpretation goes on, some results of which form the basis of this book.

## BOOKS OF THE HEBREW BIBLE ( תנ״ך )—OLD TESTAMENT

### I. TORAH (FIVE BOOKS OF MOSES)—PENTATEUCH ( חוּמָשׁ )    תּוֹרָה

1. Genesis — בְּרֵאשִׁית
2. Exodus — שְׁמוֹת
3. Leviticus — וַיִּקְרָא
4. Numbers — בְּמִדְבַּר
5. Deuteronomy — דְּבָרִים

### II. PROPHETS    נְבִיאִים רִאשׁוֹנִים

#### A. FORMER PROPHETS

6. Joshua — יְהוֹשֻׁעַ
7. Judges — שׁוֹפְטִים
8. Samuel, I and II — שְׁמוּאֵל א, ב
9. Kings, I and II — מְלָכִים א, ב

#### B. LATTER PROPHETS    נְבִיאִים אַחֲרוֹנִים

#### The Major Prophets

10. Isaiah — יְשַׁעְיָה
11. Jeremiah — יִרְמְיָה
12. Ezekiel — יְחֶזְקֵאל

#### 13. The Minor Prophets    תְּרֵי עָשָׂר

| | | | |
|---|---|---|---|
| Hosea | הוֹשֵׁעַ | Nahum | נַחוּם |
| Joel | יוֹאֵל | Habakkuk | חֲבַקּוּק |
| Amos | עָמוֹס | Zephaniah | צְפַנְיָה |
| Obadiah | עוֹבַדְיָה | Haggai | חַגַּי |
| Jonah | יוֹנָה | Zechariah | זְכַרְיָה |
| Micah | מִיכָה | Malachi | מַלְאָכִי |

### III. WRITINGS—HAGIOGRAPHA    כְּתוּבִים

#### WISDOM BOOKS

14. Psalms — תְּהִלִּים
15. Proverbs — מִשְׁלֵי
16. Job — אִיּוֹב

#### FIVE MEGILLOTH—SCROLLS

17 Song Of Songs—Canticles — שִׁיר הַשִּׁירִים
18 Ruth — רוּת
19 Lamentations — אֵיכָה
20 Ecclesiastes—Koheleth — קֹהֶלֶת
21 Esther — אֶסְתֵּר

22 Daniel — דָּנִיֵּאל
23 Ezra-Nehemiah — עֶזְרָא—נְחֶמְיָה
24 Chronicles, I and II — דִּבְרֵי הַיָּמִים א, ב

If the Twelve "Minor" Prophets and Ezra-Nehemiah are counted individually, there are thirty-six rather than twenty-four Books in the Hebrew Holy Scriptures. It may be noted here that the Christian titles of the Biblical Books, e.g., Genesis, Exodus, Leviticus, etc., are all Jewish to begin with; see H. M. Orlinsky, "The Masoretic Text: A Critical Evaluation," Prolegomenon in the KTAV reissue (1966) of C. D. Ginsburg, *Introduction to the Massoretico-Critical Edition of the Hebrew Bible*, pp. XVIII-XX.

9

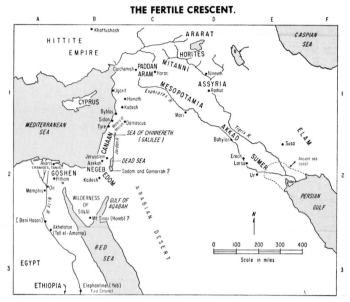

**THE FERTILE CRESCENT.**

James Henry Breasted, famed Egyptologist and first Director of the University of Chicago's Oriental Institute, coined the term "Fertile Crescent." From earliest times, this was the route of caravans, armies, travelers, etc.

Wadi el-Mughara, where three of the famous "Carmel Caves" are located. It is in caves such as these that stratified levels of Old Stone Age (Palaeolithic) and Middle Stone Age (Mesolithic) habitations have been found, and continue to be found, superimposed upon each other. Especially prevalent in the remains of the Old Stone Age are varieties of tools of the Levalloiso-Mousterian type, used by Neanderthal and Neanderthaloid man.

Chapter I

# THE FERTILE CRESCENT: HEBREW ORIGINS

THE Near East, that quadrangle of land lying between the Mediterranean, the Caspian, and Red Seas, and the Persian Gulf, and connecting Asia with Africa, is in general a barren and uninviting area. Running across it, however, from the alluvial flatlands of the Tigris and Euphrates in the southeast through Syria in the northwest, and then curving down along the coast of Palestine to the Nile Delta, lies a crescent-shaped region of rich, well-watered land.

In this Fertile Crescent the first great civilizations appeared, and man as an individual first made the transition from hunting, fishing, and cave dwelling to systematic hunting and farming within an organized community of his fellow kind. From this focus, the new mode of civilization extended to lower Mesopotamia, and from there to the Syro-Palestinian coast, to Egypt, to the Anatolian plateau, to the Indus Valley in Pakistan, to Crete, and to Greece. The caves of Mount Carmel in modern Israel have provided the best materials for identifying the stage at which food-gathering man began systematically to abandon the cave to establish food-producing villages.

*Ancient Israel was well aware of the Near East quadrangle as a geo-graphical unit, as witness* Gen. 2.10-14 *and* 15.18 *(quoted here), as well as* Deut. 1.7; 11.24; *and* Josh. 1.4.

[10]A river issues from Eden to water the garden, and it then divides and becomes four branches. [11]The name of the first is Pishon, the one that winds through the whole land of Havilah, where the gold is. ([12]The gold of that land is good; bdellium is there, and lapis lazuli.) [13]The name of the second river is Gihon, the one that winds through the whole land of Cush. [14]The name of the third river is Tigris, the one that flows east of Asshur. And the fourth river is the Euphrates.

*Genesis 2.10-14*

וְנָהָר יֹצֵא מֵעֵדֶן לְהַשְׁקוֹת אֶת־הַגָּן וּמִשָּׁם יִפָּרֵד
וְהָיָה לְאַרְבָּעָה רָאשִׁים: שֵׁם הָאֶחָד פִּישׁוֹן הוּא
הַסֹּבֵב אֵת כָּל־אֶרֶץ הַחֲוִילָה אֲשֶׁר־שָׁם הַזָּהָב:
וּזֲהַב הָאָרֶץ הַהִוא טוֹב שָׁם הַבְּדֹלַח וְאֶבֶן הַשֹּׁהַם:
וְשֵׁם הַנָּהָר הַשֵּׁנִי גִּיחוֹן הוּא הַסּוֹבֵב אֵת כָּל־אֶרֶץ
כּוּשׁ: וְשֵׁם־הַנָּהָר הַשְּׁלִישִׁי חִדֶּקֶל הוּא הַהֹלֵךְ
קִדְמַת אַשּׁוּר וְהַנָּהָר הָרְבִיעִי הוּא פְרָת:
בְּרֵאשִׁית ב:י—יד

[18]On that day the Lord made a covenant with Abram, saying, "To your offspring I give this land, from the river of Egypt to the great river, the river Euphrates: [19]the Kenites, the Kenizzites, the Kadmonites, [20]the Hittites, the Perizzites, the Rephaim, [21]the Amorites, the Canaanites, the Girgash-ites, and the Jebusites.

*Genesis 15.18-21*

בַּיּוֹם הַהוּא כָּרַת יְהֹוָה אֶת־אַבְרָם בְּרִית לֵאמֹר
לְזַרְעֲךָ נָתַתִּי אֶת־הָאָרֶץ הַזֹּאת מִנְּהַר מִצְרַיִם
עַד־הַנָּהָר הַגָּדֹל נְהַר־פְּרָת: אֶת־הַקֵּינִי וְאֶת־
הַקְּנִזִּי וְאֵת הַקַּדְמֹנִי: וְאֶת־הַחִתִּי וְאֶת־הַפְּרִזִּי
וְאֶת־הָרְפָאִים: וְאֶת־הָאֱמֹרִי וְאֶת־הַכְּנַעֲנִי וְאֶת־
הַגִּרְגָּשִׁי וְאֶת־הַיְבוּסִי:
בְּרֵאשִׁית טו:יח—כא

[30]Lot went up from Zoar and settled in the hill country with his two daughters, for he was afraid to dwell in Zoar; and he and his two daughters lived in a cave.

*Genesis 19.30*

וַיַּעַל לוֹט מִצּוֹעַר וַיֵּשֶׁב בָּהָר וּשְׁתֵּי בְנֹתָיו עִמּוֹ
כִּי יָרֵא לָשֶׁבֶת בְּצוֹעַר וַיֵּשֶׁב בַּמְּעָרָה הוּא וּשְׁתֵּי
בְנֹתָיו:
בְּרֵאשִׁית יט:ל

*Caves were occasionally inhabited in Israel even after community liv-ing in villages and towns had become the norm. The famous Dead Sea Scrolls were hidden in caves, where a considerable body of Jews lived and worked about 2,000 years ago. It used to be believed that the Horites of the Bible* (Gen. 14.6; 36.20; Deut. 2.12) *were troglodytes or cave dwellers (Hebrew* ḥorim *from* ḥor *"hole, cave"); we now know that the Horites were part of a great, non-Semitic civilization, the Hurrian, whose center was in Mesopotamia (about 2000-1400* B.C.E.*). See in general, E. Anati,* Palestine Before the Hebrews *(1963).*

[4]When Jezebel was killing off the prophets of the Lord, Obadiah had taken a hundred prophets and hidden them, fifty to a cave, and provided them with bread and water.

*I Kings 18.4*

וַיְהִי בְּהַכְרִית אִיזֶבֶל אֵת נְבִיאֵי יְהֹוָה וַיִּקַּח
עֹבַדְיָהוּ מֵאָה נְבִיאִים וַיַּחְבִּיאֵם חֲמִשִּׁים אִישׁ
בַּמְּעָרָה וְכִלְכְּלָם לֶחֶם וָמָיִם.
מְלָכִים א׳ יח:ד

Spearheads and axeheads made of cast and hammered bronze, dating from the early part of the Early Bronze Period (ca. 3100 to 2600 B.C.E.). These well-made objects show the high technical advancement of which the Early Bronze craftsmen were capable as a result of the centuries of trial and testing by the Chalcolithic smiths. Spearheads (above): from about 13 to 26 inches long; axeheads (below): about 7 inches and 5⅛ inches long. From Kfar Monash (near modern Netanya).

## The Ancient Near East

This change began during the latter stages of the Neolithic or Late Stone Age, about 5500-4000 B.C.E. In ever-increasing numbers people learned to cultivate cereal grasses and prepare more grain than was immediately needed. Once there were food surpluses, latent human energies were released. The arts of animal husbandry, of making wattle huts from mud smeared on sticks—these and other advances occurred in this period. The first crude villages appeared sometimes, as at Jericho, in association with a shrine.

A series of metallurgical discoveries accelerated this process of social organization. During the Chalcolithic, or Copper-Stone Age, about 4000–3200 B.C.E., man learned how to smelt copper for use in tools, weapons, and ornaments, and gradually this malleable, if none-too-plentiful, substance superseded stone. Silver and lead came into use in several parts of the Near East, and tin (in bronze) had been discovered, though it was only rarely used, before 3000 B.C.E. Other technical advances followed. The wheel and the plough were invented, and a rudimentary division of labor was introduced. Houses made of mud brick replaced mud-walled huts, and in the manufacture of bricks themselves fine stone aggregate eventually replaced chopped straw. Houses came to have wooden roofs, and even smoothly plastered walls sometimes decorated with geometric patterns in several colors.

During the Early Bronze Age, about 3200–2000 B.C.E., the general population increased, and large groups of people shifted about. Sumer, Akkad, Egypt, and other dynastic civilizations emerged. In this period, villages grew into cities, canals were dug to irrigate the land, architecture became monumental, men labored in organized groups. The early Egyptian dynasts built pyramid tombs, and

<sup>18</sup>Thorns and thistles shall it sprout for you,
But your feed shall be the grasses of the field.
<sup>19</sup>By the sweat of your brow shall you get bread
to eat,
Until you return to the ground—
For from it you were taken.
For dust you are,
And to dust you shall return.

*Genesis 3.18–19*

[<sup>1</sup> Now the man knew his wife Eve, and she conceived and bore Cain. . .] <sup>2</sup>She then bore his brother Abel. Abel became a keeper of sheep, and Cain a tiller of the soil.

*Genesis 4.1–2*

<sup>17</sup>Cain knew his wife, and she conceived and bore Enoch. And he then founded a city, and named the city after his son Enoch. <sup>18</sup>To Enoch was born Irad, and Irad begot Mehujael, and Mehujael begot Methusael, and Methusael begot Lamech. <sup>19</sup>Lamech took to himself two wives . . . Adah, and . . . Zillah. <sup>20</sup>Adah bore Jabal; he was the ancestor of those who dwell in tents and amidst herds. <sup>21</sup>And the name of his brother was Jubal; he was the ancestor of all who play the lyre and the pipe. <sup>22</sup>As for Zillah, she bore Tubal-cain, who forged all the implements of copper and iron. . . .

*Genesis 4.17–22*

<sup>1</sup>All the earth had the same language and the same words. <sup>2</sup>And as men migrated from the east, they came upon a valley in the land of Shinar and settled there. <sup>3</sup>They said to one another, "Come, let us make bricks and burn them hard . . . <sup>4</sup>. . . let us build us a city, and a tower with its top in the sky . . . else we shall be scattered all over the world." <sup>5</sup>The LORD came down to look at the city and tower . . . <sup>6</sup>And the LORD said, "If, as one people with one language for all, this is how they have begun to act, then nothing that they may propose to do will be out of their reach. <sup>7</sup>Let us, then, go down and confound their speech there, so that they shall not understand one another's speech." <sup>8</sup>Thus the LORD scattered them from there over the face of the whole earth; and they stopped building the city. <sup>9</sup>That is why it was called Babel. . . .

*Genesis 11.1-9*

וְקוֹץ וְדַרְדַּר תַּצְמִיחַ לָךְ וְאָכַלְתָּ אֶת־עֵשֶׂב הַשָּׂדֶה:
בְּזֵעַת אַפֶּיךָ תֹּאכַל לֶחֶם עַד שׁוּבְךָ אֶל־הָאֲדָמָה
כִּי מִמֶּנָּה לֻקָּחְתָּ כִּי־עָפָר אַתָּה וְאֶל־עָפָר תָּשׁוּב:

בְּרֵאשִׁית ג:יח-יט

וַתֹּסֶף לָלֶדֶת אֶת־אָחִיו אֶת־הָבֶל וַיְהִי־הֶבֶל
רֹעֵה צֹאן וְקַיִן הָיָה עֹבֵד אֲדָמָה: בְּרֵאשִׁית ד:ב

וַיֵּדַע קַיִן אֶת־אִשְׁתּוֹ וַתַּהַר וַתֵּלֶד אֶת־חֲנוֹךְ
וַיְהִי בֹּנֶה עִיר וַיִּקְרָא שֵׁם הָעִיר כְּשֵׁם בְּנוֹ חֲנוֹךְ:
וַיִּוָּלֵד לַחֲנוֹךְ אֶת־עִירָד וְעִירָד יָלַד אֶת־מְחוּיָאֵל
וּמְחִיָּיאֵל יָלַד אֶת מְתוּשָׁאֵל וּמְתוּשָׁאֵל יָלַד אֶת־
לָמֶךְ: וַיִּקַּח־לוֹ לֶמֶךְ שְׁתֵּי נָשִׁים שֵׁם הָאַחַת עָדָה
וְשֵׁם הַשֵּׁנִית צִלָּה: וַתֵּלֶד עָדָה אֶת־יָבָל הוּא הָיָה
אֲבִי יֹשֵׁב אֹהֶל וּמִקְנֶה: וְשֵׁם אָחִיו יוּבָל הוּא הָיָה
אֲבִי כָּל־תֹּפֵשׂ כִּנּוֹר וְעוּגָב: וְצִלָּה גַם־הִוא יָלְדָה
אֶת־תּוּבַל קַיִן לֹטֵשׁ כָּל־חֹרֵשׁ נְחֹשֶׁת וּבַרְזֶל ...

בְּרֵאשִׁית ד: יז-כב

וַיְהִי כָל־הָאָרֶץ שָׂפָה אֶחָת וּדְבָרִים אֲחָדִים:
וַיְהִי בְּנָסְעָם מִקֶּדֶם וַיִּמְצְאוּ בִקְעָה בְּאֶרֶץ שִׁנְעָר
וַיֵּשְׁבוּ שָׁם: וַיֹּאמְרוּ אִישׁ אֶל־רֵעֵהוּ הָבָה נִלְבְּנָה
לְבֵנִים וְנִשְׂרְפָה לִשְׂרֵפָה ... הָבָה נִבְנֶה־לָּנוּ
עִיר וּמִגְדָּל וְרֹאשׁוֹ בַשָּׁמַיִם וְנַעֲשֶׂה־לָּנוּ שֵׁם
פֶּן־נָפוּץ עַל־פְּנֵי כָל־הָאָרֶץ: וַיֵּרֶד יְהוָה לִרְאֹת
אֶת־הָעִיר וְאֶת־הַמִּגְדָּל אֲשֶׁר בָּנוּ בְּנֵי הָאָדָם:
וַיֹּאמֶר יְהוָה הֵן עַם אֶחָד וְשָׂפָה אַחַת לְכֻלָּם וְזֶה
הַחִלָּם לַעֲשׂוֹת וְעַתָּה לֹא־יִבָּצֵר מֵהֶם כֹּל אֲשֶׁר
יָזְמוּ לַעֲשׂוֹת: הָבָה נֵרְדָה וְנָבְלָה שָׁם שְׂפָתָם אֲשֶׁר
לֹא יִשְׁמְעוּ אִישׁ שְׂפַת רֵעֵהוּ: וַיָּפֶץ יְהוָה אֹתָם
מִשָּׁם עַל־פְּנֵי כָל־הָאָרֶץ וַיַּחְדְּלוּ לִבְנֹת הָעִיר:
עַל־כֵּן קָרָא שְׁמָהּ בָּבֶל ...

בְּרֵאשִׁית יא:א-ט

13

Seated statuette of Gudea, ensi (governor) of Lagash. The cuneiform inscription, written in the Sumerian language, covers the front of Gudea's mantle and identifies him as the builder of the temple of Ningirsu, god of Lagash. The inscription is a request for life which is carried to Ningirsu by Gudea's patron god Ningishzida. The statuette is 18 inches high.

Ziggurat (partly reconstructed), the central structure of the temple complex of the moon god Nanna, patron god of Ur, as built by King Ur-Nammu of Ur, at the end of the 22nd Century B.C.E.

the rulers of Mesopotamia erected structures in the form of tiered brick mounds, the ziggurats. Pictographic and cuneiform writing were invented, enabling the priestly and ruling classes to keep records and other professional data, such as magical spells. Henceforth, too, knowledge could be stored for the use of posterity. These early civilizations bred others as they interpenetrated and competed. Mesopotamian influences became apparent in Egypt, by way of Syria and Canaan; and Egypt, in turn, began to extend political dominion to Canaan and Syria.

## Growth of Cities

By this time man had become in every sense a thinking, planning, and articulate human being, with a clear idea of hierarchy in respect of class and occupation. As we have noted, villages which once had consisted of patriarchal family groups coalesced into cities, and these cities merged into "city-states," that is, urban centers controlling satellite territory. The family commune was replaced by a governing assembly of adult freemen, this assembly usually headed by a council of elders. Women, children, slaves, and the unpropertied were excluded from the assemblies. Slavery had become an economic institution, the earliest known instance of human chattels. These earliest slaves were foreign captives of war.

As the population increased, the elders began to assume the right, particularly in times of crisis, of electing a king, while retaining at all times the legal right to depose him. But with still further increase in the size and complexity of human settlements, kings became a permanent feature of the prevailing social order. The idea of a dynasty, or kingly line, followed in due course. Fixed rules for adjudicating anarchic private differences appeared, and collections of laws began to be

# Growth of Cities

*Slavery, far from unknown in our own days, was a common and legitimate institution throughout the ancient world. (Indeed, many a clergyman justified it during the past few centuries in the United States as biblically ordained.) At the same time, the slave had certain rights, and most legal codes in Western Asia contained clauses spelling out these rights—interestingly, more so in antiquity than in recent times. See I. Mendelsohn,* Slavery in the Ancient Near East *(1949).*

[14] When Abram heard that his kinsman had been taken captive, he mustered his retainers, born into his household, numbering three hundred and eighteen, and went in pursuit as far as Dan. [15] At night, he and his servants deployed against them and defeated them . . . [16] He brought back all the possessions; he also brought back his kinsman Lot and his possessions, and the women and the rest of the people.

*Genesis 14.14-16*

וַיִּשְׁמַע אַבְרָם כִּי נִשְׁבָּה אָחִיו וַיָּרֶק אֶת־חֲנִיכָיו יְלִידֵי בֵיתוֹ שְׁמֹנָה עָשָׂר וּשְׁלֹשׁ מֵאוֹת וַיִּרְדֹּף עַד־דָּן: וַיֵּחָלֵק עֲלֵיהֶם לַיְלָה הוּא וַעֲבָדָיו וַיַּכֵּם וַיִּרְדְּפֵם עַד־חוֹבָה אֲשֶׁר מִשְּׂמֹאל לְדַמָּשֶׂק: וַיָּשֶׁב אֵת כָּל־הָרְכֻשׁ וְגַם אֶת־לוֹט אָחִיו וּרְכֻשׁוֹ הֵשִׁיב וְגַם אֶת־הַנָּשִׁים וְאֶת־הָעָם:

בְּרֵאשִׁית יד:יד-טז

[1] These are the rules that you shall set before them: [2] When you acquire a Hebrew slave, he shall serve six years; in the seventh year he shall go free, without payment. [3] If he came single, he shall leave single; if he had a wife, his wife shall leave with him. [4] If his master gave him a wife, and she has borne him children, the wife and her children shall belong to the master, and he shall leave alone. [5] But if the slave declares, "I love my master, and my wife and children: I do not wish to go free," [6] his master shall take him before the God. He shall be brought to the door or the doorpost, and his master shall pierce his ear with an awl; and he shall then remain his slave for life.

*Exodus 21.1-6*

וְאֵלֶּה הַמִּשְׁפָּטִים אֲשֶׁר תָּשִׂים לִפְנֵיהֶם: כִּי תִקְנֶה עֶבֶד עִבְרִי שֵׁשׁ שָׁנִים יַעֲבֹד וּבַשְּׁבִעִת יֵצֵא לַחָפְשִׁי חִנָּם: אִם־בְּגַפּוֹ יָבֹא בְּגַפּוֹ יֵצֵא אִם־בַּעַל אִשָּׁה הוּא וְיָצְאָה אִשְׁתּוֹ עִמּוֹ: אִם־אֲדֹנָיו יִתֶּן־לוֹ אִשָּׁה וְיָלְדָה־לּוֹ בָנִים אוֹ בָנוֹת הָאִשָּׁה וִילָדֶיהָ תִּהְיֶה לַאדֹנֶיהָ וְהוּא יֵצֵא בְגַפּוֹ: וְאִם־אָמֹר יֹאמַר הָעֶבֶד אָהַבְתִּי אֶת־אֲדֹנִי אֶת־אִשְׁתִּי וְאֶת־בָּנָי לֹא אֵצֵא חָפְשִׁי: וְהִגִּישׁוֹ אֲדֹנָיו אֶל־הָאֱלֹהִים וְהִגִּישׁוֹ אֶל־הַדֶּלֶת אוֹ אֶל־הַמְּזוּזָה וְרָצַע אֲדֹנָיו אֶת־אָזְנוֹ בַּמַּרְצֵעַ וַעֲבָדוֹ לְעֹלָם:

שְׁמוֹת כא:א-ו

[1] When Samuel grew old, he appointed his sons chieftains for Israel. . . . [3] His sons, however, did not follow his ways; they preferred gain and took bribes, and they perverted justice. [4] So all the elders of Israel assembled and went to Samuel in Ramah, [5] and they said to him, "Since you have grown old and your sons have not followed your ways, appoint a king for us, to rule us like all other nations." [6] The matter distressed Samuel. . . . [7] But the Lord said to Samuel, "Obey the people in everything they say to you . . ."

*I Samuel 8.1-7*

וַיְהִי כַּאֲשֶׁר זָקֵן שְׁמוּאֵל וַיָּשֶׂם אֶת־בָּנָיו שֹׁפְטִים לְיִשְׂרָאֵל: . . . וְלֹא־הָלְכוּ בָנָיו בִּדְרָכָו וַיִּטּוּ אַחֲרֵי הַבָּצַע וַיִּקְחוּ־שֹׁחַד וַיַּטּוּ מִשְׁפָּט: וַיִּתְקַבְּצוּ כֹּל זִקְנֵי יִשְׂרָאֵל וַיָּבֹאוּ אֶל־שְׁמוּאֵל הָרָמָתָה: וַיֹּאמְרוּ אֵלָיו הִנֵּה אַתָּה זָקַנְתָּ וּבָנֶיךָ לֹא הָלְכוּ בִדְרָכֶיךָ עַתָּה שִׂימָה־לָּנוּ מֶלֶךְ לְשָׁפְטֵנוּ כְּכָל־הַגּוֹיִם: וַיֵּרַע הַדָּבָר בְּעֵינֵי שְׁמוּאֵל . . . וַיֹּאמֶר יְהוָה אֶל־שְׁמוּאֵל שְׁמַע בְּקוֹל הָעָם לְכֹל אֲשֶׁר־יֹאמְרוּ אֵלֶיךָ . . .

שְׁמוּאֵל א' ח:א, ג-ז

✗ this was disastrous, for any יהוה could be King— Samuel was in a most difficult epoch

15

Design on a cylinder seal of the Akkadian period (from about 2350-2200 B.C.E.) depicting a mythological scene in which several deities participate in the return or freeing of a sun deity from a cave or grave in a mountain.

A mathematical cuneiform tablet upon which is drawn a square with its two diagonals; this indicates the existence of a remarkably accurate estimate in sexagesimal form of the $\sqrt{2}$.

compiled, of which three (Ur-Nammu, Eshnunna, and Lipit-Ishtar), dating from about 2050 to about 1850 B.C.E., that is about 350–150 years before the great code of Hammurabi (or Hammurapi), have now been excavated.

## Mythology, Religion, and Science

When not warring, building, tilling the soil, and tending his flocks, man began to inquire about the nature of the universe and his place in it. Literary masterpieces were created in Sumerian, Akkadian (the cuneiform Semitic language of the Babylonians and Assyrians), and Egyptian. They represented an effort to determine the origin and to evaluate the activity of the sun, the moon, the planets, the other heavenly bodies; of the rain, wind, storm, and similar phenomena; of farming and shepherding; of human life and death, of the relationships among men, of the career of man on earth and thereafter; of justice, of good and evil, of reward and punishment. In brief, as today, so then too, man attempted to learn who really ruled the universe, and how to get the most out of it for himself during his relatively brief stay in this world.

In this early period, the existence of the gods in the upper and nether worlds and their intervention in human affairs on the earth played a dominant role in the thinking of the people. They knew little or nothing of the why and how of natural phenomena. The all-important cycle of the growth, death, and rebirth of vegetation upon which their agricultural economy depended was attributed to supernatural powers of different gradations, to higher gods and lower gods. Men explained the origin of the gods and of their functions to the best of their rather meager knowledge in the light of their geographical environment and social experience.

# Mythology, Religion, and Science

*Biblical Israel shared with its ancient neighbors many of the details as to how creation came to be. Thus when God gave names to everything that He created (Day, Night, Sky, Earth, Seas; and cf. 2.20, "And the man gave names to all the cattle and birds of the sky and to all the wild beasts"), this signified that the things named acquired recognized existence. Compare, e.g., the first two lines of the great Babylonian epic, Enuma Elish (an account of the rise of the god Marduk and his role in creation):*

> *When above, the heaven had not been named,*
> *(And) below, the earth had not been called by name,*

*that is, when heaven and earth did not yet exist. However, where the other versions of creation involved many gods and their consorts and assistants, the biblical version of creation is in a class by itself in that God alone is creator, without consort and without aid.*

¹When God began to create the heaven and the earth—²the earth being unformed and void, with darkness over the surface of the deep and a wind from God sweeping over the water—³God said, "Let there be light"; and there was light. ⁴God saw that the light was good, and God separated the light from the darkness. ⁵God called the light Day, and the darkness He called Night. And there was evening and there was morning, a first day.

⁶God said, "Let there be an expanse in the midst of the water, that it may separate water from water," ⁷ . . . And it was so. ⁸God called the expanse Sky. And there was evening and there was morning, a second day.

⁹God said, "Let the water below the sky be gathered into one area, that the dry land may appear." And it was so. . . . ¹¹And God said, "Let the earth sprout vegetation: seed-bearing plants, fruit trees of every kind on earth that bear fruit with the seed in it." And it was so. . . . ¹³And there was evening and there was morning, a third day.

¹⁴God said, "Let there be lights in the expanse of the sky to separate day from night; they shall serve as signs for the set times—the days and the years; ¹⁵and they shall serve as lights in the expanse of the sky to shine upon the earth." . . . ¹⁸and to dominate the day and the night, and to separate light from darkness. And God saw that this was good. ¹⁹And there was evening and there was morning, a fourth day.

²⁰God said, "Let the waters bring forth swarms of living creatures, and birds that fly above the earth across the expanse of the sky." . . . ²³And there was evening and there was morning, a fifth day.

בְּרֵאשִׁית בָּרָא אֱלֹהִים אֵת הַשָּׁמַיִם וְאֵת הָאָרֶץ:
וְהָאָרֶץ הָיְתָה תֹהוּ וָבֹהוּ וְחֹשֶׁךְ עַל־פְּנֵי תְהוֹם
וְרוּחַ אֱלֹהִים מְרַחֶפֶת עַל־פְּנֵי הַמָּיִם: וַיֹּאמֶר
אֱלֹהִים יְהִי אוֹר וַיְהִי־אוֹר: וַיַּרְא אֱלֹהִים אֶת־
הָאוֹר כִּי־טוֹב וַיַּבְדֵּל אֱלֹהִים בֵּין הָאוֹר וּבֵין
הַחֹשֶׁךְ: וַיִּקְרָא אֱלֹהִים לָאוֹר יוֹם וְלַחֹשֶׁךְ קָרָא
לָיְלָה וַיְהִי־עֶרֶב וַיְהִי־בֹקֶר יוֹם אֶחָד: וַיֹּאמֶר
אֱלֹהִים יְהִי רָקִיעַ בְּתוֹךְ הַמָּיִם וִיהִי מַבְדִּיל בֵּין
מַיִם לָמָיִם: . . . וַיְהִי־כֵן: וַיִּקְרָא אֱלֹהִים לָרָקִיעַ
שָׁמָיִם וַיְהִי־עֶרֶב וַיְהִי־בֹקֶר יוֹם שֵׁנִי: וַיֹּאמֶר אֱלֹהִים
יִקָּווּ הַמַּיִם מִתַּחַת הַשָּׁמַיִם אֶל־מָקוֹם אֶחָד וְתֵרָאֶה
הַיַּבָּשָׁה וַיְהִי־כֵן: . . . וַיֹּאמֶר אֱלֹהִים תַּדְשֵׁא הָאָרֶץ
דֶּשֶׁא עֵשֶׂב מַזְרִיעַ זֶרַע עֵץ פְּרִי עֹשֶׂה פְּרִי לְמִינוֹ
אֲשֶׁר זַרְעוֹ־בוֹ עַל־הָאָרֶץ וַיְהִי־כֵן: . . . וַיְהִי־עֶרֶב
וַיְהִי־בֹקֶר יוֹם שְׁלִישִׁי: וַיֹּאמֶר אֱלֹהִים יְהִי מְאֹרֹת
בִּרְקִיעַ הַשָּׁמַיִם לְהַבְדִּיל בֵּין הַיּוֹם וּבֵין הַלָּיְלָה
וְהָיוּ לְאֹתֹת וּלְמוֹעֲדִים וּלְיָמִים וְשָׁנִים: וְהָיוּ לִמְאוֹרֹת
בִּרְקִיעַ הַשָּׁמַיִם לְהָאִיר עַל־הָאָרֶץ . . . וְלִמְשֹׁל
בַּיּוֹם וּבַלַּיְלָה וּלְהַבְדִּיל בֵּין הָאוֹר וּבֵין הַחֹשֶׁךְ
וַיַּרְא אֱלֹהִים כִּי־טוֹב: וַיְהִי־עֶרֶב וַיְהִי־בֹקֶר יוֹם
רְבִיעִי: וַיֹּאמֶר אֱלֹהִים יִשְׁרְצוּ הַמַּיִם שֶׁרֶץ נֶפֶשׁ
חַיָּה וְעוֹף יְעוֹפֵף עַל־הָאָרֶץ עַל־פְּנֵי רְקִיעַ
הַשָּׁמָיִם: . . . וַיְהִי־עֶרֶב וַיְהִי־בֹקֶר יוֹם חֲמִישִׁי:

17

*(continued)*

Part of an illustration from a copy of the Egyptian Book of the Dead made for Queen Maatkare, a queen of the Twenty-First Dynasty (ca. 1087-945 B.C.E.). The scene depicts the judgment of the dead queen.

From left to right: The queen; the scales of judgment, balancing truth and the heart, and tended by Anubis, the god in charge of mortuary embalming; Thoth, the divine scribe, writing down the judgment; next to Thoth is the monster who consumes those judged unfit to enter the next world; the raised throne of Osiris, king of the world of the dead. He sits on the throne tended by his consort, Isis.

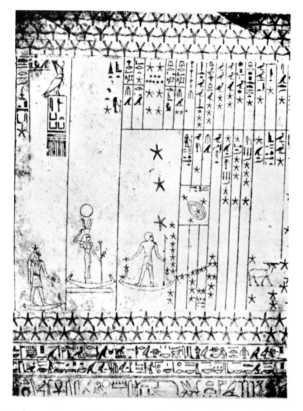

Part of an astronomical painting on the ceiling of the tomb of Senenmut (first half of 15th cent. B.C.E.), an official of the Eighteenth Dynasty. The chart depicts the various positions of the configurations of the stars (shown by symbols and divine figures) over a specified period of time as explained in the hieroglyphic inscription.

18

Mythology and religion came to be important factors in the personal and social life of men, and myths, like religions, were seized upon by those in power, as well as by those who sought to attain power, in their own interests. Kings, priest-diviners, government and military officials, landowners, merchants, craftsmen—all strove to make the religious and mythological thinking of the people serve their own ends. Eventually, a self-perpetuating priest-diviner class took shape, an intelligentsia which devoted all its time to exploring and exploiting divinity. Pantheons of gods, with appropriate mythologies and rituals of appeasement and propitiation, crystallized out of the primitive animism of prehistory, or that kind of subreligion in which all natural forces and objects are indiscriminately endowed with demonic power. Deity, like humanity, became organized.

An agricultural society needed a way of measuring time, in order to prepare for flood, drought, heat, cold, and other seasonal fluctuations. The obvious clock was the sun, moon, and the conspicuous stars, which never vary, as shepherds since time immemorial must have observed during the watches of the night. The empirical data derived from the observation of the heavenly bodies were utilized for omens. Star watching as a regular occupation naturally fell to the priests, the superior ones who could read, write, and use numbers. Thus astronomy was incorporated into the religious apparatus, and acquired ceremonial significance, both in Egypt and Mesopotamia. A knowledge of time measurement also sharpened the chronological, or historical, sense.

## Empires and Nomads

Western Asia was being constantly overrun and crisscrossed by many vigorous unsettled groups of people from 2200 to 1800 B.C.E. The Fertile Crescent, producing as it did surplus wealth, frequently attracted the more

<sup></sup>24God said, "Let the earth bring forth every kind of living creature: cattle, creeping things, and wild beasts of every kind." And it was so. 26And God said, "Let us make man in our image, after our likeness. They shall rule the fish of the sea, the birds of the sky, the cattle, the whole earth, and all the creeping things that creep on earth." 27And God created man in His image, in the image of God He created him; male and female He created them. 28God Blessed them and God said to them, "Be fertile and increase, fill the earth and master it; and rule the fish of the sea, the birds of the sky, and all the living things that creep on earth."

29God said, "See, I give you every seed-bearing plant that is upon all the earth, and every tree that has seed-bearing fruit; they shall be yours for food. 30And to all the animals on land, to all the birds of the sky, and to everything that creeps on earth, in which there is breath of life, [I give] all the green plants for food." And it was so. 31And God saw all that He had made, and found it very good. And there was evening and there was morning, the sixth day.

*Genesis 1.1-31*

וַיֹּאמֶר אֱלֹהִים תּוֹצֵא הָאָרֶץ נֶפֶשׁ חַיָּה לְמִינָהּ בְּהֵמָה
וָרֶמֶשׂ וְחַיְתוֹ־אֶרֶץ לְמִינָהּ וַיְהִי־כֵן: . . . וַיֹּאמֶר
אֱלֹהִים נַעֲשֶׂה אָדָם בְּצַלְמֵנוּ כִּדְמוּתֵנוּ וְיִרְדּוּ בִדְגַת
הַיָּם וּבְעוֹף הַשָּׁמַיִם וּבַבְּהֵמָה וּבְכָל־הָאָרֶץ וּבְכָל־
הָרֶמֶשׂ הָרֹמֵשׂ עַל־הָאָרֶץ: וַיִּבְרָא אֱלֹהִים אֶת־
הָאָדָם בְּצַלְמוֹ בְּצֶלֶם אֱלֹהִים בָּרָא אֹתוֹ זָכָר
וּנְקֵבָה בָּרָא אֹתָם: וַיְבָרֶךְ אֹתָם אֱלֹהִים וַיֹּאמֶר
לָהֶם אֱלֹהִים פְּרוּ וּרְבוּ וּמִלְאוּ אֶת־הָאָרֶץ וְכִבְשֻׁהָ
וּרְדוּ בִּדְגַת הַיָּם וּבְעוֹף הַשָּׁמַיִם וּבְכָל־חַיָּה
הָרֹמֶשֶׂת עַל־הָאָרֶץ: וַיֹּאמֶר אֱלֹהִים הִנֵּה נָתַתִּי
לָכֶם אֶת־כָּל־עֵשֶׂב זֹרֵעַ זֶרַע אֲשֶׁר עַל־פְּנֵי
כָל־הָאָרֶץ וְאֶת־כָּל־הָעֵץ אֲשֶׁר־בּוֹ פְרִי־עֵץ
זֹרֵעַ זָרַע לָכֶם יִהְיֶה לְאָכְלָה: וּלְכָל־חַיַּת הָאָרֶץ
וּלְכָל־עוֹף הַשָּׁמַיִם וּלְכֹל רוֹמֵשׂ עַל־הָאָרֶץ אֲשֶׁר־
בּוֹ נֶפֶשׁ חַיָּה אֶת־כָּל־יֶרֶק עֵשֶׂב לְאָכְלָה וַיְהִי־כֵן:
וַיַּרְא אֱלֹהִים אֶת־כָּל־אֲשֶׁר עָשָׂה וְהִנֵּה־טוֹב מְאֹד
וַיְהִי־עֶרֶב וַיְהִי־בֹקֶר יוֹם הַשִּׁשִּׁי:    בְּרֵאשִׁית א:א־לא

*Like the rest of the Near East, Israel too had its priest-diviners who were in charge of shrines (e.g., Eli and Samuel) and constituted guilds with masters and apprentices; or who were court diviners (e.g., Nathan in relation to David, Jehu the visionary in relation to Jehoshaphat). But unlike their equivalents elsewhere, Israel's seers do not seem to have practised divination by livers, entrails, the flight of birds, the spirits of the dead, star-gazing, and the like; dreams, and the use of objects, sounds, and lots (apparently the underlying function of the Urim and Thummim) were their main sources of interpretation. The rise of the prophetic movement (about 750 B.C.E. on) and the consequences of the destruction of the First Temple (586 B.C.E.) spelled the doom of the priest-diviner. See H. M. Orlinsky, "The Seer-Priest," pp. 268-279, 338-344, 353 in* The World History of the Jewish People, *Vol. III:* Judges (1971).

priest - diviners<br>forerunners of<br>Prophets

20Saul sent messengers to seize David. But when they saw the company of prophets prophesying . . . the spirit of God came upon Saul's messengers and they began to prophesy. 21This was reported to Saul, and he sent out other messengers; and they also began to prophesy. Then Saul sent messengers a third time, and they too began to prophesy . . . 23And when he set out to go there, to Naioth in Ramah, the spirit of God came upon

וַיִּשְׁלַח שָׁאוּל מַלְאָכִים לָקַחַת אֶת־דָּוִד וַיַּרְא
אֶת־לַהֲקַת הַנְּבִיאִים נִבְּאִים וּשְׁמוּאֵל עֹמֵד נִצָּב
עֲלֵיהֶם וַתְּהִי עַל־מַלְאֲכֵי שָׁאוּל רוּחַ אֱלֹהִים
וַיִּתְנַבְּאוּ גַּם־הֵמָּה: וַיַּגִּדוּ לְשָׁאוּל וַיִּשְׁלַח מַלְאָכִים
אֲחֵרִים וַיִּתְנַבְּאוּ גַּם־הֵמָּה וַיֹּסֶף שָׁאוּל וַיִּשְׁלַח
מַלְאָכִים שְׁלִשִׁים וַיִּתְנַבְּאוּ גַּם־הֵמָּה: . . . וַיֵּלֶךְ שָׁם
אֶל־נָיוֹת בָּרָמָה וַתְּהִי עָלָיו גַּם־הוּא רוּחַ אֱלֹהִים

(*continued*)

Stele commemorating a battle of King Naram-Sin, grandson of Sargon I, against a mountain people, the Lullube. The victorious king leads his soldiers up the mountain, the enemy falling away before the power of the onslaught. The uppermost figure of the enemy pleads for mercy. Found at Susa. Red sandstone; about 6½ feet high.

"cave-dwellers"

2300

One side of a broken stone monument (stele) commemorating a battle which King Sargon of Akkad successfully fought. Lower register shows the king, his servant behind him, leading soldiers. Upper register shows a line of bound and naked captives marching in a procession. On the other side (not shown) are traces of a battle scene and corpses of soldiers attacked by beasts of prey. Found at Susa. About 20 inches high.

20

primitive peoples living in the grasslands and in the highlands. The archaeological work accomplished in recent decades in this area has produced a generally clear picture of the situation. The first identifiable people to settle permanently in Mesopotamia were the Sumerians, about 3000 B.C.E.. In the earlier part of the third millennium, many Sumerian city-states were overrun by groups of Semites, and about 2300 B.C.E. the first empire in history was established by King Sargon of Akkad. About a century later a number of groups of people north and east of Akkad formed a coalition, and destroyed this Semitic empire. From about 2070 until 1960 B.C.E. the Sumerians succeeded in recapturing a goodly portion of their former glory, only to disappear forever as a sovereign people before the onslaught of several peoples from different directions. Chief among these were the Semitic Amorites from western Asia and the Elamites from the region southeast of Mesopotamia. The Amorites proceeded increasingly to dominate much of western Asia, including Syria and Palestine, and reached the peak of their influence first in Mari on the Middle Euphrates (near the modern Iraq-Syria border) and then in Babylon in the days of Hammurabi (about 1728-1686).

Another important ethnic element in the Fertile Crescent in the first half of the second millennium was the Hurrians (Biblical Horites). Shortly before 2000 B.C.E. they began to come down in ever-increasing numbers from the mountainous regions northeast of Mesopotamia, and by the end of the fifteenth century they were to be found in every part of western Asia, including Syria and Palestine, in many instances alongside the Amorites. The Hurrians attained their greatest prominence in the Mitanni Kingdom (about 1470-1350 B.C.E.), which extended from the region east of the upper part of the Tigris to the Mediterranean coast of Syria.

him also, so that he went along prophesying until he reached Naioth in Ramah. <sup>24</sup>He too stripped off his clothes and kept prophesying before Samuel; and he lay naked all that day and night. . . .

*I Samuel 19.20-24*

וַיֵּלֶךְ הָלוֹךְ וַיִּתְנַבֵּא עַד־בֹּאוֹ בְּנָיֹת בָּרָמָה: וַיִּפְשַׁט
גַּם־הוּא בְּגָדָיו וַיִּתְנַבֵּא גַם־הוּא לִפְנֵי שְׁמוּאֵל
וַיִּפֹּל עָרֹם כָּל־הַיּוֹם הַהוּא וְכָל־הַלָּיְלָה . . .

שְׁמוּאֵל א׳ יט:כ—כד

## Empires and Nomads

<sup>1</sup>These are the lines of Shem, Ham, and Japheth, the sons of Noah: sons were born to them after the flood.

<sup>2</sup>The descendants of Japheth: Gomer, Magog, Madai, Javan, Tubal, Meshech, and Tiras. . . . <sup>5</sup>From these the maritime nations branched out. [These are the descendants of Japheth] by their lands—each with its language—their clans and their nations.

<sup>6</sup>The descendants of Ham: Cush, Mizraim, Put, and Canaan...

<sup>8</sup>Cush also begot Nimrod, who was the first man of might on earth. <sup>9</sup>He was a mighty hunter by the grace of the LORD; hence the saying, "Like Nimrod a mighty hunter by the grace of the LORD." <sup>10</sup>The mainstays of his kingdom were Babylon, Erech, Accad, and Calneh in the land of Shinar. <sup>11</sup>From that land Asshur went forth and built Nineveh, Rehoboth-ir, Calah, <sup>12</sup>and Resen between Nineveh and Calah, that is the great city.

<sup>13</sup>And Mizraim begot the Ludim, the Anamim, the Lehabim, the Naphtuhim, <sup>14</sup>the Pathrusim, the Casluhim, and the Caphtorim, whence the Philistines came forth.

<sup>15</sup>Canaan begot Sidon, his first-born, and Heth; <sup>16</sup>and the Jebusites, the Amorites, the Girgashites. . . . (<sup>19</sup>The [original] Canaanite territory extended from Sidon as far as Gerar, near Gaza, and as far as Sodom, Gomorrah, Admah, and Zeboiim, near Lasha.) <sup>20</sup>These are the descendants of Ham, according to their clans and languages, by their lands and nations.

<sup>21</sup>Sons were also born to Shem, ancestor of all the descendants of Eber and older brother of Japheth. <sup>22</sup>The descendants of Shem: Elam, Asshur, Arpachshad, Lud, and Aram. <sup>23</sup>The descendants of Aram: Uz, Hul, Gether, and Mash. <sup>24</sup>Arpachshad begot Shelah, and Shelah begot Eber...

<sup>32</sup>These are the groupings of Noah's descendants, according to their origins, by their nations; and from these the nations branched out over the earth after the Flood.

*Genesis 10.1-32*

וְאֵלֶּה תּוֹלְדֹת בְּנֵי־נֹחַ שֵׁם חָם וָיָפֶת וַיִּוָּלְדוּ לָהֶם
בָּנִים אַחַר הַמַּבּוּל: בְּנֵי יֶפֶת גֹּמֶר וּמָגוֹג וּמָדַי וְיָוָן
וְתֻבָל וּמֶשֶׁךְ וְתִירָס: . . . מֵאֵלֶּה נִפְרְדוּ אִיֵּי הַגּוֹיִם
בְּאַרְצֹתָם אִישׁ לִלְשֹׁנוֹ לְמִשְׁפְּחֹתָם בְּגוֹיֵהֶם: וּבְנֵי
חָם כּוּשׁ וּמִצְרַיִם וּפוּט וּכְנָעַן: . . . וְכוּשׁ יָלַד
אֶת־נִמְרֹד הוּא הֵחֵל לִהְיוֹת גִּבֹּר בָּאָרֶץ: הוּא־
הָיָה גִבֹּר־צַיִד לִפְנֵי יְהוָה עַל־כֵּן יֵאָמַר כְּנִמְרֹד
גִּבּוֹר צַיִד לִפְנֵי יְהוָה: וַתְּהִי רֵאשִׁית מַמְלַכְתּוֹ
בָּבֶל וְאֶרֶךְ וְאַכַּד וְכַלְנֶה בְּאֶרֶץ שִׁנְעָר: מִן־
הָאָרֶץ הַהִוא יָצָא אַשּׁוּר וַיִּבֶן אֶת־נִינְוֵה וְאֶת־
רְחֹבֹת עִיר וְאֶת־כָּלַח: וְאֶת־רֶסֶן בֵּין נִינְוֵה וּבֵין
כָּלַח הִוא הָעִיר הַגְּדֹלָה: וּמִצְרַיִם יָלַד אֶת־לוּדִים
וְאֶת־עֲנָמִים וְאֶת־לְהָבִים וְאֶת־נַפְתֻּחִים: וְאֶת־
פַּתְרֻסִים וְאֶת־כַּסְלֻחִים אֲשֶׁר יָצְאוּ מִשָּׁם פְּלִשְׁתִּים
וְאֶת־כַּפְתֹּרִים: וּכְנַעַן יָלַד אֶת־צִידֹן בְּכֹרוֹ וְאֶת־
חֵת: וְאֶת־הַיְבוּסִי וְאֶת־הָאֱמֹרִי וְאֶת הַגִּרְגָּשִׁי: . . .
וַיְהִי גְּבוּל הַכְּנַעֲנִי מִצִּידֹן בֹּאֲכָה גְרָרָה עַד־
עַזָּה בֹּאֲכָה סְדֹמָה וַעֲמֹרָה וְאַדְמָה וּצְבֹיִם עַד־
לָשַׁע: אֵלֶּה בְנֵי־חָם לְמִשְׁפְּחֹתָם לִלְשֹׁנֹתָם בְּאַרְצֹתָם
בְּגוֹיֵהֶם: וּלְשֵׁם יֻלַּד גַּם־הוּא אֲבִי כָּל־בְּנֵי־עֵבֶר
אֲחִי יֶפֶת הַגָּדוֹל: בְּנֵי שֵׁם עֵילָם וְאַשּׁוּר וְאַרְפַּכְשַׁד
וְלוּד וַאֲרָם: וּבְנֵי אֲרָם עוּץ וְחוּל וְגֶתֶר וָמַשׁ:
וְאַרְפַּכְשַׁד יָלַד אֶת־שָׁלַח וְשֶׁלַח יָלַד אֶת־עֵבֶר: . . .
אֵלֶּה מִשְׁפְּחֹת בְּנֵי־נֹחַ לְתוֹלְדֹתָם בְּגוֹיֵהֶם וּמֵאֵלֶּה
נִפְרְדוּ הַגּוֹיִם בָּאָרֶץ אַחַר הַמַּבּוּל:

בְּרֵאשִׁית י:א-לב

21

**A LETTER FROM THE AMARNA ARCHIVES.**

Abimilki of Tyre writes to the king of Egypt (Akhenaton?) about the state of affairs in Northern Palestine. Among the various statements, there is the following remark: "The King of Hazor has left his fortress and has joined forces with the Habiru."

## Hebrew Beginnings and the Habiru

In this period and area of ethnic movements, the group from which the Hebrews of the Bible finally emerged took its place in documented history. From about the twentieth century B.C.E. to the twelfth a group of people appear in Near Eastern documents. They are called Habiru or Hapiru, and with them are associated the names SA.GAZ and Apiru; neither the original forms of the names nor their meanings have yet been determined. These documents derive from Mesopotamia, Asia Minor, Syria, Palestine, and Egypt.

To the limited extent that these sporadic and incomplete data permit one to draw some conclusions, it would seem that at about 2000 B.C.E. there arose a term Habiru as a name for various unsettled groups of people, Semitic and non-Semitic, chiefly the former. They wandered about as semi-nomads from one area to another, sometimes with their own flocks and sometimes as skilled craftsmen, as smiths, musicians, and the like. At other times they made sudden raids on caravans and on weak, outlying communities, or else hired themselves out for specific functions and periods of time, for example, as mercenaries and as private or government slaves. Not infrequently they became prisoners of war and state slaves doing forced labor (*corvée*). In several instances, individual Habiru rose to prominent status—for example, in the land of the Hurrians in northern Mesopotamia (about 1400 B.C.E.), in Assyria (about 1150), and in Babylonia (about 1050). Some of the Habiru settled down in conquered towns and regions and ceased to wander.

There appears to be good reason for associating the Biblical Hebrews with some of these far-flung Habiru. The Biblical account places the career of the Hebrews within the

# Hebrew Beginnings and the Habiru

*While the date of Abraham is uncertain, the kind of life that he led is known to be seminomadic, traveling up and down the land from one important center to another, when he was not pasturing his flocks for longer periods in a single region. As a seminomad, Abraham not only possessed flocks and probably had skilled craftsmen among his household, but he also trafficked in goods and articles; this would explain the source of the wealth he had amassed:* Now Abraham was very rich in cattle, silver, and gold *(Gen. 13.2)*.

[1]The LORD said to Abram, "Go forth from your native land and from your father's house to the land that I will show you.

[2]I will make of you a great nation, and I will bless you; I will make your name great, and you shall be a blessing.[a] [3]I will bless those who bless you and curse him that curses you; And all the families of the earth shall bless themselves by you.

*Genesis 12.1-3*

[5]Abram took his wife Sarai and his brother's son Lot, and all the wealth that they had amassed, and the persons that they had acquired in Haran; and they set out for the land of Canaan. When they arrived in the land of Canaan, [6]Abram passed through the land as far as the site of Shechem, at the terebinth of Moreh. The Canaanites were then in the land.

[7]The LORD appeared to Abram and said, "I will give this land to your offspring." And he built an altar there to the LORD who had appeared to him. [8]From there he moved on to the hill country east of Bethel and pitched his tent, with Bethel on the west and Ai on the east; and he built there an altar to the LORD and invoked the LORD by name. [9]Then Abram journeyed by stages toward the Negeb.

[10]There was a famine in the land, and Abram went down to Egypt to sojourn there, for the famine was severe in the land.

*Genesis 12.5-10*

[1]From Egypt, Abram went up into the Negeb, with his wife and all that he possessed, together with Lot. [2]Now Abram was very rich in cattle, silver, and gold. [3]And he proceeded by stages from the Negeb as far as Bethel, to the place where his tent had been formerly, between Bethel and Ai, [4]the site of the altar which he had built there at first; and there Abram invoked the LORD by name. [5]Lot, who went with Abram, also had flocks and herds and tents.

*Genesis 13.1-5*

וַיֹּאמֶר יְהֹוָה אֶל־אַבְרָם לֶךְ־לְךָ מֵאַרְצְךָ וּמִמּוֹלַדְתְּךָ וּמִבֵּית אָבִיךָ אֶל־הָאָרֶץ אֲשֶׁר אַרְאֶךָּ: וְאֶעֶשְׂךָ לְגוֹי גָּדוֹל וַאֲבָרֶכְךָ וַאֲגַדְּלָה שְׁמֶךָ וֶהְיֵה בְּרָכָה: וַאֲבָרֲכָה מְבָרֲכֶיךָ וּמְקַלֶּלְךָ אָאֹר וְנִבְרְכוּ בְךָ כֹּל מִשְׁפְּחֹת הָאֲדָמָה:

בְּרֵאשִׁית יב:א–ג

וַיִּקַּח אַבְרָם אֶת־שָׂרַי אִשְׁתּוֹ וְאֶת־לוֹט בֶּן־אָחִיו וְאֶת־כָּל־רְכוּשָׁם אֲשֶׁר רָכָשׁוּ וְאֶת־הַנֶּפֶשׁ אֲשֶׁר־עָשׂוּ בְחָרָן וַיֵּצְאוּ לָלֶכֶת אַרְצָה כְּנַעַן וַיָּבֹאוּ אַרְצָה כְּנָעַן: וַיַּעֲבֹר אַבְרָם בָּאָרֶץ עַד מְקוֹם שְׁכֶם עַד אֵלוֹן מוֹרֶה וְהַכְּנַעֲנִי אָז בָּאָרֶץ: וַיֵּרָא יְהֹוָה אֶל־אַבְרָם וַיֹּאמֶר לְזַרְעֲךָ אֶתֵּן אֶת־הָאָרֶץ הַזֹּאת וַיִּבֶן שָׁם מִזְבֵּחַ לַיהֹוָה הַנִּרְאֶה אֵלָיו: וַיַּעְתֵּק מִשָּׁם הָהָרָה מִקֶּדֶם לְבֵית־אֵל וַיֵּט אָהֳלֹה בֵּית־אֵל מִיָּם וְהָעַי מִקֶּדֶם וַיִּבֶן־שָׁם מִזְבֵּחַ לַיהֹוָה וַיִּקְרָא בְּשֵׁם יְהֹוָה: וַיִּסַּע אַבְרָם הָלוֹךְ וְנָסוֹעַ הַנֶּגְבָּה: וַיְהִי רָעָב בָּאָרֶץ וַיֵּרֶד אַבְרָם מִצְרַיְמָה לָגוּר שָׁם כִּי־כָבֵד הָרָעָב בָּאָרֶץ:

בְּרֵאשִׁית יב:ה–י

וַיַּעַל אַבְרָם מִמִּצְרַיִם הוּא וְאִשְׁתּוֹ וְכָל־אֲשֶׁר־לוֹ וְלוֹט עִמּוֹ הַנֶּגְבָּה: וְאַבְרָם כָּבֵד מְאֹד בַּמִּקְנֶה בַּכֶּסֶף וּבַזָּהָב: וַיֵּלֶךְ לְמַסָּעָיו מִנֶּגֶב וְעַד־בֵּית־אֵל עַד־הַמָּקוֹם אֲשֶׁר־הָיָה שָׁם אָהֳלֹה בַּתְּחִלָּה בֵּין בֵּית־אֵל וּבֵין הָעָי: אֶל־מְקוֹם הַמִּזְבֵּחַ אֲשֶׁר עָשָׂה שָׁם בָּרִאשֹׁנָה וַיִּקְרָא שָׁם אַבְרָם בְּשֵׁם יְהֹוָה: וְגַם־לְלוֹט הַהֹלֵךְ אֶת־אַבְרָם הָיָה צֹאן־וּבָקָר וְאֹהָלִים:

בְּרֵאשִׁית יג:א–ה

23

Stele cut for King Hammurabi of Babylon (18th century B.C.E.). On the relief at the top, the king is shown worshiping (or approaching as an adorant) the seated figure of the god Shamash, the divine judge. The text, which is a collection of laws given by Shamash to Hammurabi for the Babylonians, is engraved below the relief. About 7 feet 4 inches high.

From the Prologue of Hammurabi's "Code"

When Lofty Anum (sky god), king of the Anunnaki (lesser gods),
and Enlil (storm god), lord of heaven and earth,
the determiner of the destinies of the land,
determined for Marduk (god of Babylon[ia]) . . .
the Enlil functions over all mankind . . .
at that time Anum and Enlil named me
to promote the welfare of the people,
me, Hammurabi, the devout, god-fearing prince,
to cause justice to prevail in the land,
to destroy the wicked and the evil,
that the strong might not oppress the weak . . .

general orbit of the activities of some of the Habiru groups in the different lands of the Near East and in the different epochs of the second millennium B.C.E.; this can scarcely be merely a series of many remarkable coincidences.

Hebrew origins begin essentially with Abraham the son of Terah (Genesis 11), whose origin is located in the region of Ur in southern Mesopotamia, less than thirty miles from Larsa, where Habiru are found about 1900 B.C.E. Ur was an extremely important center in this very period. Terah is said to have moved with his household about six hundred miles to Haran (or Harran) in northwestern Mesopotamia, and after Terah died Abraham took his own immediate family and began the long journey to Canaan. Abraham retained contact with his family in Haran, to the point of seeking out a wife for his son Isaac from the family of Laban, grandson of Abraham's brother Nahor. Isaac's son Jacob also went to this region to acquire a wife, of the family of the same Laban. Haran was a flourishing city in the Balikh Valley at this time, and Habiru were found there in this period.

Habiru dwelt in the northwest part of the Babylonian empire during the eighteenth and seventeenth centuries B.C.E., the period made famous by King Hammurabi, and in the succeeding centuries they inhabited many of the Hurrian-controlled parts of western Asia. The Book of Genesis especially, dealing with the ideas and customs of the patriarchal period of the Hebrews, reflects clearly this early milieu of the Babylonians, Amorites (western Semites), and Hurrians. The prophet Ezekiel, in the sixth century B.C.E., knew well this fact when he addressed Jerusalem in the following words: "Your origin and your birth are of the land of the Canaanite; your father was an Amorite, and

*Biblical Israel was always conscious of its Mesopotamian origins and early contacts—contrast its abhorrence for the Egyptian way of life!—and all three Patriarchs married Mesopotamian girls of Hebraic stock. It is likely that the constant trade with the regions north and east of Israel—with its resultant cultural interplay—was a major factor in this attitude. See S. Yeivin, "The Patriarchs in the Land of Canaan," pp. 201-218, 282-4, 296 in* The World History of the Jewish People, *Vol. III:* Judges *(1971).*

[31]Terah took his son Abram, his grandson Lot the son of Haran, and his daughter-in-law Sarai, the wife of his son Abram, and they set out together from Ur of the Chaldeans for the land of Canaan; but when they had come as far as Haran, they settled there. [32]The days of Terah came to 205 years; and Terah died in Haran.

*Genesis 11.31-32*

וַיִּקַּח תֶּרַח אֶת־אַבְרָם בְּנוֹ וְאֶת־לוֹט בֶּן־הָרָן
בֶּן־בְּנוֹ וְאֵת שָׂרַי כַּלָּתוֹ אֵשֶׁת אַבְרָם בְּנוֹ וַיֵּצְאוּ אִתָּם
מֵאוּר כַּשְׂדִּים לָלֶכֶת אַרְצָה כְּנַעַן וַיָּבֹאוּ עַד־חָרָן
וַיֵּשְׁבוּ שָׁם: וַיִּהְיוּ יְמֵי־תֶרַח חָמֵשׁ שָׁנִים וּמָאתַיִם שָׁנָה
וַיָּמָת תֶּרַח בְּחָרָן:

בְּרֵאשִׁית יא:לא-לב

[4]The word of the LORD came to him in reply, "That one shall not be your heir; none but your very own issue shall be your heir."

*Genesis 15.4*

וְהִנֵּה דְבַר־יְהוָה אֵלָיו לֵאמֹר לֹא יִירָשְׁךָ זֶה
כִּי־אִם אֲשֶׁר יֵצֵא מִמֵּעֶיךָ הוּא יִירָשֶׁךָ:

בְּרֵאשִׁית טו:ד

[1]Abraham was now old, advanced in years, and the LORD had blessed Abraham in all things. [2]And Abraham said to the senior servant of his household, who had charge of all that he owned, "Put your hand under my thigh [3]and I will make you swear by the LORD, the God of heaven and the God of the earth, that you will not take a wife for my son from the daughters of the Canaanites among whom I dwell, [4]but will go to my native land and get a wife for my son Isaac." . . . [10]. . .Then the servant took ten of his master's camels and set out, taking with him all the bounty of his master; and he made his way to Aram-naharaim, to the city of Nahor. . . .

[ [57]And they said, "Let us call the girl and ask for her reply."] [58]They called Rebekah and said to her, "Will you go with this man?" And she said, "I will." [59]So they sent off their sister Rebekah and her nurse along with Abraham's servant and his men. [60]And they blessed Rebekah and said to her,

"Oh sister!
May you grow into thousands of myriads;
May your offspring seize the gates of their foes."

. . .[67]Isaac then brought her into the tent of his mother Sarah, and he took Rebekah as his wife. Isaac loved her, and thus found comfort after his mother's death.

*Genesis 24.1-67*

וְאַבְרָהָם זָקֵן בָּא בַּיָּמִים וַיהוָה בֵּרַךְ אֶת־
אַבְרָהָם בַּכֹּל: וַיֹּאמֶר אַבְרָהָם אֶל־עַבְדּוֹ זְקַן בֵּיתוֹ
הַמֹּשֵׁל בְּכָל־אֲשֶׁר־לוֹ שִׂים־נָא יָדְךָ תַּחַת יְרֵכִי:
וְאַשְׁבִּיעֲךָ בַּיהוָה אֱלֹהֵי הַשָּׁמַיִם וֵאלֹהֵי הָאָרֶץ
אֲשֶׁר לֹא־תִקַּח אִשָּׁה לִבְנִי מִבְּנוֹת הַכְּנַעֲנִי אֲשֶׁר
אָנֹכִי יוֹשֵׁב בְּקִרְבּוֹ: כִּי אֶל־אַרְצִי וְאֶל־מוֹלַדְתִּי
תֵּלֵךְ וְלָקַחְתָּ אִשָּׁה לִבְנִי לְיִצְחָק: . . . וַיִּקַּח הָעֶבֶד
עֲשָׂרָה גְמַלִּים מִגְּמַלֵּי אֲדֹנָיו וַיֵּלֶךְ וְכָל־טוּב אֲדֹנָיו
בְּיָדוֹ וַיָּקָם וַיֵּלֶךְ אֶל־אֲרַם נַהֲרַיִם אֶל־עִיר נָחוֹר:
. . . וַיִּקְרְאוּ לְרִבְקָה וַיֹּאמְרוּ אֵלֶיהָ הֲתֵלְכִי עִם־
הָאִישׁ הַזֶּה וַתֹּאמֶר אֵלֵךְ: וַיְשַׁלְּחוּ אֶת־רִבְקָה
אֲחֹתָם וְאֶת־מֵנִקְתָּהּ וְאֶת־עֶבֶד אַבְרָהָם וְאֶת־
אֲנָשָׁיו: וַיְבָרֲכוּ אֶת־רִבְקָה וַיֹּאמְרוּ לָהּ אֲחֹתֵנוּ אַתְּ
הֲיִי לְאַלְפֵי רְבָבָה וְיִירַשׁ זַרְעֵךְ אֵת שַׁעַר שֹׂנְאָיו: . . .
וַיְבִאֶהָ יִצְחָק הָאֹהֱלָה שָׂרָה אִמּוֹ וַיִּקַּח אֶת־רִבְקָה
וַתְּהִי־לוֹ לְאִשָּׁה וַיֶּאֱהָבֶהָ וַיִּנָּחֵם יִצְחָק אַחֲרֵי אִמּוֹ:

בְּרֵאשִׁית כד:א-סז

## TRADITIONAL LINEAGE OF ABRA(HA)M THE HEBREW

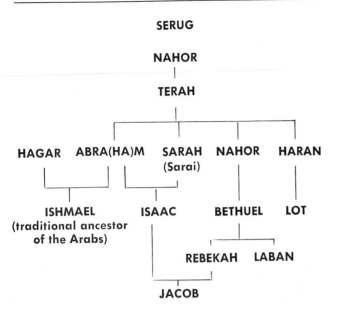

SERUG

NAHOR

TERAH

HAGAR · ABRA(HA)M · SARAH (Sarai) · NAHOR · HARAN

ISHMAEL (traditional ancestor of the Arabs) · ISAAC · BETHUEL · LOT

REBEKAH · LABAN

JACOB

According to this tradition, Abraham, Nahor, and Haran are all brothers, sons of Terah, and Sarah who married Abraham, is their half-sister. Ishmael, Isaac, Bethuel, and Lot are all first cousins, sons of the three brothers: Abraham, Nahor, and Haran. Rebekah is Isaac's niece.

### THE HILL COUNTRY IN CANAAN-ISRAEL

As seminomads in a land whose fertile lowlands and valleys were already occupied, the patriarchal clans would pitch their tents in the relatively unoccupied parts of the Hill Country that were close to permanent settlements; thus they had pasturage for their flocks and herds and commercial dealings with their sedentary neighbors.

A typical area of the Hill Country in central Canaan-Israel, where the patriarchal families encamped.

26

your mother was a Hittite" (Ezekiel 16:3, 45). It is now believed that when Rachel took the "teraphim" (household objects, perhaps gods) of her father Laban (Genesis 31), it was probably to give her husband Jacob some kind of authority, perhaps property rights; among the Hurrians, possession of the household gods went from father to son.

Many of the Biblical personal names in the patriarchal period are typical of the names employed in western Asia, especially among the Amorites, in the first half of the second millennium. Among these names may be cited Terah, Serug his grandfather, Nahor his father and his son, Haran and perhaps Abraham (or Abram), his other sons, as well as Jacob and Benjamin.

The Biblical writers recognized many groups of Hebrews in different times and lands, just as the contemporaneous, extra-Biblical records indicate the existence of many groups of Habiru throughout the Fertile Crescent during the second millennium B.C.E. When Terah left Ur for Haran, he left behind him the Hebrew family of his married son Nahor, from whom ultimately there came such peoples as the Arameans (Genesis 11:26 ff.; 22:20–24). In fact, Nahor's son Bethuel, Abraham's nephew, is referred to in the Bible (Genesis 25:20) as an Aramean; and Abraham's grandson Jacob, who married Bethuel's granddaughters, Leah and Rachel, is described once as "a nomad (or, fugitive) Aramean" (Deuteronomy 26:5). In Canaan, Abraham's nephew Lot raised a considerable Hebrew family, from which there developed, among others, the two kindred nations of the Hebrews, the Moabites and the Ammonites (Genesis 19). Abraham's son Ishmael (since Mohammed, the traditional ancestor of the Arabs), born to him by Hagar the Egyptian maidservant

³You shall say, "So said the Lord God to Jerusalem: Your origin and your kindred are from the land of the Canaanites—your father an Amorite, and your mother a Hittite."

*Ezekiel 16.3*

²⁷Now this is the line of Terah: Terah begot Abram, Nahor, and Haran; and Haran begot Lot. ²⁸Haran died in the lifetime of his father Terah, in his native land, Ur of the Chaldeans. ²⁹Abram and Nahor took to themselves wives, the name of Abram's wife being Sarai and that of Nahor's wife, Milcah, the daughter of Haran, the father of Milcah and Iscah. . . . ³¹Terah took his son Abram, his grandson Lot the son of Haran, and his daughter-in-law Sarai, the wife of his son Abram, and they set out together from Ur of the Chaldeans for the land of Canaan; but when they had come as far as Haran, they settled there.

*Genesis 11.27-31*

²⁰Some time later, Abraham was told, "Milcah too has borne children to your brother Nahor: ²¹Uz the first-born, and Buz his brother, and Kemuel the father of Aram;²² . . . and Bethuel"— ²³Bethuel being the father of Rebekah. . . .

*Genesis 22.20-23*

²⁰Isaac was forty years old when he took to wife Rebekah, daughter of Bethuel the Aramean of Paddan-aram, sister of Laban the Aramean.

*Genesis 25.20*

⁵You shall then recite as follows before the LORD your God: "My father was a fugitive Aramean. He went down to Egypt with meager numbers and sojourned there; but there he became a great and very populous nation.

*Deuteronomy 26.5*

[³⁶Thus the two daughters of Lot came to be with child by their father.]³⁷The older one bore a son and named him Moab; he is the father of the Moabites of today. ³⁸And the younger also bore a son, and she called him Ben-ammi; he is the father of the Ammonites of today.

*Genesis 19.36-38*

וְאָמַרְתָּ כֹּה־אָמַר אֲדֹנָי יֱהוִה לִירוּשָׁלַ͏ִם מְכֹרֹתַיִךְ וּמֹלְדֹתַיִךְ מֵאֶרֶץ הַכְּנַעֲנִי אָבִיךְ הָאֱמֹרִי וְאִמֵּךְ חִתִּית:

יְחֶזְקֵאל טז:ג

וְאֵלֶּה תּוֹלְדֹת תֶּרַח תֶּרַח הוֹלִיד אֶת־אַבְרָם אֶת־נָחוֹר וְאֶת־הָרָן וְהָרָן הוֹלִיד אֶת־לוֹט: וַיָּמָת הָרָן עַל־פְּנֵי תֶּרַח אָבִיו בְּאֶרֶץ מוֹלַדְתּוֹ בְּאוּר כַּשְׂדִּים: וַיִּקַּח אַבְרָם וְנָחוֹר לָהֶם נָשִׁים שֵׁם אֵשֶׁת־אַבְרָם שָׂרָי וְשֵׁם אֵשֶׁת־נָחוֹר מִלְכָּה בַּת־הָרָן אֲבִי־מִלְכָּה וַאֲבִי יִסְכָּה: . . . וַיִּקַּח תֶּרַח אֶת־אַבְרָם בְּנוֹ וְאֶת־לוֹט בֶּן־הָרָן בֶּן־בְּנוֹ וְאֵת שָׂרַי כַּלָּתוֹ אֵשֶׁת אַבְרָם בְּנוֹ וַיֵּצְאוּ אִתָּם מֵאוּר כַּשְׂדִּים לָלֶכֶת אַרְצָה כְּנַעַן וַיָּבֹאוּ עַד־חָרָן וַיֵּשְׁבוּ שָׁם:

בְּרֵאשִׁית יא:כז־לא

וַיְהִי אַחֲרֵי הַדְּבָרִים הָאֵלֶּה וַיֻּגַּד לְאַבְרָהָם לֵאמֹר הִנֵּה יָלְדָה מִלְכָּה גַם־הִוא בָּנִים לְנָחוֹר אָחִיךָ: אֶת־עוּץ בְּכֹרוֹ וְאֶת־בּוּז אָחִיו וְאֶת־קְמוּאֵל אֲבִי אֲרָם: . . . וְאֵת בְּתוּאֵל: וּבְתוּאֵל יָלַד אֶת־רִבְקָה . . .

בְּרֵאשִׁית כב:כ־כג

וַיְהִי יִצְחָק בֶּן־אַרְבָּעִים שָׁנָה בְּקַחְתּוֹ אֶת־רִבְקָה בַּת־בְּתוּאֵל הָאֲרַמִּי מִפַּדַּן אֲרָם אֲחוֹת לָבָן הָאֲרַמִּי לוֹ לְאִשָּׁה:

בְּרֵאשִׁית כה:כ

poss.

וְעָנִיתָ וְאָמַרְתָּ לִפְנֵי יְהֹוָה אֱלֹהֶיךָ אֲרַמִּי אֹבֵד אָבִי וַיֵּרֶד מִצְרַיְמָה וַיָּגָר שָׁם בִּמְתֵי מְעָט וַיְהִי־שָׁם לְגוֹי גָּדוֹל עָצוּם וָרָב:

דְּבָרִים כו:ה

וַתֵּלֶד הַבְּכִירָה בֵּן וַתִּקְרָא שְׁמוֹ מוֹאָב הוּא אֲבִי־מוֹאָב עַד־הַיּוֹם: וְהַצְּעִירָה גַם־הִוא יָלְדָה בֵּן וַתִּקְרָא שְׁמוֹ בֶּן־עַמִּי הוּא אֲבִי בְנֵי־עַמּוֹן עַד־הַיּוֹם:

בְּרֵאשִׁית יט:לז־לח

## THE PATRIARCHS AND MATRIARCHS OF ISRAEL

( Biblical lineage of the Patriarchal families.)

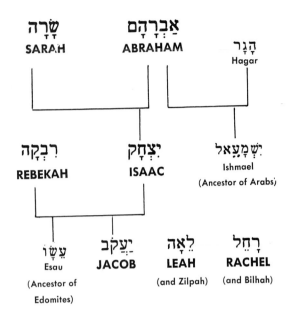

PATRIARCHS: ABRAHAM, ISAAC, AND JACOB

MATRIARCHS: SARAH, REBEKAH, LEAH , AND RACHEL

## ABRAHAM'S WANDERINGS AND THE HABIRU

The regions and cities in Western Asia associated in the Book of Genesis with the journeys and sojourns of Abraham, Isaac, and Jacob fall within the orbit of Habiru activity. Whether as Habiru, Hapiru, SA-GAZ., or Apiru, they are found from the 21st to the 11th cent. B.C.E. in such places as Ur, Larsa, Alishar, Mari, Nuzu, and Alalakh.

28

of Sarah, gave rise to a large and varied number of tribes (Genesis 25:12–18); and the same is true of the progeny born to Abraham by his second wife, Keturah—notably, the Midianites (25:1–4). Isaac's older son Esau was the progenitor of a very abundant and important number of tribes and peoples, including the Amalekites and the Edomites (Genesis 36).

There is considerable similarity between the Hebrews and a number of the non-Hebrew descendants of Abraham in the kinds of personal names employed by them. Such names as Bela, Saul, and Achbor are Edomite as well as Hebrew (Israelite). Jobab is an Arabian, an Edomite, and also an Israelite name. Reuel is the name borne by a son of Esau (by his wife Bosnath, a daughter of Ishmael), by Moses' Midianite father-in-law, and by a member of the tribe of Gad; in abbreviated form, Reu, it is the name also of Abraham's great-grandfather. But this point need not be labored here further.

It is an interesting fact that the term Habiru ceased to occur in extra-Biblical sources at about the same time that the term Hebrew ceased to be used in the Bible. Before the end of the second millennium, those of the Habiru groups which had conquered and become associated with specific territories acquired new, national names; the rest of the Habiru had become absorbed by the various settled communities in which they found themselves. The story of the name "Hebrews" is about the same. Originally associated with some of these far-flung Habiru groups, the Hebrews of the Bible came in time to lead a career of their own in a specific region, namely, Canaan; and the name Hebrews gave way to the name Israelites (literally, "Children of Israel") when the nation came into being. The other Habiru groups which had become nations in their

*While the kind of genealogies cited here cannot be checked in detail, they may be accepted as reliable overall; for Israel would hardly have gone out of its way in a later period to create such close ethnic relationship with the generally unfriendly Midianites, Amalekites, Edomites, Moabites, and the like.*

*Interestingly, out of the entire Hebrew Bible, it is precisely the genealogy of Genesis 10—where the descendants of Noah's three sons, Shem, Ham, and Japheth, are listed—that the widely-publicized historian, Arnold Toynbee, found inspiring. It is not Moses, or David, or Elijah, or Amos, or Micah, or the Psalmist, or Job, among others, who aroused in him something to remember and recall gratefully, but the "begats!" But then Toynbee had confessed to a "dim spot . . . I am ignorant of the Rabbinical Jewish literature . . . my neglect of Israel, Judah, the Jews, and Judaism. . . . Since childhood, Hebrew had left me cold. . . . This partiality is evidently irrational. . . ." Evidently, a confessedly ignorant and irrational disparager of the Jewish people regards himself as qualified to write about them! (From H. M. Orlinsky, "On Toynbee's Use of the Term 'Syriac' for One of His Societies," pp. 255-269 in A. H. Silver Jubilee Volume, Macmillan, N.Y., 1963.)*

<sup>12</sup>This is the line of Ishmael, Abraham's son, whom Hagar the Egyptian, Sarah's slave, bore to Abraham. <sup>13</sup>These are the names of the sons of Ishmael, by their names, in the order of their birth: Nebaioth, the first-born of Ishmael, Kedar . . . <sup>16</sup> . . . by their villages and their encampments: twelve chieftains of as many tribes. . . . <sup>18</sup>They dwelt from Havilah, by Shur, which is close to Egypt, all the way to Asshur; they camped alongside their kinsmen.

*Genesis 25.12-18*

וְאֵלֶּה תֹּלְדֹת יִשְׁמָעֵאל בֶּן־אַבְרָהָם אֲשֶׁר יָלְדָה הָגָר הַמִּצְרִית שִׁפְחַת שָׂרָה לְאַבְרָהָם: וְאֵלֶּה שְׁמוֹת בְּנֵי יִשְׁמָעֵאל בִּשְׁמֹתָם לְתוֹלְדֹתָם בְּכֹר יִשְׁמָעֵאל נְבָיֹת וְקֵדָר . . . בְּחַצְרֵיהֶם וּבְטִירֹתָם שְׁנֵים־עָשָׂר נְשִׂיאִם לְאֻמֹּתָם: . . . וַיִּשְׁכְּנוּ מֵחֲוִילָה עַד־שׁוּר אֲשֶׁר עַל־פְּנֵי מִצְרַיִם בֹּאֲכָה אַשּׁוּרָה עַל־פְּנֵי כָל־אֶחָיו נָפָל:

בְּרֵאשִׁית כה:יב–יח

<sup>1</sup>Abraham took another wife, whose name was Keturah. <sup>2</sup>She bore him Zimran, Jokshan, Medan, Midian . . . <sup>3</sup>Jokshan begot Sheba and Dedan . . . <sup>4</sup>The descendants of Midian were Ephah, Epher, Enoch. . . .

*Genesis 25.1-4*

וַיֹּסֶף אַבְרָהָם וַיִּקַּח אִשָּׁה וּשְׁמָהּ קְטוּרָה: וַתֵּלֶד לוֹ אֶת־זִמְרָן וְאֶת־יָקְשָׁן וְאֶת־מְדָן וְאֶת־מִדְיָן . . . וְיָקְשָׁן יָלַד אֶת־שְׁבָא וְאֶת־דְּדָן . . . וּבְנֵי מִדְיָן עֵיפָה וָעֵפֶר וַחֲנֹךְ . . .

בְּרֵאשִׁית כה:א–ד

<sup>18</sup>When Peleg had lived 30 years, he begot Reu.

*Genesis 11.18*

וַיְחִי־פֶלֶג שְׁלֹשִׁים שָׁנָה וַיּוֹלֶד אֶת־רְעוּ:

בְּרֵאשִׁית יא:יח

<sup>10</sup>These are the names of Esau's sons: Eliphaz, the son of Esau's wife Adah; Reuel, the son of Esau's wife Basemath.

*Genesis 36.10*

אֵלֶּה שְׁמוֹת בְּנֵי־עֵשָׂו אֱלִיפַז בֶּן־עָדָה אֵשֶׁת עֵשָׂו רְעוּאֵל בֶּן־בָּשְׂמַת אֵשֶׁת עֵשָׂו:

בְּרֵאשִׁית לו:י

<sup>13</sup>A fugitive brought the news to Abram the Hebrew, who was dwelling at the terebinths of Mamre the Amorite, kinsman of Eshkol and Aner, these being Abram's allies.

*Genesis 14.13*

וַיָּבֹא הַפָּלִיט וַיַּגֵּד לְאַבְרָם הָעִבְרִי וְהוּא שֹׁכֵן בְּאֵלֹנֵי מַמְרֵא הָאֱמֹרִי אֲחִי אֶשְׁכֹּל וַאֲחִי עָנֵר וְהֵם בַּעֲלֵי בְרִית־אַבְרָם:

בְּרֵאשִׁית יד:יג

29

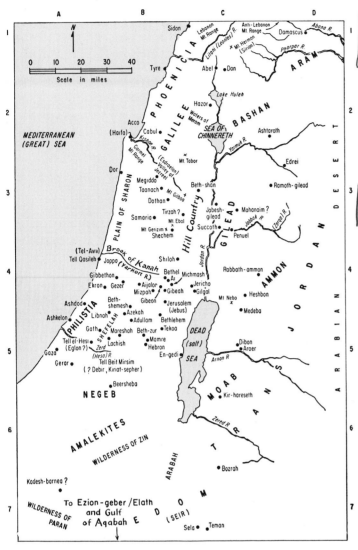

**MAP OF CANAAN SHOWING MAJOR RIVERS, MOUNTAIN RANGES, RIVER VALLEYS, AND COASTAL PLAINS.**

own right acquired new names too: Moabites, Ammonites, Edomites, and Midianites. Thus the Biblical term Hebrew was never employed for the nation any more than the term Habiru was.

A notable similarity between the Habiru and the Hebrews is to be found in the expressions "the gods of the Habiru" among the former, and "the God of the Hebrews" among the latter (Exodus 3:18; 5:3; etc.). When the Habiru entered into an agreement with another party, "the gods of the Habiru" were sometimes invoked, together with the gods of the other parties, as divine witnesses. Since the term "Hebrew" did not become associated with a sovereign land any more than "Habiru," the expression "The God of the Hebrews" is perfectly analogous.

## The Patriarchs in Canaan

Abraham and his immediate descendants and relatives, including his nephew Lot, led a career which was characteristic of those days. They constituted a seminomadic group which settled for a while in a convenient region among the Semitic and non-Semitic (especially Hurrian and Hittite) people of the land, and then, as shepherds, artisans, or merchants went on to another region. The land of the Canaanites, southern Syria and Palestine, was eminently suited to such free movement at that time. About 1800 B.C.E., western Palestine and southern Syria were generally occupied by city-states, largely under Egyptian control. Because the lowlands had the best soil and water supply, the cities of Palestine were located mostly along the Mediterranean coastal plain, in the valley of Jezreel (Esdraelon), and in the valley of the Jordan.

Central Palestine, the hilly region between the Jordan Valley and the coastal plain, was only sporadically settled. Though ill-suited for agriculture, it was inviting enough to

30

<sup>16</sup>And God said further to Moses. . . . <sup>17</sup>"Go
and assemble the elders of Israel . . .

<sup>18</sup>. . . then you shall go with the elders of Israel
to the king of Egypt and you shall say to him,
'The Lord, the God of the Hebrews, manifested
Himself to us. Now therefore, let us go a distance
of three days into the wilderness to sacrifice to
the Lord our God.' . . ."

*Exodus 3.16-18*

וַיֹּאמֶר עוֹד אֱלֹהִים אֶל־מֹשֶׁה . . . לֵךְ וְאָסַפְתָּ
אֶת־זִקְנֵי יִשְׂרָאֵל . . . וּבָאתָ אַתָּה וְזִקְנֵי יִשְׂרָאֵל
אֶל־מֶלֶךְ מִצְרַיִם וַאֲמַרְתֶּם אֵלָיו יְהֹוָה אֱלֹהֵי
הָעִבְרִיִּים נִקְרָה עָלֵינוּ וְעַתָּה נֵלְכָה־נָּא דֶּרֶךְ
שְׁלֹשֶׁת יָמִים בַּמִּדְבָּר וְנִזְבְּחָה לַיהֹוָה אֱלֹהֵינוּ:
שְׁמוֹת ג:טז–יח

<sup>3</sup>They answered "The God of the Hebrews has
manifested Himself to us. Let us go, we pray, a
distance of three days into the wilderness to sacrifice to the Lord our God, lest He strike us with
pestilence or sword."

*Exodus 5.3*

וַיֹּאמְרוּ אֱלֹהֵי הָעִבְרִים נִקְרָא עָלֵינוּ נֵלְכָה נָּא
דֶּרֶךְ שְׁלֹשֶׁת יָמִים בַּמִּדְבָּר וְנִזְבְּחָה לַיהֹוָה אֱלֹהֵינוּ
פֶּן־יִפְגָּעֵנוּ בַּדֶּבֶר אוֹ בֶחָרֶב:
שְׁמוֹת ה:ג

## The Patriarchs in Canaan

<sup>1</sup>From Egypt, Abram went up into the Negeb,
with his wife and all that he possessed, together
with Lot. <sup>2</sup>Now Abram was very rich in cattle,
silver, and gold. <sup>3</sup>And he proceeded by stages
from the Negeb as far as Bethel, to the place
where his tent had been formerly, between Bethel
and Ai, <sup>4</sup>the site of the altar which he had built
there at first; and there Abram invoked the Lord
by name.

<sup>5</sup>Lot, who went with Abram, also had flocks
and herds and tents, <sup>6</sup>so that the land could not
support them staying together; for their possessions were so great that they could not remain together. <sup>7</sup>And there was quarreling between the
herdsmen of Abram's cattle and those of Lot's
cattle. The Canaanites and Perizzites were then
dwelling in the land. <sup>8</sup>Abram said to Lot, "Let
there be no strife between you and me, between
my herdsmen and yours, for we are kinsmen. <sup>9</sup>Is
not the whole land before you? Let us separate:
if you go north, I will go south; and if you go
south, I will go north." . . .

<sup>11</sup>So Lot chose for himself the whole plain of
the Jordan, and Lot journeyed eastward. Thus
they parted from each other; <sup>12</sup>Abram remained
in the land of Canaan, while Lot settled in the
cities of the Plain, pitching his tents near Sodom.

*Genesis 13.1-12*

וַיַּעַל אַבְרָם מִמִּצְרַיִם הוּא וְאִשְׁתּוֹ וְכָל־אֲשֶׁר־
לוֹ וְלוֹט עִמּוֹ הַנֶּגְבָּה: וְאַבְרָם כָּבֵד מְאֹד בַּמִּקְנֶה
בַּכֶּסֶף וּבַזָּהָב: וַיֵּלֶךְ לְמַסָּעָיו מִנֶּגֶב וְעַד־בֵּית־אֵל
עַד־הַמָּקוֹם אֲשֶׁר־הָיָה שָׁם אָהֳלֹה בַּתְּחִלָּה בֵּין
בֵּית־אֵל וּבֵין הָעָי: אֶל־מְקוֹם הַמִּזְבֵּחַ אֲשֶׁר־עָשָׂה
שָׁם בָּרִאשֹׁנָה וַיִּקְרָא שָׁם אַבְרָם בְּשֵׁם יְהֹוָה:
וְגַם־לְלוֹט הַהֹלֵךְ אֶת־אַבְרָם הָיָה צֹאן־וּבָקָר
וְאֹהָלִים: וְלֹא־נָשָׂא אֹתָם הָאָרֶץ לָשֶׁבֶת יַחְדָּו
כִּי־הָיָה רְכוּשָׁם רָב וְלֹא־יָכְלוּ לָשֶׁבֶת יַחְדָּו:
וַיְהִי־רִיב בֵּין רֹעֵי מִקְנֵה־אַבְרָם וּבֵין רֹעֵי מִקְנֵה־
לוֹט וְהַכְּנַעֲנִי וְהַפְּרִזִּי אָז יֹשֵׁב בָּאָרֶץ: וַיֹּאמֶר
אַבְרָם אֶל־לוֹט אַל־נָא תְהִי מְרִיבָה בֵּינִי וּבֵינֶךָ
וּבֵין רֹעַי וּבֵין רֹעֶיךָ כִּי־אֲנָשִׁים אַחִים אֲנָחְנוּ:
הֲלֹא כָל־הָאָרֶץ לְפָנֶיךָ הִפָּרֶד נָא מֵעָלָי אִם־
הַשְּׂמֹאל וְאֵימִנָה וְאִם־הַיָּמִין וְאַשְׂמְאִילָה: . . .
וַיִּבְחַר־לוֹ לוֹט אֵת כָּל־כִּכַּר הַיַּרְדֵּן וַיִּסַּע לוֹט
מִקֶּדֶם וַיִּפָּרְדוּ אִישׁ מֵעַל אָחִיו: אַבְרָם יָשַׁב
בְּאֶרֶץ־כְּנַעַן וְלוֹט יָשַׁב בְּעָרֵי הַכִּכָּר וַיֶּאֱהַל
עַד־סְדֹם:
בְּרֵאשִׁית יג:א–יב

Painted wooden figure of Sen-Usert I, in whose reign Sinuhe returned from exile in Syria to Egypt. Height about 24 inches.

**THE TALE OF SINUHE**

A portion of the Egyptian text written on papyrus in hieratic (a simplified cursive form of hieroglyphics), which tells about the sojourn of the author, an Egyptian official named Sinuhe, in Upper Retenu (Syria) in the days of Nefru, daughter of Amenemhet I and wife of her brother Sen-Usert I (ca. 1971-1928 B.C.E.).

32

nomads with sheep and goats to graze. And so it was to this hill country, and to the even emptier and drier Negeb below, that Abraham and his family tended. In the Hill Country the patriarchs were associated with such places as Mamre, Bethel, Shechem, and Dothan (Map p. 30). It is now known archaeologically that the last three places existed in this period; and Mamre, it would seem, was employed as the place-name in Abraham's time only because the better known Hebron was not yet founded (about 1700 B.C.E.).

In the Negeb, Beersheba was the focal point, as it has remained ever since. In Abraham's time Sodom and Gomorrah and other towns in the Vale of Siddim, at the southern end of the Dead Sea, were flourishing, and archaeology supports the Biblical story of their catastrophic end.

The patriarchal seminomadic mode of life required a relatively simple social structure. The father was the head of the family. The sons and daughters, with their spouses and children, were all subject to the authority of the patriarch. By tribal law, the oldest son succeeded the father upon his death. The tribe lived from its herds and flocks and from the itinerant labor of its craftsmen members —for example, the smiths and musicians.

Two Egyptian sources reproduce extraordinarily well the social atmosphere breathed in Genesis. An Egyptian by the name of Sinuhe tells of his experiences in southern Syria and northern Palestine during the latter half of the twentieth century B.C.E. He relates, in the "Tale of Sinuhe," how an important Amorite ruler in Syria took him in and married him to his oldest daughter:

He set me at the head of his children. He married me to his eldest daughter. . . . He made me ruler of a tribe of the choicest of the country. Bread was made for me as daily fare, wine as daily provision, cooked meat and roast fowl, beside the

*The more important towns in pre-patriarchal Canaan were not only commercial and political but also religious centers. Old sites with names that began with Beth, e.g., Beth-shemesh, Beth-dagon, Beth-shean, and Beth-lehem, contained a shrine (beth, literally "house") of the god indicated by the rest of the name, namely, of the god Shemesh, or Dagon, or Shean, or Lehem. Abraham is said in Gen. 18 to have given the place called Luz the new name of Beth-el, House of God (El).*

¹⁰Lot looked about him and saw how well watered was the whole plain of the Jordan, all of it—this was before the LORD had destroyed Sodom and Gomorrah—all the way to Zoar, like the garden of the LORD, like the land of Egypt.

*Genesis 13.10*

וַיִּשָּׂא־לוֹט אֶת־עֵינָיו וַיַּרְא אֶת־כָּל־כִּכַּר הַיַּרְדֵּן כִּי כֻלָּהּ מַשְׁקֶה לִפְנֵי שַׁחֵת יְהֹוָה אֶת־סְדֹם וְאֶת־עֲמֹרָה כְּגַן־יְהֹוָה כְּאֶרֶץ מִצְרַיִם בֹּאֲכָה צֹעַר:

בְּרֵאשִׁית יג:י

⁸From there he moved on to the hill country east of Bethel and pitched his tent, with Bethel on the west and Ai on the east; and he built there an altar to the LORD and invoked the LORD by name. ⁹Then Abraham journeyed by stages toward the Negeb.

*Genesis 12.8-9*

וַיַּעְתֵּק מִשָּׁם הָהָרָה מִקֶּדֶם לְבֵית־אֵל וַיֵּט אָהֳלֹה בֵּית־אֵל מִיָּם וְהָעַי מִקֶּדֶם וַיִּבֶן־שָׁם מִזְבֵּחַ לַיהֹוָה וַיִּקְרָא בְּשֵׁם יְהֹוָה: וַיִּסַּע אַבְרָם הָלוֹךְ וְנָסוֹעַ הַנֶּגְבָּה:

בְּרֵאשִׁית יב:ח-ט

¹⁹He named that site Bethel; but previously the name of the city had been Luz.

*Genesis 28.19*

וַיִּקְרָא אֶת־שֵׁם־הַמָּקוֹם הַהוּא בֵּית־אֵל וְאוּלָם לוּז שֵׁם־הָעִיר לָרִאשֹׁנָה:

בְּרֵאשִׁית כח:יט

*The ancient world, like the modern, was full of incidents involving family authority, inheritance rights, fratricide, patricide, and the like.*

⁴"As for Me, this is My covenant with you: You shall be the father of a multitude of nations. ⁵And you shall no longer be called Abram, but your name shall be Abraham, for I make you the father of a multitude of nations.

*Genesis 17.4-5*

אֲנִי הִנֵּה בְרִיתִי אִתָּךְ וְהָיִיתָ לְאַב הֲמוֹן גּוֹיִם: וְלֹא־יִקָּרֵא עוֹד אֶת־שִׁמְךָ אַבְרָם וְהָיָה שִׁמְךָ אַבְרָהָם כִּי אַב־הֲמוֹן גּוֹיִם נְתַתִּיךָ:

בְּרֵאשִׁית יז:ד-ה

*goyim - of rent-a-goy!*

¹⁵And God said to Abraham, "As for your wife Sarai, you shall not call her Sarai, but her name shall be Sarah. ¹⁶I will bless her; indeed, I will give you a son by her. I will bless her so that she shall give rise to nations; rulers of peoples shall issue from her."

*Genesis 17.15-16*

וַיֹּאמֶר אֱלֹהִים אֶל־אַבְרָהָם שָׂרַי אִשְׁתְּךָ לֹא־תִקְרָא אֶת־שְׁמָהּ שָׂרָי כִּי שָׂרָה שְׁמָהּ: וּבֵרַכְתִּי אֹתָהּ וְגַם נָתַתִּי מִמֶּנָּה לְךָ בֵּן וּבֵרַכְתִּיהָ וְהָיְתָה לְגוֹיִם מַלְכֵי עַמִּים מִמֶּנָּה יִהְיוּ:

בְּרֵאשִׁית יז:טו-טז

³Reuben, you are my first-born,
My might and first fruit of my vigor,
Exceeding in rank and exceeding in honor.

*Genesis 49.3*

רְאוּבֵן בְּכֹרִי אַתָּה כֹּחִי וְרֵאשִׁית אוֹנִי יֶתֶר שְׂאֵת וְיֶתֶר עָז:

בְּרֵאשִׁית מט:ג

One of the painted registers on the wall of the tomb of Khnum-hotep III at Beni Hasan, Egypt. The scene records the arrival in Egypt of Asiatics led by the foreign prince Abishar. These foreigners are dressed in many-colored garments and carry weapons, tools, and musical instruments characteristic of bedouin life. The inscription informs us that they have brought stibium, the eye cosmetic, for trade. Nefer-hotep, a scribe, is shown on the far right holding a register of the event (ca. 1900 B.C.E.). The original consists of one long register, here divided (beginning with the left end) into four segments for the sake of convenience. About 2½ feet high.

wild beasts of the desert, for they hunted for me. . . . I spent many years [there], and my children grew up to be strong men, each man as the chief of his own tribe. The messenger who went north or who went south to the Residence City tarried with me, for I used to make everybody stop over. I gave water to the thirsty. I put him who strayed, [back] on the road. I rescued him who had been robbed. . . . Every foreign country against which I went forth, when I had made my attack on it, was driven away from its pasturage and its wells. I plundered its cattle, carried off its inhabitants, took away their food, and slew people in it. ("The Story of Sinuhe," trans. J. A. Wilson, in *Ancient Near Eastern Texts relating to the Old Testament,* ed. J. B. Pritchard [Princeton, 1950], pp. 18-22.)

The other Egyptian source is pictorial. A scene painted about 1900 B.C.E. on the wall of a noble's tomb at Beni Hasan, on the Nile in Middle Egypt, depicts a family of thirty-seven Semites from western Asia, seminomads come to Egypt to sell stibium, the popular black eye cosmetic. Several elements in the scene are common to the Biblical material. One is reminded of the families of the patriarchs; Jacob's family which went down to Egypt numbered seventy persons, including the children and grandchildren. The clothes are striped lengthwise and very colorful, and recall Joseph's so-called "coat of many colors." The lyre, the javelin, the bows and arrows, and the portable bellows are all characteristic of the occupations of the seminomadic groups. The little donkeys in the scene were the principal means of travel before the domestication of the camel.

The Biblical and the archaeological data dovetail so well in this picture of the patriarchal period that one authority has been moved to say that the "Hebrew national tradition excels all others in its clear picture of tribal and family origins. In Egypt and Babylonia, in Assyria and Phoenicia, in Greece and Rome, we look in vain for anything comparable. There is nothing like it

*The mention of camels in the patriarchal narratives has long presented a problem to scholars. On the one hand, the Patriarchs are generally dated about the middle of the Middle Bronze Age (about 2000-1500 B.C.E.), whereas our present knowledge hardly permits the dating of the domestication of the camel before about 1200 B.C.E. The nomads in the first half of the second millennium B.C.E. were ass. nomads, as can be seen from the accompanying Beni Hasan painting (and from such passages as Gen. 22.3; 42.26; 43.24; and 44.13); they'd have had to walk much more than a mile for a camel.*

¹These are the names of the sons of Israel who came to Egypt with Jacob, each coming with his household: ²Reuben, Simeon, Levi, and Judah; ³Issachar, Zebulun, and Benjamin; ⁴Dan and Naphtali, Gad and Asher. ⁵The total number of persons that were of Jacob's issue came to seventy, Joseph being already in Egypt. ⁶Joseph died, and all his brothers, and all that generation .

*Exodus 1.1-6*

וְאֵלֶּה שְׁמוֹת בְּנֵי יִשְׂרָאֵל הַבָּאִים מִצְרָיְמָה אֵת יַעֲקֹב אִישׁ וּבֵיתוֹ בָּאוּ: רְאוּבֵן שִׁמְעוֹן לֵוִי וִיהוּדָה: יִשָּׂשכָר זְבוּלֻן וּבִנְיָמִן: דָּן וְנַפְתָּלִי גָּד וְאָשֵׁר: וַיְהִי כָּל־נֶפֶשׁ יֹצְאֵי יֶרֶךְ־יַעֲקֹב שִׁבְעִים נָפֶשׁ וְיוֹסֵף הָיָה בְמִצְרָיִם: וַיָּמָת יוֹסֵף וְכָל־אֶחָיו וְכֹל הַדּוֹר הַהוּא:

שְׁמוֹת א:א-ו

²¹And the name of his brother was Jubal; he was the ancestor of all who play the lyre and the pipe. ²²As for Zillah, she bore Tubal-cain, who forged all implements of copper and iron. And the sister of Tubal-cain was Naamah.

*Genesis 4.21-22*

וְשֵׁם אָחִיו יוּבָל הוּא הָיָה אֲבִי כָּל־תֹּפֵשׂ כִּנּוֹר וְעוּגָב: וְצִלָּה גַם־הִוא יָלְדָה אֶת־תּוּבַל קַיִן לֹטֵשׁ כָּל־חֹרֵשׁ נְחֹשֶׁת וּבַרְזֶל וַאֲחוֹת תּוּבַל־קַיִן נַעֲמָה:

בְּרֵאשִׁית ד:כא-כב

*camels* — *could be an anachronism*

¹⁰Then the servant took ten of his master's camels and set out, taking with him all the bounty of his master; and he made his way to Aram-naharaim, to the city of Nahor. ¹¹He made the camels kneel down by the well outside the city, at evening time, the time when women come out to draw water. . .

¹⁴"Let the maiden to whom I say, 'Please, lower your jar that I may drink,' and who replies, 'Drink, and I will also water your camels'—let her be the one whom You have decreed for Your servant Isaac. Thereby shall I know that You have dealt graciously with my master."

*Genesis 24.10–14*

וַיִּקַּח הָעֶבֶד עֲשָׂרָה גְמַלִּים מִגְּמַלֵּי אֲדֹנָיו וַיֵּלֶךְ וְכָל־טוּב אֲדֹנָיו בְּיָדוֹ וַיָּקָם וַיֵּלֶךְ אֶל־אֲרַם נַהֲרַיִם אֶל־עִיר נָחוֹר: וַיַּבְרֵךְ הַגְּמַלִּים מִחוּץ לָעִיר אֶל־בְּאֵר הַמָּיִם לְעֵת עֶרֶב לְעֵת צֵאת הַשֹּׁאֲבֹת: . . . וְהָיָה הַנַּעֲרָה אֲשֶׁר אֹמַר אֵלֶיהָ הַטִּי־נָא כַדֵּךְ וְאֶשְׁתֶּה וְאָמְרָה שְׁתֵה וְגַם־גְּמַלֶּיךָ אַשְׁקֶה אֹתָהּ הֹכַחְתָּ לְעַבְדְּךָ לְיִצְחָק וּבָהּ אֵדַע כִּי־עָשִׂיתָ חֶסֶד עִם־אֲדֹנִי:

בְּרֵאשִׁית כד:י - יד

*i.e. Jacob*

³Now Israel loved Joseph best of all his sons, for he was the child of his old age; and he had made him an ornamented tunic.

*Genesis 37.3*

וְיִשְׂרָאֵל אָהַב אֶת־יוֹסֵף מִכָּל־בָּנָיו כִּי־בֶן־ זְקֻנִים הוּא לוֹ וְעָשָׂה לוֹ כְּתֹנֶת פַּסִּים:

בְּרֵאשִׁית לז:ג

The Weld-Blundell prism, a box-shaped tablet of clay, on the four sides of which are listed, in double columns, the kings of Sumer. The list begins with an account the origin of kingship as an institution in the ancient city of Eridu, in Southern Mesopotamia, and ends with King Sin-Magir, the fourteenth (and next to last) king of the First Dynasty of Isin (ca. 1827-1817 B.C.E.). The list records the names of the kings and how long they reigned. When the dominating dynasty changed from one city or family line to another, the usual reason given was that it was "smitten with weapons."

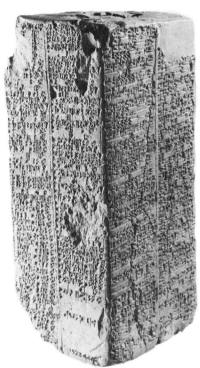

Excerpts from the Sumerian King List, column I.

1) When kingship was lowered from heaven,
2) kingship was (first) in Eridu;
3) (In) Eridu, A-lulim (became) king
4) and ruled 28,800 years,
5) Alalgar ruled 36,000 years,
6) Two kings,
7) (thus) ruled it for 64,800 years.
8) I drop (the topic) Eridu,
9) (because) its kingship to Bad-tibira
10) was brought;
11) (In) Bad-tibira, En-men-lu-Anna
12) ruled 43,200 years,
13) En-men-gal-Anna ruled 28,8000 years; . . .
36) These are five cities;
37) eight kings,
38) ruled them for 241,000 years;
39) (Then) the Flood swept over (the earth);
40) After the Flood had swept over (the earth),
41) (and) when kingship was lowered (again) from heaven
42) kingship was (first) in Kish.

in the tradition of the Germanic peoples. Neither India nor China can produce anything similar." (W. F. Albright, "The Biblical Period," in *The Jews: Their History, Culture and Religion,* ed. L. Finkelstein New York, 1949], I, p. 3.)

## The Biblical Cosmogony

All religions have a cosmogony, an explanation of how the world and mankind came to be. The Biblical cosmogony in the Book of Genesis (Chapters 1–11), dealing with Creation, the Garden of Eden (Paradise), the Fall of Man, the antediluvian (pre-Flood) patriarchs, the Flood and Noah's Ark, the Tower of Babel and the dispersion of man over the earth—all these came from the earlier part of the second millennium, when the Hebrews had direct contact with Mesopotamian society. A relationship between the most important Babylonian story of creation, found in the composition designated from its first two words, *Enûma Elish* ("When Above"), and the Biblical Genesis has long been recognized. Thus the two share in common the concept of a primeval watery chaos and the subsequent creation of order among the sky, the earth, and the seas. Both accounts speak of the existence of light prior to the creation of the sun, the moon, and the other heavenly bodies, which, in turn, made possible the regulation of time.

The Babylonian and the Hebrew versions both regard man as the final and most important act of creation, after which the creators rested. The Bible (Genesis 5) records ten patriarchs from Adam through Noah, who lived a total of 8,575 years, although the actual elapsed time was just over 1,000 years. Methuselah died at the ripest old age of them all, in his 969th year. Yet even these high numbers pale into insignificance in the light of one Sumerian list, which tells of eight antediluvian kings who reigned a total

Enûma Elish = when above

## The Biblical Cosmogony

*Like their Near Eastern neighbors, the Israelites frequently explained names by what we call popular (that is, false) etymology. Thus Hebrew* bavel *does not really derive from a root* balal *"mix up"—as we might say, "be balled up"—but is simply the Babylonian name; interestingly, the Babylonians themselves were guilty of popular etymology in explaining the name as from* bab-ili *"the gate of god." (Actually, we don't know the origin of the name.) Similarly, the name* Mosheh *"Moses" does not come from the root* mashah *(Ex. 2.10), but is an Egyptian word meaning "born of, offspring."*

⁴. . . When the LORD God made earth and heaven—⁵when no shrub of the field was yet on earth and no grasses of the field had yet sprouted, because the LORD God had not sent rain upon the earth and there was no man to till the soil, ⁶but a flow would well up from the ground and water the whole surface of the earth—⁷the LORD God formed man from the dust of the earth. He blew into his nostrils the breath of life, and man became a living being.

⁸The LORD God planted a garden in Eden, in the east, and placed there the man whom He had formed. ⁹And from the ground the LORD God caused to grow every tree that was pleasing to the sight and good for food, with the tree of life in the middle of the garden, and the tree of knowledge of good and bad.

*Genesis 2.4-9*

¹⁵The LORD God took the man and placed him in the garden of Eden, to till it and tend it. ¹⁶And the LORD God commanded the man, saying, "Of every tree of the garden you are free to eat; ¹⁷but as for the tree of knowledge of good and bad, you must not eat of it; for as soon as you eat of it, you shall die."

*Genesis 2.15-17*

⁶When the woman saw that the tree was good for eating and a delight to the eyes, and that the tree was desirable as a source of wisdom, she took of its fruit and ate. She also gave some to her husband, and he ate. . .

²²And the LORD God said, "Now that the man has become like one of us, knowing good and bad, what if he should stretch out his hand and take also from the tree of life and eat, and live forever!" . . . ²⁴He drove the man out, and stationed east of the garden of Eden the cherubim and the fiery ever-turning sword, to guard the way to the tree of life.

*Genesis 3.6, 22-24*

אֵלֶּה תוֹלְדוֹת הַשָּׁמַיִם וְהָאָרֶץ בְּהִבָּרְאָם) בְּיוֹם עֲשׂוֹת יְהוָה אֱלֹהִים אֶרֶץ וְשָׁמָיִם: וְכֹל שִׂיחַ הַשָּׂדֶה טֶרֶם יִהְיֶה בָאָרֶץ וְכָל־עֵשֶׂב הַשָּׂדֶה טֶרֶם יִצְמָח כִּי לֹא הִמְטִיר יְהוָה אֱלֹהִים עַל־הָאָרֶץ וְאָדָם אַיִן לַעֲבֹד אֶת־הָאֲדָמָה: וְאֵד יַעֲלֶה מִן־הָאָרֶץ וְהִשְׁקָה אֶת־כָּל־פְּנֵי הָאֲדָמָה: וַיִּיצֶר יְהוָה אֱלֹהִים אֶת־הָאָדָם עָפָר מִן־הָאֲדָמָה וַיִּפַּח בְּאַפָּיו נִשְׁמַת חַיִּים וַיְהִי הָאָדָם לְנֶפֶשׁ חַיָּה: וַיִּטַּע יְהוָה אֱלֹהִים גַּן־בְּעֵדֶן מִקֶּדֶם וַיָּשֶׂם שָׁם אֶת־הָאָדָם אֲשֶׁר יָצָר: וַיַּצְמַח יְהוָה אֱלֹהִים מִן־הָאֲדָמָה כָּל־עֵץ נֶחְמָד לְמַרְאֶה וְטוֹב לְמַאֲכָל וְעֵץ הַחַיִּים בְּתוֹךְ הַגָּן וְעֵץ הַדַּעַת טוֹב וָרָע:

בְּרֵאשִׁית ב:ד-ט

וַיִּקַּח יְהוָה אֱלֹהִים אֶת־הָאָדָם וַיַּנִּחֵהוּ בְגַן־עֵדֶן לְעָבְדָהּ וּלְשָׁמְרָהּ: וַיְצַו יְהוָה אֱלֹהִים עַל־הָאָדָם לֵאמֹר מִכֹּל עֵץ־הַגָּן אָכֹל תֹּאכֵל: וּמֵעֵץ הַדַּעַת טוֹב וָרָע לֹא תֹאכַל מִמֶּנּוּ כִּי בְּיוֹם אֲכָלְךָ מִמֶּנּוּ מוֹת תָּמוּת:

בְּרֵאשִׁית ב:טו-יז

וַתֵּרֶא הָאִשָּׁה כִּי טוֹב הָעֵץ לְמַאֲכָל וְכִי תַאֲוָה־הוּא לָעֵינַיִם וְנֶחְמָד הָעֵץ לְהַשְׂכִּיל וַתִּקַּח מִפִּרְיוֹ וַתֹּאכַל וַתִּתֵּן גַּם־לְאִישָׁהּ עִמָּהּ וַיֹּאכַל: . . . וַיֹּאמֶר יְהוָה אֱלֹהִים הֵן הָאָדָם הָיָה כְּאַחַד מִמֶּנּוּ לָדַעַת טוֹב וָרָע וְעַתָּה פֶּן־יִשְׁלַח יָדוֹ וְלָקַח גַּם מֵעֵץ הַחַיִּים וְאָכַל וָחַי לְעֹלָם: . . . וַיְגָרֶשׁ אֶת־הָאָדָם וַיַּשְׁכֵּן מִקֶּדֶם לְגַן־עֵדֶן אֶת־הַכְּרֻבִים וְאֵת לַהַט הַחֶרֶב הַמִּתְהַפֶּכֶת לִשְׁמֹר אֶת־דֶּרֶךְ עֵץ־הַחַיִּים:

בְּרֵאשִׁית ג:ו, כב-כד

A portion of a series of clay tablets which tell the epic story of King Gilgamesh of Sumer (ca. 2700 B.C.E.). This tablet tells of Utnapishtim boarding the boat, the coming of the storm flood, the landing on Mt. Nisir, the first sacrifice to the gods after the flood, the apotheosis of Utnapishtim, and the divine regret for sending the flood in the first place. The story of Gilgamesh then continues.

From Ashurbanipal's library, seventh cent. B.C.E., Nineveh. Clay 137 by 130 MM.

Below is a hand-copy, transliteration, and word-for-word translation of lines 127-131 of Tablet XI of the Epic.

127    6 ur·ra      ù 6 mu·ša·a ti

**6    days      and 6   nights**

il·lak ša·a·ru a·bu·bu me·hu·u i· sàp·pan KUR

**blows    the wind; the flood, the south-storm sweeps the land.**

129. si·bu·ú u₄·mu i·na ka·ša·a·di ...... šu·ú abubu qab·la

**the 7th day,    when it came, ..    the flood, the battle**

ša im·tah·ṣu         ki·ma ha·a·a·al·ti

**which he had fought      like,   an army;**

131 i·nu·uh A·AB·BA uš·ha·ri·ir·ma im·hul·lu a·bu·bu ik·la

**grew quiet the sea,    and was still the storm, the flood ceased.**

of 241,200 years, and a Babylonian list, compiled in the third century B.C.E. from much older sources, which records ten such rulers who reigned a total of 432,000 years.

The Biblical account of the Flood, with which God destroyed a world grown wicked, saving only enough of it to make a fresh start, is powerfully foreshadowed in the famous Gilgamesh Epic, which came down to the Babylonians from the earlier Sumerian civilization. Warned by the god Ea, Utnapishtim, the tenth antediluvian king in Babylonia, builds an ark in the shape of a cube, 120 cubits on each side. Into this ship he loads his family, his possessions, and "the seed of all living creatures." The epic relates how

Six days and nights
The wind blew, the downpour, the tempest, the flood overwhelmed the land,
When the seventh day arrived, the tempest, the flood,
Which had fought like an army, subsided in its onslaught.
The sea grew quiet, the storm abated, the flood ceased.
I opened a window, and light fell upon my face.
I looked upon the sea, (all) was silence,
And all mankind had turned to clay.

On Mount Nisir (or Nimush) the ship landed.
Mount Nisir held the ship fast, and did not let it move.

. . . . .

When the seventh day arrived,
I sent forth a dove and let her go.
The dove went away and came back to me;
There was no resting-place, and so she returned.
I sent forth a swallow and let her go.
The swallow went away and came back to me;
There was no resting-place, and so she returned.
I sent forth a raven and let her go.
The raven went away, and when she saw that the waters had abated,
She ate, she flew about, she cawed, and did not return.
I sent forth (everything) to the four winds and offered a sacrifice.
I poured out a libation on the peak of the mountain. (A. Heidel, *The Gilgamesh Epic and Old Testament Parallels* [Chicago, 1946], pp. 81 ff.)

*Israel shared with its older Mesopotamian neighbors the tradition of a long prehistoric past in which outstanding personages lived to an unusually old age. The origin of the names of these ten antediluvian (pre-Flood) patriarchs and of the number of years that each lived—while probably Mesopotamian—has not yet been determined.*

[1]This is the record of Adam's line. When God created man, He made him in the likeness of God; [2]male and female He created them. And when they were created, He blessed them and called them Man. [3]When Adam had lived 130 years, be begot a son in his likeness after his image, and he named him Seth . . . [5]All the days that Adam lived came to 930 years; then he died.

[6]When Seth had lived 105 years, he begot Enosh. . . . [8]All the days of Seth came to 912 years; then he died.

[9]When Enosh had lived 90 years, he begot Kenan. . . . [11]All the days of Enosh came to 905 years; then he died.

[12]When Kenan had lived 70 years, he begot Mahalalel. . . . [14]All the days of Kenan came to 910 years; then he died.

[15]When Mahalalel had lived 65 years, he begot Jared. . . . [17]All the days of Mahalalel came to 895 years; then he died.

[18]When Jared had lived 162 years, he begot Enoch. . . . [20]All the days of Jared came to 962 years; then he died.

[21]When Enoch had lived 65 years, he begot Methuselah. . . . [23]All the days of Enoch came to 365 years. [24]Enoch walked with God; then he was no more, for God took him.

[25]When Methuselah had lived 187 years, he begot Lamech. . . . [27]All the days of Methuselah came to 969; then he died.

[28]When Lamech had lived 182 years; he begot a son. [29]And he named him Noah. . . . [31]All the days of Lamech came to 777 years; then he died.

[32]When Noah had lived 500 years, Noah begot Shem, Ham, and Japheth.

זֶה סֵפֶר תּוֹלְדֹת אָדָם בְּיוֹם בְּרֹא אֱלֹהִים אָדָם
בִּדְמוּת אֱלֹהִים עָשָׂה אֹתוֹ: זָכָר וּנְקֵבָה בְּרָאָם
וַיְבָרֶךְ אֹתָם וַיִּקְרָא אֶת־שְׁמָם אָדָם בְּיוֹם הִבָּרְאָם:
וַיְחִי אָדָם שְׁלֹשִׁים וּמְאַת שָׁנָה וַיּוֹלֶד בִּדְמוּתוֹ
כְּצַלְמוֹ וַיִּקְרָא אֶת־שְׁמוֹ שֵׁת: . . . וַיִּהְיוּ כָּל־יְמֵי
אָדָם אֲשֶׁר־חַי תְּשַׁע מֵאוֹת שָׁנָה וּשְׁלֹשִׁים שָׁנָה
וַיָּמֹת: וַיְחִי־שֵׁת חָמֵשׁ שָׁנִים וּמְאַת שָׁנָה וַיּוֹלֶד
אֶת־אֱנוֹשׁ: . . . וַיִּהְיוּ כָּל־יְמֵי־שֵׁת שְׁתֵּים עֶשְׂרֵה
שָׁנָה וּתְשַׁע מֵאוֹת שָׁנָה וַיָּמֹת: וַיְחִי אֱנוֹשׁ תִּשְׁעִים
שָׁנָה וַיּוֹלֶד אֶת־קֵינָן: . . . וַיִּהְיוּ כָּל־יְמֵי אֱנוֹשׁ
חָמֵשׁ שָׁנִים וּתְשַׁע מֵאוֹת שָׁנָה וַיָּמֹת: וַיְחִי קֵינָן
שִׁבְעִים שָׁנָה וַיּוֹלֶד אֶת־מַהֲלַלְאֵל: . . . וַיִּהְיוּ כָּל־
יְמֵי קֵינָן עֶשֶׂר שָׁנִים וּתְשַׁע מֵאוֹת שָׁנָה וַיָּמֹת: וַיְחִי
מַהֲלַלְאֵל חָמֵשׁ שָׁנִים וְשִׁשִּׁים שָׁנָה וַיּוֹלֶד אֶת־
יָרֶד: . . . וַיִּהְיוּ כָּל־יְמֵי מַהֲלַלְאֵל חָמֵשׁ וְתִשְׁעִים
שָׁנָה וּשְׁמֹנֶה מֵאוֹת שָׁנָה וַיָּמֹת: וַיְחִי־יֶרֶד שְׁתַּיִם
וְשִׁשִּׁים שָׁנָה וּמְאַת שָׁנָה וַיּוֹלֶד אֶת־חֲנוֹךְ: . . . וַיִּהְיוּ
כָּל־יְמֵי־יֶרֶד שְׁתַּיִם וְשִׁשִּׁים שָׁנָה וּתְשַׁע מֵאוֹת
שָׁנָה וַיָּמֹת: וַיְחִי חֲנוֹךְ חָמֵשׁ וְשִׁשִּׁים שָׁנָה וַיּוֹלֶד
אֶת־מְתוּשָׁלַח: . . . וַיְהִי כָּל־יְמֵי חֲנוֹךְ חָמֵשׁ וְשִׁשִּׁים
שָׁנָה וּשְׁלֹשׁ מֵאוֹת שָׁנָה: וַיִּתְהַלֵּךְ חֲנוֹךְ אֶת־הָאֱלֹהִים
וְאֵינֶנּוּ כִּי־לָקַח אֹתוֹ אֱלֹהִים: וַיְחִי מְתוּשֶׁלַח שֶׁבַע
וּשְׁמֹנִים שָׁנָה וּמְאַת שָׁנָה וַיּוֹלֶד אֶת־לָמֶךְ: . . .
וַיִּהְיוּ כָּל־יְמֵי מְתוּשֶׁלַח תֵּשַׁע וְשִׁשִּׁים שָׁנָה וּתְשַׁע
מֵאוֹת שָׁנָה וַיָּמֹת: וַיְחִי־לֶמֶךְ שְׁתַּיִם וּשְׁמֹנִים שָׁנָה
וּמְאַת שָׁנָה וַיּוֹלֶד בֵּן: וַיִּקְרָא אֶת־שְׁמוֹ נֹחַ לֵאמֹר . . .
וַיְהִי כָּל־יְמֵי־לֶמֶךְ שֶׁבַע וְשִׁבְעִים שָׁנָה וּשְׁבַע מֵאוֹת
שָׁנָה וַיָּמֹת: וַיְהִי־נֹחַ בֶּן־חֲמֵשׁ מֵאוֹת שָׁנָה וַיּוֹלֶד
נֹחַ אֶת־שֵׁם אֶת־חָם וְאֶת־יָפֶת:

*Genesis 5.1-32*        בְּרֵאשִׁית ה:א–לב

Fragment of a tablet containing a Neo-Assyrian version of the epic of Atrakhasis, a flood story. This part of the epic tells of the god Ea completing his instructions to Atrakhasis to prepare himself for the coming deluge. Ea will tell him to enter the boat he is to build, together with his family and skilled artisans. Waiting to enter the boat with him will be herbivorous wild animals sent by the god.

Atrakhasis then asks for directions on how to build the boat and Ea draws the plan on the ground. About 1⅓ by 1¾ inches.

Preserved portion of a clay tablet upon which has been drawn a map of the world as conceived by a scribe who lived between 700 and 500 B.C.E. He has divided the map into the two political entities which dominated his world: Babylonia (upper rectangle) and Chaldea (lower rectangle). The Tigris and Euphrates rivers flow through these two countries into the world river which surrounds all known land. The triangles on the outer banks of the river indicate the unknown portions of the world. About 4¾ by 2 inches.

Although the resemblances between the Gilgamesh Epic and the Biblical account of Noah—who is also the tenth antediluvian patriarch—are numerous and varied, including such details as the Ark, the Flood, and the like, the differences are no less notable. It is frequently difficult to determine precisely what concepts the Hebrews derived from the various milieus in which they found themselves before about 1500 B.C.E. What is fundamental, however, is that the Hebrews infused whatever concepts they did borrow with their own spirit and thinking, thus endowing them with a content of ethics and morals which lifted the primitive mythology of their Asiatic neighbors to a wholly new spiritual level.

The moral emphasis achieved in the Biblical cosmogony, as contrasted with the naturalism of the prototypes, is sharply illustrated by yet another Babylonian flood legend, the Atrakhasis Epic. Here we are told how

The god [Enlil] became disturbed by their gatherings.
The god heard their noise
And said to the great gods:
"Great has become the noise of mankind;
With their tumult they make sleep impossible."

In other words, the gods are moved to reprisal by simple personal annoyance, whereas in Genesis God's anger is stirred by man's moral decline. As the Bible says: "The Lord saw that the wickedness of man on earth was great, and that every plan devised by his mind was only evil all the time" (Genesis 6:5).

## The Patriarchal Conception of God and the Covenant

Some features in the patriarchal stage of Israelite history stand out with especial significance. While the picture in detail is still far from clear, the Biblical and the newer

*Atrakhasis Epic*

<sup>29</sup>And all the days of Noah came to 950 years; then he died.

*Genesis 9.29*

וַיְהִי כָּל־יְמֵי־נֹחַ תְּשַׁע מֵאוֹת שָׁנָה וַחֲמִשִּׁים שָׁנָה וַיָּמֹת:

בְּרֵאשִׁית ט:כט

*Although the resemblances between the Gilgamesh Epic and the Biblical account of Noah—who is also the tenth antediluvian patriarch—are numerous and varied, including such details as the Ark, the Flood, and the like, the differences are no less notable.*

<sup>5</sup>The LORD saw how great was man's wickedness on earth, and how every plan devised by his mind was nothing but evil all the time. <sup>6</sup>And the LORD regretted that He had made man on earth, and His heart was saddened. <sup>7</sup>The LORD said, "I will blot out from the earth the men whom I created—men together with beasts, creeping things, and birds of the sky; for I regret that I made them." <sup>8</sup>But Noah found favor with the LORD. <sup>9</sup>. . . Noah was a righteous man; he was blameless in his age; Noah walked with God...

<sup>14</sup>"Make yourself an ark of gopher wood; make it an ark with compartments, and cover it inside and out with pitch...

<sup>17</sup>For My part, I am about to bring a Flood-of waters upon the earth to destroy all flesh under the sky in which there is breath of life; everything on earth shall perish."

*Genesis 6.5-17*

וַיַּרְא יְהוָה כִּי רַבָּה רָעַת הָאָדָם בָּאָרֶץ וְכָל־יֵצֶר מַחְשְׁבֹת לִבּוֹ רַק רַע כָּל־הַיּוֹם: וַיִּנָּחֶם יְהוָה כִּי־עָשָׂה אֶת־הָאָדָם בָּאָרֶץ וַיִּתְעַצֵּב אֶל־לִבּוֹ: וַיֹּאמֶר יְהוָה אֶמְחֶה אֶת־הָאָדָם אֲשֶׁר־בָּרָאתִי מֵעַל פְּנֵי הָאֲדָמָה מֵאָדָם עַד־בְּהֵמָה עַד־רֶמֶשׂ וְעַד־עוֹף הַשָּׁמַיִם כִּי נִחַמְתִּי כִּי עֲשִׂיתִם: וְנֹחַ מָצָא חֵן בְּעֵינֵי יְהוָה: . . . נֹחַ אִישׁ צַדִּיק תָּמִים הָיָה בְּדֹרֹתָיו אֶת־הָאֱלֹהִים הִתְהַלֶּךְ־נֹחַ: . . . עֲשֵׂה לְךָ תֵּבַת עֲצֵי־גֹפֶר קִנִּים תַּעֲשֶׂה אֶת־הַתֵּבָה וְכָפַרְתָּ אֹתָהּ מִבַּיִת וּמִחוּץ בַּכֹּפֶר: . . . וַאֲנִי הִנְנִי מֵבִיא אֶת־הַמַּבּוּל מַיִם עַל־הָאָרֶץ לְשַׁחֵת כָּל־בָּשָׂר אֲשֶׁר־בּוֹ רוּחַ חַיִּים מִתַּחַת הַשָּׁמָיִם כֹּל אֲשֶׁר־בָּאָרֶץ יִגְוָע:

בְּרֵאשִׁית ו:ה־יז

<sup>1</sup>Then the LORD said to Noah, "Go into the ark, with all your household, for you alone have I found righteous before Me in this generation."

<sup>10</sup>And . . . the waters of the Flood came upon the earth."

<sup>11</sup>All the fountains of the great deep burst apart, And the floodgates of the sky broke open.

*Genesis 7.1, 10-11*

וַיֹּאמֶר יְהוָה לְנֹחַ בֹּא־אַתָּה וְכָל־בֵּיתְךָ אֶל־הַתֵּבָה כִּי־אֹתְךָ רָאִיתִי צַדִּיק לְפָנַי בַּדּוֹר הַזֶּה: . . . וּמֵי הַמַּבּוּל הָיוּ עַל־הָאָרֶץ: . . . נִבְקְעוּ כָּל־מַעְיְנֹת תְּהוֹם רַבָּה וַאֲרֻבֹּת הַשָּׁמַיִם נִפְתָּחוּ:

בְּרֵאשִׁית ז:א, י־יא

<sup>6</sup>At the end of forty days, Noah opened the window of the ark that he had made <sup>7</sup>and sent out the raven; it went to and fro until the waters had dried up from the earth... 

<sup>10</sup>He waited another seven days, and again sent out the dove from the ark. <sup>11</sup>The dove came back to him toward evening, and there in its bill was a plucked-off olive leaf! Then Noah knew that the waters had decreased on the earth. <sup>12</sup>He waited still another seven days and sent the dove forth; and it did not return to him any more.

*Genesis 8.6-12*

וַיְהִי מִקֵּץ אַרְבָּעִים יוֹם וַיִּפְתַּח נֹחַ אֶת־חַלּוֹן הַתֵּבָה אֲשֶׁר עָשָׂה: וַיְשַׁלַּח אֶת־הָעֹרֵב וַיֵּצֵא יָצוֹא וָשׁוֹב עַד־יְבֹשֶׁת הַמַּיִם מֵעַל הָאָרֶץ: . . . וַיָּחֶל עוֹד שִׁבְעַת יָמִים אֲחֵרִים וַיֹּסֶף שַׁלַּח אֶת־הַיּוֹנָה מִן־הַתֵּבָה: וַתָּבֹא אֵלָיו הַיּוֹנָה לְעֵת עֶרֶב וְהִנֵּה עֲלֵה־זַיִת טָרָף בְּפִיהָ וַיֵּדַע נֹחַ כִּי־קַלּוּ הַמַּיִם מֵעַל הָאָרֶץ: וַיִּיָּחֶל עוֹד שִׁבְעַת יָמִים אֲחֵרִים וַיְשַׁלַּח אֶת־הַיּוֹנָה וְלֹא־יָסְפָה שׁוּב־אֵלָיו עוֹד:

בְּרֵאשִׁית ח:ו־יב

Spouted cup, probably used for pouring liquid offerings, which, according to the inscription on it, was dedicated by Gudea to his god, Ningishzida, for the purpose of prolonging his life. The meaning of the composition carved on the body of this vessel is unknown. What is shown is a composite monster (bird, lion, and reptile) standing with a long staff in its hand, on guard as if beside a door. Before him are two serpents coiled around a staff. The same figure is repeated facing in the opposite direction on the other side of the cup, creating the balanced composition favored in many ancient works of the Near East. 9 inches high.

Alabaster statuette (head lost) of Urningirsu, son of the Gudea mentioned above. He stands, solemnly before his god. Around the base of his statuette, are seen kneeling figures, dressed in long tunics. They are bringing offerings to the gods for Urningirsu. The statuette has a name which itself is a prayer: "I am he who loves his god, that he may prolong my life." 18½ inches high.

archaeological data combine to indicate that the patriarchs practiced a religion which, while not monotheistic in our sense of the term, was yet not polytheistic either.

Its basic concept, later to develop into national significance, was the "covenant." This was the tribal practice of entering into an agreement with one particular god, so that the deity would devote himself entirely to the covenanters, in return for their exclusive obedience and loyal trust. Abraham entered into a mutually exclusive agreement with God, "the God of Abraham," whereby Abraham was to recognize and worship no other deity and God was to protect and seek the welfare of Abraham and his family exclusively.

When Isaac renewed Abraham's covenant, God became "the Kinsman (or, Fear) of Isaac." For Jacob, God was "the Champion (or, Mighty One) of Jacob." Abraham's brother, Nahor, the one left behind in Haran, likewise adopted a personal god. When Abraham's grandson Jacob and Nahor's grandson Laban settled a dispute between themselves, Jacob said to Laban, "If the God of my father, the God of Abraham and the Kinsman of Isaac, had not been with me, you would have sent me away empty-handed" (Genesis 31:42). Whereupon Laban answered, "May the God of Abraham and the god of Nahor . . . judge between us" (verse 53).

It would be going too far to attribute to the patriarchal Hebrews a belief in the existence of one and only one God. In a sense they may be said to have practiced—but without defining—monotheism. While they probably did not think of denying the existence of other gods, and some mighty ones among them at that, the patriarchs attached themselves to one God, and Him alone they worshiped. With Him, they entered voluntarily into a covenant which was binding forever,

*In making a covenant with Noah and all who came out of the ark with him, man and beast, God set up what may be designated Natural Law, the laws by which the whole universe had to abide (cf. Gen. 1.26-30); these came to be called the Noahide (that is, Universal) Laws. Thus murder, sexual lewdness, wanton cruelty, and treacherous extermination of an entire people (genocide), and the like, were forbidden by this universal covenant. It is for transgressing these universal laws that Amos condemned Aram (Damascus) 1.3; Philistia (Gaza) 1.6; Phoenicia (Tyre) 1.9; Edom 1.11; Ammon 1.13; and Moab 2.1— whereas it is for transgressing the exclusive, national covenant with God (initiated with Abraham, Isaac, and Jacob, and their descendants) that Amos condemned Judah-Israel (2.4 ff.): ". . . because they spurned the Instruction (torah) of the Lord and disobeyed His laws . . ."*

21The LORD smelled the pleasing odor, and the LORD said to Himself: "Never again will I doom the earth because of man, since the devisings of man's mind are evil from his youth; nor will I ever again destroy every living being, as I have done.

*Genesis 8.21*

וַיָּרַח יְהֹוָה אֶת־רֵיחַ הַנִּיחֹחַ וַיֹּאמֶר יְהֹוָה אֶל־לִבּוֹ לֹא־אֹסִף לְקַלֵּל עוֹד אֶת־הָאֲדָמָה בַּעֲבוּר הָאָדָם כִּי יֵצֶר לֵב הָאָדָם רַע מִנְּעֻרָיו וְלֹא־אֹסִף עוֹד לְהַכּוֹת אֶת־כָּל־חַי כַּאֲשֶׁר עָשִׂיתִי: בְּרֵאשִׁית ח:כא

8And God said to Noah and to his sons with him, 9"I now establish My covenant with you and your offspring to come, 10and with every living thing that is with you—birds, cattle, and every wild beast as well—all that have come out of the ark, every living thing on earth. 11I will maintain My covenant with you: never again shall all flesh be cut off by the waters of a flood, and never again shall there be a flood to destroy the earth."

*Genesis 9.8-11*

וַיֹּאמֶר אֱלֹהִים אֶל־נֹחַ וְאֶל־בָּנָיו אִתּוֹ לֵאמֹר: וַאֲנִי הִנְנִי מֵקִים אֶת־בְּרִיתִי אִתְּכֶם וְאֶת־זַרְעֲכֶם אַחֲרֵיכֶם: וְאֵת כָּל־נֶפֶשׁ הַחַיָּה אֲשֶׁר אִתְּכֶם בָּעוֹף בַּבְּהֵמָה וּבְכָל־חַיַּת הָאָרֶץ אִתְּכֶם מִכֹּל יֹצְאֵי הַתֵּבָה לְכֹל חַיַּת הָאָרֶץ: וַהֲקִמֹתִי אֶת־בְּרִיתִי אִתְּכֶם וְלֹא־יִכָּרֵת כָּל־בָּשָׂר עוֹד מִמֵּי הַמַּבּוּל וְלֹא־יִהְיֶה עוֹד מַבּוּל לְשַׁחֵת הָאָרֶץ: בְּרֵאשִׁית ט:ח–יא

## The Patriarchal Conception of God and the Covenant

1The LORD said to Abram, "Go forth from your native land, and from your father's house to the land that I will show you. 2I will make of you a great nation, and I will bless you; I will make your name great. . . . 7The LORD appeared to Abram and said, "I will give this land to your offspring." And he built an altar there to the LORD who had appeared to him.

*Genesis 12.1-2, 7*

וַיֹּאמֶר יְהֹוָה אֶל־אַבְרָם לֶךְ־לְךָ מֵאַרְצְךָ וּמִמּוֹלַדְתְּךָ וּמִבֵּית אָבִיךָ אֶל־הָאָרֶץ אֲשֶׁר אַרְאֶךָּ: וְאֶעֶשְׂךָ לְגוֹי גָּדוֹל וַאֲבָרֶכְךָ וַאֲגַדְּלָה שְׁמֶךָ וֶהְיֵה בְּרָכָה: . . . וַיֵּרָא יְהֹוָה אֶל־אַבְרָם וַיֹּאמֶר לְזַרְעֲךָ אֶתֵּן אֶת־הָאָרֶץ הַזֹּאת וַיִּבֶן שָׁם מִזְבֵּחַ לַיהֹוָה הַנִּרְאֶה אֵלָיו: בְּרֵאשִׁית יב:א–ב, ז

42Had not the God of my father, the God of Abraham and the Fear of Isaac, been with me, you would have sent me away empty-handed. . . . 53"May the God of Abraham and the god of Nahor"—their ancestral deities—"judge between us." And Jacob swore by the Fear of his father Isaac.

*Genesis 31.42, 53*

לוּלֵי אֱלֹהֵי אָבִי אֱלֹהֵי אַבְרָהָם וּפַחַד יִצְחָק הָיָה לִי כִּי עַתָּה רֵיקָם שִׁלַּחְתָּנִי: . . . אֱלֹהֵי אַבְרָהָם וֵאלֹהֵי נָחוֹר יִשְׁפְּטוּ בֵינֵינוּ אֱלֹהֵי אֲבִיהֶם וַיִּשָּׁבַע יַעֲקֹב בְּפַחַד אָבִיו יִצְחָק: בְּרֵאשִׁית לא:מב, נג

Bronze statuette (early 2nd mill. B.C.E.) of a kneeling worshiper. It was originally covered with gold leaf, traces of which can still be seen on the hands and face. The inscription states that this statuette of a praying man was made by one Lu-anna, a servant of Hammurabi (of Babylon?), for his own life and that of his master, and that he dedicated it to Amurru (the patron god of the Amorites).

The cup attached to the base is probably to receive libations; the couchant ram is probably a symbol of sacrifice. On the other side of the base is a scene showing a similar praying figure, kneeling before an enthroned deity. The statuette is about 7⅝ inches high.

Upper half of a steatite statuette of a woman adorant, dated about the time of Gudea of Lagash (22nd century B.C.E.). She wears a cap, several rings around her neck, and a shawl with a decorated edge over her dress. Found at Tello in southern Mesopotamia. It is 6¾ inches high.

44

never to be broken under penalty of severe punishment and, theoretically at least, even complete rejection. It is not possible to understand the subsequent career of Israel without understanding these two inseparable concepts which arose in patriarchal times: practical monotheism and the personal covenant between the patriarchal families and their God.

## The Questioning Spirit

Another phenomenon which apparently struck root in the patriarchal period is the fundamentally questioning and antidogmatic character and outlook of ancient Israel. It is characteristic of ancient Near Eastern saga that the heroes talked back to their god (s). Within the patriarchal structure, the patriarch was the chief figure, and no one was free from his final authority. In actual life, however, the matriarch too was a dominant figure, for example, Abraham's wife Sarah and Isaac's wife Rebekah. And within the household at large there was considerable freedom of action. In the domestic sphere, the woman's ameliorative counsels and her motherly feelings were taken seriously. An important check on patriarchal authority was economically grounded. By custom, the land was regarded as ultimately inalienable, so that family and tribal rather than private rights were the norm.

God, too, was conceived in patriarchal terms, theoretically omnipotent but actually subject to considerable questioning. He was not regarded as a faraway, impersonal deity. The very notion of a covenant implies the equality of the covenanters, and the devotion exacted from God by the patriarchs was no less thorough than that exacted from them by Him. He was near at hand whenever needed, a member of the patriarchal household and available for extended question-and-answer periods. Beginning with the semi-nomadic family structure of patriarchal soci-

# The Questioning Spirit

<sup>11</sup>Who is like You, O LORD, among the celestials ;
Who is like You, majestic in holiness,
Awesome in splendor, working wonders!

*Exodus 15.11*

מִי־כָמֹכָה בָּאֵלִם יְהֹוָה מִי כָּמֹכָה נֶאְדָּר בַּקֹּדֶשׁ
נוֹרָא תְהִלֹּת עֹשֵׂה־פֶלֶא:

שְׁמוֹת טו:יא

---

<sup>4</sup>Hear, O Israel! The LORD is our God, the LORD alone.

*Deuteronomy 6.4*

שְׁמַע יִשְׂרָאֵל יְהֹוָה אֱלֹהֵינוּ יְהֹוָה אֶחָד:

דְּבָרִים ו:ד

---

<sup>12</sup>But God said to Abraham, "Do not be distressed over the boy or your slave; whatever Sarah tells you, do as she says, for it is through Isaac that offspring shall be continued for you."

*Genesis 21.12*

וַיֹּאמֶר אֱלֹהִים אֶל־אַבְרָהָם אַל־יֵרַע בְּעֵינֶיךָ
עַל־הַנַּעַר וְעַל־אֲמָתֶךָ כֹּל אֲשֶׁר תֹּאמַר אֵלֶיךָ שָׂרָה
שְׁמַע בְּקֹלָהּ כִּי בְיִצְחָק יִקָּרֵא לְךָ זָרַע:

בְּרֵאשִׁית כא:יב

---

<sup>15</sup>If you reject My laws and spurn My rules, so that you do not observe all My commandments and you break My covenant, <sup>16</sup>I in turn will do this to you: I will wreak misery upon you — consumption and fever, which cause the eyes to pine and the body to languish; you shall sow your seed to no purpose, for your enemies shall eat it.

*Leviticus 26.15-16*

וְאִם־בְּחֻקֹּתַי תִּמְאָסוּ וְאִם אֶת־מִשְׁפָּטַי תִּגְעַל
נַפְשְׁכֶם לְבִלְתִּי עֲשׂוֹת אֶת־כָּל־מִצְוֹתַי לְהַפְרְכֶם
אֶת־בְּרִיתִי: אַף־אֲנִי אֶעֱשֶׂה־זֹּאת לָכֶם וְהִפְקַדְתִּי
עֲלֵיכֶם בֶּהָלָה אֶת־הַשַּׁחֶפֶת וְאֶת־הַקַּדַּחַת מְכַלּוֹת
עֵינַיִם וּמְדִיבֹת נָפֶשׁ וּזְרַעְתֶּם לָרִיק זַרְעֲכֶם וַאֲכָלֻהוּ
אֹיְבֵיכֶם:

וַיִּקְרָא כו:טו־טז

---

<sup>42</sup>When the words of her older son Esau were reported to Rebekah, she sent for her younger son Jacob and said to him, "Your brother Esau is consoling himself by planning to kill you. <sup>43</sup>Now then, my son, listen to me. Flee at once to Haran, to my brother Laban. <sup>44</sup>Stay with him a while, until your brother's fury subsides—<sup>45</sup>until your brother's anger against you subsides—and he forgets what you have done to him. Then I will fetch you from there. Let me not lose you both in one day!"
<sup>46</sup>Rebekah said to Isaac, "I am disgusted with my life because of the Hittite women. If Jacob marries a Hittite woman like these, from among the native women, what good will life be to me?"

*Genesis 27.42-46*

וַיֻּגַּד לְרִבְקָה אֶת־דִּבְרֵי עֵשָׂו בְּנָהּ הַגָּדֹל וַתִּשְׁלַח
וַתִּקְרָא לְיַעֲקֹב בְּנָהּ הַקָּטָן וַתֹּאמֶר אֵלָיו הִנֵּה
עֵשָׂו אָחִיךָ מִתְנַחֵם לְךָ לְהָרְגֶךָ: וְעַתָּה בְנִי שְׁמַע
בְּקֹלִי וְקוּם בְּרַח־לְךָ אֶל־לָבָן אָחִי חָרָנָה: וְיָשַׁבְתָּ
עִמּוֹ יָמִים אֲחָדִים עַד אֲשֶׁר־תָּשׁוּב חֲמַת אָחִיךָ:
עַד־שׁוּב אַף־אָחִיךָ מִמְּךָ וְשָׁכַח אֵת אֲשֶׁר־עָשִׂיתָ
לּוֹ וְשָׁלַחְתִּי וּלְקַחְתִּיךָ מִשָּׁם לָמָה אֶשְׁכַּל גַּם־שְׁנֵיכֶם
יוֹם אֶחָד: וַתֹּאמֶר רִבְקָה אֶל־יִצְחָק קַצְתִּי בְחַיַּי
מִפְּנֵי בְּנוֹת חֵת אִם־לֹקֵחַ יַעֲקֹב אִשָּׁה מִבְּנוֹת־חֵת
כָּאֵלֶּה מִבְּנוֹת הָאָרֶץ לָמָה לִּי חַיִּים:

בְּרֵאשִׁית כז:מב־מו

ety, and down to the time of the composition of the latest books in the Bible, there runs through Hebrew literature the characteristic and persistent feature of questioning authority. The Hebrew mind expressed its deepest self in its oppostion to the absolute rule of any one man or tribe, be it kinsman or alien. This attitude extended even to the rule of God. Thus, in the famous dialogue between Abraham and God in Genesis 18:16–33, Abraham flatly objected when God proposed to obliterate Sodom, on the grounds that it was not fair to punish good men along with the bad. And Abraham would not rest content until God promised not to vent His anger, so long as there were as few as ten righteous men left. Which, however, seems not to have been the case.

The Book of Job provides an even more famous example of putting God to the question. But it is worth noting that neither Abraham nor Job partook of the character of a Promethean rebel. They were not insurrectionaries against God; they wanted only to see justice done, to understand and define God's powers, to have the contract properly drawn up and fulfilled on both sides.

<sup>17</sup>Now the LORD had said, "Shall I hide from Abraham what I am about to do? . . .

<sup>20</sup>The outrage of Sodom and Gomorrah is so great, and their sin so grave! . . ." <sup>23</sup>Abraham came forward and said, "Will You sweep away the innocent along with the guilty? . . . <sup>25</sup>Far be it from You to do such a thing, to bring death upon the innocent as well as the guilty, so that innocent and guilty fare alike. Far be it from You! Shall not the Judge of all the earth deal justly?" . . .<sup>32</sup> . . . And He answered, "I will not destroy, for the sake of the ten."

*Genesis 18.17–25, 32*

וַיהֹוָה אָמָר הַמְכַסֶּה אֲנִי מֵאַבְרָהָם אֲשֶׁר אֲנִי עֹשֶׂה: . . . זַעֲקַת סְדֹם וַעֲמֹרָה כִּי־רָבָּה וְחַטָּאתָם כִּי כָבְדָה מְאֹד: . . . וַיִּגַּשׁ אַבְרָהָם וַיֹּאמַר הַאַף תִּסְפֶּה צַדִּיק עִם־רָשָׁע: . . . חָלִלָה לְּךָ מֵעֲשֹׂת כַּדָּבָר הַזֶּה לְהָמִית צַדִּיק עִם־רָשָׁע וְהָיָה כַצַּדִּיק כָּרָשָׁע חָלִלָה לָּךְ הֲשֹׁפֵט כָּל־הָאָרֶץ לֹא יַעֲשֶׂה מִשְׁפָּט: . . . וַיֹּאמֶר אַל־נָא יִחַר לַאדֹנָי וַאֲדַבְּרָה אַךְ־הַפַּעַם אוּלַי יִמָּצְאוּן שָׁם עֲשָׂרָה וַיֹּאמֶר לֹא אַשְׁחִית בַּעֲבוּר הָעֲשָׂרָה:

בְּרֵאשִׁית יח:יז-כה, לב

<sup>9</sup>The LORD further said to Moses, "I see that this is a stiffnecked people. <sup>10</sup>Now, let Me be, that My anger may blaze forth against them and that I may destroy them and make of you a great nation." <sup>11</sup>But Moses implored the LORD his God, saying, "Let not Your anger, O LORD, blaze forth against Your people, whom You delivered from the land of Egypt with great power and with a mighty hand. <sup>12</sup>Let not the Egyptians say, 'It was with evil intent that He delivered them, only to kill them off in the mountains and annihilate them from the face of the earth.' Turn from Your blazing anger, and renounce the plan to punish Your people. <sup>13</sup>Remember Your servants, Abraham, Isaac, and Jacob, how You swore to them by Your Self and said to them: I will make your offspring as numerous as the stars of heaven, and I will give to your offspring this whole land of which I spoke, to possess forever." <sup>14</sup>And the LORD renounced the punishment He had planned to bring upon His people.

*Exodus 32.9-14*

וַיֹּאמֶר יְהֹוָה אֶל־מֹשֶׁה רָאִיתִי אֶת־הָעָם הַזֶּה וְהִנֵּה עַם־קְשֵׁה־עֹרֶף הוּא: וְעַתָּה הַנִּיחָה לִּי וְיִחַר־אַפִּי בָהֶם וַאֲכַלֵּם וְאֶעֱשֶׂה אוֹתְךָ לְגוֹי גָּדוֹל: וַיְחַל מֹשֶׁה אֶת־פְּנֵי יְהֹוָה אֱלֹהָיו וַיֹּאמֶר לָמָה יְהֹוָה יֶחֱרֶה אַפְּךָ בְּעַמֶּךָ אֲשֶׁר הוֹצֵאתָ מֵאֶרֶץ מִצְרַיִם בְּכֹחַ גָּדוֹל וּבְיָד חֲזָקָה: לָמָּה יֹאמְרוּ מִצְרַיִם לֵאמֹר בְּרָעָה הוֹצִיאָם לַהֲרֹג אֹתָם בֶּהָרִים וּלְכַלֹּתָם מֵעַל פְּנֵי הָאֲדָמָה שׁוּב מֵחֲרוֹן אַפֶּךָ וְהִנָּחֵם עַל־הָרָעָה לְעַמֶּךָ: זְכֹר לְאַבְרָהָם לְיִצְחָק וּלְיִשְׂרָאֵל עֲבָדֶיךָ אֲשֶׁר נִשְׁבַּעְתָּ לָהֶם בָּךְ וַתְּדַבֵּר אֲלֵהֶם אַרְבֶּה אֶת־זַרְעֲכֶם כְּכוֹכְבֵי הַשָּׁמַיִם וְכָל־הָאָרֶץ הַזֹּאת אֲשֶׁר אָמַרְתִּי אֶתֵּן לְזַרְעֲכֶם וְנָחֲלוּ לְעֹלָם: וַיִּנָּחֶם יְהֹוָה עַל־הָרָעָה אֲשֶׁר דִּבֶּר לַעֲשׂוֹת לְעַמּוֹ:

שְׁמוֹת לב:ט-יד

<sup>1</sup>The word of the LORD came to Jonah son of Amittai: <sup>2</sup>"Go at once to Nineveh, that great city, and proclaim judgment upon it; for their wickedness has come up before Me." <sup>3</sup>But Jonah set out to flee from the LORD to Tarshish. He went down to Joppa and found a ship going to Tarshish. He paid the fare and went aboard to sail with the others to Tarshish, to escape the LORD.

*Jonah 1.1-3*

וַיְהִי דְּבַר־יְהֹוָה אֶל־יוֹנָה בֶן־אֲמִתַּי לֵאמֹר: קוּם לֵךְ אֶל־נִינְוֵה הָעִיר הַגְּדוֹלָה וּקְרָא עָלֶיהָ כִּי־עָלְתָה רָעָתָם לְפָנָי: וַיָּקָם יוֹנָה לִבְרֹחַ תַּרְשִׁישָׁה מִלִּפְנֵי יְהֹוָה וַיֵּרֶד יָפוֹ וַיִּמְצָא אֳנִיָּה בָּאָה תַרְשִׁישׁ וַיִּתֵּן שְׂכָרָהּ וַיֵּרֶד בָּהּ לָבוֹא עִמָּהֶם תַּרְשִׁישָׁה מִלִּפְנֵי יְהֹוָה:

יוֹנָה א:א-ג

## Chapter II

# BONDAGE, EXODUS, AND THE NATIONAL COVENANT

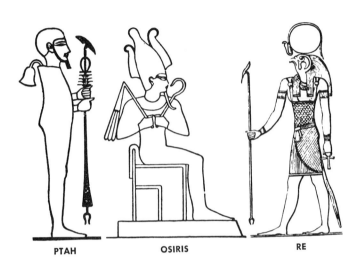

PTAH      OSIRIS      RE

ISIS      HATHOR      SETH
(suckling her son Horus)

Some of the important Egyptian gods during the period of Israel's bondage and eventual exodus.

THE second important epoch in the career of ancient Israel began with the descent of a group of Hebrews into Egypt sometime around 1700 B.C.E. By the time their descendants had found their way back to Canaan, several centuries later, they were on the verge of nationhood.

The Egyptian experience was a decisive factor in the development of Israel as a people. Here the Hebrew families grew in number, and their conception of God and His covenant with them was extended to cover the entire Hebrew folk. Here also they continued to oppose state autocracy, in contrast to the abject submission by the Egyptian people at large. The ancient custom of deifying kings, nowhere more elaborately developed than in Egypt, left them fundamentally untouched. In this great episode, the heroic figure of Moses stands out in epic grandeur.

### Eisodus: Egypt and the Hyksos

Whenever a drought and famine desolated the region of Canaan, it was common for whole clans to pick up their belongings and seek refuge in Egypt. There the periodic overflow of the Nile gave life to the land, as is does today, and helped to regulate the agriculture of the country. The Egyptians learned early to dig channels for the seasonal flood and to irrigate the grain-producing land. Migration into Egypt was therefore an ancient expedient.

In Canaan, on the other hand, the rains did not always come when needed. A late-thirteenth century Egyptian document, for example, tells how the seminomadic inhabitants of Edom, south of Canaan, left their homes in time of drought to come to Egypt

<sup>8</sup>A new king arose over Egypt, who did not know Joseph. <sup>9</sup>And he said to his people, "Look, the Israelite people are much too numerous for us. <sup>10</sup>Let us deal shrewdly with them, so that they may not increase; otherwise in the event of war they may join our enemies in fighting against us and rise from the ground."

*Exodus 1.8-10*

וַיָּקָם מֶלֶךְ־חָדָשׁ עַל־מִצְרָיִם אֲשֶׁר לֹא־יָדַע
אֶת־יוֹסֵף: וַיֹּאמֶר אֶל־עַמּוֹ הִנֵּה עַם בְּנֵי יִשְׂרָאֵל
רַב וְעָצוּם מִמֶּנּוּ: הָבָה נִתְחַכְּמָה לוֹ פֶּן־יִרְבֶּה וְהָיָה
כִּי־תִקְרֶאנָה מִלְחָמָה וְנוֹסַף גַּם־הוּא עַל־שֹׂנְאֵינוּ
וְנִלְחַם־בָּנוּ וְעָלָה מִן־הָאָרֶץ: שְׁמוֹת א:ח—י

<sup>3</sup>Moses went up to God, and the LORD called to him from the mountain, saying, "Thus shall you say to the house of Jacob and declare to the children of Israel: <sup>4</sup>'You have seen what I did to the Egyptians, how I bore you on eagles' wings and brought you to Me. <sup>5</sup>Now then, if you will obey Me faithfully and keep My covenant, you shall be My treasured possession among all the peoples. Indeed, all the earth is Mine, <sup>6</sup>but you shall be to Me a kingdom of priests and a holy nation.' These are the words that you shall speak to the children of Israel."

*Exodus 19.3-6*

וּמֹשֶׁה עָלָה אֶל־הָאֱלֹהִים וַיִּקְרָא אֵלָיו יְהֹוָה
מִן־הָהָר לֵאמֹר כֹּה תֹאמַר לְבֵית יַעֲקֹב וְתַגֵּיד לִבְנֵי
יִשְׂרָאֵל: אַתֶּם רְאִיתֶם אֲשֶׁר עָשִׂיתִי לְמִצְרָיִם וָאֶשָּׂא
אֶתְכֶם עַל־כַּנְפֵי נְשָׁרִים וָאָבִא אֶתְכֶם אֵלָי: וְעַתָּה
אִם־שָׁמוֹעַ תִּשְׁמְעוּ בְּקֹלִי וּשְׁמַרְתֶּם אֶת־בְּרִיתִי
וִהְיִיתֶם לִי סְגֻלָּה מִכָּל־הָעַמִּים כִּי־לִי כָּל־הָאָרֶץ:
וְאַתֶּם תִּהְיוּ־לִי מַמְלֶכֶת כֹּהֲנִים וְגוֹי קָדוֹשׁ אֵלֶּה
הַדְּבָרִים אֲשֶׁר תְּדַבֵּר אֶל־בְּנֵי יִשְׂרָאֵל: שְׁמוֹת יט:ג—ו

<sup>1</sup>There was a famine in the land—aside from the previous famine that had occurred in the days of Abraham—and Isaac went to Abimelech, king of the Philistines, in Gerar. <sup>2</sup>The LORD had appeared to him and said "Do not go down to Egypt; stay in the land which I point out to you."

*Genesis 26.1-2*

וַיְהִי רָעָב בָּאָרֶץ מִלְּבַד הָרָעָב הָרִאשׁוֹן אֲשֶׁר
הָיָה בִּימֵי אַבְרָהָם וַיֵּלֶךְ יִצְחָק אֶל־אֲבִימֶלֶךְ
מֶלֶךְ־פְּלִשְׁתִּים גְּרָרָה: וַיֵּרָא אֵלָיו יְהֹוָה וַיֹּאמֶר
אַל־תֵּרֵד מִצְרָיְמָה שְׁכֹן בָּאָרֶץ אֲשֶׁר אֹמַר אֵלֶיךָ:
בְּרֵאשִׁית כו:א—ב

<sup>1</sup>When Jacob saw that there were food rations to be had in Egypt, he said to his sons, "Why do you keep looking at one another? <sup>2</sup>Now I hear," he went on, "that there are rations to be had in Egypt. Go down and procure rations for us there, that we may live and not die."

*Genesis 42.1-2*

וַיַּרְא יַעֲקֹב כִּי יֶשׁ־שֶׁבֶר בְּמִצְרָיִם וַיֹּאמֶר יַעֲקֹב
לְבָנָיו לָמָּה תִּתְרָאוּ: וַיֹּאמֶר הִנֵּה שָׁמַעְתִּי כִּי יֶשׁ־
שֶׁבֶר בְּמִצְרָיִם רְדוּ־שָׁמָּה וְשִׁבְרוּ־לָנוּ מִשָּׁם וְנִחְיֶה
וְלֹא נָמוּת: בְּרֵאשִׁית מב:א—ב

49

Incised relief of an emaciated, scantily dressed, impoverished herdsman from the registers on the south wall of the tomb of Ukh-hotep at Meir, Egypt. He cannot even afford a well-hewn staff, but must use the branch of a tree. He leads three fatted oxen as gifts to the deceased occupant of the tomb. His general physical bearing perhaps alludes to the way of life and general human condition of those who live on the periphery of settled Egyptian life. Height of herdsman about 16½ inches.

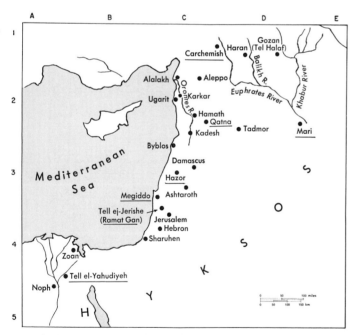

The far-flung territory of the Hyksos was kept under control by strategically located garrison cities which were usually surrounded by sloped ramparts (glacis) of beaten earth for ready access by the famed Hyksos chariots. These major cities are underlined in the map.

"to keep themselves alive and to keep their cattle alive." It was famine, too, as the Bible says, which compelled Abraham and Isaac in an earlier period to go south (Genesis 12 and 26), and the same reason is given for Jacob's sending his sons to Egypt, where grain could still be procured even in a time of general drought (Genesis 42 ff.). As a result of this mission, the entire family finally settled there.

At the same time, this Eisodus—the "going into," as distinguished from the Exodus, the "going out of"—may also have been encouraged by certain ethnic disturbances which for a period disrupted Egyptian control of Canaan and reduced the sovereignty of the Egyptian homeland as well. Following upon the increasing disintegration of the Egyptian state, a mixed group of Asiatics, apparently mostly Semites, and known generally as Hyksos (literally, "rulers of foreign countries"), appeared in the north and swarmed down through Syria and Canaan. By about 1720 B.C.E. they had crossed the land bridge into Africa and conquered much of Egypt, a domination that was not to be completely broken until about 1550 B.C.E. .

Between the Hyksos and the Hebrews there appear to be a number of points of contact. It is known, for instance, that a certain Hyksos chieftain in Egypt bore the name Jacob-el, or perhaps Jacob-har, which means "May El, or Har [the mountain god] Give Protection." The verbal element, Jacob which means "protect," is identical with the name of the Hebrew patriarch Jacob who settled in Egypt. Again, the historical kernel which resides in the dramatic story of the career of Joseph in Egypt, of the coming to power of a Hebrew in the Egyptian court, could well have derived from the period of the Hyksos, when Semites, and in all probability Habiru among them, were prominent among the new rulers of Egypt. For it was not Egyptian habit to nourish the ambitions of strangers in their

50

¹When Joseph was taken down to Egypt, a certain Egyptian, Potiphar, a courtier of Pharaoh and his chief steward, bought him from the Ishmaelites who had brought him there. ²The LORD was with Joseph, and he was a successful man; and he stayed in the house of his Egyptian master. ³And when his master saw that the LORD was with him and that the LORD lent success to everything he undertook, ⁴he took a liking to Joseph. He made him his personal attendant and put him in charge of his household, placing in his hands all that he owned. ⁵And from the time that the Egyptian put him in charge of his household and of all that he owned, the LORD blessed his house for Joseph's sake, so that the blessing of the LORD was upon everything that he owned, in the house and outside. ⁶He left all that he had in Joseph's hands and, with him there, he paid attention to nothing save the food that he ate. Now Joseph was well built and handsome.

*Genesis 39.1-6*

וְיוֹסֵף הוּרַד מִצְרָיְמָה וַיִּקְנֵהוּ פּוֹטִיפַר סְרִיס
פַּרְעֹה שַׂר הַטַּבָּחִים אִישׁ מִצְרִי מִיַּד הַיִּשְׁמְעֵאלִים
אֲשֶׁר הוֹרִדֻהוּ שָׁמָּה: וַיְהִי יְהוָה אֶת־יוֹסֵף וַיְהִי אִישׁ
מַצְלִיחַ וַיְהִי בְּבֵית אֲדֹנָיו הַמִּצְרִי: וַיַּרְא אֲדֹנָיו
כִּי יְהוָה אִתּוֹ וְכֹל אֲשֶׁר־הוּא עֹשֶׂה יְהוָה מַצְלִיחַ
בְּיָדוֹ: וַיִּמְצָא יוֹסֵף חֵן בְּעֵינָיו וַיְשָׁרֶת אֹתוֹ וַיַּפְקִדֵהוּ
עַל־בֵּיתוֹ וְכָל־יֶשׁ־לוֹ נָתַן בְּיָדוֹ: וַיְהִי מֵאָז הִפְקִיד
אֹתוֹ בְּבֵיתוֹ וְעַל כָּל־אֲשֶׁר יֶשׁ־לוֹ וַיְבָרֶךְ יְהוָה
אֶת־בֵּית הַמִּצְרִי בִּגְלַל יוֹסֵף וַיְהִי בִּרְכַּת יְהוָה
בְּכָל־אֲשֶׁר יֶשׁ־לוֹ בַּבַּיִת וּבַשָּׂדֶה: וַיַּעֲזֹב כָּל־
אֲשֶׁר־לוֹ בְּיַד יוֹסֵף וְלֹא־יָדַע אִתּוֹ מְאוּמָה כִּי
אִם־הַלֶּחֶם אֲשֶׁר־הוּא אוֹכֵל וַיְהִי יוֹסֵף יְפֵה־
תֹאַר וִיפֵה מַרְאֶה:

בְּרֵאשִׁית לט:א-ו

⁴⁴Pharaoh said to Joseph, "I am Pharaoh; yet without you, no one shall lift up hand or foot in all the land of Egypt." ⁴⁵Pharaoh then gave Joseph the name Zaphenath-paneah; and he gave him for a wife Asenath daughter of Poti-phera, priest of On. Thus Joseph emerged in charge of the land of Egypt.

*Genesis 41.44-45*

וַיֹּאמֶר פַּרְעֹה אֶל־יוֹסֵף אֲנִי פַרְעֹה וּבִלְעָדֶיךָ
לֹא־יָרִים אִישׁ אֶת־יָדוֹ וְאֶת־רַגְלוֹ בְּכָל־אֶרֶץ
מִצְרָיִם: וַיִּקְרָא פַרְעֹה שֵׁם־יוֹסֵף צָפְנַת פַּעְנֵחַ
וַיִּתֶּן־לוֹ אֶת־אָסְנַת בַּת־פּוֹטִי פֶרַע כֹּהֵן אֹן לְאִשָּׁה
וַיֵּצֵא יוֹסֵף עַל־אֶרֶץ מִצְרָיִם:

בְּרֵאשִׁית מא:מד-מה

⁶They took along their livestock and the wealth that they had amassed in the land of Canaan. Thus Jacob and all his offspring with him came to Egypt . . .

²⁶All the persons belonging to Jacob who came to Egypt—his own issue, aside from the wives of Jacob's sons—all these persons numbered 66. ²⁷And Joseph's sons who were born to him in Egypt were two in number. Thus the total of Jacob's household who came to Egypt was 70 persons.

²⁸He had sent Judah ahead of him to Joseph, to point the way before him to Goshen. And so they came to the region of Goshen.

*Genesis 46.6, 26-28*

וַיִּקְחוּ אֶת־מִקְנֵיהֶם וְאֶת־רְכוּשָׁם אֲשֶׁר רָכְשׁוּ
בְּאֶרֶץ כְּנַעַן וַיָּבֹאוּ מִצְרָיְמָה יַעֲקֹב וְכָל־זַרְעוֹ
אִתּוֹ: . . .

כָּל־הַנֶּפֶשׁ הַבָּאָה לְיַעֲקֹב מִצְרַיְמָה יֹצְאֵי יְרֵכוֹ
מִלְּבַד נְשֵׁי בְנֵי־יַעֲקֹב כָּל־נֶפֶשׁ שִׁשִּׁים וָשֵׁשׁ: וּבְנֵי
יוֹסֵף אֲשֶׁר־יֻלַּד־לוֹ בְמִצְרַיִם נֶפֶשׁ שְׁנָיִם כָּל־
הַנֶּפֶשׁ לְבֵית־יַעֲקֹב הַבָּאָה מִצְרַיְמָה שִׁבְעִים: וְאֶת־
יְהוּדָה שָׁלַח לְפָנָיו אֶל־יוֹסֵף לְהוֹרֹת לְפָנָיו גֹּשְׁנָה
וַיָּבֹאוּ אַרְצָה גֹּשֶׁן:

בְּרֵאשִׁית מו:ו, כו-כח

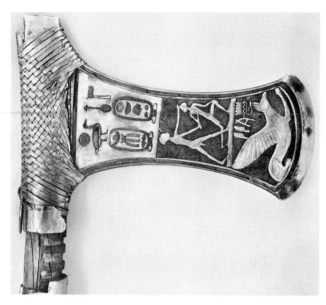

Axe from the burial furniture of Queen Mother Akh-hotep, of the Eighteenth Dynasty. The designs are made of gold and lapis lazuli inlay. The figures, which are part of the design, depict the symbolic defeat inflicted by the pharaoh upon the Asiatic enemy.

The so-called "Stele of the Year 400," portraying the god Seth, was set up by Ramses II to commemorate the 400 years since Seth became king of Egypt, and to support the hoary legitimacy of Seth's city as Ramses' own new capital. Actually, Seth was a West Semitic deity and had been introduced to Egyptian worshipers by a king of Egypt, probably of foreign extraction. The city was re-named "Ramses" (cf. Ex. 1.8-11) by the king.

midst. Furthermore, it would seem to be more than a mere coincidence that the Hebrews, according to the Bible, settled in Goshen in the Delta, the very area which the Hyksos built up around their new capital Avaris, the later Tanis.

In this connection it is also interesting to note that Josephus, the Jewish historian of the first century c.e., quotes the Egyptian historian Manetho (about 275 b.c.e.), to the effect that a large number of Hyksos made their way from Avaris to Canaan and there built Jerusalem. These Hyksos, according to Manetho, were "not fewer in number than 240,000," a figure which recalls the Biblical statement (Numbers 1:46) that 603,550 Hebrew males, exclusive of Levites, women, and children, participated in the Exodus from Egypt.

All these facts suggest that the Hebrews and the Hyksos may have been on terms of considerable intimacy; so that the entry of the Hebrews into Egypt would have been facilitated by the presence of Hyksos in positions of power, and the Bondage accounted for by the enslavement of foreign elements after the fall of the Hyksos invaders. If this hypothesis has substance, it provides evidence that the Biblical version of the Hebrew sojourn in Egypt (Genesis 39-50; Exodus 1 ff.) derives from the same period as the events which it describes. For the Egyptians themselves, humiliated by their conquest at the hands of the Hyksos, avoided and suppressed any reference to the events of the period, and it would have been well-nigh impossible for anyone to learn the historical details very much later.

## The Sojourn

The Bible itself elaborates only on the final period of the Bondage in Egypt. But what was there to say? After the Egyptians had overthrown the Hyksos, they enslaved those foreigners who had not fled, thus re-

*Scholars can no longer determine the approximate figures either of the Hyksos or of the Hebrews; for the Hebrews, a figure of about 6,000 has sometimes been suggested. See in general, B. Mazar, "The Exodus and the Conquest," pp. 69-93, 304-307, 348-349 in* The World History of the Jewish People, *Vol. III:* Judges *(1971).*

[1]On the first day of the second month, in the second year following the exodus from the land of Egypt, the LORD spoke to Moses in the wilderness of Sinai, in the Tent of Meeting, saying: [2]Take a census of the whole Israelite community by the clans of its ancestral houses, listing the names, every male, head by head. [3]You and Aaron shall record them by their groups, from the age of twenty years up, all those in Israel who are able to bear arms .

*Numbers 1.1-3*

וַיְדַבֵּר יְהֹוָה אֶל־מֹשֶׁה בְּמִדְבַּר סִינַי בְּאֹהֶל מוֹעֵד בְּאֶחָד לַחֹדֶשׁ הַשֵּׁנִי בַּשָּׁנָה הַשֵּׁנִית לְצֵאתָם מֵאֶרֶץ מִצְרַיִם לֵאמֹר: שְׂאוּ אֶת־רֹאשׁ כָּל־עֲדַת בְּנֵי־יִשְׂרָאֵל לְמִשְׁפְּחֹתָם לְבֵית אֲבֹתָם בְּמִסְפַּר שֵׁמוֹת כָּל־זָכָר לְגֻלְגְּלֹתָם: מִבֶּן עֶשְׂרִים שָׁנָה וָמַעְלָה כָּל־יֹצֵא צָבָא בְּיִשְׂרָאֵל תִּפְקְדוּ אֹתָם לְצִבְאֹתָם אַתָּה וְאַהֲרֹן:

בְּמִדְבָּר א:א–ג

[46]All who were enrolled came to 603,550. [47]The Levites, however, were not recorded among them by their ancestral tribe.

*Numbers 1.46–47*

וַיִּהְיוּ כָּל־הַפְּקֻדִים שֵׁשׁ־מֵאוֹת אֶלֶף וּשְׁלֹשֶׁת אֲלָפִים וַחֲמֵשׁ מֵאוֹת וַחֲמִשִּׁים: וְהַלְוִיִּם לְמַטֵּה אֲבֹתָם לֹא הָתְפָּקְדוּ בְּתוֹכָם:

בְּמִדְבָּר א:מו–מז

[37]The Israelites journeyed from Raamses to Succoth, about six hundred thousand men on foot, aside from children. [38]Moreover, a mixed multitude went up with them, and very much livestock, both flocks and herds.

*Exodus 12.37–38*

וַיִּסְעוּ בְנֵי־יִשְׂרָאֵל מֵרַעְמְסֵס סֻכֹּתָה כְּשֵׁשׁ־מֵאוֹת אֶלֶף רַגְלִי הַגְּבָרִים לְבַד מִטָּף: וְגַם־עֵרֶב רַב עָלָה אִתָּם וְצֹאן וּבָקָר מִקְנֶה כָּבֵד מְאֹד:

שְׁמוֹת יב:לז–לח

## The Sojourn

[11]So they set taskmasters over them to oppress them with forced labor; and they built garrison cities for Pharaoh: Pithom and Raamses. [12]But the more they were oppressed, the more they increased and spread out, so that the [Egyptians] came to dread the Israelites. [13]The Egyptians ruthlessly imposed upon the Israelites [14]the various labots that they made them perform. Ruthlessly they made life bitter for them with harsh labor at mortar and bricks and with all sorts of tasks in the field.

*Exodus 1.11-14*

וַיָּשִׂימוּ עָלָיו שָׂרֵי מִסִּים לְמַעַן עַנֹּתוֹ בְּסִבְלֹתָם וַיִּבֶן עָרֵי מִסְכְּנוֹת לְפַרְעֹה אֶת־פִּתֹם וְאֶת־רַעַמְסֵס: וְכַאֲשֶׁר יְעַנּוּ אֹתוֹ כֵּן יִרְבֶּה וְכֵן יִפְרֹץ וַיָּקֻצוּ מִפְּנֵי בְּנֵי יִשְׂרָאֵל: וַיַּעֲבִדוּ מִצְרַיִם אֶת־בְּנֵי יִשְׂרָאֵל בְּפָרֶךְ: וַיְמָרְרוּ אֶת־חַיֵּיהֶם בַּעֲבֹדָה קָשָׁה בְּחֹמֶר וּבִלְבֵנִים וּבְכָל־עֲבֹדָה בַּשָּׂדֶה אֵת כָּל־עֲבֹדָתָם אֲשֶׁר־עָבְדוּ בָהֶם בְּפָרֶךְ:

שְׁמוֹת א:יא–יד

Brickmaking. Painted register from the tomb of Rekh-mi-Re at Thebes (ca. 1450). The major steps of this work are shown (approximately from left to right): drawing water; kneading the wet clay; transporting the prepared clay to the brick makers; fashioning the bricks and setting them out to dry in the sun. To the far right the stacked bricks await removal for usage.

Farming. Painted registers from the tomb of Nakht at Thebes (late 15th cent.) Nakht sits viewing the activities. Below—preparing the ground; above—harvesting. The products are displayed before him.

versing the status of the non-Egyptians in the land. The Bible records: "A new king arose in Egypt who did not know Joseph. . . . And they [the Egyptians] set taskmasters over them [the Hebrews] to oppress them with forced labor. And they built for Pharaoh store-cities, Pithom and Ramses" (Ex. 1:8–11).

Under the Hyksos domination, Egyptian culture had sunk so low that the period has been described as "The Great Humiliation." But the successful war of liberation against the Hyksos led to an Egyptian revival on such a grand scale that the period of the New Kingdom which followed, especially during the Eighteenth and Nineteenth Dynasties (about 1570–1200 B.C.E.), has been called the Golden Age, and was the subject of a recent book which bore the suggestive title, *When Egypt Ruled the East*. The development of literature, art, and building, the inculcation of individual physical prowess in sport and in battle, the marked extension of the influence of women in the royal court and in upper-class circles generally—all of these manifested a new cosmopolitanism, and even secularism, brought on by imperial expansion abroad and increased urbanization at home.

There was much in the Egyptian environment that the Hebrews could emulate. But the kind of life which they and others led in the Egyptian slave camps did not encourage cultural apprenticeship. "Slave troops on a government building project," as one authority put it, "have no opportunity for discussion with priests and scribes. Their simple desert souls would see and shrink from some of the abominations of the effete civilization and long to escape dreary enslavement rather than admire the cultural triumph of the land of bondage." (J. A. Wilson, *The Burden of Egypt* [Chicago, 1951], p. 256.)

## Moses, Leader of the Exodus

It was probably sometime in the thirteenth

²²Then Pharaoh charged all his people, saying, "Every boy that is born you shall throw into the Nile, but let every girl live."

*Exodus 1.22*

²³A long time after that, the king of Egypt died. The Israelites were groaning under the bondage and cried out; and their cry for help from the bondage rose up to God. ²⁴God heard their moaning, and God remembered His covenant with Abraham and Isaac and Jacob. ²⁵God looked upon the Israelites; and God took notice of them.

*Exodus 2.23-25*

וַיְצַו פַּרְעֹה לְכָל־עַמּוֹ לֵאמֹר כָּל־הַבֵּן הַיִּלּוֹד הַיְאֹרָה תַּשְׁלִיכֻהוּ וְכָל־הַבַּת תְּחַיּוּן:
שְׁמוֹת א:כב

וַיְהִי בַיָּמִים הָרַבִּים הָהֵם וַיָּמָת מֶלֶךְ מִצְרַיִם וַיֵּאָנְחוּ בְנֵי־יִשְׂרָאֵל מִן־הָעֲבֹדָה וַיִּזְעָקוּ וַתַּעַל שַׁוְעָתָם אֶל־הָאֱלֹהִים מִן־הָעֲבֹדָה: וַיִּשְׁמַע אֱלֹהִים אֶת־נַאֲקָתָם וַיִּזְכֹּר אֱלֹהִים אֶת־בְּרִיתוֹ אֶת־אַבְרָהָם אֶת־יִצְחָק וְאֶת־יַעֲקֹב: וַיַּרְא אֱלֹהִים אֶת־בְּנֵי יִשְׂרָאֵל וַיֵּדַע אֱלֹהִים:
שְׁמוֹת ב:כג־כה

## Moses, Leader of the Exodus

*The ancients, like the moderns, were given to embellishing the birth and early life of their heroes. Thus King Sargon I of Akkad (about 2300 B.C.E.), in a later epic called "The King of Battle," was said to have been saved in the manner that recalls the rescue of Moses.*

¹A certain man of the house of Levi went and married a Levite woman. ²The woman conceived and bore a son; and when she saw how beautiful he was, she hid him for three months. ³When she could hide him no longer, she got a wicker basket for him and calked it with bitumen and pitch. She put the child into it and placed it among the reeds by the bank of the Nile. ⁴And his sister stationed herself at a distance, to learn what would befall him.

⁵The daughter of Pharaoh came down to bathe in the Nile, while her maidens walked along the Nile. She spied the basket among the reeds and sent her slave girl to fetch it. ⁶When she opened it, she saw that it was a child, a boy crying. She took pity on it and said, "This must be a Hebrew child." ⁷Then his sister said to Pharaoh's daughter, "Shall I go and get you a Hebrew nurse to suckle the child for you?" ⁸And Pharaoh's daughter answered, "Yes." So the girl went and called the child's mother. ⁹And Pharaoh's daughter said to her, "Take this child and nurse it for me, and I will pay your wages." So the woman took the child and nursed it. ¹⁰When the child grew up, she brought him to Pharaoh's daughter, who made him her son. She named him Moses, explaining, "I drew him out of the water."

*Exodus 2.1-10*

וַיֵּלֶךְ אִישׁ מִבֵּית לֵוִי וַיִּקַּח אֶת־בַּת־לֵוִי: וַתַּהַר הָאִשָּׁה וַתֵּלֶד בֵּן וַתֵּרֶא אֹתוֹ כִּי־טוֹב הוּא וַתִּצְפְּנֵהוּ שְׁלֹשָׁה יְרָחִים: וְלֹא־יָכְלָה עוֹד הַצְּפִינוֹ וַתִּקַּח־לוֹ תֵּבַת גֹּמֶא וַתַּחְמְרָה בַחֵמָר וּבַזָּפֶת וַתָּשֶׂם בָּהּ אֶת־הַיֶּלֶד וַתָּשֶׂם בַּסּוּף עַל־שְׂפַת הַיְאֹר: וַתֵּתַצַּב אֲחֹתוֹ מֵרָחֹק לְדֵעָה מַה־יֵּעָשֶׂה לוֹ: וַתֵּרֶד בַּת־פַּרְעֹה לִרְחֹץ עַל־הַיְאֹר וְנַעֲרֹתֶיהָ הֹלְכֹת עַל־יַד הַיְאֹר וַתֵּרֶא אֶת־הַתֵּבָה בְּתוֹךְ הַסּוּף וַתִּשְׁלַח אֶת־אֲמָתָהּ וַתִּקָּחֶהָ: וַתִּפְתַּח וַתִּרְאֵהוּ אֶת־הַיֶּלֶד וְהִנֵּה־נַעַר בֹּכֶה וַתַּחְמֹל עָלָיו וַתֹּאמֶר מִיַּלְדֵי הָעִבְרִים זֶה: וַתֹּאמֶר אֲחֹתוֹ אֶל־בַּת־פַּרְעֹה הַאֵלֵךְ וְקָרָאתִי לָךְ אִשָּׁה מֵינֶקֶת מִן הָעִבְרִיֹּת וְתֵינִק לָךְ אֶת־הַיָּלֶד: וַתֹּאמֶר־לָהּ בַּת־פַּרְעֹה לֵכִי וַתֵּלֶךְ הָעַלְמָה וַתִּקְרָא אֶת־אֵם הַיָּלֶד: וַתֹּאמֶר לָהּ בַּת־פַּרְעֹה הֵילִיכִי אֶת־הַיֶּלֶד הַזֶּה וְהֵינִקִהוּ לִי וַאֲנִי אֶתֵּן אֶת־שְׂכָרֵךְ וַתִּקַּח הָאִשָּׁה הַיֶּלֶד וַתְּנִיקֵהוּ: וַיִּגְדַּל הַיֶּלֶד וַתְּבִאֵהוּ לְבַת־פַּרְעֹה וַיְהִי־לָהּ לְבֵן וַתִּקְרָא שְׁמוֹ מֹשֶׁה וַתֹּאמֶר כִּי מִן־הַמַּיִם מְשִׁיתִהוּ:
שְׁמוֹת ב:א־י

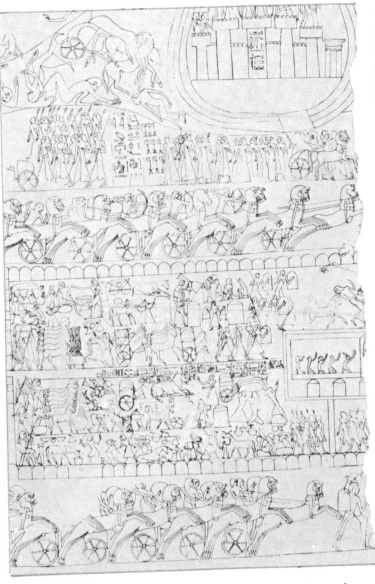

The camp of Ramses II of Egypt at the battle of Kadesh (on the Orontes River in Syria), showing the mustering and drilling of the troops, and some of the battle action against the Hittite enemy. Detail of the rock relief at Abu Simbel, near Aswan on the Nile (early 13th cent.).

century B.C.E. that a group of Hebrews and others united under the leadership of Moses to escape from Egypt. They were already state slaves who were willing to chance the break for freedom. Several outstanding leaders bore Egyptian names, for example, Moses, Miriam, Hophni, Phinehas, Merari, Puti-el, and perhaps Aaron. This alone indicates a considerable period of residence in Egypt; also a surprising degree of resistance and determination to be free, despite a long period of slavery.

The Bible makes it amply clear that some non-Hebrew elements, "the mixed multitude" of Exodus 12:38 and Numbers 11:4 accompanied Moses and the Hebrews out of Egypt. The Egyptian sources, in turn, provide a very clear background for this circumstance. Tens of thousands of workers, natives of many countries and members of different ethnic groups, labored for the Egyptian state. Already in the fifteenth century, as a result of the military conquests of Amenhotep II in Syria and Palestine, large numbers of Semitic and non-Semitic captives of war, including 3,600 Apiru (Habiru), were brought to Egypt as state slaves. The military campaigns of other Egyptian kings, from the fourteenth to the twelfth centuries, produced similar results. The great building projects of Ramses II (about 1301–1234 B.C.E.), at such places as Pithom and Ramses, employed these "mixed multitudes," many of whom were eager to escape from slavery.

Scholars have long been troubled by the fact that Egyptian records make no mention of Moses and the Exodus, and some have expressed the belief that a document or two may yet turn up with reference to them. Yet the modern student of ancient Egyptian history should share neither this worry nor this optimism. First, when the Egyptians lost a battle, they customarily either recorded it as a victory or else passed over it in silence.

<sup>11</sup>Some time after that, when Moses had grown up, he went out to his kinsfolk and witnessed their labor. He saw an Egyptian beating a Hebrew, one of his kinsmen. <sup>12</sup>He turned this way and that and, seeing no one about, he struck down the Egyptian and hid him in the sand. <sup>13</sup>When he went out the next day, he found two Hebrews fighting; so he said to the offender, "Why do you strike your fellow?" <sup>14</sup>He retorted, "Who made you chief and ruler over us? Do you mean to kill me as you killed the Egyptian?" Moses was frightened, and thought: Then the matter is known! <sup>15</sup>When Pharaoh learned of the matter, he sought to kill Moses; but Moses fled from Pharaoh. He arrived in the land of Midian, and sat down beside a well.

*Exodus 2.11-15*

<sup>1</sup>Now Moses, tending the flock of his father-in-law Jethro, the priest of Midian, drove the flock into the wilderness; and came to Horeb, the mountain of God. <sup>2</sup>An angel of the LORD appeared to him in a blazing fire out of a bush. He gazed, and there was a bush all aflame, yet the bush was not consumed. <sup>3</sup>Moses said, "I must turn aside to look at this marvelous sight; why doesn't the bush burn up?" <sup>4</sup>When the LORD saw that he had turned aside to look, God called to him out of the bush: "Moses! Moses!" He answered, "Here I am." <sup>5</sup>And He said, "Do not come closer. Remove your sandals from your feet, for the place on which you stand is holy ground. <sup>6</sup>I am," He said, "the God of your father, the God of Abraham, the God of Isaac, and the God of Jacob." And Moses hid his face, for he was afraid to look at God.

<sup>7</sup>And the LORD continued, . . . <sup>9</sup>Now the cry of the Israelites has reached Me; moreover, I have seen how the Egyptians oppress them. <sup>10</sup>Come, therefore, I will send you to Pharaoh, and you shall free My people, the Israelites, from Egypt."

*Exodus 3.1-10*

<sup>4</sup>The riffraff in their midst felt a gluttonous craving; and then the Israelites too wept and said, "If only we had meat to eat! <sup>5</sup>We remember the fish that we used to eat free in Egypt, the cucumbers, the melons, the leeks, the onions, and the garlic. <sup>6</sup>Now our gullets are shriveled. There is nothing at all! Nothing but this manna to look to!"

*Numbers 11.4-6*

וַיְהִי בַּיָּמִים הָהֵם וַיִּגְדַּל מֹשֶׁה וַיֵּצֵא אֶל־אֶחָיו
וַיַּרְא בְּסִבְלֹתָם וַיַּרְא אִישׁ מִצְרִי מַכֶּה אִישׁ־עִבְרִי
מֵאֶחָיו: וַיִּפֶן כֹּה וָכֹה וַיַּרְא כִּי־אֵין אִישׁ וַיַּךְ אֶת־
הַמִּצְרִי וַיִּטְמְנֵהוּ בַּחוֹל: וַיֵּצֵא בַּיּוֹם הַשֵּׁנִי וְהִנֵּה
שְׁנֵי־אֲנָשִׁים עִבְרִים נִצִּים וַיֹּאמֶר לָרָשָׁע לָמָּה תַכֶּה
רֵעֶךָ: וַיֹּאמֶר מִי שָׂמְךָ לְאִישׁ שַׂר וְשֹׁפֵט עָלֵינוּ
הַלְהָרְגֵנִי אַתָּה אֹמֵר כַּאֲשֶׁר הָרַגְתָּ אֶת־הַמִּצְרִי
וַיִּירָא מֹשֶׁה וַיֹּאמַר אָכֵן נוֹדַע הַדָּבָר: וַיִּשְׁמַע
פַּרְעֹה אֶת־הַדָּבָר הַזֶּה וַיְבַקֵּשׁ לַהֲרֹג אֶת־מֹשֶׁה
וַיִּבְרַח מֹשֶׁה מִפְּנֵי פַרְעֹה וַיֵּשֶׁב בְּאֶרֶץ־מִדְיָן וַיֵּשֶׁב
עַל־הַבְּאֵר:

שְׁמוֹת ב:יא-טו

וּמֹשֶׁה הָיָה רֹעֶה אֶת־צֹאן יִתְרוֹ חֹתְנוֹ כֹּהֵן
מִדְיָן וַיִּנְהַג אֶת־הַצֹּאן אַחַר הַמִּדְבָּר וַיָּבֹא אֶל־
הַר הָאֱלֹהִים חֹרֵבָה: וַיֵּרָא מַלְאַךְ יְהֹוָה אֵלָיו
בְּלַבַּת־אֵשׁ מִתּוֹךְ הַסְּנֶה וַיַּרְא וְהִנֵּה הַסְּנֶה בֹּעֵר
בָּאֵשׁ וְהַסְּנֶה אֵינֶנּוּ אֻכָּל: וַיֹּאמֶר מֹשֶׁה אָסֻרָה־נָּא
וְאֶרְאֶה אֶת־הַמַּרְאֶה הַגָּדֹל הַזֶּה מַדּוּעַ לֹא־יִבְעַר
הַסְּנֶה: וַיַּרְא יְהֹוָה כִּי סָר לִרְאוֹת וַיִּקְרָא אֵלָיו
אֱלֹהִים מִתּוֹךְ הַסְּנֶה וַיֹּאמֶר מֹשֶׁה מֹשֶׁה וַיֹּאמֶר הִנֵּנִי:
וַיֹּאמֶר אַל־תִּקְרַב הֲלֹם שַׁל־נְעָלֶיךָ מֵעַל רַגְלֶיךָ
כִּי הַמָּקוֹם אֲשֶׁר אַתָּה עוֹמֵד עָלָיו אַדְמַת־קֹדֶשׁ
הוּא: וַיֹּאמֶר אָנֹכִי אֱלֹהֵי אָבִיךָ אֱלֹהֵי אַבְרָהָם
אֱלֹהֵי יִצְחָק וֵאלֹהֵי יַעֲקֹב וַיַּסְתֵּר מֹשֶׁה פָּנָיו כִּי
יָרֵא מֵהַבִּיט אֶל־הָאֱלֹהִים: וַיֹּאמֶר יְהֹוָה . . . וְעַתָּה
הִנֵּה צַעֲקַת בְּנֵי־יִשְׂרָאֵל בָּאָה אֵלָי וְגַם־רָאִיתִי
אֶת־הַלַּחַץ אֲשֶׁר מִצְרַיִם לֹחֲצִים אֹתָם: וְעַתָּה
לְכָה וְאֶשְׁלָחֲךָ אֶל־פַּרְעֹה וְהוֹצֵא אֶת־עַמִּי בְנֵי־
יִשְׂרָאֵל מִמִּצְרָיִם:

שְׁמוֹת ג:א-י

וְהָאסַפְסֻף אֲשֶׁר בְּקִרְבּוֹ הִתְאַוּוּ תַּאֲוָה וַיָּשֻׁבוּ
וַיִּבְכּוּ גַּם בְּנֵי יִשְׂרָאֵל וַיֹּאמְרוּ מִי יַאֲכִלֵנוּ בָּשָׂר:
זָכַרְנוּ אֶת־הַדָּגָה אֲשֶׁר־נֹאכַל בְּמִצְרַיִם חִנָּם אֵת
הַקִּשֻּׁאִים וְאֵת הָאֲבַטִּחִים וְאֶת־הֶחָצִיר וְאֶת־
הַבְּצָלִים וְאֶת־הַשּׁוּמִים: וְעַתָּה נַפְשֵׁנוּ יְבֵשָׁה אֵין
כֹּל בִּלְתִּי אֶל־הַמָּן עֵינֵינוּ:

בַּמִּדְבָּר יא:ד-ו

57

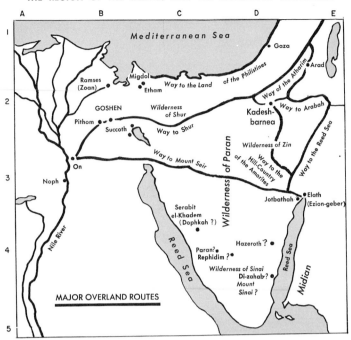

The exact route that the Israelites followed from Egypt to Canaan is uncertain, since most of the Biblical sites mentioned in connection with it cannot be identified.

The Sinai Peninsula. Satellite photograph of the Sinai Peninsula taken from a point over the coast of East Africa. On the right—Egypt, the Suez, the Red Sea, and the Peninsula itself, with Israel above and to the right. The dark line of the Jordan Valley Rift is plainly visible. Syria, Transjordan, and Saudi Arabia lie on the right margin of the picture.

(If the Egyptian king was himself a god, how could a god be permitted to suffer defeat?) Thus the prolonged Hyksos rule was not mentioned in contemporaneous Egyptian sources until the Hyksos were expelled, and even the victory over them was apparently not officially recorded. And second, the scope of the Exodus and the significance of it for the Egyptian government were so meager as not to merit any documentary mention.

## The Wandering in the Wilderness

The peninsula of Sinai is a smaller replica of the Arabian peninsula, which lies farther east and south of it. On the west, Sinai is bounded by a deep-reaching arm of the Red Sea, and on the east by the Gulf of Aqabah, as the Persian Gulf forms the eastern bound of the Arabian peninsula. It was into this burning desert upland that Moses led the way.

Here, in the wilderness of Sinai, Israel was forged, hammered into shape amid appalling hardship. The weak and weary perished, leaving the young and strong to drift yet another mile toward the Land of Promise, the ancestral home.

There was endless and violent struggle for power within this group that Moses had led from Egypt. Korah and his faction challenged the authority of Moses himself (Numbers 16). Aaron, in the incident of the Golden Calf, was accused of permitting himself to be used by another faction in a similar struggle (Exodus 32). There was the additional difficulty that the "mixed multiude" reminded themselves in the wilderness of Sinai of "the fish which we used to eat in Egypt free; the cucumbers, and the melons, and the leeks, and the onions and the garlic; but now our strength is dried up" (Numbers 11:4–5). Only a man of iron will could have endured this endless bickering, scheming, and backsliding. Moses was that man.

¹Now Korah, son of Izhar son of Kohath son of Levi, betook himself, along with Dathan and Abiram sons of Eliab, and On son of Peleth—descendants of Reuben—²to rise up against Moses, together with two hundred and fifty Israelites, chieftains of the community, chosen in the assembly, men of repute. ³They combined against Moses and Aaron and said to them, "You have gone too far! For all the community are holy, all of them, and the LORD is in their midst. Why then do you raise yourselves above the LORD's congregation?"

⁴When Moses heard this, he fell on his face. ⁵Then he spoke to Korah and all his company, saying, "Come morning, the LORD will make known who is His and who is holy, and will grant him access to Himself; He will grant access to the one He has chosen."

*Numbers 16.1-5*

וַיִּקַּח קֹרַח בֶּן־יִצְהָר בֶּן־קְהָת בֶּן־לֵוִי וְדָתָן
וַאֲבִירָם בְּנֵי אֱלִיאָב וְאוֹן בֶּן־פֶּלֶת בְּנֵי רְאוּבֵן:
וַיָּקֻמוּ לִפְנֵי מֹשֶׁה וַאֲנָשִׁים מִבְּנֵי־יִשְׂרָאֵל חֲמִשִּׁים
וּמָאתַיִם נְשִׂיאֵי עֵדָה קְרִאֵי מוֹעֵד אַנְשֵׁי־שֵׁם: וַיִּקָּהֲלוּ
עַל־מֹשֶׁה וְעַל־אַהֲרֹן וַיֹּאמְרוּ אֲלֵהֶם רַב־לָכֶם
כִּי כָל־הָעֵדָה כֻּלָּם קְדֹשִׁים וּבְתוֹכָם יְהוָה וּמַדּוּעַ
תִּתְנַשְּׂאוּ עַל־קְהַל יְהוָה: וַיִּשְׁמַע מֹשֶׁה וַיִּפֹּל עַל־
פָּנָיו: וַיְדַבֵּר אֶל־קֹרַח וְאֶל־כָּל־עֲדָתוֹ לֵאמֹר
בֹּקֶר וְיֹדַע יְהוָה אֶת־אֲשֶׁר־לוֹ וְאֶת־הַקָּדוֹשׁ
וְהִקְרִיב אֵלָיו וְאֵת אֲשֶׁר יִבְחַר־בּוֹ יַקְרִיב אֵלָיו:

בְּמִדְבָּר טז:א–ה

---

¹Miriam and Aaron spoke against Moses because of the Cushite woman he had married. . . .

*Numbers 12.1*

וַתְּדַבֵּר מִרְיָם וְאַהֲרֹן בְּמֹשֶׁה עַל־אֹדוֹת הָאִשָּׁה
הַכֻּשִׁית אֲשֶׁר לָקָח כִּי־אִשָּׁה כֻשִׁית לָקָח:
בְּמִדְבָּר יב:א

---

¹When the people saw that Moses was so long in coming down from the mountain, the people gathered against Aaron and said to him, "Come, make us a god who shall go before us, for that man Moses, who brought us from the land of Egypt—we do not know what has happened to him." ²Aaron said to them, "Take off the gold rings that are on the ears of your wives, your sons, and your daughters, and bring them to me." ³And all the people took off the gold rings that were in their ears and brought them to Aaron. ⁴This he took from them and cast in a mold, and made it into a molten calf. And they exclaimed, "This is your god, O Israel, who brought you out of the land of Egypt!" ⁵When Aaron saw this, he built an altar before it; and Aaron announced: "Tomorrow shall be a festival of the LORD!" ⁶Early next day, the people offered up burnt offerings and brought sacrifices of well-being; they sat down to eat and drink, and then rose to dance.

*Exodus 32.1-6*

וַיַּרְא הָעָם כִּי־בֹשֵׁשׁ מֹשֶׁה לָרֶדֶת מִן־הָהָר
וַיִּקָּהֵל הָעָם עַל־אַהֲרֹן וַיֹּאמְרוּ אֵלָיו קוּם עֲשֵׂה־
לָנוּ אֱלֹהִים אֲשֶׁר יֵלְכוּ לְפָנֵינוּ כִּי־זֶה מֹשֶׁה הָאִישׁ
אֲשֶׁר הֶעֱלָנוּ מֵאֶרֶץ מִצְרַיִם לֹא יָדַעְנוּ מֶה־הָיָה
לוֹ: וַיֹּאמֶר אֲלֵהֶם אַהֲרֹן פָּרְקוּ נִזְמֵי הַזָּהָב אֲשֶׁר
בְּאָזְנֵי נְשֵׁיכֶם בְּנֵיכֶם וּבְנֹתֵיכֶם וְהָבִיאוּ אֵלָי:
וַיִּתְפָּרְקוּ כָּל־הָעָם אֶת־נִזְמֵי הַזָּהָב אֲשֶׁר בְּאָזְנֵיהֶם
וַיָּבִיאוּ אֶל־אַהֲרֹן: וַיִּקַּח מִיָּדָם וַיָּצַר אֹתוֹ בַּחֶרֶט
וַיַּעֲשֵׂהוּ עֵגֶל מַסֵּכָה וַיֹּאמְרוּ אֵלֶּה אֱלֹהֶיךָ יִשְׂרָאֵל
אֲשֶׁר הֶעֱלוּךָ מֵאֶרֶץ מִצְרָיִם: וַיַּרְא אַהֲרֹן וַיִּבֶן מִזְבֵּחַ
לְפָנָיו וַיִּקְרָא אַהֲרֹן וַיֹּאמַר חַג לַיהוָה מָחָר:
וַיַּשְׁכִּימוּ מִמָּחֳרָת וַיַּעֲלוּ עֹלֹת וַיַּגִּשׁוּ שְׁלָמִים וַיֵּשֶׁב
הָעָם לֶאֱכֹל וְשָׁתוֹ וַיָּקֻמוּ לְצַחֵק:
שְׁמוֹת לב:א–ו

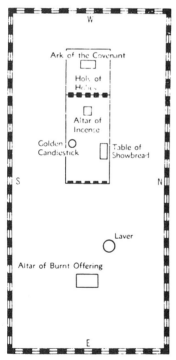

Plan of the tabernacle and its courts.

It was in the wilderness of Sinai, and not in Egypt, that this struggle for power took place, and the subsequent welding together of a heterogeneous, inexperienced, and uncultured mass of individuals into something of a unified force and social group. That about a generation—the traditional "forty years" of wandering—should have elapsed before the goal was approached is not only reasonable, but also accounts for the fact that virtually none of the leaders of the Exodus, such as Moses, Aaron, and Miriam, lived to enter the Promised Land.

Until recently the Bible has been virtually the only source for the history of the wandering in the Wilderness. As a result, the significance of this stage in Israel's history has been minimized, when its very authenticity has not been questioned.

A central feature of the Biblical account is the movable Tabernacle, or Tent of Meeting, around which the political and religious life of the wandering Hebrews revolved. This institution used to be regarded as a late fiction, projected back into the past. Recently, however, archaeological and literary parallels have been accumulating which not only explain the origin of this structure and institution in the wilderness of Sinai, but also clarify its history as the "Tent of the Lord" at Shiloh, following the conquest of Canaan. It was ultimately replaced by the Temple which David planned and Solomon built.

Much the same thing happened in the case of the Ark, the acacia chest in which, according to tradition, Moses placed and kept the two stone tablets recording the Ten Commandments. Furthermore, the traditional route of the Wandering, as described in the books of Exodus and Numbers, accords well with the topography of Sinai and with what has been learned of the location of the copper and turquoise mines which were being worked and garrisoned in the thirteenth

³²Thus was completed all the work of the Tabernacle of the Tent of Meeting . . . ²¹and he brought the ark inside the Tabernacle . . . just as the LORD had commanded Moses.

*Exodus 39.32; 40.21*

וַתֵּכֶל כָּל־עֲבֹדַת מִשְׁכַּן אֹהֶל מוֹעֵד . . . וַיָּבֵא אֶת־הָאָרֹן אֶל־הַמִּשְׁכָּן . . . כַּאֲשֶׁר צִוָּה יְהֹוָה אֶת־מֹשֶׁה:

שְׁמוֹת לט:לב; מ:כא

¹⁰Thereupon the LORD was incensed and He swore, ¹¹'None of the men from twenty years up who came out of Egypt shall see the land that I promised on oath to Abraham, Isaac, and Jacob, for they did not remain loyal to Me—¹²none except Caleb son of Jephunneh the Kenizzite and Joshua son of Nun, for they remained loyal to the LORD.' ¹³The LORD was incensed at Israel, and for forty years He made them wander in the wilderness, until the whole generation that had provoked the LORD's displeasure was gone. ¹⁴And now you, a breed of sinful men, have replaced your fathers, to add still further to the LORD's wrath against Israel. ¹⁵If you turn away from Him and He abandons them once more in the wilderness, you will bring calamity upon all this people."

*Numbers 32.10-15*

וַיִּחַר־אַף יְהֹוָה בַּיּוֹם הַהוּא וַיִּשָּׁבַע לֵאמֹר: אִם־יִרְאוּ הָאֲנָשִׁים הָעֹלִים מִמִּצְרַיִם מִבֶּן עֶשְׂרִים שָׁנָה וָמַעְלָה אֵת הָאֲדָמָה אֲשֶׁר נִשְׁבַּעְתִּי לְאַבְרָהָם לְיִצְחָק וּלְיַעֲקֹב כִּי לֹא־מִלְאוּ אַחֲרָי: בִּלְתִּי כָּלֵב בֶּן־יְפֻנֶּה הַקְּנִזִּי וִיהוֹשֻׁעַ בִּן־נוּן כִּי מִלְאוּ אַחֲרֵי יְהֹוָה: וַיִּחַר־אַף יְהֹוָה בְּיִשְׂרָאֵל וַיְנִעֵם בַּמִּדְבָּר אַרְבָּעִים שָׁנָה עַד־תֹּם כָּל־הַדּוֹר הָעֹשֶׂה הָרַע בְּעֵינֵי יְהֹוָה: וְהִנֵּה קַמְתֶּם תַּחַת אֲבֹתֵיכֶם תַּרְבּוּת אֲנָשִׁים חַטָּאִים לִסְפּוֹת עוֹד עַל חֲרוֹן אַף־יְהֹוָה אֶל־יִשְׂרָאֵל: כִּי תְשׁוּבֻן מֵאַחֲרָיו וְיָסַף עוֹד לְהַנִּיחוֹ בַּמִּדְבָּר וְשִׁחַתֶּם לְכָל־הָעָם הַזֶּה:

בַּמִּדְבָּר לב: י־טו

⁹You stand this day, all of you, before the LORD your God—your tribal heads, your elders and your officials, all the men of Israel, ¹⁰your children, your wives, even the stranger within your camp, from woodchopper to waterdrawer—¹¹to enter into the covenant of the LORD your God, which the LORD your God is concluding with you this day, with its sanctions; ¹²to the end that He may establish you this day as His people and be your God, as He promised you and as He swore to your fathers, Abraham, Isaac, and Jacob. ¹³I make this covenant, with its sanctions, not with you alone, ¹⁴but both with those who are standing here with us this day before the LORD our God and with those who are not with us here this day.

*Deuteronomy 29.9-14*

אַתֶּם נִצָּבִים הַיּוֹם כֻּלְּכֶם לִפְנֵי יְהֹוָה אֱלֹהֵיכֶם רָאשֵׁיכֶם שִׁבְטֵיכֶם זִקְנֵיכֶם וְשֹׁטְרֵיכֶם כֹּל אִישׁ יִשְׂרָאֵל: טַפְּכֶם נְשֵׁיכֶם וְגֵרְךָ אֲשֶׁר בְּקֶרֶב מַחֲנֶיךָ מֵחֹטֵב עֵצֶיךָ עַד שֹׁאֵב מֵימֶיךָ: לְעָבְרְךָ בִּבְרִית יְהֹוָה אֱלֹהֶיךָ וּבְאָלָתוֹ אֲשֶׁר יְהֹוָה אֱלֹהֶיךָ כֹּרֵת עִמְּךָ הַיּוֹם: לְמַעַן הָקִים־אֹתְךָ הַיּוֹם לוֹ לְעָם וְהוּא יִהְיֶה־לְּךָ לֵאלֹהִים כַּאֲשֶׁר דִּבֶּר־לָךְ וְכַאֲשֶׁר נִשְׁבַּע לַאֲבֹתֶיךָ לְאַבְרָהָם לְיִצְחָק וּלְיַעֲקֹב: וְלֹא אִתְּכֶם לְבַדְּכֶם אָנֹכִי כֹּרֵת אֶת־הַבְּרִית הַזֹּאת וְאֶת־הָאָלָה הַזֹּאת: כִּי אֶת־אֲשֶׁר יֶשְׁנוֹ פֹּה עִמָּנוּ עֹמֵד הַיּוֹם לִפְנֵי יְהֹוָה אֱלֹהֵינוּ וְאֵת אֲשֶׁר אֵינֶנּוּ פֹּה עִמָּנוּ הַיּוֹם:

דְּבָרִים כט: ט־יד

61

**THE NAME OF THE GOD OF ISRAEL**

Because the Hebrew term consists of four letters, YHWH, it is called the Tetragrammaton. Some time after about the fifth century B.C.E., the original pronunciation of the name ceased to be employed for ordinary purposes, and the term Adonai, "Lord," came to be substituted for it. The term Jehovah is a relatively recent creation (about fourteenth century C.E.), by a Christian who erroneously read the vowels of Adonai together with the consonants of YHWH. The Revised Standard Version (New York, 1952) follows the tradition of the King James (so-called Authorized) Version, the Revised Version, and the Jewish Publication Society Translation in rejecting the term Jehovah, usually in favor of LORD; so all modern translations.

Many scholars believe that the original pronunciation of YHWH was Yahweh. The evidence for this belief, however, is not decisive, and there are also very considerable differences of opinion as to what the term meant originally

century B.C.E. These garrisoned sites, in the hands of the Egyptians, appear to have been situated at just those points which the Hebrews were careful to avoid in their trek through Sinai.

## Moses and the Covenant

The concept of the Covenant between God and the new nation, a factor of the most fundamental importance in Israel's career, came into being during this period. The relationship between the patriarchs and their God had begun, according to the social patterns of seminomadic family life, as a personal arrangement. In Moses' first experience with the Deity, at the theophany in the burning bush (Exodus 3), the relationship was also personal; and in accord with the patriarchal tradition, the Deity Himself acquired a new personal name, YHWH, which is usually rendered "Lord" (or "Jehovah").

The experiences of the Exodus and the Wandering gradually forged the more individualistic elements into a new cohesive unit. The purpose of the Exodus was not merely to free a group of slaves for their own sake, but for something far greater in scope and significance, the creation of a new nation. The direct relationship between God and the Nation was the new element created by the forces of history and circumstances. From that point on, and throughout the entire Bible henceforth, the new Covenant, a national pact between God and His people, sealed by the act of the Exodus, replaced the older, individual covenants between God and the patriarchal leaders.

The personality of Moses so dominated Israel's formative years that later centuries came to credit him with authorship of the Pentateuch. This honor is justified in a figurative sense, and perhaps even in a factual sense as well. Research has now shown that an important part of the legal code of ancient

<sup></sup>45I will abide among the Israelites, and I will be their God. <sup></sup>46And they shall know that I the LORD am their God, who brought them out from the land of Egypt that I might abide among them, I the LORD their God.

*Exodus 29.45–46*

וְשָׁכַנְתִּי בְּתוֹךְ בְּנֵי יִשְׂרָאֵל וְהָיִיתִי לָהֶם לֵאלֹהִים: וְיָדְעוּ כִּי אֲנִי יְהֹוָה אֱלֹהֵיהֶם אֲשֶׁר הוֹצֵאתִי אֹתָם מֵאֶרֶץ מִצְרַיִם לְשָׁכְנִי בְתוֹכָם אֲנִי יְהֹוָה אֱלֹהֵיהֶם:

שְׁמוֹת כט: מה–מו

<sup></sup>12I will be ever present in your midst: I will be your God, and you shall be My people. <sup></sup>13I the LORD am your God who brought you out from the land of the Egyptians to be their slaves no more, who broke the bars of your yoke and made you walk erect.

*Leviticus 26.12-13*

וְהִתְהַלַּכְתִּי בְּתוֹכְכֶם וְהָיִיתִי לָכֶם לֵאלֹהִים וְאַתֶּם תִּהְיוּ־לִי לְעָם: אֲנִי יְהֹוָה אֱלֹהֵיכֶם אֲשֶׁר הוֹצֵאתִי אֶתְכֶם מֵאֶרֶץ מִצְרַיִם מִהְיֹת לָהֶם עֲבָדִים וָאֶשְׁבֹּר מֹטֹת עֻלְּכֶם וָאוֹלֵךְ אֶתְכֶם קוֹמְמִיּוּת:

וַיִּקְרָא כו: יב–יג

<sup></sup>2 . . . Thus said the LORD:
I remembered, in your favor the devotion of
  your youth, your love as a bride—
How you followed Me in the wilderness, in a
  land not sown.
<sup></sup>3Israel was holy to the LORD, first fruits of
  His harvest
All who partook of it were punished, disaster
  befell them. . . .

*Jeremiah 2.2–3*

. . . כֹּה אָמַר יְהֹוָה
זָכַרְתִּי לָךְ חֶסֶד נְעוּרַיִךְ אַהֲבַת כְּלוּלֹתָיִךְ
לֶכְתֵּךְ אַחֲרַי בַּמִּדְבָּר בְּאֶרֶץ לֹא זְרוּעָה:
קֹדֶשׁ יִשְׂרָאֵל לַיהֹוָה רֵאשִׁית תְּבוּאָתֹה
כָּל־אֹכְלָיו יֶאְשָׁמוּ רָעָה תָּבֹא אֲלֵיהֶם . . .

יִרְמְיָהוּ ב:ב–ג

*To such an extent was Moses associated with the Torah of God, that the expression* torath-mosheh *("the torah of Moses") is used in the Bible somewhat more than half as often as* torath-adonay/elohim *("the torah of the Lord/God"). See H. M. Orlinsky, "Moses," pp. 3-32 in* Molders of the Jewish Mind *(B'nai B'rith, Washington, 1966; = pp. 10-39 in* Great Jewish Personalities in Ancient and Medieval Times, *1959).*

<sup></sup>24When Moses had put down in writing the words of this Teaching to the very end. . . .

*Deuteronomy 31.24*

וַיְהִי כְּכַלּוֹת מֹשֶׁה לִכְתֹּב אֶת־דִּבְרֵי הַתּוֹרָה־הַזֹּאת עַל־סֵפֶר עַד תֻּמָּם:

דְּבָרִים לא: כד

<sup></sup>4When Moses charged us with the Teaching
As the heritage of the congregation of Jacob.

*Deuteronomy 33.4*

תּוֹרָה צִוָּה־לָנוּ מֹשֶׁה מוֹרָשָׁה קְהִלַּת יַעֲקֹב:

דְּבָרִים לג:ד

63

Section of a carved limestone relief from Tell el-Amarna (ancient Akhetaton) in Egypt. The scene depicted here has sometimes been called the "manifesto" of the solar cult of Akhenaton. The Pharaoh Akhenaton (left) and his queen, Nefertiti (right), and their three children receive the beneficent rays of the sun disk, the god Aton, the object of their worship. Each ray ends in a stylized hand; some of the hands hold the ankh sign, symbol of life. The relief indicates the very personal relationship between the king and the god. About 17 inches high.

Akhenaton's Queen Nefertiti

Israel clearly derives from the pre-Canaanite period which coincides with the Hebrew wandering in the Wilderness (see below in Chapter III). And the Sinaitic origin of the Tabernacle, noted above, implies the development of numerous religious and cultic regulations under the leadership of Moses.

Great intelligence and character were required to solve the many vexing problems, to take advantage fully and wisely of the new and changing circumstances, to know when to follow and when to lead the unorganized Hebrews and their fellow travelers. When the mixed tribal following had emerged from the wilderness, they were all bound to one God. Moses alone provided that essential leadership, and he well deserves his traditional reputation of having brought Israel into being as a nation.

The question of who would succeed Moses in authority was of prime importance; there appears to have been no opposition to Moses' selection of Joshua, identified with the tribe of Ephraim, as his successor.

## Moses and the Atonism of Akh-en-Aton

According to a much-quoted theory, Moses could have acquired the concept of monotheism which he introduced to the Hebrews only from the Egyptian environment in which he had grown up, specifically from the so-called monotheism of the Aton. This worship of the round disk of the sun, while known previously in Egypt, found an ardent devotee in Amenhotep IV, who changed his name to Akh-en-Aton (Egyptian for "It is Well with the Aton," or the like; about 1369–1353 B.C.E.).

Two important facts, however, each independent of the other, disprove this theory. First, in sponsoring monotheism, Moses was actually not introducing a new concept to the

*Important as the activities and leadership of Joshua were made to be in later times (see, e.g., Ex. 17.8-16; 24.12-13; Num. 14.5-10; Deut. 3.28; 31.14)—indeed, he was attributed full succession to Moses—the honorific title* navi *("prophet") was denied him; if Moses had indeed been a* navi, *that title would naturally have been Joshua's too.*

[1]After the death of Moses, the servant of the LORD, the LORD said to Joshua son of Nun, Moses' attendant, [2]"Moses My servant is dead. Prepare to cross the Jordan, together with all this people, into the land which I am giving to the Israelites. [3]Every spot on which your foot treads I give to you—as I promised Moses."

*Joshua 1.1-3*

וַיְהִי אַחֲרֵי מוֹת מֹשֶׁה עֶבֶד יְהֹוָה וַיֹּאמֶר יְהֹוָה אֶל־יְהוֹשֻׁעַ בִּן־נוּן מְשָׁרֵת מֹשֶׁה לֵאמֹר: מֹשֶׁה עַבְדִּי מֵת וְעַתָּה קוּם עֲבֹר אֶת־הַיַּרְדֵּן הַזֶּה אַתָּה וְכָל־הָעָם הַזֶּה אֶל־הָאָרֶץ אֲשֶׁר אָנֹכִי נֹתֵן לָהֶם לִבְנֵי יִשְׂרָאֵל: כָּל־מָקוֹם אֲשֶׁר תִּדְרֹךְ כַּף־רַגְלְכֶם בּוֹ לָכֶם נְתַתִּיו כַּאֲשֶׁר דִּבַּרְתִּי אֶל־מֹשֶׁה:

יְהוֹשֻׁעַ א:א-ג

[9]Joshua son of Nun was filled with the spirit of wisdom because Moses had laid his hands upon him; and the Israelites heeded him, doing as the LORD had commanded Moses.
[10]Never again did there arise in Israel a prophet likes Moses . . .

*Deuteronomy 34.9-10*

וִיהוֹשֻׁעַ בִּן־נוּן מָלֵא רוּחַ חָכְמָה כִּי־סָמַךְ מֹשֶׁה אֶת־יָדָיו עָלָיו וַיִּשְׁמְעוּ אֵלָיו בְּנֵי־יִשְׂרָאֵל וַיַּעֲשׂוּ כַּאֲשֶׁר צִוָּה יְהֹוָה אֶת־מֹשֶׁה: וְלֹא־קָם נָבִיא עוֹד בְּיִשְׂרָאֵל . . . :

דְּבָרִים לד:ט-י

## Moses and the Atonism of Akh-en-aton

[15]For your own sake, therefore, be most careful—since you saw no shape when the LORD your God spoke to you at Horeb out of the fire—[16]not to act wickedly and make for yourselves a sculptured image in any likeness whatever: the form of a man or a woman, [17]the form of any beast on earth, the form of any winged bird that flies in the sky, [18]the form of anything that creeps on the ground, the form of any fish that is in the waters below the earth. [19]And when you look up to the sky and behold the sun and the moon and the stars, the whole heavenly host, you must not be lured into bowing down to them or serving them. These the LORD your God allotted to the other peoples everywhere under heaven; [20]but you the LORD took and brought out of Egypt, that iron blast furnace, to be His very own people, as is now the case.

*Deuteronomy 4.15-20*

וְנִשְׁמַרְתֶּם מְאֹד לְנַפְשֹׁתֵיכֶם כִּי לֹא רְאִיתֶם כָּל־תְּמוּנָה בְּיוֹם דִּבֶּר יְהֹוָה אֲלֵיכֶם בְּחֹרֵב מִתּוֹךְ הָאֵשׁ: פֶּן־תַּשְׁחִתוּן וַעֲשִׂיתֶם לָכֶם פֶּסֶל תְּמוּנַת כָּל־סָמֶל תַּבְנִית זָכָר אוֹ נְקֵבָה: תַּבְנִית כָּל־בְּהֵמָה אֲשֶׁר בָּאָרֶץ תַּבְנִית כָּל־צִפּוֹר כָּנָף אֲשֶׁר תָּעוּף בַּשָּׁמָיִם: תַּבְנִית כָּל־רֹמֵשׂ בָּאֲדָמָה תַּבְנִית כָּל־דָּגָה אֲשֶׁר־בַּמַּיִם מִתַּחַת לָאָרֶץ: וּפֶן־תִּשָּׂא עֵינֶיךָ הַשָּׁמַיְמָה וְרָאִיתָ אֶת־הַשֶּׁמֶשׁ וְאֶת־הַיָּרֵחַ וְאֶת־הַכּוֹכָבִים כֹּל צְבָא הַשָּׁמַיִם וְנִדַּחְתָּ וְהִשְׁתַּחֲוִיתָ לָהֶם וַעֲבַדְתָּם אֲשֶׁר חָלַק יְהֹוָה אֱלֹהֶיךָ אֹתָם לְכֹל הָעַמִּים תַּחַת כָּל־הַשָּׁמָיִם: וְאֶתְכֶם לָקַח יְהֹוָה וַיּוֹצִא אֶתְכֶם מִכּוּר הַבַּרְזֶל מִמִּצְרָיִם לִהְיוֹת לוֹ לְעַם נַחֲלָה כַּיּוֹם הַזֶּה:

דְּבָרִים ד:טו-כ

[3]You shall have no other gods beside Me.

*Exodus 20.3*

לֹא־יִהְיֶה לְךָ אֱלֹהִים אֲחֵרִים עַל־פָּנָי:

שְׁמוֹת כ:ג

65

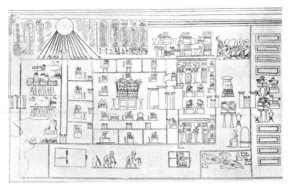

A temple of Aton as depicted in the tomb of Meryre.

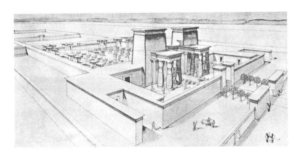

A reconstruction of the solar temple of the god Aton at Akhetaton. Note the extensive area taken up in the complex by open courts. Only storerooms seem to be covered. The openness of the temple, which contrasts with some other known Egyptian temples, would go well with the sun-disk worship.

Hebrews. He had a familiar, developable Hebraic idea of monotheism to work with, and there was nothing fundamental in his approach to the Deity which was not already to be found in the patriarchal period. Even the Covenant of Sinai represented not so much a change in kind as a change in degree from the old way of binding oneself to the Deity. Second, Moses could hardly have been affected by Atonism, since this worship was limited to Akh-en-Aton and his family and was crushed immediately after Akh-en-Aton's death. Indeed, Akh-en-Aton's own courtiers had worshiped Akh-en-Aton himself, and Atonism itself was not truly monotheistic.

J. A. Wilson has recently declared (*op. cit.*, pp. 224 ff.): "As to whether Atonism was ancestral to Hebrew monotheism . . . it may be stated flatly that the mechanism of transmission from the faith of Akh-en-Aton to the monotheism of Moses is not apparent. This was the personal religion of a Pharaoh who later became a heretic within one generation. . . ." Finally, the Bible makes it clear that the Hebrews brought with them from Egypt little or no cultural baggage, while from the Egyptian side the question is well summed up in the statement, "Our argument then is that there certainly were bondages and that there certainly was an exodus, but that neither of these experiences was an effective instrument for cultural transmission, but was rather a barrier to such transmission." (Wilson, p. 256.)

<sup>14</sup>For you must not worship any other god, be- כִּי לֹא תִשְׁתַּחֲוֶה לְאֵל אַחֵר כִּי יְהֹוָה קַנָּא שְׁמוֹ
cause the LORD, whose name is Impassioned, is אֵל קַנָּא הוּא:
an impassioned God.

*Exodus 34.14* שְׁמוֹת לד:יד

<sup>6</sup>"I am," He said, "the God of your father, the וַיֹּאמֶר אָנֹכִי אֱלֹהֵי אָבִיךָ אֱלֹהֵי אַבְרָהָם אֱלֹהֵי
God of Abraham, the God of Isaac, and the God יִצְחָק וֵאלֹהֵי יַעֲקֹב וַיַּסְתֵּר מֹשֶׁה פָּנָיו כִּי יָרֵא
of Jacob." And Moses hid his face, for he was מֵהַבִּיט אֶל־הָאֱלֹהִים:
afraid to look at God.

*Exodus 3.6* שְׁמוֹת ג:ו

<sup>2</sup>God spoke to Moses and said to him, "I am וַיְדַבֵּר אֱלֹהִים אֶל־מֹשֶׁה וַיֹּאמֶר אֵלָיו אֲנִי
the LORD. <sup>3</sup>I appeared to Abraham, Isaac, and יְהֹוָה: וָאֵרָא אֶל־אַבְרָהָם אֶל־יִצְחָק וְאֶל־יַעֲקֹב
Jacob as El Shaddai, but I did not make Myself בְּאֵל שַׁדָּי וּשְׁמִי יְהֹוָה לֹא נוֹדַעְתִּי לָהֶם: וְגַם
known to them by My name יהוה <sup>a</sup>. <sup>4</sup>I also es- הֲקִמֹתִי אֶת־בְּרִיתִי אִתָּם לָתֵת לָהֶם אֶת־אֶרֶץ
tablished My covenant with them, to give them כְּנָעַן אֵת אֶרֶץ מְגֻרֵיהֶם אֲשֶׁר־גָּרוּ בָהּ:
the land of Canaan, the land in which they lived
as sojourners.

*Exodus 6.2-4* שְׁמוֹת ו:ב־ד

a *This divine name is traditionally not pronounced; instead, Adonai,
"(the) Lord," is regularly substituted for it.*

*The Oracles of Balaam reflect an ancient ( priest-diviner, probably
Mesopotamian) manner of viewing and helping determine the future
of a group; Balaam would be representative of the Mesopotamian
diviner. However, God and Israel, in their covenanted relationship, are
considered as being too powerful for any enemy; and this is the central
theme of the Bible—Israel is secure against any threat so long as it
heeds its covenant with God.*

<sup>7</sup>He [Balaam] took up his theme, and said: וַיִּשָּׂא מְשָׁלוֹ וַיֹּאמַר
From Aram has Balak brought me, מִן־אֲרָם יַנְחֵנִי בָלָק מֶלֶךְ־מוֹאָב מֵהַרְרֵי־קֶדֶם
Moab's king from the hills of the East: לְכָה אָרָה־לִּי יַעֲקֹב וּלְכָה זֹעֲמָה יִשְׂרָאֵל:
Come, curse me Jacob, מָה אֶקֹּב לֹא קַבֹּה אֵל וּמָה אֶזְעֹם לֹא זָעַם יְהֹוָה:
Come, tell Israel's doom! כִּי־מֵרֹאשׁ צֻרִים אֶרְאֶנּוּ וּמִגְּבָעוֹת אֲשׁוּרֶנּוּ
<sup>8</sup>How can I damn when God has not damned, הֶן־עָם לְבָדָד יִשְׁכֹּן וּבַגּוֹיִם לֹא יִתְחַשָּׁב:
How doom when the LORD has not doomed? מִי מָנָה עֲפַר יַעֲקֹב וּמִסְפָּר אֶת־רֹבַע יִשְׂרָאֵל
<sup>9</sup>As I see them from the mountain tops, תָּמֹת נַפְשִׁי מוֹת יְשָׁרִים וּתְהִי אַחֲרִיתִי כָּמֹהוּ:
Gaze on them from the heights,
There is a people that dwells apart,
Not reckoned among the nations.
<sup>10</sup>Who can count the dust of Jacob,
Number the dust-cloud of Israel?
May I die the death of the upright,
May my fate be like theirs!

*Numbers 23.7-10* בַּמִּדְבָּר כג:ז־י

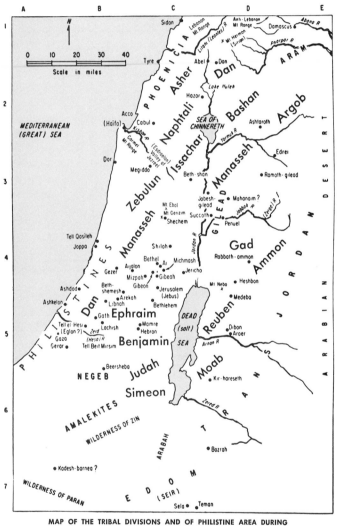

**MAP OF THE TRIBAL DIVISIONS AND OF PHILISTINE AREA DURING
THE PERIOD OF THE JUDGES (CA. 12th-11th CENT. B.C.E.)**

## Chapter III

# ISRAEL IN CANAAN: THE PERIOD OF THE JUDGES

CANAAN was the home of the patriarchs, and it was with this land that the God of the patriarchs was associated. Moses and all later leaders recognized this fundamental fact, and it was to Canaan that they led the Hebrews through the wilderness. During the period of the Judges, in the twelfth and eleventh centuries, the term "Israelites" replaced that of "Hebrews," and the relationship of God, Israel and the Land of Israel became intertwined and indissoluble, as it has remained ever since. In the view of the Biblical writers, there could have been no Israel without God and the Holy Land.

## The Geography of the Land of Israel

The Land of Israel, as envisaged in the Bible, covered approximately 10,000 square miles spread over an area that stretches from Dan in the north, at the foot of the Anti-Lebanon mountain range, to below Beersheba in the south, and from the Mediterranean Sea in the west to the desert fringes of Transjordan in the east. The whole territory, of which about three-fifths lies west of Jordan, resembles in size and shape the state of New Hampshire, the forty-fifth state in area in the Union. This little country is broken up into some eight natural geographical units.

<sup>19</sup>. . . Choose life—if you and your offspring would live—<sup>20</sup>by loving the LORD your God, heeding His commands, and holding fast to Him. For thereby you shall have life and shall long endure upon the soil that the LORD your God swore to Abraham, Isaac, and Jacob to give to them.

*Deuteronomy 30.19-20*

When you enter the land that the LORD your God is giving you as a heritage, and you occupy it and settle in it . . . <sup>11</sup>You shall enjoy, together with the Levite and the stranger in your midst, all the bounty that the LORD your God has bestowed upon you and your household.

*Deuteronomy 26.1, 11*

<sup>1</sup>The word that came to Jeremiah from the LORD: <sup>2</sup>Hear the terms of this covenant and proclaim them to the men of Judah and the inhabitants of Jerusalem. <sup>3</sup>You shall say to them: Thus said the LORD, the God of Israel, "Cursed be the man who will not carry out the terms of this covenant, <sup>4</sup>with which I charged your ancestors when I freed them from the land of Egypt, that iron blast furnace, when I said: Heed My commands and fulfill them, just as I have charged you, and you shall be My people and I, in turn, will be your God—<sup>5</sup>thus fulfilling the vow that I swore to your ancestors, to give them a land flowing with milk and honey, as is now the case . . .

*Jeremiah 11.1-5*

וּבָחַרְתָּ בַּחַיִּים לְמַעַן תִּחְיֶה אַתָּה וְזַרְעֶךָ:
לְאַהֲבָה אֶת־יְהוָה אֱלֹהֶיךָ לִשְׁמֹעַ בְּקֹלוֹ וּלְדָבְקָה־
בוֹ כִּי הוּא חַיֶּיךָ וְאֹרֶךְ יָמֶיךָ לָשֶׁבֶת עַל־הָאֲדָמָה
אֲשֶׁר נִשְׁבַּע יְהוָה לַאֲבֹתֶיךָ לְאַבְרָהָם לְיִצְחָק
וּלְיַעֲקֹב לָתֵת לָהֶם:     דברים ל: יט–כ

וְהָיָה כִּי־תָבוֹא אֶל־הָאָרֶץ אֲשֶׁר יְהוָה אֱלֹהֶיךָ
נֹתֵן לְךָ נַחֲלָה וִירִשְׁתָּהּ וְיָשַׁבְתָּ בָּהּ: . . . וְשָׂמַחְתָּ
בְכָל־הַטּוֹב אֲשֶׁר נָתַן־לְךָ יְהוָה אֱלֹהֶיךָ וּלְבֵיתֶךָ
אַתָּה וְהַלֵּוִי וְהַגֵּר אֲשֶׁר בְּקִרְבֶּךָ:
דְּבָרִים כו:א, יא

הַדָּבָר אֲשֶׁר־הָיָה אֶל־יִרְמְיָהוּ מֵאֵת יְהוָה
לֵאמֹר: שִׁמְעוּ אֶת־דִּבְרֵי הַבְּרִית הַזֹּאת וְדִבַּרְתֶּם
אֶל־אִישׁ יְהוּדָה וְעַל־יֹשְׁבֵי יְרוּשָׁלָ‍ִם: וְאָמַרְתָּ
אֲלֵיהֶם כֹּה־אָמַר יְהוָה אֱלֹהֵי יִשְׂרָאֵל אָרוּר הָאִישׁ
אֲשֶׁר לֹא יִשְׁמַע אֶת־דִּבְרֵי הַבְּרִית הַזֹּאת: אֲשֶׁר
צִוִּיתִי אֶת־אֲבוֹתֵיכֶם בְּיוֹם הוֹצִיאִי־אוֹתָם מֵאֶרֶץ־
מִצְרַיִם מִכּוּר הַבַּרְזֶל לֵאמֹר שִׁמְעוּ בְקוֹלִי וַעֲשִׂיתֶם
אוֹתָם כְּכֹל אֲשֶׁר־אֲצַוֶּה אֶתְכֶם וִהְיִיתֶם לִי לְעָם
וְאָנֹכִי אֶהְיֶה לָכֶם לֵאלֹהִים: לְמַעַן הָקִים אֶת־
הַשְּׁבוּעָה אֲשֶׁר־נִשְׁבַּעְתִּי לַאֲבוֹתֵיכֶם לָתֵת לָהֶם
אֶרֶץ זָבַת חָלָב וּדְבַשׁ כַּיּוֹם הַזֶּה . . . יִרְמְיָהוּ יא:א–ה

## The Geography of the Land of Israel

<sup>1</sup>Moses went up from the steppes of Moab to Mount Nebo, to the summit of Pisgah, opposite Jericho, and the LORD showed him the whole land: Gilead as far as Dan; <sup>2</sup>all Naphtali; the land of Ephraim and Manasseh; the whole land of Judah as far as the Western Sea; <sup>3</sup>the Negeb; and the Plain—the valley of Jericho, the city of palm trees—as far as Zoar. <sup>4</sup>And the LORD said to him, "This is the land of which I swore to Abraham, Isaac, and Jacob: 'I will give it to your offspring.' . . ."

*Deuteronomy 34.1-4*

וַיַּעַל מֹשֶׁה מֵעַרְבֹת מוֹאָב אֶל־הַר נְבוֹ רֹאשׁ
הַפִּסְגָּה אֲשֶׁר עַל־פְּנֵי יְרֵחוֹ וַיַּרְאֵהוּ יְהוָה אֶת־
כָּל־הָאָרֶץ אֶת־הַגִּלְעָד עַד־דָּן: וְאֵת כָּל־נַפְתָּלִי
וְאֶת־אֶרֶץ אֶפְרַיִם וּמְנַשֶּׁה וְאֵת כָּל־אֶרֶץ יְהוּדָה
עַד הַיָּם הָאַחֲרוֹן: וְאֶת־הַנֶּגֶב וְאֶת־הַכִּכָּר בִּקְעַת
יְרֵחוֹ עִיר הַתְּמָרִים עַד־צֹעַר: וַיֹּאמֶר יְהוָה אֵלָיו
זֹאת הָאָרֶץ אֲשֶׁר נִשְׁבַּעְתִּי לְאַבְרָהָם לְיִצְחָק
וּלְיַעֲקֹב לֵאמֹר לְזַרְעֲךָ אֶתְּנֶנָּה . . . דְּבָרִים לד:א–ד

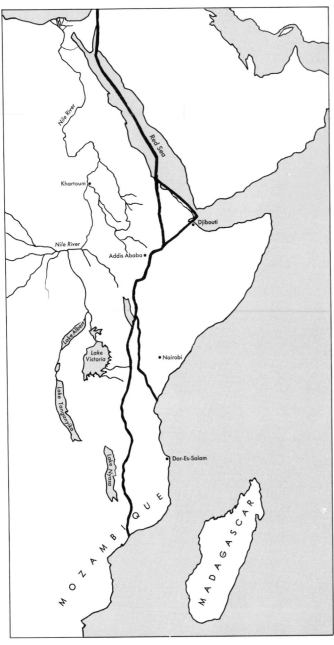

**THE GREAT RIFT**

Along with such other geological formations as the Hill Country, the Mediterranean Coastal Plain and the Shefelah between these two, the "Great Rift" helped determine the climate, the economy, and the history of Israel. The map above exhibits the extent of the "Rift," which begins between the Lebanon and Anti-Lebanon Ranges in Syria, then becomes the Jordan Valley and the Arabah to the Red (Reed) Sea, and continues south into East Africa in the form of the African Lakes (e.g., Lake Nyasa) as far as Mozambique. About 4000 miles in length, the "Great Rift" is longer than the boundary that divides the United States and Canada from Maine to the Pacific—the longest unfortified frontier in the world in the past century. The Valley of Jezreel is one of the smaller rifts in Israel.

First there is the coastal plain along the Mediterranean, about ten miles wide and divided in half approximately at Joppa, near modern Tel Aviv. The Plain of Sharon lies to the north as far as the Carmel range near modern Haifa, and the more important Philistine plain, Philistia, lies to the south. The Plain of Acco extends north of Sharon, from the Carmel mountains to Acco and somewhat beyond. Further along the coast lay Phoenicia, separated from Acco and the rest of western Palestine by mountains of the region.

To the east of and paralleling Philistia rises the Shefelah, the second principal area, which is separated by longitudinal valleys from the central Hill Country and forms the transition to it. The Hill Country begins in southern Syria and in the form of hills and mountains extends down the length of Palestine until it begins to peter out in the extreme south.

The third part, the northern Hill Country, is called Galilee, and is usually subdivided into Upper and Lower Galilee. The fourth unit is the Valley of Jezreel, or Esdraelon (or simply "The Valley"), which cuts right across Galilee and constitutes the easy road for traders and invaders to reach Transjordan. Central Palestine, the fifth part, consisted of Samaria in the north, with the southern sector constituting Judah. The sixth division, formed by the rest of western Palestine, was the vast semiarid area in the south, the Negeb.

The territory west of the Jordan, the seventh section, was separated from Transjordan by a geologically marvellous "rift valley," the corollary of the long range of hills which forms the Hill Country. This rift begins in Syria, separates and forms Mount Lebanon and Mount Anti-Lebanon (Biblical Hermon), and continues south in the form of the Jordan Valley and the Ara-

*It is difficult to reconstruct the precise boundaries of most of the various Israelite groups prior to the rise of the Monarchy. The meaning of the Hebrew text itself is often enough unclear, and much of the geographical data given here was not recorded until long after the events that they deal with. At the same time, it should be observed that Biblical Israel was extremely interested in every part of its little territory, an interest and love that can be witnessed in Modern Israel. See Y. Aharoni, "The Settlement of Canaan," pp. 94-128, 308-313, 349 in* The World History of the Jewish People, *Vol. III:* Judges *(1971).*

מֵהַמִּדְבָּר וְהַלְּבָנוֹן הַזֶּה וְעַד־הַנָּהָר הַגָּדוֹל
נְהַר־פְּרָת כֹּל אֶרֶץ הַחִתִּים וְעַד־הַיָּם הַגָּדוֹל
מְבוֹא הַשֶּׁמֶשׁ יִהְיֶה גְּבוּלְכֶם:
יְהוֹשֻׁעַ א:ד

[4]Your territory shall extend from the wilderness and Lebanon to the Great River, the Euphrates River [on the east]—the whole Hittite country—and up to the Mediterranean Sea on the west.

*Joshua 1.4*

[1]Joshua was now old, advanced in years. The LORD said to him, "You have grown old, you are advanced in years; and very much of the land still remains to be occupied. [2]This is the territory that remains: All the districts of the Philistines and all those of the Geshurites, [3]from the Shihor, which is close to Egypt, to the territory of Ekron on the north, are accounted Canaanite, namely, those of the five lords of the Philistines—the Gazites, the Ashdodites, the Ashkelonites, the Gittites, and the Ekronites—and that of the Avvim [4]on the south. Further, all of the Canaanite country from Mearah of the Sidonians to Aphek by the Amorite border [5]and the land of the Gebalites, with the whole [Valley of] Lebanon, from Baalgad at the foot of Mount Hermon to Lebo-hamath, on the east, [6]with all the inhabitants of the hill country from the [Valley of] Lebanon to Misrephoth-maim and all the Sidonians. I will dispossess them for the Israelites; you have only to apportion it by lot among Israel, as I have commanded you.

*Joshua 13.1-6*

וִיהוֹשֻׁעַ זָקֵן בָּא בַּיָּמִים וַיֹּאמֶר יְהוָה אֵלָיו אַתָּה
זָקַנְתָּה בָּאתָ בַיָּמִים וְהָאָרֶץ נִשְׁאֲרָה הַרְבֵּה־מְאֹד
לְרִשְׁתָּהּ: זֹאת הָאָרֶץ הַנִּשְׁאָרֶת כָּל־גְּלִילוֹת
הַפְּלִשְׁתִּים וְכָל־הַגְּשׁוּרִי: מִן־הַשִּׁיחוֹר אֲשֶׁר עַל־
פְּנֵי מִצְרַיִם וְעַד גְּבוּל עֶקְרוֹן צָפוֹנָה לַכְּנַעֲנִי תֵּחָשֵׁב
חֲמֵשֶׁת סַרְנֵי פְלִשְׁתִּים הָעַזָּתִי וְהָאַשְׁדּוֹדִי הָאֶשְׁקְלוֹנִי
הַגִּתִּי וְהָעֶקְרוֹנִי וְהָעַוִּים: מִתֵּימָן כָּל־אֶרֶץ הַכְּנַעֲנִי
וּמְעָרָה אֲשֶׁר לַצִּידֹנִים עַד־אֲפֵקָה עַד גְּבוּל
הָאֱמֹרִי: וְהָאָרֶץ הַגִּבְלִי וְכָל־הַלְּבָנוֹן מִזְרַח הַשֶּׁמֶשׁ
מִבַּעַל גָּד תַּחַת הַר־חֶרְמוֹן עַד לְבוֹא חֲמָת:
כָּל־יֹשְׁבֵי הָהָר מִן־הַלְּבָנוֹן עַד־מִשְׂרְפֹת מַיִם
כָּל־צִידֹנִים אָנֹכִי אוֹרִישֵׁם מִפְּנֵי בְּנֵי יִשְׂרָאֵל רַק
הַפִּלֶהָ לְיִשְׂרָאֵל בְּנַחֲלָה כַּאֲשֶׁר צִוִּיתִךָ:

יְהוֹשֻׁעַ יג:א–ו

[1]These are the kings of the land whom the Israelites defeated and whose territories they occupied. East of the Jordan, from the wadi Arnon to Mount Hermon, including the eastern half of Arabah: [2]King Sihon of the Amorites, who resided in Heshbon and ruled [over the territory] from Aroer on the bank of the wadi Arnon and the wadi proper—part of Gilead—up to the wadi

וְאֵלֶּה מַלְכֵי הָאָרֶץ אֲשֶׁר הִכּוּ בְנֵי־יִשְׂרָאֵל
וַיִּרְשׁוּ אֶת־אַרְצָם בְּעֵבֶר הַיַּרְדֵּן מִזְרְחָה הַשֶּׁמֶשׁ
מִנַּחַל אַרְנוֹן עַד־הַר חֶרְמוֹן וְכָל־הָעֲרָבָה מִזְרָחָה:
סִיחוֹן מֶלֶךְ הָאֱמֹרִי הַיּוֹשֵׁב בְּחֶשְׁבּוֹן מֹשֵׁל מֵעֲרוֹעֵר
אֲשֶׁר עַל־שְׂפַת־נַחַל אַרְנוֹן וְתוֹךְ הַנַּחַל וַחֲצִי

71

The three pictures below are intended to illustrate the varied climate of Israel.

Snow-capped **Mount Hermon** about 9100 feet high.

**Valley of Jezreel,** about 200-250 feet above sea level.

**Jericho,** about 100 miles south of Mount Hermon and about 800 feet below sea level.

bah, to the Gulf of Aqabah and the Red Sea—indeed, as far as Mozambique and into the great depressions filled by the African lakes. The Jordan River runs through the valley, pooled en route in Lake Huleh (not far from the Waters of Merom) and the Sea of Galilee (or Chinnereth), and terminates to the south in the *cul-de-sac* which is the Dead, or Salt, Sea. The last two bodies of water fill below-sea-level troughs in the valley floor. The Dead Sea, about 1,275 feet below the Mediterranean, is the lowest depression in the world.

Finally, eastern Palestine, or Transjordan, is essentially a plateau, and is divided up by four rivers into five main regions. The Yarmuk River, flowing into the Jordan just south of the Sea of Galilee, made up the dividing line between Bashan and Gilead. The Jabbok, or Wadi Zerqa, emptying into the Jordan about two-thirds of the way down, constituted the boundary between Gilead and Ammon. The Arnon, or Wadi Mojib, in turn, sometimes served as the natural barrier between Ammon and Moab, at the middle of the Dead Sea. The boundary between the two countries varied during Biblical times, usually lying north of the Arnon. Finally, at the southern end of the Dead Sea, the Zered, or Wadi Hesa, separated Moab from Edom. When it rained, these wadis became real streams. Otherwise they were mostly dry riverbeds.

## The Climate of the Holy Land

Small as it is, Palestine has always had the advantages of many kinds of climate, owing in part to the variety of the terrain. In general, the land resembles the drier parts of Southern California, but everything is on a much smaller scale. Mount Hermon in the north, which is over 9,000 feet high, tends to be cold, whereas just over one hundred miles to the south, in the Jordan Valley, Jericho

Jabbok, the border of the Ammonites, ³and over the Arabah up to the Sea of Chinereth on the east, and down to the Sea of the Arabah—the Dead Sea—on the east, by way of Beth-jeshimoth which is in the south at the foot of the slopes of Pisgah. ⁴Also the territory of King Og of Bashan, one of the last of the Rephaim, who resided in Ashtaroth and in Edrei . . .

⁷These are the kings of the land whom Joshua and the Israelites defeated on the west side of the Jordan, from Baal-gad in the Valley of Lebanon to Mount Halak which ascends to Seir, which Joshua assigned as a possession to the tribal divisions of Israel: ⁸in the hill country, in the Shefelah, in the Arabah, in the slopes, in the wilderness, and in the Negeb—[in the territories of] the Hittites, the Amorites, the Canaanites, the Perizzites, the Hivites, and the Jebusites.

*Joshua 12.1-8 (followed in vv. 9-24*
*by a list of 31 kings).*

הַגִּלְעָד וְעַד יַבֹּק הַנַּחַל גְּבוּל בְּנֵי עַמּוֹן: וְהָעֲרָבָה
עַד־יָם כִּנְרוֹת מִזְרָחָה וְעַד יָם הָעֲרָבָה יָם־
הַמֶּלַח מִזְרָחָה דֶּרֶךְ בֵּית הַיְשִׁמוֹת וּמִתֵּימָן תַּחַת
אַשְׁדּוֹת הַפִּסְגָּה: וּגְבוּל עוֹג מֶלֶךְ הַבָּשָׁן מִיֶּתֶר
הָרְפָאִים הַיּוֹשֵׁב בְּעַשְׁתָּרוֹת וּבְאֶדְרֶעִי: . . . וְאֵלֶּה
מַלְכֵי הָאָרֶץ אֲשֶׁר הִכָּה יְהוֹשֻׁעַ וּבְנֵי יִשְׂרָאֵל
בְּעֵבֶר הַיַּרְדֵּן יָמָּה מִבַּעַל גָּד בְּבִקְעַת הַלְּבָנוֹן
וְעַד־הָהָר הֶחָלָק הָעֹלֶה שֵׂעִירָה וַיִּתְּנָהּ יְהוֹשֻׁעַ
לְשִׁבְטֵי יִשְׂרָאֵל יְרֻשָּׁה כְּמַחְלְקֹתָם: בָּהָר וּבַשְּׁפֵלָה
וּבָעֲרָבָה וּבָאֲשֵׁדוֹת וּבַמִּדְבָּר וּבַנֶּגֶב הַחִתִּי הָאֱמֹרִי
וְהַכְּנַעֲנִי הַפְּרִזִּי הַחִוִּי וְהַיְבוּסִי:

יְהוֹשֻׁעַ יב:א–ח

¹The portion that fell by lot to the various clans of the tribe of Judah lay farthest south, from the border of Edom, at the Wilderness of Zin. ²Their southern boundary began from the tip of the Dead Sea, from the tongue that turns southward . . . ⁵The boundary on the east was the Dead Sea up to the mouth of the Jordan . . . ⁸Then the boundary ascended into the Valley of Ben-hinnon, along the southern flank of the Jebusites—that is, Jerusalem. The border then ran up to the top of the hill which flanks the Valley of Hinnom on the west . . . ⁹From that hilltop the boundary curves to the fountain of the Waters of Nephtoah and ran on . . . ¹¹The boundary then proceeded to the northern flank of Ekron and . . . the boundary ran on to the Sea. ¹²And the western boundary was the Mediterranean Sea. These were the boundaries of the territory of the various clans of the Judites on all sides.

*Joshua 15.1–12*

וַיְהִי הַגּוֹרָל לְמַטֵּה בְּנֵי יְהוּדָה לְמִשְׁפְּחֹתָם
אֶל־גְּבוּל אֱדוֹם מִדְבַּר־צִן נֶגְבָּה מִקְצֵה תֵימָן:
וַיְהִי לָהֶם גְּבוּל נֶגֶב מִקְצֵה יָם הַמֶּלַח מִן־הַלָּשֹׁן
הַפֹּנֶה נֶגְבָּה: . . . וּגְבוּל קֵדְמָה יָם הַמֶּלַח עַד־קְצֵה
הַיַּרְדֵּן . . . וְעָלָה הַגְּבוּל גֵּי בֶן־הִנֹּם אֶל־כֶּתֶף
הַיְבוּסִי מִנֶּגֶב הִיא יְרוּשָׁלָ͏ִם וְעָלָה הַגְּבוּל אֶל־רֹאשׁ
הָהָר אֲשֶׁר עַל־פְּנֵי גֵי־הִנֹּם יָמָּה . . . וְתָאַר הַגְּבוּל
מֵרֹאשׁ הָהָר אֶל־מַעְיַן מֵי נֶפְתּוֹחַ וְיָצָא . . . וְיָצָא
הַגְּבוּל אֶל־כֶּתֶף עֶקְרוֹן צָפוֹנָה . . . וְהָיוּ תֹצְאוֹת
הַגְּבוּל . . . יָמָּה: וּגְבוּל יָם הַיָּמָּה הַגָּדוֹל וּגְבוּל
זֶה גְּבוּל בְּנֵי־יְהוּדָה סָבִיב לְמִשְׁפְּחֹתָם:

יְהוֹשֻׁעַ טו:א–יב

## The Climate of the Holy Land

*If the Bible abounds in allusions to the various aspects of nature—climate, wind, rain, drought, clouds, and the like—it is the awareness that derives in large measure from the chiefly agricultural character of the economy in that period. See in general, D. Baly,* The Geography of the Bible *(1957).*

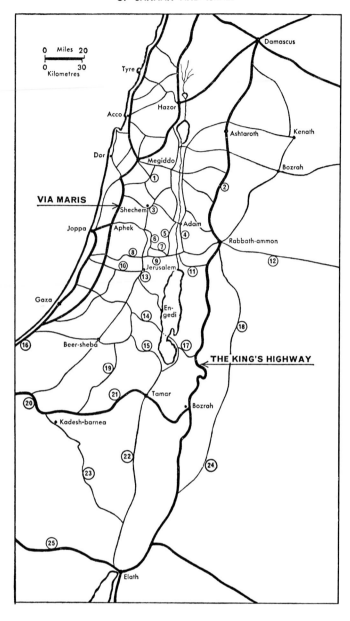

0   Miles   20
0            30
Kilometres

Damascus

Tyre

Hazor

Acco

Ashtaroth    Kenath

Dor

Megiddo    Bozrah

VIA MARIS

Shechem ③

Joppa    Aphek    Adam

Rabbath-ammon

Jerusalem ⑨ ⑪    ⑫

⑬

Gaza

En-
gedi

Beer-sheba    ⑮    ⑰    THE KING'S HIGHWAY

⑯    ⑱

⑲

⑳    ㉑    Tamar

Kadesh-barnea    Bozrah

㉒

㉓    ㉔

㉕

Elath

1. The way (to) Beth-haggan
2. The road to Bashan
3. The way (to) the Diviners Oak
4. The way of the plain
5. The way to the Jordan
6. The way (to) Ophrah
7. The way to the wilderness
8. The way of Beth-horon
9. The way of the Arabah
10. The way (to) Beth-shemesh/the
    road to Timnah
11. The way (to) Beth-jeshimoth
12. The way of the tent dwellers
13. The way to Ephrath
14. The way to Moab

15. The way (to) Edom
16. The way (to) the land of
    the Philistines
17. The road to Horonaim
18. The way of the wilderness
    of Moab
19. The way of the Atharim
20. The way to Shur
21. The way (to) the Arabah
22. The way to the Reed Sea
23. The way to the hill country of
    the Amorites
24. The way of the wilderness
    of Edom
25. The way (to) Mount Seir

74

swelters in tropical heat. Jerusalem, although less than fifteen miles to the southwest of Jericho, is about 3400 feet higher, and its inhabitants have usually found its climate temperate.

From Jerusalem to the coast the distance is just over thirty miles, and the descent ranges from about 2,600 feet to sea level. The coastal climate is of course much warmer, although never so unbearable in summer as the Jordan Valley. The temperatures in the Transjordan plateau approximate those of Jerusalem.

There is another important element, the winds. The winds from the east are usually hot and dry, coming as they do from the desert. Those from the north, on the other hand, and especially from the west across the Mediterranean, are much more gentle, bringing with them cool air and rain. The all-important rainy season usually begins in October and ends in March or April. One of God's greatest blessings to Israel was His promise: "I will give the rain of your land in its season, the early rain and the later rain, that you may gather in your grain, your wine, and your oil" (Deuteronomy 11:14; 28:12). The threat of drought was a curse and a disaster (28:23–24).

## Geography and Economy

A network of valleys provided avenues of settlement as well as commercial and military traffic. This made for the historical interplay between hill and valley peoples that figures so prominently in the books of Joshua, Judges, and Samuel.

Geography made Biblical Israel primarily an agricultural, and only secondarily a commercial, society. The coastal plains of Sharon and Philistia, the Jezreel and Jordan valleys, and a considerable part of the Hill Country of Samaria and Judah lent themselves to successful farming. Even the nearly waterless Negeb was tilled profitably when the inhabitants diligently exploited the available

¹³So Moses held out his rod over the land of Egypt, and the LORD drove an east wind over the land all that day and all night; and when morning came, the east wind had brought the locusts. ¹⁴Locusts invaded all the land of Egypt and settled within all the territory of Egypt in a thick mass; never before had there been so many, nor will there ever be so many again.

*Exodus 10.13–14*

וַיֵּ֨ט מֹשֶׁ֜ה אֶת־מַטֵּהוּ֮ עַל־אֶ֣רֶץ מִצְרַיִם֒ וַֽיהֹוָ֗ה נִהַ֣ג רֽוּחַ־קָדִים֮ בָּאָ֨רֶץ֙ כָּל־הַיּ֣וֹם הַה֔וּא וְכָל־הַלָּ֑יְלָה הַבֹּ֣קֶר הָיָ֔ה וְר֙וּחַ֙ הַקָּדִ֔ים נָשָׂ֖א אֶת־הָאַרְבֶּֽה: וַיַּ֣עַל הָֽאַרְבֶּ֗ה עַ֚ל כָּל־אֶ֣רֶץ מִצְרַ֔יִם וַיָּ֕נַח בְּכֹ֖ל גְּב֣וּל מִצְרָ֑יִם כָּבֵ֣ד מְאֹ֔ד לְ֠פָנָ֠יו לֹא־הָ֨יָה כֵ֤ן אַרְבֶּה֙ כָּמֹ֔הוּ וְאַחֲרָ֖יו לֹ֥א יִֽהְיֶה־כֵּֽן:

                              שְׁמוֹת י:יג–יד

⁴⁵In no time at all, the sky grew dark with clouds and storm, and a heavy rain began to fall. So Ahab mounted [his chariot] and set out for Jezreel.

*I Kings 18.45*

וַיְהִ֣י ׀ עַד־כֹּ֣ה וְעַד־כֹּ֗ה וְהַשָּׁמַ֙יִם֙ הִֽתְקַדְּרוּ֙ עָבִ֔ים וְר֖וּחַ וַיְהִ֣י גֶּ֣שֶׁם גָּד֑וֹל וַיִּרְכַּ֥ב אַחְאָ֖ב וַיֵּ֥לֶךְ יִזְרְעֶֽאלָה:

                              מְלָכִים א' יח:מה

⁴The Lord cast a mighty wind upon the sea and a heavy storm came upon the sea, and the ship was in danger of breaking up.

*Jonah 1.4*

וַֽיהֹוָ֗ה הֵטִ֤יל רֽוּחַ־גְּדוֹלָה֙ אֶל־הַיָּ֔ם וַיְהִ֥י סַֽעַר־גָּד֖וֹל בַּיָּ֑ם וְהָ֣אֳנִיָּ֔ה חִשְּׁבָ֖ה לְהִשָּׁבֵֽר:

                              יוֹנָה א:ד

¹³If, then, you obey the commandments that I enjoin upon you this day, loving the LORD your God and serving Him with all your heart and soul, ¹⁴I will grant the rain for your land in season, the early rain and the late. You shall gather in your new grain and wine and oil—¹⁵I will also provide grass in the fields for your cattle —and thus you shall eat your fill.

*Deuteronomy 11.13-15*

וְהָיָ֗ה אִם־שָׁמֹ֤עַ תִּשְׁמְעוּ֙ אֶל־מִצְוֺתַ֔י אֲשֶׁ֧ר אָנֹכִ֛י מְצַוֶּ֥ה אֶתְכֶ֖ם הַיּ֑וֹם לְאַֽהֲבָ֞ה אֶת־יְהֹוָ֤ה אֱלֹֽהֵיכֶם֙ וּלְעָבְד֔וֹ בְּכָל־לְבַבְכֶ֖ם וּבְכָל־נַפְשְׁכֶֽם: וְנָתַתִּ֧י מְטַֽר־אַרְצְכֶ֛ם בְּעִתּ֖וֹ יוֹרֶ֣ה וּמַלְק֑וֹשׁ וְאָֽסַפְתָּ֣ דְגָנֶ֔ךָ וְתִֽירֹֽשְׁךָ֖ וְיִצְהָרֶֽךָ: וְנָֽתַתִּ֛י עֵ֥שֶׂב בְּשָֽׂדְךָ֖ לִבְהֶמְתֶּ֑ךָ וְאָֽכַלְתָּ֖ וְשָׂבָֽעְתָּ:

                              דְּבָרִים יא:יג–טו

¹²The LORD will open for you His bounteous store, the heavens, to provide rain for your land in season and to bless all your undertakings. You will be creditor to many nations, but debtor to none.

*Deuteronomy 28.12*

יִפְתַּ֣ח יְהֹוָ֣ה ׀ לְךָ֡ אֶת־אֽוֹצָר֣וֹ הַטּוֹב֩ אֶת־הַשָּׁמַ֨יִם לָתֵ֤ת מְטַֽר־אַרְצְךָ֙ בְּעִתּ֔וֹ וּלְבָרֵ֕ךְ אֵ֖ת כָּל־מַֽעֲשֵׂ֣ה יָדֶ֑ךָ וְהִלְוִ֙יתָ֙ גּוֹיִ֣ם רַבִּ֔ים וְאַתָּ֖ה לֹ֥א תִלְוֶֽה:

                              דְּבָרִים כח:יב

²³The skies above your head shall be copper and the earth under you iron. ²⁴The LORD will make the rain of your land dust, and sand shall drop on you from the sky, until you are wiped out.

*Deuteronomy 28.23–24*

… וְהָי֥וּ שָׁמֶ֛יךָ אֲשֶׁ֥ר עַל־רֹֽאשְׁךָ֖ נְחֹ֑שֶׁת וְהָאָ֥רֶץ אֲשֶׁר־תַּחְתֶּ֖יךָ בַּרְזֶֽל: יִתֵּ֧ן יְהֹוָ֛ה אֶת־מְטַ֥ר אַרְצְךָ֖ אָבָ֣ק וְעָפָ֑ר מִן־הַשָּׁמַ֙יִם֙ יֵרֵ֣ד עָלֶ֔יךָ עַ֖ד הִשָּֽׁמְדָֽךְ:

                              דְּבָרִים כח: כג–כד

## Geography and Economy

³But Jonah set out to flee from the Lord to Tarshish. He went down to Joppa and found a ship going to Tarshish. He paid the fare and went aboard to sail with the others to Tarshish to escape from the Lord.

*Jonah 1.3*

וַיָּ֣קָם יוֹנָ֗ה לִבְרֹ֤חַ תַּרְשִׁ֙ישָׁה֙ מִלִּפְנֵ֣י יְהֹוָ֔ה וַיֵּ֨רֶד יָפ֜וֹ וַיִּמְצָ֧א אֳנִיָּ֣ה ׀ בָּאָ֣ה תַרְשִׁ֗ישׁ וַיִּתֵּ֨ן שְׂכָרָ֜הּ וַיֵּ֤רֶד בָּהּ֙ לָב֤וֹא עִמָּהֶם֙ תַּרְשִׁ֔ישָׁה מִלִּפְנֵ֖י יְהֹוָֽה:

                              יוֹנָה א:ג

                                                                75

The tree, its fruit and its wood, constituted an important element in Israel's essentially agricultural economy. The Bible will frequently mention figs, olives, grapes, nuts, cedar wood, and the like.

Cedar tree.

Nut tree (almond).

Olive tree.

supply of water by terracing and irrigating the land.

Ancient Israel, with its few and inadequate harbors, derived slight commercial advantage from its Mediterranean coast. Even Dor and Joppa, the nation's best ports, could be used only when the sea was calm. Such better harbors as were to be found along the coast, Byblos, Sidon, Tyre, and usually even Acco, were in Phoenician hands. In the days of Solomon, considerable maritime trade centered about Ezion-geber (or, Elath) on the Gulf of Aqabah and continued at least sporadically for some time after his reign.

It was as the land-bridge between Asia and Africa that the land of Israel acquired commercial significance. Its plains and valleys, notably Jezreel and the Mediterranean coast, were commercial and military highways from time immemorial; and this fact explains why the sites which guarded and controlled these routes played so important a role in Biblical history. Beth-shan, Megiddo, Shechem, Gaza, and Beersheba were among the better-known cities in the west, and in Transjordan such sites as Ashtaroth, Ramoth-gilead, Rabbath-ammon, Heshbon, and Kir-hareseth dominated the main road from Damascus through Bashan, Gilead, Ammon, and Moab, to Edom in the south.

Israel was not rich in natural resources. The copper and iron ores in the south were exploited by the Israelites only when Edom was under their control and Egypt was weak. Limited both in area and water supply, the country could not support a large population; but in spite of that, the Israelites might well have succeeded in turning their domain into "a land flowing with milk and honey" (Exodus 3:8) if it had not fallen directly across the path of invasion and conquest at the hands of the expanding empires of western Asia and Egypt.

<sup>26</sup>King Solomon built a navy at Ezion-geber, which is near Eloth (Elath), on the shore of the Reed Sea, in the land of Edom.

*I Kings 9.26*

וַאֳנִי עָשָׂה הַמֶּלֶךְ שְׁלֹמֹה בְּעֶצְיוֹן־גֶּבֶר אֲשֶׁר
אֶת־אֵלוֹת עַל־שְׂפַת יַם־סוּף בְּאֶרֶץ אֱדוֹם:

מְלָכִים א׳ ט:כו

<sup>25</sup>Then they sat down to a meal. Looking up, they saw a caravan of Ishmaelites coming from Gilead, their camels bearing gum, balm, and ladanum to be taken to Egypt.

*Genesis 37.25*

וַיֵּשְׁבוּ לֶאֱכָל־לֶחֶם וַיִּשְׂאוּ עֵינֵיהֶם וַיִּרְאוּ וְהִנֵּה
אֹרְחַת יִשְׁמְעֵאלִים בָּאָה מִגִּלְעָד וּגְמַלֵּיהֶם נֹשְׂאִים
נְכֹאת וּצְרִי וָלֹט הוֹלְכִים לְהוֹרִיד מִצְרָיְמָה:

בְּרֵאשִׁית לז:כה

<sup>16</sup>Solomon sent a message to Hiram, as follows: ". . . <sup>19</sup>I now intend to build a House for the name of the Lord my God . . . <sup>20</sup>So issue orders that cedars of Lebanon be cut down for me . . ." <sup>22</sup>Hiram returned word to Solomon, as follows: ". . . I will do just as you requested in the matter of the cedar and cypress timber. <sup>23</sup>My servants will bring them down from Lebanon to the Sea, and I shall have them towed by sea as rafts to whatever place you let me know . . ."

*I Kings 5.16–23*

וַיִּשְׁלַח שְׁלֹמֹה אֶל־חִירָם לֵאמֹר: . . . זְהִנְנִי אֹמֵר
לִבְנוֹת בַּיִת לְשֵׁם יְהוָה אֱלֹהָי . . . וְעַתָּה צַוֵּה
וְיִכְרְתוּ־לִי אֲרָזִים מִן־הַלְּבָנוֹן . . . וַיִּשְׁלַח חִירָם
אֶל־שְׁלֹמֹה לֵאמֹר שָׁמַעְתִּי אֵת אֲשֶׁר־שָׁלַחְתָּ אֵלִי
אֲנִי אֶעֱשֶׂה אֶת־כָּל־חֶפְצְךָ בַּעֲצֵי אֲרָזִים וּבַעֲצֵי
בְרוֹשִׁים: עֲבָדַי יֹרִדוּ מִן־הַלְּבָנוֹן יָמָּה וַאֲנִי אֲשִׂימֵם
דֹבְרוֹת בַּיָּם עַד־הַמָּקוֹם אֲשֶׁר־תִּשְׁלַח אֵלַי . . .

מְלָכִים א׳, ה:טז־כג

*Much useful information on the geography and economy of ancient Israel may be found in D. Baly,* Geographical Companion to the Bible *(1963).*

<sup>7</sup>For the Lord your God is bringing you into a good land, a land with streams and springs and fountains issuing from plain and hill; <sup>8</sup>a land of wheat and barley, of vines, figs, and pomegranates, a land of olive trees and honey; <sup>9</sup>a land where you may eat food without stint, where you will lack nothing; a land whose rocks are iron and from whose hills you can mine copper.

*Deuteronomy 8.7-9*

כִּי יְהוָה אֱלֹהֶיךָ מְבִיאֲךָ אֶל־אֶרֶץ טוֹבָה אֶרֶץ
נַחֲלֵי מָיִם עֲיָנֹת וּתְהֹמֹת יֹצְאִים בַּבִּקְעָה וּבָהָר:
אֶרֶץ חִטָּה וּשְׂעֹרָה וְגֶפֶן וּתְאֵנָה וְרִמּוֹן אֶרֶץ־זֵית
שֶׁמֶן וּדְבָשׁ: אֶרֶץ אֲשֶׁר לֹא בְמִסְכֵּנֻת תֹּאכַל־בָּהּ
לֶחֶם לֹא תֶחְסַר כֹּל בָּהּ אֶרֶץ אֲשֶׁר אֲבָנֶיהָ בַרְזֶל
וּמֵהֲרָרֶיהָ תַּחְצֹב נְחֹשֶׁת:

דְּבָרִים ח:ז־ט

Fragments of pottery from Megiddo, painted with figures of soldiers. The almost complete figure on the sherd is identified as Canaanite by his full head of black hair and his short black beard. He carries a shield and wields a battle axe. He may wear chest armor. Late Bronze Age (ca. 1200).

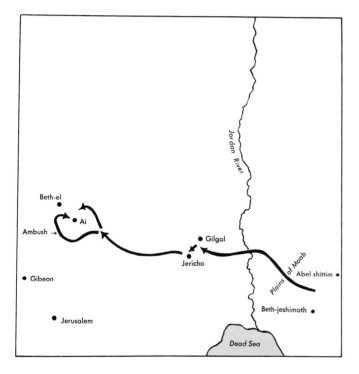

**AI AND BETHEL**

According to the account in Joshua 8.1-29, the Israelite forces marched from Jericho to Ai and destroyed that Canaanite community. Archaeologically, however, it is known that Ai had lain in ruins for about a thousand years prior to Joshua, whereas the important town of Bethel, only a few miles to the northwest of Ai, was destroyed in precisely this period but receives no mention in the account of Joshua's campaign of conquest. Many scholars believe, therefore, that it is the battle of Bethel, rather than Ai, which Joshua 8.1-29 originally described.

## Joshua and the Conquest of Canaan: The Ideal and the Reality

According to the traditional understanding of the Biblical account, the taking of Canaan was accomplished in a single spectacularly successful invasion, with Joshua smiting one-and-thirty kings. In this picture, the Hebrew tribes, led by Joshua, crossed the Jordan near the Dead Sea and took the key point of Jericho, "whose walls came tumbling down." The next objective was Ai, up in the Hill Country, just over ten miles west of Jericho as the crow flies, but twice as far by foot. This fortified place Joshua took by stratagem.

Thereafter, in a series of forays down the valleys—on one occasion, the lost Book of Jashar tells us (Joshua 10:12–14), he commanded the sun in Gibeon and the moon in the valley of Aijalon to stand still, so that he could mop up remnants of Canaanite resistance—Joshua took and razed a series of fortified towns, Libnah, Lachish, Eglon, Hebron, and Debir. This done, he conquered all the highland of southern Canaan, a section of the coastal strip as far as Gaza, and then in the north by the Waters of Merom, a hundred miles more or less from his base at Gilgal, he routed a Canaanite army.

Reuben, Gad, and half of the tribe of Manasseh occupied Transjordan; the other half of Manasseh settled on the Plain of Sharon just south of Esdraelon. The tribe of Levi, consisting entirely of religious functionaries, received no single fixed territory. The rest of the tribes shared in the partition of Canaan according to their population.

The author of Chapters 10–11 in the Book of Joshua provides the basis for this traditional view, Joshua, he recounts (10:40; 11:23):
conquered the whole country: the hill country, the Negeb, the Shefelah, and the slopes, with all their kings; he left none remaining; but utterly destroyed all that breathed . . . So Joshua con-

²⁰So the people shouted and the horns were sounded; and when the people heard the sound of the horns, the people raised a mighty war spot. The people rushed into the city, every man straight ahead, and captured the city.

*Joshua 6.20*

וַיָּרַע הָעָם וַיִּתְקְעוּ בַּשּׁוֹפָרוֹת וַיְהִי כִשְׁמֹעַ הָעָם
אֶת־קוֹל הַשּׁוֹפָר וַיָּרִיעוּ הָעָם תְּרוּעָה גְדוֹלָה
וַתִּפֹּל הַחוֹמָה תַּחְתֶּיהָ וַיַּעַל הָעָם הָעִירָה אִישׁ נֶגְדּוֹ
וַיִּלְכְּדוּ אֶת־הָעִיר:

יְהוֹשֻׁעַ ו:כ

¹²Then Joshua addressed the LORD, when the LORD routed the Amorites before the Israelites, saying in the presence of the Israelites:
"O sun, stand still at Gibeon,
O moon, in the valley of Aijalon!"
¹³And the sun stood still
And the moon halted,
Till the nation took vengence on its foes.

It is so recorded in the Book of Jashar. Thus the sun halted in the middle of the sky, and did not press on to set for about a full day. ¹⁴Never before or since was there a day like that, when the LORD heeded the plea of a man—for the LORD was fighting for Israel.

⁴⁰Thus Joshua conquered the whole region: the hill country, the Negeb, the Shefelah, and the slopes, with all their kings—he let none escape. He proscribed every soul, as the LORD, the God of Israel , commanded.

*Joshua 10.12-14, 40*

אָז יְדַבֵּר יְהוֹשֻׁעַ לַיהוָה בְּיוֹם תֵּת יְהוָה אֶת־
הָאֱמֹרִי לִפְנֵי בְּנֵי יִשְׂרָאֵל וַיֹּאמֶר לְעֵינֵי יִשְׂרָאֵל
שֶׁמֶשׁ בְּגִבְעוֹן דּוֹם וְיָרֵחַ בְּעֵמֶק אַיָּלוֹן: וַיִּדֹּם
הַשֶּׁמֶשׁ וְיָרֵחַ עָמָד עַד־יִקֹּם גּוֹי אֹיְבָיו הֲלֹא־הִיא
כְתוּבָה עַל־סֵפֶר הַיָּשָׁר וַיַּעֲמֹד הַשֶּׁמֶשׁ בַּחֲצִי
הַשָּׁמַיִם וְלֹא־אָץ לָבוֹא כְּיוֹם תָּמִים: וְלֹא הָיָה
כַּיּוֹם הַהוּא לְפָנָיו וְאַחֲרָיו לִשְׁמֹעַ יְהוָה בְּקוֹל
אִישׁ כִּי יְהוָה נִלְחָם לְיִשְׂרָאֵל: . . . וַיַּכֶּה יְהוֹשֻׁעַ אֶת־
כָּל־הָאָרֶץ הָהָר וְהַנֶּגֶב וְהַשְּׁפֵלָה וְהָאֲשֵׁדוֹת וְאֵת
כָּל־מַלְכֵיהֶם לֹא הִשְׁאִיר שָׂרִיד וְאֵת כָּל־הַנְּשָׁמָה
הֶחֱרִים כַּאֲשֶׁר צִוָּה יְהוָה אֱלֹהֵי יִשְׂרָאֵל:

יְהוֹשֻׁעַ י:יב-יד, מ

¹⁰Joshua then turned back and captured Hazor, and put her king to the sword—for Hazor in the past was the capital of all those kingdoms. ¹¹They put to the sword every person in it, because of the proscription; not a soul survived. And Hazor itself was burned down . . . ¹³But all the towns that have remained standing on their mounds were not burned down by Israel . . . ²³Thus Joshua captured the whole country, exactly as the LORD had promised Moses, and Joshua assigned it to Israel to share according to their tribal divisions. And the land had rest from war.

*Joshua 11.10—23*

וַיָּשָׁב יְהוֹשֻׁעַ בָּעֵת הַהִיא וַיִּלְכֹּד אֶת־חָצוֹר
וְאֶת־מַלְכָּהּ הִכָּה בֶחָרֶב כִּי־חָצוֹר לְפָנִים הִיא
רֹאשׁ כָּל־הַמַּמְלָכוֹת הָאֵלֶּה: וַיַּכּוּ אֶת־כָּל־הַנֶּפֶשׁ
אֲשֶׁר־בָּהּ לְפִי־חֶרֶב הַחֲרֵם לֹא נוֹתַר כָּל־נְשָׁמָה
וְאֶת־חָצוֹר שָׂרַף בָּאֵשׁ: . . . רַק כָּל־הֶעָרִים
הָעֹמְדוֹת עַל־תִּלָּם לֹא־שְׂרָפָם יִשְׂרָאֵל . . . וַיִּקַּח
יְהוֹשֻׁעַ אֶת־כָּל־הָאָרֶץ כְּכֹל אֲשֶׁר דִּבֶּר יְהוָה
אֶל־מֹשֶׁה וַיִּתְּנָהּ יְהוֹשֻׁעַ לְנַחֲלָה לְיִשְׂרָאֵל כְּמַחְלְקֹתָם
לְשִׁבְטֵיהֶם וְהָאָרֶץ שָׁקְטָה מִמִּלְחָמָה:

יְהוֹשֻׁעַ יא:י-כג

79

## THE TRIBES OF ISRAEL

Although the Bible offers several variant lists of the number of tribes in ancient Israel, the traditional number, found in most of the lists, is twelve; see most recently J. Liver, "The Israelite Tribes," in *The World History of the Jewish People*, Vol. III: *Judges* (1971), 183-211, 326-331, 351-352. The following scheme derives from Genesis 29-30 (cf. 35.23-29 and chap. 49); and note that Joseph is said to have given rise to Ephraim and Manasseh (Genesis 48.15-22) who participate in the division of Canaan in place of Levi and Joseph, thus retaining the number 12 for both the sons of Jacob-Israel and the tribes of Israel.

| לֵאָה | | יַעֲקֹב | | רָחֵל |
| --- | --- | --- | --- | --- |
| **LEAH** | | **JACOB** | | **RACHEL** |

| | | | אֶפְרַיִם | |
| --- | --- | --- | --- | --- |
| רְאוּבֵן | Reuben | יוֹסֵף | | Ephraim |
| שִׁמְעוֹן | Simeon | Joseph | מְנַשֶּׁה | |
| לֵוִי | Levi | | | Manasseh |
| יְהוּדָה | Judah | בִּנְיָמִין | | Benjamin |
| יִשָּׂשׁכָר | Issachar | | | |
| זְבֻלוּן | Zebulun | | | |
| | Dinah | (Bilhah, maidservant) | | |
| | | דָּן | | Dan |
| | | נַפְתָּלִי | | Naphtali |
| (Zilpah maidservant) | | | | |
| גָּד | Gad | | | |
| אָשֵׁר | Asher | | | |

### THE TWELVE TRIBES OF ISRAEL (cf. Numbers 1)

| | |
| --- | --- |
| Reuben | Manasseh |
| Simeon | Benjamin |
| Judah | Dan |
| Issachar | Asher |
| Zebulun | Gad |
| Ephraim | Naphtali |

quered the whole country, exactly as the Lord said to Moses; and Joshua assigned it to Israel according to their tribal divisions. And the land had rest from war.

Chapters 15–19 in Joshua and Chapter I in Judges, however, give a different picture both of the conquest and of the role that Joshua played in it. This version describes the conquest as a slow piecemeal affair, accomplished largely after Joshua and his generation were gone, by individual tribes and clans seldom acting even in partial unison. Thus Judges 1:1 would indicate that the land was not at rest from war, in fact was never pacified: "After the death of Joshua, the Israelites inquired of the Lord, 'Which of us shall be the first to go up and attack the Canaanites?'"

The latter picture of the conquest was generally taken by scholars to be correct and the former thrown into discard, together with Joshua's traditional career, as myth. The truth of the matter, however, appears to comprehend both versions. Excavations at Lachish, Tell Beit Mirsim (=Kiriat-sepher?), Gibeon, Hazor, Eglon, Beth-shemesh, Gibeah, Bethel, Shiloh, Megiddo, Beth-shan, etc., indicate that these places were destroyed or occupied, then were sometimes retaken and rebuilt by the Canaanites, only to change hands again, during the thirteenth, twelfth, and eleventh centuries B.C.E. The Biblical version of the Joshuan conquest would seem to be "a collection of miscellaneous fragments *of varying dates and of varying reliability...* There was a campaign by Joshua which achieved an amazing success in attacking certain key Canaanite royal cities but . . . there was also a long period of struggle for possession which continued after Joshua's death." (Quoted from G. E. Wright, in *Journal of Near Eastern Studies*, V [1946], 105–114. Joshua's capture of Ai was probably confused with that of Bethel. The archaeological story of Jericho is not clear.)

<sup>1</sup>After the death of Joshua, the Israelites inquired of the LORD, "Which of us shall be the first to go up against the Canaanites and attack them?" <sup>2</sup>The LORD replied, "Judah shall go up. I now deliver the country into his hands." <sup>13</sup>Judah then said to its brother-tribe Simeon, "Come up with me to my allotment and let us attack the Canaanites; and I, in turn, will go with you to your allotment." So Simeon went with him. <sup>4</sup>Judah went up, and the LORD delivered the Canaanites and the Perizzites into his hands; they defeated ten thousand men at Bezek.

*Judges 1.1-4*

וַיְהִי אַחֲרֵי מוֹת יְהוֹשֻׁעַ וַיִּשְׁאֲלוּ בְּנֵי יִשְׂרָאֵל
בַּיהֹוָה לֵאמֹר מִי־יַעֲלֶה־לָּנוּ אֶל־הַכְּנַעֲנִי בַּתְּחִלָּה
לְהִלָּחֶם בּוֹ: וַיֹּאמֶר יְהֹוָה יְהוּדָה יַעֲלֶה הִנֵּה נָתַתִּי
אֶת־הָאָרֶץ בְּיָדוֹ: וַיֹּאמֶר יְהוּדָה לְשִׁמְעוֹן אָחִיו עֲלֵה
אִתִּי בְגוֹרָלִי וְנִלָּחֲמָה בַּכְּנַעֲנִי וְהָלַכְתִּי גַם־אֲנִי אִתְּךָ
בְּגוֹרָלֶךָ וַיֵּלֶךְ אִתּוֹ שִׁמְעוֹן: וַיַּעַל יְהוּדָה וַיִּתֵּן יְהֹוָה
אֶת־הַכְּנַעֲנִי וְהַפְּרִזִּי בְּיָדָם וַיַּכּוּם בְּבֶזֶק עֲשֶׂרֶת
אֲלָפִים אִישׁ:

שׁוֹפְטִים א:א–ד

<sup>9</sup>After that the Judites went down to attack the Canaanites who lived in the hill country, the Negeb, and the Shefelah. <sup>10</sup>Judah marched against the Canaanites who lived in Hebron—the name of Hebron was formerly Kiriath-arba—and defeated Sheshai, Ahiman, and Talmai.

*Judges 1.9-10*

וְאַחַר יָרְדוּ בְּנֵי יְהוּדָה לְהִלָּחֵם בַּכְּנַעֲנִי יוֹשֵׁב
הָהָר וְהַנֶּגֶב וְהַשְּׁפֵלָה: וַיֵּלֶךְ יְהוּדָה אֶל־הַכְּנַעֲנִי
הַיּוֹשֵׁב בְּחֶבְרוֹן וְשֵׁם־חֶבְרוֹן לְפָנִים קִרְיַת אַרְבַּע
וַיַּכּוּ אֶת־שֵׁשַׁי וְאֶת־אֲחִימָן וְאֶת־תַּלְמָי:

שׁוֹפְטִים א:ט–י

<sup>21</sup>The Benjaminites did not dispossess the Jebusites who inhabited Jerusalem; so the Jebusites have lived in Jerusalem to this day.

*Judges 1.21*

וְאֶת־הַיְבוּסִי יֹשֵׁב יְרוּשָׁלַם לֹא הוֹרִישׁוּ בְּנֵי
בִנְיָמִן וַיֵּשֶׁב הַיְבוּסִי אֶת־בְּנֵי בִנְיָמִן בִּירוּשָׁלַם עַד
הַיּוֹם הַזֶּה:

שׁוֹפְטִים א:כא

<sup>27</sup>Manasseh did not dispossess [the inhabitants of] Beth-shean and its villages, or [of] Taanach and its villages, or the inhabitants of Dor and its villages, or the inhabitants of Ibleam and its villages, or the inhabitants of Megiddo and its villages. The Canaanites persisted in dwelling in this region.

*Judges 1.27*

וְלֹא־הוֹרִישׁ מְנַשֶּׁה אֶת־בֵּית־שְׁאָן וְאֶת־בְּנוֹתֶיהָ
וְאֶת־תַּעְנַךְ וְאֶת־בְּנֹתֶיהָ וְאֶת־יֹשְׁבֵי דוֹר וְאֶת־
בְּנוֹתֶיהָ וְאֶת־יוֹשְׁבֵי יִבְלְעָם וְאֶת־בְּנֹתֶיהָ וְאֶת־
יוֹשְׁבֵי מְגִדּוֹ וְאֶת־בְּנוֹתֶיהָ וַיּוֹאֶל הַכְּנַעֲנִי לָשֶׁבֶת
בָּאָרֶץ הַזֹּאת:

שׁוֹפְטִים א:כז

<sup>29</sup>Nor did Ephraim dispossess the Canaanites who lived in Gezer; so the Canaanites remained among them in Gezer. <sup>30</sup>Zebulun did not dispossess the inhabitants of Kitron or the inhabitants of Nahalol; so the Canaanites remained among them, but became subject to forced labor. <sup>31</sup>Asher did not dispossess the inhabitants of Acco or the inhabitants of Sidon, Ahlab, Achzib, Helbah, Aphik, and Rehob.

*Judges 1.29-31*

וְאֶפְרַיִם לֹא הוֹרִישׁ אֶת־הַכְּנַעֲנִי הַיּוֹשֵׁב בְּגָזֶר
וַיֵּשֶׁב הַכְּנַעֲנִי בְּקִרְבּוֹ בְּגָזֶר: זְבוּלֻן לֹא הוֹרִישׁ
אֶת־יוֹשְׁבֵי קִטְרוֹן וְאֶת־יוֹשְׁבֵי נַהֲלֹל וַיֵּשֶׁב הַכְּנַעֲנִי
בְּקִרְבּוֹ וַיִּהְיוּ לָמַס: אָשֵׁר לֹא הוֹרִישׁ אֶת־יֹשְׁבֵי
עַכּוֹ וְאֶת־יוֹשְׁבֵי צִידוֹן וְאֶת־אַחְלָב וְאֶת־אַכְזִיב
וְאֶת־חֶלְבָּה וְאֶת־אֲפִיק וְאֶת־רְחֹב:

שׁוֹפְטִים א:כט–לא

The so-called "Israel Stele." Commemorative stele celebrating Pharaoh Merneptah's victory over the Libyan enemy (ca. 1230). In the last poetic stanza, the pharaoh also refers to victories over such enemies as the Hittites, Canaanites, and Horites, and to the destruction of such cities as Ashkelon, Gezer, and Yanoam.

The figures carved at the top of the stele are (right to left): the god Horus, Pharaoh Merneptah, the god Amun, the god Amun again (facing the other way), the pharaoh again (facing the other way), and the goddess Mun. Most interesting for us is the only mention of Israel known to date in ancient Egyptian literature:

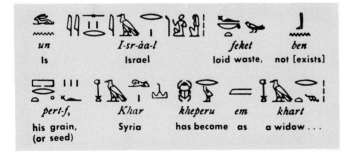

| *un* | *I-sr-àa-l* | | *feket* | *ben* |
|------|-------------|--|---------|-------|
| Is | Israel | | laid waste, | not [exists] |
| *pert-f,* | *Khar* | *kheperu* | *em* | *khart* |
| his grain, (or seed) | Syria | has become | as | a widow ... |

Biblical authors tended to telescope accounts of long campaigns—a device by no means abandoned even today—and to give all the credit for victory to well-established military heroes such as Joshua. Their purpose, after all, was not merely to chronicle but to dramatize the past and to edify and influence their readers. To achieve this end they naturally tended to lump weary details under one splendid name. Thus Joshua acquires once again an association with the conquest of Canaan no less deserving and prominent in its way than that of Moses with the Exodus and the Wilderness Wandering.

## Hebrews and Israelites

During the Period of the Judges, the term "Israel" (or "Israelites") came to replace the term "Hebrew," just as the term "Israelites" was later replaced by "Judeans" and "Jews," after the Exile in Babylon (see Chapter VI). There is good historical reason for this change.

The term "Hebrew," according to the Bible, is older than "Israel." The latter, we are told, is said to have originated with the superhuman being who, after wrestling all night without being able to overcome him, bestowed it on Jacob (Genesis 32:23–33). Outside the Bible, the term Habiru is likewise found earlier than Israel, the latter occurring for the first time in the extant literature about 1230 B.C.E., when King Merneptah of Egypt celebrated victory over numerous foes in an alleged campaign in western Asia. The Pharaoh boasted:

Israel is laid waste, its seed is not,
Palestine (Hurru) is become a widow for Egypt.

The origin of the terms "Israel" and "Hebrew," not to mention the relationship between the two, is as obscure as the early history of the tribes which bore these names. The fragmentary character of the Biblical data concerning this problem permits little

# Hebrews and Israelites

*See the survey by M. Greenberg, "Hab/piru and the Hebrews," pp. 188-200, 279-281, 296 in* The World History of the Jewish People, *Vol. II:* Patriarchs *(1970).*

[23] That same night he arose, and taking his two wives, his two maidservants, and his eleven children, he crossed the ford of the Jabbok. [24] After taking them across the stream, he sent across all his possessions. [25] Jacob was left alone. And a man wrestled with him untill the break of dawn. [26] When he saw that he had not prevailed against him, he wrenched Jacob's hip at its socket, so that the socket of his hip was strained as he wrestled with him. [27] Then he said, "Let me go, for dawn is breaking." But he answered, "I will not let you go, unless you bless me." [28] Said the other, "What is your name?" He replied, "Jacob." [29] Said he, "Your name shall no longer be Jacob, but Israel, for you have striven[a] with [b]beings divine and human,[b] and have prevailed." [30] Jacob asked, "Pray tell me your name." But he said, "You must not ask my name!" And he took leave of him there.

*Genesis 32.23-30*

a *Heb.* saritha, *connected with first part of* Israel.
b-b Or *"God* (Elohim, *connected with second part of* Israel) *and* men."

וַיָּקָם בַּלַּיְלָה הוּא וַיִּקַּח אֶת־שְׁתֵּי נָשָׁיו וְאֶת־שְׁתֵּי שִׁפְחֹתָיו וְאֶת־אַחַד עָשָׂר יְלָדָיו וַיַּעֲבֹר אֵת מַעֲבַר יַבֹּק: וַיִּקָּחֵם וַיַּעֲבִרֵם אֶת־הַנָּחַל וַיַּעֲבֵר אֶת־אֲשֶׁר־לוֹ: וַיִּוָּתֵר יַעֲקֹב לְבַדּוֹ וַיֵּאָבֵק אִישׁ עִמּוֹ עַד עֲלוֹת הַשָּׁחַר: וַיַּרְא כִּי לֹא יָכֹל לוֹ וַיִּגַּע בְּכַף־יְרֵכוֹ וַתֵּקַע כַּף־יֶרֶךְ יַעֲקֹב בְּהֵאָבְקוֹ עִמּוֹ: וַיֹּאמֶר שַׁלְּחֵנִי כִּי עָלָה הַשָּׁחַר וַיֹּאמֶר לֹא אֲשַׁלֵּחֲךָ כִּי אִם־בֵּרַכְתָּנִי: וַיֹּאמֶר אֵלָיו מַה־שְּׁמֶךָ וַיֹּאמֶר יַעֲקֹב: וַיֹּאמֶר לֹא יַעֲקֹב יֵאָמֵר עוֹד שִׁמְךָ כִּי אִם־ יִשְׂרָאֵל כִּי־שָׂרִיתָ עִם־אֱלֹהִים וְעִם־אֲנָשִׁים וַתּוּכָל: וַיִּשְׁאַל יַעֲקֹב וַיֹּאמֶר הַגִּידָה־נָּא שְׁמֶךָ וַיֹּאמֶר לָמָּה זֶּה תִּשְׁאַל לִשְׁמִי וַיְבָרֶךְ אֹתוֹ שָׁם:

בְּרֵאשִׁית לב:כג־ל

[15] For in truth, I was kidnapped from the land of the Hebrews; nor have I done anything here that they should have put me in the dungeon.

*Genesis 40.15*

כִּי־גֻנֹּב גֻּנַּבְתִּי מֵאֶרֶץ הָעִבְרִים וְגַם־פֹּה לֹא־ עָשִׂיתִי מְאוּמָה כִּי־שָׂמוּ אֹתִי בַּבּוֹר:

בְּרֵאשִׁית מ:טו

[32] They served him by himself, and them by themselves, and the Egyptians who ate with him by themselves; for the Egyptians could not dine with the Hebrews, since that would be abhorrent to the Egyptians.

*Genesis 43.32*

וַיָּשִׂימוּ לוֹ לְבַדּוֹ וְלָהֶם לְבַדָּם וְלַמִּצְרִים הָאֹכְלִים אִתּוֹ לְבַדָּם כִּי לֹא יוּכְלוּן הַמִּצְרִים לֶאֱכֹל אֶת־הָעִבְרִים לֶחֶם כִּי־תוֹעֵבָה הִוא לְמִצְרָיִם:

בְּרֵאשִׁית מג:לב

[15] The king of Egypt spoke to the Hebrew midwives, one of whom was named Shiphrah and the other Puah, [16] saying, "When you deliver the Hebrew women, look at the birthstool: if it is a boy, kill him; if it is a girl, let her live."

*Exodus 1.15-16*

וַיֹּאמֶר מֶלֶךְ מִצְרַיִם לַמְיַלְּדֹת הָעִבְרִיֹּת אֲשֶׁר שֵׁם הָאַחַת שִׁפְרָה וְשֵׁם הַשֵּׁנִית פּוּעָה: וַיֹּאמֶר בְּיַלֶּדְכֶן אֶת־הָעִבְרִיּוֹת וּרְאִיתֶן עַל־הָאָבְנָיִם אִם־בֵּן הוּא וַהֲמִתֶּן אֹתוֹ וְאִם־בַּת הִוא וָחָיָה:

שְׁמוֹת א:טו־טז

83

Upper part of a small limestone plaque inscribed in Archaic Hebrew script, excavated by R. A. S. Macalister at Gezer in 1908. While it cannot be dated exactly, it is generally acknowledged as being the earliest of Hebrew inscriptions. (10th cent. B.C.E.?).

The text list schematically the yearly cycle of the agricultural beginning, interestingly enough, with the fall harvest season, when late summer crops are gathered for storage in the winter.

| | |
|---|---|
| ירחו אסף ירחו ז | 1 (Its?) 2 months of ingathering 2 months of sow- |
| רע ירחו לקש | 2 ing 2 months of late sowing |
| ירח עצד פסת | 3 The month of pulling flax |
| ירח קצר שערם | 4 The month of barley harvest |
| ירח קצר ו[כ]ל[ל]ה | 5 The month when everything (else) is harvested |
| ירחו זמר | 6 2 months of vine-pruning |
| ירח קץ | 7 The month of summer fruit |

more than scholarly speculation; but what does appear clear is that Biblical writers began to use the term "Israelites" (literally, "the Children of Israel") approximately when the Hebrews began to constitute something of a nation, that is, at the time of the Conquest.

The last reference to the Hebrews as a distinct group occurs in connection with the bitter struggle between the Philistine hosts and the Israelite forces of King Saul (I Samuel 14:21 and 29:3). The Hebrew text (14:21) appears to say that the Hebrews had sided with the Philistines and were now deserting to the Israelites; but the text is really not as clear as the English translations would make it appear.

## The Canaanite Civilization

When the Hebrews and Israelites entered Canaan, they found there a highly developed and sophisticated society. Thanks to recent discoveries of inscriptions and other archaeological evidence, part of this highly significant culture has been recovered. Indeed, the Canaanite civilization was so advanced that it nearly absorbed the desert invaders. Thus it was when the Semitic Akkadians swept into the non-Semitic society of Sumer. Thus, too, when Rome conquered Greece, the visitors were in turn conquered by the superior culture of their victims.

There is no doubt that the Israelites of the time of Joshua and the Judges were quite unable to match the material techniques of Canaan, at least until the period of Solomon in the tenth century. Israelite fortifications, Saul's strong point at Gibeah for example, did not compare with those of contemporary Canaan. The foundations and masonry found in Canaanite towns are clearly superior to Israelite remains. Canaanite Bethel had a drainage system, which was unknown in Israelite towns. Canaanite pottery of the

²¹Now the Hebrews were with the Philistines as in the past, with whom they had gone up in the camp . . . but they too [turned] to be with the Israelites who were with Saul and Jonathan.

*I Samuel 14.21*

וְהָעִבְרִים הָיוּ לַפְּלִשְׁתִּים כְּאֶתְמוֹל שִׁלְשׁוֹם אֲשֶׁר עָלוּ עִמָּם בַּמַּחֲנֶה סָבִיב וְגַם־הֵמָּה לִהְיוֹת עִם־יִשְׂרָאֵל אֲשֶׁר עִם־שָׁאוּל וְיוֹנָתָן:

שְׁמוּאֵל א׳ יד:כא

³The commanders of the Philistines asked, "What are these Hebrews doing here?" And Achish replied to the Philistine commanders, "Why, this is David, the servant of King Saul of Israel, who has been with me a long time [lit. these days or these years]; I have found no fault in him from the day he deserted to the present."

*I Samuel 29.3*

וַיֹּאמְרוּ שָׂרֵי פְלִשְׁתִּים מָה הָעִבְרִים הָאֵלֶּה וַיֹּאמֶר אָכִישׁ אֶל־שָׂרֵי פְלִשְׁתִּים הֲלוֹא־זֶה דָוִד עֶבֶד | שָׁאוּל מֶלֶךְ־יִשְׂרָאֵל אֲשֶׁר הָיָה אִתִּי זֶה יָמִים אוֹ־זֶה שָׁנִים וְלֹא־מָצָאתִי בוֹ מְאוּמָה מִיּוֹם נָפְלוֹ עַד־הַיּוֹם־הַזֶּה:

שְׁמוּאֵל א׳ : כט, ג

## The Canaanite Civilization

*See I. Mendelsohn, "Society and Economic Conditions," pp. 39-51, 301-2, 347-8 in* The World History of the Jewish People, *Vol. III:* Judges *(1971).*

²⁷This is what they told him: "We came to the land you sent us to; it does indeed flow with milk and honey, and this is its fruit. ²⁸However, the people who inhabit the country are powerful, and the cities are fortified and very large; moreover, we saw the Anakites there."

*Numbers 13.27-28*

וַיְסַפְּרוּ־לוֹ וַיֹּאמְרוּ בָּאנוּ אֶל־הָאָרֶץ אֲשֶׁר שְׁלַחְתָּנוּ וְגַם זָבַת חָלָב וּדְבַשׁ הִוא וְזֶה־פִּרְיָהּ: אֶפֶס כִּי־עַז הָעָם הַיֹּשֵׁב בָּאָרֶץ וְהֶעָרִים בְּצֻרוֹת גְּדֹלֹת מְאֹד וְגַם־יְלִדֵי הָעֲנָק רָאִינוּ שָׁם:

בַּמִּדְבָּר יג:כז—כח

¹⁹Not a smith was to be found throughout the land of Israel, for the Philistines said, "The Hebrews must not make swords or spears." ²⁰And every Israelite had to go down to the Philistines to sharpen his plowshare, or mattock, or axe, or sickle.

*I Samuel 13.19-20*

וְחָרָשׁ לֹא יִמָּצֵא בְּכֹל אֶרֶץ יִשְׂרָאֵל כִּי־אָמַר פְּלִשְׁתִּים פֶּן יַעֲשׂוּ הָעִבְרִים חֶרֶב אוֹ חֲנִית: וַיֵּרְדוּ כָל־יִשְׂרָאֵל הַפְּלִשְׁתִּים לִלְטוֹשׁ אִישׁ אֶת־מַחֲרַשְׁתּוֹ וְאֶת־אֵתוֹ וְאֶת־קַרְדֻּמּוֹ וְאֵת מַחֲרֵשָׁתוֹ:

שְׁמוּאֵל א׳ יג:יט—כ

¹⁸These entered Micah's house and took the sculptured image of the ephod, the household gods, and the molten image. The priest said to them. "What are you doing?" ¹⁹But they answered him, "Be quiet! Put your hand on your mouth and come with us, and be our father and priest. Would you rather be priest to one man's household, or be priest to a tribe and clan in Israel?" ²⁰The priest was delighted. He took the ephod, the household gods, and the sculptured image, and he joined the group.

*Judges 18.18-20*

וְאֵלֶּה בָּאוּ בֵּית מִיכָה וַיִּקְחוּ אֶת־פֶּסֶל הָאֵפוֹד וְאֶת־הַתְּרָפִים וְאֶת־הַמַּסֵּכָה וַיֹּאמֶר אֲלֵיהֶם הַכֹּהֵן מָה אַתֶּם עֹשִׂים: וַיֹּאמְרוּ לוֹ הַחֲרֵשׁ שִׂים־יָדְךָ עַל־פִּיךָ וְלֵךְ עִמָּנוּ וֶהְיֵה־לָנוּ לְאָב וּלְכֹהֵן הֲטוֹב הֱיוֹתְךָ כֹהֵן לְבֵית אִישׁ אֶחָד אוֹ הֱיוֹתְךָ כֹהֵן לְשֵׁבֶט וּלְמִשְׁפָּחָה בְּיִשְׂרָאֵל: וַיִּיטַב לֵב הַכֹּהֵן וַיִּקַּח אֶת־הָאֵפוֹד וְאֶת־הַתְּרָפִים וְאֶת־הַפֶּסֶל וַיָּבֹא בְּקֶרֶב הָעָם:

שׁוֹפְטִים יח:יח—כ

Sarcophagus prepared for Ahiram of Byblos by his son Ittobaal (Ethbaal). The scenes on the sides of the sarcophagus shown here are well-known motifs in Ancient Near Eastern art. A ruler sits on a throne which is decorated with winged, human-headed lions (perhaps the Biblical cherub). A table is set with food before him. His attendants, officials, and subjects approach him, bearing gifts or taxes. There are bare-breasted dancing girls at one end. The depiction of these scenes on a sarcophagus may point to their funerary function—the last respects. In other contexts, the scenes would have more joyous meaning.

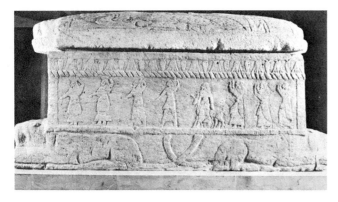

Carved on the sarcophagus is the oldest Phoenician inscription extant; it is written in the dialect of Byblos (ca. 1000).

The ancient harbor of Byblos in 1928.

Middle and Late Bronze Ages (about 2000–1200 B.C.E.) compared with the best, but the products of early Israel were crude.

The origin of the alphabet cannot as yet be determined with precision. It is the Canaanites, however, who may well have been associated with its invention, who gave this great cultural force to the world at large. It is likewise uncertain exactly what Semitic language or languages the Hebrews and Israelites spoke in the patriarchal period; but after they settled in Canaan, they adopted a variety of Canaanite alphabets and dialects. For good reason, then, the Bible itself refers to the Hebrew language as "the tongue of Canaan" (Isaiah 19:18), recognizing Biblical Hebrew as originally a dialect of Canaanite.

Canaanite literature was notable for its mythological and religious compositions. The Greeks and Romans owed much more than their alphabet to the Canaanites, whom the Greeks began to call Phoenicians after about 1000 B.C.E.; they derived also considerable and important elements in their mythologies from them.

The religious system was a highly organized and central element in every aspect of the daily life of the Canaanites, and its influence extended widely into the economic, political, and social spheres. The diviner-priests—for, as in early Israel too, the diviner (or seer) and the priest were one and the same—constituted an important and powerful group in the upper class of Canaanite society. They were landowners, slaveowners, and moneylenders on a large scale, while operating temples and shrines under the protection of the gods. In Canaan, as in Mesopotamia and Egypt, the temples "were heavily endowed with landed properties and received a tremendous income. At certain periods they probably owned nearly all the land of the country and acquired almost an economic strangle-hold over the people."

86

*Interestingly, ancient Israel's national language is not called "Hebrew" (ivrith) in the Bible, but either "Canaanite" (as in Isa. 19.18 quoted below) or "Judean" (yehudith) (II Ki. 18.26, 28; Isa. 36.11, 13; Neh. 13.24; and II Chron. 32.18).*

<sup>18</sup>In that day, there shall be several (*lit.* five) towns in the land of Egypt speaking the language of Canaan and worshiping (*lit.* swearing to) the LORD of Hosts . . .

*Isaiah 19.18*

בַּיּוֹם הַהוּא יִהְיוּ חָמֵשׁ עָרִים בְּאֶרֶץ מִצְרַיִם
מְדַבְּרוֹת שְׂפַת כְּנַעַן וְנִשְׁבָּעוֹת לַיהֹוָה צְבָאוֹת עִיר
הַהֶרֶס יֵאָמֵר לְאֶחָת:
יְשַׁעְיָהוּ יט:יח

<sup>18</sup>He [Elijah] answered, "It is not I who have brought trouble on Israel, but you [King Ahab] and your father's house, by forsaking the commandments of the LORD and going after the Baalim. <sup>19</sup>Now, send orders for all Israel to join me at Mount Carmel, together with the four hundred and fifty prophets of Baal and the four hundred prophets of Asherah, who eat at Jezebel's table." . . . <sup>21</sup>Elijah approached all the people and said, "How long will you keep hopping on both sides? If the LORD is God, follow Him; and if Baal, follow him!" But the people didn't so much as answer him a word. <sup>22</sup>Then Elijah said to the people, "I alone am left a prophet of the LORD, while the prophets of Baal are four hundred and fifty . . . <sup>24</sup>You invoke your god by name, and then I shall invoke the LORD by name; and whichever god responds with fire, that one is God." And all the people answered, "Good!"

*I Kings 18.18-24*

וַיֹּאמֶר לֹא עָכַרְתִּי אֶת־יִשְׂרָאֵל כִּי אִם־אַתָּה
וּבֵית אָבִיךָ בַּעֲזָבְכֶם אֶת־מִצְוֹת יְהֹוָה וַתֵּלֶךְ אַחֲרֵי
הַבְּעָלִים: וְעַתָּה שְׁלַח קְבֹץ אֵלַי אֶת־כָּל־יִשְׂרָאֵל
אֶל־הַר הַכַּרְמֶל וְאֶת־נְבִיאֵי הַבַּעַל אַרְבַּע־מֵאוֹת
וַחֲמִשִּׁים וּנְבִיאֵי הָאֲשֵׁרָה אַרְבַּע מֵאוֹת אֹכְלֵי
שֻׁלְחַן אִיזָבֶל: . . . וַיִּגַּשׁ אֵלִיָּהוּ אֶל־כָּל־הָעָם
וַיֹּאמֶר עַד־מָתַי אַתֶּם פֹּסְחִים עַל־שְׁתֵּי הַסְּעִפִּים
אִם־יְהֹוָה הָאֱלֹהִים לְכוּ אַחֲרָיו וְאִם־הַבַּעַל לְכוּ
אַחֲרָיו וְלֹא־עָנוּ הָעָם אֹתוֹ דָּבָר: וַיֹּאמֶר אֵלִיָּהוּ
אֶל־הָעָם אֲנִי נוֹתַרְתִּי נָבִיא לַיהֹוָה לְבַדִּי וּנְבִיאֵי
הַבַּעַל אַרְבַּע־מֵאוֹת וַחֲמִשִּׁים אִישׁ: . . .
וּקְרָאתֶם בְּשֵׁם אֱלֹהֵיכֶם וַאֲנִי אֶקְרָא בְשֵׁם־
יְהֹוָה וְהָיָה הָאֱלֹהִים אֲשֶׁר־יַעֲנֶה בָאֵשׁ הוּא הָאֱלֹהִים
וַיַּעַן כָּל־הָעָם וַיֹּאמְרוּ טוֹב הַדָּבָר:
מְלָכִים א' יח: יח–כד

<sup>5</sup>They said to him, "Please inquire of God, so that we may know whether the mission on which we are going will be successful." <sup>6</sup>And he replied, "Go in peace; the LORD is observing the mission in which you are engaged."

*Judges 18.5-6*

וַיֹּאמְרוּ לוֹ שְׁאַל־נָא בֵאלֹהִים וְנֵדְעָה הֲתַצְלִיחַ
דַּרְכֵּנוּ אֲשֶׁר אֲנַחְנוּ הֹלְכִים עָלֶיהָ: וַיֹּאמֶר לָהֶם
הַכֹּהֵן לְכוּ לְשָׁלוֹם נֹכַח יְהֹוָה דַּרְכְּכֶם אֲשֶׁר
תֵּלְכוּ־בָהּ:
שׁוֹפְטִים יח:ה–ו

<sup>9</sup>The makers of idols all work to no purpose; / And their choicest works are useless, / As they themselves can bear witness. / They see nothing and know nothing, / And so they shall be shamed. / <sup>10</sup>Who would fashion a god or cast a statue / That can do no good? / <sup>11</sup>Lo, all its adherents shall be shamed . . .

*Isaiah 44.9-11*

יֹצְרֵי־פֶסֶל כֻּלָּם תֹּהוּ וַחֲמוּדֵיהֶם בַּל־יוֹעִילוּ
וְעֵדֵיהֶם הֵמָּה בַּל־יִרְאוּ וּבַל־יֵדְעוּ לְמַעַן יֵבֹשׁוּ:
מִי־יָצַר אֵל וּפֶסֶל נָסָךְ לְבִלְתִּי הוֹעִיל: הֵן כָּל־
חֲבֵרָיו יֵבֹשׁוּ . . .
יְשַׁעְיָהוּ מד:ט–יא

Canaanite deities were many and varied. They could be shown anthropormorphically, worshiped through symbols and steles, or, as the Bible tells us, through certain trees (e.g., asherah). Below are some representations of divinities known in the Canaanite world.

Storm god
(Ras Shamra, Middle Bronze Age).
About 5 feet tall.

War god with sword (bent out of shape) and shield (Megiddo, Bronze Age).

The inner sanctum of the (13th cent.) temple at Hazor. Note, among the steles which perhaps symbolize divinity, a stele with two raised hands beneath a star or sun in a disk. Perhaps this is a symbol of the astral or solar god.

(From a symposium on "The Significance of the Temple in the Ancient Near East," *The Biblical Archaeologist*, VII [Sept. and Dec., 1944], 41–88.)

The religious beliefs and practices of the Canaanites revolved about the predominantly agricultural character of their economy. The Canaanites were polytheists, regarding the forces of nature as divine beings and giving to them personal names. These deities personified the heavenly bodies—the sun, moon, stars, and planets—and such manifestations of nature as rain, thunder, lightning, vegetation, death, and wisdom, the last mentioned including the arts and inventions.

Mythological stories and qualities were woven about the careers of the gods, and much of the ritual at the shrines of Canaanite cults was intended primarily to ensure the fertility of the soil. Foremost among the gods was Baal, to whom there is so much derogatory reference in the Bible. The Canaanite Baal was a god of rain, prime mover of the agricultural world. Periodically Baal was killed by the forces of Mot, the god of drought and death, so that the rains and vegetation ceased. However, Baal came to life in the fall, and the all-important rains came down again. In the spring Baal and his half-sister Anath, goddess of fertility and war, cohabited, so that fecundity came to the land and its inhabitants. The Canaanite worship of their gods was characterized by idolatry and sexual rites.

## Israel and Canaan

The manner in which the Israelites reacted to the Canaanite civilization forms one of the vivid periods in their dramatic career. It will be remembered that not all the Hebrews left Canaan for Egypt in the days of Jacob and Joseph. The stay-at-homes inclined to feel indifferent about a Bondage and Exodus in

*It is generally overlooked that the* bamoth *"shrines" (traditional "high places") that are here condemned as idolatrous were actually from the beginning—already in the period of the Judges—as "kosher" in the service of Israel's God as the royal shrine (the Temple) in Jerusalem. It was only in the late seventh century, when the government of King Josiah attempted to seize control of the scores of shrines all over the country, and their income, that these shrines came to be designated as idolatrous and hence deserving elimination.*

<sup>13</sup>In addition, he removed his (grand) mother Maacah as queen mother for making an abomination for the sacred post (Asherah); he burned her abomination in the Kidron Valley.

*I Kings 15:13*

וְגַם אֶת־מַעֲכָה אִמּוֹ וַיְסִרֶהָ מִגְּבִירָה אֲשֶׁר־עָשְׂתָה מִפְלֶצֶת לָאֲשֵׁרָה וַיִּכְרֹת אָסָא אֶת־מִפְלַצְתָּהּ וַיִּשְׂרֹף בְּנַחַל קִדְרוֹן:

מְלָכִים א' טו:יג

<sup>23</sup>The lords of the Philistines gathered to offer a great sacrifice to their god Dagon and to make merry. They declared:

Our god has delivered into our hands
Samson our enemy.

*Judges 16.23*

וְסַרְנֵי פְלִשְׁתִּים נֶאֶסְפוּ לִזְבֹּחַ זֶבַח־גָּדוֹל לְדָגוֹן אֱלֹהֵיהֶם וּלְשִׂמְחָה וַיֹּאמְרוּ נָתַן אֱלֹהֵינוּ בְּיָדֵנוּ אֵת שִׁמְשׁוֹן אוֹיְבֵנוּ:

שׁוֹפְטִים טז:כג

<sup>31</sup>It was not enough for him [King Ahab] to follow the sinful acts of Jeroboam son of Nebat; he married Jezebel daughter of King Ethbaal of the Phoenicians (lit. Sidonians), and he went and served Baal and worshiped him.

*I Kings 16.31*

וַיְהִי הֲנָקֵל לֶכְתּוֹ בְּחַטֹּאות יָרָבְעָם בֶּן־נְבָט וַיִּקַּח אִשָּׁה אֶת־אִיזֶבֶל בַּת־אֶתְבַּעַל מֶלֶךְ צִידֹנִים וַיֵּלֶךְ וַיַּעֲבֹד אֶת־הַבַּעַל וַיִּשְׁתַּחוּ לוֹ:

מְלָכִים א' טז:לא

<sup>9</sup>. . . And they [the Israelites] built shrines for themselves in all their settlements, from watchmen's tower to fortified city. <sup>10</sup> They set up pillars and sacred posts (Asherim) for themselves on every high hill and under every luxuriant tree.

*II Kings 17.9-10*

. . . וַיִּבְנוּ לָהֶם בָּמוֹת בְּכָל־עָרֵיהֶם מִמִּגְדַּל נוֹצְרִים עַד־עִיר מִבְצָר: וַיַּצִּבוּ לָהֶם מַצֵּבוֹת וַאֲשֵׁרִים עַל כָּל־גִּבְעָה גְבֹהָה וְתַחַת כָּל־עֵץ רַעֲנָן:

מְלָכִים ב' יז:ט–י

<sup>16</sup>They forsook all the commandments of the LORD their God and made a molten image for themselves, two calves; and they made a sacred pole, they worshiped all the host of heaven, and served Baal. <sup>17</sup>They passed their sons and daughters through the fire and resorted to augury and divination—they devoted themselves to doing what displeased the LORD and vexed Him.

*II Kings 17.16–17*

וַיַּעַזְבוּ אֶת־כָּל־מִצְוֹת יְהוָה אֱלֹהֵיהֶם וַיַּעֲשׂוּ לָהֶם מַסֵּכָה שְׁנֵי עֲגָלִים וַיַּעֲשׂוּ אֲשֵׁרָה וַיִּשְׁתַּחֲווּ לְכָל־צְבָא הַשָּׁמַיִם וַיַּעַבְדוּ אֶת־הַבָּעַל: וַיַּעֲבִירוּ אֶת־בְּנֵיהֶם וְאֶת־בְּנוֹתֵיהֶם בָּאֵשׁ וַיִּקְסְמוּ קְסָמִים וַיְנַחֲשׁוּ וַיִּתְמַכְּרוּ לַעֲשׂוֹת הָרַע בְּעֵינֵי יְהוָה לְהַכְעִיסוֹ:

מְלָכִים ב' יז:טז–יז

## Israel and Canaan

[<sup>26</sup>How long will . . .] <sup>27</sup>they [the false prophets] scheme to cause My people to forget My name through the dreams that they keep telling one another, as their ancestors forgot My name through Baal?

*Jeremiah 23.27*

הַחֹשְׁבִים לְהַשְׁכִּיחַ אֶת־עַמִּי שְׁמִי בַּחֲלוֹמֹתָם אֲשֶׁר יְסַפְּרוּ אִישׁ לְרֵעֵהוּ כַּאֲשֶׁר שָׁכְחוּ אֲבוֹתָם אֶת־שְׁמִי בַּבָּעַל:

יִרְמְיָהוּ כג:כז

Reaching a height of about 1850 ft. above sea level, its isolation in the Valley Jezreel, and its steep sides and dome-shaped summit give Mt. Tabor a grandeur that invites comparison with Mt. Carmel and Mt. Hermon (Jer. 46.18; Ps. 89.13). It controls one of the two eastern passages between the Valley and the Jordan, and the borders of the three tribes, Naphtali, Zebulun, and Issachar meet here. The men of Naphtali and Zebulun gathered at Mt. Tabor, and then came down to join forces with Deborah-Barak against Sisera.

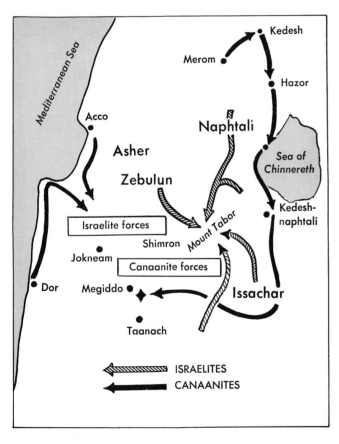

The decisive battle between the Israelite forces of Deborah-Barak and the Canaanite army of Sisera—a battle made memorable by the Song of Deborah (Judges 5).

which their own ancestors had not participated. While their kinsmen had been off adventuring and finding God, they themselves had acquired land, herds, and status. And to this end they had compromised, in great measure or small, with the culture and religion of Canaan. Not for them the harsh dedications of the Law, the admonition from on high, "Be very strong and courageous, being mindful to observe all the Teaching which Moses My servant commanded you . . . This Book of Teaching shall not cease from your lips: you shall recite it day and night . . . for only then will you prosper in your undertakings, and only then will you be successful" (Joshua 1:7–8). These people had already feathered their nests without the assistance of the national Covenant.

Among the new settlers too there developed different points of view. Some of those fresh from the Mosaic scene, once they were comfortably ensconced, found it desirable to wink an eye and look away from the Law. On several occasions the Israelites in Trans-Jordan had to be ordered to help their fellow tribesmen secure their allotments in western Palestine (Joshua 1:12–18). When the crucial struggle between the Israelites and the Canaanites came to a head in the battle near Taanach in the valley of Jezreel (about 1125 B.C.E.), an event made famous by the triumphal Song of Deborah (Judges 5), several tribes refused to join in the battle and accordingly were cursed. A whole century of indecision and wavering passed before the reluctant tribes, faced with a common danger, were able to bring themselves to make a common cause. The individualism and desert ways of these tribes died hard.

The same process is reflected in the religious picture painted in the Book of Judges. The Israelite population at large, even the

<sup></sup>7"But you must be very strong and resolute to observe faithfully all the Teaching which My servant Moses enjoined upon you. Do not turn from it right or left, that you may be successful wherever you go. 8Let not this Book of Teaching cease from your lips, but recite it day and night, so that you may observe faithfully all that is written in it. Only then will you prosper in your undertakings and only then will you be successful. "

*Joshua 1.7–8*

12Then Joshua said to the Reubenites, the Gadites, and the half-tribe of Manasseh: 13Remember what Moses, the servant of the LORD, charged you with, when he said, "The LORD your God is granting you a haven and is assigning this territory to you.14. . . But every one of the fighting men shall go across armed, in the van of your kinsmen, and you shall assist them 15 until the Lord has given your kinsmen a haven, such as you have, and until they too have gained possession of the land which the Lord your God assigned to them. Then you may return to the land allotted to you and occupy it. . . ."

*Joshua 1.12-15*

1Deborah and Barak son of Abinoam sang that day:

2 When in Israel locks are untrimmed,
When people dedicate themselves—
Bless the LORD!
3Hear, O kings! Give ear, O potentates!
I will sing, will sing to the LORD,
Will hymn the LORD, the God of Israel.
4O LORD, when You came forth from Seir,
Advanced from the country of Edom,
The earth trembled,
Yea, the heavens sagged,
Yea, the clouds dripped water,
5The mountains streamed—
Before the LORD, Him of Sinai,
Before the LORD, God of Israel.
6In the days of Shamgar son of Anath,
In Jael's days, caravans ceased,
And wayfarers went
By roundabout paths.
7Unwalled towns ceased,
Ceased in Israel,
Till you arose, O Deborah,
Arose, O mother, in Israel!

*Judges 5.1-7*

רַק חֲזַק וֶאֱמַץ מְאֹד לִשְׁמֹר לַעֲשׂוֹת כְּכָל־
הַתּוֹרָה אֲשֶׁר צִוְּךָ מֹשֶׁה עַבְדִּי אַל־תָּסוּר מִמֶּנּוּ
יָמִין וּשְׂמֹאול לְמַעַן תַּשְׂכִּיל בְּכֹל אֲשֶׁר תֵּלֵךְ:
לֹא־יָמוּשׁ סֵפֶר הַתּוֹרָה הַזֶּה מִפִּיךָ וְהָגִיתָ בּוֹ
יוֹמָם וָלַיְלָה לְמַעַן תִּשְׁמֹר לַעֲשׂוֹת כְּכָל־הַכָּתוּב
בּוֹ כִּי־אָז תַּצְלִיחַ אֶת־דְּרָכֶךָ וְאָז תַּשְׂכִּיל:

יְהוֹשֻׁעַ א:ז–ח

וְלָרֽאוּבֵנִי וְלַגָּדִי וְלַחֲצִי שֵׁבֶט הַמְנַשֶּׁה אָמַר
יְהוֹשֻׁעַ לֵאמֹר: זָכוֹר אֶת־הַדָּבָר אֲשֶׁר צִוָּה אֶתְכֶם
מֹשֶׁה עֶבֶד־יְהוָֹה לֵאמֹר יְהוָֹה אֱלֹהֵיכֶם מֵנִיחַ לָכֶם
וְנָתַן לָכֶם אֶת־הָאָרֶץ הַזֹּאת: . . .
וְאַתֶּם תַּעַבְרוּ חֲמֻשִׁים לִפְנֵי אֲחֵיכֶם כֹּל גִּבּוֹרֵי
הַחַיִל וַעֲזַרְתֶּם אוֹתָם: עַד אֲשֶׁר־יָנִיחַ יְהוָֹה לַאֲחֵיכֶם
כָּכֶם וְיָרְשׁוּ גַם־הֵמָּה אֶת־הָאָרֶץ אֲשֶׁר־יְהוָֹה
אֱלֹהֵיכֶם נֹתֵן לָהֶם וְשַׁבְתֶּם לְאֶרֶץ יְרֻשַּׁתְכֶם
וִירִשְׁתֶּם אוֹתָהּ . . .

יְהוֹשֻׁעַ א:יב–טו

וַתָּשַׁר דְּבוֹרָה וּבָרָק בֶּן־אֲבִינֹעַם בַּיּוֹם הַהוּא
לֵאמֹר: בִּפְרֹעַ פְּרָעוֹת בְּיִשְׂרָאֵל בְּהִתְנַדֵּב עָם בָּרְכוּ
יְהוָֹה: שִׁמְעוּ מְלָכִים הַאֲזִינוּ רֹזְנִים אָנֹכִי לַיהוָֹה
אָנֹכִי אָשִׁירָה אֲזַמֵּר לַיהוָֹה אֱלֹהֵי יִשְׂרָאֵל: יְהוָֹה
בְּצֵאתְךָ מִשֵּׂעִיר בְּצַעְדְּךָ מִשְּׂדֵה אֱדוֹם אֶרֶץ רָעָשָׁה
גַּם־שָׁמַיִם נָטָפוּ גַּם־עָבִים נָטְפוּ מָיִם: הָרִים נָזְלוּ
מִפְּנֵי יְהוָֹה זֶה סִינַי מִפְּנֵי יְהוָֹה אֱלֹהֵי יִשְׂרָאֵל:
בִּימֵי שַׁמְגַּר בֶּן־עֲנָת בִּימֵי יָעֵל חָדְלוּ אֳרָחוֹת
וְהֹלְכֵי נְתִיבוֹת יֵלְכוּ אֳרָחוֹת עֲקַלְקַלּוֹת: חָדְלוּ
פְרָזוֹן בְּיִשְׂרָאֵל חָדֵלּוּ עַד שַׁקַּמְתִּי דְּבוֹרָה שַׁקַּמְתִּי
אֵם בְּיִשְׂרָאֵל:

שׁוֹפְטִים ה:א–ז

Two incense altars dating from the period of Israel's settlement in Canaan (Early Iron Age) and the establishment of the early monarchy. Common to both these objects is the concept of open rather than closed pottery, which manifests itself in fenestration (or pseudo-fenestration) in the case of both altars.

**Above: From Taanach.** This altar shows several common motifs current in the Ancient Near East.

Master of animals (bottom row); winged, human-headed lions (first register up; see the Ahiram sarcophagus p. 86; lion flanking goats nibbling from a "sacred" tree (2nd register up); winged disk above goat or ibex between vegetal motifs (3rd register up); winged animals (on the sides of the third register up).

**From Megiddo.** The altar is simpler in construction and was probably used for burning incense. The simple applied designs are pinched protuberances which surround the bowl, and a wavy ledge which surrounds the upper stalk of the stand. The applied decoration may represent leaves, especially the bowl decorations. About 26½ inches tall.

newcomers in the land, conveniently adapted their way of life to the Canaanite practices, especially those which were aimed at the maintenance and improvement of their well-being. Local shrines, with guilds of seer-priests in charge, sprang up everywhere. While they did not go so far as to produce idols to represent the Lord, many Israelites did acquire figurines of the Canaanite goddess of fertility. They also added to the worship of the Lord ritualistic features from the cults of Baal, Asherah, Ashtoreth, and the other gods of Canaan. Such heroes as Saul and David (about 1000 B.C.E.), it should be noted, gave some of their children names which included the element "Baal."

But some, the Gideons of Israel, would not take the pagan bait. Thus Gideon risked his life in the dark of the night by smashing a Baal altar and cutting down the Asherah beside it for firewood for burning an Israelite sacrificial bull. "And when the townspeople rose early in the morning," the Bible tells us, "they found that the altar of Baal had been torn down, and the sacred pole that was beside it had been cut down, and the second bull had been offered [to the Lord] on the newly-built altar" (Judges 6:28).

The authors of the Book of Judges openly blamed Israel's misfortunes during the period of settlement upon this widespread religious defection. When Midianite camel raiders and the better-organized forces of Ammon and Moab overran Israelite communities, their depredations were explained as punishment for Israel's desertion of the Lord. Israel would not have experienced these sufferings, the Biblical writers maintained (Judges 2:11 ff.), if she had held together under the Covenant. Israel's strength lay in united devotion to the Lord, and the worship of Baal was the most divisive and destructive force that Israel had to face. It threatened to destroy the Covenant between God and His chosen people.

*Personal names are often an excellent clue to the time and place in which their owners lived. Thus Mordecai and Esther (from the Babylonian names Marduk and Ishtar) derive from a Babylonian milieu; during the Golden Era in Spain, Jews will have names which include the word "ibn" (Arabic for "son of"); in more recent times, if a Jewish boy's Hebrew name was, say, Tzvi ("reindeer," Yiddish "Hirsh"), his name in Eastern Europe would often be "Hirsh, Hershel," in Germany "Heinrich," in English-speaking countries "Harry, Henry, Harold"; and the like. See above on the Egyptian origin of such biblical names as Moses, Miriam, Hophni, Phinehas, Merari, and perhaps Aaron.*

39Ner begot Kish, Kish begot Saul, and Saul begot Jonathan, Malchi-shua, Abinadab, and Eshbaal. 40Jonathan's son: Merib-baal; and Meri(b)-baal begot Micah.

*I Chronicles 9.39-40*

וְנֵר הוֹלִיד אֶת־קִישׁ וְקִישׁ הוֹלִיד אֶת־שָׁאוּל וְשָׁאוּל הוֹלִיד אֶת־יְהוֹנָתָן וְאֶת־מַלְכִּי־שׁוּעַ וְאֶת־אֲבִינָדָב וְאֶת־אֶשְׁבָּעַל: וּבֶן־יְהוֹנָתָן מְרִיב בָּעַל וּמְרִי־בַעַל הוֹלִיד אֶת־מִיכָה:

דִּבְרֵי הַיָּמִים א׳ ט:לט-מ

3David took more wives in Jerusalem, and David begot more sons and daughters.
[The names of 13 children follow, vv. 4-7.]
*I Chronicles 14.3*

וַיִּקַּח דָּוִיד עוֹד נָשִׁים בִּירוּשָׁלָ͏ִם וַיּוֹלֶד דָּוִיד עוֹד בָּנִים וּבָנוֹת:

דִּבְרֵי הַיָּמִים א׳ יד:ג

11The Israelites did what displeased the LORD; they served the Baalim. 12They forsook the LORD, the God of their fathers, who had freed them from the land of Egypt, and followed alien gods from among the peoples around them and worshiped them; they provoked the LORD. 13They forsook the LORD and served Baal and the Ashtaroth.

*Judges 2.11-13*

וַיַּעֲשׂוּ בְנֵי־יִשְׂרָאֵל אֶת־הָרַע בְּעֵינֵי יְהֹוָה וַיַּעַבְדוּ אֶת־הַבְּעָלִים: וַיַּעַזְבוּ אֶת־יְהֹוָה אֱלֹהֵי אֲבוֹתָם הַמּוֹצִיא אוֹתָם מֵאֶרֶץ מִצְרַיִם וַיֵּלְכוּ אַחֲרֵי אֱלֹהִים אֲחֵרִים מֵאֱלֹהֵי הָעַמִּים אֲשֶׁר סְבִיבוֹתֵיהֶם וַיִּשְׁתַּחֲווּ לָהֶם וַיַּכְעִסוּ אֶת־יְהֹוָה: וַיַּעַזְבוּ אֶת־יְהֹוָה וַיַּעַבְדוּ לַבַּעַל וְלָעַשְׁתָּרוֹת:

שׁוֹפְטִים ב:יא-יג

25That night the LORD said to him [Gideon]: "Take the young bull belonging to your father and another bull seven years old; pull down the altar of Baal which belongs to your father, and cut down the sacred pole which is beside it ."
28When the townspeople rose the next morning, the altar of Baal had been torn down, the sacred pole that was beside it cut down, and the second bull offered on the newly-built altar.

*Judges 6.25, 28*

וַיְהִי בַּלַּיְלָה הַהוּא וַיֹּאמֶר לוֹ יְהֹוָה קַח אֶת־פַּר־הַשּׁוֹר אֲשֶׁר לְאָבִיךָ וּפַר הַשֵּׁנִי שֶׁבַע שָׁנִים וְהָרַסְתָּ אֶת־מִזְבַּח הַבַּעַל אֲשֶׁר לְאָבִיךָ וְאֶת־הָאֲשֵׁרָה אֲשֶׁר־עָלָיו תִּכְרֹת: וַיַּשְׁכִּימוּ אַנְשֵׁי הָעִיר בַּבֹּקֶר וְהִנֵּה נֻתַּץ מִזְבַּח הַבַּעַל וְהָאֲשֵׁרָה אֲשֶׁר־עָלָיו כֹּרָתָה וְאֵת הַפָּר הַשֵּׁנִי הֹעֲלָה עַל־הַמִּזְבֵּחַ הַבָּנוּי:

שׁוֹפְטִים ו:כה, כח

An Israelite altar unearthed at Megiddo.

## THE JUDGES OF ISRAEL

The — essentially — *military* chieftains (*shofeṭim*, traditional Judges) of Israel can no longer be listed in chronological sequence; indeed, it is not even possible to determine with confidence the number of Judges. Part of the difficulty stems from the fact that no one is specifically referred to as a *shofeṭ* (judge); instead, it is a verbal form, *shafaṭ / wa-yishpoṭ* or *wa-yósha'*—both used in the military sense of "triumph, deliver, bring victory to"—that is regularly employed, *shofeṭim* and *moshi'a* being the general terms used for "deliverer, military leader." Typical sentences will read: "The Lord raised up chieftains (*shofeṭim*) who delivered them (*wa-yoshi'um*) from their plunderers" (Judges 2.16); "The Israelites cried out to the Lord, and the Lord raised a champion (or: deliverer, *moshi'a*) for the Israelites who delivered them (*wa-yoshi'em*): Othniel son of Kenaz . . . The spirit of the Lord descended upon him and he became Israel's chieftain (*wa-yishpoṭ eth-Yisra'el*). He went forth in battle (*wa-yeṣe la-milḥamah*) . . ." (Judges 3.9-10).

The "Judges" of Israel are generally reckoned to be twelve in number, perhaps by design, conforming to the traditional number of tribes (and of the sons of Jacob):

| | | | |
|---|---|---|---|
| 1. Othniel | עָתְנִיאֵל | 7. Jair | יָאִיר |
| 2. Ehud | אֵהוּד | 8. Jephthah | יִפְתָּח |
| 3. Shamgar | שַׁמְגַּר | 9. Ibzan | אִבְצָן |
| 4. Barak-Deborah | בָּרָק-דְּבוֹרָה | 10. Elon | אֵלֹן |
| 5. Gideon | גִּדְעוֹן | 11. Abdon | עַבְדּוֹן |
| (Abimelech) | אֲבִימֶלֶךְ | 12. Samson | שִׁמְשׁוֹן |
| 6. Tola | תּוֹלָע | (Eli; Samuel) | עֵלִי-שְׁמוּאֵל |

## The Judges (or Chieftains)

The period that preceded the rise of the monarchy is described in the Bible as "the days when the judges (or chieftains) ruled." These "judges" were primarily local military heroes and dominated Israel during the period of pacification and adjustment. When an alien force attacked a segment of Israel, men of uncommon mettle frequently stepped forward from among the people to rally and lead their fellows. Such natural leaders, if they proved successful, became chieftains and were accepted as rulers within the area of resistance (Judges 2:14 ff.).

The Bible records some twelve judges in all, some of them contemporaries, as in the case of Ehud and Shamgar. The most famous judges were Ehud, Gideon, Jephthah, and Samson. These successful military chieftains sometimes acquired a kind of judicial authority—approximately that of an arbiter—alongside the seer-priests of the local sanctuaries, but only secondarily, and they held it only so long as "the land had rest" from the enemy. Unlike the judges of the later monarchy, these judges were brought into being by external, military needs.

Not more than three leaders in the Period of the Judges really adjudicated; they were Deborah, Eli, and Samuel. Eli, however, was specifically a priest. And Deborah and Samuel, unlike the others, are described as "prophets"; indeed, neither one ever served as military leader for any of the tribes.

## Tribal Structure of Israel and her Neighbors

Except for occasional brief emergency alliances, the Israelite tribes maintained complete autonomy during the Period of the Judges and recognized no central capital or shrine for all Israel. "In those days there was no king in Israel; every man did as he

# The Judges

²The LORD raised up chieftains who delivered them from those who plundered them. ¹⁷But they did not heed their chieftains either; they went astray after other gods and worshiped them. They were quick to turn aside from the way which their fathers had followed in obedience to the commandments of the LORD; they did not do right. ¹⁸When the LORD raised up chieftains for them, the LORD was with the chieftain and saved them from their enemies during the chieftain's lifetime; for the LORD would be moved to pity by their moanings because of those who oppressed and crushed them.

*Judges 2.16-18*

וַיָּקֶם יְהֹוָה שֹׁפְטִים וַיּוֹשִׁיעוּם מִיַּד שֹׁסֵיהֶם: וְגַם אֶל־שֹׁפְטֵיהֶם לֹא שָׁמֵעוּ כִּי זָנוּ אַחֲרֵי אֱלֹהִים אֲחֵרִים וַיִּשְׁתַּחֲווּ לָהֶם סָרוּ מַהֵר מִן־הַדֶּרֶךְ אֲשֶׁר הָלְכוּ אֲבוֹתָם לִשְׁמֹעַ מִצְוֺת־יְהֹוָה לֹא־עָשׂוּ כֵן: וְכִי־הֵקִים יְהֹוָה לָהֶם שֹׁפְטִים וְהָיָה יְהֹוָה עִם־הַשֹּׁפֵט וְהוֹשִׁיעָם מִיַּד אֹיְבֵיהֶם כֹּל יְמֵי הַשּׁוֹפֵט כִּי־יִנָּחֵם יְהֹוָה מִנַּאֲקָתָם מִפְּנֵי לֹחֲצֵיהֶם וְדֹחֲקֵיהֶם:

שׁוֹפְטִים ב:טז–יח

¹³Gideon said to him, "Please, my lord, if the LORD is with us, why has all this befallen us, and where are all His wondrous deeds about which our fathers told us: 'Truly the LORD brought us up from Egypt?' Now the LORD has abandoned us and delivered us into the hands of Midian!" ¹⁴The LORD turned to him and said, "Go in this strength of yours, and you shall deliver Israel from the power of the Midianites. I now send you forth."

*Judges 6.13-14*

וַיֹּאמֶר אֵלָיו גִּדְעוֹן בִּי אֲדֹנִי וְיֵשׁ יְהֹוָה עִמָּנוּ וְלָמָּה מְצָאַתְנוּ כָּל־זֹאת וְאַיֵּה כָל־נִפְלְאֹתָיו אֲשֶׁר סִפְּרוּ־לָנוּ אֲבוֹתֵינוּ לֵאמֹר הֲלֹא מִמִּצְרַיִם הֶעֱלָנוּ יְהֹוָה וְעַתָּה נְטָשָׁנוּ יְהֹוָה וַיִּתְּנֵנוּ בְּכַף מִדְיָן: וַיִּפֶן אֵלָיו יְהֹוָה וַיֹּאמֶר לֵךְ בְּכֹחֲךָ זֶה וְהוֹשַׁעְתָּ אֶת־יִשְׂרָאֵל מִכַּף מִדְיָן הֲלֹא שְׁלַחְתִּיךָ:

שׁוֹפְטִים ו:יג–יד

²There was a certain man from Zorah, of the clan of Dan, whose name was Manoah. His wife was barren, she had borne no children. ³An angel of the LORD appeared to the woman and said to her, "You are barren and have had no child; but you shall conceive and bear a son. ⁴You must now be careful not to drink wine or other intoxicant, or to eat anything unclean. ⁵For you are about to conceive and bear a son; let no razor touch his head, for the boy is to be a nazirite to God from the womb on. He shall be the first to deliver Israel from the power of the Philistines."

*Judges 13.2-5*

וַיְהִי אִישׁ אֶחָד מִצָּרְעָה מִמִּשְׁפַּחַת הַדָּנִי וּשְׁמוֹ מָנוֹחַ וְאִשְׁתּוֹ עֲקָרָה וְלֹא יָלָדָה: וַיֵּרָא מַלְאַךְ־יְהֹוָה אֶל־הָאִשָּׁה וַיֹּאמֶר אֵלֶיהָ הִנֵּה־נָא אַתְּ־עֲקָרָה וְלֹא יָלַדְתְּ וְהָרִית וְיָלַדְתְּ בֵּן: וְעַתָּה הִשָּׁמְרִי נָא וְאַל־תִּשְׁתִּי יַיִן וְשֵׁכָר וְאַל־תֹּאכְלִי כָּל־טָמֵא: כִּי הִנָּךְ הָרָה וְיֹלַדְתְּ בֵּן וּמוֹרָה לֹא־יַעֲלֶה עַל־רֹאשׁוֹ כִּי־נְזִיר אֱלֹהִים יִהְיֶה הַנַּעַר מִן־הַבָּטֶן וְהוּא יָחֵל לְהוֹשִׁיעַ אֶת־יִשְׂרָאֵל מִיַּד־פְּלִשְׁתִּים:

שׁוֹפְטִים יג:ב–ה

95

Bronze plaque of a Canaanite. Found at Hazor in a Late Bronze Age context. About 4 inches high.

The most important criterion for dating one group of excavated objects in relation to another in ancient Palestine is the differences in pottery style and manufacture. Illustrated here is a complete jar with painted decoration dating to the Late Bronze Period (ca. 1550-1200). The very sophisticated arrangement of figures is called the "Palm tree and Ibex motif;" it is believed to be very characteristic of this period, when Canaanite civilization was at its height.

pleased" (Judges 17:6, 21:25). The hilly terrain, netted by a maze of valleys and wadis, made for political disjunction. Since no enemy was powerful enough to threaten more than a small part of Israel at any one time, the pressure from without was not great enough to produce any effective integration.

The Canaanite society, moreover, consisted of independent fortified townships without any tradition of commonwealth or of mutual assistance. Canaanite political example, if anything, tended to retard the development of the nationalism latent in the Mosaic Covenant. Customs both old and new thus militated against unity among the Israelite tribes. Dwellers on the plains ignored the plight of the hill people, who returned the compliment. And intertribal warfare itself was not unknown, despite a common religion (Judges 12:19–21).

Across the valley, on the Transjordan plateau, lived other Semitic peoples, in all probability of the same Habiru origin as the Israelites. If the Biblical account is taken literally, at least one of these countries was a monarchy. "These are the kings who reigned in the land of Edom," the Scriptures tell us, "before any king reigned over the Israelites" (Genesis 36:31–39; I Chronicles 1:43–51). Whereupon eight kings are listed.

It appears that the Edomite term "king" meant something essentially different from what it came to mean later on, since none of these "kings" was ever succeeded by a son or by any relative or even any fellow townsman. As a matter of fact, the Edomite kings are listed in the same manner as the local chieftains in the above-mentioned chapters in Genesis and Chronicles and exactly like the list of judges in Judges 10:1–3 and 12:8–15. It would seem that an Edomite "king" was about the same sort of personage as "King" Abimelech of Shechem, son of Gid-

[1]In the days when the chieftains ruled, there was a famine in the land, and a man from Bethlehem of Judah, together with his wife and two sons, went to reside in the country of Moab.

*Ruth 1.1*

וַיְהִי בִּימֵי שְׁפֹט הַשֹּׁפְטִים וַיְהִי רָעָב בָּאָרֶץ וַיֵּלֶךְ אִישׁ מִבֵּית לֶחֶם יְהוּדָה לָגוּר בִּשְׂדֵי מוֹאָב הוּא וְאִשְׁתּוֹ וּשְׁנֵי בָנָיו:

רוּת א:א

## Tribal Structure of Israel and her Neighbors

In those days there was no king in Israel; every man did as he pleased.

*Judges 17.6*

בַּיָּמִים הָהֵם ־אֵין מֶלֶךְ בְּיִשְׂרָאֵל אִישׁ הַיָּשָׁר בְּעֵינָיו יַעֲשֶׂה:

שׁוֹפְטִים יז:ו

[12]And the tribes of Israel sent men through the whole tribe of Benjamin, saying, "What is this evil thing that has happened among you? [13]Now, hand over those scoundrels in Gibeah, so that we may put them to death and stamp out the evil from Israel." But the Benjaminites would not listen to their brother Israelites. [48]The men of Israel then turned back to the rest of the Benjaminites and put them to the sword: towns, men, cattle—everything that remained. And they set fire to all the towns that were left.

*Judges 20.12–13, 48*

וַיִּשְׁלְחוּ שִׁבְטֵי יִשְׂרָאֵל אֲנָשִׁים בְּכָל־שִׁבְטֵי בִנְיָמִן לֵאמֹר מָה הָרָעָה הַזֹּאת אֲשֶׁר נִהְיְתָה בָּכֶם: וְעַתָּה תְּנוּ אֶת־הָאֲנָשִׁים בְּנֵי־בְלִיַּעַל אֲשֶׁר בַּגִּבְעָה וּנְמִיתֵם וּנְבַעֲרָה רָעָה מִיִּשְׂרָאֵל וְלֹא אָבוּ בְּנֵי בִנְיָמִן לִשְׁמֹעַ בְּקוֹל אֲחֵיהֶם בְּנֵי־יִשְׂרָאֵל:
וְאִישׁ יִשְׂרָאֵל שָׁבוּ אֶל־בְּנֵי בִנְיָמִן וַיַּכּוּם לְפִי־חֶרֶב מֵעִיר מְתֹם עַד־בְּהֵמָה עַד כָּל־הַנִּמְצָא גַּם כָּל־הֶעָרִים הַנִּמְצָאוֹת שִׁלְּחוּ בָאֵשׁ:

שׁוֹפְטִים כ:יב־יג, מח

[31]These are the kings who reigned in the land of Edom before any king reigned over the Israelites. [32]Bela son of Beor reigned in Edom, and the name of his city was Dinhabah. [33]When Bela died, Jobab son of Zerah, from Bozrah, succeeded him as king. [34]When Jobab died, Husham of the land of the Temanites succeeded him as king. [35]When Husham died, Hadad son of Bedad, who defeated the Midianites in the country of Moab, succeeded him as king; the name of his city was Avith. [36]When Hadad died, Samlah of Masrekah succeeded him as king. [37]When Samlah died, Saul of Rehoboth-on-the-river succeeded him as king. [38]When Saul died, Baal-hanan son of Achbor succeeded him as king. [39]And when Baal-hanan son of Achbor died, Hadar succeeded him as king; the name of his city was Pau, and his wife's name was Mehetabel daughter of Matred daughter of Mezahab.

[40]The following are the name of the clans of Esau, each with its families and locality, name by name: the clans Timna, Alvah, Jetheth . . .

*Genesis 36.31-40*

וְאֵלֶּה הַמְּלָכִים אֲשֶׁר מָלְכוּ בְּאֶרֶץ אֱדוֹם לִפְנֵי מְלָךְ־מֶלֶךְ לִבְנֵי יִשְׂרָאֵל: וַיִּמְלֹךְ בֶּאֱדוֹם בֶּלַע בֶּן־בְּעוֹר וְשֵׁם עִירוֹ דִּנְהָבָה: וַיָּמָת בָּלַע וַיִּמְלֹךְ תַּחְתָּיו יוֹבָב בֶּן־זֶרַח מִבָּצְרָה: וַיָּמָת יוֹבָב וַיִּמְלֹךְ תַּחְתָּיו חֻשָׁם מֵאֶרֶץ הַתֵּימָנִי: וַיָּמָת חֻשָׁם וַיִּמְלֹךְ תַּחְתָּיו הֲדַד בֶּן־בְּדַד הַמַּכֶּה אֶת־מִדְיָן בִּשְׂדֵה מוֹאָב וְשֵׁם עִירוֹ עֲוִית: וַיָּמָת הֲדָד וַיִּמְלֹךְ תַּחְתָּיו שַׂמְלָה מִמַּשְׂרֵקָה: וַיָּמָת שַׂמְלָה וַיִּמְלֹךְ תַּחְתָּיו שָׁאוּל מֵרְחֹבוֹת הַנָּהָר: וַיָּמָת שָׁאוּל וַיִּמְלֹךְ תַּחְתָּיו בַּעַל חָנָן בֶּן־עַכְבּוֹר: וַיָּמָת בַּעַל חָנָן בֶּן־עַכְבּוֹר וַיִּמְלֹךְ תַּחְתָּיו הֲדַר וְשֵׁם עִירוֹ פָּעוּ וְשֵׁם אִשְׁתּוֹ מְהֵיטַבְאֵל בַּת־מַטְרֵד בַּת מֵי זָהָב: וְאֵלֶּה שְׁמוֹת אַלּוּפֵי עֵשָׂו לְמִשְׁפְּחֹתָם לִמְקֹמֹתָם בִּשְׁמֹתָם אַלּוּף תִּמְנָע אַלּוּף עַלְוָה אַלּוּף יְתֵת:

בְּרֵאשִׁית לו:לא־מ

## INSTALLATIONS OF AGRICULTURAL AND ECONOMIC LIFE

One of the many small dyeing installations from the Iron Age, excavated at Tell Beit Mirsim (Debir?). The most prominent and easily recognizeable feature is the stone container in which only small quantities of cloth or the like could be placed with the dye solution, perhaps to insure consistent color and easily regulated hues.

The floor of a pressing vat for grapes with its drainage channel to lead the juices off to small storage containers. This vat was found at Beth-shemesh in an Iron Age level.

eon the Judge (Judges 9). In other words, he was a mere chieftain with some additional powers of a provisional and local nature.

Nor did the Ammonites or the Moabites, any more than the Edomites, have a centralized form of government at the time of the Judges. If the Ammonites could not overcome the small forces of Jephthah (Judges 11), and if Ammon, Moab, and Amalek had to combine to establish power even in a small part of Israel (Judges 3), and if Israel, in turn, could dominate Moab, it is extremely unlikely that any of these Transjordanian territories was monarchized or, by virtue of a central government, capable of presenting a united front. But soon events came to pass which corrected this irregular situation.

## Israelite Economy and Government

The Israelites, meanwhile, raised cattle, sheep, and goats, and tilled the soil. Artisans organized guilds, practiced weaving, dyeing, tanning, smithing, pottery making, and other crafts, even though on a very small scale. Private ownership of land, including wells, gradually replaced the communal ownership of patriarchal days.

Even though there was a concentration of wealth among the Canaanites, rich families among the Israelites did not appear to dominate the communities in the time of the Judges. Imposing palaces and elaborate fortifications discovered in the Canaanite levels of Palestinian mounds are not equaled in the Israelite levels until the days of Solomon. The lack of concentrated wealth also helped hold back the development of a nationally conscious leadership.. This circumstance accounts also for the absence from Israel, at least up to the time of David, of the *corvée*, or forced labor.

It would seem that during the Period of the Judges a form of primitive democracy

98

Abimelech son of Jerubbaal went to his mother's brothers in Shechem and spoke to them and to the whole clan of his mother's family. He said, ²"Announce publicly to all the citizens of Shechem: Which is better for you, that seventy men rule you, all the sons of Jerubbaal, or that one man rule you? And remember, I am your flesh and blood!"

*Judges 9.1-2*

וַיֵּלֶךְ אֲבִימֶלֶךְ בֶּן־יְרֻבַּעַל שְׁכֶמָה אֶל־אֲחֵי אִמּוֹ
וַיְדַבֵּר אֲלֵיהֶם וְאֶל־כָּל־מִשְׁפַּחַת בֵּית־אֲבִי אִמּוֹ
לֵאמֹר: דַּבְּרוּ־נָא בְּאָזְנֵי כָל־בַּעֲלֵי שְׁכֶם מַה־טּוֹב
לָכֶם הַמְשֹׁל בָּכֶם שִׁבְעִים אִישׁ כֹּל בְּנֵי יְרֻבַּעַל
אִם־מְשֹׁל בָּכֶם אִישׁ אֶחָד וּזְכַרְתֶּם כִּי־עַצְמְכֶם
וּבְשַׂרְכֶם אָנִי:

שׁוֹפְטִים ט: א־ב

Jephthah crossed over to the Ammonites to attack them, and the LORD delivered them into his hands. ³³He utterly routed them . . . and the Ammonites were subdued by the Israelites.

*Judges 11.32-33*

וַיַּעֲבֹר יִפְתָּח אֶל־בְּנֵי עַמּוֹן לְהִלָּחֶם בָּם וַיִּתְּנֵם
יְהוָה בְּיָדוֹ: וַיַּכֵּם . . . מַכָּה גְדוֹלָה מְאֹד וַיִּכָּנְעוּ
בְּנֵי עַמּוֹן מִפְּנֵי בְּנֵי יִשְׂרָאֵל:

שׁוֹפְטִים יא: לב־לג

The Israelites again did what was offensive to the LORD, and the LORD gave King Eglon of Moab the upper hand over Israel . . . ¹³In alliance with the Ammonites and the Amalekites, he went and defeated Israel, and occupied the City of Palms.

*Judges 3.12-13*

וַיֹּסִפוּ בְּנֵי יִשְׂרָאֵל לַעֲשׂוֹת הָרַע בְּעֵינֵי יְהוָה
וַיְחַזֵּק יְהוָה אֶת־עֶגְלוֹן מֶלֶךְ־מוֹאָב . . . : וַיֶּאֱסֹף אֵלָיו
אֶת־בְּנֵי־עַמּוֹן וַעֲמָלֵק וַיֵּלֶךְ וַיַּךְ אֶת־יִשְׂרָאֵל וַיִּירְשׁוּ
אֶת־עִיר הַתְּמָרִים:

שׁוֹפְטִים ג: יב־יג

## Israelite Economy and Government

*Much is now known about guilds in ancient Mesopotamia and Canaan-Israel, including the terminology; thus* ben *(lit. "son") means a member of a guild, and* mishpahah *(lit. "family, clan") denotes "guild" —clearly because the son frequently followed the craft of the father, and a guild revolved about a number of related families. These guilds were located in places where the raw materials for their craft were readily available, so that the superior clay in the Shefelah determined the location of the royal potteries in Netaim and Gederah. (These and related matters are discussed by I. Mendelsohn in* Bulletin of the American Schools of Oriental Research, *No. 97, Dec. 1940, pp. 17-21.)*

When he gave the silver back to his mother, his mother took two hundred shekels of silver and gave it to a smith, who made a sculptured and molten image of it; and it was placed in the house of Micah.

*Judges 17.4*

וַיָּשֶׁב אֶת־הַכֶּסֶף לְאִמּוֹ וַתִּקַּח אִמּוֹ מָאתַיִם
כֶּסֶף וַתִּתְּנֵהוּ לַצּוֹרֵף וַיַּעֲשֵׂהוּ פֶּסֶל וּמַסֵּכָה וַיְהִי
בְּבֵית מִיכָיְהוּ:

שׁוֹפְטִים יז:ד

Sons of Shelah son of Judah: Er the father of Lecah, Laadah the father of Mareshah, and the family guild of the weavers of Beth-ashbea; ²²also Jokim, the men of Cozeba, and Joash and Saraph . . .²³These were the potters living at Netaim and Gederah; they dwelt there with the king in his service.

*I Chron. 4.21-23*

בְּנֵי שֵׁלָה בֶן־יְהוּדָה עֵר אֲבִי לֵכָה וְלַעְדָּה אֲבִי
מָרֵשָׁה וּמִשְׁפְּחוֹת בֵּית־עֲבֹדַת הַבֻּץ לְבֵית אַשְׁבֵּעַ:
וְיוֹקִים וְאַנְשֵׁי כֹזֵבָא וְיוֹאָשׁ וְשָׂרָף . . . : הֵמָּה הַיּוֹצְרִים
וְיֹשְׁבֵי נְטָעִים וּגְדֵרָה עִם־הַמֶּלֶךְ בִּמְלַאכְתּוֹ יָשְׁבוּ
שָׁם:

דִּבְרֵי הַיָּמִים א׳ ד: כא־כג

99

The stele of Hammurabi, king of the city of Babylon and its possessions during the greater part of the eighteenth century. The bas-relief at the top of the monument shows the king presenting himself before the god Shamash. Shamash, as constant as the sun of which he is an anthropomorphic personification, is the god of immutable justice. As such, he is the logical divinity to be chosen for a monument listing laws that are given to the king for his people.

Head of a statuette carved out of diorite depicting a Mesopotamian ruler of the early part of the Second Millennium B.C.E. The hat and beard style are similar to those of Hammurabi (above). About 6 inches high.

functioned among the Israelites. There does not appear to have been any centralized authority within the tribal unit capable of dominating the rest of the population. The heads of wealthy and important families constituted a group of "elders," and they met—usually in the town gate, the common meeting place in those days—whenever the occasion demanded. In conjunction with the elders, although the precise relationship remains obscure, there also functioned a public assembly of all the free adult males of the community. The elders and the assembly made their authority felt in every aspect of the community's activities, the military, political, religious, economic, legal, and social. In Israelite society it was not easy to separate the religious from the secular aspects of these activities.

## Israel's Legal Codes

During the Period of the Judges the legal system of Israel began to take on some definite shape. It is now generally agreed that the formulation of the legal enactments in the Pentateuch fall into two main groups. Numerous laws are introduced by a direct command or prohibition of the Lord, "You shall (or, shall not). . . ." The Ten Commandments (Exodus 20:1–17) are a case in point, e.g., "You shall have no other gods beside Me," etc. Laws expressed so dogmatically and directly are called *apodictic*.

The second major group of laws, called *casuistic*, is characterized by a conditional clause ("If; Provided that"). The Book of the Covenant (Exodus 20:22–23:33; 24:7) is a good example of this formulation, e.g., "If a thief is found breaking in, and he is beaten to death, there shall be no bloodguilt for him" (22:1). Or, "If a foreigner sojourns with you in your land, you shall not wrong him. The foreigner who sojourns with you

All the elders of Israel came to the king at Hebron; and King David made a pact with them in Hebron in the presence of the LORD, and they anointed David king over Israel.

*II Samuel 5.3*

וַיָּבֹאוּ כָּל־זִקְנֵי יִשְׂרָאֵל אֶל־הַמֶּלֶךְ חֶבְרוֹנָה
וַיִּכְרֹת לָהֶם הַמֶּלֶךְ דָּוִד בְּרִית בְּחֶבְרוֹן לִפְנֵי יְהֹוָה
וַיִּמְשְׁחוּ אֶת־דָּוִד לְמֶלֶךְ עַל־יִשְׂרָאֵל:

שְׁמוּאֵל ב׳ ה: ג

## Israel's Legal Codes

*See S. E. Loewenstamm, "Law," pp. 231-267, 334-7, 351 in* The World History of the Jewish People, *Vol. III:* Judges *(1971).*

[1]God spoke all these words, saying:
[2]I the LORD am your God who brought you out of the land of Egypt, the house of bondage: [3]You shall have no other gods beside Me.
[4]You shall not make for yourself a sculptured image, or any likeness of what is in the heavens above, or on the earth below, or in the waters below the earth. [5]You shall not bow down to them or serve them. For I the LORD your God am an impassioned God, visiting the guilt of the fathers upon the children, upon the third and upon the fourth generations of those who reject Me, [6]but showing kindness to the thousandth generation of those who love Me and keep My commandments.
[7]You shall not utter the name of the LORD your God improperly; for the LORD will not clear one who utters His name improperly.
[8]Remember the sabbath day and keep it holy. [9]Six days you shall labor and do all your work, [10]but the seventh day is a sabbath of the LORD your God: you shall not do any work—you, your son or daughter, your male or female slave, or your cattle, or the stranger who is within your settlements. [11]For in six days the LORD made heaven and earth and sea, and all that is in them, and He rested on the seventh day; therefore the LORD blessed the sabbath day and hallowed it.
[12]Honor your father and your mother, that you may long endure on the land which the LORD your God is giving you.
[13]You shall not murder.
You shall not commit adultery.
You shall not steal.
You shall not bear false witness against your neighbor.
[14]You shall not covet your neighbor's house: you shall not covet your neighbor's wife, or his male or female slave, or his ox or his ass, or anything that is your neighbor's.

*Exodus 20.1-14*

וַיְדַבֵּר אֱלֹהִים אֵת כָּל־הַדְּבָרִים הָאֵלֶּה לֵאמֹר:
אָנֹכִי יְהֹוָה אֱלֹהֶיךָ אֲשֶׁר הוֹצֵאתִיךָ מֵאֶרֶץ מִצְרַיִם
מִבֵּית עֲבָדִים: לֹא־יִהְיֶה לְךָ אֱלֹהִים אֲחֵרִים
עַל־פָּנָי: לֹא־תַעֲשֶׂה לְךָ פֶסֶל וְכָל־תְּמוּנָה אֲשֶׁר
בַּשָּׁמַיִם מִמַּעַל וַאֲשֶׁר בָּאָרֶץ מִתַּחַת וַאֲשֶׁר בַּמַּיִם
מִתַּחַת לָאָרֶץ: לֹא־תִשְׁתַּחֲוֶה לָהֶם וְלֹא תָעָבְדֵם
כִּי אָנֹכִי יְהֹוָה אֱלֹהֶיךָ אֵל קַנָּא פֹּקֵד עֲוֹן אָבֹת
עַל־בָּנִים עַל־שִׁלֵּשִׁים וְעַל־רִבֵּעִים לְשֹׂנְאָי: וְעֹשֶׂה
חֶסֶד לַאֲלָפִים לְאֹהֲבַי וּלְשֹׁמְרֵי מִצְוֹתָי: לֹא תִשָּׂא
אֶת־שֵׁם־יְהֹוָה אֱלֹהֶיךָ לַשָּׁוְא כִּי לֹא יְנַקֶּה יְהֹוָה
אֵת אֲשֶׁר־יִשָּׂא אֶת־שְׁמוֹ לַשָּׁוְא: זָכוֹר אֶת־יוֹם
הַשַּׁבָּת לְקַדְּשׁוֹ: שֵׁשֶׁת יָמִים תַּעֲבֹד וְעָשִׂיתָ כָּל־
מְלַאכְתֶּךָ: וְיוֹם הַשְּׁבִיעִי שַׁבָּת לַיהֹוָה אֱלֹהֶיךָ לֹא־
תַעֲשֶׂה כָל־מְלָאכָה אַתָּה וּבִנְךָ וּבִתֶּךָ עַבְדְּךָ
וַאֲמָתְךָ וּבְהֶמְתֶּךָ וְגֵרְךָ אֲשֶׁר בִּשְׁעָרֶיךָ: כִּי שֵׁשֶׁת־
יָמִים עָשָׂה יְהֹוָה אֶת־הַשָּׁמַיִם וְאֶת־הָאָרֶץ אֶת־
הַיָּם וְאֶת־כָּל־אֲשֶׁר־בָּם וַיָּנַח בַּיּוֹם הַשְּׁבִיעִי עַל־
כֵּן בֵּרַךְ יְהֹוָה אֶת־יוֹם הַשַּׁבָּת וַיְקַדְּשֵׁהוּ: כַּבֵּד
אֶת־אָבִיךָ וְאֶת־אִמֶּךָ לְמַעַן יַאֲרִכוּן יָמֶיךָ עַל
הָאֲדָמָה אֲשֶׁר־יְהֹוָה אֱלֹהֶיךָ נֹתֵן לָךְ: לֹא תִרְצָח:
לֹא תִנְאָף: לֹא תִגְנֹב: לֹא־תַעֲנֶה בְרֵעֲךָ עֵד שָׁקֶר:
לֹא תַחְמֹד בֵּית רֵעֶךָ לֹא־תַחְמֹד אֵשֶׁת רֵעֶךָ
וְעַבְדּוֹ וַאֲמָתוֹ וְשׁוֹרוֹ וַחֲמֹרוֹ וְכֹל אֲשֶׁר לְרֵעֶךָ:

שְׁמוֹת כ:א – יד

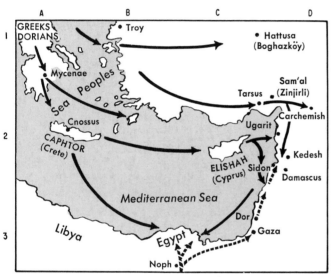

▪◆▪▪▪▪▪ EGYPTIAN FORCES

◀━━━ SEA PEOPLES

**MAP WITH SUGGESTED MOVEMENTS OF AEGEAN AND OTHER PEOPLES AT THE END OF THE 13TH AND BEGINNING OF THE 12TH CENTURY.**

shall be to you like the native born among you; you shall love him as yourself, for you were foreigners in the land of Egypt. I the Lord am your God" (Leviticus 19:33–34). In general, Israelite civil law was expressed casuistically, and the ritual law apodictically.

It would seem that the Israelites borrowed to some extent from the legal compilations of the Babylonians, Hurrians, and Canaanites. This is apparent especially in the casuistic group of laws. The apodictic group derived primarily from their own experiences in their nomadic wanderings in Canaan and in the wilderness of Sinai. But by and large, the Israelites made and compiled their own laws to suit their own way of life, and what they did borrow from others they adapted to their own needs. The result was, as a well-known scholar recently remarked, "Hebrew legislation suited to Hebrew needs. . . . Herein, as so often, the pupil surpassed the teacher." (T. J. Meek, *Hebrew Origins*, rev. ed. [New York, 1950; now a Harper Torchbook], p. 81 of the useful chapter on "The Origin of Hebrew Law.")

## The Philistines

About 1175 B.C.E. a number of Aegean peoples were driven by northern invaders from their homes on Crete and the shores of Asia Minor and took to the sea. They failed to penetrate Egypt, but they did gain a hold on the Palestinian coast. These "sea peoples," as the Egyptians called them, had a superior military and political organization. Despite their lack of numbers, they gradually got a grip on the coastal plain. Among these migrant sea peoples were the Philistines. Indeed, it is from them that the name "Palestine" derives, by way of the Latinized Greek word "Palaestina," as finally impressed on the whole region by the Roman conquerors of Judah over a thousand years later.

<sup>1</sup>If the thief is seized while tunneling, and he is beaten to death, there is no bloodguilt in his case.

*Exodus 22.1*

<sup>33</sup>When a stranger resides with you in your land, you shall not wrong him. <sup>34</sup>The stranger who resides with you shall be to you as one of your citizens; you shall love him as yourself, for you were strangers in the land of Egypt: I the LORD am your God.

*Leviticus 19.33-34*

<sup>23</sup>But if other damage ensues, the penalty shall be life for life, <sup>24</sup>eye for eye, tooth for tooth, hand for hand, foot for foot, <sup>25</sup>burn for burn, wound for wound, bruise for bruise.

*Exodus 21.23-25*

אִם־בַּמַּחְתֶּרֶת יִמָּצֵא הַגַּנָּב וְהֻכָּה וָמֵת אֵין לוֹ
דָּמִים: שְׁמוֹת כב:א

וְכִי־יָגוּר אִתְּךָ גֵּר בְּאַרְצְכֶם לֹא תוֹנוּ אֹתוֹ:
כְּאֶזְרָח מִכֶּם יִהְיֶה לָכֶם הַגֵּר הַגָּר אִתְּכֶם וְאָהַבְתָּ
לוֹ כָּמוֹךָ כִּי־גֵרִים הֱיִיתֶם בְּאֶרֶץ מִצְרָיִם אֲנִי
יְהוָה אֱלֹהֵיכֶם: וַיִּקְרָא יט:לג--לד

וְאִם־אָסוֹן יִהְיֶה וְנָתַתָּה נֶפֶשׁ תַּחַת נָפֶשׁ: עַיִן
תַּחַת עַיִן שֵׁן תַּחַת שֵׁן יָד תַּחַת יָד רֶגֶל תַּחַת רָגֶל:
כְּוִיָּה תַּחַת כְּוִיָּה פֶּצַע תַּחַת פָּצַע חַבּוּרָה תַּחַת
חַבּוּרָה: שְׁמוֹת כא:כג--כה

## The Philistines

The Israelites again did what was offensive to the LORD. They served the Baalim, and the Ashtaroth, and the gods of Aram, the gods of Sidon, the gods of Moab, the gods of the Ammonites, and the gods of the Philistines; they forsook the LORD and did not serve Him.

*Judges 10.6*

וַיֹּסִפוּ בְּנֵי יִשְׂרָאֵל לַעֲשׂוֹת הָרַע בְּעֵינֵי יְהוָה
וַיַּעַבְדוּ אֶת־הַבְּעָלִים וְאֶת־הָעַשְׁתָּרוֹת וְאֶת־אֱלֹהֵי
אֲרָם וְאֶת־אֱלֹהֵי צִידוֹן וְאֵת אֱלֹהֵי מוֹאָב וְאֵת
אֱלֹהֵי בְנֵי־עַמּוֹן וְאֵת אֱלֹהֵי פְלִשְׁתִּים וַיַּעַזְבוּ
אֶת־יְהוָה וְלֹא עֲבָדוּהוּ: שׁוֹפְטִים י:ו

The Israelites again did what was offensive to the LORD, and the LORD delivered them into the hands of the Philistines for forty years.

*Judges 13.1*

וַיֹּסִפוּ בְּנֵי יִשְׂרָאֵל לַעֲשׂוֹת הָרַע בְּעֵינֵי יְהוָה
וַיִּתְּנֵם יְהוָה בְּיַד־פְּלִשְׁתִּים אַרְבָּעִים שָׁנָה:
שׁוֹפְטִים יג: א

Samuel's order went out to all Israel, and Israel marched out to engage the Philistines in battle; they encamped near Ebenezer, while the Philistines encamped at Aphek. <sup>2</sup>The Philistines arrayed themselves opposite Israel and the battle was joined; and Israel was routed by the Philistines, who slew about four thousand men on the battlefield.

*I Samuel 4.1-2*

וַיְהִי דְבַר־שְׁמוּאֵל לְכָל־יִשְׂרָאֵל וַיֵּצֵא יִשְׂרָאֵל
לִקְרַאת פְּלִשְׁתִּים לַמִּלְחָמָה וַיַּחֲנוּ עַל־הָאֶבֶן
הָעֵזֶר וּפְלִשְׁתִּים חָנוּ בַאֲפֵק: וַיַּעַרְכוּ פְלִשְׁתִּים
לִקְרַאת יִשְׂרָאֵל וַתִּטֹּשׁ הַמִּלְחָמָה וַיִּנָּגֶף יִשְׂרָאֵל
לִפְנֵי פְלִשְׁתִּים וַיַּכּוּ בַמַּעֲרָכָה בַּשָּׂדֶה כְּאַרְבַּעַת
אֲלָפִים אִישׁ: שְׁמוּאֵל א' ד:א-ב

The Philistines captured the Ark of God and brought it from Ebenezer to Ashdod; <sup>2</sup>the Philistines took the Ark of God and carried it into the temple of Dagon and placed it beside Dagon.

*I Samuel 5.1-2*

וּפְלִשְׁתִּים לָקְחוּ אֵת אֲרוֹן הָאֱלֹהִים וַיְבִאֻהוּ
מֵאֶבֶן הָעֵזֶר אַשְׁדּוֹדָה: וַיִּקְחוּ פְלִשְׁתִּים אֶת־אֲרוֹן
הָאֱלֹהִים וַיָּבִאוּ אֹתוֹ בֵּית דָּגוֹן וַיַּצִּיגוּ אֹתוֹ אֵצֶל
דָּגוֹן: שְׁמוּאֵל א' ה:א-ב

Here is one of several scenes in relief from Medinet Habu which depict Ramses III protecting Egypt from invaders, who come by land and sea. The enemy is represented by two distinctive types of headdress, one with a horned helmet, the other with a head ornament of vertical lines which droop over in the front and the back. The former helmet is known also from the "Warrior Vase," dated to the 12th cent. and found at Mycenae on mainland Greece; the latter has been found on the clay anthropoid coffins from Beth-shan. Whether the latter headdress—the hair treatment has also been called the "feather crown"—is to be assigned exclusively to the Philistines is a problem not yet solved by scholars.

Warrior Vase

Anthropoid Coffin. About 6½ feet tall.

Their closely knit political structure, coupled with the need for mercantile expansion, brought the Philistines into the hinterland. Philistine society was divided up into five important city-states, with a "tyrant," or chieftain, at the head of each. These city-states knew how to combine for military attack. Moreover, the Philistines had a virtual monopoly on the important new metal, iron, and used it for swords, ax heads, and chariots, as well as for plough tips and sickles.

The Israelites were squarely in the path of the Philistine drive to the east. Various Israelite tribes were badly hit by the systematic depredations of the strangers from the coast. Eventually the situation reached such a pass that the tribes most seriously affected were driven to submit to a central authority of their own. This novelty, however, was not introduced without bitter resistance from diehards to whose advantage it was to maintain an extremely literal interpretation of the meaning of the Sinaitic Covenant. The man chosen to be "king" was Saul; the opposition to him was led by Samuel, the seer-priest.

## King Saul

Speaking before the elders and assembled freemen, Samuel argued that if they elected Saul to be their king they would be flouting the primacy of God. It was not his own judgeship and authority that he was worrying about, Samuel insisted, but that of the Lord. In addition he warned the Israelites that a king would take their sons and daughters, the best of their fields, and one-tenth of their seed and flocks. The Israelites, he said, would become the king's servants, which, in effect, meant his slaves. "And you shall cry out on that day," he said, "because of the king whom you chose for yourselves; but the Lord will not answer you on that day" (I Samuel 8:18).

Joshua was now old, advanced in years. The LORD said to him, ". . . ²This is the territory that remains [to be occupied]: All the districts of the Philistines . . . ³those of the five lords of the Philistines—the Gazites, the Ashdodites, the Ashkelonites, the Gittites, and the Ekronites . . ."

*Joshua 13.1-3*

וִיהוֹשֻׁעַ זָקֵן בָּא בַּיָּמִים וַיֹּאמֶר יְהֹוָה אֵלָיו... זֹאת הָאָרֶץ הַנִּשְׁאָרֶת כָּל־גְּלִילוֹת הַפְּלִשְׁתִּים... חֲמֵשֶׁת סַרְנֵי פְלִשְׁתִּים הָעַזָּתִי וְהָאַשְׁדּוֹדִי הָאֶשְׁקְלוֹנִי הַגִּתִּי וְהָעֶקְרוֹנִי...

יְהוֹשֻׁעַ יג: א-ג

## King Saul

Not a smith was to be found throughout the land of Israel, for the Philistines said, "The Hebrews must not make swords or spears." ²⁰And every Israelite had to go down to the Philistines to sharpen his plowshare, or mattock, or axe, or sickle. ²¹It cost a *pim* for the plowshares and mattocks, and a third of a shekel for sharpening the axes and for setting the goads. ²²So on the day of the battle, neither dagger nor spear was to be found among the troops with Saul and Jonathan, with the exception of Saul and his son Jonathan.

*I Samuel 13.19-22*

וְחָרָשׁ לֹא יִמָּצֵא בְּכֹל אֶרֶץ יִשְׂרָאֵל כִּי־אָמַר פְּלִשְׁתִּים פֶּן יַעֲשׂוּ הָעִבְרִים חֶרֶב אוֹ חֲנִית: וַיֵּרְדוּ כָל־יִשְׂרָאֵל הַפְּלִשְׁתִּים לִלְטוֹשׁ אִישׁ אֶת־מַחֲרַשְׁתּוֹ וְאֶת־אֵתוֹ וְאֶת־קַרְדֻּמּוֹ וְאֵת מַחֲרֵשָׁתוֹ: וְהָיְתָה הַפְּצִירָה פִים לַמַּחֲרֵשׁוֹת וְלָאֵתִים וְלִשְׁלֹשׁ קִלְּשׁוֹן וּלְהַקַּרְדֻּמִּים וּלְהַצִּיב הַדָּרְבָן: וְהָיָה בְּיוֹם מִלְחֶמֶת וְלֹא נִמְצָא חֶרֶב וַחֲנִית בְּיַד כָּל־הָעָם אֲשֶׁר אֶת־שָׁאוּל וְאֶת־יוֹנָתָן וַתִּמָּצֵא לְשָׁאוּל וּלְיוֹנָתָן בְּנוֹ:

שְׁמוּאֵל א׳ יג:יט-כב

Samuel reported all the words of the LORD to the people who were asking him for a king. ¹¹He said, "This will be the rule of the king who will reign over you: he will take your sons and assign them to his chariots and horsemen, and they shall escort his chariots as outrunners; ¹²also to serve him as chiefs of thousands and as chiefs of fifties; also, to plow his ground and to reap his harvest, and to make his tools of war and the equipment for his chariots . . . ¹⁸When that day comes, you will cry out because of the king that you have chosen for yourselves, but the LORD will not answer you on that day."

*I Samuel 8.10-12, 18*

וַיֹּאמֶר שְׁמוּאֵל אֵת כָּל־דִּבְרֵי יְהֹוָה אֶל־הָעָם הַשֹּׁאֲלִים מֵאִתּוֹ מֶלֶךְ: וַיֹּאמֶר זֶה יִהְיֶה מִשְׁפַּט הַמֶּלֶךְ אֲשֶׁר יִמְלֹךְ עֲלֵיכֶם אֶת־בְּנֵיכֶם יִקַּח וְשָׂם לוֹ בְּמֶרְכַּבְתּוֹ וּבְפָרָשָׁיו וְרָצוּ לִפְנֵי מֶרְכַּבְתּוֹ: וְלָשׂוּם לוֹ שָׂרֵי אֲלָפִים וְשָׂרֵי חֲמִשִּׁים וְלַחֲרֹשׁ חֲרִישׁוֹ וְלִקְצֹר קְצִירוֹ וְלַעֲשׂוֹת כְּלֵי־מִלְחַמְתּוֹ וּכְלֵי רִכְבּוֹ: ... וּזְעַקְתֶּם בַּיּוֹם הַהוּא מִלִּפְנֵי מַלְכְּכֶם אֲשֶׁר בְּחַרְתֶּם לָכֶם וְלֹא־יַעֲנֶה יְהֹוָה אֶתְכֶם בַּיּוֹם הַהוּא:

שְׁמוּאֵל א׳ ח: י-יב, יח

But the people refused to heed Samuel, and said, "No! We want a king over us. ²⁰We want to be like all the other nations; let our king be our leader, marching at our head and fighting our battles . . ."

*I Samuel 8.19-20*

וַיְמָאֲנוּ הָעָם לִשְׁמֹעַ בְּקוֹל שְׁמוּאֵל וַיֹּאמְרוּ לֹא כִּי אִם־מֶלֶךְ יִהְיֶה עָלֵינוּ: וְהָיִינוּ גַם־אֲנַחְנוּ כְּכָל־הַגּוֹיִם וּשְׁפָטָנוּ מַלְכֵּנוּ וְיָצָא לְפָנֵינוּ וְנִלְחַם אֶת־מִלְחֲמֹתֵנוּ:

שְׁמוּאֵל א׳ ח: יט-כ

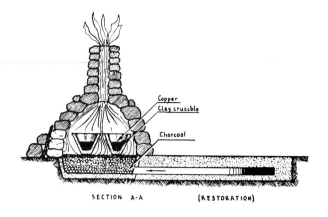

COPPER FURNACE
STRATUM XI

Copper
Clay crucible

Charcoal

SECTION A-A          (RESTORATION)

Plan of the reconstruction of the Early Iron Age copper-smelting furnace found at Tell Qasile.

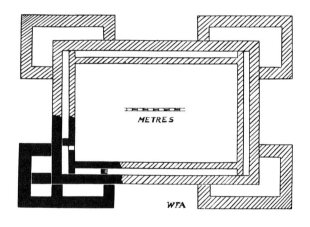

METRES

WFA

Outline plan of the citadel of Gibeah (modern Tell el-Ful), built by Saul as his capital.

In his home town Gibeah, on a hill three miles north of Jebus (Jerusalem), Saul built upon the ruins of an earlier settlement a palace-fortress that constituted his capital. Befitting his new status in Israel, the structure was at least 170 feet long and 115 feet wide, and two or three stories high. A double wall—the outer one being 7 feet thick—surrounded the building, and the corners, the weakest parts of the enclosure, were protected by strong towers. But the structure suffered destruction, probably by the Philistines, and was rebuilt shortly thereafter along the same lines as before.

The Israelite assembly rejected this Catonian warning, and chose Saul son of Kish, a native of Benjamin, to be their first king. Saul was a striking figure, a man among men. "There was no better person among the Israelites than he," we are told, "from his shoulders and upward he was taller than any of the people" (I Samuel 9:2). When Samuel saw that further protest was useless, he anointed Saul, and thus the kingship over Israel was sanctified.

## Trials of King Saul

Almost at once Saul's royal authority was tested; shortly after assuming office, he summoned all Israel to raise the Ammonite siege of Jabesh-gilead in Transjordan. Saul threatened to destroy the herds of every able-bodied Israelite who failed to answer the call. He raised a force large enough to beat off the Ammonites, but the response of the tribes was still far from unanimous. Saul's close followers proposed that he destroy the slackers, but he refused. Again, in battle against the Philistines at Michmash, part of Saul's army deserted, and but for a clever stratagem devised by Jonathan, the crown prince, the day would have been lost.

Then, after another victory, this time over the Amalekites, Saul's political star began to fade. The conservative element led by Samuel consistently undercut the king. Their support was grudging; they gave him little credit when he won and loudly condemned him when he lost. And meanwhile Saul was the prey of his own tempestuous and moody nature, which from time to time floundered in fits of fear and rage.

On one occasion Saul suddenly lost confidence in himself, when he was faced, in the Shefelah foothills near Azekah, by a Philistine army led by a giant of a man named Goliath. The once-powerful monarch was

And he (Kish) had a son whose name was Saul, a handsome young man; there was no one among the Israelites more handsome than he, taller by a head than the rest of the people.

*I Samuel 9.2*

וְלוֹ־הָיָה בֵן וּשְׁמוֹ שָׁאוּל בָּחוּר וָטוֹב וְאֵין אִישׁ מִבְּנֵי יִשְׂרָאֵל טוֹב מִמֶּנּוּ מִשִּׁכְמוֹ וָמַעְלָה גָּבֹהַּ מִכָּל־הָעָם:

שְׁמוּאֵל א׳ ט:ב

## Trials of King Saul

Nahash the Ammonite came up and encamped against Jabesh-gilead. And all the men of Jabesh-gilead said to Nahash, "Make a pact with us and we will serve you." ²But Nahash the Ammonite said in reply, "I will do so on this condition, that I gouge out all your right eyes and thus bring shame on all Israel."

*I Samuel 11.1-2*

וַיַּעַל נָחָשׁ הָעַמּוֹנִי וַיִּחַן עַל־יָבֵישׁ גִּלְעָד וַיֹּאמְרוּ כָּל־אַנְשֵׁי יָבֵישׁ אֶל־נָחָשׁ כְּרָת־לָנוּ בְרִית וְנַעַבְדֶךָ: וַיֹּאמֶר אֲלֵיהֶם נָחָשׁ הָעַמּוֹנִי בְּזֹאת אֶכְרֹת לָכֶם בִּנְקוֹר לָכֶם כָּל־עֵין יָמִין וְשַׂמְתִּיהָ חֶרְפָּה עַל־כָּל־יִשְׂרָאֵל:

שְׁמוּאֵל א, יא:א-ב

And (Saul) took a yoke of oxen and cut them in pieces which he sent by messengers throughout the territory of Israel with this message: This will be done to the oxen of everyone who fails to come out behind Saul and Samuel! And the fear of the LORD fell upon the people and they came out as one man . . . ¹¹The next day Saul deployed the troops in three columns, and they penetrated the center of the camp at the morning watch and struck down the Ammonites until midday . . . ¹²The people then said to Samuel, "Whoever said, 'Will Saul be king over us?'—let those men be surrendered that we may put them to death." ¹³But Saul said, "No man shall be put to death this day, for the LORD has wrought victory in Israel today."

*I Samuel 11.7, 11-13*

וַיִּקַּח צֶמֶד בָּקָר וַיְנַתְּחֵהוּ וַיְשַׁלַּח בְּכָל־גְּבוּל יִשְׂרָאֵל בְּיַד הַמַּלְאָכִים לֵאמֹר אֲשֶׁר אֵינֶנּוּ יֹצֵא אַחֲרֵי שָׁאוּל וְאַחַר שְׁמוּאֵל כֹּה יֵעָשֶׂה לִבְקָרוֹ וַיִּפֹּל פַּחַד־יְהוָה עַל־הָעָם וַיֵּצְאוּ כְּאִישׁ אֶחָד: . . . וַיְהִי מִמָּחֳרָת וַיָּשֶׂם שָׁאוּל אֶת־הָעָם שְׁלֹשָׁה רָאשִׁים וַיָּבֹאוּ בְתוֹךְ־הַמַּחֲנֶה בְּאַשְׁמֹרֶת הַבֹּקֶר וַיַּכּוּ אֶת־עַמּוֹן עַד־חֹם הַיּוֹם... וַיֹּאמֶר הָעָם אֶל־שְׁמוּאֵל מִי הָאֹמֵר שָׁאוּל יִמְלֹךְ עָלֵינוּ תְּנוּ הָאֲנָשִׁים וּנְמִיתֵם: וַיֹּאמֶר שָׁאוּל לֹא־יוּמַת אִישׁ בַּיּוֹם הַזֶּה כִּי הַיּוֹם עָשָׂה־יְהוָה תְּשׁוּעָה בְּיִשְׂרָאֵל:

שמואל א׳ יא:ז, יא-יג

The Philistine garrison went out to the Pass of Michmash . . . ¹¹The two of them showed themselves to the Philistine garrison, and the Philistines said, "Look, the Hebrews are coming out of the holes in which they hid." ¹²The men of the garrison then shouted to Jonathan and his armor-bearer, "Come up here, we have something to tell you." Thereupon Jonathan said to his armor-bearer, "Follow behind me, for the LORD has delivered them into the hands of Israel." ¹³Jonathan climbed up on hands and feet, followed by his armor-bearer, and the Philistines fell before Jonathan, while his armor-bearer behind him finished them off . . . ¹⁵Then consternation broke out in the camp . . .

*I Samuel 13.23; 14.11-15*

וַיֵּצֵא מַצַּב פְּלִשְׁתִּים אֶל־מַעֲבַר מִכְמָשׂ: . . . וַיִּגָּלוּ שְׁנֵיהֶם אֶל־מַצַּב פְּלִשְׁתִּים וַיֹּאמְרוּ פְלִשְׁתִּים הִנֵּה עִבְרִים יֹצְאִים מִן־הַחֹרִים אֲשֶׁר הִתְחַבְּאוּ־שָׁם: וַיַּעֲנוּ אַנְשֵׁי הַמַּצָּבָה אֶת־יוֹנָתָן וְאֶת־נֹשֵׂא כֵלָיו וַיֹּאמְרוּ עֲלוּ אֵלֵינוּ וְנוֹדִיעָה אֶתְכֶם דָּבָר וַיֹּאמֶר יוֹנָתָן אֶל־נֹשֵׂא כֵלָיו עֲלֵה אַחֲרַי כִּי־נְתָנָם יְהוָה בְּיַד יִשְׂרָאֵל: וַיַּעַל יוֹנָתָן עַל־יָדָיו וְעַל־רַגְלָיו וְנֹשֵׂא כֵלָיו אַחֲרָיו וַיִּפְּלוּ לִפְנֵי יוֹנָתָן וְנֹשֵׂא כֵלָיו מְמוֹתֵת אַחֲרָיו: . . . וַתְּהִי חֲרָדָה בַמַּחֲנֶה. . .

שמואל א׳ יג: כג: יד: יא-טו

Warrior shown in the act of hurling a missile with his sling. Excavated at Tel Halaf (Biblical Gozan) on the upper regions of the Khabur River, this is one of a small group of carved orthostats showing war pursuits. Basalt; about 25 inches high.

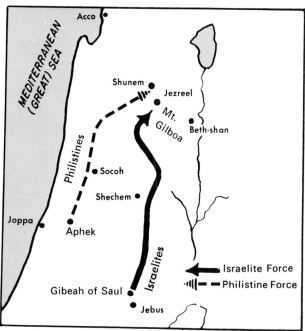

THE ISRAELITES AND THE PHILISTINES AT MT. GILBOA.

"overcome by dismay and fear" (I Samuel 17:11). The opportunity presented itself for an unknown lad, David, son of Jesse of Bethlehem, to step into the breach. A popular tradition had it that he slew the monster Goliath with a slingshot and became the boy hero of all Israel. Thereafter David's rise was meteoric. He could do no wrong, fortune smiled on him at every turn. Saul made David a military chieftain and, because of his additional talents, also personal court musician, to play soothing music when "the evil spirit of God" came upon the king.

## The King Comes to Grief

Saul soon realized that David was becoming the center of popular favor and was threatening to reap the political rewards of fame. "Saul has slain his thousands," the people sang, "but David—his ten thousands!" Even Jonathan, the king's son, regarded David as his bosom friend. Saul tried several times to kill his younger rival. The jealous idea became fixed in Saul's head, the Biblical authors tell us (I Samuel 18–30), that if he could only rid himself of the upstart, David, all would go well with him.

Saul died where he had first made his name, on the field of battle. Against Philistines assembled in the valley of Jezreel, Saul and his forces took up counterpositions at near-by Mount Gilboa. In the ensuing engagement the Philistines overwhelmed the Israelites, and Saul "took the sword and fell upon it," rather than fall into the hands of his enemies.

Thus died Saul, the aging champion, battered to his knees, one of the most human and touching figures in all literature. His was a heroic and tragic role in a crucial

When Saul and all Israel heard these taunts of the Philistine, they were overcome by dismay and fear.

*I Samuel 17.11*

וַיִּשְׁמַע שָׁאוּל וְכָל־יִשְׂרָאֵל אֶת־דִּבְרֵי הַפְּלִשְׁתִּי
הָאֵלֶּה וַיֵּחַתּוּ וַיִּרְאוּ מְאֹד:
שְׁמוּאֵל א׳ יז:יא

Thus David triumphed over the Philistine with a sling and stone, striking down the Philistine and slaying him; David had no dagger with him.

*I Samuel 17.50*

וַיֶּחֱזַק דָּוִד מִן־הַפְּלִשְׁתִּי בַּקֶּלַע וּבָאֶבֶן וַיַּךְ
אֶת־הַפְּלִשְׁתִּי וַיְמִתֵהוּ וְחֶרֶב אֵין בְּיַד־דָּוִד:
שְׁמוּאֵל א׳ יז:נ

## The King Comes to Grief

. . . When David returned after defeating the Philistine, the women came out singing and dancing from all the towns of Israel, to welcome King Saul . . . ⁷As they were disporting themselves, the women kept chanting:

Saul has slain his thousands,
And David—his tens of thousands!

⁸Saul was much aggrieved; the matter displeased him. "To David," he said, "they have given tens of thousands, and me they have given the thousands. He lacks now only the throne." ⁹Saul kept a watchful eye on David from that day on. ¹⁰The next day, an evil spirit of God rushed upon Saul, and he began to act like a prophet [that is, like a diviner in frenzy] in his house, while David was playing the musical instrument in his hand as usual; Saul had a spear in his hand. ¹¹Saul hurled the spear shouting, "I will pierce David through into the wall!" But David eluded him twice.

*I Samuel 18.6-11*

וַיְהִי בְּבוֹאָם בְּשׁוּב דָּוִד מֵהַכּוֹת אֶת־הַפְּלִשְׁתִּי
וַתֵּצֶאנָה הַנָּשִׁים מִכָּל־עָרֵי־יִשְׂרָאֵל לָשִׁיר וְהַמְּחֹלוֹת
לִקְרַאת שָׁאוּל הַמֶּלֶךְ . . . וַתַּעֲנֶינָה הַנָּשִׁים הַמְשַׂחֲקוֹת
וַתֹּאמַרְןָ הִכָּה שָׁאוּל בַּאֲלָפָיו וְדָוִד בְּרִבְבֹתָיו:
וַיִּחַר לְשָׁאוּל מְאֹד וַיֵּרַע בְּעֵינָיו הַדָּבָר הַזֶּה וַיֹּאמֶר
נָתְנוּ לְדָוִד רְבָבוֹת וְלִי נָתְנוּ הָאֲלָפִים וְעוֹד לוֹ אַךְ
הַמְּלוּכָה: וַיְהִי שָׁאוּל עוֹיֵן אֶת־דָּוִד מֵהַיּוֹם הַהוּא
וָהָלְאָה: וַיְהִי מִמָּחֳרָת וַתִּצְלַח רוּחַ אֱלֹהִים רָעָה
אֶל־שָׁאוּל וַיִּתְנַבֵּא בְתוֹךְ־הַבַּיִת וְדָוִד מְנַגֵּן בְּיָדוֹ
כְּיוֹם בְּיוֹם וְהַחֲנִית בְּיַד־שָׁאוּל: וַיָּטֶל שָׁאוּל אֶת־
הַחֲנִית וַיֹּאמֶר אַכֶּה בְדָוִד וּבַקִּיר וַיִּסֹּב דָּוִד מִפָּנָיו
פַּעֲמָיִם:

שְׁמוּאֵל א׳ יח: ו–יא

David was successful in all his actions, the LORD being with him; ¹⁵and when Saul saw that he was very successful, he grew afraid of him. ¹⁶All Israel and Judah favored David for he served them well as leader (lit. went out and came in before them).

*I Samuel 18.14-16*

וַיְהִי דָוִד לְכָל־דְּרָכָו מַשְׂכִּיל וַיהֹוָה עִמּוֹ:
וַיַּרְא שָׁאוּל אֲשֶׁר־הוּא מַשְׂכִּיל מְאֹד וַיָּגָר מִפָּנָיו:
וְכָל־יִשְׂרָאֵל וִיהוּדָה אֹהֵב אֶת־דָּוִד כִּי־הוּא יוֹצֵא
וָבָא לִפְנֵיהֶם:
שְׁמוּאֵל א׳ יח:יד–טז

And Jonathan spoke favorably to his father Saul about David. He said to him, "Let not the king wrong his servant David, for he has done you no wrong and his undertakings are greatly to your advantage."

*I Samuel 19.4*

וַיְדַבֵּר יְהוֹנָתָן בְּדָוִד טוֹב אֶל־שָׁאוּל אָבִיו
וַיֹּאמֶר אֵלָיו אַל־יֶחֱטָא הַמֶּלֶךְ בְּעַבְדּוֹ בְדָוִד כִּי
לוֹא חָטָא לָךְ וְכִי מַעֲשָׂיו טוֹב־לְךָ מְאֹד:
שְׁמוּאֵל א׳ יט:ד

109

period in Israel's career. It was his hard lot to bear the brunt of the reaction which is always evoked by deep social change. His sick nature, moreover, was a scourge. Yet the fact remains that Saul laid the foundation for an effective opposition to the Philistine advance, for an attack on their valuable monopoly of iron, and, perhaps most important, for a measurable degree of unification among the individualistic tribes of Israel.

The Philistines attacked Israel, and the men of Israel fled before the Philistines and fell mortally wounded on Mount Gilboa. [2]The Philistines caught up with Saul and his sons, and the Philistines struck down Jonathan, Abinadab, and Malchishua, Saul's sons. [3]The battle grew severe about Saul, and the archers came upon him, the men with the bow; he was in great dread of the archers. [4]Saul said to his armor-bearer, "Draw your dagger and run me through with it; else those uncircumcised ones will come and run me through after making sport of me." But the armor-bearer refused, for he was afraid. Thereupon Saul seized the dagger and fell on it. [5]When his armor-bearer saw that Saul was dead, he too fell on his dagger and died with him. [6]So Saul, his three sons, and his armor-bearer, along with his men, died together that day. [7]When the men of Israel who were on the other side of the valley and those beyond the Jordan saw that the men of Israel had fled and that Saul and his sons were dead, they abandoned their towns and fled. The Philistines then came and occupied them.

*I Samuel 31.1-7*

וּפְלִשְׁתִּים נִלְחָמִים בְּיִשְׂרָאֵל וַיָּנֻסוּ אַנְשֵׁי יִשְׂרָאֵל מִפְּנֵי פְלִשְׁתִּים וַיִּפְּלוּ חֲלָלִים בְּהַר הַגִּלְבֹּעַ: וַיַּדְבְּקוּ פְלִשְׁתִּים אֶת־שָׁאוּל וְאֶת־בָּנָיו וַיַּכּוּ פְלִשְׁתִּים אֶת־יְהוֹנָתָן וְאֶת־אֲבִינָדָב וְאֶת־מַלְכִּישׁוּעַ בְּנֵי שָׁאוּל: וַתִּכְבַּד הַמִּלְחָמָה אֶל־שָׁאוּל וַיִּמְצָאֻהוּ הַמּוֹרִים אֲנָשִׁים בַּקָּשֶׁת וַיָּחֶל מְאֹד מֵהַמּוֹרִים: וַיֹּאמֶר שָׁאוּל לְנֹשֵׂא כֵלָיו שְׁלֹף חַרְבְּךָ וְדָקְרֵנִי בָהּ פֶּן־יָבוֹאוּ הָעֲרֵלִים הָאֵלֶּה וּדְקָרֻנִי וְהִתְעַלְּלוּ־בִי וְלֹא אָבָה נֹשֵׂא כֵלָיו כִּי יָרֵא מְאֹד וַיִּקַּח שָׁאוּל אֶת־הַחֶרֶב וַיִּפֹּל עָלֶיהָ: וַיַּרְא נֹשֵׂא־כֵלָיו כִּי־מֵת שָׁאוּל וַיִּפֹּל גַּם־הוּא עַל־חַרְבּוֹ וַיָּמָת עִמּוֹ: וַיָּמָת שָׁאוּל וּשְׁלֹשֶׁת בָּנָיו וְנֹשֵׂא כֵלָיו גַּם כָּל־אֲנָשָׁיו בַּיּוֹם הַהוּא יַחְדָּו: וַיִּרְאוּ אַנְשֵׁי־יִשְׂרָאֵל אֲשֶׁר־בְּעֵבֶר הָעֵמֶק וַאֲשֶׁר בְּעֵבֶר הַיַּרְדֵּן כִּי־נָסוּ אַנְשֵׁי יִשְׂרָאֵל וְכִי־מֵתוּ שָׁאוּל וּבָנָיו וַיַּעַזְבוּ אֶת־הֶעָרִים וַיָּנֻסוּ וַיָּבֹאוּ פְלִשְׁתִּים וַיֵּשְׁבוּ בָּהֶן:

שְׁמוּאֵל א' לא:א–ז

*The tribal structure of Israel was too loose for Saul to achieve control over all Israel; the theory that Israel constituted a sort of amphictyony in the Period of the Judges was first attacked by H. M. Orlinsky, "The Tribal System of Israel and Related Groups in the Period of the Judges"* (in Studies and Essays in Honor of Abraham A. Neuman, *1962, pp. 375-387 [= pp. 11-20 in* Oriens Antiquus, *1 (1962)]), and it has been abandoned by several other scholars since (e.g., J. G. Vink, in* Oudtestamentische Studiën, *XV [1969]; G. W. Anderson, in the H. G. May volume:* Translating and Understanding the Old Testament [1970], *pp. 135-151; and R. de Vaux,* Harvard Theological Review, *64 [1971], pp. 415-436), so that it is now all but dead. See also M. A. Cohen, "The Role of the Shilonite Priesthood in the United Monarchy of Ancient Israel,"* Hebrew Union College Annual, *36 (1965), 59-98.*

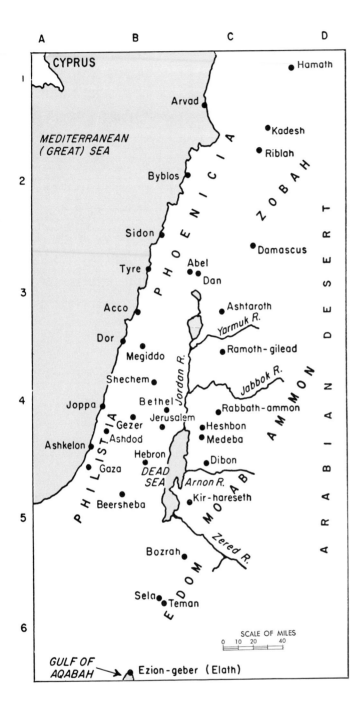

MAP OF ISRAELITE EMPIRE UNDER DAVID AND SOLOMON.

## Chapter IV

# THE ISRAELITE EMPIRE UNDER DAVID AND SOLOMON

ANCIENT Israel's Golden Era came during the tenth century B.C.E. when David and Solomon ruled Israel and Israel dominated western Asia. It was this period that the prophets had in mind, later, when they urged the restoration of a united Israel and called for vengeance on the foes about them. And it was among the descendants of David that they assumed the leader would be found who could make possible this achievement. Thus Isaiah affirmed: "A shoot shall come forth out of the stock of Jesse (the father of David). . . . And the spirit of the Lord shall descend upon him. . . . And in that day the root of Jesse that has remained standing shall become an ensign to the peoples; to him shall the nations go for counsel, and his abode shall be glorious (Isaiah 11:1–10).

And now, say thus to My servant David, "Thus said the LORD of Hosts: I took you from the pasture, from following the flocks, to be prince over My people Israel; ⁹I have been with you wherever you went, and have cut down all your enemies before you; and I will give you great renown like that of the greatest men on earth. ¹⁰I will establish a home for My people Israel, and I will plant them firm so that they shall dwell secure; they shall tremble no more, and evil men shall not oppress them any more, as in the past . . . ¹²And when your days are done and you lie with your fathers, I will raise up your offspring after you, one of your own issue, and I will establish his kingship. ¹³He shall build a House for My name, and I will establish his royal throne forever. ¹⁴I will be a father to him, and he shall be a son to Me: when he does wrong, I will chastise him with the rod of man and the afflictions of mortals . . . ¹⁶Your House and your kingship shall ever be secure before you, your throne shall be established forever."

*II Samuel 7.8-16*

A shoot shall grow out of the stock of Jesse,
A twig shall branch off from his roots.
²The spirit of the LORD shall descend upon him:
A spirit of wisdom and insight,
A spirit of counsel and valor,
A spirit of acknowledgment and awe of the Lord.
⁴ . . . He shall judge the poor with equity
And decide with justice for the lowly of the land.
He shall strike down a land with the rod of his mouth,
And slay the wicked with the breath of his lips.
⁵Justice shall be the girdle of his loins,
And faithfulness the girdle of his waist.
⁶The wolf shall dwell with the lamb,
The leopard lie down with the kid;
The calf, the beast of prey, and the fatling together,
With a little boy to lead them.
⁷The cow and the bear shall graze,
Their young shall lie down together;
And the lion, like the ox, shall eat straw.
⁸A babe shall play over a viper's hole,
And an infant pass his hand over an adder's den.
⁹Nothing evil or vile shall be done
In all of My sacred mount,
For the land shall be filled with acknowledgment of the Lord,
As waters cover the sea.

*Isaiah 11.1-9*

וְעַתָּה כֹּה־תֹאמַר לְעַבְדִּי לְדָוִד כֹּה אָמַר יְהֹוָה צְבָאוֹת אֲנִי לְקַחְתִּיךָ מִן־הַנָּוֶה מֵאַחַר הַצֹּאן לִהְיוֹת נָגִיד עַל־עַמִּי עַל־יִשְׂרָאֵל: וָאֶהְיֶה עִמְּךָ בְּכֹל אֲשֶׁר הָלַכְתָּ וָאַכְרִתָה אֶת־כָּל־אֹיְבֶיךָ מִפָּנֶיךָ וְעָשִׂתִי לְךָ שֵׁם גָּדוֹל כְּשֵׁם הַגְּדֹלִים אֲשֶׁר בָּאָרֶץ: וְשַׂמְתִּי מָקוֹם לְעַמִּי לְיִשְׂרָאֵל וּנְטַעְתִּיו וְשָׁכַן תַּחְתָּיו וְלֹא יִרְגַּז עוֹד וְלֹא־יֹסִיפוּ בְנֵי־עַוְלָה לְעַנּוֹתוֹ כַּאֲשֶׁר בָּרִאשׁוֹנָה: ... כִּי יִמְלְאוּ יָמֶיךָ וְשָׁכַבְתָּ אֶת־אֲבֹתֶיךָ וַהֲקִימֹתִי אֶת־זַרְעֲךָ אַחֲרֶיךָ אֲשֶׁר יֵצֵא מִמֵּעֶיךָ וַהֲכִינֹתִי אֶת־מַמְלַכְתּוֹ: הוּא יִבְנֶה־בַּיִת לִשְׁמִי וְכֹנַנְתִּי אֶת־כִּסֵּא מַמְלַכְתּוֹ עַד־עוֹלָם: אֲנִי אֶהְיֶה־לּוֹ לְאָב וְהוּא יִהְיֶה־לִּי לְבֵן אֲשֶׁר בְּהַעֲוֹתוֹ וְהֹכַחְתִּיו בְּשֵׁבֶט אֲנָשִׁים וּבְנִגְעֵי בְּנֵי אָדָם: ... וְנֶאְמַן בֵּיתְךָ וּמַמְלַכְתְּךָ עַד־עוֹלָם לְפָנֶיךָ כִּסְאֲךָ יִהְיֶה נָכוֹן עַד־עוֹלָם:

שְׁמוּאֵל ב׳ ז:ח–טז

וְיָצָא חֹטֶר מִגֵּזַע יִשָׁי וְנֵצֶר מִשָּׁרָשָׁיו יִפְרֶה: וְנָחָה עָלָיו רוּחַ יְהֹוָה רוּחַ חָכְמָה וּבִינָה רוּחַ עֵצָה וּגְבוּרָה רוּחַ דַּעַת וְיִרְאַת יְהֹוָה: ... וְשָׁפַט בְּצֶדֶק דַּלִּים וְהוֹכִיחַ בְּמִישׁוֹר לְעַנְוֵי־אָרֶץ וְהִכָּה־אֶרֶץ בְּשֵׁבֶט פִּיו וּבְרוּחַ שְׂפָתָיו יָמִית רָשָׁע: וְהָיָה צֶדֶק אֵזוֹר מָתְנָיו וְהָאֱמוּנָה אֵזוֹר חֲלָצָיו: וְגָר זְאֵב עִם־כֶּבֶשׂ וְנָמֵר עִם־גְּדִי יִרְבָּץ וְעֵגֶל וּכְפִיר וּמְרִיא יַחְדָּו וְנַעַר קָטֹן נֹהֵג בָּם: וּפָרָה וָדֹב תִּרְעֶינָה יַחְדָּו יִרְבְּצוּ יַלְדֵיהֶן וְאַרְיֵה כַּבָּקָר יֹאכַל־תֶּבֶן: וְשִׁעֲשַׁע יוֹנֵק עַל־חֻר פָּתֶן וְעַל מְאוּרַת צִפְעוֹנִי גָּמוּל יָדוֹ הָדָה: לֹא־יָרֵעוּ וְלֹא־יַשְׁחִיתוּ בְּכָל־הַר קָדְשִׁי כִּי־מָלְאָה הָאָרֶץ דֵּעָה אֶת־יְהֹוָה כַּמַּיִם לַיָּם מְכַסִּים:

יְשַׁעְיָהוּ יא:א–ט

113

The hunt and the battle were very important activities of the monarch in the ancient Near East. The stories of David's heroism belong to this category.

In the two carved orthostats from Tel Halaf reproduced here (10th-8th cent.), one shows a warrior-hero killing a lion which has fastened a hold on his arm, and the other depicts two warriors fighting a battle in which they stab each other with short swords held in one hand while they hold their opponent's forelock with the other.

114

Recent discoveries have greatly enhanced the historical value of the Biblical account, and even enriched its three-thousand-year-old story with considerable new material. The Queen of Sheba, after she met Solomon, is reported to have exclaimed, "It was a true report that I heard in my country concerning your achievements and your wisdom. But I did not believe the reports until I came and my own eyes saw. Indeed, the half of it was not told me. You have wisdom and prosperity exceeding the report that I heard" (I Kings 10:6–7). The same words might well express the mood of modern scholars rereading the Biblical history of the reigns of David and Solomon in the light of the recent revelations.

## David the Favorite

David, having achieved military distinction at an early age, began to assume the stature of a legendary figure almost before his mature life was well begun. Thus he was credited with having killed a lion and a bear even before his dramatic conquest of the Philistine Goliath (I Samuel 16–17).

Saul at first made David his protégé, married him to his daughter Michal, and acknowledged him favorite of the court. But David's popularity could know no bounds, and as it continued to swell among important segments of the population, the king realized the danger of rising opposition to his rule and finally turned on him with pent-up fury. Driven from the court, David maintained his place in the hearts of the people by his gallant and resourceful acts. He sent his parents to Moab for safety, while he himself sought refuge, now at the sanctuary of Nob near Jerusalem, now at the court of Achish, the Philistine king of Gath and enemy of Saul. For a time, too, he led a band of several hundred outlaws in the Shefelah foothills in the region of Adullam. And again he proved

She said to the king, "It was a true report that I heard in my country about your achievements and your wisdom. [7]But I did not believe the reports until I came and my own eyes saw that not even the half had been told me. You have wisdom and wealth exceeding the reports that I heard."

*I Kings 10.6-7*

וַתֹּאמֶר אֶל־הַמֶּלֶךְ אֱמֶת הָיָה הַדָּבָר אֲשֶׁר שָׁמַעְתִּי בְּאַרְצִי עַל־דְּבָרֶיךָ וְעַל־חָכְמָתֶךָ: וְלֹא־הֶאֱמַנְתִּי לַדְּבָרִים עַד אֲשֶׁר־בָּאתִי וַתִּרְאֶינָה עֵינַי וְהִנֵּה לֹא־הֻגַּד־לִי הַחֵצִי הוֹסַפְתָּ חָכְמָה וָטוֹב אֶל־הַשְּׁמוּעָה אֲשֶׁר שָׁמָעְתִּי:

מְלָכִים א׳ י׃ו–ז

## David the Favorite

Samuel said to Jesse, "Are these all the boys?" "There is still the youngest one," he answered, "but he is taking care of the flock." "Send for him," Samuel said to Jesse, "for we will not begin our feast until he comes." [12]So he had him brought. (Now he was of ruddy complexion and with striking eyes, and he was handsome.) Then the LORD said, "Come, anoint him, for he is the one."

*I Samuel 16.11-12*

וַיֹּאמֶר שְׁמוּאֵל אֶל־יִשַׁי הֲתַמּוּ הַנְּעָרִים וַיֹּאמֶר עוֹד שָׁאַר הַקָּטָן וְהִנֵּה רֹעֶה בַּצֹּאן וַיֹּאמֶר שְׁמוּאֵל אֶל־יִשַׁי שִׁלְחָה וְקָחֶנּוּ כִּי לֹא־נָסֹב עַד־בֹּאוֹ פֹה: וַיִּשְׁלַח וַיְבִיאֵהוּ וְהוּא אַדְמוֹנִי עִם־יְפֵה עֵינַיִם וְטוֹב רֹאִי וַיֹּאמֶר יְהוָה קוּם מְשָׁחֵהוּ כִּי־זֶה הוּא:

שְׁמוּאֵל א׳ טז׃יא–יב

One of the young men spoke up, saying, "I have seen a son of Jesse the Bethlehemite who is a musician, a brave man, a warrior, discerning, and handsome, and the LORD is with him.

*I Samuel 16.18*

וַיַּעַן אֶחָד מֵהַנְּעָרִים וַיֹּאמֶר הִנֵּה רָאִיתִי בֵּן לְיִשַׁי בֵּית הַלַּחְמִי יֹדֵעַ נַגֵּן וְגִבּוֹר חַיִל וְאִישׁ מִלְחָמָה וּנְבוֹן דָּבָר וְאִישׁ תֹּאַר וַיהוָה עִמּוֹ:

שְׁמוּאֵל א׳ טז׃יח

Whenever the spirit of God came upon Saul, David took the lyre in his hand and played it; so Saul would find relief and feel better, and the evil spirit would depart from him.

*I Samuel 16.23*

וְהָיָה בִּהְיוֹת רוּחַ־אֱלֹהִים אֶל־שָׁאוּל וְלָקַח דָּוִד אֶת־הַכִּנּוֹר וְנִגֵּן בְּיָדוֹ וְרָוַח לְשָׁאוּל וְטוֹב לוֹ וְסָרָה מֵעָלָיו רוּחַ הָרָעָה:

שְׁמוּאֵל א׳ טז׃כג

Saul said to David, "Here is my older daughter Merab; I will give her to you for a wife. And you shall be my warrior, and fight the LORD's battles . . ." [18]David answered Saul, "Who am I and what is my career, my father's clan in Israel, that I should be the king's son-in-law?" [19]But when the time came for Saul's daughter Merab to be given to David, she was given instead to Adriel the Meholathite for a wife. [20]However Saul's daughter Michal had fallen in love with David; and when this was reported to Saul, it pleased him. [21]Saul thought: I will give her to him, and she will become a snare for him, and the hand of the Philistines will be against him . . .

*I Samuel 18.17-21*

וַיֹּאמֶר שָׁאוּל אֶל־דָּוִד הִנֵּה בִתִּי הַגְּדוֹלָה מֵרַב אֹתָהּ אֶתֶּן־לְךָ לְאִשָּׁה אַךְ הֱיֵה־לִי לְבֶן־חַיִל וְהִלָּחֵם מִלְחֲמוֹת יְהוָה וְשָׁאוּל אָמַר אַל־תְּהִי יָדִי בּוֹ וּתְהִי־בוֹ יַד־פְּלִשְׁתִּים: וַיֹּאמֶר דָּוִד אֶל־שָׁאוּל מִי אָנֹכִי וּמִי חַיַּי מִשְׁפַּחַת אָבִי בְּיִשְׂרָאֵל כִּי־אֶהְיֶה חָתָן לַמֶּלֶךְ: וַיְהִי בְּעֵת תֵּת אֶת־מֵרַב בַּת־שָׁאוּל לְדָוִד וְהִיא נִתְּנָה לְעַדְרִיאֵל הַמְּחֹלָתִי לְאִשָּׁה: וַתֶּאֱהַב מִיכַל בַּת־שָׁאוּל אֶת־דָּוִד וַיַּגִּדוּ לְשָׁאוּל וַיִּשַׁר הַדָּבָר בְּעֵינָיו: וַיֹּאמֶר שָׁאוּל אֶתְּנֶנָּה לוֹ וּתְהִי־לוֹ לְמוֹקֵשׁ וּתְהִי־בוֹ יַד־פְּלִשְׁתִּים וַיֹּאמֶר שָׁאוּל אֶל־דָּוִד בִּשְׁתַּיִם תִּתְחַתֵּן בִּי הַיּוֹם:

שְׁמוּאֵל א׳ יח׃ יז–כא

**THE GREAT POOL OF GIBEON**

The only specific reference to a battle in the long struggle between the supporters of Saul and those of David is the encounter between Abner's men and Joab's men at the "Great Pool" of Gibeon (II Sam. 2.12-17; 3.1; Jer. 41.12). The hand-to-hand combat having ended indecisively ("they felled one another," v. 16), a major battle ensued, in which David's forces were victorious (v. 17). The photo above shows the Pool, cut out of rock in cylindrical shape, 42 steps leading down to the bottom, from where a tunnel and another spiral stairway led to the water-level 45 feet farther down.

In the days of Saul, the composite bow—made up of layers of wood, sinew, and horn glued together and first introduced by the Hyksos—was the chief long-range weapon, and bowmen were intensively trained. In this restored wall painting from a Tomb in Thebes (Eighteenth Dynasty), two instructors are shown standing behind their students, teaching them how to hold the arrow and stretch the bowstring with the right hand, while holding the bow in the left.

his mettle by serving as border guard in the south for the Philistines (I Samuel 21–30). Several times during his banishment he could have killed Saul, but his deep nobility of character—and perhaps also his reverence for Saul as God's anointed one—prevented this final desperate act.

Defeated by the Philistines at Mount Gilboa, the Israelites were left leaderless and vulnerable. By this victory the Philistines had secured the valley of Jezreel, the principal commercial and military highway from the sea into the valley of the Jordan. As a result of their defeat the Israelites seemed poised on the verge of complete disintegration, like the Canaanites before them. From this fate they were saved by David and his followers.

## David Acquires the Throne of Saul

Immediately on the death of Saul, a struggle broke out for the succession to his power. Some supported Ishbosheth (Esh-baal), a son of Saul, while others, particularly the Shilonite seer-priesthood headed by Samuel, demanded David as king (II Samuel 2–4). (The role of Samuel in anointing David king even before Saul died [I Samuel 16] is quite obscure. It is sometimes no longer possible to separate and to date the various strands that came to be woven together to form the Biblical Book of Samuel.) To seize and consolidate the royal power David had to resolve both domestic and foreign problems. On the one hand he had to acquire sole authority in Israel, and on the other hand he had to unite Israel and check the Philistine drive.

In the bloody battle which ensued, David and his followers left no room for doubt as to which group was to rule in Israel. To some supporters of Ishbosheth, death was meted out—not always, perhaps, with David's knowledge or consent; to others, such as Mephibosheth, the crippled son of Jonathan, mercy was shown (II Samuel 9). Not relying completely on his fellow-Israelites, David hired

The men of Judah came and anointed David there as king over the House of Judah. And they told David, "It was the men of Jabesh-gilead who buried Saul."

*II Samuel 2.4*

וַיָּבֹאוּ אַנְשֵׁי יְהוּדָה וַיִּמְשְׁחוּ־שָׁם אֶת־דָּוִד לְמֶלֶךְ עַל־בֵּית יְהוּדָה וַיַּגִּדוּ לְדָוִד לֵאמֹר אַנְשֵׁי יָבֵישׁ גִּלְעָד אֲשֶׁר קָבְרוּ אֶת־שָׁאוּל:

שְׁמוּאֵל ב׳ ב:ד

When Abner son of Ner and the followers of Ish-bosheth son of Saul marched out of Mahanaim to Gibeon, 13Joab son of Zeruiah and David's followers marched out, and they confronted one another at the Pool of Gibeon; one group remained on one side of the pool, and the other on the other side . . . 15Then an agreed upon number went and crossed the lines, twelve representing Benjamin and Ish-bosheth son of Saul, and twelve of David's followers. 16Each seized his opponent by the head, with his dagger in his opponent's side, and they felled one another . . . 17The battle raged all that day, and Abner and the men of Israel were routed by David's followers.

*II Samuel 2.12-17*

וַיֵּצֵא אַבְנֵר בֶּן־נֵר וְעַבְדֵי אִישׁ־בֹּשֶׁת בֶּן־שָׁאוּל מִמַּחֲנָיִם גִּבְעוֹנָה: וְיוֹאָב בֶּן־צְרוּיָה וְעַבְדֵי דָוִד יָצְאוּ וַיִּפְגְּשׁוּם עַל־בְּרֵכַת גִּבְעוֹן יַחְדָּו וַיֵּשְׁבוּ אֵלֶּה עַל־הַבְּרֵכָה מִזֶּה וְאֵלֶּה עַל־הַבְּרֵכָה מִזֶּה: ...וַיָּקֻמוּ וַיַּעַבְרוּ בְּמִסְפָּר שְׁנֵים עָשָׂר לְבִנְיָמִן וּלְאִישׁ־בֹּשֶׁת בֶּן־שָׁאוּל וּשְׁנֵים עָשָׂר מֵעַבְדֵי דָוִד: וַיַּחֲזִקוּ אִישׁ בְּרֹאשׁ רֵעֵהוּ וְחַרְבּוֹ בְּצַד רֵעֵהוּ וַיִּפְּלוּ יַחְדָּו:... וַתְּהִי הַמִּלְחָמָה קָשָׁה עַד־מְאֹד בַּיּוֹם הַהוּא וַיִּנָּגֶף אַבְנֵר וְאַנְשֵׁי יִשְׂרָאֵל לִפְנֵי עַבְדֵי דָוִד:

שְׁמוּאֵל ב׳ ב:יב־יז

## David Acquires the Throne of Saul

The struggle between the Houses of Saul and David continued a long time; but David grew stronger, while the House of Saul grew weaker.

*II Samuel 3.1*

וַתְּהִי הַמִּלְחָמָה אֲרֻכָּה בֵּין בֵּית שָׁאוּל וּבֵין בֵּית דָּוִד וְדָוִד הֹלֵךְ וְחָזֵק וּבֵית שָׁאוּל הֹלְכִים וְדַלִּים:

שְׁמוּאֵל ב׳ ג:א

Mephibosheth son of Jonathan son of Saul came to David and flung himself down in obeisance. And David said, "Mephibosheth!" And he answered, "Your servant is at your service." 7Then David said, "Do not be afraid. I will treat you kindly for the sake of your father Jonathan; I will restore to you all the property of your father Saul, and you shall henceforth eat at my table."

*II Samuel 9.6-7*

וַיָּבֹא מְפִיבֹשֶׁת בֶּן־יְהוֹנָתָן בֶּן־שָׁאוּל אֶל־דָּוִד וַיִּפֹּל עַל־פָּנָיו וַיִּשְׁתָּחוּ וַיֹּאמֶר דָּוִד מְפִיבֹשֶׁת וַיֹּאמֶר הִנֵּה עַבְדֶּךָ: וַיֹּאמֶר לוֹ דָוִד אַל־תִּירָא כִּי עָשֹׂה אֶעֱשֶׂה עִמְּךָ חֶסֶד בַּעֲבוּר יְהוֹנָתָן אָבִיךָ וַהֲשִׁבֹתִי לְךָ אֶת־כָּל־שְׂדֵה שָׁאוּל אָבִיךָ וְאַתָּה תֹּאכַל לֶחֶם עַל־שֻׁלְחָנִי תָּמִיד:

שְׁמוּאֵל ב׳ ט:ו־ז

All his (David's) followers marched past him; and all the Cherethites and Pelethites, and all the Gathites, six hundred men who came from Gath as infantry, marched past the king.

*II Samuel 15.18*

וְכָל־עֲבָדָיו עֹבְרִים עַל־יָדוֹ וְכָל־הַכְּרֵתִי וְכָל־הַפְּלֵתִי וְכָל־הַגִּתִּים שֵׁשׁ־מֵאוֹת אִישׁ אֲשֶׁר־בָּאוּ בְרַגְלוֹ מִגַּת עֹבְרִים עַל־פְּנֵי הַמֶּלֶךְ:

שְׁמוּאֵל ב׳ טו:יח

Joab was in command of the whole army of Israel, and Benaiah son of Jehoiada was in charge of the Cherethites and Pelethites.

*II Samuel 20.23*

וְיוֹאָב אֶל־כָּל־הַצָּבָא יִשְׂרָאֵל וּבְנָיָה בֶּן־יְהוֹיָדָע עַל־הַכְּרֵתִי וְעַל־הַפְּלֵתִי:

שְׁמוּאֵל ב׳ כ:כג

117

The Canaanite terraces of the fourteenth and thirteenth centuries were built on Jerusalem's Ophel Hill with the aid of a series of retaining walls. Each retaining wall held in a fill of stones upon which were constructed some of the city's buildings. The Ophel Hill is the site of the main known occupation of pre-exilic Jerusalem. Such terracing, however, is not sturdy, and there is much evidence of collapse due to flooding, earthquake, and probably the vicissitudes of war.

The two photographs shown here, from Miss Kathleen M. Kenyon's excavations outside the present city wall on the Ophel Hill, show these terraces, some in good repair, but mostly in various stages of collapse.

mercenaries from Crete and elsewhere, the traditional "Cherethites and Pelethites" (II Samuel 8:18; 15:18), who served as his bodyguard.

Even more important and spectacular in this swift consolidation of power and prestige were David's military triumphs. Jerusalem, then also known as Jebus, the stronghold of the Jebusites, fell before his attack. Then, on several occasions, he checked the Philistines, and finally he cut them up so badly, particularly at Gath, that they never recovered their power to threaten Israel (II Samuel 21:15–22). It is interesting to note that some of these battles seem to have been decided by a fight between one or more picked warriors of the two sides, as in the case of David and Goliath, or the twelve-man teams which represented the forces of David and Ishbosheth. (See Y. Yadin, *Journal of the Palestine Oriental Society*, XXI [1948], 110–116.)

Having secured his western and southern flanks, David sent his forces east across the Jordan as far as Damascus and Zobah, and in a long series of battles he subdued some of the vigorous Aramean groups, as well as the Ammonites, Moabites, and Edomites. He even completed the destruction, which Saul had begun, of the elusive Amalekites in the south.

By the time David's astonishing military force had spent itself, the Israelites were in control of territories running from Kadesh on the Orontes river in Syria to Ezion-geber at the head of the Gulf of Aqabah. The Mediterranean coast, except for Phoenicia and small segments of Philistia, had been made tributary, and Transjordan, as far as the Arabian desert on the east, also acknowledged David as king. These military triumphs, moreover, greatly furthered regional and tribal coalescence and the composition of ancient quarrels. Already Israel was becoming a kingdom in fact, as it had been only in title under Saul.

Again the Philistines made war on Israel, and David went down together with his followers and fought the Philistines. David grew weary, [16]and Ishbi-benob, who was one of the descendants of the Rephaites . . . thought to kill David. [17]But Abishai son of Zeruiah came to his aid; he struck down the Philistine and slew him. Thereupon David's men vowed to him, "You shall not go out again with us in battle, lest you quench the lamp of Israel." [18]After this, war broke out again with the Philistines, at Gob; on that occasion Sibbecai the Hushathite slew Saph, who was one of the descendants of the Rephaites. [19]Again there was war with the Philistines at Gob; and Elhanan son of Jaare-oregim the Bethlehemite slew Goliath the Gathite, whose spear was like a weaver's beam. [20]War broke out again, at Gath. There was a giant of a man who had six fingers on each hand and six toes on each foot, twenty-four in all, and who was also a descendant of the Rephaites. [21]And when he challenged Israel, Jonathan son of Shimea, David's brother, slew him. [22]All four of these were descendants of the Rephaites of Gath, and they fell at the hand of David and his followers.

*II Samuel 21.15-22*
*(compare I Chronicles 20.1-8)*

וַתְּהִי־עוֹד מִלְחָמָה לַפְּלִשְׁתִּים אֶת־יִשְׂרָאֵל וַיֵּרֶד דָּוִד וַעֲבָדָיו עִמּוֹ וַיִּלָּחֲמוּ אֶת־פְּלִשְׁתִּים וַיָּעַף דָּוִד: וְיִשְׁבּוֹ בְּנֹב אֲשֶׁר בִּילִידֵי הָרָפָה וּמִשְׁקַל קֵינוֹ שְׁלֹשׁ מֵאוֹת מִשְׁקַל נְחֹשֶׁת וְהוּא חָגוּר חֲדָשָׁה וַיֹּאמֶר לְהַכּוֹת אֶת־דָּוִד: וַיַּעֲזָר־לוֹ אֲבִישַׁי בֶּן־צְרוּיָה וַיַּךְ אֶת־הַפְּלִשְׁתִּי וַיְמִתֵהוּ אָז נִשְׁבְּעוּ אַנְשֵׁי־דָוִד לוֹ לֵאמֹר לֹא־תֵצֵא עוֹד אִתָּנוּ לַמִּלְחָמָה וְלֹא תְכַבֶּה אֶת־נֵר יִשְׂרָאֵל: וַיְהִי אַחֲרֵי־כֵן וַתְּהִי־עוֹד הַמִּלְחָמָה בְּגוֹב עִם־פְּלִשְׁתִּים אָז הִכָּה סִבְּכַי הַחֻשָׁתִי אֶת־סַף אֲשֶׁר בִּילִדֵי הָרָפָה: וַתְּהִי־עוֹד הַמִּלְחָמָה בְּגוֹב עִם־פְּלִשְׁתִּים וַיַּךְ אֶלְחָנָן בֶּן־יַעְרֵי אֹרְגִים בֵּית הַלַּחְמִי אֵת גָּלְיָת הַגִּתִּי וְעֵץ חֲנִיתוֹ כִּמְנוֹר אֹרְגִים: וַתְּהִי־עוֹד מִלְחָמָה בְּגַת וַיְהִי אִישׁ מָדוֹן וְאֶצְבְּעֹת יָדָיו וְאֶצְבְּעוֹת רַגְלָיו שֵׁשׁ וָשֵׁשׁ עֶשְׂרִים וְאַרְבַּע מִסְפָּר וְגַם־הוּא יֻלַּד לְהָרָפָה: וַיְחָרֵף אֶת־יִשְׂרָאֵל וַיַּכֵּהוּ יְהוֹנָתָן בֶּן־שִׁמְעָי אֲחִי דָוִד: אֶת־אַרְבַּעַת אֵלֶּה יֻלְּדוּ לְהָרָפָה בְּגַת וַיִּפְּלוּ בְיַד־דָּוִד וּבְיַד עֲבָדָיו:

שְׁמוּאֵל ב׳ כא:טו-כב

But the king was adamant in his order to Joab and the army officers; so Joab and the army officers left the king's presence to take a census of the Israelite people. [5]They crossed the Jordan, and after encamping at Aroer, on the right (i.e. south) side of the town that is in the middle of the valley, [they continued on to] Gad and Jazer. [6]They went on to Gilead and to the region of Tahtim-hodshi, and then continued to Dan-jaan and round toward Sidon. [7]They went to the fortress of Tyre and all the Hivite and Canaanite towns, and then proceeded to the Negeb of Judah, at Beer-sheba. [8]Thus they traversed the whole country, and at the end of nine months and twenty days they arrived at Jerusalem.

*II Samuel 24.4-8*

וַיֶּחֱזַק דְּבַר־הַמֶּלֶךְ אֶל־יוֹאָב וְעַל שָׂרֵי הֶחָיִל וַיֵּצֵא יוֹאָב וְשָׂרֵי הַחַיִל לִפְנֵי הַמֶּלֶךְ לִפְקֹד אֶת־הָעָם אֶת־יִשְׂרָאֵל: וַיַּעַבְרוּ אֶת־הַיַּרְדֵּן וַיַּחֲנוּ בַעֲרוֹעֵר יְמִין הָעִיר אֲשֶׁר בְּתוֹךְ־הַנַּחַל הַגָּד וְאֶל־יַעְזֵר: וַיָּבֹאוּ הַגִּלְעָדָה וְאֶל־אֶרֶץ תַּחְתִּים חָדְשִׁי וַיָּבֹאוּ דָּנָה יַּעַן וְסָבִיב אֶל־צִידוֹן: וַיָּבֹאוּ מִבְצַר־צֹר וְכָל־עָרֵי הַחִוִּי וְהַכְּנַעֲנִי וַיֵּצְאוּ אֶל־נֶגֶב יְהוּדָה בְּאֵר שָׁבַע: וַיָּשֻׁטוּ בְּכָל־הָאָרֶץ וַיָּבֹאוּ מִקְצֵה תִשְׁעָה חֳדָשִׁים וְעֶשְׂרִים יוֹם יְרוּשָׁלָ͏ִם:

שְׁמוּאֵל ב׳ כד:ד-ח

*The passage quoted immediately above is far from clear in detail; indeed, the Hebrew text of verses 5-7 simply cannot be translated correctly to make sense as it stands. (Thus it is most dubious that such places as "Tahtim-hodshi" and "Dan-jaan" ever existed, or that* ha-nahal ha-gad *and even* yemin ha-'ir *in v. 5 constitute acceptable Biblical Hebrew.) Yet the passage as a whole makes it amply clear that David's reign witnessed the conquest of much of what had previously been the land empire of Canaan and Egypt.*

Figure of a divine, protecting warrior carved on the inner face of the doorway of the King's Gate at Boghazkoy (ancient Hattusha, capital of the Hittite Empire), Turkey.

Armed with an axe, and with a short sword in his belt, the warrior shakes his fist at any enemy who would dare enter the inner city of the capital. Over 7½ feet high.

## The Setting for International Expansion

The rise of the Israelite empire can be understood properly only in the context of the entire Near East. At the turn of the second millennium not a single state in Mesopotamia, Asia Minor, Syria, and Egypt—the aggressive forces normally active within the historic constellation of which Israel was a part—was powerful enough to interfere with David's plans for expansion. Babylonia had been in decline since the downfall of the Hammurabi dynasty in the sixteenth century B.C.E. The Hurrian state, in northeast Iraq, had been destroyed by Assyria in the thirteenth century. The latter, in turn (except briefly about 1100 under Tiglath-pileser I), was too weak to seek empire and adventure outside its territory until after 900 B.C.E. The Hittites, who had taken over northern Syria and the Hurrian state early in the fourteenth century, and whose power in the entire Near East at the time was equaled only by that of Egypt, collapsed before the onslaught of the Aegean peoples at about 1200 B.C.E.

Egypt's power, too, had waned. The disintegration which had begun during the Twentieth Dynasty, especially after 1150, was not alleviated when the Amon priesthood and their wealthy associates assumed control of the land, about 1100. Except for a brief period under Sheshonk I, the Biblical Shishak (about 925), Egypt was in no position to challenge anyone outside its borders until over four centuries later, when her power revived under Necho of the Twenty-sixth Dynasty. As for the Arameans (Syrians), their ascendancy in upper Transjordan, where they eventually founded a number of city-states, had only just begun.

In the context of this political void which was western Asia about 1000 B.C.E., the Biblical account of the rise of David's empire

*Except for sporadic bursts of energy, which faded almost as quickly as they appeared, Egypt was no longer a nation but was broken into smaller states, which were independent of each other but loosely related by trade relationships. The Twenty-First Dynasty rule was divided by common consent between the merchant princes of Tanis in the Delta and the Heri-Hor dynasty at Thebes, those army commanders who had moved through the high priesthood of Amon into the kingship. This period saw the flowering of a new power, a family of Libyan descent from the Faiyum. Toward the end of the Twentieth Dynasty a Libyan bearing some such outlandish name as Buyuwawa or Beywaw had settled down at Herakleopolis in the Faiyum. The following five generations served as high priests of the local god Harsaphes, but continued to cling proudly to a hereditary title, "Great Chief of the Me," that is, the Meshwesh tribes of western Libyans. Perhaps they had originally been mercenary soldiers, settled upon the land when Egypt withdrew from empire. Around 950 B.C. one of these princes held sway as far south as Abydos and was so powerful that the last king of the Twenty-First Dynasty invited him "to participate in the festivals of his majesty, jointly receiving victory." It was well to be respectful to this Libyan-Egyptian Sheshonk because in a few years he seized the throne of Egypt and started the Twenty-Second Dynasty.*

*The Libyan dynasty had an initial spurt of triumphant energy, marked by a military raid into Palestine, but later lapsed into relative stagnation, punctured by civil war and with increasing local separatism.*

*From John A. Wilson,* The Burden of Egypt *(Chicago, 1951), p. 292*

Table showing how the forms of the Hebrew and Phoenician alphabets relate to each other and to the Greek and Latin-English alphabets.

| Hebrew | Old Hebrew | Phoenician | Early Greek | Later Greek | Latin | English |
|---|---|---|---|---|---|---|
| א | ✦✦✦ | ✦ | A | A | A | A |
| ב | 99 | 9 | ξ 9 | B | B | B |
| ג | ־־ | 1 | ٦ | Γ | C G | C.G |
| ד | ٩ | △ | △ | △ | D | D |
| ה | ヨヨℲ | ヨ | ζ | ε | E | E |
| ו | Υ۷٦٦ | Υ | Υ | Υ | F V | F.V.U |
| ז | 工工工工 | 工 | 工 | 工 | ... | Z |
| ח | BBHB | H | 日 | 日 | H | E.H |
| ט | ⊕ ⊕ | ⊕ | ⊗ | ⊗ | ... | TH.PH |
| י | ₹₹₹₹ | ₹ | ₹ | ₹ | I | I |
| כ | ५५५ | ५ | ⅄ | K | ... | K.KH |
| ל | ՄՄՄՄ | Ⴑ | ✓٦٦ | ┗Λ | L | L |
| מ | ५५५५ | ५ | М | М | M | M |
| נ | ٦٦٦٦ | ٦ | ५ | N | N | N |
| ס | ₹ ₹ | ≢ | ≢ | ≢ | X | X |
| ע | ○ | ○ | ○ | ○ | O | O |
| פ | ١ | ١ | ٦ | Γ | P | P |
| צ | トฦ | ١٦ | ٦ | М | ... | S |
| ק | φ | φ | φ | 9 | Q | Q |
| ר | ٩ 4 | ٩ | ٩ | P | R | R |
| ש | w v | w | ₹ | ₹ | S | S |
| ת | ✕ ✝ | ✕ | ⊤ | ⊤ | T | T |

## Israel and Phoenicia

bears eloquent testimony to the skillful manner in which the Israelites moved to fill the vacuum.

Only against Phoenicia David did not go to battle; to do so was neither necessary nor desirable. The once-great Canaanite civilization had been reduced to a narrow coastal strip running northward from near modern Haifa to beyond Byblos. Here the Phoenician remnant flourished.

The Israelites under David and the Phoenicians under Hiram I entered into a mutually beneficial military and political understanding. The Phoenicians agreed to provide the Israelites with skilled engineers and craftsmen, and with cedar and cypress timber from Lebanon. As a matter of fact they built David a palace (II Samuel 5:11), for which he, in turn, probably paid more in protection and non-aggression than in silver and gold. After all, Phoenicia was, in effect, militarily and economically at the mercy of Israel, and it could hope to retain its independence and increase its wealth only so long as it was useful to Israel's kings.

This situation made it possible, as well as geographically necessary, for the Phoenicians to concentrate on maritime expansion. Within a very brief period they had reached almost every part of the Mediterranean basin —Spain, Sardinia, Corsica, Sicily, and north-central Africa (later Carthage)—with their commercial undertakings, colonial activity, or cultural influence. In fact, Greece and Rome (and through them ultimately a great proportion of the entire world) acquired from the Phoenicians an alphabet in which to record the *Odyssey* and the *Iliad* and the other epics which had come into being, orally perhaps, during the era corresponding to the Biblical Period of the Judges.

King Hiram of Tyre (i.e., Phoenicia) sent envoys to David, with cedar wood, carpenters, and stone-masons, and they built David a palace.

*II Samuel 5.11*

וַיִּשְׁלַח חִירָם מֶלֶךְ־צֹר מַלְאָכִים אֶל־דָּוִד וַעֲצֵי אֲרָזִים וְחָרָשֵׁי עֵץ וְחָרָשֵׁי אֶבֶן קִיר וַיִּבְנוּ־בַיִת לְדָוִד:

שְׁמוּאֵל ב' ה׃יא

At the end of the twenty years during which Solomon built the two buildings, the LORD's House and the royal palace—[11]since King Hiram of Tyre had supplied Solomon with all the cedar and cypress timber and gold that he required—King Solomon, in turn, gave Hiram twenty towns in the region of Galilee. [12]But when Hiram came from Tyre to see the towns which Solomon had given him, he was not pleased with them. [13]"My brother," he said, "what kind of towns have you given me?" So they were named the land of Cabul, as is still the case. [14]However, Hiram sent the king one hundred and twenty talents of gold. [15]This is the account of the forced levy which Solomon imposed for building the House of the LORD, his own palace, the Millo, the wall of Jerusalem, Hazor, Megiddo, and Gezer. ([16]Pharaoh king of Egypt had come up and captured Gezer, and after burning it down and killing the Canaanites who dwelt in the town, had given it as dowry to his daughter, Solomon's wife.) [17]Solomon fortified Gezer, Lower Beth-Horon, [18]Baalath, Tadmor in the wilderness, in the home land, [19]and all the garrison towns of Solomon, the chariot and cavalry towns—everything that Solomon set his heart on building in Jerusalem, in the Lebanon, and throughout the territory of his domain.

*I Kings 9.10-19*

וַיְהִי מִקְצֵה עֶשְׂרִים שָׁנָה אֲשֶׁר־בָּנָה שְׁלֹמֹה אֶת שְׁנֵי הַבָּתִּים אֶת־בֵּית יְהוָה וְאֶת־בֵּית הַמֶּלֶךְ: חִירָם מֶלֶךְ צֹר נִשָּׂא אֶת־שְׁלֹמֹה בַּעֲצֵי אֲרָזִים וּבַעֲצֵי בְרוֹשִׁים וּבַזָּהָב לְכָל־חֶפְצוֹ אָז יִתֵּן הַמֶּלֶךְ שְׁלֹמֹה לְחִירָם עֶשְׂרִים עִיר בְּאֶרֶץ הַגָּלִיל: וַיֵּצֵא חִירָם מִצֹּר לִרְאוֹת אֶת־הֶעָרִים אֲשֶׁר נָתַן־לוֹ שְׁלֹמֹה וְלֹא יָשְׁרוּ בְּעֵינָיו: וַיֹּאמֶר מָה הֶעָרִים הָאֵלֶּה אֲשֶׁר נָתַתָּה לִּי אָחִי וַיִּקְרָא לָהֶם אֶרֶץ כָּבוּל עַד הַיּוֹם הַזֶּה: וַיִּשְׁלַח חִירָם לַמֶּלֶךְ מֵאָה וְעֶשְׂרִים כִּכַּר זָהָב: וְזֶה דְבַר־הַמַּס אֲשֶׁר־הֶעֱלָה הַמֶּלֶךְ שְׁלֹמֹה לִבְנוֹת אֶת־בֵּית יְהוָה וְאֶת־בֵּיתוֹ וְאֶת־הַמִּלּוֹא וְאֵת חוֹמַת יְרוּשָׁלָם וְאֶת־חָצֹר וְאֶת־מְגִדּוֹ וְאֶת־גָּזֶר: פַּרְעֹה מֶלֶךְ־מִצְרַיִם עָלָה וַיִּלְכֹּד אֶת־גֶּזֶר וַיִּשְׂרְפָהּ בָּאֵשׁ וְאֶת־הַכְּנַעֲנִי הַיֹּשֵׁב בָּעִיר הָרָג וַיִּתְּנָהּ שִׁלֻּחִים לְבִתּוֹ אֵשֶׁת שְׁלֹמֹה: וַיִּבֶן שְׁלֹמֹה אֶת־גָּזֶר וְאֶת־בֵּית חֹרֹן תַּחְתּוֹן: וְאֶת־בַּעֲלָת וְאֶת־תַּדְמֹר בַּמִּדְבָּר בָּאָרֶץ: וְאֵת כָּל־עָרֵי הַמִּסְכְּנוֹת אֲשֶׁר הָיוּ לִשְׁלֹמֹה וְאֵת עָרֵי הָרֶכֶב וְאֵת עָרֵי הַפָּרָשִׁים וְאֵת חֵשֶׁק שְׁלֹמֹה אֲשֶׁר חָשַׁק לִבְנוֹת בִּירוּשָׁלַם וּבַלְּבָנוֹן וּבְכֹל אֶרֶץ מֶמְשַׁלְתּוֹ:

מְלָכִים א' ט' י—יט

You shall say to Tyre, that sits at the gateway of the Sea, the merchant of the peoples on many coastlands: Thus said the Lord God,
"O Tyre, you have boasted,
'I am perfect in beauty.'
[4]Your frontiers were on the high seas,
Your builders made you perfect in beauty."

*Ezekiel 27.3-4*

וְאָמַרְתָּ לְצוֹר הַיֹּשֶׁבֶת עַל־מְבוֹאֹת יָם רֹכֶלֶת הָעַמִּים אֶל־אִיִּים רַבִּים כֹּה אָמַר אֲדֹנָי יֱהוִה צוֹר אַתְּ אָמַרְתְּ אֲנִי כְּלִילַת יֹפִי: בְּלֵב יַמִּים גְּבוּלָיִךְ בֹּנַיִךְ כָּלְלוּ יָפְיֵךְ:

יְחֶזְקֵאל כז׃ג—ד

123

Fragment of ivory inlay found at Megiddo showing two major scenes: a prince returning from a successful battle, and a court scene where he sits, receives his queen, and feasts to the accompaniment of music. No specific historical experience can be attached to this particular scene, and what is probably shown is the common, every-day pursuits of a reigning noble during the Late Bronze Age. Length about 10¼ inches.

A bronze cart for wheeling around large vessels. The scene on the side shown here depicts a vignette from court life: a man bringing food or drink in a bowl, and two musicians. (Compare the Megiddo ivory inlay above.) From Cyprus, Early Iron Age (ca. 1000).

124

## The New Administration

Thus within one generation the tribes of Israel came into imperial splendor and created a national capital where none had previously existed. Shifting his headquarters from Hebron in the territory of Judah to newly conquered Jerusalem, David made this the private domain of his royal court. Existing outside all tribal jurisdiction, and belonging solely to the king, it came frequently to be called "The City of David."

The centralization of political authority in the abode of the king called for a corresponding focus for religious jurisdiction, and David's ministers began to plan the erection of a royal chapel, a magnificent edifice which would represent the earthly dwelling of Israel's invisible God. To provide fitting service for the Temple, a priesthood was established and musical guilds were organized, the latter in all likelihood by David, who was a distinguished musician and composer in his own right. Abiathar, who had assisted David at Nob, and Zadok, both of whom boasted ancient and distinguished ancestry, were appointed priests to David. Later the Zadokites, descendants real or nominal of this same Zadok, were to become the principal caste of Temple priests.

The centralization of power in David's hands was implemented further by the creation of new administrative and military systems. The boundaries of a number of tribes were altered on the excuse—plausible enough—of increasing fiscal and administrative efficiency, but more likely for the larger purpose of weakening tribal independence. The new units were to be represented at the court in Jerusalem, not in the traditional manner by the heads of the tribes and families, but by royal officials. And thus the way was paved for the collection of the taxes which were the price of monarchy.

# The New Administration

Solomon became the son-in-law of (or: formed a marriage-alliance with) Pharaoh king of Egypt; he married Pharaoh's daughter and brought her to the City of David, until he had finished building his palace, the House of the LORD, and the wall about Jerusalem.

*I Kings 3.1*

וַיִּתְחַתֵּן שְׁלֹמֹה אֶת־פַּרְעֹה מֶלֶךְ מִצְרָיִם וַיִּקַּח אֶת־בַּת־פַּרְעֹה וַיְבִיאֶהָ אֶל־עִיר דָּוִד עַד כַּלֹּתוֹ לִבְנוֹת אֶת־בֵּיתוֹ וְאֶת־בֵּית יְהֹוָה וְאֶת־חוֹמַת יְרוּשָׁלַם סָבִיב:

מְלָכִים א׳ ג:א

This is the account of his (Jeroboam's) revolt against the king. Solomon had built the Millo, closing up the breach of the City of David his father.

*I Kings 11.27*

וְזֶה הַדָּבָר אֲשֶׁר־הֵרִים יָד בַּמֶּלֶךְ שְׁלֹמֹה בָּנָה אֶת־הַמִּלּוֹא סָגַר אֶת־פֶּרֶץ עִיר דָּוִד אָבִיו:

מְלָכִים א׳ יא:כז

At the Fountain Gate they (Nehemiah and his followers) went up straight ahead by the stairs of the City of David at the ascent of the wall, above the House of David, as far as the Water Gate on the east.

*Nehemiah 12.37*

וְעַל שַׁעַר הָעַיִן וְנֶגְדָּם עָלוּ עַל־מַעֲלוֹת עִיר דָּוִד בַּמַּעֲלֶה לַחוֹמָה מֵעַל לְבֵית דָּוִיד וְעַד שַׁעַר הַמַּיִם מִזְרָח:

נְחֶמְיָה יב:לז

Then the king (David) said to the prophet Nathan, "Look, here I am dwelling in a house of cedar while the Ark of God dwells inside tent-curtains."

*II Samuel 7.2*

וַיֹּאמֶר הַמֶּלֶךְ אֶל־נָתָן הַנָּבִיא רְאֵה נָא אָנֹכִי יוֹשֵׁב בְּבֵית אֲרָזִים וַאֲרוֹן הָאֱלֹהִים יֹשֵׁב בְּתוֹךְ הַיְרִיעָה:

שְׁמוּאֵל ב׳ ז:ב

After this, David defeated the Philistines . . . [2]He defeated Moab . . . and Moab came under the rule of David, subject to tribute. [3]David defeated King Hadadezer, son of Rehob, of Zobah . . . [5]And when the Arameans of Damascus came to the aid of King Hadadezer of Zobah, David defeated the Arameans . . . [6]David appointed governors over the Arameans of Damascus . . . [14]and he appointed governors over Edom . . . [15]So David became king over all Israel; and David administered law and justice to all his people. [16]Joab son of Zeruriah was in command of the army, Jehoshaphat son of Ahilud was recorder, [17]Zadok son of Ahitub and Ahimelech son of Abiathar were priests, Seraiah was secretary, [18]and Benaiah son of Johoiada was [over] the Cherethites and the Pelethites . . .

*II Samuel 8.1-18*

וַיְהִי אַחֲרֵי־כֵן וַיַּךְ דָּוִד אֶת־פְּלִשְׁתִּים . . . וַיַּךְ אֶת־מוֹאָב . . . וַתְּהִי מוֹאָב לְדָוִד לַעֲבָדִים נֹשְׂאֵי מִנְחָה: וַיַּךְ דָּוִד אֶת־הֲדַדְעֶזֶר בֶּן־רְחֹב מֶלֶךְ־צוֹבָה . . . וַתָּבֹא אֲרַם דַּמֶּשֶׂק לַעְזֹר לַהֲדַדְעֶזֶר מֶלֶךְ צוֹבָה וַיַּךְ דָּוִד בַּאֲרָם . . . וַיָּשֶׂם דָּוִד נְצִבִים בַּאֲרַם דַּמֶּשֶׂק . . . וַיָּשֶׂם בֶּאֱדוֹם נְצִבִים . . . וַיִּמְלֹךְ דָּוִד עַל־כָּל־יִשְׂרָאֵל וַיְהִי דָוִד עֹשֶׂה מִשְׁפָּט וּצְדָקָה לְכָל־עַמּוֹ: וְיוֹאָב בֶּן־צְרוּיָה עַל־הַצָּבָא וִיהוֹשָׁפָט בֶּן־אֲחִילוּד מַזְכִּיר: וְצָדוֹק בֶּן־אֲחִיטוּב וַאֲחִימֶלֶךְ בֶּן־אֶבְיָתָר כֹּהֲנִים וּשְׂרָיָה סוֹפֵר: וּבְנָיָהוּ בֶּן־יְהוֹיָדָע וְהַכְּרֵתִי וְהַפְּלֵתִי וּבְנֵי דָוִד כֹּהֲנִים הָיוּ:

שְׁמוּאֵל ב׳ ח:א—יח

Bas-relief orthostat from the palace of King Sennacherib of Assyria (704-681) at Nineveh. This relief is one of a series depicting activities connected with the building of his palace. It portrays the hard labor that foreign workers had to perform as they transported a protective genius (lamassu) [on an adjoining slab] to its position at a doorway of the palace. Height of orthostat about 4 ft. 5 inches.

Commemorative stele for the restoration of Marduk's temple in Babylon by King Ashurbanipal of Assyria (668-627). The king is shown with a basket on his head, symbolizing his participation, at least spiritually—for he probably considered the reconstruction his duty. Height about 14½ inches.

The army was transformed into a permanent professional body, and the command reorganized to centralize control in Jerusalem directly under the king's authority. Abner, the commander-in-chief under Saul and Ishbosheth, was killed, and he was replaced by David's colorful nephew and devoted friend, Joab, one of the most underrated personalities in the Bible.

For the first time in Israelite history, the government introduced forced labor. Every able-bodied resident in Israel was made subject to labor service without compensation. This innovation, in turn, was probably the chief motivation behind the census which David caused to be taken throughout the land.

Imperial consolidation went on apace. Plans were projected for building the Temple and the government palaces in Jerusalem. David recognized the need for fortified sites scattered through the land and for administrative centers such as Megiddo. All of this involved a great building program, which, taken together with the development of the new army, the expansion of administrative services, the reorganization of the royal household, and the like, required unprecedented quantities of money, men, and supervision.

The supervision was provided by the newly created court bureaucracy composed of scribes, heralds, recorders, priest-diviners, ministers, stewards, and clerks, assembled in such numbers that not all of them were Israelites. To find sufficient money and manpower it was necessary to resort to booty and tribute from conquered peoples and to taxation and forced labor at home. This vast program set the stage for David to become the great builder and organizer, as well as the military hero of Israel.

Joab left David and sent messengers after Abner, and they brought him back from the Cistern of Sirah. David knew nothing of this. ²⁷When Abner returned to Hebron, Joab drew him apart inside the gate to speak to him in private, and there stabbed him in the ribs(?); so he died for shedding the blood of his (Joab's) brother Asahel. ²⁸Afterward, when David heard of it he said, "I and my kingdom are forever innocent before the LORD of the bloodshed of Abner son of Ner." . . . ³⁰Thus Joab and his brother Abishai slew Abner because he killed their brother Asahel at the battle of Gibeon.

*II Samuel 3.26-30*

וַיֵּצֵא יוֹאָב מֵעִם דָּוִד וַיִּשְׁלַח מַלְאָכִים אַחֲרֵי
אַבְנֵר וַיָּשִׁבוּ אֹתוֹ מִבּוֹר הַסִּרָה וְדָוִד לֹא יָדָע:
וַיָּשָׁב אַבְנֵר חֶבְרוֹן וַיַּטֵּהוּ יוֹאָב אֶל־תּוֹךְ הַשַּׁעַר
לְדַבֵּר אִתּוֹ בַּשֶּׁלִי וַיַּכֵּהוּ שָׁם הַחֹמֶשׁ וַיָּמָת בְּדַם
עֲשָׂהאֵל אָחִיו: וַיִּשְׁמַע דָּוִד מֵאַחֲרֵי כֵן וַיֹּאמֶר נָקִי
אָנֹכִי וּמַמְלַכְתִּי מֵעִם יְהוָה עַד־עוֹלָם מִדְּמֵי אַבְנֵר
בֶּן־נֵר: . . . וְיוֹאָב וַאֲבִישַׁי אָחִיו הָרְגוּ לְאַבְנֵר עַל
אֲשֶׁר הֵמִית אֶת־עֲשָׂהאֵל אֲחִיהֶם בְּגִבְעוֹן בַּמִּלְחָמָה:

שְׁמוּאֵל ב׳ : ג׳ : כו–ל

He (Samuel) said, "This will be the rule of the king who will reign over you: he will take your sons and assign them to his chariotry and cavalry, and they will become outrunners for his chariots . . . ¹³He will take your daughters as perfumers, cooks, and bakers. ¹⁴He will take your choice fields, vineyards, and olive groves . . . ¹⁶He will take your choice male and female slaves and young men, and your asses . . . ¹⁷He will take a tenth of your flocks and you yourselves shall become his slaves ."

*I Samuel 8.11-17*

וַיֹּאמֶר זֶה יִהְיֶה מִשְׁפַּט הַמֶּלֶךְ אֲשֶׁר יִמְלֹךְ
עֲלֵיכֶם אֶת־בְּנֵיכֶם יִקָּח וְשָׂם לוֹ בְּמֶרְכַּבְתּוֹ וּבְפָרָשָׁיו
וְרָצוּ לִפְנֵי מֶרְכַּבְתּוֹ: . . . וְאֶת־בְּנוֹתֵיכֶם יִקָּח
לְרַקָּחוֹת וּלְטַבָּחוֹת וּלְאֹפוֹת: וְאֶת־שְׂדוֹתֵיכֶם וְאֶת
־כַּרְמֵיכֶם וְזֵיתֵיכֶם הַטּוֹבִים יִקָּח . . . וְאֶת־עַבְדֵיכֶם
וְאֶת־שִׁפְחוֹתֵיכֶם וְאֶת־בַּחוּרֵיכֶם הַטּוֹבִים וְאֶת
חֲמוֹרֵיכֶם יִקָּח . . . צֹאנְכֶם יַעְשֹׂר וְאַתֶּם תִּהְיוּ לוֹ
לַעֲבָדִים:

שְׁמוּאֵל א׳ : ח : א–יז

Again the LORD's anger flared up against Israel, and He incited David against them: "Go, number Israel and Judah." ²Thereupon the king said to Joab, his commander in chief, "Make your way throughout the tribes of Israel, from Dan to Beersheba, and take a census of the people, that I may know the total population." ³But Joab replied to the king, "May the LORD your God increase the number of the people a hundredfold in my lord the king's lifetime (lit. the eyes of my lord the king seeing)—but why does my lord the king insist on this act?"

*II Samuel 24.1-3*

וַיֹּסֶף אַף־יְהוָה לַחֲרוֹת בְּיִשְׂרָאֵל וַיָּסֶת אֶת־
דָּוִד בָּהֶם לֵאמֹר לֵךְ מְנֵה אֶת־יִשְׂרָאֵל וְאֶת־
יְהוּדָה: וַיֹּאמֶר הַמֶּלֶךְ אֶל־יוֹאָב שַׂר־הַחַיִל אֲשֶׁר־
אִתּוֹ שׁוּט־נָא בְּכָל־שִׁבְטֵי יִשְׂרָאֵל מִדָּן וְעַד־בְּאֵר
שֶׁבַע וּפִקְדוּ אֶת־הָעָם וְיָדַעְתִּי אֵת מִסְפַּר הָעָם:
וַיֹּאמֶר יוֹאָב אֶל־הַמֶּלֶךְ וְיוֹסֵף יְהוָה אֱלֹהֶיךָ אֶל־
הָעָם כָּהֵם וְכָהֵם מֵאָה פְעָמִים וְעֵינֵי אֲדֹנִי־
הַמֶּלֶךְ רֹאוֹת וַאדֹנִי הַמֶּלֶךְ לָמָּה חָפֵץ בַּדָּבָר הַזֶּה:

שְׁמוּאֵל ב׳ : כד : א–ג

Let a house be built for Baal like the gods',
And a court like the children of Asherah's!"
Quoth Lady Asherah of the Sea:
"Art great indeed, O El, and wise,
Thy beard's gray hair instructs thee . . .
Now, too, the *seasons* of his rains will Baal *observe*,
The *seasons* of . . . with *snow*;
And [he will] peal his thunder in the clouds,
Flashing his lightnings to the earth.
The house of cedar—*let him burn it*;
Yea, the house of brick—*remove it*.
Be it told to Puissant Baal:
Summon *weeds* into thy house,
*Herbs* into the midst of thy palace.
The mountains shall bring thee much silver,
The hills a treasure of gold;
They'll bring thee *god's grandeur aplenty.*
So build thou a silver and gold house,
A house of most pure lapis lazuli."

The Maiden Anath rejoices,
*Stamps* with her foot so the earth *quakes*.
There, she is off on her way
Unto Baal upon Zaphon's summit,
O'er a thousand fields, ten thousand acres.
Laughing, the Maiden Anath
Lifts up her voice and cries:
"Receive, Baal, the glad tidings I bring thee.
They will build thee a house like thy brethren's
And a court like unto they kindred's.
Summon *weeds* into thy house,
*Herbs* into the midst of thy palace.
The mountains shall bring thee much silver,
The hills a treasure of gold;
They'll bring thee *god's grandeur aplenty.*
So build thou a silver and gold house,
A house of most pure lapis lazuli."

Puissant Baal rejoiced.
He summoned *weeds* into his house,
*Herbs* into the midst of his palace.
The mountains did bring him much silver,
The hills a treasure of gold;
They brought him *god's grandeur aplenty.*
Then he [se]nt unto Kothar wa-Khasis.
(Direction to the reciter):
Now turn to the account of the sending of the lads.

Before he could put all these magnificent plans into action, however, David died, so that his actual building was limited to the fortification of a few key sites against the Philistines, such as Tell Beit Mirsim (perhaps Biblical Kiriat-sepher) in the southern Shefelah, Beth-shemesh in the northern Shefelah, and Tell Qasileh (inside modern Tel Aviv) near the Mediterranean Sea, and to the erection of royal buildings in Jerusalem and perhaps also in Megiddo.

## King David, the Personality

The Biblical tradition attributes to David many qualities, but none more endearing, perhaps, than his gift for poetry and music. In all probability he must have composed at least some parts of the psalms which the Bible attributes to him, in addition to the famous lament over Saul and Jonathan (II Samuel 1:17–27). David's reputation was so great, however, that many psalms composed either before or after his reign came to be associated with his name. Indeed, the official collection of the first 72 psalms—though not the entire book of 150 psalms, as popular belief has since assumed—was attached to his name.

David's loves and hates have gripped the emotions and imaginations of people from his day down through the ages. Most famous of all, perhaps, was his deep affection for Jonathan, but the mere mention of David conjures up the names of Absalom, of Abigail, and the beautiful Bath-sheba. In each of these stories, kingly grandeur is blended with human weakness in a way that has touched and captivated each succeeding generation of readers.

On one of the rare occasions when a significant portion of the population sided with an armed revolt against David's rule, there was among the leaders David's favorite son,

# King David, the Personality

David uttered this lament over Saul and his son Jonathan; [18]. . . it is recorded in the Book of Jashar.

[19]O glory of Israel
Slain in your heights;
How your heroes have fallen!
[20]Tell not in Gath,
Do not announce in Ashkelon's squares,
Or the daughters of the Philistines will rejoice,
The daughters of the uncircumcised will exult.
[21]O mountains of Gilboa,
Let no dew or rain (fall) upon you . . .
For there the shield of warriors was dishonored,
The shield of Saul,
No more anointed with oil.
[22]From the blood of the slain,
From the fat of the warriors,
Jonathan's bow never fell back
And Saul's sword never returned empty.
[23]Saul and Jonathan, beloved and lovely,
In life and in death never divided;
Swifter than eagles, stronger than lions.
[24]Daughters of Israel, weep for Saul
Who clothed you in finery of purple,
Adorned your robes with jewels of gold.
[25]How the heroes have fallen in battle,
Jonathan slain on your heights!
[26]I grieve for you, O my brother Jonathan;
You were very dear to me,
Your love more wonderful to me
Than the love of women.
[27]How the heroes have fallen,
The weapons of war stilled!

*II Samuel 1.17-27*

When he (David) had finished speaking to Saul, Jonathan became deeply attached to David; Jonathan loved him as himself . . . [3]And Jonathan and David made a pact, for he loved him as himself.

*I Samuel 18.1-3*

Absalom said to Joab, ". . . Come, let me confront the king, and if there be any wrong in me let him put me to death." [33]Joab went to the king and reported this to him. He summoned Absalom who came to the king and bowed low with his face to the ground before the king; and the king kissed Absalom.

*II Samuel 14.32-33*

וַיְקֹנֵן דָּוִד אֶת־הַקִּינָה הַזֹּאת עַל־שָׁאוּל וְעַל־יְהוֹנָתָן בְּנוֹ: וַיֹּאמֶר לְלַמֵּד בְּנֵי־יְהוּדָה קָשֶׁת הִנֵּה כְתוּבָה עַל־סֵפֶר הַיָּשָׁר: הַצְּבִי יִשְׂרָאֵל עַל־בָּמוֹתֶיךָ חָלָל אֵיךְ נָפְלוּ גִבּוֹרִים: אַל־תַּגִּידוּ בְגַת אַל־תְּבַשְּׂרוּ בְּחוּצֹת אַשְׁקְלוֹן פֶּן־תִּשְׂמַחְנָה בְּנוֹת פְּלִשְׁתִּים פֶּן־תַּעֲלֹזְנָה בְּנוֹת הָעֲרֵלִים: הָרֵי בַגִּלְבֹּעַ אַל־טַל וְאַל־מָטָר עֲלֵיכֶם וּשְׂדֵי תְרוּמֹת כִּי שָׁם נִגְעַל מָגֵן גִּבּוֹרִים מָגֵן שָׁאוּל בְּלִי מָשִׁיחַ בַּשָּׁמֶן: מִדַּם חֲלָלִים מֵחֵלֶב גִּבּוֹרִים קֶשֶׁת יְהוֹנָתָן לֹא נָשׂוֹג אָחוֹר וְחֶרֶב שָׁאוּל לֹא תָשׁוּב רֵיקָם: שָׁאוּל וִיהוֹנָתָן הַנֶּאֱהָבִים וְהַנְּעִימִם בְּחַיֵּיהֶם וּבְמוֹתָם לֹא נִפְרָדוּ מִנְּשָׁרִים קַלּוּ מֵאֲרָיוֹת גָּבֵרוּ: בְּנוֹת יִשְׂרָאֵל אֶל־שָׁאוּל בְּכֶינָה הַמַּלְבִּשְׁכֶם שָׁנִי עִם־עֲדָנִים הַמַּעֲלֶה עֲדִי זָהָב עַל לְבוּשְׁכֶן: אֵיךְ נָפְלוּ גִבֹּרִים בְּתוֹךְ הַמִּלְחָמָה יְהוֹנָתָן עַל־בָּמוֹתֶיךָ חָלָל: צַר־לִי עָלֶיךָ אָחִי יְהוֹנָתָן נָעַמְתָּ לִּי מְאֹד נִפְלְאַתָה אַהֲבָתְךָ לִי מֵאַהֲבַת נָשִׁים: אֵיךְ נָפְלוּ גִבּוֹרִים וַיֹּאבְדוּ כְּלֵי מִלְחָמָה:

שְׁמוּאֵל ב' א:יז–כז

וַיְהִי כְּכַלֹּתוֹ לְדַבֵּר אֶל־שָׁאוּל וְנֶפֶשׁ יְהוֹנָתָן נִקְשְׁרָה בְּנֶפֶשׁ דָּוִד וַיֶּאֱהָבֵהוּ יְהוֹנָתָן כְּנַפְשׁוֹ: . . . וַיִּכְרֹת יְהוֹנָתָן וְדָוִד בְּרִית בְּאַהֲבָתוֹ אֹתוֹ כְּנַפְשׁוֹ:

שְׁמוּאֵל א' יח: א–ג

וְעַתָּה . . . וַיֹּאמֶר אַבְשָׁלוֹם אֶל־יוֹאָב אֶרְאֶה פְּנֵי הַמֶּלֶךְ וְאִם־יֶשׁ־בִּי עָוֹן וֶהֱמִתָנִי: וַיָּבֹא יוֹאָב אֶל־הַמֶּלֶךְ וַיַּגֶּד־לוֹ וַיִּקְרָא אֶל־אַבְשָׁלוֹם וַיָּבֹא אֶל־הַמֶּלֶךְ וַיִּשְׁתַּחוּ לוֹ עַל־אַפָּיו אַרְצָה לִפְנֵי הַמֶּלֶךְ וַיִּשַּׁק הַמֶּלֶךְ לְאַבְשָׁלוֹם:

שְׁמוּאֵל ב' יד: לב–לג

129

**Quotations from the poetic imagery of Canaan and Egypt reminiscent of Hebrew psalms.**

**From the Baal Epic in the Ugaritic Language (composed ca. 18th cent.).**

I tell you, O Prince Baal,
I declare, O Rider of the Clouds:
Now your enemy, O Baal,
Now your enemy will you strike down,
Now will you cut off your adversary.
You shall possess your eternal kingdom,
Your everlasting dominion.

**The Aton Hymn, period of Ikhnaton (18th Dynasty, ca. 1370).**

When you set in the western horizon,
The land is in darkness like death . . .
Every lion comes forth from his den . . .

At daybreak, when you arise in the horizon . . .
You drive away the darkness . . .
Men awake and stand upon their feet . . .
All the world, they do their labor.

How manifold are your works!
They are hidden from man's sight.
O sole god, like whom there is no other,
You have made the earth according to your desire.

**Psalm 104**

¹ Bless the Lord, O my soul.
O Lord my God, You are great indeed,
Clothed in majesty and splendor . . .
¹⁰ You who set springs gushing in the wadis,
They run between the hills;
¹¹ They provide drink for all wild beasts,
The wild asses quench their thirst . . .
¹⁹ You make the moon to mark the seasons.
The sun knows its place of setting.
²⁰ You make the darkness, and it is night,
When all the wild animals creep forth;
²¹ The lions roar for prey,
They claim their food from God.
²² When the sun rises, they slink away
And lie down in their lairs;
²³ But man goes forth to his tasks,
And to his labors until the evening . . .

the charming but vacillating Absalom. Out-witted and outfought by David's well-trained militia, the rebels were defeated, although not yet crushed, when the implacable Joab brought the whole revolt to its final dénouement by killing Absalom with his own hands. It was altogether characteristic of David's ofttimes unpredictable mood that he did not want any harm to come to his rebellious son and that when he heard the tragic news, "He was much moved, and went up to the chamber over the gate, and wept; and as he went, thus he said, 'O my son Absalom, my son, my son Absalom! would that I died for you, O Absalom, my son, my son!'" (II Samuel 19:1).

On those other famous occasions when he was unable to repress his passion for Abigail, whose husband he did not attempt to save from death, or for Bath-sheba, whose husband he brutally caused to be killed, David nevertheless was genuinely repentant for having caused the death of his rivals in love, and humbly accepted the bitter rebuke of Nathan the prophet. It would be difficult to find another such intense, compulsive, dramatic, practical, talented personality in the wide range of human history, or so simple and powerful a delineation of character in all our literature.

To the Israelites after him, David was the key figure in the Golden Era of their history, a figure beyond reproach and beyond compare. After all, it was not he but his son and successor, Solomon, who carried out his projects to their ultimate, and frequently distasteful, conclusions. David fully deserved his place of honor in his people's history but, at the same time, it was largely a matter of good fortune that his good lived after him, whereas his evil was interred with Solomon's bones.

130

*See now M. A. Cohen's fine analysis of "The Rebellions During the Reign of David: An Inquiry into Social Dynamics of Ancient Israel"* (in Studies in Jewish Bibliography, History, and Literature in Honor of I. Edward Kiev, ed. C. Berlin [KTAV, 1971], 91–112).

The king was deeply moved. He wept as he went up to the chamber above the gate, crying as he went, "O my son Absalom, my son, my son Absalom! Would that I had died for you. O Absalom, my son, my son!" [2]Joab was told that the king was weeping and in mourning for Absalom. [3]So the victory that day turned to mourning for all the troops, for the troops heard that day: "The king is grieving for his son."

*II Samuel 19.1-3*

וַיִּרְגַּז הַמֶּלֶךְ וַיַּעַל עַל־עֲלִיַּת הַשַּׁעַר וַיֵּבְךְּ
וְכֹה אָמַר בְּלֶכְתּוֹ בְּנִי אַבְשָׁלוֹם בְּנִי בְנִי אַבְשָׁלוֹם
מִי־יִתֵּן מוּתִי אֲנִי תַחְתֶּיךָ אַבְשָׁלוֹם בְּנִי בְנִי:
וַיֻּגַּד לְיוֹאָב הִנֵּה הַמֶּלֶךְ בֹּכֶה וַיִּתְאַבֵּל עַל־
אַבְשָׁלֹם: וַתְּהִי הַתְּשֻׁעָה בַּיּוֹם הַהוּא לְאֵבֶל
לְכָל־הָעָם כִּי־שָׁמַע הָעָם בַּיּוֹם הַהוּא לֵאמֹר
נֶעֱצַב הַמֶּלֶךְ עַל־בְּנוֹ:

שְׁמוּאֵל ב׳ יט:א־ג

David's servants went to Abigail at Carmel and said to her, "David has sent us to you to bring you to him as his wife."

*I Samuel 25.40*

וַיָּבֹאוּ עַבְדֵי דָוִד אֶל־אֲבִיגַיִל הַכַּרְמֶלָה וַיְדַבְּרוּ
אֵלֶיהָ לֵאמֹר דָּוִד שְׁלָחָנוּ אֵלַיִךְ לְקַחְתֵּךְ לוֹ לְאִשָּׁה:

שְׁמוּאֵל א׳ כה: מ

When the period of mourning (of Bathsheba for her husband Uriah) was over, David had her brought to his house; she became his wife and bore him a son. But David's act displeased the LORD.

*II Samuel 11.27*

וַיַּעֲבֹר הָאֵבֶל וַיִּשְׁלַח דָּוִד וַיַּאַסְפָהּ אֶל־בֵּיתוֹ
וַתְּהִי־לוֹ לְאִשָּׁה וַתֵּלֶד לוֹ בֵּן וַיֵּרַע הַדָּבָר אֲשֶׁר
עָשָׂה דָוִד בְּעֵינֵי יְהוָה:

שְׁמוּאֵל ב׳ יא: כז

The LORD sent Nathan to David. He came to him and said to him, "There were two men in a town, one was rich and the other poor. [2]The rich man had very many sheep and cattle, [3]but the poor man had nothing but a little ewe lamb which he had bought. He raised it, and it grew up together with him and his children, eating his bread and drinking from his cup and nestling in his bosom; it was like a daughter to him. [4]A traveler once came to the rich man, who out of pity did not take one of his own flock or herds to prepare a meal for the wayfarer who had come to him, but took instead the poor man's lamb and prepared it for the man who had come to him. [5]David's anger flared up against the man. "As the LORD lives," he cried out to Nathan, "the man who did this deserves to die; [6]and he must pay fourfold for the lamb, because he committed this act, and showed no pity!" [7]"You are the man!" Nathan replied to David . . .

*II Samuel 12.1-7*

וַיִּשְׁלַח יְהוָה אֶת־נָתָן אֶל־דָּוִד וַיָּבֹא אֵלָיו
וַיֹּאמֶר לוֹ שְׁנֵי אֲנָשִׁים הָיוּ בְּעִיר אֶחָת אֶחָד עָשִׁיר
וְאֶחָד רָאשׁ: לֶעָשִׁיר הָיָה צֹאן וּבָקָר הַרְבֵּה מְאֹד:
וְלָרָשׁ אֵין־כֹּל כִּי אִם־כִּבְשָׂה אַחַת קְטַנָּה אֲשֶׁר
קָנָה וַיְחַיֶּהָ וַתִּגְדַּל עִמּוֹ וְעִם־בָּנָיו יַחְדָּו מִפִּתּוֹ
תֹאכַל וּמִכֹּסוֹ תִשְׁתֶּה וּבְחֵיקוֹ תִשְׁכָּב וַתְּהִי־לוֹ
כְּבַת: וַיָּבֹא הֵלֶךְ לְאִישׁ הֶעָשִׁיר וַיַּחְמֹל לָקַחַת
מִצֹּאנוֹ וּמִבְּקָרוֹ לַעֲשׂוֹת לָאֹרֵחַ הַבָּא לוֹ וַיִּקַּח
אֶת־כִּבְשַׂת הָאִישׁ הָרָאשׁ וַיַּעֲשֶׂהָ לָאִישׁ הַבָּא אֵלָיו:
וַיִּחַר־אַף דָּוִד בָּאִישׁ מְאֹד וַיֹּאמֶר אֶל־נָתָן חַי־
יְהוָה כִּי בֶן־מָוֶת הָאִישׁ הָעֹשֶׂה זֹאת: וְאֶת־הַכִּבְשָׂה
יְשַׁלֵּם אַרְבַּעְתָּיִם עֵקֶב אֲשֶׁר עָשָׂה אֶת־הַדָּבָר
הַזֶּה וְעַל אֲשֶׁר לֹא־חָמָל: וַיֹּאמֶר נָתָן אֶל־דָּוִד
אַתָּה הָאִישׁ...

שְׁמוּאֵל ב׳ יב:א־ז

Model of the 10th and 9th cent. sanctuary discovered at Tell Arad. The plan is similar to the description of Solomon's Temple, with its main features: an open court, a porticoed entrance, a hall, and a holy of holies. Note the altar in the courtyard.

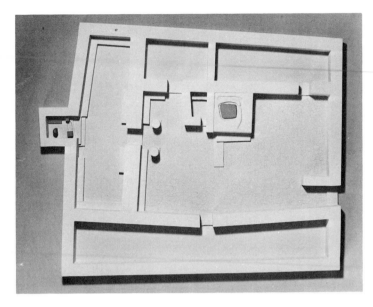

The holy of holies at Arad, raised above the level of the rest of the sanctuary, with two incense altars at the top of the stairs and a pillar.

## King Solomon

When David's end drew near, there was another contest for the royal succession, just as there had been at the death of Saul. In this characteristic the history of Israel is no different from that of any other comparable kingdoms in Assyria, Babylonia, or Egypt. The penalty for coming out second best in such a power struggle, normally, was death. So it was with Adonijah, the oldest son of David, who had prior claim over his half-brother, Solomon. Adonijah, indeed, had already been proclaimed king by his followers, including the redoubtable Joab, when Solomon's backers began a counterattack. Bath-sheba, David's favorite wife and Solomon's mother, joined with the prophet Nathan to persuade the aged king to name Solomon his legal heir. Bath-sheba pointed out that if Adonijah had his way she and her son would be as good as dead.

David let himself be swayed, and gave the decisive order: "Let Zadok the priest and Nathan the prophet anoint him . . . king over Israel; and sound the ram's horn, and shout 'Long live King Solomon!'" (I Kings 1:34). Adonijah's followers deserted him, and Solomon later found a pretext for killing Adonijah. Other supporters of Adonijah were likewise killed or banished, until "the kingship was established firmly in the hand of Solomon" (I Kings 2:46; I Chronicles 29).

## Solomon's Building Program: The Temple

Solomon inherited the task of fulfilling the plans that time and circumstances had permitted his father David only to formulate and dream about; and to this program he added plans and dreams of his own. Continuing and extending the pact with Phoenicia, Solomon imported vast amounts of timber from Lebanon and recruited large

# King Solomon

The king gave an order to Benaiah son of Jehoiada, and he went out and struck him (Shimei) down, and he died. So the kingdom was secured in Solomon's hand.

*I Kings 2.46*

וַיְצַו הַמֶּלֶךְ אֶת־בְּנָיָהוּ בֶן־יְהוֹיָדָע וַיֵּצֵא וַיִּפְגַּע־בּוֹ וַיָּמֹת וְהַמַּמְלָכָה נָכוֹנָה בְּיַד שְׁלֹמֹה:

מְלָכִים א׳ ב:מו

---

[32]King David said, ". . . [33]mount my son Solomon on my mule and bring him down to Gihon. [34]Let the priest Zadok and the prophet Nathan anoint him there king over Israel. Then sound the ram's horn and shout, 'Long live King Solomon!'"

*I Kings 1.32-34*

וַיֹּאמֶר הַמֶּלֶךְ דָּוִד... וְהִרְכַּבְתֶּם אֶת־שְׁלֹמֹה בְנִי עַל־הַפִּרְדָּה אֲשֶׁר־לִי וְהוֹרַדְתֶּם אֹתוֹ אֶל־גִּחוֹן: וּמָשַׁח אֹתוֹ שָׁם צָדוֹק הַכֹּהֵן וְנָתָן הַנָּבִיא לְמֶלֶךְ עַל־יִשְׂרָאֵל וּתְקַעְתֶּם בַּשּׁוֹפָר וַאֲמַרְתֶּם יְחִי הַמֶּלֶךְ שְׁלֹמֹה:

מְלָכִים א׳, א: לב–לד

---

Adonijah and all the guests who were with him, who had just finished eating, heard it. When Joab heard the sound of the ram's horn, he asked, "Why is the city in an uproar?" [42]While he was still speaking, the priest Jonathan son of Abiathar arrived. "Come in," said Adonijah, "you are a worthy man and you surely bring good news." [43]But Jonathan replied to Adonijah, "To the contrary, our lord King David has made Solomon king. [44]The king sent with him the priest Zadok, the prophet Nathan, Benaiah son of Jehoiada, and the Cherethites and Pelethites. They mounted him on the king's mule [45]and the priest Zadok and the prophet Nathan have anointed him king at Gihon. They have come up from there rejoicing and the city is in an uproar, That is the noise that you have heard. [46]Moreover, Solomon is seated on the royal throne . . ." [49]Thereupon all of Adonijah's guests rose in terror and each went his own way. [50]Adonijah himself, in fear of Solomon, ran off at once and grasped the horns of the altar. [51]Solomon was informed as follows, "Adonijah is in fear of King Solomon, and he has grasped the horns of the altar, saying, 'Let King Solomon first swear to me that he will not slay his servant with the sword.'"

*I Kings 1.41-51*

וַיִּשְׁמַע אֲדֹנִיָּהוּ וְכָל־הַקְּרֻאִים אֲשֶׁר אִתּוֹ וְהֵם כִּלּוּ לֶאֱכֹל וַיִּשְׁמַע יוֹאָב אֶת־קוֹל הַשּׁוֹפָר וַיֹּאמֶר מַדּוּעַ קוֹל־הַקִּרְיָה הוֹמָה: עוֹדֶנּוּ מְדַבֵּר וְהִנֵּה יוֹנָתָן בֶּן־אֶבְיָתָר הַכֹּהֵן בָּא וַיֹּאמֶר אֲדֹנִיָּהוּ בֹּא כִּי אִישׁ חַיִל אַתָּה וְטוֹב תְּבַשֵּׂר: וַיַּעַן יוֹנָתָן וַיֹּאמֶר לַאֲדֹנִיָּהוּ אֲבָל אֲדֹנֵינוּ הַמֶּלֶךְ־דָּוִד הִמְלִיךְ אֶת־שְׁלֹמֹה: וַיִּשְׁלַח אִתּוֹ הַמֶּלֶךְ אֶת־צָדוֹק הַכֹּהֵן וְאֶת־נָתָן הַנָּבִיא וּבְנָיָהוּ בֶּן־יְהוֹיָדָע וְהַכְּרֵתִי וְהַפְּלֵתִי וַיַּרְכִּבוּ אֹתוֹ עַל פִּרְדַּת הַמֶּלֶךְ: וַיִּמְשְׁחוּ אֹתוֹ צָדוֹק הַכֹּהֵן וְנָתָן הַנָּבִיא לְמֶלֶךְ בְּגִחוֹן וַיַּעֲלוּ מִשָּׁם שְׂמֵחִים וַתֵּהֹם הַקִּרְיָה הוּא הַקּוֹל אֲשֶׁר שְׁמַעְתֶּם: וְגַם יָשַׁב שְׁלֹמֹה עַל כִּסֵּא הַמְּלוּכָה: ... וַיֶּחֶרְדוּ וַיָּקֻמוּ כָּל־הַקְּרֻאִים אֲשֶׁר לַאֲדֹנִיָּהוּ וַיֵּלְכוּ אִישׁ לְדַרְכּוֹ: וַאֲדֹנִיָּהוּ יָרֵא מִפְּנֵי שְׁלֹמֹה וַיָּקָם וַיֵּלֶךְ וַיַּחֲזֵק בְּקַרְנוֹת הַמִּזְבֵּחַ: וַיֻּגַּד לִשְׁלֹמֹה לֵאמֹר הִנֵּה אֲדֹנִיָּהוּ יָרֵא אֶת־הַמֶּלֶךְ שְׁלֹמֹה וְהִנֵּה אָחַז בְּקַרְנוֹת הַמִּזְבֵּחַ לֵאמֹר יִשָּׁבַע־לִי כַיּוֹם הַמֶּלֶךְ שְׁלֹמֹה אִם־יָמִית אֶת־עַבְדּוֹ בֶּחָרֶב:

מְלָכִים א׳–א–מ:א–נא

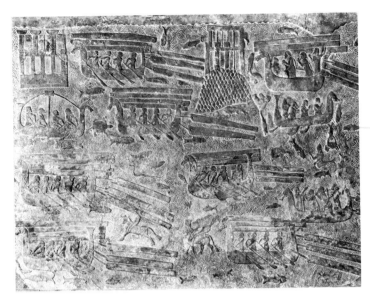

numbers of engineers, overseers, and artisans for the building of the Temple.

Solomon is best remembered for his Temple. In becoming the national shrine, as David had intended that it should, the Temple completed the process of making Jerusalem the spiritual as well as the political capital of Israel; but its cost was tremendous. To finish the magnificent edifice, Solomon was obliged to levy taxes without mercy, to force tens of thousands of his subjects to serve in labor gangs, to chop cedar and cypress in Lebanon, to raft timber from Phoenicia to Joppa, and to bear it log by log to the heights of Jerusalem.

The complex of the Temple and its associated buildings formed a magnificent architectural unit. Built by Canaanite architects, it followed the style of their native temple tradition. The two free-standing columns called Jachin and Boaz (I Kings 7:21), and the three main divisions of vestibule, holy place, and holy of holies, all sprang from the Canaanite convention. Their respective Hebrew names, *ulam, hekhal,* and *debir*—likewise the term *bayit* (house) for the whole Temple, which was "The House of the Lord" —also appear to have been borrowed from the Canaanites.

Solomon's regime was further distinguished by the erection of government buildings, and the building or rebuilding of key fortifications. It is a frequent archaeological experience to uncover the material remains of the Solomonic (Early Iron) level of Israelite towns—for example, at Megiddo, Gezer, Tell Qasileh, Ezion-geber, Hazor, and Lachish. Like the Temple, these structures were generally Phoenician in concept and in such details as the pattern of masonry, the use of capitals (which the Greeks also borrowed from the Phoenicians a couple of centuries later), and the style of gateways. A note-

Details of two scenes from bas-reliefs, from the palace of King Sargon II of Assyria (721-705) at Dur-Sharrukin (modern Khorsabad), depicting the transportation of timber along the Mediterranean coast and then the unloading.

## Solomon's Building Program: The Temple

King Solomon imposed forced labor (corvée) on all Israel; the levy came to 30,000 men. [28]He sent them to the Lebanon in shifts of 10,000 a month: they spent one month in the Lebanon and two months at home. Adoniram was in charge of the corvée. [29]Solomon also had 70,000 porters and 80,000 quarriers in the hills, [30]apart from Solomon's 3,300 officials who were in charge of the work and supervised the gangs engaged in the work.

*I Kings 5.27-30*

וַיַּעַל הַמֶּלֶךְ שְׁלֹמֹה מַס מִכָּל־יִשְׂרָאֵל וַיְהִי הַמַּס שְׁלֹשִׁים אֶלֶף אִישׁ: וַיִּשְׁלָחֵם לְבָנוֹנָה עֲשֶׂרֶת אֲלָפִים בַּחֹדֶשׁ חֲלִיפוֹת חֹדֶשׁ יִהְיוּ בַלְּבָנוֹן שְׁנַיִם חֳדָשִׁים בְּבֵיתוֹ וַאֲדֹנִירָם עַל־הַמַּס: וַיְהִי לִשְׁלֹמֹה שִׁבְעִים אֶלֶף נֹשֵׂא סַבָּל וּשְׁמֹנִים אֶלֶף חֹצֵב בָּהָר: לְבַד מִשָּׂרֵי הַנִּצָּבִים לִשְׁלֹמֹה אֲשֶׁר עַל־הַמְּלָאכָה שְׁלֹשֶׁת אֲלָפִים וּשְׁלֹשׁ מֵאוֹת הָרֹדִים בָּעָם הָעֹשִׂים בַּמְּלָאכָה:

מְלָכִים א' ה: כז-ל

So Solomon completed the construction of the House. [15]He constructed the walls of the House on the inside with planks of cedar, and overlaid the inside with wood from the floor of the House to where the walls [touched] the ceiling; and he overlaid the floor of the House with planks of cypress. [16]The twenty cubits from the rear of the House he constructed with planks of cedar from the floor to the walls; and he built its interior as a shrine, as the Holy of Holies. [17]The House, that is the Temple, measured forty cubits along the front part . . . [19]He prepared a shrine in the innermost part of the House in which to place the Ark of the Covenant of the LORD . . . [23]In the shrine he made two cherubim of olive wood, each ten cubits high. [24]Each of the two wings of one cherub was five cubits across . . .

*I Kings 6.14-24*

וַיִּבֶן שְׁלֹמֹה אֶת־הַבַּיִת וַיְכַלֵּהוּ: וַיִּבֶן אֶת־קִירוֹת הַבַּיִת מִבַּיְתָה בְּצַלְעוֹת אֲרָזִים מִקַּרְקַע הַבַּיִת עַד קִירוֹת הַסִּפֻּן צִפָּה עֵץ מִבַּיִת וַיְצַף אֶת־קַרְקַע הַבַּיִת בְּצַלְעוֹת בְּרוֹשִׁים: וַיִּבֶן אֶת־עֶשְׂרִים אַמָּה מִיַּרְכְּתֵי הַבַּיִת בְּצַלְעוֹת אֲרָזִים מִן־הַקַּרְקַע עַד־הַקִּירוֹת וַיִּבֶן לוֹ מִבַּיִת לִדְבִיר לְקֹדֶשׁ הַקֳּדָשִׁים: וְאַרְבָּעִים בָּאַמָּה הָיָה הַבָּיִת הוּא הַהֵיכָל לִפְנָי: . . . וּדְבִיר בְּתוֹךְ־הַבַּיִת מִפְּנִימָה הֵכִין לְתִתֶּן שָׁם אֶת־אֲרוֹן בְּרִית יְהוָה: . . . וַיַּעַשׂ בַּדְּבִיר שְׁנֵי כְרוּבִים עֲצֵי־שֶׁמֶן עֶשֶׂר אַמּוֹת קוֹמָתוֹ: וְחָמֵשׁ אַמּוֹת כְּנַף הַכְּרוּב הָאֶחָת . . .

מְלָכִים א' ו: יד-כד

He set up the columns at the porch of the great hall; he set up one column on the right and named it Jachin, and he set up the other column on the left and called it Boaz. [22]Upon the top of the columns there was a (capital of) lily design . . .

*I Kings 7.21-22*

וַיָּקֶם אֶת־הָעַמֻּדִים לְאֻלָם הַהֵיכָל וַיָּקֶם אֶת־הָעַמּוּד הַיְמָנִי וַיִּקְרָא אֶת־שְׁמוֹ יָכִין וַיָּקֶם אֶת־הָעַמּוּד הַשְּׂמָאלִי וַיִּקְרָא אֶת־שְׁמוֹ בֹּעַז: וְעַל רֹאשׁ הָעַמּוּדִים מַעֲשֵׂה שׁוֹשָׁן . . .

מְלָכִים א' ז: כא-כב

*From the considerable archaeological material now available, it is possible to understand that the two columns did not have the function of supporting any roof or structure, and that the names probably constituted the first words of an inscription on the columns, perhaps something like "May He (God) establish the House of David" (cf. I Kings 2.24) for Jachin, and "In the strength (of God) may the House of David rejoice" (cf. Psalm 21.2) for Boaz. (See R. B. Y. Scott's article on "Jachin and Boaz" in Interpreter's Dictionary of the Bible, vol. II, pp. 780-81, with its references to the earlier articles by W. F. Albright and H. G. May in Bulletin of the American Schools of Oriental Research, Nos. 85 and 88, both in 1942.)*

Aerial view of the excavation of Ezion-geber (Tell el-Kheleifeh) on the Gulf of Aqabah.

The so-called "Solomon's Pillars" near Timna, in the immediate vicinity of the open-pit copper refining plant of the Israelite period.

136

worthy achievement was the water-tunnel constructed at Megiddo.

## Solomon the Merchant Prince: Ezion-geber

Of particular interest is the famous copper refinery and seaport at Ezion-geber, on the Gulf of Aqabah, rediscovered in the 1930's, about a third of a mile north of the present coastline. Although the site of the port had long been sought by scholars and travelers, no one was prepared for the discovery of the extraordinary structure built specifically to smelt the copper ore which was dug from the mines of near-by Sinai and Edom. Its excavator called Ezion-geber "the Pittsburgh of Palestine, in addition to being its most important port," and described Solomon "as a great copper king." Ezion-geber, like the corresponding levels from the period of Solomon at Megiddo and Tell Qasileh, "was planned in advance, and built with considerable architectural and engineering skill at one time as an integral whole."

Solomon's great enterprise at Ezion-geber, with its seaport and fleet of merchant ships, would seem to clarify an intriguing Biblical problem of long standing. It has often been asked: Did the Queen of Sheba really visit Solomon, and if so, why should she, a woman, have made the arduous and even dangerous trip of some 1,300 miles from her country in southwest Arabia to Jerusalem, bringing with her gifts of fabulous worth? The Bible explains: "Now when the Queen of Sheba heard of the fame of Solomon . . ." She came to test him with hard questions . . ." (I Kings 10:1–13). This explanation is clearly diplomatic. The "hard questions" very likely revolved about matters of the pocketbook. Our authority on Ezion-geber points out:

Solomon's shipping line evidently made such inroads in the lucrative caravan trade controlled by the Queen of Sheba, that she hastened to Jerusalem

The one tank (traditional "sea") with the twelve oxen underneath the tank, [45]the pails, the scrapers, and the sprinkling bowls—all these vessels in the House of the Lord which Hiram made for King Solomon were of burnished copper. [46]The king had them cast in the plain of the Jordan in earthen molds (lit. "in the thick of the earth"), between Succoth and Zarethan. [47]Solomon left all the vessels unweighed because of their very great quantity; the weight of the copper was not reckoned.

*I Kings 7.44-47*

וְאֶת־הַיָּם הָאֶחָד וְאֶת־הַבָּקָר שְׁנֵים־עָשָׂר תַּחַת הַיָּם: וְאֶת־הַסִּירוֹת וְאֶת־הַיָּעִים וְאֶת־הַמִּזְרָקוֹת וְאֵת כָּל־הַכֵּלִים הָאֵלֶּה אֲשֶׁר עָשָׂה חִירָם לַמֶּלֶךְ שְׁלֹמֹה בֵּית יְהוָה נְחֹשֶׁת מְמֹרָט: בְּכִכַּר הַיַּרְדֵּן יְצָקָם הַמֶּלֶךְ בְּמַעֲבֵה הָאֲדָמָה בֵּין סֻכּוֹת וּבֵין צָרְתָן: וַיַּנַּח שְׁלֹמֹה אֶת־כָּל־הַכֵּלִים מֵרֹב מְאֹד מְאֹד לֹא נֶחְקַר מִשְׁקַל הַנְּחֹשֶׁת:

מְלָכִים א׳ ז:מד–מז

## Solomon the Merchant Prince: Ezion-geber

King Solomon built a navy in Ezion-geber, which is near Eloth (=Elath) on the shore of the Sea of Reeds in the land of Edom.

*I Kings 9.26*

וָאֳנִי עָשָׂה הַמֶּלֶךְ שְׁלֹמֹה בְּעֶצְיוֹן־גֶּבֶר אֲשֶׁר אֶת־אֵלוֹת עַל־שְׂפַת יַם־סוּף בְּאֶרֶץ אֱדוֹם:

מְלָכִים א׳ ט:כו

For the king had a Tarshish fleet in the (Mediterranean) Sea along with Hiram's fleet; once every three years the Tarshish fleet put in, bearing gold and silver, ivory, apes, and peacocks.

*I Kings 10.22*

כִּי אֳנִי תַרְשִׁישׁ לַמֶּלֶךְ בַּיָּם עִם אֳנִי חִירָם אַחַת לְשָׁלֹשׁ שָׁנִים תָּבוֹא אֳנִי תַרְשִׁישׁ נֹשְׂאֵת זָהָב וָכֶסֶף שֶׁנְהַבִּים וְקֹפִים וְתֻכִּיִּים:

מְלָכִים א׳ י:כב

Now the queen of Sheba heard of Solomon's fame . . . and she came to test him with hard questions. [2]She arrived in Jerusalem with a very large retinue, with camels bearing spices, a great quantity of gold, and precious stones . . . [4]When the queen of Sheba observed all of Solomon's wisdom, the palace that he had built, [5]the food of his table, the seating of his courtiers, the service and attire of his attendants, his cupbearers, and the burnt offerings which he presented at the House of the Lord, she was left breathless. [6]She said to the king, "The report that I heard in my own country about your accomplishments and your wisdom is indeed true. [7]I could not believe the reports until I came and saw with my own eyes; as a matter of fact, not even the half had been told me: in wisdom and wealth you exceed the reports that I heard."

*I Kings 10.1-7*

וּמַלְכַּת־שְׁבָא שֹׁמַעַת אֶת־שֵׁמַע שְׁלֹמֹה לְשֵׁם יְהוָה וַתָּבֹא לְנַסֹּתוֹ בְּחִידוֹת: וַתָּבֹא יְרוּשָׁלְַמָה בְּחַיִל כָּבֵד מְאֹד גְּמַלִּים נֹשְׂאִים בְּשָׂמִים וְזָהָב רַב־מְאֹד וְאֶבֶן יְקָרָה וַתָּבֹא אֶל־שְׁלֹמֹה וַתְּדַבֵּר אֵלָיו אֵת כָּל־אֲשֶׁר הָיָה עִם־לְבָבָהּ: . . . וַתֵּרֶא מַלְכַּת־שְׁבָא אֵת כָּל־חָכְמַת שְׁלֹמֹה וְהַבַּיִת אֲשֶׁר בָּנָה: וּמַאֲכַל שֻׁלְחָנוֹ וּמוֹשַׁב עֲבָדָיו וּמַעֲמַד מְשָׁרְתָו וּמַלְבֻּשֵׁיהֶם וּמַשְׁקָיו וְעֹלָתוֹ אֲשֶׁר יַעֲלֶה בֵּית יְהוָה וְלֹא־הָיָה בָהּ עוֹד רוּחַ: וַתֹּאמֶר אֶל־הַמֶּלֶךְ אֱמֶת הָיָה הַדָּבָר אֲשֶׁר שָׁמַעְתִּי בְּאַרְצִי עַל־דְּבָרֶיךָ וְעַל־חָכְמָתֶךָ: וְלֹא־הֶאֱמַנְתִּי לַדְּבָרִים עַד אֲשֶׁר־בָּאתִי וַתִּרְאֶינָה עֵינַי וְהִנֵּה לֹא־הֻגַּד־לִי הַחֵצִי הוֹסַפְתָּ חָכְמָה וָטוֹב אֶל־הַשְּׁמוּעָה אֲשֶׁר שָׁמָעְתִּי:

מְלָכִים א׳ י:א–ז

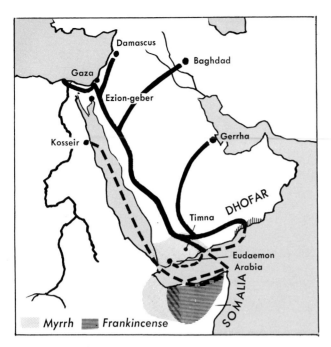

Map of the trade routes of the first millennium B.C.E. over which myrrh, frankincense, etc. were carried from South Arabia to its northern neighbors. (Note that Ezion-geber is on the natural overland route.) The shaded areas show the extent of the natural habitat of the two trees. This Timna is the capital of Qataban, one of the five ancient kingdoms of South Arabia. Sheba of the Bible is located in this region.

An almost life-size head of a statue of a woman, found at Timna. The artist has created the head out of several materials: the head itself is alabaster, the hair is plaster, the eyes are lapis lazuli set in blue paste.

with all manner of presents in order to conclude an amicable trade agreement with him. . . . A satisfactory commercial treaty was evidently negotiated between the two sovereigns, because we are informed that "King Solomon gave to the Queen of Sheba all that it pleased her to ask, besides that which he gave her according to his royal bounty" [I Kings 10:13]. (N. Glueck, in *Biblical Archaeologist*, I [September, 1938] 14.)

The commercial enterprises of Solomon, handled by "the king's merchants," extended in all directions. Thus he virtually monopolized the strategic as well as lucrative horse and chariot trade; his agents bought up the horses in Cilicia and the chariots in Egypt and sold them to the Hittites, Arameans, and other peoples of the Near East (I Kings 10: 28–29) .

## Relations with Phoenicia

The details of the economic relations between Israel and Phoenicia (cf. I Kings 5) will probably never be wholly recovered. It may be doubted that Solomon, at least in the early part of his reign, paid much into Phoenicia's governmental coffers for the men and materials that he received from Hiram. After all, Phoenicia was at the mercy of Solomon no less than of David; it was not Phoenicia but Israel which bought horses in Cilicia. On the other hand, Solomon would have had no port, refinery, fleet, or crews at Ezion-geber were it not for Phoenicia, and the latter did not make this possible out of sheer good will. The Phoenicians would have preferred to direct these projects themselves, or at least to share in the profits.

In this connection the Cabul transaction is illuminating. In return for considerable material assistance in the building of the Temple and palace complexes, Solomon offered Hiram the Galilean district of Cabul, containing twenty towns; Hiram, dissatisfied with this exchange, rejected it outright. Solomon

King Solomon, in turn, gave the queen of Sheba whatever it pleased her to ask for—in addition to the bounty that King Solomon himself gave her. Then she and her attendants set out to return to her country.

*I Kings 10.13*

וְהַמֶּלֶךְ שְׁלֹמֹה נָתַן לְמַלְכַּת־שְׁבָא אֶת־כָּל־
חֶפְצָהּ אֲשֶׁר שָׁאָלָה מִלְּבַד אֲשֶׁר נָתַן־לָהּ כְּיַד
הַמֶּלֶךְ שְׁלֹמֹה וַתֵּפֶן וַתֵּלֶךְ לְאַרְצָהּ הִיא וַעֲבָדֶיהָ׃
מְלָכִים א' י:יג

## Relations with Phoenicia

*It has now been determined from extra-biblical sources that the word, מִקְוֵה in I Ki. 10.28, traditionally and incorrectly translated as "linen yarn; company (of merchants); droves (of horses); Keveh," etc., actually represents the place name "Kue" (or Coa) in the plains of Cilicia in Asia Minor. Further, the term מִצְרַיִם in the same verse as a source of horses may represent not Egypt but Musru, a neighboring region of Kue in Asia Minor. (See J. A. Montgomery,* The Book of Kings, *1961, pp. 226-228; A. S. Kapelrud, article "Kue," in* Interpreter's Dictionary of the Bible, *III, p. 50.)*

Solomon amassed chariots and horses. He had 1400 chariots and 12,000 horses, which were quartered in the chariot-towns or near the king in Jerusalem . . . [28]Egypt and Kue were the source of Solomon's horses; the royal merchants would make the purchase in Kue at a fixed price. [29]A chariot was imported from Musru for 600 shekels of silver and a horse for 150; these, in turn, were exported by them to all the kings of the Hittites and the kings of the Arameans.

*I Kings 10.26-29*

וַיֶּאֱסֹף שְׁלֹמֹה רֶכֶב וּפָרָשִׁים וַיְהִי־לוֹ אֶלֶף
וְאַרְבַּע־מֵאוֹת רֶכֶב וּשְׁנֵים־עָשָׂר אֶלֶף פָּרָשִׁים
וַיַּנְחֵם בְּעָרֵי הָרֶכֶב וְעִם־הַמֶּלֶךְ בִּירוּשָׁלָ͏ִם׃ . . .
וּמוֹצָא הַסּוּסִים אֲשֶׁר לִשְׁלֹמֹה מִמִּצְרָיִם וּמִקְוֵה סֹחֲרֵי
הַמֶּלֶךְ יִקְחוּ מִקְוֵה בִּמְחִיר׃ וַתַּעֲלֶה וַתֵּצֵא מֶרְכָּבָה
מִמִּצְרַיִם בְּשֵׁשׁ־מֵאוֹת כֶּסֶף וְסוּס בַּחֲמִשִּׁים וּמֵאָה וְכֵן
לְכָל־מַלְכֵי הַחִתִּים וּלְמַלְכֵי אֲרָם בְּיָדָם יֹצִאוּ׃
מְלָכִים א' י: כו—כט

King Hiram of Tyre sent his courtiers to Solomon when he heard that he had been anointed king as successor to his father, for Hiram had always been an ally of David. [16]Solomon sent this message to Hiram: [17]"You know that my father David could not build a House for the name of the LORD his God because of the wars which encompassed him, until the LORD had placed them (i.e., his enemies) under the soles of his feet. [18]Now, however, that the LORD my God has given me respite all around, without adversary and without threat of attack, [19]I propose to build a House for the name of the LORD my God, as the LORD had promised my father David: 'Your son, whom I will set on the throne to succeed you—he will build the House for My name.' [20]So please issue orders for cedars to be cut down for me in the Lebanon. My servants will work with yours, and I will pay you whatever hire you set for your servants. For you know that there is none among us who knows how to cut timber like the Sidonians."

*I Kings 5.15-20*
*(= 5. 1-6 in the English versions)*

וַיִּשְׁלַח חִירָם מֶלֶךְ־צוֹר אֶת־עֲבָדָיו אֶל־שְׁלֹמֹה
כִּי שָׁמַע כִּי אֹתוֹ מָשְׁחוּ לְמֶלֶךְ תַּחַת אָבִיהוּ כִּי
אֹהֵב הָיָה חִירָם לְדָוִד כָּל־הַיָּמִים׃ וַיִּשְׁלַח שְׁלֹמֹה
אֶל־חִירָם לֵאמֹר׃ אַתָּה יָדַעְתָּ אֶת־דָּוִד אָבִי כִּי
לֹא יָכֹל לִבְנוֹת בַּיִת לְשֵׁם יְהוָה אֱלֹהָיו מִפְּנֵי
הַמִּלְחָמָה אֲשֶׁר סְבָבֻהוּ עַד תֵּת־יְהוָה אֹתָם תַּחַת
כַּפּוֹת רַגְלָו׃ וְעַתָּה הֵנִיחַ יְהוָה אֱלֹהַי לִי מִסָּבִיב
אֵין שָׂטָן וְאֵין פֶּגַע רָע׃ וְהִנְנִי אֹמֵר לִבְנוֹת בַּיִת
לְשֵׁם יְהוָה אֱלֹהָי כַּאֲשֶׁר דִּבֶּר יְהוָה אֶל־דָּוִד אָבִי
לֵאמֹר בִּנְךָ אֲשֶׁר אֶתֵּן תַּחְתֶּיךָ עַל־כִּסְאֶךָ הוּא־
יִבְנֶה הַבַּיִת לִשְׁמִי׃ וְעַתָּה צַוֵּה וְיִכְרְתוּ־לִי אֲרָזִים
מִן־הַלְּבָנוֹן וַעֲבָדַי יִהְיוּ עִם־עֲבָדֶיךָ וּשְׂכַר עֲבָדֶיךָ
אֶתֵּן לְךָ כְּכֹל אֲשֶׁר תֹּאמֵר כִּי אַתָּה יָדַעְתָּ כִּי אֵין
בָּנוּ אִישׁ יֹדֵעַ לִכְרָת־עֵצִים כַּצִּדֹנִים׃
מְלָכִים א' ה:טו—כ

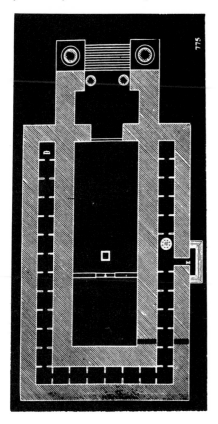

Ground plan of the Temple of Solomon as reconstructed from the Biblical descriptions and pertinent archaeological data.

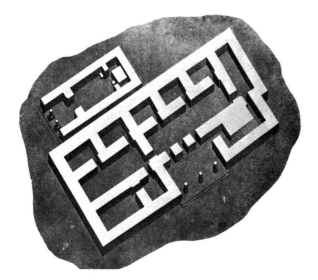

Ground plan of the palace and accompanying sanctuary at Tell Tainat (on the Orontes River, in Syria). Note the resemblances among this sanctuary, the plan suggested for Solomon's sanctuary (above), and the layout of the Arad sanctuary (p. 132). They all follow a similar plan: court, porticoed entrance, hall, and inner sanctum.

simply took back Cabul and settled it with Israelites (I Kings 9:10–13; II Chronicles 8:1–2), leaving with the historian, as apparently with the Phoenicians, the feeling that Solomon could do just about as he pleased.

This relationship between Israel and Phoenicia changed radically after the death of Solomon. Israel's united kingdom split into two, and the military balance in the Near East changed with the rise of Shishak in Egypt and with the growth of the rival empires of Assyria and Aram. Phoenicia continued to grow rich in her maritime and colonial ventures and ceased to grant to Israel any more concessions or favors.

## The Administration of Solomon

Solomon perfected and extended the administrative organization initiated by his father, David (I Kings 4), and so facilitated even more the collection of taxes and the recruitment of forced labor. At the same time, he weakened further the tribal loyalties.

For administrative purposes Israel was divided into twelve districts, each with its own governor. But the areas of jurisdiction, it should be noted, did not necessarily coincide with tribal territories. The territories said to have been assigned to Reuben and Gad, for instance, were merged into one district. Manasseh in Transjordan was split into two districts, and the northern part of the Plain of Sharon was taken away from the tribe and made a separate district. In the case of Zebulun and Simeon, these territories had ceased to represent tribal domains even before the rise of the monarchy.

Excavations indicate that some of the governors, perhaps all, lived in palaces, to which were attached storehouses for the grain, olive oil, and cattle collected as taxes in kind. Each governor was required to provide food for the royal household one month out of the

King Hiram of Tyre supplied Solomon with all the cedar and cypress timber and the gold that he desired, and King Solomon, in turn, gave Hiram twenty towns in the region of Galilee. <sup>12</sup>But when Hiram came from Tyre to inspect the towns which Solomon had given him, he was not pleased with them.

*I Kings 9.11-12*

חִירָם מֶלֶךְ־צֹר נִשָּׂא אֶת־שְׁלֹמֹה בַּעֲצֵי אֲרָזִים וּבַעֲצֵי בְרוֹשִׁים וּבַזָּהָב לְכָל־חֶפְצוֹ אָז יִתֵּן הַמֶּלֶךְ שְׁלֹמֹה לְחִירָם עֶשְׂרִים עִיר בְּאֶרֶץ הַגָּלִיל: וַיֵּצֵא חִירָם מִצֹּר לִרְאוֹת אֶת־הֶעָרִים אֲשֶׁר נָתַן־לוֹ שְׁלֹמֹה וְלֹא יָשְׁרוּ בְּעֵינָיו:

מְלָכִים א׳ ט׳: יא־יב

## The Administration of Solomon

*The full significance of the administrative data in I Kings 4—incomplete as they are—is only recently coming to be appreciated. Scholars have sought, and found, Egyptian, Mesopotamian, and Canaanite origins and parallels for the civil service structure initiated by David and developed far more fully by Solomon. It has not yet been determined the extent to which Solomon followed or disregarded tribal regions in his administrative division of the land. Some of the top level administrators were close relatives by marriage; thus Ben-abinadab, governor of Dor (the coastal region below Acco), and Ahimaaz, governor of Naphtali, were sons-in-law of King Solomon (verses 11 and 15 below).*

And so King Solomon reigned over all Israel. <sup>2</sup>These were his officials: Azariah son of Zadok—the priest; <sup>3</sup>Elihoreph and Ahijah, sons of Shisha—scribes; Jehoshaphat son of Ahilud—the recorder; <sup>4</sup>Benaiah son of Jehoiada—head of the army; Zadok and Abiathar—priests; <sup>5</sup>Azariah son of Nathan—in charge of the governors; Zabud son of Nathan—priest, Friend of the king; <sup>6</sup>Ahishar —steward of the household; and Adoniram son of Abda—in charge of the corvée. <sup>7</sup>Solomon also had twelve governors over all Israel, who supplied the provisions for the king and his household; each one supplied provisions for one month of the year. <sup>8</sup>These were their names: Ben-hur, in the hill country of Ephraim . . . <sup>11</sup>Ben-abinadab, in the whole district of Dor; he had married Taphath daughter of Solomon . . . <sup>15</sup>Ahimaaz, in Naphtali; he too took a daughter of Solomon as a wife, Bosmath . . .

*I Kings 4.1-19*

וַיְהִי הַמֶּלֶךְ שְׁלֹמֹה מֶלֶךְ עַל־כָּל־יִשְׂרָאֵל: וְאֵלֶּה הַשָּׂרִים אֲשֶׁר־לוֹ עֲזַרְיָהוּ בֶן־צָדוֹק הַכֹּהֵן: אֱלִיחֹרֶף וַאֲחִיָּה בְּנֵי שִׁישָׁא סֹפְרִים יְהוֹשָׁפָט בֶּן־אֲחִילוּד הַמַּזְכִּיר: וּבְנָיָהוּ בֶן־יְהוֹיָדָע עַל־הַצָּבָא וְצָדוֹק וְאֶבְיָתָר כֹּהֲנִים: וַעֲזַרְיָהוּ בֶן־נָתָן עַל־הַנִּצָּבִים וְזָבוּד בֶּן־נָתָן כֹּהֵן רֵעֶה הַמֶּלֶךְ: וַאֲחִישָׁר עַל־הַבָּיִת וַאֲדֹנִירָם בֶּן־עַבְדָּא עַל־הַמַּס:

וְלִשְׁלֹמֹה שְׁנֵים־עָשָׂר נִצָּבִים עַל־כָּל־יִשְׂרָאֵל וְכִלְכְּלוּ אֶת־הַמֶּלֶךְ וְאֶת־בֵּיתוֹ חֹדֶשׁ בַּשָּׁנָה יִהְיֶה עַל־*אֶחָד לְכַלְכֵּל: וְאֵלֶּה שְׁמוֹתָם בֶּן־חוּר בְּהַר אֶפְרָיִם . . . בֶּן־אֲבִינָדָב כָּל־נָפַת דֹּאר טָפַת בַּת־שְׁלֹמֹה הָיְתָה לּוֹ לְאִשָּׁה: . . . אֲחִימַעַץ בְּנַפְתָּלִי גַּם־הוּא לָקַח אֶת־בָּשְׂמַת בַּת־שְׁלֹמֹה לְאִשָּׁה: . . .

מְלָכִים א׳ ד׳: א־יט

At the end of the twenty years that it took Solomon to build the House of the LORD and his palace, <sup>2</sup>Solomon rebuilt the towns which Huram (Hiram) had given Solomon, and he settled Israelites in them.

*II Chronicles 8.1-2*

וַיְהִי מִקֵּץ עֶשְׂרִים שָׁנָה אֲשֶׁר בָּנָה שְׁלֹמֹה אֶת־בֵּית יְהוָה וְאֶת־בֵּיתוֹ: וְהֶעָרִים אֲשֶׁר נָתַן חוּרָם לִשְׁלֹמֹה בָּנָה שְׁלֹמֹה אֹתָם וַיּוֹשֶׁב שָׁם אֶת־בְּנֵי

דִּבְרֵי הַיָּמִים ב׳ ח׳: א־ב

General view of a portion of the excavations of Hazor covering the period of the Late Bronze and Iron Ages. Note the gateway and casemate wall of the 10th century city (to be seen in the foreground of the picture), the wall itself stretching vertically up the left side of the picture. Bronze Age structures are to be seen beneath the gateway and wall. The gate, which was the outer gate of the Solomonic city, became an inner gate when the city expanded in the 9th century. Similar gates are to be found at Gezer and Megiddo. The pillared building of the 9th century and buildings of the later periods are to be seen in the upper center and at the top of the picture.

year. But the district of Judah, because it provided the principal backers and lieutenants of the royal house—as well as because Jerusalem, the capital and chief city of the nation was located within its boundaries—occupied a specially privileged position, directly under the king. At least two of the twelve governors were not only natives of Judah but sons-in-law of Solomon himself.

The population of the land increased. The Bible tells how David's census takers found "in Israel eight hundred thousand warriors that drew the sword; and the men of Judah were five hundred thousand men" (II Samuel 24:9. I Chronicles 21:5 gives a variant total). When Solomon counted heads to plan for his labor levies, he is reported (II Chronicles 2:16–17) to have found 153,600 aliens alone. However, there is no way of determining whether these figures are even approximately correct, and all estimates of Israel's population are essentially but learned guesses.

## Culture and Religion

Increased prosperity and growth had marked impact on the culture and religion of the country. Writing, uncommon although far from unknown in the times of Moses and the Judges, spread widely in Solomon's day. Royal secretaries recorded the affairs of state, and royal archives are referred to repeatedly in the books of Kings and Chronicles, with some variation of the formula: "And the rest of the acts of King So-and-So and all that he did are inscribed in the records of the royal chronicles of Israel and Judah." Unfortunately, however, these records have not yet been recovered by excavators.

The royal annals, in keeping with the classical Hebrew narrative style of such other books as Judges and Samuel, were written in a highly developed Hebrew prose. Israel's poets, moreover, stood on the same high level

142

Joab gave to the king (David) the figures of the census of the people: Israel numbered 800,000 able-bodied fighting men (lit., able men who draw the sword), and Judah 500,000.

*II Samuel 24.9*

וַיִּתֵּן יוֹאָב אֶת־מִסְפַּר מִפְקַד־הָעָם אֶל־הַמֶּלֶךְ
וַתְּהִי יִשְׂרָאֵל שְׁמֹנֶה מֵאוֹת אֶלֶף אִישׁ־חַיִל שֹׁלֵף
חֶרֶב וְאִישׁ יְהוּדָה חֲמֵשׁ־מֵאוֹת אֶלֶף אִישׁ:
שְׁמוּאֵל ב׳ כד:ט

(Joab gave David the figures of the census of the people:) all Israel numbered 1,100,000 fighting men, and Judah 470,000 fighting men.

*I Chronicles 21.5*

וַיִּתֵּן יוֹאָב אֶת־מִסְפַּר מִפְקַד־הָעָם אֶל־דָּוִיד
וַיְהִי כָל־יִשְׂרָאֵל אֶלֶף אֲלָפִים וּמֵאָה אֶלֶף אִישׁ
שֹׁלֵף חֶרֶב וִיהוּדָה אַרְבַּע מֵאוֹת וְשִׁבְעִים אֶלֶף אִישׁ
שֹׁלֵף חָרֶב:
דִּבְרֵי הַיָּמִים א׳ כא:ה

Solomon took a census of all the resident aliens in the land of Israel, following the census that his father David had taken: they came to 153,600. [17]He made 70,000 of them porters, 80,000 quarriers in the hills, and 3600 overseers to supervise the work of the people.

*II Chronicles 2.16-17*

וַיִּסְפֹּר שְׁלֹמֹה כָּל־הָאֲנָשִׁים הַגֵּירִים אֲשֶׁר בְּאֶרֶץ
יִשְׂרָאֵל אַחֲרֵי הַסְּפָר אֲשֶׁר סְפָרָם דָּוִיד אָבִיו
וַיִּמָּצְאוּ מֵאָה וַחֲמִשִּׁים אֶלֶף וּשְׁלֹשֶׁת אֲלָפִים וְשֵׁשׁ
מֵאוֹת: וַיַּעַשׂ מֵהֶם שִׁבְעִים אֶלֶף סַבָּל וּשְׁמֹנִים
אֶלֶף חֹצֵב בָּהָר וּשְׁלֹשֶׁת אֲלָפִים וְשֵׁשׁ מֵאוֹת מְנַצְּחִים
לְהַעֲבִיד אֶת־הָעָם:
דִּבְרֵי הַיָּמִים ב׳ ב:טז־יז

The LORD struck the king (Uzziah-Azariah) so that he became a leper until the day he died; he lived in the leper(?) house while Prince Jotham, who was in charge of the palace, ruled the populace (lit., the people of the land). [6]The rest of the acts of Azariah and all that he did are recorded in the annals of the kings of Judah.

*II Kings 15.5-6*

וַיְנַגַּע יְהוָה אֶת־הַמֶּלֶךְ וַיְהִי מְצֹרָע עַד־יוֹם מֹתוֹ
וַיֵּשֶׁב בְּבֵית הַחָפְשִׁית וְיוֹתָם בֶּן־הַמֶּלֶךְ עַל־הַבַּיִת
שֹׁפֵט אֶת־עַם הָאָרֶץ: וְיֶתֶר דִּבְרֵי עֲזַרְיָהוּ וְכָל־
אֲשֶׁר עָשָׂה הֲלֹא־הֵם כְּתוּבִים עַל־סֵפֶר דִּבְרֵי
הַיָּמִים לְמַלְכֵי יְהוּדָה:
מְלָכִים ב׳ טו:ה־ו

*The Book of Chronicles had long been regarded by scholars as consisting of generally unreliable and one-sided data. Thus it records (see II Chron. 2.16-17 above) only non-Israelites ("resident aliens") as subjected to forced labor by Solomon when the Book of Kings (I Ki. 5.27-30; see p. 135) refers to "all Israel"—thereby attempting to remove a stain from the record of the Davidic dynasty; the favoritism shown to David and his line is especially apparent. On the other hand, Chronicles is being increasingly recognized as having preserved much reliable material; thus whereas II Ki. 15.1-7 records for the long reign of King Azariah (Uzziah) of Judah (about 780-740 B.C.E.) merely the fact that he was leprous—or whatever the skin disease really was—II Chron. 26 has included—doubtlessly from ancient royal annals—important facts about Uzziah's considerable military, construction, and economic activities.*

By the time of the Divided Monarchy, the winged sphinx was a well-known and time-honored motif from Egypt to Assyria and beyond. This type of figured representation might have been the precursor of the Biblical notion of the cherub.

A fragment of ivory inlay showing a winged sphinx wearing an Egyptian hair mantle and a crown. From the excavations at Nimrud (Calah), an ancient capital of Assyria. About 7½ by 6 inches.

The throne on which the prince is seated. Detail from an ivory inlay. from Megiddo (cf. p. 124 above).

The throne on which the prince is seated. Detail from the sarcophagus of Ahiram (cf. p. 86a above).

as her writers of prose, as can readily be seen from the few samples that have been preserved, for example: Moses' Song of Triumph at the Red Sea (Exodus 15, in part), the Blessing of Moses (Deuteronomy 33, in part), the Oracles of Balaam (Numbers 23–24), and the Song of Deborah (Judges 5).

The books of the Pentateuch began to take shape from material that for centuries had been orally transmitted from generation to generation. Solomon himself was a patron of literature and the arts, and it is not accidental that his name became intimately associated with such classics as Proverbs, Canticles, and Ecclesiastes. These books crystallized in their present written form after the Babylonian Exile.

Increasing economic and political contact between the Israelites and the other peoples in the Near East led inevitably to some changes in the realm of Israelite religion. It does not appear that religious syncretism was practiced in Israel, nor that basic non-Israelite beliefs found any integral place in the worship of the Lord. Israel's God remained the unique and supreme Deity; but some ceremonial practices and even theological concepts of foreign origin were absorbed into His worship. It was during Solomon's reign that this tendency toward toleration and assimilation of alien religious ideas first increased to prominence.

Canaanite elements were responsible for the main divergences from the worship of the Lord. Economic and political co-operation between Israel and Phoenicia led to the free exchange of cultural and religious practices as well. The worship of Baal and other prominent Phoenician deities, including some of their orgiastic elements, spread in Israel. Intermarriage with Phoenician and other non-Israelite peoples also became less rare. The king himself "loved many foreign women—

# Culture and Religion

⁵How fair are your tents, O Jacob,
Your dwellings. O Israel!
⁶Like palm-groves that stretch out,
Like gardens beside a river,
Like aloes planted by the LORD,
Like cedars beside the water;
⁷Their boughs drip with moisture,
Their roots have abundant water.
Their king shall rise above Agag,
Their kingdom shall be exalted.
⁸God who freed them from Egypt
Is for them like the horns of the wild ox.
They shall devour enemy nations,
Crush their bones,
And smash their arrows.
⁹They crouch, they lie down like a lion,
Like the king of beasts; who dare rouse them?
Blessed are they who bless you,
Accursed they who curse you!

*Numbers 24.5-9*

מַה־טֹּבוּ אֹהָלֶיךָ יַעֲקֹב מִשְׁכְּנֹתֶיךָ יִשְׂרָאֵל:
כִּנְחָלִים נִטָּיוּ כְּגַנֹּת עֲלֵי נָהָר כַּאֲהָלִים נָטַע יְהוָה
כַּאֲרָזִים עֲלֵי־מָיִם: יִזַּל־מַיִם מִדָּלְיָו וְזַרְעוֹ בְּמַיִם
רַבִּים וְיָרֹם מֵאֲגַג מַלְכּוֹ וְתִנַּשֵּׂא מַלְכֻתוֹ: אֵל מוֹצִיאוֹ
מִמִּצְרַיִם כְּתוֹעֲפֹת רְאֵם לוֹ יֹאכַל גּוֹיִם צָרָיו
וְעַצְמֹתֵיהֶם יְגָרֵם וְחִצָּיו יִמְחָץ: כָּרַע שָׁכַב כַּאֲרִי
וּכְלָבִיא מִי יְקִימֶנּוּ מְבָרֲכֶיךָ בָרוּךְ וְאֹרֲרֶיךָ אָרוּר:

בְּמִדְבָּר כד: ה־ט

Hear, O kings! Give ear, O potentates!
I will sing, will sing to the LORD,
I will hymn the Lord, the God of Israel.

*Judges 5.3*

שִׁמְעוּ מְלָכִים הַאֲזִינוּ רֹזְנִים אָנֹכִי לַיהוָה אָנֹכִי
אָשִׁירָה אֲזַמֵּר לַיהוָה אֱלֹהֵי יִשְׂרָאֵל:

שׁוֹפְטִים ה:ג

The Proverbs of Solomon, son of David, king of Israel—
²To learn wisdom and discipline,
To understand words of discernment,
³To acquire the discipline of reason,
Justice, equity, and right.

*Proverbs 1.1-3*

מִשְׁלֵי שְׁלֹמֹה בֶן־דָּוִד מֶלֶךְ יִשְׂרָאֵל: לָדַעַת
חָכְמָה וּמוּסָר לְהָבִין אִמְרֵי בִינָה: לָקַחַת מוּסַר
הַשְׂכֵּל צֶדֶק וּמִשְׁפָּט וּמֵישָׁרִים:

מִשְׁלֵי א:א־ג

The Song of Songs, which is Solomon's.
²Oh that he might give me of the kisses of his
mouth—
For your love is better than wine.

*Song of Songs 1.1-2*

שִׁיר הַשִּׁירִים אֲשֶׁר לִשְׁלֹמֹה: יִשָּׁקֵנִי מִנְּשִׁיקוֹת
פִּיהוּ כִּי־טוֹבִים דֹּדֶיךָ מִיָּיִן:

שִׁיר הַשִּׁירִים א:א־ב

The words of Koheleth, son of David, king in
Jerusalem:
²"Utter futility," said Koheleth,
"Utter futility! All is futility!"

*Ecclesiastes 1.1-2*

דִּבְרֵי קֹהֶלֶת בֶּן־דָּוִד מֶלֶךְ בִּירוּשָׁלִָם: הֲבֵל
הֲבָלִים אָמַר קֹהֶלֶת הֲבֵל הֲבָלִים הַכֹּל הָבֶל:

קֹהֶלֶת א:א־ב

²⁹O happy Israel! Who is like you,
A people delivered by the LORD,
Your protecting Shield, your Sword triumphant!
Your enemies shall come cringing before you,
And you shall tread on their backs.

*Deuteronomy 33.29*

אַשְׁרֶיךָ יִשְׂרָאֵל מִי כָמוֹךָ עַם נוֹשַׁע בַּיהוָה מָגֵן
עֶזְרֶךָ וַאֲשֶׁר־חֶרֶב גַּאֲוָתֶךָ וְיִכָּחֲשׁוּ אֹיְבֶיךָ לָךְ וְאַתָּה
עַל־בָּמוֹתֵימוֹ תִדְרֹךְ:

דְּבָרִים לג: כט

Following a tradition dating back as early as the Hittite empire, the Assyrians sometimes adopted the practice of portraying their gods standing on the backs of animals, real or mythological. Each animal belonged to or characterized the divine master.

Relief (above) at Maltaya, north of Mosul in Iraq, shows a procession of gods portrayed in this manner. An Assyrian king, most probably Sennacherib (704-681), stands in an attitude of worship both before and behind them.

Limestone orthostat from Carchemish (ca. 8th cent. B.C.E.) upon which has been carved in relief a scene which depicts an important figure at a banquet. From left to right: Attendant holding fly whisk; bearded man seated on a camp stool and raising a cup; the banquet table laden with foods; an attendant with vessel; and a musician playing a lute. About 4½ feet high.

beside the daughter of Pharaoh—Moabite, Ammonite, Edomite, Sidonian, and Hittite women" (I Kings 11:1 ff.). It is true that Solomon's acquisition of many of the alleged total of "seven hundred princesses and three hundred concubines" was motivated, as royal marriages so frequently are, by the dictates of diplomacy. But these casual marriages with foreigners brought in their wake additional concessions to alien gods. The Biblical writers did not overlook the fact that Solomon built idolatrous shrines for Ashtoreth, Milcom, Chemosh, Molech, Asherah, and other deities of the foreign princesses, just as he permitted Phoenician novelties to intrude among various aspects of the Temple cult and paraphernalia.

Tens of thousands of Israelites of the border regions of northern Israel mingled busily with the Phoenicians. Also in commercial towns such as Tell Qasileh and border towns such as Beth-shemesh, Israelites and non-Israelites freely mixed. Small wonder that the Biblical historians of the Book of Kings blamed Solomon for this apostasy from the Lord, which, in their opinion, accounted largely for the disruption of the kingdom and the other disasters which followed his death (I Kings 11:9–13).

## The Last Days of the United Kingdom

The opulence and power of Solomon's kingdom was doomed to deteriorate. Under the increasing pressure of this decline, tensions, both foreign and domestic, produced a split between politically favored Judah in the south and the northern districts which came to call themselves Israel—with "Israel" here representing a political and not a spiritual unit. It was during Solomon's reign, for example, that the regime of Pharaoh Shishak I began to restore to Egypt, if only temporarily, some of its former imperial pre-

King Solomon loved many foreign women as well as the daughter of Pharaoh—Moabite, Ammonite, Edomite, Sidonian (i.e., Phoenician), and Hittite women [2]from the nations of whom the LORD had said to the Israelites, "You shall not intermarry with one another (lit., you shall not enter into marriage with them or they with you), for they will turn away your heart to their gods"; but Solomon clung to them in love. [3]He had seven hundred wives and three hundred concubines; and his wives turned away his heart . . . [5]Solomon followed Ashtoreth, the goddess of the Sidonians, and Milcom, the abomination of the Ammonites . . . [7]At that time, Solomon built a shrine for Chemosh, the abomination of Moab, on the hill near Jerusalem, and for Molech, the abomination of the Ammonites. [8]And thus he did for all his foreign wives, who presented offerings and sacrifices to their gods.

*I Kings 11.1-8*

וְהַמֶּלֶךְ שְׁלֹמֹה אָהַב נָשִׁים נָכְרִיּוֹת רַבּוֹת וְאֶת־
בַּת־פַּרְעֹה מוֹאֲבִיּוֹת עַמֳּנִיּוֹת אֲדֹמִית צֵדְנִית חִתִּית:
מִן־הַגּוֹיִם אֲשֶׁר אָמַר־יְהֹוָה אֶל־בְּנֵי יִשְׂרָאֵל לֹא־
תָבֹאוּ בָהֶם וְהֵם לֹא־יָבֹאוּ בָכֶם אָכֵן יַטּוּ אֶת־
לְבַבְכֶם אַחֲרֵי אֱלֹהֵיהֶם בָּהֶם דָּבַק שְׁלֹמֹה לְאַהֲבָה:
וַיְהִי־לוֹ נָשִׁים שָׂרוֹת שְׁבַע מֵאוֹת וּפִילַגְשִׁים שְׁלֹשׁ
מֵאוֹת וַיַּטּוּ נָשָׁיו אֶת־לִבּוֹ:... וַיֵּלֶךְ שְׁלֹמֹה אַחֲרֵי
עַשְׁתֹּרֶת אֱלֹהֵי צִדֹנִים וְאַחֲרֵי מִלְכֹּם שִׁקֻּץ עַמֹּנִים:
... אָז יִבְנֶה שְׁלֹמֹה בָּמָה לִכְמוֹשׁ שִׁקֻּץ מוֹאָב בָּהָר
אֲשֶׁר עַל־פְּנֵי יְרוּשָׁלָ͏ִם וּלְמֹלֶךְ שִׁקֻּץ בְּנֵי עַמּוֹן:
וְכֵן עָשָׂה לְכָל־נָשָׁיו הַנָּכְרִיּוֹת מַקְטִירוֹת וּמְזַבְּחוֹת
לֵאלֹהֵיהֶן:

מְלָכִים א' יא:א-ח

## The Last Days of the United Kingdom

One time Jeroboam went out of Jerusalem and the prophet Ahijah of Shilo encountered him on the way; he (Ahijah) was wrapped in a new garment, and the two were alone in the open country. [30]Ahijah took hold of the new garment he was wearing and tore it into twelve pieces. [31]He said to Jeroboam, "Take ten pieces. For thus said the LORD, the God of Israel: I am going to tear the kingdom out of Solomon's hands and give you ten tribes. [32]But one tribe [Judah, apparently including Benjamin] shall remain his—for the sake of My servant David and for the sake of Jerusalem, the city which I have chosen out of all the tribes of Israel. [33]For they have forsaken Me; they have worshiped Ashtoreth the goddess of the Sidonians, Chemosh the god of Moab, and Milcom the god of the Ammonites. They have not walked in My ways, to do what is right in My sight—My laws and My rules—as his father David did.

*I Kings 11.29-33*

וַיְהִי בָּעֵת הַהִיא וְיָרָבְעָם יָצָא מִירוּשָׁלָ͏ִם וַיִּמְצָא
אֹתוֹ אֲחִיָּה הַשִּׁילֹנִי הַנָּבִיא בַּדֶּרֶךְ וְהוּא מִתְכַּסֶּה
בְּשַׂלְמָה חֲדָשָׁה וּשְׁנֵיהֶם לְבַדָּם בַּשָּׂדֶה: וַיִּתְפֹּשׂ
אֲחִיָּה בַּשַּׂלְמָה הַחֲדָשָׁה אֲשֶׁר עָלָיו וַיִּקְרָעֶהָ שְׁנֵים
עָשָׂר קְרָעִים: וַיֹּאמֶר לְיָרָבְעָם קַח־לְךָ עֲשָׂרָה
קְרָעִים כִּי כֹה אָמַר יְהֹוָה אֱלֹהֵי יִשְׂרָאֵל הִנְנִי קֹרֵעַ
אֶת־הַמַּמְלָכָה מִיַּד שְׁלֹמֹה וְנָתַתִּי לְךָ אֵת עֲשָׂרָה
הַשְּׁבָטִים: וְהַשֵּׁבֶט הָאֶחָד יִהְיֶה־לּוֹ לְמַעַן עַבְדִּי
דָוִד וּלְמַעַן יְרוּשָׁלַ͏ִם הָעִיר אֲשֶׁר בָּחַרְתִּי בָהּ מִכֹּל
שִׁבְטֵי יִשְׂרָאֵל: יַעַן אֲשֶׁר עֲזָבוּנִי וַיִּשְׁתַּחֲווּ לְעַשְׁתֹּרֶת
אֱלֹהֵי צִדֹנִין לִכְמוֹשׁ אֱלֹהֵי מוֹאָב וּלְמִלְכֹּם אֱלֹהֵי
בְּנֵי־עַמּוֹן וְלֹא־הָלְכוּ בִדְרָכַי לַעֲשׂוֹת הַיָּשָׁר בְּעֵינַי
וְחֻקֹּתַי וּמִשְׁפָּטַי כְּדָוִד אָבִיו:

מְלָכִים א' יא:כט-לג

147

Drawing of a limestone relief from the south wall of the Amon Temple at Karnak in Egypt which records the conquests that Sheshonk I (10th cent.) claimed to have achieved during his Syrian and Palestinian campaigns. The large figure in the center, wearing the tall feathered crown, is the god Amon. He leads the captives of the listed cities by their bonds. Several towns mentioned here are known to us from the historical books of the Bible, e.g., Beth-horon, Beth-shan, Gibeon, Megiddo, and Taanach. The lower half of the body of each captive has been replaced with a symbol, which means walled town, inside of which is written the name of the town in hieroglyphics.

eminence. Shishak gave political refuge to rebels, both Israelite and non-Israelite, who quarreled with the royal house in Jerusalem —for example, to Jeroboam of the tribe of Ephraim and to Hadad of the royal house of Edom (I Kings 11:14 ff.). The kingdom of Aram too, under Rezon in Damascus, was becoming powerful enough to be "an adversary to Solomon all the days of his life" (I Kings 11:23–25).

In Israel, Solomon's rule brought great prosperity and prestige to the land as a whole, but it was only in a limited degree that the common people shared with the aristocracy in this new wealth and status. Forced labor, high taxes, and political corruption bred a host of enemies for the king's regime, particularly among the heavily burdened lower classes.

These grievances further aggravated the ancient distrust and resentment of the northern tribes for the Judean newcomers and their assumed superiority. Even before Solomon's reign had drawn to its close, the situation had become critical. When Rehoboam, Solomon's son and successor, sent his tax collector, Adoniram, to treat with the Israelites under Jeroboam, he was confronted with open revolt. Adoniram was stoned to death, and Rehoboam himself barely escaped with his life (I Kings 12; II Chronicles 10). This act of violence ushered in the Divided Kingdom.

The rebel leaders of northern Israel did not oppose a monarchy, nor did they care about the kind of worship that went on in the Temple and the shrines. They were willing to support one of their own as king, in the hope and belief that this would lighten the heavy burden of taxation and increase their share in the common wealth. But the lower classes who made up the backbone of the rebellion in the North had yet to learn

The Lord raised up an adversary to Solomon, Hadad the Edomite, who was of the royal family of Edom. ¹⁵When David held sway over (lit. was in) Edom, Joab, the army commander, went up to bury the slain and killed every male in Edom; ¹⁶for Joab and all Israel remained there for six months, until he had slain all the males in Edom. ¹⁷But Adad (Hadad), together with some Edomite servants of his father, escaped, and headed for Egypt; Hadad was then a young boy.

*I Kings 11.14-17*

וַיָּקֶם יְהֹוָה שָׂטָן לִשְׁלֹמֹה אֵת הֲדַד הָאֲדֹמִי מִזֶּרַע הַמֶּלֶךְ הוּא בֶּאֱדוֹם: וַיְהִי בִּהְיוֹת דָּוִד אֶת־אֱדוֹם בַּעֲלוֹת יוֹאָב שַׂר הַצָּבָא לְקַבֵּר אֶת־הַחֲלָלִים וַיַּךְ כָּל־זָכָר בֶּאֱדוֹם: כִּי שֵׁשֶׁת חֳדָשִׁים יָשַׁב־שָׁם יוֹאָב וְכָל־יִשְׂרָאֵל עַד־הִכְרִית כָּל־זָכָר בֶּאֱדוֹם: וַיִּבְרַח אֲדַד הוּא וַאֲנָשִׁים אֲדֹמִיִּים מֵעַבְדֵי אָבִיו אִתּוֹ לָבוֹא מִצְרָיִם וַהֲדַד נַעַר קָטָן:

מְלָכִים א׳ יא:יד–יז

God raised up another adversary for him (Solomon), Rezon son of Eliada, who had fled from his lord, King Hadadezer of Zobah. ²⁴When David was slaughtering them [the Arameans; II Samuel 8.3-8], he gathered men about him and became a captain over a troop; they went to Damascus and settled there and reigned in Damascus. ²⁵He was an adversary for Israel all the days of Solomon . . .

*I Kings 11.23-25*

וַיָּקֶם אֱלֹהִים לוֹ שָׂטָן אֶת־רְזוֹן בֶּן־אֶלְיָדָע אֲשֶׁר בָּרַח מֵאֵת הֲדַדְעֶזֶר מֶלֶךְ־צוֹבָה אֲדֹנָיו: וַיִּקְבֹּץ עָלָיו אֲנָשִׁים וַיְהִי שַׂר־גְּדוּד בַּהֲרֹג דָּוִד אֹתָם וַיֵּלְכוּ דַמֶּשֶׂק וַיֵּשְׁבוּ בָהּ וַיִּמְלְכוּ בְּדַמָּשֶׂק: וַיְהִי שָׂטָן לְיִשְׂרָאֵל כָּל־יְמֵי שְׁלֹמֹה ...

מְלָכִים א׳ יא:כג–כה

King Rehoboam sent Adoram (Adoniram), who was head of the forced labor, but all Israel pelted him to death with stones; and King Rehoboam himself had to mount his chariot in a hurry to flee to Jerusalem. ¹⁹So Israel revolted against the House of David, as is still the case.

*I Kings 12.18-19*

וַיִּשְׁלַח הַמֶּלֶךְ רְחַבְעָם אֶת־אֲדֹרָם אֲשֶׁר עַל־הַמַּס וַיִּרְגְּמוּ כָל־יִשְׂרָאֵל בּוֹ אֶבֶן וַיָּמֹת וְהַמֶּלֶךְ רְחַבְעָם הִתְאַמֵּץ לַעֲלוֹת בַּמֶּרְכָּבָה לָנוּס יְרוּשָׁלָ͏ִם: וַיִּפְשְׁעוּ יִשְׂרָאֵל בְּבֵית דָּוִד עַד הַיּוֹם הַזֶּה:

מְלָכִים א׳ יב:יח–יט

Rehoboam went to Shechem, for all Israel had come to Shechem to proclaim him king. ²When Jeroboam son of Nebat heard this—he was still in Egypt, having fled from King Solomon—Jeroboam remained in Egypt; ³So they sent messengers and summoned him. And Jeroboam and all the assembly of Israel came and spoke to

וַיֵּלֶךְ רְחַבְעָם שְׁכֶם כִּי שְׁכֶם בָּא כָל־יִשְׂרָאֵל לְהַמְלִיךְ אֹתוֹ: וַיְהִי כִּשְׁמֹעַ יָרָבְעָם בֶּן־נְבָט וְהוּא עוֹדֶנּוּ בְמִצְרַיִם אֲשֶׁר בָּרַח מִפְּנֵי הַמֶּלֶךְ שְׁלֹמֹה וַיֵּשֶׁב יָרָבְעָם בְּמִצְרָיִם: וַיִּשְׁלְחוּ וַיִּקְרְאוּ־לוֹ וַיָּבֹא יָרָבְעָם וְכָל־קְהַל יִשְׂרָאֵל וַיְדַבְּרוּ אֶל־רְחַבְעָם

*(continued)*

149

Occasionally in the art of the Ancient Near East, princes and kings chose to be shown with their sons. The following are two examples:

King Esarhaddon of Assyria (680-669) has perhaps chosen to show here his two sons on the sides, rather than on the face of his memorial stele, to indicate that his victory was the important event in this case. The stele is over 10½ feet high.

that what Jeroboam and the other northern leaders intended was nothing more than replacing the Judean monarchy of Solomon with another equally harsh monarchy of their own.

The Biblical historian makes it clear that if the ruling group behind Rehoboam had been willing to share the considerable wealth of the kingdom with the leading supporters of Jeroboam, the united kingdom of Solomon would have endured (I Kings 12:1–19). Whether there simply was not enough wealth to satsify both groups, or whether Rehoboam overestimated his strength, the fact remains that the North broke forever with the South.

King Darius of Persia (521-486), seated on the throne; his son Xerxes stands behind him in attendance. The convention of seated King and standing Prince is used here to show the difference in importance between the two men. The relief is over 8 feet 2 inches tall.

Rehoboam as follows, ⁴Your father made our yoke heavy. Now lighten your father's harsh labor and the heavy yoke which he laid on us, and we will serve you." ⁵He answered them, "Leave me for three days, and then come back to me." So the people went away. ⁶King Rehoboam then took counsel with the elders who had been in his father's service during his lifetime. He asked, "How do you advise to reply to this people?" ⁷They answered him, "If you will be a servant to this people today and serve them, and if you respond by speaking to them with kind words, they will be your servants forever." ⁸But he rejected the advice that the elders gave him, and took counsel with the young men who had grown up with him and had been in his service. ⁹He asked them, "What do you advise that we reply to the people who said to me, 'Lighten the yoke that your father placed upon us'?" ¹⁰The young men who had grown up with him answered him, "Say thus to the people who said to you, 'Your father made our yoke heavy, now you lighten it for us'; tell them this: My little finger is thicker than my father's loins. ¹¹Yes, my father laid a heavy yoke on you; but I will add to your yoke. My father disciplined you with whips; but I will discipline you with scorpions!"

*I Kings 12.1-11*

לֵאמֹר: אָבִיךָ הִקְשָׁה אֶת־עֻלֵּנוּ וְאַתָּה עַתָּה הָקֵל מֵעֲבֹדַת אָבִיךָ הַקָּשָׁה וּמֵעֻלּוֹ הַכָּבֵד אֲשֶׁר־נָתַן עָלֵינוּ וְנַעַבְדֶךָ: וַיֹּאמֶר אֲלֵיהֶם לְכוּ־עֹד שְׁלֹשָׁה יָמִים וְשׁוּבוּ אֵלָי וַיֵּלְכוּ הָעָם: וַיִּוָּעַץ הַמֶּלֶךְ רְחַבְעָם אֶת־הַזְּקֵנִים אֲשֶׁר־הָיוּ עֹמְדִים אֶת־פְּנֵי שְׁלֹמֹה אָבִיו בִּהְיֹתוֹ חַי לֵאמֹר אֵיךְ אַתֶּם נוֹעָצִים לְהָשִׁיב אֶת־הָעָם־הַזֶּה דָּבָר:

וַיְדַבְּרוּ אֵלָיו לֵאמֹר אִם־הַיּוֹם תִּהְיֶה־עֶבֶד לָעָם הַזֶּה וַעֲבַדְתָּם וַעֲנִיתָם וְדִבַּרְתָּ אֲלֵיהֶם דְּבָרִים טוֹבִים וְהָיוּ לְךָ עֲבָדִים כָּל־הַיָּמִים: וַיַּעֲזֹב אֶת־עֲצַת הַזְּקֵנִים אֲשֶׁר יְעָצֻהוּ וַיִּוָּעַץ אֶת־הַיְלָדִים אֲשֶׁר גָּדְלוּ אִתּוֹ אֲשֶׁר הָעֹמְדִים לְפָנָיו: וַיֹּאמֶר אֲלֵהֶם מָה אַתֶּם נוֹעָצִים וְנָשִׁיב דָּבָר אֶת־הָעָם הַזֶּה אֲשֶׁר דִּבְּרוּ אֵלַי לֵאמֹר הָקֵל מִן־הָעֹל אֲשֶׁר־נָתַן אָבִיךָ עָלֵינוּ: וַיְדַבְּרוּ אֵלָיו הַיְלָדִים אֲשֶׁר גָּדְלוּ אִתּוֹ לֵאמֹר כֹּה־תֹאמַר לָעָם הַזֶּה אֲשֶׁר דִּבְּרוּ אֵלֶיךָ לֵאמֹר אָבִיךָ הִכְבִּיד אֶת־עֻלֵּנוּ וְאַתָּה הָקֵל מֵעָלֵינוּ כֹּה תְּדַבֵּר אֲלֵיהֶם קָטָנִּי עָבָה מִמָּתְנֵי אָבִי: וְעַתָּה אָבִי הֶעְמִיס עֲלֵיכֶם עֹל כָּבֵד וַאֲנִי אֹסִיף עַל־עֻלְּכֶם אָבִי יִסַּר אֶתְכֶם בַּשּׁוֹטִים וַאֲנִי אֲיַסֵּר אֶתְכֶם בָּעַקְרַבִּים:

מְלָכִים א׳ יב:א–יא

151

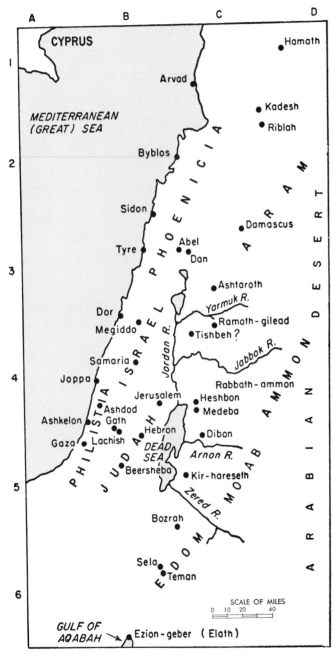

**MAP OF THE DIVIDED KINGDOM**

## Chapter V

# THE DIVIDED KINGDOM: ISRAEL AND JUDAH

ISRAELITE civilization was not destined to make any important contributions to mankind's material progress. The physical and economic geography of the land constituted a formidable obstacle to any such achievement. The natural resources of the region lying between Dan and Beersheba were few, its population small, and economic surpluses, therefore, negligible. Unlike the Egyptians, Phoenicians, and such peoples of western Asia as the Sumerians, Babylonians, and Assyrians, the Israelites never won a major place among the great builders, merchants, or warriors of the ancient Near East.

Israel's defensive situation was not more fortunate. Having made their home in a buffer area amid stronger civilizations, the Israelites were under almost constant pressure or attack from neighbors striving, if not to conquer them outright, at least to use their land as a highway or base for invasion of some rival. Once David's reign was over, the momentary lull in the imperial struggles of western Asia came to an end. Without such a lull the Israelite empire could hardly have

<sup>12</sup>Jeroboam and all the people came to Rehoboam on the third day, as the king had spoken, "Come back on the third day." <sup>13</sup>The king answered the people harshly, rejecting the advice that the elders had given him. <sup>14</sup>He spoke to them in accordance with the advice of the young men, and said, "My father made your yoke heavy; but I will add to your yoke. My father disciplined you with whips; but I will discipline you with scorpions." —<sup>15</sup>The king did not listen to the people; for the LORD had brought it about in order to fulfill the promise which the LORD had made through Ahijah the Shilonite to Jeroboam son of Nebat.—<sup>16</sup>When all Israel saw that the king had not listened to them, the people answered the king:

We have no portion in David,
No share in the son of Jesse!
To your tents, O Israel!
Now look to your own house, O David.

So Israel left for their homes. <sup>17</sup>As for the Israelites who lived in the towns of Judah, Rehoboam continued to reign over them.

*I Kings 12.12-17*

וַיָּבֹא יָרׇבְעָם וְכׇל־הָעָם אֶל־רְחַבְעָם בַּיּוֹם הַשְּׁלִישִׁי כַּאֲשֶׁר דִּבֶּר הַמֶּלֶךְ לֵאמֹר שׁוּבוּ אֵלַי בַּיּוֹם הַשְּׁלִישִׁי: וַיַּעַן הַמֶּלֶךְ אֶת־הָעָם קָשָׁה וַיַּעֲזֹב אֶת־עֲצַת הַזְּקֵנִים אֲשֶׁר יְעָצֻהוּ: וַיְדַבֵּר אֲלֵיהֶם כַּעֲצַת הַיְלָדִים לֵאמֹר אָבִי הִכְבִּיד אֶת־עֻלְּכֶם וַאֲנִי אֹסִיף עַל־עֻלְּכֶם אָבִי יִסַּר אֶתְכֶם בַּשּׁוֹטִים וַאֲנִי אֲיַסֵּר אֶתְכֶם בָּעַקְרַבִּים: וְלֹא־שָׁמַע הַמֶּלֶךְ אֶל־הָעָם כִּי־הָיְתָה סִבָּה מֵעִם יְהֹוָה לְמַעַן הָקִים אֶת־דְּבָרוֹ אֲשֶׁר דִּבֶּר יְהֹוָה בְּיַד אֲחִיָּה הַשִּׁילֹנִי אֶל־יָרׇבְעָם בֶּן־נְבָט: וַיַּרְא כׇּל־יִשְׂרָאֵל כִּי לֹא־שָׁמַע הַמֶּלֶךְ אֲלֵהֶם וַיָּשִׁבוּ הָעָם אֶת־הַמֶּלֶךְ דָּבָר ׀ לֵאמֹר מַה־לָּנוּ חֵלֶק בְּדָוִד וְלֹא־נַחֲלָה בְּבֶן־יִשַׁי לְאֹהָלֶיךָ יִשְׂרָאֵל עַתָּה רְאֵה בֵיתְךָ דָּוִד וַיֵּלֶךְ יִשְׂרָאֵל לְאֹהָלָיו: וּבְנֵי יִשְׂרָאֵל הַיֹּשְׁבִים בְּעָרֵי יְהוּדָה וַיִּמְלֹךְ עֲלֵיהֶם רְחַבְעָם:

מְלָכִים א׳ יב: יב—יז

153

In the 9th century, after several centuries of imperialistic inactivity, Assyria renewed its expansion efforts to conquer lands as far west as the Mediterranean Sea. Foremost in these efforts of expansion were Ashurnasirpal II and Shalmeneser III.

As a prelude to what the Divided Monarchy of the Israelites was to expect, the Assyrians exacted tribute from cities like Tyre (a), accepted surrender from cities like Hama (b), and massacred the inhabitants of those cities that resisted (c).

Bronze overlay for gates at the town of Imgur-Bel (modern Balawat), between Nineveh and Nimrud, made for Shalmeneser III (858-824) and now in the British Museum. Each strip is about 10½ inches high.

A

B

C

emerged at all; and when it was over, Judah and Israel had no rest. Actual invasions were not uncommon, and the threat of possible or impending attack was almost constant. These same conditions, on the other hand, provided the setting for the Israelite genius which came to express itself in the realm of culture and religion; and it was largely during the period of the Divided Kingdom that the Israelite civilization took on its definite shape and character.

## The Two Kingdoms in Equilibrium

The split between Judah and Israel, following the revolt of Jeroboam, leader of the northern rebels, against Rehoboam, successor to Solomon, resulted in a stalemate. Israel, the northern segment, being larger both in total arable land and population; and more favorably situated in regard to the caravan-commercial routes connecting western Asia and Egypt, was wealthier than its rival. But if Judah, from whose soil the state of David had sprung, was smaller and geographically more concentrated, it was for that very reason, at least in part, more efficiently administered and far less torn by regional conflicts. Israel was united in large measure by its opposition to Judah. Several powerful groups sought the control of the country, and Jeroboam held the discordant segments of the newborn kingdom together largely because its independent existence was threatened by Rehoboam and his son and successor, Abijah (Abijam).

Had the two kingdoms been left to themselves, either might have gained the ascendancy over its opponent. But the major factors in preserving an equilibrium were external. Egypt, for a short time, and then Aram and Assyria, managed to preserve a balance of power between the two.

# The Two Kingdoms in Equilibrium

<sup>20</sup>When all Israel heard that Jeroboam had returned, they sent messengers and summoned him to the assembly and made him king over all Israel. Only the tribe of Judah remained loyal to the House of David. <sup>21</sup>When Rehoboam reached Jerusalem, he mustered all the House of Judah and the tribe of Benjamin, 180,000 picked warriors, to fight against the House of Israel and restore the kingship to Rehoboam son of Solomon. <sup>22</sup>But the word of God came to Shemaiah, the man of God: <sup>23</sup>Say to Rehoboam . . . and to all the House of Judah and Benjamin . . . <sup>24</sup>"Thus said the LORD: You shall not set out to wage war against your fellow Israelites. Let every man return to his home, for this thing has been brought about by Me." They heeded the word of the LORD, and turned back in accordance with the word of the LORD.

<sup>25</sup>Jeroboam fortified Shechem in the hill country of Ephraim and settled there; and he went out from there and fortified Penuel. <sup>26</sup>Jeroboam said to himself, "As things are, the kingdom will revert to the House of David. <sup>27</sup>If this people continues to go up to offer sacrifices at the House of the LORD in Jerusalem, the heart of this people will turn back to their master, King Rehoboam of Judah, and they will kill me and go back to King Rehoboam of Judah." <sup>28</sup>The king took counsel, and made two golden calves. He said to them (the people), "You have been going up to Jerusalem long enough. Here are your gods, O Israel, who brought you up from the land of Egypt." <sup>29</sup>He set one up in Bethel, and placed the other in Dan. <sup>30</sup>This became a cause of sin, for the people went to worship the one (at Bethel or the other) at Dan.

*1 Kings 12.20-30*

כְּשְׁמֹעַ כָּל־יִשְׂרָאֵל כִּי־שָׁב יָרָבְעָם וַיִּשְׁלְחוּ וַיִּקְרְאוּ אֹתוֹ אֶל־הָעֵדָה וַיַּמְלִיכוּ אֹתוֹ עַל־כָּל־יִשְׂרָאֵל לֹא הָיָה אַחֲרֵי בֵית־דָּוִד זוּלָתִי שֵׁבֶט־יְהוּדָה לְבַדּוֹ: וַיָּבֹאוּ רְחַבְעָם יְרוּשָׁלִַם וַיַּקְהֵל אֶת־כָּל־בֵּית יְהוּדָה וְאֶת־שֵׁבֶט בִּנְיָמִן מֵאָה וּשְׁמֹנִים אֶלֶף בָּחוּר עֹשֵׂה מִלְחָמָה לְהִלָּחֵם עִם־בֵּית יִשְׂרָאֵל לְהָשִׁיב אֶת־הַמְּלוּכָה לִרְחַבְעָם בֶּן־שְׁלֹמֹה: וַיְהִי דְּבַר הָאֱלֹהִים אֶל־שְׁמַעְיָה אִישׁ־הָאֱלֹהִים לֵאמֹר: אֱמֹר אֶל־רְחַבְעָם . . . וְאֶל־כָּל־בֵּית יְהוּדָה וּבִנְיָמִין . . . לֵאמֹר: כֹּה אָמַר יְהֹוָה לֹא־תַעֲלוּ וְלֹא־תִלָּחֲמוּן עִם־אֲחֵיכֶם בְּנֵי־יִשְׂרָאֵל שׁוּבוּ אִישׁ לְבֵיתוֹ כִּי מֵאִתִּי נִהְיָה הַדָּבָר הַזֶּה וַיִּשְׁמְעוּ אֶת־דְּבַר יְהֹוָה וַיָּשֻׁבוּ לָלֶכֶת כִּדְבַר יְהֹוָה: וַיִּבֶן יָרָבְעָם אֶת־שְׁכֶם בְּהַר אֶפְרַיִם וַיֵּשֶׁב בָּהּ וַיֵּצֵא מִשָּׁם וַיִּבֶן אֶת־פְּנוּאֵל: וַיֹּאמֶר יָרָבְעָם בְּלִבּוֹ עַתָּה תָּשׁוּב הַמַּמְלָכָה לְבֵית־דָּוִד: אִם־יַעֲלֶה הָעָם הַזֶּה לַעֲשׂוֹת זְבָחִים בְּבֵית־יְהֹוָה בִּירוּשָׁלִַם וְשָׁב לֵב הָעָם הַזֶּה אֶל־אֲדֹנֵיהֶם אֶל־רְחַבְעָם מֶלֶךְ יְהוּדָה וַהֲרָגֻנִי וְשָׁבוּ אֶל־רְחַבְעָם מֶלֶךְ־יְהוּדָה: וַיִּוָּעַץ הַמֶּלֶךְ וַיַּעַשׂ שְׁנֵי עֶגְלֵי זָהָב וַיֹּאמֶר אֲלֵהֶם רַב־לָכֶם מֵעֲלוֹת יְרוּשָׁלִַם הִנֵּה אֱלֹהֶיךָ יִשְׂרָאֵל אֲשֶׁר הֶעֱלוּךָ מֵאֶרֶץ מִצְרָיִם: וַיָּשֶׂם אֶת־הָאֶחָד בְּבֵית־אֵל וְאֶת־הָאֶחָד נָתַן בְּדָן: וַיְהִי הַדָּבָר הַזֶּה לְחַטָּאת וַיֵּלְכוּ הָעָם לִפְנֵי הָאֶחָד עַד־דָּן:

מְלָכִים א׳: י"ב: כ-ל

    *While he has traditionally been accused of setting up idols ("golden calves")—the Hebrew text itself makes it clear that Jeroboam's purpose was political—most scholars now tend to believe that what Jeroboam set up was really pedestals in the form of golden calves upon which the invisible God of Israel was enthroned. These pedestals are the* cherubim *of the Bible, and when God is described as* יֹשֵׁב הַכְּרֻבִים *(Isaiah 37.16; Psalms 80.2; 99.1), it means that He is "Enthroned on the Cherubim." These* cherubim *are common in the ancient Near East, and are not to be confused with the medieval notion of them. (See T. H. Gaster's article on "Angel," §3, "Cherubim and Seraphim," in* Interpreter's Dictionary of the Bible, *I, pp. 131-32.)*

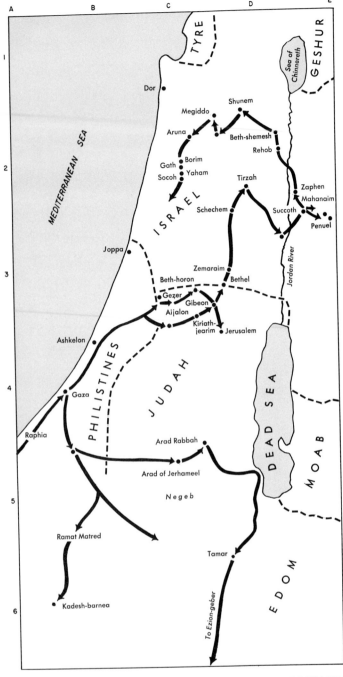

CAMPAIGN OF KING SHISHAK (SHESHONK) OF EGYPT (ABOUT 920 B.C.E.).

## The International Setting: Egypt, Aram, Assyria

After lying dormant several centuries, Egypt began to show renewed signs of imperial vigor under Shishak, founder of the Twenty-second Dynasty. By harboring such enemies of Solomon as Jeroboam and Hadad the Edomite, Shishak had helped split united Israel and then, exploiting the break, he moved at once to invade the southern kingdom of Judah.

Anticipating an Egyptian invasion, Rehoboam shelved the idea of challenging the secessionist government of Israel and instead made a feverish attempt to strengthen his own defenses (II Chronicles 11:5–12). These efforts proved of no avail when Shishak's army began to march (about 920 B.C.E.): fortified cities of Judah fell one after another, and the treasures of the palace and Temple in Jerusalem fell into the enemy's hands.

At first, northern Israel welcomed the breathing spell provided by Egypt's invasion of Judah. But Shishak's mixed hordes did not stop at the boundaries of Judah; they pushed on into the territory of Israel, as well as south into Edom and west into Philistia. Difficulties at home, however, prevented Shishak from exploiting this brilliant beginning; and except for an unsuccessful attack against Rehoboam's grandson Asa, at Mareshah, Egypt did not again disturb western Asia seriously for several centuries. Yet in one respect, at least, this isolated imperialist irruption was of great significance: it left Judah unable to re-establish its old predominance over Israel.

The split between Israel and Judah considerably facilitated the emergence of several Aramean states in the northern part of the area that lay between Israel and the Euphrates, i.e., Syria. The two most prominent

156

Rehoboam resided in Jerusalem,	and rebuilt
towns for defense in Judah. ⁶He fortified Bethlehem . . . ⁷Beth-zur . . . ⁸Gath . . . ⁹ . . . Lachish,
Azekah, ¹⁰. . . and Hebron . . . ¹¹ . . . He placed
commanders in them, and stores of food, oil, wine,
¹² . . . shields, and spears . . .

*II Chronicles 11.5-12*

וַיֵּשֶׁב רְחַבְעָם בִּירוּשָׁלָ͏ִם וַיִּבֶן עָרִים לְמָצוֹר
בִּיהוּדָה: וַיִּבֶן אֶת־בֵּית־לָחֶם... וְאֶת־בֵּית־צוּר...
וְאֶת־גַּת... וְאֶת־לָכִישׁ וְאֶת־עֲזֵקָה...וְאֶת־חֶבְרוֹן...
וַיִּתֵּן בָּהֶם נְגִידִים וְאֹצְרוֹת מַאֲכָל וְשֶׁמֶן וָיָיִן:...
צִנּוֹת וּרְמָחִים...

דִּבְרֵי הַיָּמִים ב' יא:ה-יב

In the fifth year of King Rehoboam, King Shishak of Egypt marched against Jerusalem. ²⁶He
took (as tribute) the treasures of the House of
the LORD and the treasures of the royal palace;
he took everything, even taking all the golden
shields that Solomon had made. ²⁷King Rehoboam had bronze shields made instead, and put
them in the charge of the officers of the guard
(or outrunners), who stood guard at the entrance
of the royal palace.

*I Kings 14.25-27*

וַיְהִי בַּשָּׁנָה הַחֲמִישִׁית לַמֶּלֶךְ רְחַבְעָם עָלָה שׁוּשַׁק
מֶלֶךְ־מִצְרַיִם עַל־יְרוּשָׁלָ͏ִם: וַיִּקַּח אֶת־אֹצְרוֹת
בֵּית־יְהוָה וְאֶת־אוֹצְרוֹת בֵּית־הַמֶּלֶךְ וְאֶת־הַכֹּל
לָקָח וַיִּקַּח אֶת־כָּל־מָגִנֵּי הַזָּהָב אֲשֶׁר עָשָׂה שְׁלֹמֹה:
וַיַּעַשׂ הַמֶּלֶךְ רְחַבְעָם תַּחְתָּם מָגִנֵּי נְחֹשֶׁת וְהִפְקִיד
עַל־יַד שָׂרֵי הָרָצִים הַשֹּׁמְרִים פֶּתַח בֵּית הַמֶּלֶךְ:

מְלָכִים א' יד:כה-כז

There was war between Asa and King Baasha . . .
all their days. ¹⁷King Baasha of Israel marched
against Judah, and he fortified Ramah to prevent
anyone belonging to King Asa of Judah from going out or coming in. ¹⁸Asa took all the silver and
gold left in the treasures of the House of the LORD
and in those of the king's palace and, handing
them over to his officials, King Asa sent them to
Ben-hadad son of Tabrimmon son of Hezion,
king of Aram, who resided in Damascus, with
this message: ¹⁹"There is a pact between you and
me, between your father and my father. I herewith send you a gift of silver and gold. Go
and break your pact with King Baasha of Israel, so that he will lift his siege (lit., withdraw
from me)." ²⁰Ben-hadad heeded King Asa; he
sent his army commanders against the towns of
Israel, and captured Ijon, Dan, Abel-beth-maacah, and all Chinneroth, as well as all the territory of Naphtali. ²¹When Baasha heard about it,
he stopped fortifying Ramah and settled in Tirzah.

*I Kings 15.16-21*

וּמִלְחָמָה הָיְתָה בֵּין אָסָא וּבֵין בַּעְשָׁא מֶלֶךְ־
יִשְׂרָאֵל כָּל־יְמֵיהֶם:
וַיַּעַל בַּעְשָׁא מֶלֶךְ־יִשְׂרָאֵל עַל־יְהוּדָה וַיִּבֶן
אֶת־הָרָמָה לְבִלְתִּי תֵּת יֹצֵא וָבָא לְאָסָא מֶלֶךְ
יְהוּדָה: וַיִּקַּח אָסָא אֶת־כָּל־הַכֶּסֶף וְהַזָּהָב הַנּוֹתָרִים
בְּאוֹצְרוֹת בֵּית־יְהוָה וְאֶת־אוֹצְרוֹת בֵּית הַמֶּלֶךְ
וַיִּתְּנֵם בְּיַד עֲבָדָיו וַיִּשְׁלָחֵם הַמֶּלֶךְ אָסָא אֶל־בֶּן־
הֲדַד בֶּן־טַבְרִמֹּן בֶּן־חֶזְיוֹן מֶלֶךְ אֲרָם הַיֹּשֵׁב
בְּדַמֶּשֶׂק לֵאמֹר: בְּרִית בֵּינִי וּבֵינֶךָ בֵּין אָבִי וּבֵין
אָבִיךָ הִנֵּה שָׁלַחְתִּי לְךָ שֹׁחַד כֶּסֶף וְזָהָב לֵךְ הָפֵרָה
אֶת־בְּרִיתְךָ אֶת־בַּעְשָׁא מֶלֶךְ־יִשְׂרָאֵל וְיַעֲלֶה
מֵעָלָי: וַיִּשְׁמַע בֶּן־הֲדַד אֶל־הַמֶּלֶךְ אָסָא וַיִּשְׁלַח
אֶת־שָׂרֵי הַחֲיָלִים אֲשֶׁר־לוֹ עַל־עָרֵי יִשְׂרָאֵל וַיַּךְ
אֶת־עִיּוֹן וְאֶת־דָּן וְאֵת אָבֵל בֵּית־מַעֲכָה וְאֵת
כָּל־כִּנְרוֹת עַל כָּל־אֶרֶץ נַפְתָּלִי: וַיְהִי כִּשְׁמֹעַ
בַּעְשָׁא וַיֶּחְדַּל מִבְּנוֹת אֶת־הָרָמָה וַיֵּשֶׁב בְּתִרְצָה:

מְלָכִים א' טו:טז-כא

157

Upper half of a statuette of King Ashurnasirpal II of Assyria (883-859) on a bas-relief, originally in his palace at Nimrud (ancient Calah).

Two beardless (Aramean?) figures from a procession carved on a series of orthostats which were excavated at Zinjirli (ancient Samal). The figure on the right wears his hair in shoulder-length curls and has an earlock. The stone is about 37 inches high.

Foundation course of a city wall of Samaria (9th cent.). The bossed masonry, arranged alternately in headers (short sides) and stretchers (long side), is characteristic of the period.

of these were Aram Zobah and Aram Damascus. The former controlled the area which lay east of Damascus and Hamath, and the latter, as the name would indicate, revolved essentially about the ancient and commercially important city of Damascus.

The powerful state of David and Solomon had held the various Aramean states in check. Divided, Israel and Judah were less successful. Now and then they joined forces against the Arameans, and at other times one or the other entered into a coalition with an Aramean state against her sister state. When Israel under King Baasha overran the northern part of Judah, the latter paid Ben-hadad of Aram to invade Israel and thus draw off her troops. A few decades later, however, King Jehoshaphat of Judah and King Ahab of Israel once more joined forces against Aram.

Phoenicia, too, failed to maintain its independence. Faced by the growing power first of the Arameans and later of the Assyrians, the Phoenicians continued to cultivate their neighborly relations with Israel. This policy led, among other things, to the marriage of Ahab, son of King Omri of Israel, to Jezebel, daughter of King Ittobaal of Phoenicia. Early in the ninth century, the Assyrian Ashurnasirpal II (about 883–859 B.C.E.) managed to reduce parts of Phoenicia to a tributary status and at the same time to establish the reputation of the Assyrian armies for merciless brutality. Ashurnasirpal himself boasted over his vanquished foes, "With their blood I dyed the mountain red like wool." Under Shalmaneser III (about 858–824 B.C.E.) Assyria continued its drive westward with ever-increasing military and economic pressure.

The Assyrian menace provoked a reaction in the form of a defensive coalition in the region headed by the Israelites and Arameans. The royal Assyrian chronicle recounts that

158

Ahab son of Omri became king over Israel in the thirty-eighth year of King Asa of Judah; and Ahab son of Omri reigned over Israel in Samaria for twenty-two years. ³⁰Ahab son of Omri did what was evil in the sight of the LORD, more than everyone else before him. ³¹As if it were not enough that he followed in the sinful ways of Jeroboam son of Nebat, he took for a wife Jezebel daughter of Ethbaal of the Sidonians (Phoenicians), and he went and served Baal and worshiped him. ³²He erected an altar to Baal in the temple of Baal which he built in Samaria.

*I Kings 16.29-32*

וְאַחְאָב בֶּן־עָמְרִי מָלַךְ עַל־יִשְׂרָאֵל בִּשְׁנַת
שְׁלֹשִׁים וּשְׁמֹנֶה שָׁנָה לְאָסָא מֶלֶךְ יְהוּדָה וַיִּמְלֹךְ
אַחְאָב בֶּן־עָמְרִי עַל־יִשְׂרָאֵל בְּשֹׁמְרוֹן עֶשְׂרִים
וּשְׁתַּיִם שָׁנָה:
וַיַּעַשׂ אַחְאָב בֶּן־עָמְרִי הָרַע בְּעֵינֵי יְהוָה מִכֹּל
אֲשֶׁר לְפָנָיו: וַיְהִי הֲנָקֵל לֶכְתּוֹ בְּחַטֹּאות יָרָבְעָם
בֶּן־נְבָט וַיִּקַּח אִשָּׁה אֶת־אִיזֶבֶל בַּת־אֶתְבַּעַל מֶלֶךְ
צִידֹנִים וַיֵּלֶךְ וַיַּעֲבֹד אֶת־הַבַּעַל וַיִּשְׁתַּחוּ לוֹ: וַיָּקֶם
מִזְבֵּחַ לַבַּעַל בֵּית הַבַּעַל אֲשֶׁר בָּנָה בְּשֹׁמְרוֹן:

מְלָכִים א׳ טז: כט –לב

Three years went by without war between Aram and Israel. ²Then, in the third year, King Jehoshaphat of Judah went down to (visit) the king of Israel. ³The king of Israel said to his officials, "Do you realize that Ramoth-gilead is ours, yet we sit idle and do not wrest it from the hands of the king of Aram? ⁴And he said to Jehoshaphat, "Will you come with me to attack Ramoth-gilead?" Jehoshaphat replied to the king of Israel, "I am one with you, my troops are one with your troops, my horses one with your horses . . ." ²⁹So the king of Israel and King Jehoshaphat of Judah marched against Ramoth-gilead.

*I Kings 22.1-4, 29*

וַיֵּשְׁבוּ שָׁלֹשׁ שָׁנִים אֵין מִלְחָמָה בֵּין אֲרָם וּבֵין
יִשְׂרָאֵל: וַיְהִי בַּשָּׁנָה הַשְּׁלִישִׁית וַיֵּרֶד יְהוֹשָׁפָט מֶלֶךְ־
יְהוּדָה אֶל־מֶלֶךְ יִשְׂרָאֵל: וַיֹּאמֶר מֶלֶךְ יִשְׂרָאֵל
אֶל־עֲבָדָיו הַיְדַעְתֶּם כִּי־לָנוּ רָמֹת גִּלְעָד וַאֲנַחְנוּ
מַחְשִׁים מִקַּחַת אֹתָהּ מִיַּד מֶלֶךְ אֲרָם: וַיֹּאמֶר
אֶל־יְהוֹשָׁפָט הֲתֵלֵךְ אִתִּי לַמִּלְחָמָה רָמֹת גִּלְעָד
וַיֹּאמֶר יְהוֹשָׁפָט אֶל־מֶלֶךְ יִשְׂרָאֵל כָּמוֹנִי כָמוֹךָ
כְּעַמִּי כְעַמֶּךָ כְּסוּסַי כְּסוּסֶיךָ:...וַיַּעַל מֶלֶךְ־יִשְׂרָאֵל
וִיהוֹשָׁפָט מֶלֶךְ־יְהוּדָה רָמֹת גִּלְעָד:

מְלָכִים א׳ כב: א–ד, כט

The Black Obelisk commemorating the campaigns of Shalmeneser III (858-824). The scenes follow the circumference of the monument, each register describing a different event—in this case tribute offerings of different rulers and countries. About 6 feet 8 inches high.

Detail of the second register of the Black Obelisk, showing King Jehu, son of Omri, of the Northern Kingdom of Israel, capitulating to the Assyrian ruler in the presence of court officials and of the symbols of two divinities. Above the panel runs part of the explanatory description in the cuneiform characters of the Assyrian language. The signs visible on this side of the obelisk read:

tribute of Jehu son of Omri.

ma-da-tu ša ᵐya-u-a mar ᵐhu-um-ri-i

On the other three sides, the inscription goes on to say: gold, a golden bowl, a golden vase with pointed base, golden tumblers, golden buckets, tin, a staff for a king . . .

King Ahab of Israel contributed 2,000 chariots and 10,000 foot soldiers to the coalition; but, in spite of this magnificence, its forces were defeated at the battle of Karkar, near Hamath (about 853). It does not appear that the Assyrian army was able to exploit the victory at once; but within ten years Shalmaneser's government was collecting tribute from states as far west as Israel and Phoenicia. From then until the Medes and a resurgent Babylonia brought her to heel some two and a half centuries later (612–605 B.C.E.), Assyria held not only Judah and Israel but all of western Asia in her sway.

## The Northern Kingdom of Israel

No single major group within Israel ever became strong enough to dominate the entire kingdom for more than a generation or two at a time. Chronic plotting for the succession —the sign and result of internal imbalances —repeatedly brought kings and would-be kings to bloody ends. The dynasty of Jeroboam ended abruptly with the murder of his son Nadab. After ruling only two years, he was murdered while battling to take Gibbethon from the Philistines (about 905). His assassin, Baasha of the tribe of Issachar, seized the throne; but Baasha's son and successor, Elah, was in his turn assassinated after a reign of two years. Again the murderer, this time a certain Zimri, "commander of one-half of the chariotry," succeeded his victim, but for only seven days! To avoid the humiliation of being killed by Omri, commander-in-chief of Elah's forces, Zimri set fire to his headquarters in Tirzah and died in the holocaust.

During the next several years civil war raged in Israel between forces led by Omri and the followers of his rival, Tibni. About 878 B.C.E. Omri finally gained the upper hand and established what the Assyrian royal chronicles called the "House of Omri" (I Kings 15:9 ff.; 16:1–23).

# The Northern Kingdom of Israel

Nadab son of Jeroboam became king over Israel in the second year of King Asa of Judah, and he reigned over Israel for two years. [26]He did what was evil in the sight of the Lord, and he continued the sinful acts of his father by which he had led Israel to sin. [27]Then Baasha son of Ahijah of the house of Issacher conspired against him; and Baasha struck him down in Gibbethon, which belonged to the Philistines, while Nadab and all Israel were laying siege to Gibbethon. [28]Baasha killed him in the third year of King Asa of Judah, and succeeded him as king. [29]As soon as he became king, he struck down all the House of Jeroboam, sparing no one, until he had destroyed it—in accordance with the word that the LORD had spoken by His servant Ahijah the Shilonite.

*I Kings 15.25-29*

וְנָדָב בֶּן־יָרָבְעָם מָלַךְ עַל־יִשְׂרָאֵל בִּשְׁנַת שְׁתַּיִם לְאָסָא מֶלֶךְ יְהוּדָה וַיִּמְלֹךְ עַל־יִשְׂרָאֵל שְׁנָתָיִם: וַיַּעַשׂ הָרַע בְּעֵינֵי יְהוָה וַיֵּלֶךְ בְּדֶרֶךְ אָבִיו וּבְחַטָּאתוֹ אֲשֶׁר הֶחֱטִיא אֶת־יִשְׂרָאֵל: וַיִּקְשֹׁר עָלָיו בַּעְשָׁא בֶן־אֲחִיָּה לְבֵית יִשָּׂשכָר וַיַּכֵּהוּ בַעְשָׁא בְּגִבְּתוֹן אֲשֶׁר לַפְּלִשְׁתִּים וְנָדָב וְכָל־יִשְׂרָאֵל צָרִים עַל־גִּבְּתוֹן: וַיְמִתֵהוּ בַעְשָׁא בִּשְׁנַת שָׁלֹשׁ לְאָסָא מֶלֶךְ יְהוּדָה וַיִּמְלֹךְ תַּחְתָּיו: וַיְהִי כְמָלְכוֹ הִכָּה אֶת־כָּל־בֵּית יָרָבְעָם לֹא־הִשְׁאִיר כָּל־נְשָׁמָה לְיָרָבְעָם עַד־הִשְׁמִדוֹ כִּדְבַר יְהוָה אֲשֶׁר דִּבֶּר בְּיַד־עַבְדּוֹ אֲחִיָּה הַשִּׁילֹנִי:

מְלָכִים א׳ טו:כה–כט

Zimri destroyed the whole House of Baasha in accordance with the word that the LORD had spoken concerning Baasha through the prophet Jehu—[13]because of all the sinful acts which Baasha and his son Elah committed and led Israel to commit, provoking the LORD, the God of Israel, with their idols (lit., futilities) . . . [17]Omri and all Israel with him raised the siege of Gibbethon and laid siege to Tirzah; [18]and when Zimri saw that the town was captured, he went into the citadel of the royal palace and burnt down the royal palace over himself, and he died.

*I Kings 16.12-18*

וַיַּשְׁמֵד זִמְרִי אֵת כָּל־בֵּית בַּעְשָׁא כִּדְבַר יְהוָה אֲשֶׁר דִּבֶּר אֶל־בַּעְשָׁא בְּיַד יֵהוּא הַנָּבִיא: אֶל כָּל־חַטֹּאות בַּעְשָׁא וְחַטֹּאות אֵלָה בְנוֹ אֲשֶׁר חָטְאוּ וַאֲשֶׁר הֶחֱטִיאוּ אֶת־יִשְׂרָאֵל לְהַכְעִיס אֶת־יְהוָה אֱלֹהֵי יִשְׂרָאֵל בְּהַבְלֵיהֶם: . . . וַיַּעֲלֶה עָמְרִי וְכָל־יִשְׂרָאֵל עִמּוֹ מִגִּבְּתוֹן וַיָּצֻרוּ עַל־תִּרְצָה: וַיְהִי כִּרְאוֹת זִמְרִי כִּי־נִלְכְּדָה הָעִיר וַיָּבֹא אֶל־אַרְמוֹן בֵּית־הַמֶּלֶךְ וַיִּשְׂרֹף עָלָיו אֶת־בֵּית־מֶלֶךְ בָּאֵשׁ וַיָּמֹת:

מְלָכִים א׳ טז:יב–יח

Then the people of Israel split into two: one part followed Tibni son of Ginath to proclaim him king, the other followed Omri. [22]The people who followed Omri prevailed against those who followed Tibni son of Ginath; Tibni died and Omri became king.

*I Kings 16.21-22*

אָז יֵחָלֵק הָעָם יִשְׂרָאֵל לַחֵצִי חֲצִי הָעָם הָיָה אַחֲרֵי תִבְנִי בֶן־גִּינַת לְהַמְלִיכוֹ וְהַחֲצִי אַחֲרֵי עָמְרִי: וַיֶּחֱזַק הָעָם אֲשֶׁר אַחֲרֵי עָמְרִי אֶת־הָעָם אֲשֶׁר אַחֲרֵי תִבְנִי בֶן־גִּינַת וַיָּמָת תִּבְנִי וַיִּמְלֹךְ עָמְרִי:

מְלָכִים א׳ טז: כא–כב

Ninth-century buildings at Megiddo, formerly called "Solomon's Stables" but most probably built following the division of the United Kingdom. The upper picture shows the remains after excavation; the lower attempts to reconstruct its original appearance.

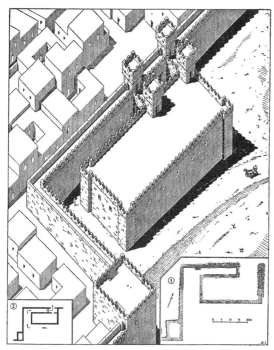

A reconstruction of the city-gate on the eastern part of the summit of Samaria. The construction at Samaria was essentially the work of King Omri and his son Ahab.

## The Omride Dynasty

It was under Omri that the northern kingdom acquired, for the first time, a permanent and impressive capital. Abandoning Tirzah, which had served as a kind of capital for several decades, Omri built a new political center, which he named Samaria. From the excavations at this site, a good picture is gained of the magnificent palace and fortifications which he and his son Ahab erected there. And at Megiddo, 20 miles to the north of Samaria, excavations have uncovered the remains of what were the mammoth stables that housed some 480 of Ahab's countless horses. (These used to be known as "Solomon's Stables," but recent study seems to have set the record straight.)

The house of Omri brought prosperity to the northern kingdom. Aram for the time being had ceased to threaten, Moab in Transjordan was under control, and relations with rapidly expanding Phoenicia developed along lines of mutual economic interest. This prosperity, however, was restricted almost exclusively to Israel's upper class. The common people, those who worked with their hands in the towns and on the land, derived little enough from this increasing wealth. The petty farmer increasingly lost his crops and his land to the big landowner. The apprentices and artisans found the economic and social gap widening between themselves and their masters. The merchant class became richer and more influential than before. Freemen were becoming slaves, and the poor were being compelled to sell their children into bondage. Where members of the lower classes were able to obtain loans from the rich, it was usually at exorbitant rates of interest. Nor was the economic and social structure helped by the periodic droughts which came upon the land, such as the drought and famine recorded in the days of Ahab.

## The Omride Dynasty

He bought the hill of Samaria from Shemer for two talents of silver, and fortified the hill; and he named the city which he built Samaria, after the name, Shemer, of the owner of the hill.

*I Kings 16.24*

וַיִּקֶן אֶת־הָהָר שֹׁמְרוֹן מֵאֶת שֶׁמֶר בְּכִכְּרַיִם כָּסֶף וַיִּבֶן אֶת־הָהָר וַיִּקְרָא אֶת־שֵׁם הָעִיר אֲשֶׁר בָּנָה עַל שֶׁם־שֶׁמֶר אֲדֹנֵי הָהָר שֹׁמְרוֹן:

מְלָכִים א׳ טז:כד

[Elijah asked the widow at the Phoenician town of Zarephath to fetch him some water.] ¹¹When she went to fetch it, he called out to her, "Please bring with you a piece of bread for me." ¹²But she replied, "As the LORD your God lives, I have nothing baked, only a handful of flour in a jar and a little oil in a cruse; I am gathering a couple of sticks, and I shall go and prepare this for my son and myself to eat, and then we shall die."

*I Kings 17.11-12*

וַתֵּלֶךְ לָקַחַת וַיִּקְרָא אֵלֶיהָ וַיֹּאמַר לִקְחִי־נָא לִי פַת־לֶחֶם בְּיָדֵךְ: וַתֹּאמֶר חַי־יְהֹוָה אֱלֹהֶיךָ אִם־יֶשׁ־לִי מָעוֹג כִּי אִם־מְלֹא כַף־קֶמַח בַּכַּד וּמְעַט־שֶׁמֶן בַּצַּפָּחַת וְהִנְנִי מְקֹשֶׁשֶׁת שְׁנַיִם עֵצִים וּבָאתִי וַעֲשִׂיתִיהוּ לִי וְלִבְנִי וַאֲכַלְנֻהוּ וָמָתְנוּ:

מְלָכִים א׳ יז:יא–יב

Elijah set out to appear before Ahab; and the famine was severe in Samaria . . . ⁵Ahab said to Obadiah, "Go through the land to all the springs of water and to all the wadis. Perhaps we shall find some grass to keep horses and mules alive, so that we are not left without animals."

*I Kings 18.2,5*

וַיֵּלֶךְ אֵלִיָּהוּ לְהֵרָאוֹת אֶל־אַחְאָב וְהָרָעָב חָזָק בְּשֹׁמְרוֹן: וַיֹּאמֶר אַחְאָב אֶל־עֹבַדְיָהוּ לֵךְ בָּאָרֶץ אֶל־כָּל־מַעְיְנֵי הַמַּיִם וְאֶל כָּל־הַנְּחָלִים אוּלַי נִמְצָא חָצִיר וּנְחַיֶּה סוּס וָפֶרֶד וְלוֹא נַכְרִית מֵהַבְּהֵמָה:

מְלָכִים א׳ יח:ב, ה

## Ahab, Naboth, and Elijah

It was sometime afterward. Naboth the Jezreelite had a vineyard in Jezreel, near the palace of King Ahab of Samaria. ²Ahab spoke to Naboth. "Give me your vineyard," he said, "that I may have it for a vegetable garden, since it is next to my house. In exchange I'll give you a better vineyard, or if you prefer, I will give you its equivalent in silver." ³But Naboth replied to Ahab, "The LORD forbid that I should give you my ancestral property!" ⁴Ahab went home sullen and seething because of the reply that Naboth the Jezreelite gave him when he said, "I will not give you my ancentral property." He lay down on his couch, turned away his face and refused to eat.

וַיְהִי אַחַר הַדְּבָרִים הָאֵלֶּה כֶּרֶם הָיָה לְנָבוֹת הַיִּזְרְעֵאלִי אֲשֶׁר בְּיִזְרְעֶאל אֵצֶל הֵיכַל אַחְאָב מֶלֶךְ שֹׁמְרוֹן: וַיְדַבֵּר אַחְאָב אֶל־נָבוֹת לֵאמֹר תְּנָה־לִי אֶת־כַּרְמְךָ וִיהִי־לִי לְגַן־יָרָק כִּי הוּא קָרוֹב אֵצֶל בֵּיתִי וְאֶתְּנָה לְךָ תַּחְתָּיו כֶּרֶם טוֹב מִמֶּנּוּ אִם טוֹב בְּעֵינֶיךָ אֶתְּנָה־לְךָ כֶסֶף מְחִיר זֶה: וַיֹּאמֶר נָבוֹת אֶל־אַחְאָב חָלִילָה לִּי מֵיהֹוָה מִתִּתִּי אֶת־נַחֲלַת אֲבֹתַי לָךְ: וַיָּבֹא אַחְאָב אֶל־בֵּיתוֹ סַר וְזָעֵף עַל־הַדָּבָר אֲשֶׁר־דִּבֶּר אֵלָיו נָבוֹת הַיִּזְרְעֵאלִי וַיֹּאמֶר לֹא־אֶתֵּן לְךָ אֶת־נַחֲלַת אֲבוֹתָי וַיִּשְׁכַּב עַל־מִטָּתוֹ וַיַּסֵּב אֶת־פָּנָיו וְלֹא־אָכַל לָחֶם:

*(continued)*

163

Inscription of King Mesha of Moab (about 830 B.C.E.); 34 lines preserved, several toward the bottom incompletely. It reads: (Lines 1-9.)

I (am) Mesha, son of Chemosh-[ . . . ], king of Moab, the Dibonite—my father (had) reigned over Moab thirty years, and I reigned after my father,—(who) made this high place for Chemosh in Qarhoh [ . . . ] because he saved me from all the kings and caused me to triumph over all my adversaries. As for Omri, (5) king of Israel, he humbled Moab many years (lit., days), for Chemosh was angry at his land. And his son followed him and he also said, "I will humble Moab." In my time he spoke (thus), but I have triumphed over him and over his house, while Israel hath perished for ever! (Now) Omri had occupied the land of Medeba, and (Israel) had dwelt there in his time and half the time of his son (Ahab), forty years; but Chemosh dwelt there in my time.

## Ahab, Naboth, and Elijah

It was during this period that the event occurred which is recorded in I Kings 21, and is now celebrated in the annals of justice and literature. Naboth, a commoner, owned a vineyard which lay next to King Ahab's palace. The king, determined to acquire the land for a vegetable garden, made the owner several offers for his vineyard. But Naboth, a man of strong ancestral sentiment, would not trade or sell the property he had inherited from his fathers. Thereupon Jezebel, Ahab's Phoenician wife, took matters into her own hands. She bribed two men to accuse Naboth falsely of having committed blasphemy to God and treason to the king. Naboth and his heirs were stoned to death, and the king got his vineyard.

At this juncture the prophet Elijah stepped forth and denounced the injustice of the royal couple in blunt terms: "Have you murdered, and you will take possession too?" And he went on to curse the king, saying, "Thus said the Lord, 'In the very place where the dogs licked the blood of Naboth, shall the dogs lick your blood too'" (I Kings 21:19).

Elijah's act recalls that of the prophet Nathan in the previous century, who, in the memorable parable of the lone lamb which the rich man took from his poor neighbor, fearlessly condemned David for causing the death of Uriah, the husband of Bath-sheba (II Samuel 11-12). Of course, both were using religious authority and language in their efforts to prevent the growing centralization of political and economic power from crushing the old order.

A combination of external and domestic developments ended the Omride dynasty when King Joram (or Jehoram), younger son of Ahab, was killed. On the death of Ahab, King Mesha of Moab rose up to shake off the Israelite yoke. In the face of this new

<sup>5</sup>His wife Jezebel came to him and asked him "Why are you so dispirited and refuse to eat?" <sup>6</sup>He replied, "I was speaking to Naboth the Jezreelite and I said to him, 'Give me your vineyard for money (lit., silver), or if you choose, I will give you a vineyard in exchange.' But he answered, 'I will not give you my vineyard.'" <sup>7</sup>Whereupon his wife Jezebel said to him, "You must now exercise royal right over Israel! Get up, eat something, and you will feel better. I myself will get you Naboth the Jezreelite's vineyard." <sup>8</sup>She wrote letters in Ahab's name which she sealed with his seal. She sent the letters to the elders and freemen of his town, Naboth's townspeople. <sup>9</sup>In the letters she wrote, "Proclaim a fast, and put Naboth at the front of the people. <sup>10</sup>Then place two scoundrels opposite him and let them testify: 'You blessed (i.e., cursed) God and king!' Then have him taken out and pelted to death with stones." <sup>11</sup>His townspeople, the elders and the freemen who lived in his town, acted in accordance with Jezebel's message to them, as was written in the letters she had sent them.

*I Kings 21.5-11*

וַתָּבֹא אֵלָיו אִיזֶבֶל אִשְׁתּוֹ וַתְּדַבֵּר אֵלָיו מַה־זֶּה רוּחֲךָ סָרָה וְאֵינְךָ אֹכֵל לָחֶם: וַיְדַבֵּר אֵלֶיהָ כִּי־אֲדַבֵּר אֶל־נָבוֹת הַיִּזְרְעֵאלִי וָאֹמַר לוֹ תְּנָה־לִּי אֶת־כַּרְמְךָ בְּכֶסֶף אוֹ אִם־חָפֵץ אַתָּה אֶתְּנָה־לְךָ כֶרֶם תַּחְתָּיו וַיֹּאמֶר לֹא־אֶתֵּן לְךָ אֶת־כַּרְמִי: וַתֹּאמֶר אֵלָיו אִיזֶבֶל אִשְׁתּוֹ אַתָּה עַתָּה תַּעֲשֶׂה מְלוּכָה עַל־יִשְׂרָאֵל קוּם אֱכָל־לֶחֶם וְיִטַב לִבֶּךָ אֲנִי אֶתֵּן לְךָ אֶת־כֶּרֶם נָבוֹת הַיִּזְרְעֵאלִי: וַתִּכְתֹּב סְפָרִים בְּשֵׁם אַחְאָב וַתַּחְתֹּם בְּחֹתָמוֹ וַתִּשְׁלַח הַסְּפָרִים אֶל־הַזְּקֵנִים וְאֶל־הַחֹרִים אֲשֶׁר בְּעִירוֹ הַיֹּשְׁבִים אֶת־נָבוֹת: וַתִּכְתֹּב בַּסְּפָרִים לֵאמֹר קִרְאוּ־צוֹם וְהוֹשִׁיבוּ אֶת־נָבוֹת בְּרֹאשׁ הָעָם וְהוֹשִׁיבוּ שְׁנַיִם אֲנָשִׁים בְּנֵי־בְלִיַּעַל נֶגְדּוֹ וִיעִדֻהוּ לֵאמֹר בֵּרַכְתָּ אֱלֹהִים וָמֶלֶךְ וְהוֹצִיאֻהוּ וְסִקְלֻהוּ וְיָמֹת: וַיַּעֲשׂוּ אַנְשֵׁי עִירוֹ הַזְּקֵנִים וְהַחֹרִים אֲשֶׁר הַיֹּשְׁבִים בְּעִירוֹ כַּאֲשֶׁר שָׁלְחָה אֲלֵיהֶם אִיזֶבֶל כַּאֲשֶׁר כָּתוּב בַּסְּפָרִים אֲשֶׁר שָׁלְחָה אֲלֵיהֶם:

מְלָכִים א׳ כא: ה—יא

When Ahab heard that Naboth was dead, Ahab started out to go down to the vineyard of Naboth the Jezreelite, to take possession of it. <sup>17</sup>But the word of the LORD came to Elijah the Tishbite: <sup>18</sup>"Go down at once to confront King Ahab of Israel, in Samaria; he is now in Naboth's vineyard, to which he has gone down to take possession of it. <sup>19</sup>You shall say to him, 'Thus said the LORD: You have murdered, and you will take possession too?' And you shall say further, 'Thus said the LORD: In the very place where dogs licked up the blood of Naboth shall dogs lick up your blood too!'"

*I Kings 21.16-19*

וַיְהִי כִּשְׁמֹעַ אַחְאָב כִּי מֵת נָבוֹת וַיָּקָם אַחְאָב לָרֶדֶת אֶל־כֶּרֶם נָבוֹת הַיִּזְרְעֵאלִי לְרִשְׁתּוֹ: וַיְהִי דְּבַר־יְהֹוָה אֶל־אֵלִיָּהוּ הַתִּשְׁבִּי לֵאמֹר: קוּם רֵד לִקְרַאת אַחְאָב מֶלֶךְ־יִשְׂרָאֵל אֲשֶׁר בְּשֹׁמְרוֹן הִנֵּה בְּכֶרֶם נָבוֹת אֲשֶׁר־יָרַד שָׁם לְרִשְׁתּוֹ: וְדִבַּרְתָּ אֵלָיו לֵאמֹר כֹּה אָמַר יְהֹוָה הֲרָצַחְתָּ וְגַם־יָרָשְׁתָּ וְדִבַּרְתָּ אֵלָיו לֵאמֹר כֹּה אָמַר יְהֹוָה בִּמְקוֹם אֲשֶׁר לָקְקוּ הַכְּלָבִים אֶת־דַּם נָבוֹת יָלֹקּוּ הַכְּלָבִים אֶת־דָּמְךָ גַּם־אָתָּה:

מְלָכִים א׳ כא:טז—יט

165

Fragments of ivory inlay, found at Arslan Tash (ancient Assyrian Hadattu) and dating to about 800 B.C.E., showing a bearded figure in a long-fringed mantle, holding his hands together like the courtiers on bas-reliefs from the palaces of the Assyrian kings. A short inscription is etched on three other unsculptured fragments, stating that something was made for a "lord Hazael in the year . . ." (broken). These ivories may have been part of the booty that the Assyrians took when they attacked Aram.

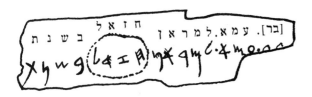

. . . Bar Ama to our lord Hazael in the year . . .

threat, Judah and Edom allied themselves with Israel and went forth in battle against Moab. The campaign was only partially successful (II Kings 3).

Aram, in the meantime, took advantage of the turmoil to make several raids on Israel, even besieging Samaria, the capital city. During one of the battles against the Arameans in Transjordan, King Joram of Israel was wounded. While recuperating in Jezreel, he was attacked and killed by a mutinous section of his own army. The leader of the revolt, Jehu, then seized the throne (about 842 B.C.E.).

## The Dynasty of Jehu

The new monarch initiated a sweeping purge of the Omride household and its chief supporters. He killed Jezebel and all of Ahab's heirs and "all who remained of the House of Ahab in Jezreel, and including all his officials, friends, and priests, until no remnant was left him" (II Kings 10:11).

Aram continued to be a constant threat during the Jehu dynasty. When King Hazael threatened Israel, Jehu paid tribute to Shalmaneser of Assyria to keep the Syrian ruler in check. This event has become famous because Shalmaneser's Black Obelisk, discovered in his palace in 1846 C.E., records and illustrates the transaction. The bas-relief clearly pictures the Israelite delegation, headed by a prostrate figure—perhaps representing either Jehu or his personal deputy—bringing the tribute to "the mighty monarch."

Later, when the Assyrians developed troubles of their own at home, their domination of Israel was replaced by that of the Arameans, under Hazael and his son Ben-hadad. But Aram, in its turn, was rent and weakened by civil war, thus giving the kingdom of

King Mesha of Moab was a sheepmaster, and he used to pay the king of Israel 100,000 lambs and the wool of 100,000 rams [or: the wool of 100,000 lambs and 100,000 rams] as tribute. [4]But when Ahab died, the king of Moab rebelled against the king of Israel.

*II Kings 3.4-5*

וּמֵישַׁע מֶלֶךְ־מוֹאָב הָיָה נֹקֵד וְהֵשִׁיב לְמֶלֶךְ־יִשְׂרָאֵל מֵאָה־אֶלֶף כָּרִים וּמֵאָה אֶלֶף אֵילִים צָמֶר: וַיְהִי כְּמוֹת אַחְאָב וַיִּפְשַׁע מֶלֶךְ־מוֹאָב בְּמֶלֶךְ יִשְׂרָאֵל:

מְלָכִים ב' ג:ד-ה

He [viz., King Ahaziah of Judah] accompanied Joram son of Ahab in battle against King Hazael of Aram in Ramoth-gilead, and the Arameans wounded Joram. [29]King Joram returned to Jezreel to recover from the wounds inflicted by the Arameans in Ramah [i.e., Ramoth] when he fought against King Hazael of Aram; and King Ahaziah of Judah, son of Jehoram, went down to visit Joram son of Ahab in Jezreel, since he was ailing.

*II Kings 8.28-29*

וַיֵּלֶךְ אֶת־יוֹרָם בֶּן־אַחְאָב לַמִּלְחָמָה עִם־חֲזָאֵל מֶלֶךְ־אֲרָם בְּרָמֹת גִּלְעָד וַיַּכּוּ אֲרַמִּים אֶת־יוֹרָם: וַיָּשָׁב יוֹרָם הַמֶּלֶךְ לְהִתְרַפֵּא בְיִזְרְעֶאל מִן־הַמַּכִּים אֲשֶׁר יַכֻּהוּ אֲרַמִּים בָּרָמָה בְּהִלָּחֲמוֹ אֶת־חֲזָהאֵל מֶלֶךְ אֲרָם וַאֲחַזְיָהוּ בֶן־יְהוֹרָם מֶלֶךְ יְהוּדָה יָרַד לִרְאוֹת אֶת־יוֹרָם בֶּן־אַחְאָב בְּיִזְרְעֶאל כִּי־חֹלֶה הוּא:

מְלָכִים ב' ח:כח-כט

## The Dynasty of Jehu

[[14]Jehu son of Jehoshaphat son of Nimshi conspired against Joram . . .] [24]Jehu drew his bow at full strength and struck Jehoram [i.e., Joram] between the shoulders. The arrow penetrated his heart and he collapsed in his chariot. [25]He [viz., Jehu] said to Bidkar his officer, "Pick him up and throw him into Naboth the Jezreelite's plot of land. For remember how you and I were driving teams [i.e., chariots] behind his father Ahab when the Lord pronounced this decree against him: [26]'As surely as I saw yesterday the blood of Naboth and the blood of his sons—declares the LORD—I will requite you in this very plot—declares the Lord.' Now pick him up and throw him into the plot, in accordance with the word of the Lord."

*II Kings 9.24-26*

[וַיִּתְקַשֵּׁר יֵהוּא בֶּן־יְהוֹשָׁפָט בֶּן־נִמְשִׁי אֶל־יוֹרָם...] וְיֵהוּא מִלֵּא יָדוֹ בַקֶּשֶׁת וַיַּךְ אֶת־יְהוֹרָם בֵּין זְרֹעָיו וַיֵּצֵא הַחֵצִי מִלִּבּוֹ וַיִּכְרַע בְּרִכְבּוֹ: וַיֹּאמֶר אֶל־בִּדְקַר שָׁלִשֹׁה שָׂא הַשְׁלִכֵהוּ בְּחֶלְקַת שְׂדֵה נָבוֹת הַיִּזְרְעֵאלִי כִּי זְכֹר אֲנִי וָאַתָּה אֵת רֹכְבִים צְמָדִים אַחֲרֵי אַחְאָב אָבִיו וַיהוָה נָשָׂא עָלָיו אֶת־הַמַּשָּׂא הַזֶּה: אִם־לֹא אֶת־דְּמֵי נָבוֹת וְאֶת־דְּמֵי בָנָיו רָאִיתִי אֶמֶשׁ נְאֻם־יְהוָה וְשִׁלַּמְתִּי לְךָ בַּחֶלְקָה הַזֹּאת נְאֻם־יְהוָה וְעַתָּה שָׂא הַשְׁלִכֵהוּ בַּחֶלְקָה כִּדְבַר יְהוָה:

מְלָכִים ב' ט:כד-כו

Jehu struck down all who were left of the House of Ahaz in Jezreel, including all his officials, friends, and priests, until no remnant was left him.

*II Kings 10.11*

וַיַּךְ יֵהוּא אֵת כָּל־הַנִּשְׁאָרִים לְבֵית־אַחְאָב בְּיִזְרְעֶאל וְכָל־גְּדֹלָיו וּמְיֻדָּעָיו וְכֹהֲנָיו עַד־בִּלְתִּי הִשְׁאִיר־לוֹ שָׂרִיד:

מְלָכִים ב' י:יא

167

Column capital found during the excavations at Jerusalem. Such capitals of columns have been found associated with Israelite buildings. They are virtually all of one basic type, with two volutes extending from a center triangle; they owe their original conception to the design of the floral motif of the Egyptian palmette.

The capitals are the window ornaments for a balustrade (late-8th cent. B.C.E.) at Ramat Rachel. The motif of the balustrade in a window is known also from ivory carvings (see below). The capitals are about 14¼ inches high.

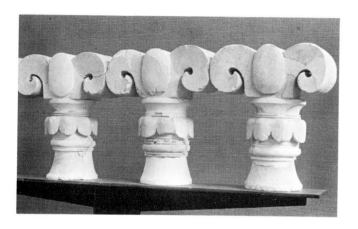

Head of a woman looking out over a window decorated with balustrades.

Israel the opportunity to embark once again on an extended period of expansion and prosperity.

The long reign of Jeroboam II witnessed the spectacular, if only temporary, reconquest of a considerable part of the area originally controlled by David and Solomon. The territory across the Jordan which had been lost to Aram was recovered. The Bible records that Jeroboam "restored the boundary of Israel from the entrance of Hamath as far as the Sea of the Arabah" (II Kings 14:25). None of Assyria, Aram, or Judah was in a position to interfere with Israel's limited objectives, and the Phoenicians profited with Israel through their long-established policy of co-operation. Excavations of such cities as Samaria and Megiddo have uncovered striking evidence of Israel's increased wealth during this period. It seemed that northern Israel was once again well on the way to prosperity and peace.

## Amos and Hosea

Once again, however, the increasing power and arrogance of the monarchy provoked a ringing challenge on the part of those who wanted a greater share of the growing economy. As Nathan had confronted David, as Elijah had berated Ahab and Jezebel, now Amos spoke out, even at the temple of Bethel in Israel. As a herdsman of Tekoa in Judah, Amos saw a most gloomy picture within the gilded frame of royal riches. As fast as the upper classes were acquiring wealth, the poorer groups were sinking into a disastrous economic and social decline. He realized that on such a foundation the stability of Israel could not long endure.

In tirades which have never been equaled in their majestic force or terrible beauty, Amos denounced King Jeroboam II. The king and his supporters, Amos warned, had

168

In the fifteenth year of King Amaziah of Judah, son of Joash, Jeroboam son of King Joash of Israel became king in Samaria, [and he reigned] forty-one years. ²⁴He did what was evil in the sight of the Lord; he did not turn away from any of the sinful acts which Jeroboam son of Nebat led Israel to commit. ²⁵It was he who restored the territory of Israel from Lebo-hamath to the sea of the Arabah . . . ²⁷For the Lord had not decreed to blot out Israel's name under heaven, and He delivered them through Jeroboam son of Joash. ²⁸The rest of the acts of Jeroboam and all that he did and his acts of bravery—how he fought and restored Damascus and Hamath . . . they are inscribed in the records of the chronicles of the kings of Israel.

*II Kings 14.23-28*

בִּשְׁנַת חֲמֵשׁ־עֶשְׂרֵה שָׁנָה לַאֲמַצְיָהוּ בֶן־יוֹאָשׁ
מֶלֶךְ יְהוּדָה מָלַךְ יָרָבְעָם בֶּן־יוֹאָשׁ מֶלֶךְ־יִשְׂרָאֵל
בְּשֹׁמְרוֹן אַרְבָּעִים וְאַחַת שָׁנָה: וַיַּעַשׂ הָרַע בְּעֵינֵי
יְהֹוָה לֹא סָר מִכָּל־חַטֹּאות יָרָבְעָם בֶּן־נְבָט אֲשֶׁר
הֶחֱטִיא אֶת־יִשְׂרָאֵל: הוּא הֵשִׁיב אֶת־גְּבוּל יִשְׂרָאֵל
מִלְּבוֹא חֲמָת עַד־יָם הָעֲרָבָה . . . : וְלֹא־דִבֶּר
יְהֹוָה לִמְחוֹת אֶת־שֵׁם יִשְׂרָאֵל מִתַּחַת הַשָּׁמָיִם
וַיּוֹשִׁיעֵם בְּיַד יָרָבְעָם בֶּן־יוֹאָשׁ: וְיֶתֶר דִּבְרֵי יָרָבְעָם
וְכָל־אֲשֶׁר עָשָׂה וּגְבוּרָתוֹ אֲשֶׁר־נִלְחָם וַאֲשֶׁר הֵשִׁיב
אֶת־דַּמֶּשֶׂק וְאֶת־חֲמָת לִיהוּדָה בְּיִשְׂרָאֵל הֲלֹא־
הֵם כְּתוּבִים עַל־סֵפֶר דִּבְרֵי הַיָּמִים לְמַלְכֵי יִשְׂרָאֵל:

מְלָכִים ב׳ יד:כג–כח

## Amos and Hosea

Thus said the Lord:
Because of three transgressions of Israel,
Because of four, I will not hold back—
Because they sold those in the right for silver,
And the needy for a pair of sandals . . .
⁹It was I who destroyed the Amorites before them,
Whose height was that of cedars
And whose strength was that of oaks;
I who destroyed their fruit above
And their roots below.
¹⁰It was I who brought you up
From the land of Egypt
And led you in the wilderness forty years
To take possession of the land of the Amorites.

*Amos 2.6-10*

כֹּה אָמַר יְהֹוָה עַל־שְׁלֹשָׁה פִּשְׁעֵי יִשְׂרָאֵל וְעַל־
אַרְבָּעָה לֹא אֲשִׁיבֶנּוּ עַל־מִכְרָם בַּכֶּסֶף צַדִּיק
וְאֶבְיוֹן בַּעֲבוּר נַעֲלָיִם: . . . וְאָנֹכִי הִשְׁמַדְתִּי אֶת־
הָאֱמֹרִי מִפְּנֵיהֶם אֲשֶׁר כְּגֹבַהּ אֲרָזִים גָּבְהוֹ וְחָסֹן
הוּא כָּאַלּוֹנִים וָאַשְׁמִיד פִּרְיוֹ מִמַּעַל וְשָׁרָשָׁיו מִתָּחַת:
וְאָנֹכִי הֶעֱלֵיתִי אֶתְכֶם מֵאֶרֶץ מִצְרָיִם וָאוֹלֵךְ אֶתְכֶם
בַּמִּדְבָּר אַרְבָּעִים שָׁנָה לָרֶשֶׁת אֶת־אֶרֶץ הָאֱמֹרִי:

עָמוֹס ב:ו–י

Hear this decree, you cows of Bashan,
Who are on lofty Samaria;
You who defraud the poor and crush the needy,
Who clamor to their husbands,
"Bring and let us feast!" . . .
⁴Go to Bethel and transgress,
To Gilgal and multiply transgression;
Bring your sacrifices each morning,
Your tithes every three days.
⁵Present your thanksgiving offerings of that
which is leavened,
And announce publicly your freewill offerings,
For that is what you love—declares the Lord GOD.

*Amos 4.1-5*

שִׁמְעוּ הַדָּבָר הַזֶּה פָּרוֹת הַבָּשָׁן אֲשֶׁר בְּהַר
שֹׁמְרוֹן הָעֹשְׁקוֹת דַּלִּים הָרֹצְצוֹת אֶבְיוֹנִים הָאֹמְרֹת
לַאֲדֹנֵיהֶם הָבִיאָה וְנִשְׁתֶּה: . . . בֹּאוּ בֵית־אֵל וּפִשְׁעוּ
הַגִּלְגָּל הַרְבּוּ לִפְשֹׁעַ וְהָבִיאוּ לַבֹּקֶר זִבְחֵיכֶם
לִשְׁלֹשֶׁת יָמִים מַעְשְׂרֹתֵיכֶם: וְקַטֵּר מֵחָמֵץ תּוֹדָה
וְקִרְאוּ נְדָבוֹת הַשְׁמִיעוּ כִּי כֵן אֲהַבְתֶּם בְּנֵי יִשְׂרָאֵל
נְאֻם אֲדֹנָי יֱהֹוִה:

עָמוֹס ד:א–ה

169

Seal stone inscribed with the figure of a roaring lion and a legend identifying the owner. The legend reads:

Belonging to Shema    לשמע

servant of Jeroboam    עבד ירבעם

Shema is known to have been a court minister of King Jeroboam II (ca. 783-749). About 1½ inches long x 1 inch wide.

**THE ARMIES OF SHALMANESER V AND SARGON II**

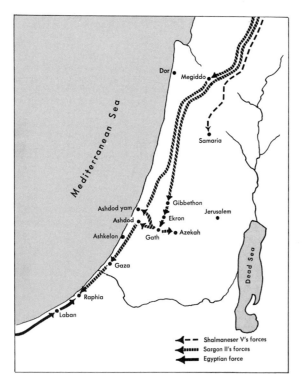

Shalmaneser V's forces
Sargon II's forces
Egyptian force

Once the Assyrian government had decided upon full domination of Western Asia, there was very little that the relatively petty Kingdom of Israel could do to stem the military tide. What the army began under Shalmaneser V (726-722) it finished under Sargon II (721-705).

broken the Covenant with God: "They sold those in the right for money, and the needy for a pair of sandals." In the name of God, Amos portrayed with thunderous phrase the mortal peril of a society in which the powerful "trample the head of the poor into the dust of the earth, and turn aside the way of the humble . . . so that they have profaned My holy name" (Amos 2:6–7).

The same dire warning was hurled at Israel by the prophet Hosea, an Israelite contemporary of Amos. Knowing intimately all phases of her life, Hosea dwelt upon Israel's faithless desertion of the Lord for the gods of the Phoenicians and the idols of the heathen. Her leaders and priests, even her prophets, he charged, shared in the common acts of sin and sacrilege. Thus to depend on fortified cities, on impotent idols, and on Assyrian might, he warned Israel—in other words, to seek foreign alliances as a means of bolstering an unsatisfactory social structure at home—was to invite disaster and exile. Only if Israel turned back to God, could the catastrophe be averted:

Samaria shall bear her guilt,
Because she had rebelled against her God.
They shall fall by the sword,
Their infants shall be dashed in pieces,
And their pregnant women shall be ripped open.
Return, O Israel, to the Lord your God,
For you have stumbled because of your iniquity
[Hosea 14.1–2; 13:16 f. in English versions].

The warnings of Amos and Hosea were fulfilled. The dynasty of Jehu, like that of Omri, came to a catastrophic end. After a rule of six months, Zachariah, son of Jeroboam, was assassinated by the adventurer Shallum, who himself was cut down a short month later by a certain Menahem of Tirzah (about 750 B.C.E.)

## The Fall of Israel

By this time, in truth, it made very little

170

*In II Kings 15.10 below, the three dots represent Hebrew.* קָבָל־עָם, *traditionally translated "before the people," i.e., publicly. But* קָבָל *is not used elsewhere in the Bible and is essentially an Aramaic word. (Forms of* קָבֵל *are used close to 30 times in the Aramaic parts of the Bible, in Ezra and Daniel; ordinarily,* קֳדָם *is the Aramaic word there used for "before.") The Hebrew preposition ordinarily used in the Bible for "before" is of course* לִפְנֵי *. Interestingly, the great nineteenth-century Jewish historian, Heinrich Graetz, suggested that* קָבָל־עָם *was an error for an original* בְּיִבְלְעָם *, "in Ibleam" (* בי *being misread as* ק *) and this clever conjecture was later confirmed by an ancient tradition preserved in the Old Greek (Septuagint) translation of the Bible. Most scholars accept "in Ibleam" as the original.*

In the thirty-eighth year of King Azariah of Judah, Zechariah son of Jeroboam became king over Israel, [and he reigned] in Samaria six months . . . ¹⁰Then Shallum son of Jabesh conspired against him and struck him down . . . and killed him, and became king in his stead . . . ¹²That was the decree of the Lord which He declared to Jehu, when He said, "The fourth generation of your line shall sit on the throne of Israel." And so it was. ¹³Shallum son of Jabesh became king in the thirty-ninth year of King Uzziah of Judah, and he reigned one month in Samaria. ¹⁴Then Menahem son of Gadi came up from Tirzah, entered Samaria, and struck down Shallum son of Jabesh in Samaria and killed him; and he became king in his stead . . . ¹⁶Then Menahem destroyed Tiphsah and everything in it . . . he ripped open all its pregnant women. ¹⁷In the thirty-ninth year of King Azariah of Judah, Menahem son of Gadi became king over Israel, [and he reigned] ten years in Samaria.

*II Kings 15.8-17*

בִּשְׁנַת שְׁלֹשִׁים וּשְׁמֹנֶה שָׁנָה לַעֲזַרְיָהוּ מֶלֶךְ יְהוּדָה מָלַךְ זְכַרְיָהוּ בֶן־יָרָבְעָם עַל־יִשְׂרָאֵל בְּשֹׁמְרוֹן שִׁשָּׁה חֳדָשִׁים: . . . וַיִּקְשֹׁר עָלָיו שַׁלֻּם בֶּן־יָבֵשׁ וַיַּכֵּהוּ קָבָל־עָם וַיְמִיתֵהוּ וַיִּמְלֹךְ תַּחְתָּיו: . . . הוּא דְבַר־יְהוָה אֲשֶׁר דִּבֶּר אֶל־יֵהוּא לֵאמֹר בְּנֵי רְבִיעִים יֵשְׁבוּ לְךָ עַל־כִּסֵּא יִשְׂרָאֵל וַיְהִי־כֵן: שַׁלּוּם בֶּן־יָבֵישׁ מָלַךְ בִּשְׁנַת שְׁלֹשִׁים וָתֵשַׁע שָׁנָה לְעֻזִיָּה מֶלֶךְ יְהוּדָה וַיִּמְלֹךְ יֶרַח־יָמִים בְּשֹׁמְרוֹן: וַיַּעַל מְנַחֵם בֶּן־גָּדִי מִתִּרְצָה וַיָּבֹא שֹׁמְרוֹן וַיַּךְ אֶת־שַׁלּוּם בֶּן־יָבֵישׁ בְּשֹׁמְרוֹן וַיְמִיתֵהוּ וַיִּמְלֹךְ תַּחְתָּיו: . . . אָז יַכֶּה־מְנַחֵם אֶת־תִּפְסַח וְאֶת־כָּל־אֲשֶׁר־בָּהּ וְאֶת־גְּבוּלֶיהָ מִתִּרְצָה כִּי לֹא פָתַח וַיַּךְ אֵת כָּל־הֶהָרוֹתֶיהָ בִּקֵּעַ: בִּשְׁנַת שְׁלֹשִׁים וָתֵשַׁע שָׁנָה לַעֲזַרְיָה מֶלֶךְ יְהוּדָה מָלַךְ מְנַחֵם בֶּן־גָּדִי עַל־יִשְׂרָאֵל עֶשֶׂר שָׁנִים בְּשֹׁמְרוֹן:

מְלָכִים ב׳ טו: ח–יז:

Hear the word of the Lord, O people of Israel,
For the Lord has a dispute
With the inhabitants of the land:
There is no truth, no loyalty,
No acknowledgment of God in the land . . .
³Therefore the land shall mourn
And all its inhabitants shall languish;
Beasts of the field, birds of the sky,
Fish of the sea—they shall all be swept away . . .
⁹The priests are not different from the people;
I will punish them for their ways,
Requite them for their deeds.

*Hosea 4.1, 3, 9*

שִׁמְעוּ דְבַר־יְהוָה בְּנֵי יִשְׂרָאֵל כִּי רִיב לַיהוָה עִם־יוֹשְׁבֵי הָאָרֶץ כִּי אֵין־אֱמֶת וְאֵין־חֶסֶד וְאֵין־דַּעַת אֱלֹהִים בָּאָרֶץ: . . . עַל־כֵּן תֶּאֱבַל הָאָרֶץ וְאֻמְלַל כָּל־יוֹשֵׁב בָּהּ בְּחַיַּת הַשָּׂדֶה וּבְעוֹף הַשָּׁמַיִם וְגַם־דְּגֵי הַיָּם יֵאָסֵפוּ: . . . וְהָיָה כָעָם כַּכֹּהֵן וּפָקַדְתִּי עָלָיו דְּרָכָיו וּמַעֲלָלָיו אָשִׁיב לוֹ:

הוֹשֵׁעַ ד׳: א, ג, ט

171

Upper half of a bas-relief, discovered at Nimrud, showing Tiglath-pileser III with his staff. The relief is part of a series showing the king at court. About 41 inches high by about 46 inches wide.

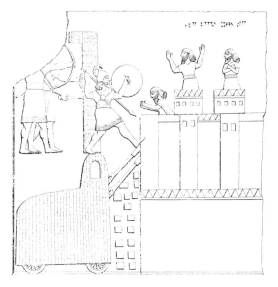

Drawing of a lost relief from Nimrud, showing the Assyrians attacking the Israelite city of Gezer in the time of Tiglath-pileser III (744-727).

difference who ruled Israel, for Assyria once again had begun its massive westward thrust in the greatest phase of its imperialist expansion. Tiglath-pileser III conquered all of western Asia and carried off to distant lands large segments of the conquered populations.

Menahem prevented the total devastation of the country only by paying heavy tribute, which he raised with a crushing levy on the people. Their plight can be read in the Assyrian annals in which Tiglath-pileser is made to boast:

As for Menahem, I overwhelmed him [like a snowstorm] and he . . . fled like a bird alone. . . . I returned him to his place [and imposed tribute upon him]. . . . Israel [literally "Omri-Land"] . . . all its inhabitants [and] their possessions I led to Assyria. They overthrew their King Pekah and I placed Hoshea as king over them. I received from them 10 talents of gold, 1,000 [?] talents of silver as their tribute and brought them to Assyria. (A. Leo Oppenheim, in *Ancient Near Eastern Texts*, ed. J. B. Pritchard [Princeton, 1950], pp. 283–284.)

The Pekah referred to in the Assyrian inscription was a military commander who had killed Menahem's son, Pekahiah, and then usurped his throne. Pekah made common cause with King Rezin of Aram against Judah. The allies advanced well into Judean territory before they were thwarted by a mercenary Assyrian army hastily summoned by King Ahaz of Judah. And soon after this check, Pekah lost both his life and throne to a rival called Hoshea.

The new Israelite administration, however, was not content to remain a mere vassal of Assyria, and withheld tribute on several occasions and began negotiations for a coalition with Egypt. Thus flouted, the Assyrians decided to put a stop, once and for all, to the spirit of resistance and intrigue which still smoldered in Israel.

The Assyrian army under Shalmaneser V

172

# The Fall of Israel

*In accordance with I Chronicles 5.26, "King Pul of Assyria and . . . King Tilgath-pileser of Assyria" were considered two distinct persons, until less than a century ago. From Mesopotamian records it became known that when King Tilgath-pileser of Assyria ascended the throne of Babylon, he also assumed the name Pul.*

When King Pul [viz., Tilgath-pileser] of Assyria marched against the country, Menahem gave Pul a thousand silver talents so that he should help him strengthen his control of the kingdom.[20] Menahem exacted the silver from Israel, from every person of means, to pay the king of Assyria, fifty silver shekels per person. Then the king of Assyria turned back, and did not remain there in the land.

*II Kings 15.19-20*

בָּא פוּל מֶלֶךְ־אַשּׁוּר עַל־הָאָרֶץ וַיִּתֵּן מְנַחֵם
לְפוּל אֶלֶף כִּכַּר־כָּסֶף לִהְיוֹת יָדָיו אִתּוֹ לְהַחֲזִיק
הַמַּמְלָכָה בְּיָדוֹ: וַיֹּצֵא מְנַחֵם אֶת־הַכֶּסֶף עַל־
יִשְׂרָאֵל עַל כָּל־גִּבּוֹרֵי הַחַיִל לָתֵת לְמֶלֶךְ אַשּׁוּר
חֲמִשִּׁים שְׁקָלִים כֶּסֶף לְאִישׁ אֶחָד וַיָּשָׁב מֶלֶךְ
אַשּׁוּר וְלֹא־עָמַד שָׁם בָּאָרֶץ:

מְלָכִים ב׳ טו:יט-כ

In the fiftieth year of King Azariah of Judah, Pekahiah son of Menahem became king over Israel, [and he reigned] in Samaria two years . . . [25]Then his officer, Pekah son of Remaliah, conspired against him and struck him down in Samaria . . . and became king in his stead . . . [27]In the fifty-second year of King Azariah of Judah, Pekah son of Remaliah became king over Israel, [and he reigned] in Samaria twenty years . . . [29]In the days ot King Pekah of Israel, King Tiglath-pileser of Assyria came and captured Ijon, Abel-beth-maacah, Janoah, Kedesh, Hazor, Gilead, Galilee, [and] all the territory of Naphtali, and exiled them to Assyria. [30]Then Hoshea son of Elah conspired against Pekah son of Remaliah; he struck him down and killed him, and became king in his stead in the twentieth year of Jotham son of Uzziah.

*II Kings 15.23-30*

בִּשְׁנַת חֲמִשִּׁים שָׁנָה לַעֲזַרְיָה מֶלֶךְ יְהוּדָה מָלַךְ
פְּקַחְיָה בֶן־מְנַחֵם עַל־יִשְׂרָאֵל בְּשֹׁמְרוֹן שְׁנָתָיִם: . . .
וַיִּקְשֹׁר עָלָיו פֶּקַח בֶּן־רְמַלְיָהוּ שָׁלִישׁוֹ וַיַּכֵּהוּ בְשֹׁמְרוֹן
. . . וַיִּמְלֹךְ תַּחְתָּיו: . . . בִּשְׁנַת חֲמִשִּׁים וּשְׁתַּיִם שָׁנָה
לַעֲזַרְיָה מֶלֶךְ יְהוּדָה מָלַךְ פֶּקַח בֶּן־רְמַלְיָהוּ עַל־
יִשְׂרָאֵל בְּשֹׁמְרוֹן עֶשְׂרִים שָׁנָה: בִּימֵי פֶּקַח
מֶלֶךְ־יִשְׂרָאֵל בָּא תִּגְלַת פִּלְאֶסֶר מֶלֶךְ אַשּׁוּר וַיִּקַּח
אֶת־עִיּוֹן וְאֶת־אָבֵל בֵּית־מַעֲכָה וְאֶת־יָנוֹחַ וְאֶת־
קֶדֶשׁ וְאֶת־חָצוֹר וְאֶת־הַגִּלְעָד וְאֶת־הַגָּלִילָה כֹּל
אֶרֶץ נַפְתָּלִי וַיַּגְלֵם אַשּׁוּרָה: וַיִּקְשָׁר־קֶשֶׁר הוֹשֵׁעַ
בֶּן־אֵלָה עַל־פֶּקַח בֶּן־רְמַלְיָהוּ וַיַּכֵּהוּ וַיְמִיתֵהוּ
וַיִּמְלֹךְ תַּחְתָּיו בִּשְׁנַת עֶשְׂרִים לְיוֹתָם בֶּן־עֻזִּיָּה:

מְלָכִים ב׳ טו:כג-ל

In the days of Ahaz son of Jotham son of Uzziah, king of Judah, King Rezin of Aram and Pekah son of Remaliah, king of Israel, marched against Jerusalem to attack it; but they could not attack it.

*Isaiah 7.1*

וַיְהִי בִּימֵי אָחָז בֶּן־יוֹתָם בֶּן־עֻזִּיָּהוּ מֶלֶךְ יְהוּדָה
עָלָה רְצִין מֶלֶךְ־אֲרָם וּפֶקַח בֶּן־רְמַלְיָהוּ מֶלֶךְ־
יִשְׂרָאֵל יְרוּשָׁלַם לַמִּלְחָמָה עָלֶיהָ וְלֹא יָכֹל לְהִלָּחֵם
עָלֶיהָ:

יְשַׁעְיָהוּ ז:א

173

Fragment of a bas-relief showing the head and shoulders of King Sargon II of Assyria (721-705 B.C.E.), probably from his capital at Dur-Sharrukin (modern Khorsabad). Height of relief about 35 inches.

Drawing of a bas-relief from Dur-Sharrukin showing Assyrian soldiers at the time of Sargon II attacking the city of Gibbethon near Gezer. The cuneiform inscription identifies the city (Gabbutunu). The city was stormed during a campaign against the Philistine coastal cities.

marched into Israel and for three years besieged the capital, Samaria. Not until Shalmaneser was succeeded by his commander-in-chief, Sargon II, did the Assyrians smash through the crumbling defenses and put the city to fire and sword. Thus the sovereignty of the northern kingdom of Israel came to a final end (about 722 B.C.E.).

Sargon always took great pride in his capture of Samaria. He records in his Annals:

At the beginning of my royal rule, I besieged and conquered Samaria, led away as booty 27,290 inhabitants of it. I formed from them a contingent of 50 chariots and made the remaining [inhabitants] assume their [social] positions. I installed over them an officer of mine and imposed upon them the tribute of the former king. (From the Annals of Sargon II, in Oppenheim, pp. 284–285.)

This depletion of Israel by forced exile had its counterpart in the resettlement throughout the land of Canaan of Babylonians, Elamites, Arameans, and others drawn from other conquered territories. This deportation has given rise to a double misconception: first, that there were ten tribes in northern Israel at the time of its destruction, and secondly, that these ten tribes were "lost," only to reappear elsewhere in the world. Time and again, peoples the world over have claimed descent from these "Ten Lost Tribes."

There were not, in fact, ten distinct tribes in Israel at the time of Sargon the Assyrian; and the exiles were lost only in the sense that they were absorbed wherever they were transplanted. Probably only a few of the descendants of the Israelite exiles remained true to the God and land of Israel and managed, nearly a century and a half later, to join in the Babylonian captivity of the exiles of Judah.

The foreigners who were thus introduced into Israel also tended to lose their cultural identity in a general amalgamation. It was

King Shalmaneser of Assyria marched against Hoshea, and he became his vassal and paid him tribute. [4]But when the king of Assyria discovered a conspiracy on the part of Hoshea—in that he had sent messengers to King So of Egypt and did not send the tribute to the Assyrian king as he had done every year—the king of Assyria arrested him and put him in prison.

*II Kings 17.3-4*

עָלָיו עָלָה שַׁלְמַנְאֶסֶר מֶלֶךְ אַשּׁוּר וַיְהִי־לוֹ
הוֹשֵׁעַ עֶבֶד וַיָּשֶׁב לוֹ מִנְחָה: וַיִּמְצָא מֶלֶךְ־אַשּׁוּר
בְּהוֹשֵׁעַ קֶשֶׁר אֲשֶׁר שָׁלַח מַלְאָכִים אֶל־סוֹא מֶלֶךְ־
מִצְרַיִם וְלֹא־הֶעֱלָה מִנְחָה לְמֶלֶךְ אַשּׁוּר כְּשָׁנָה
בְשָׁנָה וַיַּעַצְרֵהוּ מֶלֶךְ אַשּׁוּר וַיַּאַסְרֵהוּ בֵּית כֶּלֶא:

מְלָכִים ב׳ יז:ג–ד

The king of Assyria brought people from Babylon, Cuthah, Avva, Hamath, and Sepharvaim, and settled them in the towns of Samaria in place of the Israelites; they took possession of Samaria and settled in its towns. [25]When they first settled there, they did not worship the Lord; so the Lord sent lions among them, which sometimes killed some of them. [26]The king of Assyria was told: "The nations whom you deported and settled in the towns of Samaria do not know the law of the God of the land, and He has sent lions among them . . ." [27]The king of Assyria then issued an order: "Send there one of the priests whom you had deported from there . . . and let him instruct them in the law of the God of the land . . ." [28] So one of the priests who had been exiled from Samaria came and settled in Bethel, and he taught them how to worship the Lord.

*II Kings 17.24-28*

וַיָּבֵא מֶלֶךְ־אַשּׁוּר מִבָּבֶל וּמִכּוּתָה וּמֵעַוָּא וּמֵחֲמָת
וּסְפַרְוַיִם וַיָּשֶׁב בְּעָרֵי שֹׁמְרוֹן תַּחַת בְּנֵי יִשְׂרָאֵל
וַיִּרְשׁוּ אֶת־שֹׁמְרוֹן וַיֵּשְׁבוּ בְּעָרֶיהָ: וַיְהִי בִּתְחִלַּת
שִׁבְתָּם שָׁם לֹא יָרְאוּ אֶת־יְהוָה וַיְשַׁלַּח יְהוָה בָּהֶם
אֶת־הָאֲרָיוֹת וַיִּהְיוּ הֹרְגִים בָּהֶם: וַיֹּאמְרוּ לַמֶּלֶךְ
אַשּׁוּר לֵאמֹר הַגּוֹיִם אֲשֶׁר הִגְלִיתָ וַתּוֹשֶׁב בְּעָרֵי
שֹׁמְרוֹן לֹא יָדְעוּ אֶת־מִשְׁפַּט אֱלֹהֵי הָאָרֶץ וַיְשַׁלַּח־
בָּם אֶת־הָאֲרָיוֹת וְהִנָּם מְמִיתִים אוֹתָם כַּאֲשֶׁר
אֵינָם יֹדְעִים אֶת־מִשְׁפַּט אֱלֹהֵי הָאָרֶץ: וַיְצַו מֶלֶךְ־
אַשּׁוּר לֵאמֹר הֹלִיכוּ שָׁמָּה אֶחָד מֵהַכֹּהֲנִים אֲשֶׁר
הִגְלִיתֶם מִשָּׁם וְיֵלְכוּ וְיֵשְׁבוּ שָׁם וְיֹרֵם אֶת־מִשְׁפַּט
אֱלֹהֵי הָאָרֶץ: וַיָּבֹא אֶחָד מֵהַכֹּהֲנִים אֲשֶׁר הִגְלוּ
מִשֹּׁמְרוֹן וַיֵּשֶׁב בְּבֵית־אֵל וַיְהִי מוֹרֶה אֹתָם אֵיךְ
יִירְאוּ אֶת־יְהוָֹה:

מְלָכִים ב׳ יז:כד–כח

In the fourth year of King Hezekiah—which was the seventh year of King Hoshea son of Elah of Israel—King Shalmaneser of Assyria marched against Samaria and laid siege to it, [10]and he captured it at the end of three years; in the sixth year of Hezekiah—which was the ninth year of King Hoshea of Israel—Samaria was captured. [11]And the king of Assyria deported Israel to Assyria, settling them in Halah, on the Habor, the river of Gozan, and among the towns of Media.

*II Kings 18.9-11*

וַיְהִי בַּשָּׁנָה הָרְבִיעִית לַמֶּלֶךְ חִזְקִיָּהוּ הִיא הַשָּׁנָה
הַשְּׁבִיעִית לְהוֹשֵׁעַ בֶּן־אֵלָה מֶלֶךְ יִשְׂרָאֵל עָלָה
שַׁלְמַנְאֶסֶר מֶלֶךְ־אַשּׁוּר עַל־שֹׁמְרוֹן וַיָּצַר עָלֶיהָ:
וַיִּלְכְּדֻהָ מִקְצֵה שָׁלֹשׁ שָׁנִים בִּשְׁנַת־שֵׁשׁ לְחִזְקִיָּה
הִיא שְׁנַת־תֵּשַׁע לְהוֹשֵׁעַ מֶלֶךְ יִשְׂרָאֵל נִלְכְּדָה
שֹׁמְרוֹן: וַיֶּגֶל מֶלֶךְ־אַשּׁוּר אֶת־יִשְׂרָאֵל אַשּׁוּרָה
וַיַּנְחֵם בַּחְלַח וּבְחָבוֹר נְהַר גּוֹזָן וְעָרֵי מָדָי:

מְלָכִים ב׳ יח:ט–יא

175

this resettlement, with its inevitable effect on religious and social customs, which set the stage for the rise of the anti-Judean group among the Samaritans that resisted the restoration of Jerusalem and the Temple later on when the Persians had come to power.

## The Southern Kingdom of Judah

The history of Judah generally paralleled that of Israel, with the one qualification that Judah tended to be weak when Israel was strong, and prospered when Israel was weak. For one thing, the area from Dan to Beersheba, with its limited natural resources and economic advantages, did not seem able to support two prosperous kingdoms at once. Agriculture, commerce, the handicrafts, slavery, and the tribute of weaker nations formed the major sources of income of both countries. Another important factor in this relationship was the intervention of neighboring powers—whether Assyria, the Aramean states, Phoenicia, Egypt, or the Transjordan countries—that tended to keep the two divided and unequal. Only occasionally did circumstances combine to allow an effective and equal alliance between Israel and Judah.

Finally, there was one more difference: Judah lasted longer. The southern kingdom, consisting of only one major group, Judah, which had absorbed such smaller groups as Benjamin, was far more compact and therefore capable of reacting with much greater coherence and agility. Then, too, Judah did not lie directly across the path of conquerors and was much less a prize than Israel, besides being less important as an ally or as a potential foe to either Assyria or Aram.

## Under Asa and Jehoshaphat

During most of the long reigns of Asa and his son Jehoshaphat (about 912–850 B.C.E.), Judah and the dynasty of David continued to

176

Asa took all the silver and gold that was left in the treasures of the House of the Lord and those of the king's palace; King Asa then handed them over to his officials and sent them to Ben-hadad son of Tabrimmon son of Hezion, king of Aram, who resided in Damascus, with this message: [19]"There is a pact between you and me, as between your father and my father. I herewith send you a gift of silver and gold. Go, break your pact with King Baasha of Israel, so that he raises his siege." [20]Ben-hadad heeded King Asa, and sent his military officers against the towns of Israel . . .

*I Kings 15.18-20*

וַיִּקַּח אָסָא אֶת־כָּל־הַכֶּסֶף וְהַזָּהָב הַנּוֹתָרִים
בְּאוֹצְרוֹת בֵּית־יְהוָה וְאֶת־אוֹצְרוֹת בֵּית הַמֶּלֶךְ
וַיִּתְּנֵם בְּיַד־עֲבָדָיו וַיִּשְׁלָחֵם הַמֶּלֶךְ אָסָא אֶל־בֶּן־
הֲדַד בֶּן־טַבְרִמֹּן בֶּן־חֶזְיוֹן מֶלֶךְ אֲרָם הַיֹּשֵׁב
בְּדַמֶּשֶׂק לֵאמֹר: בְּרִית בֵּינִי וּבֵינֶךָ בֵּין אָבִי וּבֵין
אָבִיךָ הִנֵּה שָׁלַחְתִּי לְךָ שֹׁחַד כֶּסֶף וְזָהָב לֵךְ הָפֵרָה
אֶת־בְּרִיתְךָ אֶת־בַּעְשָׁא מֶלֶךְ־יִשְׂרָאֵל וְיַעֲלֶה
מֵעָלָי: וַיִּשְׁמַע בֶּן־הֲדַד אֶל־הַמֶּלֶךְ אָסָא וַיִּשְׁלַח
אֶת־שָׂרֵי הַחֲיָלִים אֲשֶׁר־לוֹ עַל־עָרֵי יִשְׂרָאֵל . . .

מְלָכִים א׳ טו:יח–כ

*The matter of numbers, especially in battle accounts, has long been a problem to scholars. Thus Zerah the Ethiopian (probably the leader of raiding Arabian Bedouin tribes) is said in v. 8 below to have headed 1,000,000 men (apart from 300 chariots); and in v. 7 before that, Asa is said to have mustered 300,000 Judeans and 280,000 Benjaminites. These figures bear little relationship to reality.*

Zerah the Ethiopian marched against them with 1,000,000 [lit., a thousand thousand] men and 300 chariots, and reached Mareshah. [9]Asa marched out to meet him, and they drew up their battle lines in the Valley of Zephathah at Mareshah. [10]Asa cried to the Lord his God: "O Lord, there is none but You to help the weak against the mighty. Help us, O Lord our God, for we rely on You, and in Your name we have marched against this multitude. . . ." [11]The Lord routed the Ethiopians before Asa and Judah, and the Ethiopians fled. [12]Asa and the troops with him pursued them as far as Gerar . . . and carried off very much booty.

*II Chronicles 14.8-12*

וַיֵּצֵא אֲלֵיהֶם זֶרַח הַכּוּשִׁי בְּחַיִל אֶלֶף אֲלָפִים
וּמַרְכָּבוֹת שְׁלֹשׁ מֵאוֹת וַיָּבֹא עַד־מָרֵשָׁה: וַיֵּצֵא
אָסָא לְפָנָיו וַיַּעַרְכוּ מִלְחָמָה בְּגֵיא צְפַתָה לְמָרֵשָׁה:
וַיִּקְרָא אָסָא אֶל־יְהוָה אֱלֹהָיו וַיֹּאמַר יְהוָה אֵין־
עִמְּךָ לַעְזוֹר בֵּין רַב לְאֵין כֹּחַ עָזְרֵנוּ יְהוָה אֱלֹהֵינוּ
כִּי־עָלֶיךָ נִשְׁעַנּוּ וּבְשִׁמְךָ בָאנוּ עַל־הֶהָמוֹן הַזֶּה
יְהוָה אֱלֹהֵינוּ אַתָּה אַל־יַעְצֹר עִמְּךָ אֱנוֹשׁ: וַיִּגֹּף
יְהוָה אֶת־הַכּוּשִׁים לִפְנֵי אָסָא וְלִפְנֵי יְהוּדָה וַיָּנֻסוּ
הַכּוּשִׁים: וַיִּרְדְּפֵם אָסָא וְהָעָם אֲשֶׁר־עִמּוֹ עַד־
לִגְרָר וַיִּפֹּל מִכּוּשִׁים לְאֵין־לָהֶם מִחְיָה כִּי־נִשְׁבְּרוּ
לִפְנֵי־יְהוָה וְלִפְנֵי מַחֲנֵהוּ וַיִּשְׂאוּ שָׁלָל הַרְבֵּה מְאֹד:

דִּבְרֵי הַיָּמִים ב׳ יד:ח–יב

177

Female pillar-figurines found in levels dated to the Israelite period. They are made in two parts: a handmade pillar-shaped torso, and a head (made in a mold) which was then attached to the torso. The breasts are shaped by pinching the torso, and the arms are added. All the figurines of this type wear a curly-haired, page-boy-cut coiffure. They also have aquiline noses and large staring eyes. There is an element of assembly line manufacture about these figurines. We might imagine that quantities of such figurines were made upon demand. They were all probably of the same size.

From a tomb near Hebron; About 7 inches high.

Head. From Tel Erani (about 5 miles northeast of Lachish).

178

prosper. Asa's administration stabilized the position of the land. Asa checked the Egyptian army under Zerah the Ethiopian at Mareshah (II Chronicles 14:8–14) and bribed Ben-hadad of Aram to attack Baasha of Israel, thus forcing Baasha to raise his siege of northern Judah.

Asa also carried out a program of religious reform. Early in his career he abolished male prostitution and various forms of idolatry, alien elements which had no rightful place alongside the worship of the Lord. In all of this he had the vigorous encouragement of the prophet Azariah. Later, however, the seer Hanani accused Asa of basing his policy on the favor of Ben-hadad of Aram rather than on fear of the Lord (I Kings 15; II Chronicles 15–16). For this attack, the king had the seer imprisoned; but the precise social circumstances surrounding these actions can no longer be determined.

Faced by the growing menace of the Arameans and Assyrians, Jehoshaphat then concluded a pact with Israel; and his son Joram (or Jehoram) was married to Athaliah, daughter (or sister) of Ahab. But not all the Judeans favored the alliance of the government with that of Ahab. Indeed, on one occasion when Jehoshaphat returned from an ill-starred joint military venture with Israel against Ramoth-gilead in Transjordan, then in Aramean hands, Jehu, son of Hanani the seer, denounced him: "Should you help the wicked, and favor those who hate the Lord?" (I Kings 22; II Chronicles 18; 19:2).

The Judean government levied tribute on the Philistines and Arabs, garrisoned the fortified cities of the land, and defeated a coalition of Ammonites, Moabites, and Edomites. For a time Judah held sway over the southern part of Transjordan all the way to Ezion-geber. Jehoshaphat rebuilt the harbor there and in a joint venture with Ahab's older son Ahaziah launched a new merchant

The spirit of God came upon Azariah son of Oded. [2]He went out and confronted Asa and said to him, "Listen to me, Asa and all Judah and Benjamin: The Lord is with you when you are with Him: if you seek Him, He will let Himself be found by you, but if you forsake Him, He will forsake you. [3]For a long time Israel was without the true God, without priest to teach and without instruction. [4]But when they were in trouble and they turned back to the Lord, the God of Israel, and sought Him, He let Himself be found by them . . . [7]But you, be of courage! Let not your hands grow weak, for your work will be rewarded."

*II Chronicles 15.1-7*

וַעֲזַרְיָהוּ בֶּן־עוֹדֵד הָיְתָה עָלָיו רוּחַ אֱלֹהִים:
וַיֵּצֵא לִפְנֵי אָסָא וַיֹּאמֶר לוֹ שְׁמָעוּנִי אָסָא וְכָל־
יְהוּדָה וּבִנְיָמִן יְהוָה עִמָּכֶם בִּהְיוֹתְכֶם עִמּוֹ וְאִם־
תִּדְרְשֻׁהוּ יִמָּצֵא לָכֶם וְאִם־תַּעַזְבֻהוּ יַעֲזֹב אֶתְכֶם:
וְיָמִים רַבִּים לְיִשְׂרָאֵל לְלֹא אֱלֹהֵי אֱמֶת וּלְלֹא
כֹּהֵן מוֹרֶה וּלְלֹא תוֹרָה: וַיָּשָׁב בַּצַּר־לוֹ עַל־
יְהוָה אֱלֹהֵי יִשְׂרָאֵל וַיְבַקְשֻׁהוּ וַיִּמָּצֵא לָהֶם: וּבָעִתִּים
הָהֵם אֵין שָׁלוֹם לַיּוֹצֵא וְלַבָּא כִּי מְהוּמֹת רַבּוֹת
עַל כָּל־יֹשְׁבֵי הָאֲרָצוֹת: וְכֻתְּתוּ גוֹי־בְּגוֹי וְעִיר
בְּעִיר כִּי־אֱלֹהִים הֲמָמָם בְּכָל־צָרָה: וְאַתֶּם חִזְקוּ
וְאַל־יִרְפּוּ יְדֵיכֶם כִּי יֵשׁ שָׂכָר לִפְעֻלַּתְכֶם:

דִּבְרֵי הַיָּמִים ב' טו:א–ז

At that time Hanani the seer came to King Asa of Judah and said to him, "Because you relied on the king of Aram instead of relying on the Lord your God, the army of Aram escaped your clutches. [8]The Cushites and Libyans had a large army and very many chariots and horsemen; but because you relied on the Lord, He delivered them into your hands."

*II Chronicles 16.7-8*

וּבָעֵת הַהִיא בָּא חֲנָנִי הָרֹאֶה אֶל־אָסָא מֶלֶךְ
יְהוּדָה וַיֹּאמֶר אֵלָיו בְּהִשָּׁעֶנְךָ עַל־מֶלֶךְ אֲרָם וְלֹא
נִשְׁעַנְתָּ עַל־יְהוָה אֱלֹהֶיךָ עַל־כֵּן נִמְלַט חֵיל
מֶלֶךְ־אֲרָם מִיָּדֶךָ: הֲלֹא הַכּוּשִׁים וְהַלּוּבִים הָיוּ
לְחַיִל לָרֹב לְרֶכֶב וּלְפָרָשִׁים לְהַרְבֵּה מְאֹד
וּבְהִשָּׁעֶנְךָ עַל־יְהוָה נְתָנָם בְּיָדֶךָ:

דִּבְרֵי הַיָּמִים ב' טז:ז–ח,

Some time later, the Moabites and Ammonites . . . marched against Jehoshaphat in battle . . . [22] . . . the Lord set an ambush against the Ammonites, Moab, and [the inhabitants of] Mount Seir who were marching against Judah, and they were routed. [23]The Ammonites and Moab rose against the inhabitants of Mount Seir to destroy them utterly; and when they finished off the inhabitants of Seir they set to [lit., helped] killing one another . . . [27]All the men of Judah and Jerusalem, with Jehoshaphat at their head, returned to Jerusalem . . . [28]They entered Jerusalem with lyres, harps, and trumpets, to the House of the Lord. [29]And the terror of the Lord fell upon the kingdoms of the countries when they heard that the Lord fought against the enemies of Israel. . . . [37]Then Eliezer son of Dodavahu of Mareshah prophesied against Jehoshophat: Because you allied yourself with Ahaziah, the Lord will thwart your projects. (His) ships broke up and were unable to sail to Tarshish.

*II Chronicles 20.1, 22-29, 37*

וַיְהִי אַחֲרֵי־כֵן בָּאוּ בְנֵי־מוֹאָב וּבְנֵי עַמּוֹן וְעִמָּהֶם
מֵהָעַמּוֹנִים עַל־יְהוֹשָׁפָט לַמִּלְחָמָה: . . . נָתַן יְהוָה
מְאָרְבִים עַל־בְּנֵי עַמּוֹן מוֹאָב וְהַר־שֵׂעִיר הַבָּאִים
לִיהוּדָה וַיִּנָּגֵפוּ:

וַיַּעַמְדוּ בְּנֵי עַמּוֹן וּמוֹאָב עַל־יֹשְׁבֵי הַר־שֵׂעִיר
לְהַחֲרִים וּלְהַשְׁמִיד וּכְכַלּוֹתָם בְּיוֹשְׁבֵי שֵׂעִיר עָזְרוּ
אִישׁ בְּרֵעֵהוּ לְמַשְׁחִית: . . . וַיָּשֻׁבוּ כָּל־אִישׁ יְהוּדָה
וִירוּשָׁלַם וִיהוֹשָׁפָט בְּרֹאשָׁם לָשׁוּב אֶל־יְרוּשָׁלַם . . .
וַיָּבֹאוּ יְרוּשָׁלַם בִּנְבָלִים וּבְכִנֹּרוֹת וּבַחֲצֹצְרוֹת אֶל־
בֵּית יְהוָה: וַיְהִי פַּחַד אֱלֹהִים עַל כָּל־מַמְלְכוֹת
הָאֲרָצוֹת בְּשָׁמְעָם כִּי נִלְחַם יְהוָה עִם אוֹיְבֵי
יִשְׂרָאֵל: . . .

דִּבְרֵי הַיָּמִים ב' כ:א, כב–כט

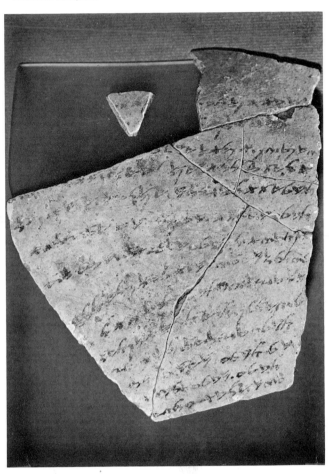

| | |
|---|---|
| 1 Let my lord the official (or, governor) hear | ישמע אדני השר |
| 2 the complaint of his servant. As for your servant— | את דבר עבדה עבדך |
| 3 your servant was reaping in Ha— | קצר היה עבדך בח |
| 4 sar Asam (?). Your servant had reaped ... | צר אסם ויקצר עבדך |
| 7 ...Then came Ḥashavyahu son of Shova— | סם כימם ויבא חשביהו |
| | בן שב |
| 8 i and took away your servant's garment ... | י ויקח את בגד עבדך ... |
| 10 All my fellow workers, who were reaping with me in the heat, will testify for me ... | וכל אחי יענו לי הקצרם |
| | אתי בחם ... |

fleet. The prophet Eliezer protested vehemently against this act of co-operation with Israel. In any case, the ships were wrecked, and the project was not repeated. But in another joint venture with Israel, that of collecting tribute from the Moabites, Jehoshaphat was somewhat more successful.

## Judicial Reforms

An important development in this period was the reorganization of the Judean judicial system. The authority of the "elders" and the "heads of the tribes" had been on the wane ever since the days of the United Kingdom. The Bible reports that David and Solomon themselves acted as judges (II Samuel 15:2–6; I Kings 3:9–12) and appointed judges who, like the district governors, were responsible directly to them. Even the priests who administered the religious law and formed a kind of civil service were personally responsible to the king.

Probably because the civil administration of justice had become corrupt and unreliable (cf. II Chronicles 19:6–7), Jehoshaphat cleaned out the old system and appointed priests and prominent laymen to administer both the religious and civil law. The Bible says of this reform:

And, finally, Amariah the chief priest shall be over you in all [religious] matters of the Lord, and Zebadiah, son of Ishmael, the leader of the house of Judah, shall be over you in all the king's [civil] matters; and the officers—the Levites—shall be before you. Act courageously, and may the Lord be with the good! [II Chronicles 19:11]

Unfortunately, the religious and civil spheres of the law and those who were charged with administering them can no longer be determined with confidence; nor is the role of the priesthood, and that of the Levites later on, clear.

180

Early in the day, Absalom would station himself beside the road to the gate, and Absalom would call to every person who had a suit to present to the king for decision, "From what town are you?" When the answer came, "Your servant is from such and such a tribe [lit., from one of the tribes] of Israel," ³Absalom would answer him, "See, your case is just and proper. But you will have no one deputed by the king to hear you." ⁴Absalom would say further, "If only I'd be made ruler [or: judge] in the land, so that every man who has a lawsuit might come to me; I would grant him justice." . . . ⁶Absalom did this to every Israelite who went to the king for decision; thus Absalom duped [lit., stole the mind of] the men of Israel.

*II Samuel 15.2-6*

וְהִשְׁכִּים אַבְשָׁלוֹם וְעָמַד עַל־יַד דֶּרֶךְ הַשָּׁעַר
וַיְהִי כָּל־הָאִישׁ אֲשֶׁר־יִהְיֶה־לּוֹ רִיב לָבוֹא אֶל־
הַמֶּלֶךְ לַמִּשְׁפָּט וַיִּקְרָא אַבְשָׁלוֹם אֵלָיו וַיֹּאמֶר אֵי־
מִזֶּה עִיר אַתָּה וַיֹּאמֶר מֵאַחַד שִׁבְטֵי־יִשְׂרָאֵל עַבְדֶּךָ:
וַיֹּאמֶר אֵלָיו אַבְשָׁלוֹם רְאֵה דְבָרֶיךָ טוֹבִים וּנְכֹחִים
וְשֹׁמֵעַ אֵין־לְךָ מֵאֵת הַמֶּלֶךְ: וַיֹּאמֶר אַבְשָׁלוֹם מִי־
יְשִׂמֵנִי שֹׁפֵט בָּאָרֶץ וְעָלַי יָבוֹא כָּל־אִישׁ אֲשֶׁר־יִהְיֶה
־לּוֹ רִיב וּמִשְׁפָּט וְהִצְדַּקְתִּיו: . . . וַיַּעַשׂ אַבְשָׁלוֹם
כַּדָּבָר הַזֶּה לְכָל־יִשְׂרָאֵל אֲשֶׁר־יָבֹאוּ לַמִּשְׁפָּט
אֶל־הַמֶּלֶךְ וַיְגַנֵּב אַבְשָׁלוֹם אֶת־לֵב אַנְשֵׁי יִשְׂרָאֵל:

שְׁמוּאֵל ב' טו:ב-ו

[⁵At Gibeon the Lord appeared to Solomon in a dream by night; and God said, "Ask, what shall I grant you?" ⁶Solomon said, ". . .] ⁹Grant Your servant an understanding mind to judge Your people, to distinguish between good and bad; for who can judge this vast people of Yours?" ¹⁰The Lord was pleased that Solomon asked for this. ¹¹And God said to him, "Because you asked for this, and did not ask for yourself long life, and did not ask for riches, and did not ask for the life of your enemies, but asked for discernment to dispense justice, ¹²I now do as you have asked: I grant you a wise and discerning mind, so that no one like you has ever been before nor will any one like you ever be again."

*I Kings 3.9-12*

וְנָתַתָּ לְעַבְדְּךָ לֵב שֹׁמֵעַ לִשְׁפֹּט אֶת־עַמְּךָ לְהָבִין
בֵּין־טוֹב לְרָע כִּי מִי יוּכַל לִשְׁפֹּט אֶת־עַמְּךָ הַכָּבֵד
הַזֶּה: וַיִּיטַב הַדָּבָר בְּעֵינֵי אֲדֹנָי כִּי שָׁאַל שְׁלֹמֹה
אֶת־הַדָּבָר הַזֶּה: וַיֹּאמֶר אֱלֹהִים אֵלָיו יַעַן אֲשֶׁר
שָׁאַלְתָּ אֶת־הַדָּבָר הַזֶּה וְלֹא־שָׁאַלְתָּ לְּךָ יָמִים
רַבִּים וְלֹא־שָׁאַלְתָּ לְּךָ עֹשֶׁר וְלֹא שָׁאַלְתָּ נֶפֶשׁ אֹיְבֶיךָ
וְשָׁאַלְתָּ לְּךָ הָבִין לִשְׁמֹעַ מִשְׁפָּט: הִנֵּה עָשִׂיתִי
כִּדְבָרֶיךָ הִנֵּה נָתַתִּי לְךָ לֵב חָכָם וְנָבוֹן אֲשֶׁר כָּמוֹךָ
לֹא־הָיָה לְפָנֶיךָ וְאַחֲרֶיךָ לֹא־יָקוּם כָּמוֹךָ:

מְלָכִים א' ג:ט-יב

[King Jehoshaphat] appointed judges in the land, in all the fortified towns of Judah, town by town. ⁶He said to the judges, "Consider what you do; for you render decision not for man but for the Lord, who is with you to render justice. ⁷And so, let the fear of the Lord rest upon you. Be careful in how you act, for iniquity, favoritism, and bribery are not part of the Lord our God."

*II Chronicles 19.5-7*

וַיַּעֲמֵד שֹׁפְטִים בָּאָרֶץ בְּכָל־עָרֵי יְהוּדָה
הַבְּצֻרוֹת לְעִיר וָעִיר: וַיֹּאמֶר אֶל־הַשֹּׁפְטִים רְאוּ
מָה־אַתֶּם עֹשִׂים כִּי לֹא לְאָדָם תִּשְׁפְּטוּ כִּי לַיהוָֹה
וְעִמָּכֶם בִּדְבַר מִשְׁפָּט: וְעַתָּה יְהִי פַחַד־יְהוָֹה
עֲלֵיכֶם שִׁמְרוּ וַעֲשׂוּ כִּי־אֵין עִם־יְהוָֹה אֱלֹהֵינוּ
עַוְלָה וּמַשֹּׂא פָנִים וּמִקַּח־שֹׁחַד:

דִּבְרֵי הַיָּמִים ב' יט:ה-ז

Corner of a fortress dated to the period of the Judaean Kingdom. The source of the photograph leaves the place unidentified, but it is possibly Horvat Uzza (near Arad). The stones are laid in header and stretcher fashion, and each course is about one foot high. The large cornerstone in the second course from the top is about one foot high, two and a half feet long, and one foot wide.

Architectural fragment dated to the Hasmonean (Late Maccabean) Period. It was inscribed in the Aramaic language for the bones of King Uzziah of Judah (ca. 780-740), which were moved to a new resting place for some unknown reason. The inscription was found on the Mount of Olives.

**The inscription reads:**

| | |
|---|---|
| To this place (lit. hither) were brought | לכה התית |
| the bones of Uzziah | טמי עזיה |
| King of Judah. | מלך יהודה |
| Do not open! | ולא למפתח |

## Conflict and Instability

During the eight-year reign of Jehoshaphat's son, Joram (or Jehoram), and during the brief reigns of Joram's successors, Ahaziah his son, and Athaliah his wife, Judah's position deteriorated steadily. Internal instability was reflected in Joram's murder of his six brothers, to whom "their father had given generous gifts of silver, gold, and precious things, along with fortified cities in Judah" (II Chronicles 21:1 ff.). Also during this period the Edomites revolted from Judah, achieving a measure of independence; and Philistine and Arabian marauders invaded the royal palace and made off with its treasures, the royal wives, and all the princes but one.

Ahaziah, the lone survivor, had reigned but one year (about 842 B.C.E.) when he was killed during a visit to his uncle, King Joram of Israel. His mother Athaliah proceeded to murder all but one of her grandsons and to usurp the throne. Thus a full-blooded Phoenician woman, Jezebel, was the power behind the throne of Ahab in Israel, and her half-Phoenician daughter was on the throne in Judah. Athaliah was deposed and killed six years later, and Joash (or Jehoash), the single grandson who had escaped her murderous net, assumed the kingship about 836 B.C.E.

Under Joash and his son Amaziah, Judah's troubles continued. Joash was defeated by Hazael of Aram, and Amaziah's conquest of Edom was nullified by a disastrous defeat at the hands of King Joash of Israel. Amaziah, like his father Joash before him, was murdered by a rival group, but the murder of Amaziah occurred twelve years after he had been dethroned in favor of his son Uzziah (or Azariah) (II Kings 14; II Chronicles 25).

## Under Uzziah

During the long reign of Uzziah and the

Jehoshaphat slept with his fathers and was buried with his fathers in the City of David; and his son Jehoram became king in his place. ²He had brothers, sons of Jehoshaphat: Azariah, Jehiel, Zechariah, Azariahu, Michael, and Shephatiah; they were all sons of King Jehoshaphat of Israel. ³Their father had given them many gifts of silver, gold, and garments, as well as fortified towns in Judah; but he gave the monarchy to Jehoram, since he was the first-born. ⁴And when Jehoram strengthened his hold over his father's kingdom, he went and put all his brothers to the sword, along with some Israelite officers . . . ⁸During his reign Edom rose in rebellion against Judah, and set up its own king . . .¹⁰ . . . At that time Libnah rose in rebellion against him [Jehoram], because he had forsaken the Lord, the God of his fathers.

*II Chronicles 21.1-10 (cf. II Kings 8.16-24)*

¹⁶The Lord stirred up against Jehoram the anger of the Philistines and Arabians . . . ¹⁷They marched against Judah and breached it, and carried off all the wealth to be found in the palace of the king, as well as his children and wives; not a child of his was left, except his youngest son, Jehoahaz.

*II Chronicles 21.16-17*

The inhabitants of Jerusalem made his [Jehoram's] youngest son, Ahaziah [=Jehoahaz], king in his place . . . ². . . and he reigned in Jerusalem one year; his mother's name was Athᵃliah daughter of Omri. ³He too followed the ways of the House of Ahab, since his mother was his counselor in evil-doing.

*II Chronicles 22.1-3*

When Athaliah, Ahaziah's mother, saw that her son was dead, she went and did away with all the royal seed . . . ¹¹But Jehoshabeath, daughter of the king, took Joash son of Ahaziah . . . and hid him . . .¹²six years . ²³.¹In the seventh year . . . ¹⁵they laid hands on her [Athaliah], and when she reached the entrance to the Horse Gate of the palace, they slew her . . .

*II Chronicles 22.10-23.15*

וַיִּשְׁכַּב יְהוֹשָׁפָט עִם־אֲבֹתָיו וַיִּקָּבֵר עִם־אֲבֹתָיו בְּעִיר דָּוִיד וַיִּמְלֹךְ יְהוֹרָם בְּנוֹ תַּחְתָּיו: וְלוֹ־אַחִים בְּנֵי יְהוֹשָׁפָט עֲזַרְיָה וִיחִיאֵל וּזְכַרְיָהוּ וַעֲזַרְיָהוּ וּמִיכָאֵל וּשְׁפַטְיָהוּ כָּל־אֵלֶּה בְּנֵי יְהוֹשָׁפָט מֶלֶךְ־יִשְׂרָאֵל: וַיִּתֵּן לָהֶם | אֲבִיהֶם מַתָּנוֹת רַבּוֹת לְכֶסֶף וּלְזָהָב וּלְמִגְדָּנוֹת עִם־עָרֵי מְצֻרוֹת בִּיהוּדָה וְאֶת־הַמַּמְלָכָה נָתַן לִיהוֹרָם כִּי־הוּא הַבְּכוֹר: וַיָּקָם יְהוֹרָם עַל־מַמְלֶכֶת אָבִיו וַיִּתְחַזַּק וַיַּהֲרֹג אֶת־כָּל־אֶחָיו בֶּחָרֶב וְגַם מִשָּׂרֵי יִשְׂרָאֵל...

בְּיָמָיו פָּשַׁע אֱדוֹם מִתַּחַת יַד־יְהוּדָה וַיַּמְלִיכוּ עֲלֵיהֶם מֶלֶךְ: ...

אָז תִּפְשַׁע לִבְנָה בָּעֵת הַהִיא מִתַּחַת יָדוֹ כִּי עָזַב אֶת־יְהוָה אֱלֹהֵי אֲבֹתָיו:

דִּבְרֵי הַיָּמִים ב' כא: א-י

וַיָּעַר יְהוָה עַל־יְהוֹרָם אֵת־רוּחַ הַפְּלִשְׁתִּים וְהָעַרְבִים... וַיַּעֲלוּ בִיהוּדָה וַיִּבְקָעוּהָ וַיִּשְׁבּוּ אֵת כָּל־הָרְכוּשׁ הַנִּמְצָא לְבֵית־הַמֶּלֶךְ וְגַם־בָּנָיו וְנָשָׁיו וְלֹא נִשְׁאַר־לוֹ בֵּן כִּי אִם־יְהוֹאָחָז קְטֹן בָּנָיו:

דִּבְרֵי הַיָּמִים ב' כא: טז-יז

וַיַּמְלִיכוּ יוֹשְׁבֵי יְרוּשָׁלַם אֶת־אֲחַזְיָהוּ בְנוֹ הַקָּטֹן תַּחְתָּיו... וּשְׁנָה אַחַת מָלַךְ בִּירוּשָׁלַם וְשֵׁם אִמּוֹ עֲתַלְיָהוּ בַּת־עָמְרִי: גַּם־הוּא הָלַךְ בְּדַרְכֵי בֵּית אַחְאָב כִּי אִמּוֹ הָיְתָה יוֹעַצְתּוֹ לְהַרְשִׁיעַ:

דִּבְרֵי הַיָּמִים ב' כב: א-ג

וַעֲתַלְיָהוּ אֵם אֲחַזְיָהוּ רָאֲתָה כִּי מֵת בְּנָהּ וַתָּקָם וַתְּדַבֵּר אֶת־כָּל־זֶרַע הַמַּמְלָכָה לְבֵית יְהוּדָה: וַתִּקַּח יְהוֹשַׁבְעַת בַּת־הַמֶּלֶךְ אֶת־יוֹאָשׁ בֶּן־אֲחַזְיָהוּ... וַתַּסְתִּירֵהוּ... שֵׁשׁ שָׁנִים... וּבַשָּׁנָה הַשְּׁבִעִית... וַיָּשִׂימוּ לָהּ יָדַיִם וַתָּבוֹא אֶל־מְבוֹא שַׁעַר־הַסּוּסִים בֵּית הַמֶּלֶךְ וַיְמִיתוּהָ שָׁם:

דִּבְרֵי הַיָּמִים ב' כב: י – כג: טו

183

Stone (in reverse) encased in its original copper setting. On the face is carved the figure of a ram, in front of which is another object variously described as a very stylized figure of a man, a vessel set upon a tripod, and a palm tree. Above the ram is a legend naming the owner, a certain Yotham. This name was borne by a Judean king (ca. 741- 734), and the seal may have actually belonged to him. Found in the vicinity of Ezion-geber. Size of stone about ¾ inch wide and ⅝ inch high.

Belonging to Jotham.

ליתם

Seal of stone carved with Egyptian symbols (sun disk, animal horns, plants, and 4 uraeus serpents) and a two-line legend identifying its owner (in reverse).

Belonging to Eshna, servant of Ahaz.

לאשנא
עבד אחז

shorter one of his son and coregent Jotham (about 775–735 B.C.E. in all), Judah reached the peak of its power and prosperity. Free of any threat of interference by Israel, Uzziah was able to effect impressive improvements in his people's position both at home and abroad. The army was enlarged, reorganized, and supplied with the latest weapons and engines of siege. Key sites were fortified. Recalcitrant Philistine cities, such as Gath, Jabneh, and Ashdod, were reduced to subjection. The Ammonites and other peoples of Transjordan were conquered and laid under tribute. In the Negeb, all the way to Ezion-geber and even beyond into Arabia, agriculture, commerce, and building flourished as never before (II Chronicles 26).

## Assyrian Domination of Judah; Isaiah

Under Tiglath-pileser III Assyria was on the march again. Judah formed a defensive coalition with Israel, Aram, and other nations against the Mesopotamian menace; but it was with the greatest difficulty that the little kingdom, now ruled by Jotham's son Ahaz (about 735-715 B.C.E.), retained some semblance of her former independence.

On two occasions Judah was able to save her territory and her population, if not her dignity and sovereignty, by submitting to Assyria; once when King Rezin of Aram and King Pekah of Israel made a joint attack against her (about 735), and again, about a decade later, during Israel's fatal revolt against Assyria.

On the first occasion Ahaz purchased Tiglath-pileser's assistance in driving off the two invaders. And again a prophet, this time Isaiah, warned Ahaz that Judah would become the arena for a struggle between the major powers. In vivid language Isaiah exhorted the king: "Be on guard and be calm; fear not, and let not your heart be faint

# Under Uzziah

God aided him [Uzziah] against the Philistines and Arabians . . . [8]The Ammonites too paid tribute to Uzziah. [9]And Uzziah built towers in Jerusalem . . . and fortified them. [10]And he built towers in the wilderness and he hewed out many cisterns, for he owned much livestock . . . he was [also] a lover of the soil . . . [11]Uzziah had a trained army . . .

*II Chronicles 26.7-11*

וַיַּעְזְרֵהוּ הָאֱלֹהִים עַל־פְּלִשְׁתִּים וְעַל־הָעַרְבִים...
וַיִּתְּנוּ הָעַמּוֹנִים מִנְחָה לְעֻזִּיָּהוּ... וַיִּבֶן עֻזִּיָּהוּ מִגְדָּלִים
בִּירוּשָׁלַ͏ִם... וַיְחַזְּקֵם: וַיִּבֶן מִגְדָּלִים בַּמִּדְבָּר וַיַּחְצֹב
בֹּרוֹת רַבִּים כִּי מִקְנֶה־רַּב הָיָה לוֹ... אֹהֵב אֲדָמָה
הָיָה: וַיְהִי לְעֻזִּיָּהוּ חַיִל עֹשֵׂה מִלְחָמָה...

דִּבְרֵי הַיָּמִים ב, כו: ז־יא

He [Jotham son of Uzziah] built the Upper Gate of the House of the Lord . . . [4]He built towns in the hill country of Judah . . . [5]He waged war against the king of the Ammonites and overcame them. And the Ammonites gave him that year 100 talents of silver, 10,000 *cor* of wheat, and 10,000 of barley; the Ammonites paid him the same amount in the second and third years. [6]Jotham became powerful because he pursued an upright life before the Lord his God.

*II Chronicles 27.3-6*

הוּא בָּנָה אֶת־שַׁעַר בֵּית־יְהֹוָה הָעֶלְיוֹן... וְעָרִים
בָּנָה בְּהַר־יְהוּדָה... וְהוּא נִלְחַם עִם־מֶלֶךְ בְּנֵי־
עַמּוֹן וַיֶּחֱזַק עֲלֵיהֶם וַיִּתְּנוּ־לוֹ בְנֵי־עַמּוֹן בַּשָּׁנָה
הַהִיא מֵאָה כִּכַּר־כֶּסֶף וַעֲשֶׂרֶת אֲלָפִים כֹּרִים חִטִּים
וּשְׂעוֹרִים עֲשֶׂרֶת אֲלָפִים זֹאת הֵשִׁיבוּ לוֹ בְּנֵי עַמּוֹן
וּבַשָּׁנָה הַשֵּׁנִית וְהַשְּׁלִשִׁית: וַיִּתְחַזֵּק יוֹתָם כִּי הֵכִין
דְּרָכָיו לִפְנֵי יְהֹוָה אֱלֹהָיו:

דִּבְרֵי הַיָּמִים ב' כז: ג־ו

## Assyrian Domination of Judah: Isaiah

During the reign of King Ahaz son of Jotham son of Uzziah of Judah, King Rezin of Aram and King Pekah son of Remaliah of Israel marched upon Jerusalem to attack it; but they were unable to attack it. [2]When it was reported to the House of David that Aram had joined with Ephraim, his [Ahaz's] heart and the heart of his people trembled as the trees of the forest tremble before the wind. [3]But the Lord said to Isaiah, "Go out and confront Ahaz . . . [4]and say to him: Be on guard and be calm. Do not fear and do not lose heart on account of those two smoking stubs [lit., tails] of firebrands . . . [5]Because Aram [and] Ephraim have plotted against you . . . [7]thus said the Lord God: It shall not come to pass, it shall never be.
[8a]For the chief city of Aram is Damascus,
And the chief of Damascus is Rezin;
[9a]The chief city of Ephraim is Samaria,
And the chief of Samaria is the son of Remaliah;
[8b]And in another sixty-five years
Ephraim shall be shattered as a people " . . .

*Isaiah 7.1-9*

וַיְהִי בִּימֵי אָחָז בֶּן־יוֹתָם בֶּן־עֻזִּיָּהוּ מֶלֶךְ יְהוּדָה
עָלָה רְצִין מֶלֶךְ־אֲרָם וּפֶקַח בֶּן־רְמַלְיָהוּ מֶלֶךְ־
יִשְׂרָאֵל יְרוּשָׁלַ͏ִם לַמִּלְחָמָה עָלֶיהָ וְלֹא יָכֹל לְהִלָּחֵם
עָלֶיהָ: וַיֻּגַּד לְבֵית דָּוִד לֵאמֹר נָחָה אֲרָם עַל־
אֶפְרָיִם וַיָּנַע לְבָבוֹ וּלְבַב עַמּוֹ כְּנוֹעַ עֲצֵי־יַעַר
מִפְּנֵי־רוּחַ: וַיֹּאמֶר יְהֹוָה אֶל־יְשַׁעְיָהוּ
צֵא־נָא לִקְרַאת אָחָז... וְאָמַרְתָּ אֵלָיו
הִשָּׁמֵר וְהַשְׁקֵט אַל־תִּירָא וּלְבָבְךָ אַל־יֵרַךְ
מִשְּׁנֵי זַנְבוֹת הָאוּדִים הָעֲשֵׁנִים הָאֵלֶּה... יַעַן כִּי־יָעַץ
עָלֶיךָ אֲרָם רָעָה אֶפְרַיִם וּבֶן־רְמַלְיָהוּ... כֹּה אָמַר
אֲדֹנָי יְהֹוִה לֹא תָקוּם וְלֹא תִהְיֶה: כִּי רֹאשׁ אֲרָם
דַּמֶּשֶׂק וְרֹאשׁ דַּמֶּשֶׂק רְצִין וּבְעוֹד שִׁשִּׁים וְחָמֵשׁ שָׁנָה
יֵחַת אֶפְרַיִם מֵעָם: וְרֹאשׁ אֶפְרַיִם שֹׁמְרוֹן וְרֹאשׁ
שֹׁמְרוֹן בֶּן־רְמַלְיָהוּ
...

יְשַׁעְיָהוּ ז: א־ט

## CHRONOLOGICAL CHART OF JUDAH AND ISRAEL.

*THE KINGDOM OF JUDAH*     *THE KINGDOM OF ISRAEL*

Horizontal lines indicate a change of dynasty. Overlapping reigns and coregencies have not been indicated. (A reminder: dates are approximate.)

| KING | REIGN | PROPHETS | KING | REIGN |
|---|---|---|---|---|
| Rehoboam | 925–914 | | Jeroboam I | 925–905 |
| Abijah (Abijam) | 914–912 | | | |
| Asa | 912–871 | | Nadab | 905–904 |
| | | | Baasha | 904–881 |
| | | | Elah | 881–880 |
| | | | Zimri (7 days) | 880 |
| | | | Tibni | 880 |
| | | | Omri | 880–873 |
| Jehoshaphat | 871–849 | ELIJAH | Ahab | 873–853 |
| J(eh)oram | 849–842 | | Ahaziah | 853–852 |
| Ahaziah (Jehohaz) | 842 | ELISHA | J(eh)oram | 852–842 |
| Athaliah (usurper) | 842–836 | | Jehu | 842–814 |
| J(eh)oash | 836–798 | | Jehoahaz | 814–800 |
| Amaziah | 798–780 | | J(eh)oash | 800–783 |
| Uzziah (Azariah) | 780–741 | AMOS HOSEA | Jeroboam II | 783–749 |
| | | | Zechariah (6 months) | 749–748 |
| | | | Shallum (1 month) | 748 |
| | | | Menahem | 748–740 |
| Jotham | 741–734 | ISAIAH | Pekahiah | 740–739 |
| | | | Pekah | 739–732 |
| Ahaz (Jehoahaz I) | 734–715 | MICAH | Hoshea | 732–724 |
| | | | Fall of Samaria to Assyria | 722–721 |
| Hezekiah | 715–687 | | | |
| Invasion of Judah by Sennacherib of Assyria, 701 | | | | |
| Manasseh | 687–642 | | | |
| Amon | 642–640 | | | |
| Josiah | 640–609/608 | | | |
| Jehoahaz II (Shallum) (3 months) | 609/608 | JEREMIAH | | |
| Jehoiakim (Eliakim) | 609/608–598/597 | | | |
| Jehoiachin (Jeconiah) (3 months) | 598/597 | | | |
| First phase of Babylonian Exile | 598/597 | | | |
| Zedekiah (Mattaniah) | 598/597–587/586 | | | |
| Fall of Jerusalem to Babylonia | 587/586 | | | |

587/586  Second (and major) phase of Babylonian Exile.
582/581  Governor Gedaliah assassinated.
         Third phase of Babylonian Exile.
592–570  Ezekiel, prophet in Babylonia.
550–540  The Second Isaiah, prophet in Babylonia.
539      First Return to Judah; Edict of Liberation by Cyrus of Persia.
         Zerubbabel and Joshua, secular and religious heads of Judea.
515      Haggai and Zechariah, prophets in Judea. Temple in Jerusalem
         rebuilt.
400      Second return to Judah, under Ezra. Jewish colonies in Egypt.
         Jewish theocracy established in Judea by Ezra and Nehemiah.
         The high priests rule Judea.
300      Hellenistic civilization overwhelms Western Asia and Egypt,
         following on the conquests of Alexander the Great.

because of these two tails of smoking fire-brands"—as he scornfully called Rezin and Pekah—and assured him that within a few years "the land before whose two kings you are in dread will be forsaken" (Isaiah 7:4). Relentlessly the prophet continued to warn that, if Ahaz stubbornly refused to heed the word of the Lord, "Then . . . in that day every place where there used to be a thousand vines worth a thousand pieces of silver will become briers and thorns. . . . It shall become a place where cattle are sent forth to pasture and where flocks tread" (Isaiah 7:23–25).

Judah's tribute to Assyria must have been considerable, yet on the surface her prosperity appeared to continue. This impression may have been due, in part at least, to the fact that her surrounding rivals had likewise been weakened by Assyria.

## Under Hezekiah and Manasseh; Micah

After Israel's fall, Merodach-baladan, king of Babylon, tried to form a coalition with Judah and organize western Asia to defy Assyria. And again Isaiah came forth and warned Hezekiah, son of Ahaz, that he would be trapped in the middle of a bitter struggle. The prophet thundered:

. . . Hear the word of the Lord: Lo, a time is coming when everything in your palace, which your fathers have stored up to this day, will be carried off to Babylon . . . and some of your sons, your own issue, who will be born to you, shall be taken away to serve as eunuchs in the palace of the king of Babylon [II Kings 20:16–18; Isaiah 39:5–7].

Isaiah was joined by another prophet, Micah, native of Moresheth, near Philistine Gath in the Shefelah. In the spirit of Hosea before him, who had described Israel as "mingling among the nations . . . like a silly dove, without understanding" (Hosea 7:8–11), Micah had already excoriated Israel for her reliance on the power of foreign allies

For in that day, every place where there used to be a thousand vines worth a thousand pieces of silver shall become briers and thorns. [24]One will have to go there with bow and arrows [viz., because of the wild beasts] . . . [25]And all the hills that had to be worked with a hoe . . . shall become a place where cattle are let loose and where flocks tread.

*Isaiah 7.23-25*

וְהָיָה בַּיּוֹם הַהוּא יִהְיֶה כָל־מָקוֹם אֲשֶׁר יִהְיֶה־שָּׁם אֶלֶף גֶּפֶן בְּאֶלֶף כָּסֶף לַשָּׁמִיר וְלַשַּׁיִת יִהְיֶה: בַּחִצִּים וּבַקֶּשֶׁת יָבֹא שָׁמָּה . . . וְכֹל הֶהָרִים אֲשֶׁר בַּמַּעְדֵּר יֵעָדֵרוּן . . . וְהָיָה לְמִשְׁלַח שׁוֹר וּלְמִרְמַס שֶׂה:

יְשַׁעְיָהוּ ז:כג–כה

## Under Hezekiah and Manasseh; Micah

At that time, King Merodach-baladan son of Baladan of Babylon sent envoys with a message and gifts to Hezekiah, for he had heard of his illness and recovery. [2]Hezekiah welcomed them and showed them his treasure house . . . and everything that was to be found in his storehouses . . . in his palace and in all his realm. [3]Then the prophet Isaiah came to King Hezekiah and said to him, "What did those men say? And where did they come from? . . . [4]And what," he continued, "did they see in your palace?" And Hezekiah replied, "They saw everything that was in my palace . . ." [5]Then Isaiah said to Hezekiah, "Hear the word of the Lord of Hosts: [6]There shall come a time when all that is in your palace and that your fathers stored up to this day will be carried off to Babylon; nothing will be left behind, said the Lord. [7]And some of your sons, your own issue whom you have fathered, shall be taken captive and be made eunuchs in the palace of the king of Babylon."

*Isaiah 39.1-7*

בָּעֵת הַהִיא שָׁלַח מְרֹאדַךְ בַּלְאֲדָן בֶּן־בַּלְאֲדָן מֶלֶךְ־בָּבֶל סְפָרִים וּמִנְחָה אֶל־חִזְקִיָּהוּ וַיִּשְׁמַע כִּי חָלָה וַיֶּחֱזָק: וַיִּשְׂמַח עֲלֵיהֶם חִזְקִיָּהוּ וַיַּרְאֵם אֶת־בֵּית נְכֹתֹה . . . וְאֵת כָּל־אֲשֶׁר נִמְצָא בְּאוֹצְרֹתָיו . . . בְּבֵיתוֹ וּבְכָל־מֶמְשַׁלְתּוֹ: וַיָּבֹא יְשַׁעְיָהוּ הַנָּבִיא אֶל־הַמֶּלֶךְ חִזְקִיָּהוּ וַיֹּאמֶר אֵלָיו מָה־אָמְרוּ | הָאֲנָשִׁים הָאֵלֶּה וּמֵאַיִן יָבֹאוּ אֵלֶיךָ . . . וַיֹּאמֶר מָה רָאוּ בְּבֵיתֶךָ וַיֹּאמֶר חִזְקִיָּהוּ אֵת כָּל־אֲשֶׁר בְּבֵיתִי רָאוּ . . . וַיֹּאמֶר יְשַׁעְיָהוּ אֶל־חִזְקִיָּהוּ שְׁמַע דְּבַר־יְהוָה צְבָאוֹת: הִנֵּה יָמִים בָּאִים וְנִשָּׂא | כָּל־אֲשֶׁר בְּבֵיתֶךָ וַאֲשֶׁר אָצְרוּ אֲבֹתֶיךָ עַד־הַיּוֹם הַזֶּה בָּבֶל לֹא־יִוָּתֵר דָּבָר אָמַר יְהוָה: וּמִבָּנֶיךָ אֲשֶׁר יֵצְאוּ מִמְּךָ אֲשֶׁר תּוֹלִיד יִקָּחוּ וְהָיוּ סָרִיסִים בְּהֵיכַל מֶלֶךְ בָּבֶל:

יְשַׁעְיָהוּ לט: א – ז

Ephraim has mingled with the peoples,
Ephraim has become a cake half baked [lit., not turned over].
[9]Aliens have devoured his strength,
And he is not aware;
Gray hairs have appeared [lit.,are sprinkled] on him,
And he is not aware.
[10]Israel's pride has confronted him,
Yet they have not turned back to the Lord their God,
They have not sought Him, for all this.
[11]Ephraim has become a dove,
Silly and stupid,
Calling to Egypt, going to Assyria.

*Hosea 7.8-11*

אֶפְרַיִם בָּעַמִּים הוּא יִתְבּוֹלָל אֶפְרַיִם הָיָה עֻגָה בְּלִי הֲפוּכָה: אָכְלוּ זָרִים כֹּחוֹ וְהוּא לֹא יָדָע גַּם־ שֵׂיבָה זָרְקָה בּוֹ וְהוּא לֹא יָדָע: וְעָנָה גְאוֹן־יִשְׂרָאֵל בְּפָנָיו וְלֹא־שָׁבוּ אֶל־יְהוָה אֱלֹהֵיהֶם וְלֹא בִקְשֻׁהוּ בְּכָל־זֹאת: וַיְהִי אֶפְרַיִם כְּיוֹנָה פוֹתָה אֵין לֵב מִצְרַיִם קָרָאוּ אַשּׁוּר הָלָכוּ:

הוֹשֵׁעַ ז: ח־יא

187

**Kings holding court and receiving tribute**

At the conclusion of each military campaign, Assyrian kings personally received the important prisoners and an account of the booty. Such meetings were commemorated by victory stele or by carved orthostats which decorated rooms of their palaces. Here is an example of the latter from the Nineveh palace of King Sennacherib of Assyria (704-681), who is receiving a report on the battle of Lachish; prisoners kneel and await audience. Real fear is portrayed by the artists, who depict the cowing prisoners already showing deference to the king before whom they are to appear.

instead of on the strength of the Lord. Now in His name he warned the people again:

> I will make Samaria a ruin in the field,
> A place for planting vineyards;
> I will roll down her stones into the valley,
> And I will uncover her foundations
>
> [Micah 1:6].

Moreover, he continued, Israel's doom would extend to Judah, for Judah was guilty of the same sins:

> The godly man has perished from the land,
> And the upright among men is no more.
> They all lie in wait for blood,
> And each stalks his brother with a net
>
> [Micah 7:2].

Judah's leaders, her prophets, her judges, her priests, and her rich men were all misleading her. Trusting in sacrifices and prayers alone—that is, while offering God His due—they ignored Micah's classic injunction:

> O man, you have been told what is good,
> And what the Lord requires of you:
> Only to do justice
> And to love loyally
> And to walk humbly with your God.
>
> [Micah 6:8].

The ominous warnings of Isaiah and Micah went unheeded. Shortly after 715 B.C.E., Assyria invaded the rebellious states and crushed them. Another major invasion took place about 701. The Assyrian forces under Sennacherib subjugated most of western Asia, and the enemy threatened Jerusalem itself. Interestingly, the Biblical account of this event (II Kings 18–19; Isaiah 36–38) is supplemented by the Assyrian chronicle. Together they paint a vivid picture of the campaign. Sennacherib, in his chronicle, boasts:

As for Hezekiah the Judean, he did not submit to my yoke, I laid siege to 46 of his strong cities, walled forts, and to the countless small villages in their vicinity, and conquered them . . . I drove out of them 200,150 people . . . [Hezekiah] himself I made a prisoner in Jerusalem, his royal residence, like a bird in a cage.

188

The word of the Lord that came to Micah of Moresheth in the days of Kings Jotham, Ahaz, [and] Hezekiah of Judah, which he prophesied concerning Samaria and Jerusalem:
²Listen, nations, every one;
Pay attention, O earth and its inhabitants! . . .
³The Lord is setting out from His place,
He will come down and stride atop the heights [or backs] of the earth.
⁴The mountains shall melt under Him,
And the valleys shall split open . . .
⁵All this because of Jacob's transgression,
Because of the sins of the House of Israel . . .
⁶I will make Samaria a ruin in the open country,
A place for planting vines;
I will roll down her stones into the valley,
And I will lay her foundations bare.

*Micah 1.1-6*

דְּבַר־יְהֹוָה | אֲשֶׁר הָיָה אֶל־מִיכָה הַמֹּרַשְׁתִּי
בִּימֵי יוֹתָם אָחָז יְחִזְקִיָּה מַלְכֵי יְהוּדָה אֲשֶׁר־חָזָה
עַל־שֹׁמְרוֹן וִירוּשָׁלָם: שִׁמְעוּ עַמִּים כֻּלָּם הַקְשִׁיבִי
אֶרֶץ וּמְלֹאָהּ... כִּי־הִנֵּה יְהֹוָה יֹצֵא מִמְּקוֹמוֹ וְיָרַד
וְדָרַךְ עַל־בָּמֳתֵי־אָרֶץ: וְנָמַסּוּ הֶהָרִים תַּחְתָּיו
וְהָעֲמָקִים יִתְבַּקָּעוּ... בְּפֶשַׁע יַעֲקֹב כָּל־זֹאת
וּבְחַטֹּאות בֵּית יִשְׂרָאֵל... וְשַׂמְתִּי שֹׁמְרוֹן לְעִי הַשָּׂדֶה
לְמַטָּעֵי כָרֶם וְהִגַּרְתִּי לַגַּי אֲבָנֶיהָ וִיסֹדֶיהָ אֲגַלֶּה:

מִיכָה א : א־ו

The godly man has perished from the land,
And the upright among men is no more.
They all lie in wait for blood,
And each stalks his brother with a net.

*Micah 7.2*

אָבַד חָסִיד מִן־הָאָרֶץ וְיָשָׁר בָּאָדָם אַיִן כֻּלָּם
לְדָמִים יֶאֱרֹבוּ אִישׁ אֶת־אָחִיהוּ יָצוּדוּ חֵרֶם:

מִיכָה ז : ב

In the fourteenth year of King Hezekiah, King Sennacherib of Assyria marched against all the fortified towns of Judah and captured them. ¹⁴King Hezekiah of Judah sent this message to the king of Assyria at Lachish: "I have done wrong. Withdraw from me; I will pay whatever you impose upon me." The king of Assyria then imposed upon King Hezekiah of Judah 300 talents of silver and 30 talents of gold. ¹⁵Hezekiah gave up all the silver that was found in the House of the Lord and in the treasuries of the king's palace. ¹⁶At the same time Hezekiah stripped the gold from [lit., cut up] the doors of the great hall of [the House of] the Lord and from the doorposts which King Hezekiah of Judah had overlaid, and he gave it to the king of Assyria.

*II Kings 18.13-16*

וּבְאַרְבַּע עֶשְׂרֵה שָׁנָה לַמֶּלֶךְ חִזְקִיָּהוּ עָלָה
סַנְחֵרִיב מֶלֶךְ־אַשּׁוּר עַל כָּל־עָרֵי יְהוּדָה הַבְּצֻרוֹת
וַיִּתְפְּשֵׂם: וַיִּשְׁלַח חִזְקִיָּה מֶלֶךְ־יְהוּדָה אֶל־מֶלֶךְ־
אַשּׁוּר | לָכִישָׁה | לֵאמֹר | חָטָאתִי שׁוּב מֵעָלַי אֵת
אֲשֶׁר־תִּתֵּן עָלַי אֶשָּׂא וַיָּשֶׂם מֶלֶךְ־אַשּׁוּר עַל־
חִזְקִיָּה מֶלֶךְ־יְהוּדָה שְׁלֹשׁ מֵאוֹת כִּכַּר־כֶּסֶף
וּשְׁלֹשִׁים כִּכַּר זָהָב: וַיִּתֵּן חִזְקִיָּה אֶת־כָּל־הַכֶּסֶף
הַנִּמְצָא בֵית־יְהֹוָה וּבְאֹצְרוֹת בֵּית הַמֶּלֶךְ: בָּעֵת
הַהִיא קִצַּץ חִזְקִיָּה אֶת־דַּלְתוֹת הֵיכַל יְהֹוָה וְאֶת־
הָאֹמְנוֹת אֲשֶׁר צִפָּה חִזְקִיָּה מֶלֶךְ יְהוּדָה וַיִּתְּנֵם
לְמֶלֶךְ אַשּׁוּר:

מְלָכִים ב יח : יג־טז

*"The duties of Israel in carrying out the covenant with the Lord, in other words, the worship of the Lord, were twofold: (1) the injunction pertaining to God directly [i.e., sacrifice and prayer], and (2) the injunctions pertaining to fellow-Israelites [i.e., social justice]. The two sets of injunctions were equally important . . ." (from H. M. Orlinsky, "Who Is the Ideal Jew: The Biblical View," Judaism, 13 [1964-65], pp. 19-28; = pp. 521-528 in the David Ben-Gurion Jubilee Volume [Hebrew], 5724-1964).*

## THE SILOAM TUNNEL AND INSCRIPTION

In order to bring water within reach of the inhabitants of Jerusalem in time of siege, King Hezekiah of Judah cut a horizontal water tunnel in the bedrock under the Ophel Hill from the spring of Gihon in the Kedron Valley to the valley west of the Ophel Hill. The water flowed through the tunnel (below) and passed into a stone-covered cistern and reservoir.

The major portion of an inscription describing the moments when the tunnel was completed. It was cut into the wall inside the entrance: Height of tunnel about 6 feet and over.

1 [תמה] הנקבה. וזה היה דבר הנקבה. בעוד [מנפם
החצבם את]
2 הגרזן אש אל רעו ובעוד שלש אמת להנק[ב נשמ]ע
קל אש ק
3 רא אל רעו כי הית זדה בצר מימן ומ[שמ]אל ובים ה
4 נקבה הכו החצבם אש לקרת רעו גרזן על [ג]רזן וילכו
5 המים מן המוצא אל הברכה במאתים ואלף אמה ומ[א]
6 ת אמה היה גבה הצר על ראש החצב [ם].

". . . and while there were still three cubits to be cut through, [there was heard] the voice of a man calling to his fellow, for there was an overlap [?] in the rock on the right [and on the left]. And when the tunnel was driven through, the quarrymen hewed [the rock], each man toward his fellow, axe against axe, and the water flowed from the spring toward the reservoir for 1,200 cubits, and the height of the rock above the heads of the quarrymen was 100 cubits."

190

The Assyrian army, however, did not take Jerusalem. A plague, achieving what the Judeans could not, laid the invaders low and spared the city. As the story is told by the Biblical chronicler: "That night the angel of the Lord went forth and struck down 185,000 in the camp of Assyria. And when men arose early in the morning, there they were, all corpses, dead. So King Sennacherib of Assyria set out to return home, and stayed at Nineveh" (II Kings 19:35–36).

During the reign of Hezekiah, a great engineering feat was accomplished. Lacking an adequate supply of water, Jerusalem was dangerously vulnerable to siege. To obviate this fatal weakness, workmen using hand tools cut a tunnel about six feet high through more than half a mile of solid rock. Starting from the two ends, the workmen met at about the middle, a remarkable feat to be performed without benefit of surveyor's instruments. Thus the pool of Siloam inside the city was connected directly with the Gihon spring outside, and the achievement was commemorated by the so-called "Siloam Inscription" which was carved in the solid rock.

Hezekiah's administration also put through several religious reforms (II Chronicles 29–30). The Temple and its paraphernalia were purified, the priestly orders were reorganized, what were designated idolatrous objects and sites throughout the land were destroyed, and the celebration of the Passover given new life. This revival was seized upon as an occasion to urge the Israelite population to make the pilgrimage to Jerusalem for the celebration of the feast and the renewal of their membership in the Judean kingdom. It is recorded, however, that "when the [Judean] couriers passed from city to city through the country of Ephraim and Manasseh and as far as Zebulun, they laughed them to scorn, and mocked them" (II Chronicles 30:10).

That very night an angel of the Lord went out and struck down 185,000 of the Assyrian camp; and early next morning, there they were, all corpses, dead. ³⁶So King Sennacherib of Assyria set out to return home, and stayed at Nineveh.

*II Kings 19.35-36*

וַיְהִי בַּלַּיְלָה הַהוּא וַיֵּצֵא | מַלְאַךְ יְהוָה וַיַּךְ
בְּמַחֲנֵה אַשּׁוּר מֵאָה שְׁמוֹנִים וַחֲמִשָּׁה אָלֶף וַיַּשְׁכִּימוּ
בַבֹּקֶר וְהִנֵּה כֻלָּם פְּגָרִים מֵתִים: וַיִּסַּע וַיֵּלֶךְ וַיָּשָׁב
סַנְחֵרִיב מֶלֶךְ־אַשּׁוּר וַיֵּשֶׁב בְּנִינְוֵה:

מְלָכִים ב׳ יט: לה־לו

The rest of the acts of Hezekiah and his exploits, and how he made the pool and the tunnel [or conduit] and brought water into the city, are recorded in the Annals of the Kings of Judah.

*II Kings 20.20*

וְיֶתֶר דִּבְרֵי חִזְקִיָּהוּ וְכָל־גְּבוּרָתוֹ וַאֲשֶׁר עָשָׂה
אֶת־הַבְּרֵכָה וְאֶת־הַתְּעָלָה וַיָּבֵא אֶת־הַמַּיִם
הָעִירָה הֲלֹא־הֵם כְּתוּבִים עַל־סֵפֶר דִּבְרֵי הַיָּמִים
לְמַלְכֵי יְהוּדָה:

מְלָכִים ב׳ כ: כ

Also, Hezekiah closed the upper outlet of the waters of Gihon and directed them down to the west side of the city of David. Thus Hezekiah prospered in all his undertakings.

*II Chronicles 32.30*

וְהוּא יְחִזְקִיָּהוּ סָתַם אֶת־מוֹצָא מֵימֵי גִיחוֹן
הָעֶלְיוֹן וַיַּישְׁרֵם לְמַטָּה־מַּעֲרָבָה לְעִיר דָּוִיד וַיַּצְלַח
יְחִזְקִיָּהוּ בְּכָל־מַעֲשֵׂהוּ:

דִּבְרֵי הַיָּמִים ב׳ לב: ל

*The Book of Chronicles has much to say here (II Chron. 29 and 30) about the role of the "Levites." Most scholars, however, continue to believe that this group did not achieve status and authority until the exilic and postexilic period, when the foreign rulers of Israel, the Persians particularly, preferred the more amenable priestly rule to the secular (i.e., monarchic).*

The king [Hezekiah], his officials, and all the assembly in Jerusalem took counsel about observing the passover in the second month . . . ⁵They reached a decision to issue a proclamation throughout Israel, from Beer-sheba to Dan, to come and observe the passover in Jerusalem to the Lord, the God of Israel . . . ⁶ . . .: "O People of Israel, turn back to the Lord, the God of Abraham, Isaac, and Israel, so that He may turn back to the remnant left of you from the hand of the kings of Assyria. ⁷Do not be like your fathers and brothers who acted faithlessly against the Lord, the God of their fathers, so that He handed them over to destruction, as you see for yourselves . . ." ¹⁰However, when the couriers [with the proclamation] went from town to town in the territory of Ephraim and Manasseh and as far as Zebulun, they were laughed and scoffed at. ¹¹But other people from Asher, Manasseh, and Zebulun acquiesced, and came to Jerusalem.

*II Chronicles 30.2-11*

וַיִּוָּעַץ הַמֶּלֶךְ וְשָׂרָיו וְכָל־הַקָּהָל בִּירוּשָׁלַםִ
לַעֲשׂוֹת הַפֶּסַח בַּחֹדֶשׁ הַשֵּׁנִי: . . .
וַיַּעֲמִידוּ דָבָר לְהַעֲבִיר קוֹל בְּכָל־יִשְׂרָאֵל
מִבְּאֵר־שֶׁבַע וְעַד־דָּן לָבוֹא לַעֲשׂוֹת פֶּסַח לַיהוָה
אֱלֹהֵי־יִשְׂרָאֵל בִּירוּשָׁלָםִ.
לֵאמֹר בְּנֵי יִשְׂרָאֵל שׁוּבוּ אֶל־יְהוָה אֱלֹהֵי
אַבְרָהָם יִצְחָק וְיִשְׂרָאֵל וְיָשֹׁב אֶל־הַפְּלֵיטָה
הַנִּשְׁאֶרֶת לָכֶם מִכַּף מַלְכֵי אַשּׁוּר: וְאַל־תִּהְיוּ
כַּאֲבוֹתֵיכֶם וְכַאֲחֵיכֶם אֲשֶׁר מָעֲלוּ בַּיהוָה אֱלֹהֵי
אֲבוֹתֵיהֶם וַיִּתְּנֵם לְשַׁמָּה כַּאֲשֶׁר אַתֶּם רֹאִים: . . . וַיִּהְיוּ
הָרָצִים עֹבְרִים מֵעִיר לָעִיר בְּאֶרֶץ־אֶפְרַיִם וּמְנַשֶּׁה
וְעַד־זְבֻלוּן וַיִּהְיוּ מַשְׂחִיקִים עֲלֵיהֶם וּמַלְעִגִים בָּם:
אַךְ אֲנָשִׁים מֵאָשֵׁר וּמְנַשֶּׁה וּמִזְּבֻלוּן נִכְנְעוּ וַיָּבֹאוּ
לִירוּשָׁלָםִ:

דִּבְרֵי הַיָּמִים ב׳ ל: ב־יא

191

Example of a vassal treaty written in cuneiform script on a large clay tablet. The treaty was imposed by King Esarhaddon of Assyria (680-669) on an Iranian princeling named Ramataia. The one-way pact stipulates that the subject will support the birthrights of his master's sons on the death of their father. The terms of the treaty are supported with lists of blessings if they are kept, and with lists of curses if they are broken. The seal of Esarhaddon was impressed on the left side of the tablet; the seal, possibly of the very famous hero-king Tukulti-Ninurta I (1244-1208), but surely Middle Assyrian in date (13th cent.), is affixed to the right-hand side of the tablet. An older seal, possibly Old Assyrian in date (19th and 18th cent.), is impressed vertically between them. The personal possession of the two older seals perhaps supports the legitimacy of Esarhaddon's rule and that of his sons. About 18½ by 11¾ inches.

The long reign of Hezekiah's son, Manasseh (about 687–642 B.C.E.), traditionally fifty-five years and the longest in the history of Judah or Israel, was remembered by the Biblical writer for "the evil that he did in the sight of the Lord" (II Kings 21:2). He reintroduced the idolatrous objects and shrines which his father had removed, and "shed . . . much innocent blood, until he had filled Jerusalem from one end to another." But it must be borne in mind that during this period Judah was a vassal of the renowned Assyrian kings, Esarhaddon and Ashurbanipal (about 681–630). (The author of II Chronicles 33 tells us that the Lord punished Manasseh for his wickedness by causing him to be taken captive to Babylon, and that when the king repented of his sins, the Lord caused him to be restored to his throne in Jerusalem, from where he instituted sweeping religious reforms. The true historical picture is not clear.)

## Josiah and the Reformation; Jeremiah

Amon, son of the long-lived Manasseh, had been on the throne only two years when he was murdered in a palace revolution. The conspirators, probably an anti-Assyrian group, were in turn killed by another group, known as "the people of the land," who then proceeded to proclaim Amon's son, Josiah, as king. These events occurred about 640 B.C.E. in the midst of the period of Assyrian domination.

Possibly with the full knowledge of Assyria, Josiah began to act with a remarkable show of independence; he seems even to have entertained hopes of taking over Israel, now an Assyrian colony. Later, the Judean government was able to reorganize and enlarge the army, as well as to nurture other bold designs, because Assyria was being challenged by powerful peoples round about her in Mesopotamia.

Manasseh was twelve years old when he became king, and he reigned fifty-five years in Jerusalem; his mother's name was Hephzibah. ²He did evil in the sight of the Lord, following the abominable acts of the nations whom the Lord had dispossessed before the Israelites. ³He rebuilt the shrines which his father Hezekiah had destroyed . . .

*II Kings 21.1-3*

בֶּן־שְׁתֵּים עֶשְׂרֵה שָׁנָה מְנַשֶּׁה בְמָלְכוֹ וַחֲמִשִּׁים
וְחָמֵשׁ שָׁנָה מָלַךְ בִּירוּשָׁלָ͏ִם וְשֵׁם אִמּוֹ חֶפְצִי־בָהּ:
וַיַּעַשׂ הָרַע בְּעֵינֵי יְהוָה כְּתוֹעֲבֹת הַגּוֹיִם אֲשֶׁר הוֹרִישׁ
יְהוָה מִפְּנֵי בְּנֵי יִשְׂרָאֵל: וַיָּשָׁב וַיִּבֶן אֶת־הַבָּמוֹת
אֲשֶׁר אִבַּד חִזְקִיָּהוּ אָבִיו...

מְלָכִים ב׳ כא:א־ג

The Lord brought against them the king of Assyria's army commanders, and they seized Manasseh with hooks and bound him in chains and brought him to Babylon. ¹²In distress, he entreated the pardon of the Lord his God . . . ¹³When he prayed to Him, He responded: He heeded his plea and restored him to his kingdom in Jerusalem . . . ¹⁴Afterwards he built an outer wall for the city of David to the west of Gihon . . . and stationed military chiefs in all the fortified towns in Judah. ¹⁵He removed the alien gods and the idol from the House of the Lord, and all the [alien] altars that had been built on the mount of the Lord's House and in Jerusalem . . . ¹⁶He rebuilt the altar of the Lord . . . and ordered Judah to serve the Lord, the God of Israel. ¹⁷But the people continued to sacrifice at the shrines, though only to the Lord their God.

*II Chronicles 33.11-17*

וַיָּבֵא יְהוָה עֲלֵיהֶם אֶת־שָׂרֵי הַצָּבָא אֲשֶׁר לְמֶלֶךְ
אַשּׁוּר וַיִּלְכְּדוּ אֶת־מְנַשֶּׁה בַּחֹחִים וַיַּאַסְרֻהוּ
בַּנְחֻשְׁתַּיִם וַיּוֹלִיכֻהוּ בָּבֶלָה: וּכְהָצֵר לוֹ חִלָּה אֶת־
פְּנֵי יְהוָה אֱלֹהָיו...וַיִּתְפַּלֵּל אֵלָיו וַיֵּעָתֶר לוֹ וַיִּשְׁמַע
תְּחִנָּתוֹ וַיְשִׁיבֵהוּ יְרוּשָׁלַ͏ִם לְמַלְכוּתוֹ... וְאַחֲרֵי־כֵן
בָּנָה חוֹמָה חִיצוֹנָה | לְעִיר־דָּוִיד מַעְרָבָה לְגִיחוֹן...
וַיָּשֶׂם שָׂרֵי־חַיִל בְּכָל־הֶעָרִים הַבְּצֻרוֹת בִּיהוּדָה:
וַיָּסַר אֶת־אֱלֹהֵי הַנֵּכָר וְאֶת־הַסֶּמֶל מִבֵּית יְהוָה
וְכָל־הַמִּזְבְּחוֹת אֲשֶׁר בָּנָה בְּהַר בֵּית־יְהוָה
וּבִירוּשָׁלָ͏ִם...וַיִּבֶן אֶת־מִזְבַּח יְהוָה...וַיֹּאמֶר לִיהוּדָה
לַעֲבוֹד אֶת־יְהוָה אֱלֹהֵי יִשְׂרָאֵל: אֲבָל עוֹד הָעָם
זֹבְחִים בַּבָּמוֹת רַק לַיהוָה אֱלֹהֵיהֶם:

דִּבְרֵי הַיָּמִים ב׳ לג:יא־יז

*It should be noted that the* bamoth *("shrines") were not in themselves any more or less idolatrous than the royal shrine in Jerusalem. It was actually only when King Josiah decided—for economic and political reasons—to abolish them in favor of his center in Jerusalem that they were branded as idolatrous, quite unjustifiably. In postexilic times, the word* bamah *came to be associated with idolatry.*

## Josiah and the Reformation: Jeremiah

He [Amon] followed all the ways pursued by his father [Manasseh], serving and prostrating himself before the idols which his father had served . . . ²³Amon's officials conspired against him, and they killed the king in his palace. ²⁴But the people of the land struck down all who had conspired against King Amon, and the people of the land proclaimed his son Josiah king in his place.

*II Kings 21.21-24*

וַיֵּלֶךְ בְּכָל־הַדֶּרֶךְ אֲשֶׁר־הָלַךְ אָבִיו וַיַּעֲבֹד
אֶת־הַגִּלֻּלִים אֲשֶׁר עָבַד אָבִיו וַיִּשְׁתַּחוּ לָהֶם:
וַיַּעֲזֹב אֶת־יְהוָה אֱלֹהֵי אֲבֹתָיו וְלֹא הָלַךְ בְּדֶרֶךְ
יְהוָה: וַיִּקְשְׁרוּ עַבְדֵי־אָמוֹן עָלָיו וַיָּמִיתוּ אֶת־הַמֶּלֶךְ
בְּבֵיתוֹ: וַיַּךְ עַם־הָאָרֶץ אֵת כָּל־הַקֹּשְׁרִים עַל־
הַמֶּלֶךְ אָמוֹן וַיַּמְלִיכוּ עַם־הָאָרֶץ אֶת־יֹאשִׁיָּהוּ בְנוֹ
תַּחְתָּיו:

מְלָכִים ב׳ כא: כא־כד

193

Ostracon from the 7th-cent. citadel at Tel Arad. The letter is addressed to a certain Eliashib, probably the commander of the citadel, asking him to provide something for Shemariahu and the Kerosites. The excavators suggest that this letter is a supply order. The site of the local sanctuary, which may have been closed down during the great reform of King Josiah, must have continued in use as a storehouse for taxes collected in kind from the local population. The taxes were later taken to Jerusalem or held as reserves against famine and war. The text reads:

(Line 1) To my lord Elia(2)shib. May the Lord *(YHWH)* gr(3)ant you well-being. And now: (4) Give to Shemariahu (5) . . . To the Kerosite(s?) (6) you shall give . . . And regarding the mat(7)ter which you com(8)manded me: the *shelem* offering (9) of the House of the Lord (10[on the back of the ostracon, not shown here]) he shall remit. [W. F. Albright, see now ANET (3rd ed., 1969), 568 f., dates the ostracon in 598/597, and translates lines 6b-10 differently.]

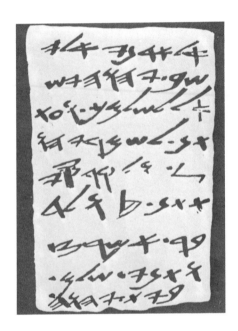

A modern impression of the stone seal (7th-6th cent.), "Belonging to Eliashib/son of Eshiahu," which was found in the citadel of Arad.

About 621, while catastrophe was brewing for Assyria, and unbeknownst to anyone, for Judah as well, Josiah effected the sweeping religious reforms subsequently known as the Reformation of Josiah. Unlike so many of its predecessors, Josiah's regime was not content merely to cleanse the Temple of idolatrous objects and rites and to reorganize its services and priesthood. Rounding up the priests who had abetted alien practices, Josiah had them slain, and at the same time he abolished all shrines except the Temple in Jerusalem. He incorporated the dislodged priests in the purged guild at Jerusalem (II Kings 22–23).

The religious occasion for this reform was the accidental discovery by the high priest Hilkiah, during a rebuilding of the Temple, of the Book of the Law (or Covenant). Hilkiah's scroll is now generally supposed to have contained a basic part of the book of Deuteronomy.

(The problems underlying Josiah's reformation, the identification of the Book of the Covenant, and the history of the high priesthood—as of the priesthood itself—are very complex.)

It was in fact at about this time that the Book of Deuteronomy seems to have taken on the form we know today. The method employed by the editor apparently was to take the older traditions, the bare bones of the Mosaic experience, the themes of national covenant and chosen people, and amplify them in terms of the prophetic tradition. The purpose was to drive home the idea that all Israel was a community bound and locked to a God who would reward those who obeyed Him and punish those who did not; and that the center of the community was the royal shrine in Jerusalem.

Jeremiah the prophet had supported and encouraged Josiah's reformation. But the reforms do not appear to have affected the

. . . and in the twelfth year [of his reign, Josiah] began to purge Judah and Jerusalem . . . ⁴In his presence, the altars of the Baals were torn down, and the incense stands that were over them were cut down. He smashed the Asherim [sacred poles], the images, and the pillars and ground them into bits which he strewed over the graves of those who had sacrificed to them; ⁵and he burned the bones of the priests on their altars . . .

*II Chronicles 34.3-5*

He [Josiah] suppressed the idolatrous priests whom the kings of Judah had appointed to make offerings [lit., and he made offerings] at the shrines in the towns of Judah and in the suburbs of Jerusalem; also those who made offerings to Baal, to the sun and moon and constellations and all the host of heaven . . . ⁷He tore down the houses of the sacred prostitutes that were in the House of the Lord, where the women wove coverings [or hangings; robes] for Asherah. ⁸He brought in [to Jerusalem] all the priests from the towns of Judah and defiled the shrines where the priests had made offerings . . .

*II Kings 23.5-8*

Hilkiah the high priest said to Shaphan the secretary, "I have found the Scroll [or Book] of Teaching in the House of the Lord"; . . .¹⁰. . . and Shaphan read it to the king. ¹¹When the king heard the text of the Scroll of the Teaching, he tore his garments.¹²The king ordered Hilkiah . . .¹³to go and inquire of the Lord . . . for the Lord's wrath is great . . . because our fathers did not heed the words of the Scroll . . .²³ ²Then the king went up to the House of the Lord, together with all the men of Judah and all the inhabitants of Jerusalem, and with the priests and prophets, and all the people, young and old, and he read out to them the text of the Covenant Scroll which had been found in the House of the Lord . . . ²¹The king ordered all the people: "Observe the passover of the Lord your God as prescribed in this Covenant Scroll." ²²Such a passover had not been observed since the days of the chieftains who ruled Israel during the days of the kings of Israel and Judah.

*II Kings 22.8-23.22*

...וּבִשְׁתֵּים | עֶשְׂרֵה שָׁנָה הֵחֵל לְטַהֵר אֶת־יְהוּדָה וִירוּשָׁלִַם... וַיְנַתְּצוּ לְפָנָיו אֵת מִזְבְּחוֹת הַבְּעָלִים וְהַחַמָּנִים אֲשֶׁר־לְמַעְלָה מֵעֲלֵיהֶם גִּדֵּעַ וְהָאֲשֵׁרִים וְהַפְּסִלִים וְהַמַּסֵּכוֹת שִׁבַּר וְהֵדַק וַיִּזְרֹק עַל־פְּנֵי הַקְּבָרִים הַזֹּבְחִים לָהֶם: וְעַצְמוֹת כֹּהֲנִים שָׂרַף עַל־מִזְבְּחוֹתָם...

דִּבְרֵי הַיָּמִים ב׳ לד: ג־ה

וְהִשְׁבִּית אֶת־הַכְּמָרִים אֲשֶׁר נָתְנוּ מַלְכֵי יְהוּדָה וַיְקַטֵּר בַּבָּמוֹת בְּעָרֵי יְהוּדָה וּמְסִבֵּי יְרוּשָׁלִַם וְאֶת־הַמְקַטְּרִים לַבַּעַל לַשֶּׁמֶשׁ וְלַיָּרֵחַ וְלַמַּזָּלוֹת וּלְכֹל צְבָא הַשָּׁמָיִם... וַיִּתֹּץ אֶת־בָּתֵּי הַקְּדֵשִׁים אֲשֶׁר בְּבֵית יְהוָה אֲשֶׁר הַנָּשִׁים אֹרְגוֹת שָׁם בָּתִּים לָאֲשֵׁרָה: וַיָּבֵא אֶת־כָּל־הַכֹּהֲנִים מֵעָרֵי יְהוּדָה וַיְטַמֵּא אֶת־הַבָּמוֹת אֲשֶׁר קִטְּרוּ־שָׁמָּה הַכֹּהֲנִים...

מְלָכִים ב׳ כג: ה־ח

וַיֹּאמֶר חִלְקִיָּהוּ הַכֹּהֵן הַגָּדוֹל עַל־שָׁפָן הַסֹּפֵר סֵפֶר הַתּוֹרָה מָצָאתִי בְּבֵית יְהוָה... וַיִּקְרָאֵהוּ שָׁפָן לִפְנֵי הַמֶּלֶךְ: וַיְהִי כִּשְׁמֹעַ הַמֶּלֶךְ אֶת־דִּבְרֵי סֵפֶר הַתּוֹרָה וַיִּקְרַע אֶת־בְּגָדָיו: וַיְצַו הַמֶּלֶךְ אֶת־חִלְקִיָּה...לְכוּ דִרְשׁוּ אֶת־יְהוָה בַּעֲדִי וּבְעַד־הָעָם... כִּי־גְדוֹלָה חֲמַת יְהוָה אֲשֶׁר־הִיא נִצְּתָה בָנוּ עַל אֲשֶׁר לֹא־שָׁמְעוּ אֲבֹתֵינוּ עַל־דִּבְרֵי הַסֵּפֶר הַזֶּה... וַיַּעַל הַמֶּלֶךְ בֵּית־יְהוָֹה וְכָל־אִישׁ יְהוּדָה וְכָל־יֹשְׁבֵי יְרוּשָׁלִַם אִתּוֹ וְהַכֹּהֲנִים וְהַנְּבִיאִים וְכָל־הָעָם לְמִקָּטֹן וְעַד־גָּדוֹל וַיִּקְרָא בְאָזְנֵיהֶם אֶת־כָּל־דִּבְרֵי סֵפֶר הַבְּרִית הַנִּמְצָא בְּבֵית יְהוָה... וַיְצַו הַמֶּלֶךְ אֶת־כָּל־הָעָם לֵאמֹר עֲשׂוּ פֶסַח לַיהוָה אֱלֹהֵיכֶם כַּכָּתוּב עַל סֵפֶר הַבְּרִית הַזֶּה: כִּי לֹא נַעֲשָׂה כַּפֶּסַח הַזֶּה מִימֵי הַשֹּׁפְטִים אֲשֶׁר שָׁפְטוּ אֶת־יִשְׂרָאֵל וְכֹל יְמֵי מַלְכֵי יִשְׂרָאֵל וּמַלְכֵי יְהוּדָה:

מְלָכִים ב׳ כב: ח־כג: כב

From a copy (in the British Museum; 21901) of a brief historical narrative of the events during the reigns of the Neo-Babylonian (Chaldean) kings. Here the allied troops of King Cyaxeres of Media, the Umman-manda, and the Chaldeans (soldiers and king of Akkad) destroy the city of Nineveh.

**Reconstructed text of lines 38-48**

[In the fourteenth year] the king of Akkad mustered his army [and marched to . . .] the king of the Umman-manda with the king of Akkad

. . . they met each other

the king of Akkad . . . [Cyaxe]res . . . he made to cross and they marched along the bank of the Tigris River and . . . against Nineveh . . . they encamped [?].

From the month of Sivan to the month of Ab three US [measures . . . they advanced (?)].

A strong attack they made against the city, and in the month of Ab [the . . . th day the city was captured . . .] a great defeat of the chief [people] was made.

View of the mound of Kuyunjik, one of the two mounds which once were the city of Nineveh, a capital of the Assyrian Empire.

196

Judean population deeply nor to have lasted long. Jeremiah found it necessary to dissociate himself from the project and to lament its deterioration. Indeed, he went so far as to praise the piety of a small group known as the Rechabites, whose mode of living revolved about such negative principles as living in tents rather than houses and shunning the vine and its products (Jeremiah 35).

In the last years of Josiah's reign, the Assyrian empire began to crumble; in 612 B.C.E. the Babylonians, Medes, and Scythians destroyed it forever and leveled its capital, the fabled Nineveh, in the dust.

This shattering event was taken by the prophet Nahum as his theme to demonstrate the retributive justice of the God of Israel. Beginning with the traditional avowal (Nahum 1:1):

The Lord is a jealous and avenging God,
The Lord avenges and is full of wrath;
The Lord takes vengeance on His adversaries,
And He reserves wrath for His enemies. . . .

he ends his Oracle concerning Nineveh with a somber, almost elegiac, triumph (3:18–19):

Your shepherds are asleep, O king of Assyria,
Your warriors slumber;
Your troops are scattered on the mountains,
And there is none to gather them.
There is no assuaging your hurt,
Your wound is grievous;
All who hear the report of you
Clap their hands over you—
For upon whom has not come
Your tireless cruelty?

Nahum's exultation over Nineveh recalls Isaiah's epic mockery of Sennacherib almost a century before (II Kings 19:20 ff.; Isaiah 37:21 ff.).

### Near Eastern Ferment and the Fall of Judah

Assyria's fall only paved the way for new

The word that came to Jeremiah from the Lord during the reign of King Jehoiakim son of Josiah of Judah: [2]"Go to the quarters of the Rechabites and speak with them, and bring them to the House of the Lord, to one of the chambers, and offer them wine to drink." . . . [6]But they replied, ". . . [8]We have obeyed our ancestor Jehonadab son of Rechab in everything that he commanded us, never [lit., all our days] drinking wine—none of us, or our wives or sons or daughters—[9]and never building houses to dwell in; nor have we ever owned vineyards or fields or seed. [10]We have lived in tents . . ."

*Jeremiah 35.1-10*

Isaiah son of Amoz sent this message to Hezekiah: Thus said the Lord, the God of Israel: "I have heard your prayer to Me [see vv. 15-19 preceding] concerning King Sennacherib of Assyria. [21]This is the word that the Lord has spoken concerning him:
Fair Maiden Zion
Despises you, scorns you;
Fair Jerusalem
Shakes her head after you.
[22]Whom have you blasphemed and reviled,
Against whom raised your voice
And lifted up insolently your eyes?
Against the Holy One of Israel!
[23] . . . Because you have said,
'With my many chariots
I was able to climb the highest mountains,
To the very limits of Lebanon;
I cut down its loftiest cedars,
Its choicest cypresses . . .
[24]I myself drew [or dug] and drank
Alien waters;
I dried out with the soles of my feet
All the streams of Egypt'. . .
[28]Because you have raged against Me
And your tumult has reached My ears,
I will put My hook through your nostrils
And My bit between your lips;
And I will make your return by the road
On which you came."

*II Kings 19.20-28*

הַדָּבָר אֲשֶׁר־הָיָה אֶל־יִרְמְיָהוּ מֵאֵת יְהֹוָה בִּימֵי יְהֹויָקִים בֶּן־יֹאשִׁיָּהוּ מֶלֶךְ יְהוּדָה לֵאמֹר: הָלוֹךְ אֶל־בֵּית הָרֵכָבִים וְדִבַּרְתָּ אוֹתָם וַהֲבִאוֹתָם בֵּית יְהֹוָה אֶל־אַחַת הַלְּשָׁכוֹת וְהִשְׁקִיתָ אוֹתָם יָיִן:.... וַנִּשְׁמַע בְּקוֹל יְהוֹנָדָב בֶּן־רֵכָב אָבִינוּ לְכֹל אֲשֶׁר צִוָּנוּ לְבִלְתִּי שְׁתוֹת־יַיִן כָּל־יָמֵינוּ אֲנַחְנוּ נָשֵׁינוּ בָּנֵינוּ וּבְנֹתֵינוּ: וּלְבִלְתִּי בְּנוֹת בָּתִּים לְשִׁבְתֵּנוּ וְכֶרֶם וְשָׂדֶה וָזֶרַע לֹא יִהְיֶה־לָּנוּ: וַנֵּשֶׁב בָּאֳהָלִים...

יִרְמְיָהוּ לה: א־י

וַיִּשְׁלַח יְשַׁעְיָהוּ בֶן־אָמוֹץ אֶל־חִזְקִיָּהוּ לֵאמֹר כֹּה־אָמַר יְהֹוָה אֱלֹהֵי יִשְׂרָאֵל אֲשֶׁר הִתְפַּלַּלְתָּ אֵלַי אֶל־סַנְחֵרִב מֶלֶךְ־אַשּׁוּר שָׁמָעְתִּי: זֶה הַדָּבָר אֲשֶׁר־דִּבֶּר יְהֹוָה עָלָיו בָּזָה לְךָ לָעֲגָה לְךָ בְּתוּלַת בַּת־צִיּוֹן אַחֲרֶיךָ רֹאשׁ הֵנִיעָה בַּת יְרוּשָׁלַ͏ִם: אֶת־מִי חֵרַפְתָּ וְגִדַּפְתָּ וְעַל־מִי הֲרִימוֹתָ קּוֹל וַתִּשָּׂא מָרוֹם עֵינֶיךָ עַל־קְדוֹשׁ יִשְׂרָאֵל: בְּיַד מַלְאָכֶיךָ חֵרַפְתָּ | אֲדֹנָי וַתֹּאמֶר בְּרֹב רִכְבִּי אֲנִי עָלִיתִי מְרוֹם הָרִים יַרְכְּתֵי לְבָנוֹן וְאֶכְרֹת קוֹמַת אֲרָזָיו מִבְחוֹר בְּרֹשָׁיו וְאָבוֹאָה מְלוֹן קִצֹּה יַעַר כַּרְמִלּוֹ: אֲנִי קַרְתִּי וְשָׁתִיתִי מַיִם זָרִים וְאַחְרִב בְּכַף פְּעָמַי כֹּל יְאֹרֵי מָצוֹר: ...יַעַן הִתְרַגֶּזְךָ אֵלַי וְשַׁאֲנַנְךָ עָלָה בְאָזְנָי וְשַׂמְתִּי חַחִי בְּאַפֶּךָ וּמִתְגִּי בִּשְׂפָתֶיךָ וַהֲשִׁבֹתִיךָ בַּדֶּרֶךְ אֲשֶׁר־בָּאתָ בָּהּ:

מְלָכִים ב' יט: כ־כח

197

Description of the battle of Carchemish from a historical chronicle of the Babylonian kings. Commencing at the end of the reign of Nabopolassar (605 B.C.E.):

1. In the twenty-first year the king of Akkad stayed in his own land. Nebuchadrezzar his oldest son, the crown-prince,

2. mustered [the Babylonian army] and took command of his troops. He marched to Carchemish, which is on the bank of the Euphrates,

3. and crossed the river [to march] against the Egyptian army which lay in Carchemish

4. ...fought with each other, and the Egyptian army withdrew before him.

5. He accomplished the defeat and to non-existence [reduced] them. As for the rest of the Egyptian army,

6. which had escaped from the defeat [so quickly that] no weapon had reached them, in the district of Hamath

7. the Babylonian troops overtook and defeated them, so that not a single man [escaped] to his own country.

Basalt orthostat at the King's Gate at Carchemish (ca. 9th cent. B.C.E.). These two soldiers, dressed in short, belted tunics and plumed helmets, carry shields slung over their backs and a long lance. They are part of a series of similarly dressed soldiers facing the entrance (perhaps to greet the comings and goings of the king). A little over 4 feet tall.

and greater disasters. The Egyptians, reviving under Necho, rushed into the vacuum left by the Assyrians and made an effort to gain control of western Asia. Fearful of this threat, Josiah moved north into the valley of Jezreel to intercept the Egyptian advance. He took his stand at strategic Megiddo, but his Judean forces were overwhelmed and Josiah himself was killed (609–8 B.C.E.; II Kings 23:29).

His son Jehoahaz II (Shallum) succeeded to the throne; but three months later Necho dragged him off in chains to the Nile and replaced him with Jehoiakim (Eliakim), another of Josiah's sons. In the meantime, however, Babylonia, the most rapidly growing power in Mesopotamia, inflicted a crushing defeat on Necho's forces at Carchemish (605) and succeeded the Assyrians as overlords of western Asia.

For a time, Jehoiakim vacillated, now looking hopefully to Babylonia, now to his Egyptian sponsors. Judah did not yet realize that Egypt would never recover from the catastrophe at Carchemish and would itself become but a dependency of other powers. Forgotten was the ancient warning: "Now, you are only relying on the support of this bruised reed, on Egypt, which will enter and pierce through the hand of anyone who leans upon it. So is Pharaoh, king of Egypt, to all who rely on him" (II Kings 18:21; Isaiah 36:6).

This indecision was rudely resolved when Babylonia, under the energetic leadership of the ascendant Chaldean minority headed by Nebuchadnezzar, dispatched an army that swiftly subdued all of Judah. Even then, however, Nebuchadnezzar had no sooner turned his back than Jehoiakim revolted in a desperate gamble on aid from Egypt. However, as Jeremiah had warned, this aid never came. The Chaldean conqueror replied by sending a punitive force back into Judah, and the enemy captured Jerusalem, though only after strenuous resistance.

# Near Eastern Ferment and the Fall of Judah

During his [Josiah's] reign, King Pharaoh-Necho of Egypt set out to meet the king of Assyria at the Euphrates River; and when King Josiah marched out to intercept him, he [Necho] slew him at Megiddo, as soon as he encountered him. [30]His servants brought his body by chariot from Megiddo to Jerusalem, and buried him in his tomb . . .

*II Kings 23.29-30*

בְּיָמָיו עָלָה פַּרְעֹה נְכֹה מֶלֶךְ־מִצְרַיִם עַל־מֶלֶךְ
אַשּׁוּר עַל־נְהַר־פְּרָת וַיֵּלֶךְ הַמֶּלֶךְ יֹאשִׁיָּהוּ לִקְרָאתוֹ
וַיְמִיתֵהוּ בִּמְגִדּוֹ כִּרְאֹתוֹ אֹתוֹ: וַיַּרְכִּבֻהוּ עֲבָדָיו
מֵת מִמְּגִדּוֹ וַיְבִאֻהוּ יְרוּשָׁלַם וַיִּקְבְּרֻהוּ בִּקְבֻרָתוֹ...

מְלָכִים ב׳ כג: כט – ל

For thus said the Lord concerning King Shallum [= Jehoahaz II] son of Josiah of Judah, who succeeded his father Josiah as king but has gone away from this place: he shall never come back. [12]He shall die in the place to which he was exiled, and he shall not see this country again.

[13]Woe to the man who builds his house without justice
And his upper chambers without equity;
Who makes his fellow man work without pay
And does not pay him his wages . . .
[17]For your eyes and your mind are only
On ill-gotten gain,
On shedding the blood of the innocent,
On committing fraud and violence.

*Jeremiah 22.11-17*

כִּי־כֹה אָמַר־יְהֹוָה אֶל־שַׁלֻּם בֶּן־יֹאשִׁיָּהוּ מֶלֶךְ
יְהוּדָה הַמֹּלֵךְ תַּחַת יֹאשִׁיָּהוּ אָבִיו אֲשֶׁר יָצָא מִן־
הַמָּקוֹם הַזֶּה לֹא־יָשׁוּב שָׁם עוֹד: כִּי בִּמְקוֹם אֲשֶׁר־
הִגְלוּ אֹתוֹ שָׁם יָמוּת וְאֶת־הָאָרֶץ הַזֹּאת לֹא־יִרְאֶה
עוֹד:
הוֹי בֹּנֶה בֵיתוֹ בְּלֹא־צֶדֶק וַעֲלִיּוֹתָיו בְּלֹא מִשְׁפָּט
בְּרֵעֵהוּ יַעֲבֹד חִנָּם וּפֹעֲלוֹ לֹא יִתֶּן־לוֹ:...
כִּי אֵין עֵינֶיךָ וְלִבְּךָ כִּי אִם־עַל־בִּצְעֶךָ וְעַל דַּם־
הַנָּקִי לִשְׁפּוֹךְ וְעַל־הָעֹשֶׁק וְעַל־הַמְּרוּצָה לַעֲשׂוֹת:

יִרְמְיָהוּ כב: יא – יז

Pharaoh-Necho imprisoned him [Jehoahaz II-Shallum] in Riblah, in the territory of Hamath—so that he ceased to reign in Jerusalem—and levied on the land a fine of one hundred talents of silver and a [a numeral is presumably missing here] talent of gold. [34]Pharaoh-Necho installed Eliakim son of Josiah as king in place of his father Josiah, and changed his name to Jehoiakim; and he took Jehoahaz down to Egypt, where he died. [35]Jehoiakim paid the silver and gold to Pharaoh; he taxed the country to raise the money demanded by Pharaoh: he exacted the silver and gold from each person according to his means [or evaluation] . . .

*II Kings 23.33-35*

וַיַּאַסְרֵהוּ פַרְעֹה נְכֹה בְרִבְלָה בְּאֶרֶץ חֲמָת
מִמְּלֹךְ בִּירוּשָׁלָם וַיִּתֶּן־עֹנֶשׁ עַל־הָאָרֶץ מֵאָה כִכַּר־
כֶּסֶף וְכִכַּר זָהָב: וַיַּמְלֵךְ פַּרְעֹה נְכֹה אֶת־אֶלְיָקִים
בֶּן־יֹאשִׁיָּהוּ תַּחַת יֹאשִׁיָּהוּ אָבִיו וַיַּסֵּב אֶת־שְׁמוֹ
יְהוֹיָקִים וְאֶת־יְהוֹאָחָז לָקָח וַיָּבֹא מִצְרַיִם וַיָּמָת שָׁם:
וְהַכֶּסֶף וְהַזָּהָב נָתַן יְהוֹיָקִים לְפַרְעֹה אַךְ הֶעֱרִיךְ
אֶת־הָאָרֶץ לָתֵת אֶת־הַכֶּסֶף עַל־פִּי פַרְעֹה אִישׁ
כְּעֶרְכּוֹ נָגַשׂ אֶת־הַכֶּסֶף וְאֶת־הַזָּהָב...

מְלָכִים ב׳ כג: לג-לה

You are relying for a staff on that splintered reed, on Egypt, which enters and pierces the palm of anyone who leans on it. That is King Pharaoh of Egypt to all who rely on him.

*Isaiah 36.6*

הִנֵּה בָטַחְתָּ עַל־מִשְׁעֶנֶת הַקָּנֶה הָרָצוּץ הַזֶּה
עַל־מִצְרַיִם אֲשֶׁר יִסָּמֵךְ אִישׁ עָלָיו וּבָא בְכַפּוֹ
וּנְקָבָהּ כֵּן פַּרְעֹה מֶלֶךְ־מִצְרַיִם לְכָל־הַבֹּטְחִים
עָלָיו:

יְשַׁעְיָהוּ לו: ו

Portion of the Babylonian historical text describing the conquest of Jerusalem by Nebuchadnezzar II (598-597), It reads:

Year 7, month Kislimu [Hebrew Kislev]: The king of Akkad moved his army into Hatti land, laid seige to the city of Judah (Ia-a-hu-du) [viz., Jerusalem] and the king took the city on the second day of the month Addaru [Heb. Adar]. He appointed in it a (new) king of his liking, took heavy booty from it, and brought it to Babylon.

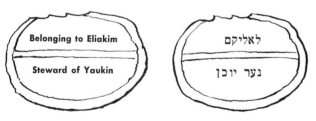

| Belonging to Eliakim | לאליקם |
| Steward of Yaukin | נער יוכן |

An ancient seal impression on a jar handle with the seal stone of Elia-kim steward of King Yaukin (Jehoiachin).

The seal was of the same type as those of Gedaliah and Jaazniah (p. 202) with the single line encircling the legend and the double line dividing it into two registers. Note also that the spelling "Yaukin" represents the later pronunciation of Jehoiachin, the king of Judah who was exiled to Babylonia in 598-597 B.C.E.

About three months before this Babylonian expedition actually breached the city, Jehoiakim was slain, apparently the victim of a palace plot. It was his young son Jehoiachin (Jeconiah), and successor on the throne, who caught the full weight of the Babylonian vengeance. He and all the royal household, together with a portion of the upper class and a great levy of craftsmen, were marched off as captives to Babylon. As puppet ruler, the conqueror left on the throne Mattaniah, a son of Josiah, and changed his name to Zedekiah (II Kings 24:17; I Chronicles 3:15).

After some ten years of Babylonian rule, Judah revolted a second time, again refusing to heed Jeremiah's dismal warnings to rely on the Lord, that is, to renew no alliances or to rely on the force of arms. This time Babylonia struck back with even greater fury, not merely to bring the rebellious province to the dust, but to dispel any dreams of like resurgence on the part of Egypt.

The Babylonians systematically took and razed all the fortified cities of Judah. Archaeological excavation has confirmed the thoroughness of this destruction. Jerusalem, the capital, held out for almost two years, but fierce hunger and the Babylonian siege engines finally broke through the defenses and forced capitulation (587–586 B.C.E.). The conquerors leveled the Temple to the ground. "They captured the king, and brought him up to the king of Babylonia at Riblah [near Kadesh], and judgment was passed on him. They slew the sons of Zedekiah before his eyes, and put out the eyes of Zedekiah, and bound him in fetters, and took him to Babylon" (II Kings 25:6–7). There followed renewed deportations of the people from their land. The sovereign state of Judah was no more.

Now the Babylonians reduced Judah to the status of an outright colony, similar to that

Therefore, thus said the Lord concerning King Jehoiakim of Judah: He shall have no one of his line sitting on the throne of David, and his corpse shall be left exposed to the heat of the day and the frost of the night.

*Jeremiah 36.30*

Jehoiachin was eighteen years old when he became king, and he reigned in Jerusalem three months . . . [11]Then King Nebuchadnezzar of Babylon marched against the city; and when his troops [lit., servants] were besieging it, [12]King Jehoiachin of Judah, together with his mother and courtiers and officials and eunuchs, surrendered [lit., went out] to the king of Babylon . . . [14]He exiled all Jerusalem and all the officials and all the soldiers —10,000 exiles—and all the artisans and smiths; only the poorest of the population [lit., people of the land] remained [25.12 reads: "The Babylonian captain of the guard left some of the poorest of the land as vinedressers and plowmen"] . . . [17]The king of Babylon made Mattaniah his [Jehoiachin's] uncle king in his place, and changed his name to Zedekiah.

*II Kings 24.8-17*

In the ninth year of his [Zedekiah's] reign, on the tenth day of the tenth month, King Nebuchadnezzar of Babylon and all his army marched upon Jerusalem and laid siege to it . . . [2]The city was under siege until King Zedekiah's eleventh year; [3]but on the ninth day of the [fourth] month, when famine was raging in the city . . . [4]the city was breached and all the military [fled] by night by way of the gate . . . [5]The Chaldean troops pursued the king . . . [6]and they captured the king and brought him to the king of Babylon at Riblah, where he was arraigned. [7]Zedekiah's two sons were slain before his eyes, and Zedekiah's eyes were put out. They then bound him in chains and brought him to Babylon. [8]On the seventh day of the fifth month . . . Nebuzaradan, captain of the guard [the Hebrew term is uncertain], came . . . [9]and burnt down the House of the Lord and the royal palace and all the houses in Jerusalem . . ., [10]and the walls around Jerusalem were torn down . . .

*II Kings 25.1-10*

לָכֵן כֹּה־אָמַר יְהוָה עַל־יְהוֹיָקִים מֶלֶךְ יְהוּדָה לֹא־יִהְיֶה־לּוֹ יוֹשֵׁב עַל־כִּסֵּא דָוִד וְנִבְלָתוֹ תִּהְיֶה מֻשְׁלֶכֶת לַחֹרֶב בַּיּוֹם וְלַקֶּרַח בַּלָּיְלָה:

יִרְמְיָהוּ לו:ל

בֶּן־שְׁמֹנֶה עֶשְׂרֵה שָׁנָה יְהוֹיָכִין בְּמָלְכוֹ וּשְׁלֹשָׁה חֳדָשִׁים מָלַךְ בִּירוּשָׁלָיִם... וַיָּבֹא נְבֻכַדְנֶאצַּר מֶלֶךְ־בָּבֶל עַל־הָעִיר וַעֲבָדָיו צָרִים עָלֶיהָ: וַיֵּצֵא יְהוֹיָכִין מֶלֶךְ־יְהוּדָה עַל־מֶלֶךְ בָּבֶל הוּא וְאִמּוֹ וַעֲבָדָיו וְשָׂרָיו וְסָרִיסָיו... וְהִגְלָה אֶת־כָּל־יְרוּשָׁלַם וְאֶת־כָּל־הַשָּׂרִים וְאֵת | כָּל־גִּבּוֹרֵי הַחַיִל עֲשֶׂרֶת אֲלָפִים גּוֹלֶה וְכָל־הֶחָרָשׁ | וְהַמַּסְגֵּר לֹא נִשְׁאַר זוּלַת דַּלַּת עַם־הָאָרֶץ:

וַיַּמְלֵךְ מֶלֶךְ־בָּבֶל אֶת־מַתַּנְיָה דֹדוֹ תַּחְתָּיו וַיַּסֵּב אֶת־שְׁמוֹ צִדְקִיָּהוּ:

מְלָכִים ב׳ כד: ח – יז

וַיְהִי בִשְׁנַת הַתְּשִׁיעִית לְמָלְכוֹ בַּחֹדֶשׁ הָעֲשִׂירִי בֶּעָשׂוֹר לַחֹדֶשׁ בָּא נְבֻכַדְנֶאצַּר מֶלֶךְ־בָּבֶל הוּא וְכָל־חֵילוֹ עַל־יְרוּשָׁלַם וַיִּחַן עָלֶיהָ... וַתָּבֹא הָעִיר בַּמָּצוֹר עַד עַשְׁתֵּי עֶשְׂרֵה שָׁנָה לַמֶּלֶךְ צִדְקִיָּהוּ: בְּתִשְׁעָה לַחֹדֶשׁ וַיֶּחֱזַק הָרָעָב בָּעִיר... וַתִּבָּקַע הָעִיר וְכָל־אַנְשֵׁי הַמִּלְחָמָה | הַלַּיְלָה דֶּרֶךְ שַׁעַר... וַיִּרְדְּפוּ חֵיל־כַּשְׂדִּים אַחַר הַמֶּלֶךְ... וַיִּתְפְּשׂוּ אֶת־הַמֶּלֶךְ וַיַּעֲלוּ אֹתוֹ אֶל־מֶלֶךְ בָּבֶל רִבְלָתָה וַיְדַבְּרוּ אִתּוֹ מִשְׁפָּט: וְאֶת־בְּנֵי צִדְקִיָּהוּ שָׁחֲטוּ לְעֵינָיו וְאֶת־עֵינֵי צִדְקִיָּהוּ עִוֵּר וַיַּאַסְרֵהוּ בַנְחֻשְׁתַּיִם וַיְבִיאֵהוּ בָּבֶל:

וּבַחֹדֶשׁ הַחֲמִישִׁי בְּשִׁבְעָה לַחֹדֶשׁ... בָּא נְבוּזַרְאֲדָן רַב־טַבָּחִים עֶבֶד מֶלֶךְ־בָּבֶל יְרוּשָׁלָם: וַיִּשְׂרֹף אֶת־בֵּית יְהוָה וְאֶת־בֵּית הַמֶּלֶךְ וְאֵת כָּל־בָּתֵּי יְרוּשָׁלַם וְאֶת־כָּל־בֵּית גָּדוֹל שָׂרַף בָּאֵשׁ: וְאֶת־חוֹמֹת יְרוּשָׁלַם סָבִיב נָתְצוּ . . .

מְלָכִים ב׳ כה: א – י

201

Seal of Gedaliah, discovered at Lachish. It belongs to the period (ca. 600 B.C.E.) of the Gedaliah of II Kings 25.23-25; but whether the same person is involved is uncertain.

| Belonging to Gedaliah | לגדליהו |
|---|---|
| In charge of (or, who is over) the House | [א]שר על הבי[ת] |

Impression of the stamp seal of onyx found in the excavations of Tell en-Nasbeh (probably ancient Mizpah). It is similar in shape to and belongs to the same period as the Gedaliah seal above. Beneath the legend is the design of a bird, usually described as a fighting cock. It may well be that the Jaazniah of the seal is the one mentioned with Gedaliah in II Kings 23. It reads:

| Belonging to Jaazniah | ליאזניהו |
|---|---|
| Steward of the King | עבד המלך |

endured by Israel since the days of the Assyrian rule. A native Judean, Gedaliah by name, was appointed governor of the despoiled and depopulated land, and he established headquarters at Mizpah. Gedaliah's administration seems to have been mild, for many Judeans who had fled into the hills, or into Egypt or Transjordan, returned from their places of refuge. But a certain Ishmael, a member of the Judean royal house, was desirous of restoring the monarchy and, abetted by the Ammonites, conspired to throw off Babylon's yoke. His well-meaning but utterly irresponsible accomplices murdered Gedaliah, together with the Judeans and Babylonians who made up his retinue, and embarked upon a reign of terror in the land. Once again the revenge of Babylon was swift and terrible. In 582 B.C.E. her troops instituted the third and final phase of Judah's depopulation and destruction (II Kings 25; Jeremiah 41–42).

Finally peace was achieved. Judah lay quiet, all the swirl and clash of centuries apparently come to naught. The period of the great Babylonian Exile descended upon the people of Judah, God's people. But the Law remained, and all that it stood for and implied.

As for the population that remained in the land of Judah, whom he had allowed to remain, King Nebuchadnezzar of Babylon appointed Gedaliah son of Ahikam son of Shaphan governor over them. [23]When all the chiefs of the troops, they and the[ir] men, heard that the king of Babylon had appointed Gedaliah governor, they went to him at Mizpah . . . [24]Gedaliah swore to them and their men; he said to them, "Do not be afraid of the officials of the Chaldeans. Dwell in the land and serve the king of Babylon, and it will go well with you." [25]But in the seventh month, Ishmael son of Nethaniah son of Elishama, who was of royal seed, came with ten men and murdered Gedaliah and all the Judeans and Chaldeans who were with him in Mizpah. [26] So the rest of the people, from the smallest to the greatest [or young and old], and the chiefs of the troops, left at once for Egypt, for they were afraid of the Chaldeans.

*II Kings 25.22-26*

וְהָעָם הַנִּשְׁאָר בְּאֶרֶץ יְהוּדָה אֲשֶׁר הִשְׁאִיר
נְבוּכַדְנֶאצַּר מֶלֶךְ בָּבֶל וַיַּפְקֵד עֲלֵיהֶם אֶת־
גְּדַלְיָהוּ בֶן־אֲחִיקָם בֶּן־שָׁפָן: וַיִּשְׁמְעוּ כָל־שָׂרֵי
הַחֲיָלִים הֵמָּה וְהָאֲנָשִׁים כִּי־הִפְקִיד מֶלֶךְ־בָּבֶל
אֶת־גְּדַלְיָהוּ וַיָּבֹאוּ אֶל־גְּדַלְיָהוּ הַמִּצְפָּה... וַיִּשָּׁבַע
לָהֶם גְּדַלְיָהוּ וּלְאַנְשֵׁיהֶם וַיֹּאמֶר לָהֶם אַל־תִּירְאוּ
מֵעַבְדֵי הַכַּשְׂדִּים שְׁבוּ בָאָרֶץ וְעִבְדוּ אֶת־מֶלֶךְ
בָּבֶל וְיִטַב לָכֶם:
וַיְהִי | בַּחֹדֶשׁ הַשְּׁבִיעִי בָּא יִשְׁמָעֵאל בֶּן־נְתַנְיָה
בֶן־אֱלִישָׁמָע מִזֶּרַע הַמְּלוּכָה וַעֲשָׂרָה אֲנָשִׁים אִתּוֹ
וַיַּכּוּ אֶת־גְּדַלְיָהוּ וַיָּמֹת וְאֶת־הַיְּהוּדִים וְאֶת־
הַכַּשְׂדִּים אֲשֶׁר־הָיוּ אִתּוֹ בַּמִּצְפָּה: וַיָּקֻמוּ כָל־הָעָם
מִקָּטֹן וְעַד־גָּדוֹל וְשָׂרֵי הַחֲיָלִים וַיָּבֹאוּ מִצְרָיִם כִּי
יָרְאוּ מִפְּנֵי כַשְׂדִּים:

מְלָכִים ב׳ כה: כב־כו

As for me, I will remain in Mizpah, to attend upon [or: to act as representative before] the Chaldeans who come to us, while you harvest your wine and summer crops and oil, and fill your storage jars . . . [11]Similarly, when all the Judeans who were in Moab, Ammon, and Edom, or who were in other countries, heard that the king of Babylon had left a remnant in Judah and had appointed Gedaliah governor over them . . ., [12]all these Judeans came back from all the places to which they had scattered.

*Jeremiah 40.10-12*

וַאֲנִי הִנְנִי יֹשֵׁב בַּמִּצְפָּה לַעֲמֹד לִפְנֵי הַכַּשְׂדִּים
אֲשֶׁר יָבֹאוּ אֵלֵינוּ וְאַתֶּם אִסְפוּ יַיִן וָקַיִץ וְשֶׁמֶן וְשִׂמוּ
בִּכְלֵיכֶם... וְגַם כָּל־הַיְּהוּדִים אֲשֶׁר־בְּמוֹאָב |
וּבִבְנֵי־עַמּוֹן וּבֶאֱדוֹם וַאֲשֶׁר בְּכָל־הָאֲרָצוֹת שָׁמְעוּ
כִּי־נָתַן | מֶלֶךְ־בָּבֶל שְׁאֵרִית לִיהוּדָה וְכִי הִפְקִיד
עֲלֵיהֶם אֶת־גְּדַלְיָהוּ... וַיָּשֻׁבוּ כָל־הַיְּהוּדִים מִכָּל־
הַמְּקֹמוֹת אֲשֶׁר נִדְּחוּ־שָׁם...

יִרְמְיָהוּ מ: י־יב

In the twenty-third year of Nebuchadrezzar [=582 B.C.E.], Nebuzaradan, captain of the guard, exiled 745 Judeans—in all: 4,600 persons.

*Jeremiah 52.30*

בִּשְׁנַת שָׁלֹשׁ וְעֶשְׂרִים לִנְבוּכַדְרֶאצַּר הֶגְלָה
נְבוּזַרְאֲדָן רַב־טַבָּחִים יְהוּדִים נֶפֶשׁ שְׁבַע מֵאוֹת
אַרְבָּעִים וַחֲמִשָּׁה כָּל־נֶפֶשׁ אַרְבַּעַת אֲלָפִים וְשֵׁשׁ
מֵאוֹת:

יִרְמְיָהוּ נב: ל

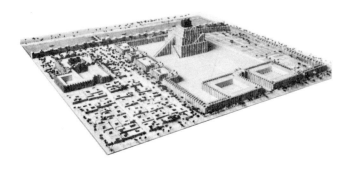

Model of some of the structures of the temple complex of the city of Babylon in the Neo-Babylonian (Chaldean) period—the period of the Babylonian Exile. At the upper right is the famous tower of Babylon, and at the left is the main temple of Marduk, chief god of Babylon. This is a good indication of the enormous power that confronted the Judean exiles in the territory of their conquerors.

204

## Chapter VI

# THE BABYLONIAN EXILE AND THE RESTORATION OF JUDAH

THE Babylonian Exile was a supreme test of Israel's vitality. The Judeans were the only people in ancient times known to have been taken wholesale into captivity and still to have retained their religious and social identity. The Exile proved that Israel—the spiritual community—could adapt itself to, and develop under, the most adverse conditions. In fact, the very adversity seems to have bred leaders whose religious experience climaxed the prophetic tradition. Many Judeans lost faith in God. According to the Covenant He was their infallible protector; but in the contest with the Babylonian gods, He obviously had been worsted. There were others, however, who believed, also on convenantal grounds, that the Lord had visited destruction on Judah as a punishment for its wickedness; and it was this idea which was championed by the prophetic movement.

The Exile, in addition, marked the beginning of a slow transition of Judaism to a form

The Lord showed me two baskets of figs set in front of the Temple of the Lord . . . ³The Lord said to me, "What do you see, Jeremiah?" I replied, "Figs—the good figs are very good, the bad ones very bad, so bad that they cannot be eaten." ⁴Then the word of the Lord came to me: ⁵"Thus said the Lord, the God of Israel: As with these good figs, so I will recognize for good the Judean exiles whom I have expelled from this place to the land of the Chaldeans. ⁶I will look upon them with favor, and bring them back to this land; I will rebuild them rather than tear down, and I will plant them rather than pluck up. ⁷I will give them the mind to acknowledge Me, that I am the Lord; then they shall be My people and I will be their God—when they turn back to Me with all their heart. ⁸And as with the bad figs, which cannot be eaten they are so bad — thus has the Lord said — so will I treat King Zedekiah of Judah and his officials, and the remnant of Judah that remains in this land, and those who live in the land of Egypt: ⁹I will make them a horror [and] a disaster to all the kingdoms of the earth, a disgrace and a proverb, a byword and a curse in all the places to which I banish them . . ." 29 ¹⁹". . . because they did not listen to My words"—declared the Lord—"when I kept sending them My servants the prophets . . ."

*Jeremiah 24.1-9; 29.19*

הֶרְאַנִי יְהֹוָה וְהִנֵּה שְׁנֵי דוּדָאֵי תְאֵנִים מוּעָדִים
לִפְנֵי הֵיכַל יְהֹוָה... וַיֹּאמֶר יְהֹוָה אֵלַי מָה־אַתָּה
רֹאֶה יִרְמְיָהוּ וָאֹמַר תְּאֵנִים הַתְּאֵנִים הַטֹּבוֹת טֹבוֹת
מְאֹד וְהָרָעוֹת רָעוֹת מְאֹד אֲשֶׁר לֹא־תֵאָכַלְנָה
מֵרֹעַ: וַיְהִי דְבַר־יְהֹוָה אֵלַי לֵאמֹר: כֹּה־אָמַר
יְהֹוָה אֱלֹהֵי יִשְׂרָאֵל כַּתְּאֵנִים הַטֹּבוֹת הָאֵלֶּה כֵּן
אַכִּיר אֶת־גָּלוּת יְהוּדָה אֲשֶׁר שִׁלַּחְתִּי מִן־הַמָּקוֹם
הַזֶּה אֶרֶץ כַּשְׂדִּים לְטוֹבָה: וְשַׂמְתִּי עֵינִי עֲלֵיהֶם
לְטוֹבָה וַהֲשִׁבֹתִים עַל־הָאָרֶץ הַזֹּאת וּבְנִיתִים וְלֹא
אֶהֱרֹס וּנְטַעְתִּים וְלֹא אֶתּוֹשׁ: וְנָתַתִּי לָהֶם לֵב לָדַעַת
אֹתִי כִּי אֲנִי יְהֹוָה וְהָיוּ־לִי לְעָם וְאָנֹכִי אֶהְיֶה לָהֶם
לֵאלֹהִים כִּי־יָשֻׁבוּ אֵלַי בְּכָל־לִבָּם: וְכַתְּאֵנִים
הָרָעוֹת אֲשֶׁר לֹא־תֵאָכַלְנָה מֵרֹעַ כִּי־כֹה | אָמַר
יְהֹוָה כֵּן אֶתֵּן אֶת־צִדְקִיָּהוּ מֶלֶךְ־יְהוּדָה וְאֶת־
שָׂרָיו וְאֵת | שְׁאֵרִית יְרוּשָׁלַ͏ִם הַנִּשְׁאָרִים בָּאָרֶץ
הַזֹּאת וְהַיֹּשְׁבִים בְּאֶרֶץ מִצְרָיִם: וּנְתַתִּים לְזַעֲוָה
לְרָעָה לְכֹל מַמְלְכוֹת הָאָרֶץ לְחֶרְפָּה וּלְמָשָׁל
לִשְׁנִינָה וְלִקְלָלָה בְּכָל־הַמְּקֹמוֹת אֲשֶׁר־אַדִּיחֵם
שָׁם: ... תַּחַת אֲשֶׁר־לֹא־שָׁמְעוּ אֶל־דְּבָרַי נְאֻם־
יְהֹוָה אֲשֶׁר שָׁלַחְתִּי אֲלֵיהֶם אֶת־עֲבָדַי הַנְּבִאִים
הַשְׁכֵּם וְשָׁלֹחַ וְלֹא שְׁמַעְתֶּם נְאֻם־יְהֹוָה:

יִרְמְיָהוּ כד: א–ט; כט:יט

The tell of Biblical Lachish, with views of the British excavations carried on in the 1930's.

Reverse side of one of some two dozen ostraca found in the latest pre-exilic levels at Lachish. Only six have meaningful texts preserved. The letter is written on both sides of a broken piece of pottery (ostracon) by Hoshaiah, commander of an observation post, to his superior, Yoash, commander at Lachish. After answering some questions regarding day-to-day business, the last lines refer to business at hand:

"And let (my lord) know that we are watching for the signals of Lachish, according to all the indications which my lord has given, for we cannot see Azekah."

206

which was destined to evolve during the period of the Second Commonwealth and set the pattern for Jewish life during the Diaspora, or great dispersion, which took place after the Romans destroyed Jerusalem in 70 C.E.

## Devastation in Judah

The land of Judah, itself, lay for a time inert, physically reduced, its remnants of population bereft of direction and spirit. Recent excavations at such sites as Lachish, Beth-shemesh, and Tell Beit Mirsim (perhaps Kiriat-sepher) bear eloquent testimony to the devastation wreaked on the rebellious kingdom of Judah by the forces of Chaldea. In 1935 C.E. a number of *ostraca*—potsherds used as writing material—were dug up at Lachish. Most of these appear to have been military dispatches written about 588 B.C.E. and record a determined struggle on the part of the Judean garrisons against the more powerful Babylonian enemy. The writer of Ostracon VI expressed deep concern about rumors of defeatism among the ruling class in Jerusalem: "And behold the words of the (princes) are not good, but to weaken our hands." Significantly, these relics were found buried deep in ashes.

Many towns in Judah were so thoroughly leveled by the Babylonians that they never were restored. The Temple, and the central religious organization too, was totally destroyed. The normal leaders of the community—the well-to-do, the well-educated, even the artisans—were either carried off to Babylon or fled to Transjordan and Egypt. Indeed, when Gedaliah was murdered, Jeremiah urged his fellow Judeans to remain in the land; but a group took Jeremiah forcibly with them into Egypt (Jeremiah 41–43).

As the Judean social order thus fell apart, the teachings associated with Moses and the

Oh, my anguish, my anguish! How I writhe!
Oh, the walls of my heart!
My heart moans within me, I cannot be silent;
For I [lit.: you, O my being] hear the blast of the
 horn,
The alarm of war.
²⁰Disaster follows on disaster,
For all the land is ravaged;
Suddenly my tents are ravaged,
In a moment, my tent-cloths.
²¹How long must I see standards,
Hear the sound of the horn?
²²For My people is stupid,
They do not acknowledge Me;
They are senseless children,
Without understanding.
They are wise—at doing wrong;
But do not know how to do right.
²³I look at the earth,
And it is unformed and void;
At the skies,
And their light is gone.
²⁴I look at the mountains,
And they are quaking,
And all the hills are rocking.
²⁵I look, and no man is left,
And all the birds of the sky have fled.
²⁶I look, and the farm land is desert,
And all its towns are in ruin—
Because of the Lord,
Because of His blazing anger.
²⁷For thus said the Lord:
"The whole land shall be desolate—
But I will not make an end of it."

*Jeremiah 4.19-27*

מֵעַי ׀ מֵעַי ׀ אוֹחִילָה קִירוֹת לִבִּי הֹמֶה־לִּי
לִבִּי לֹא אַחֲרִישׁ כִּי קוֹל שׁוֹפָר שָׁמַעַתְּ נַפְשִׁי תְּרוּעַת
מִלְחָמָה: שֶׁבֶר עַל־שֶׁבֶר נִקְרָא כִּי־שֻׁדְּדָה כָּל־
הָאָרֶץ פִּתְאֹם שֻׁדְּדוּ אֹהָלַי רֶגַע יְרִיעֹתָי: עַד־מָתַי
אֶרְאֶה־נֵּס אֶשְׁמְעָה קוֹל שׁוֹפָר: כִּי ׀ אֱוִיל עַמִּי אוֹתִי
לֹא יָדָעוּ בָּנִים סְכָלִים הֵמָּה וְלֹא נְבוֹנִים הֵמָּה
חֲכָמִים הֵמָּה לְהָרַע וּלְהֵיטִיב לֹא יָדָעוּ: רָאִיתִי
אֶת־הָאָרֶץ וְהִנֵּה־תֹהוּ וָבֹהוּ וְאֶל־הַשָּׁמַיִם וְאֵין
אוֹרָם: רָאִיתִי הֶהָרִים וְהִנֵּה רֹעֲשִׁים וְכָל־הַגְּבָעוֹת
הִתְקַלְקָלוּ: רָאִיתִי וְהִנֵּה אֵין הָאָדָם וְכָל־עוֹף
הַשָּׁמַיִם נָדָדוּ: רָאִיתִי וְהִנֵּה הַכַּרְמֶל הַמִּדְבָּר וְכָל־
עָרָיו נִתְּצוּ מִפְּנֵי יְהוָה מִפְּנֵי חֲרוֹן אַפּוֹ: כִּי־כֹה
אָמַר יְהוָה שְׁמָמָה תִהְיֶה כָּל־הָאָרֶץ וְכָלָה לֹא
אֶעֱשֶׂה:

יִרְמְיָהוּ ד : יט–כז

 

But Azariah son of Hoshaiah and Johanan son
of Kareah, and all the other arrogant men, challenged Jeremiah, saying, "You are lying! The Lord
our God did not send you to say, 'Do not go to
Egypt and settle there'." ⁵Then Johanan son of
Kareah and all the army chiefs took the remnant
of Judah . . . ⁶men, women, and children . . . and
the prophet Jeremiah, and Baruch son of Neriah,
⁷and they went to Egypt . . .

*Jeremiah 43.2-7*

וַיֹּאמֶר עֲזַרְיָה בֶן־הוֹשַׁעְיָה וְיוֹחָנָן בֶּן־קָרֵחַ
וְכָל־הָאֲנָשִׁים הַזֵּדִים אֹמְרִים אֶל־יִרְמְיָהוּ שֶׁקֶר
אַתָּה מְדַבֵּר לֹא שְׁלָחֲךָ יְהוָה אֱלֹהֵינוּ לֵאמֹר לֹא־
תָבֹאוּ מִצְרַיִם לָגוּר שָׁם:... וַיִּקַּח יוֹחָנָן בֶּן־קָרֵחַ
וְכָל־שָׂרֵי הַחֲיָלִים אֵת כָּל־שְׁאֵרִית יְהוּדָה... אֶת־
הַגְּבָרִים וְאֶת־הַנָּשִׁים וְאֶת־הַטַּף... וְאֶת יִרְמְיָהוּ
הַנָּבִיא וְאֶת־בָּרוּךְ בֶּן־נֵרִיָּהוּ: וַיָּבֹאוּ אֶרֶץ מִצְרָיִם:...

יִרְמְיָהוּ מג : ב–ז

An artist's conception of the area around the Ishtar Gate in the city of Babylon, as reconstructed by the Babylonians, in the Neo-Babylonian period. Past the gate to the left, there is visible a portion of the temple of the goddess Ninmah. To the right are the famous "hanging gardens," actually the rooftop parks of the fortified palace. In the upper right stands the ziggurat (temple tower).

Façade of the Ishtar Gate as seen today after excavation. Designs from the Gate and along the processional way leading to the Gate of bulls, lions, and dragons have been removed and some are now reconstructed in the State Museum of Berlin. The designs were made of baked bricks covered with glazes of blue, gold, and white. Height of gate about 47 feet.

utterances of the prophets were ignored and gradually forgotten. Those few remaining members of society who might have provided a nucleus of the religious and cultural stability and continuity could accomplish almost nothing in the chaotic conditions which prevailed. Edomites, Ammonites, Moabites, and others from the neighboring regions—some of whom had previously been settled by Assyria in the territory of the northern kingdom —encroached more and more on the territory of Judah. Inevitably this infiltration led to intermarriage with these alien peoples and then indirectly to their gradually increasing influence upon the religious practices and daily life of the Israelites. Thus with the general tendency toward social and intellectual deterioration, assimilation and syncretism went on apace. Finally Judah, much reduced in territory, came under the control of a governor who resided in Samaria.

## The Babylonian Captivity

In Babylonia, the exiled Jews found themselves in the midst of a flourishing and impressive civilization. The Chaldean regime of Nebuchadnezzar (605–562 B.C.E.)—currently the greatest power in western Asia—had embarked on a tremendous building campaign for the glorification of the king, his capital, and his empire. Among the new structures were the terraces of Babylon, the so-called Hanging Gardens which the Greeks made famous as one of the seven wonders of the world. In actual fact, these masonry terraces were eclipsed by the Ishtar Gate and by the Temple of Marduk built in stepped tiers like the towers of a modern skyscraper. To carry out these projects, artisans of all kinds were imported, both as captives and as highly paid skilled workers, as recorded in the Biblical statement: "And Nebuchadnezzar carried away . . . all the craftsmen and smiths" (II Kings 24:14) .

By the streams of Babylon,
There we sat and wept
When we thought of Zion.
²Upon the willow trees in her midst
We hung our harps.
³For there our captors demanded of us
Melodious songs,
And those who mocked us,
Merry tunes:
"Sing for us some songs of Zion."
⁴But how can we sing
The songs of the Lord on alien soil?
⁵If I forget you, O Jerusalem,
May my right hand wither!
⁶May my tongue stick to my palate
If I do not remember you,
If I do not regard Jerusalem above my greatest joy.

*Psalm 137.1-6*

עַל־נַהֲרוֹת ׀ בָּבֶל שָׁם יָשַׁבְנוּ גַּם־בָּכִינוּ
בְּזָכְרֵנוּ אֶת־צִיּוֹן: עַל־עֲרָבִים בְּתוֹכָהּ תָּלִינוּ
כִּנֹּרוֹתֵינוּ: כִּי שָׁם שְׁאֵלוּנוּ שׁוֹבֵינוּ דִּבְרֵי־שִׁיר
וְתוֹלָלֵינוּ שִׂמְחָה שִׁירוּ לָנוּ מִשִּׁיר צִיּוֹן: אֵיךְ נָשִׁיר
אֶת־שִׁיר־יְהוָה עַל אַדְמַת נֵכָר: אִם־אֶשְׁכָּחֵךְ
יְרוּשָׁלִָם תִּשְׁכַּח יְמִינִי: תִּדְבַּק לְשׁוֹנִי לְחִכִּי אִם־
לֹא אֶזְכְּרֵכִי אִם־לֹא אַעֲלֶה אֶת־יְרוּשָׁלִַם עַל
רֹאשׁ שִׂמְחָתִי:

תְּהִלִּים קלז: א־ו

Concerning the Ammonites. Thus said the Lord:
Has Israel no sons,
Has he no heir?
Why then has Milcom [Hebrew *malkam*] pos-
    sessed Gad
And his people live in its towns?
²Assuredly, the time will come
            —declares the Lord—
When I will cause the blast of war to be heard
Against Rabbah of the Ammonites;
It shall become a desolate mound,
And its villages shall be consumed in fire.
Then Israel shall possess those who possessed it,
Said the Lord.

*Jeremiah 49.1-2*

לִבְנֵי עַמּוֹן כֹּה אָמַר יְהוָה הֲבָנִים אֵין לְיִשְׂרָאֵל
אִם־יוֹרֵשׁ אֵין לוֹ מַדּוּעַ יָרַשׁ מַלְכָּם אֶת־גָּד וְעַמּוֹ
בְּעָרָיו יָשָׁב: לָכֵן הִנֵּה יָמִים בָּאִים נְאֻם־יְהוָה
וְהִשְׁמַעְתִּי אֶל־רַבַּת בְּנֵי־עַמּוֹן תְּרוּעַת מִלְחָמָה
וְהָיְתָה לְתֵל שְׁמָמָה וּבְנֹתֶיהָ בָּאֵשׁ תִּצַּתְנָה וְיָרַשׁ
יִשְׂרָאֵל אֶת־יֹרְשָׁיו אָמַר יְהוָה:

יִרְמְיָהוּ מט: א־ב

Alas! Lonely sits the city once great with people!
She that was great among nations
Is become like a widow;
The princess among states is become a thrall.
²Bitterly she weeps in the night,
Her cheeks wet with tears.
There is none to comfort her of all her friends.
All her allies have betrayed her;
They have become her foes.
³Judah has gone into exile
Because of misery and harsh oppression;
When she settled among the nations,
She found no rest;

אֵיכָה ׀ יָשְׁבָה בָדָד הָעִיר רַבָּתִי עָם הָיְתָה
כְּאַלְמָנָה רַבָּתִי בַגּוֹיִם שָׂרָתִי בַּמְּדִינוֹת הָיְתָה לָמַס:
בָּכוֹ תִבְכֶּה בַּלַּיְלָה וְדִמְעָתָהּ עַל לֶחֱיָהּ אֵין־לָהּ
מְנַחֵם מִכָּל־אֹהֲבֶיהָ כָּל־רֵעֶיהָ בָּגְדוּ בָהּ הָיוּ לָהּ
לְאֹיְבִים: גָּלְתָה יְהוּדָה מֵעֹנִי וּמֵרֹב עֲבֹדָה הִיא
יָשְׁבָה בַגּוֹיִם לֹא מָצְאָה מָנוֹחַ כָּל־רֹדְפֶיהָ הִשִּׂיגוּהָ
בֵּין הַמְּצָרִים: . . .

*(continued)*

209

One of a group of cuneiform texts with lists of the rations for captive kings and their retinues living in the vicinity of Babylon. Among the peoples listed are Philistines, Phoenicians, Judeans, Elamites, Medians, and Persians. These texts are basic for our knowledge of the treatment of captive foreigners by the Babylonians. This text is dated in the 13th year of Nebuchadnezzar II (592 B.C.E.). Jehoiachin and his sons are mentioned. Other names known to us from the Bible occur, for example, Samakuyama, with which compare Semachyahu (I Chronicles 26.7); the name is also found in the contemporaneous Lachish Ostraca.

Of special interest for us are lines 17-18 (on the reverse of the tablet):

17. 10 sila (a measure) [of oil] for Yakukinu (Jehoiachin) (and?) the son of the king of Jakudu (Judah).

18. 2½ sila (a measure) [of oil] for the 5 sons of the king of Jakudu through (or, in the possession of) Qana'a. (After Oppenheim, ANET², p. 308b.)

The Judean exiles were treated no differently from the other captive peoples. The common folk were generally enslaved outright, and those of higher status were given limited freedom to earn a living and choose their abode. A number of the exiled Judeans even managed to live in their own homes in a special quarter of the city of Babylon.

Especially interesting is the manner in which the Biblical and the Babylonian texts confirm and clarify one another in their statements about the Babylonian treatment of King Jehoiachin and his household. The Biblical historian tells us:

And in the thirty-seventh year of the exile of King Jehoiachin of Judah . . . King Evil-merodach of Babylon, in the year that he began to reign, lifted up the head of King Jehoiachin of Judah from prison. And he spoke kindly to him, and gave him a seat above the seats of the kings who were with him in Babylon. And Jehoiachin put off his prison garments, and he ate regularly in the king's presence all the days of his life. And for his allowance, a regular allowance was given him by the king, every day a portion, all the days of his life [II Kings 25:27–30].

Shortly after the beginning of the twentieth century, the Kaiser Friedrich Museum in Berlin received some three hundred cuneiform tablets which had been excavated by a German expedition near the Ishtar Gate in Babylon. These tablets lay for over three decades in the basement of the museum, unknown and undeciphered. Under the very thorough Nazi regime, the boxes of tablets came to the attention of the curator of the museum and he began to study them. He was astounded to discover that several of the tablets dealt precisely with this same King Jehoiachin of Judah and his family in exile in Babylon, and that these texts not only substantiated but even filled in gaps in the Biblical account. It is unusual for archaeological discoveries to confirm a Bib-

210

All her pursuers overtook her in the narrow
    places . . .
7All the precious things she had
In the days of old
Jerusalem recalled
In her days of woe and sorrow,
When her people fell by enemy hands
With none to help her;
When enemies looked on and gloated
Over her downfall.
8Jersualem has greatly sinned,
Therefore she is an outcast.
All who admired her despise her,
For they have seen her disgraced;
She can only sigh
And shrink back.
9Her uncleanness clings to her skirts.
She gave no thought to her future;
She has sunk appallingly,
With none to comfort her.—
See, O Lord, my misery;
How the enemy jeers!
10The foe has laid hands
On everything dear to her.
She has seen her Sanctuary
Invaded by nations
Which You have denied admission
Into Your community.
11All her inhabitants sigh,
As they search for bread;
They have bartered their treasures for food,
To keep themselves alive.—
See, O Lord, and behold,
How abject I have become!

*Lamentations 1.1-11*    אֵיכָה א׃א-יא

זָכְרָה יְרוּשָׁלַ͏ִם יְמֵי עׇנְיָהּ וּמְרוּדֶיהָ כֹּל מַחֲמֻדֶיהָ
אֲשֶׁר הָיוּ מִימֵי קֶדֶם בִּנְפֹל עַמָּהּ בְּיַד־צָר וְאֵין
עוֹזֵר לָהּ רָאוּהָ צָרִים שָׂחֲקוּ עַל־מִשְׁבַּתֶּהָ: חֵטְא
חָטְאָה יְרוּשָׁלַ͏ִם עַל־כֵּן לְנִידָה הָיָתָה כׇּל־
מְכַבְּדֶיהָ הִזִּילוּהָ כִּי־רָאוּ עֶרְוָתָהּ גַּם־הִיא נֶאֶנְחָה
וַתָּשׇׁב אָחוֹר: טֻמְאָתָהּ בְּשׁוּלֶיהָ לֹא זָכְרָה אַחֲרִיתָהּ
וַתֵּרֶד פְּלָאִים אֵין מְנַחֵם לָהּ רְאֵה יְהֹוָה אֶת־עׇנְיִי
כִּי הִגְדִּיל אוֹיֵב: יָדוֹ פָּרַשׂ צָר עַל כׇּל־מַחֲמַדֶּיהָ
כִּי־רָאֲתָה גוֹיִם בָּאוּ מִקְדָּשָׁהּ אֲשֶׁר צִוִּיתָה לֹא־
יָבֹאוּ בַקָּהָל לָךְ: כׇּל־עַמָּהּ נֶאֱנָחִים מְבַקְּשִׁים לֶחֶם
נָתְנוּ מַחֲמוֹדֵּיהֶם בְּאֹכֶל לְהָשִׁיב נָפֶשׁ רְאֵה יְהֹוָה
וְהַבִּיטָה כִּי הָיִיתִי זוֹלֵלָה:

This is the text of the letter that the prophet
Jeremiah sent from Jerusalem to the rest of the
elders of the exiles, to the priests, prophets, and
all the people whom Nebuchadnezzar had exiled
from Jerusalem to Babylon (2after King Jeconiah,
the Queen Mother, the eunuchs, the officials of
Judah and Jerusalem, and the craftsmen and
smiths had left Jerusalem), 3through Elasah son

וְאֵלֶּה דִּבְרֵי הַסֵּפֶר אֲשֶׁר שָׁלַח יִרְמְיָה הַנָּבִיא
מִירוּשָׁלָ͏ִם אֶל־יֶתֶר זִקְנֵי הַגּוֹלָה וְאֶל־הַכֹּהֲנִים
וְאֶל־הַנְּבִיאִים וְאֶל־כׇּל־הָעָם אֲשֶׁר הֶגְלָה
נְבוּכַדְנֶאצַּר מִירוּשָׁלַ͏ִם בָּבֶלָה: אַחֲרֵי צֵאת יְכׇנְיָה
הַמֶּלֶךְ וְהַגְּבִירָה וְהַסָּרִיסִים שָׂרֵי יְהוּדָה וִירוּשָׁלַ͏ִם
וְהֶחָרָשׁ וְהַמַּסְגֵּר מִירוּשָׁלָ͏ִם: בְּיַד אֶלְעָשָׂה בֶן־

*(continued)*

211

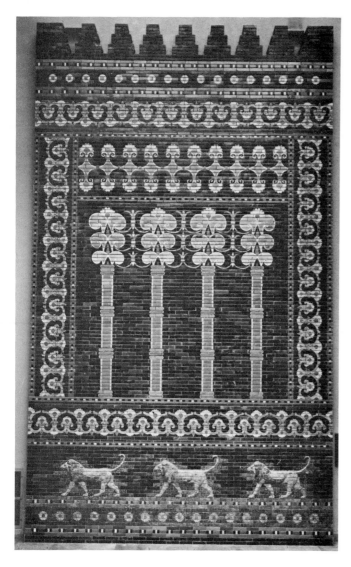

Part of the wall decoration of the throne room of the Late-Babylonian palace at Babylon. The glazed bricks of this panel incorporate within their designs architectural elements such as merlons (top), multiple capitaled pillars (center), and lions striding along a processional way (bottom). Floral elements complete the design. Yellow, green, white, turquoise, and dark blue glazes are used to create the color scheme.

lical account so specifically. (See W. F. Albright, "King Joiachin in Exile," *Biblical Archaeologist*, V [Dec., 1942], 49–55.)

Practically all the Judean exiles, except those who had been enslaved and brutalized by exhausting manual labor, longed for home. As time passed, however, and no immediate prospect of release developed, many were caught up in the colorful life of the Babylonian metropolis. These practical folk, recognizing that life went on in any case, made up their minds to "sing low in a bad tune," and to learn to adjust to Babylonian ways and customs according to the advice of Jeremiah:

Thus said the Lord of Hosts, the God of Israel, to all the exiles whom I have exiled from Jerusalem to Babylon: Build houses and settle down; plant gardens and eat their fruit. Take wives and beget sons and daughters; and take wives for your sons, and give your daughters to husbands, that they may bear sons and daughters; and multiply there and be not diminished. And seek the welfare of the city to which I have exiled you, and pray to the Lord for it; for in its welfare shall you have welfare [29:4 ff.].

It should be noted in passing that Jeremiah did not give the Babylonians any credit for having overpowered Judah. The Lord, having condemned Judah, delivered her people to Babylon to serve out their sentence of exile. Thus, according to Jeremiah, the only thing to do was to endure the captivity and build up a record for good behavior.

By about the middle of the sixth century, after some three or four decades, two generations of Judeans had grown up in exile. Those born to families that had sought assimilation had quite lost touch with Judah. For them the memory of Temple and Covenant had faded, and Jerusalem seemed remote and unimportant compared with mighty and cosmopolitan Babylon. Content to earn a living of Shaphan and Gemariah son of Hilkiah, whom King Zedekiah of Judah had despatched to Babylon to King Nebuchadnezzar of Babylon: [4]Thus said the Lord of Hosts, the God of Israel, to all those that I exiled from Jerusalem to Babylon: [5]Build houses and settle down; plant gardens and eat their fruit. [6]Take wives and beget sons and daughters; take wives for your sons and give your daughters to husbands, that they may bear sons and daughters. Multiply there, and do not decline. [7]And seek the welfare of the city to which I have exiled you . . . for your welfare shall depend on its welfare.

*Jeremiah 29.1-7*

שָׁפָן וּגְמַרְיָה בֶּן־חִלְקִיָּה אֲשֶׁר שָׁלַח צִדְקִיָּה מֶלֶךְ־יְהוּדָה אֶל־נְבוּכַדְנֶאצַּר מֶלֶךְ בָּבֶל בָּבֶלָה לֵאמֹר: כֹּה אָמַר יְהוָה צְבָאוֹת אֱלֹהֵי יִשְׂרָאֵל לְכָל־הַגּוֹלָה אֲשֶׁר־הִגְלֵיתִי מִירוּשָׁלַ͏ִם בָּבֶלָה: בְּנוּ בָתִּים וְשֵׁבוּ וְנִטְעוּ גַנּוֹת וְאִכְלוּ אֶת־פִּרְיָן: קְחוּ נָשִׁים וְהוֹלִידוּ בָּנִים וּבָנוֹת וּקְחוּ לִבְנֵיכֶם נָשִׁים וְאֶת־בְּנוֹתֵיכֶם תְּנוּ לַאֲנָשִׁים וְתֵלַדְנָה בָּנִים וּבָנוֹת וּרְבוּ־שָׁם וְאַל־תִּמְעָטוּ: וְדִרְשׁוּ אֶת־שְׁלוֹם הָעִיר אֲשֶׁר הִגְלֵיתִי אֶתְכֶם שָׁמָּה וְהִתְפַּלְלוּ בַעֲדָהּ אֶל־יְהוָה כִּי בִשְׁלוֹמָהּ יִהְיֶה לָכֶם שָׁלוֹם:

יִרְמְיָהוּ כט: א–ז

The word which came to Jeremiah from the Lord: . . . [3]For days are coming—declares the Lord—when I will restore the fortunes of My people Israel and Judah . . . and I will bring them back to the land which I gave their fathers, and they shall possess it . . . [8]In that day—declares the Lord of Hosts—I will break his [Babylon's] yoke from your neck and I will rip off your bonds. Aliens shall not treat them as slaves any more, [9]but they shall serve the Lord their God and David their king whom [i.e., a descendant] I will raise up for them.

[10]But you,
Have no fear, My servant Jacob
————declares the Lord.
Be not dismayed, O Israel!
For I will deliver you from afar,
Your descendants from their land of captivity;
Jacob shall again have calm,
Be at rest with none to trouble him.
[11]For I am with you to deliver you
————declares the Lord.
I will make an end of all the nations
Among which I have dispersed you;
But I will not make an end of you!
I will chastise you as you deserve,
I will not leave you unpunished.
31 [1][=30.25 in some Bible editions]
At that time—declares the Lord—I will be God to all the household [lit. families, clans] of Israel, and they shall be My people.

*Jeremiah 30.1-11; 31.1*

הַדָּבָר אֲשֶׁר־הָיָה אֶל־יִרְמְיָהוּ מֵאֵת יְהוָה לֵאמֹר:... כִּי הִנֵּה יָמִים בָּאִים נְאֻם־יְהוָה וְשַׁבְתִּי אֶת־שְׁבוּת עַמִּי יִשְׂרָאֵל וִיהוּדָה אָמַר יְהוָה וַהֲשִׁבֹתִים אֶל־הָאָרֶץ אֲשֶׁר־נָתַתִּי לַאֲבוֹתָם וִירֵשׁוּהָ:... וְהָיָה בַיּוֹם הַהוּא נְאֻם | יְהוָה צְבָאוֹת אֶשְׁבֹּר עֻלּוֹ מֵעַל צַוָּארֶךָ וּמוֹסְרוֹתֶיךָ אֲנַתֵּק וְלֹא־יַעַבְדוּ־בוֹ עוֹד זָרִים: וְעָבְדוּ אֵת יְהוָה אֱלֹהֵיהֶם וְאֵת דָּוִד מַלְכָּם אֲשֶׁר אָקִים לָהֶם: וְאַתָּה אַל־תִּירָא עַבְדִּי יַעֲקֹב נְאֻם־יְהוָה וְאַל־תֵּחַת יִשְׂרָאֵל כִּי הִנְנִי מוֹשִׁיעֲךָ מֵרָחוֹק וְאֶת־זַרְעֲךָ מֵאֶרֶץ שִׁבְיָם וְשָׁב יַעֲקֹב וְשָׁקַט וְשַׁאֲנַן וְאֵין מַחֲרִיד: כִּי־אִתְּךָ אֲנִי נְאֻם־יְהוָה לְהוֹשִׁיעֶךָ כִּי אֶעֱשֶׂה כָלָה בְּכָל־הַגּוֹיִם | אֲשֶׁר הֲפִצוֹתִיךָ שָּׁם אַךְ אֹתְךָ לֹא־אֶעֱשֶׂה כָלָה וְיִסַּרְתִּיךָ לַמִּשְׁפָּט וְנַקֵּה לֹא אֲנַקֶּךָ:... בָּעֵת הַהִיא נְאֻם־יְהוָה אֶהְיֶה לֵאלֹהִים לְכֹל מִשְׁפְּחוֹת יִשְׂרָאֵל וְהֵמָּה יִהְיוּ־לִי לְעָם:

יִרְמְיָהוּ ל: א –יא;לא:א

213

The inscription on this green stone tells us that it was made by Nebuchadnezzar II as a copy of a one mina weight (60 shekels) belonging to Shulgi, King of Ur (ca. 2000 B.C.E.). The weight of the stone, estimated as almost 1,000 grams, is the standard set by Shulgi at that time.

It was under King Nebuchadnezzar II (604-562 B.C.E.) that the Baby-lonian Empire attained its peak. After the battle of Carchemish (between the months of Nisan and Ab in 605 B.C.E.), only the Medes on the east and north and a weakened Egypt in the extreme southwest, stood in the way if further expansion were needed. It is in the midst of this vast empire that Ezekiel and Second Isaiah had to persuade their fellow Judean exiles that their God was still unique and omnipotent!

in peace, these people had no desire to return to the land of their fathers and grandfathers.

A minority of the exiles, however, did remain faithful. Consisting largely of priests, men of learning, landowners, functionaries of the royal administration, and the like, this group maintained the will to resist assimilation. They struggled to keep track of political developments in the world about them and to keep alive the dream of restoring the Temple and the nation of Judah. For them captivity was bitter frustration, and deliverance and return held the one great promise of life, a hope which they implanted and nursed in their children with religious fervor.

The voices of the prophets ceaselessly and tirelessly admonished the expatriates always to remember their origin, their faith, and their mission. These faithful few did not intermarry, or at least not in sufficient numbers to dilute their consciousness of kind. They studied the teachings of Moses and the prophets, and found in them not only the explanation of Judah's defeat and exile, but also a program for salvation and redemption.

## The Prophet Ezekiel

Among the Biblical writings which gave expression to this belief, the foremost were the books of Ezekiel and the so-called Second Isaiah. Ezekiel, the first prophet to receive the divine call outside the Holy Land, was visited by God Himself in a vision in Babylonia, and commanded to preach that Judah and the Temple had been overcome not by the might of Babylon, but by the wickedness of Judah which had provoked God's wrath.

Carrying on the great tradition of Jeremiah, Ezekiel contended that the God of Israel was still omnipotent and that Babylon was His mere instrument. Her pomp and might, her lion-guarded ways, her many gods who were "no-gods," all these trappings and

A Song of Ascents (or A Pilgrim Song).

When the Lord restored the fortunes of Zion,
We were like dreamers.
²Then our mouths were filled with laughter
And our tongues with joy.
Then it was said among the nations,
"The Lord has wrought great things for them."
³Yes, the Lord has wrought great things for us,
And we have been joyful.
⁴Restore our fortunes, O Lord,
Like the watercourses in the Negeb.
⁵Those who sow in tears shall reap in joy;
⁶He who goes forth in weeping,
Bearing his seed for sowing,
Shall come home in joy, bearing his sheaves.

*Psalm 126.1-6*

שִׁיר הַמַּעֲלוֹת בְּשׁוּב יְהוָה אֶת־שִׁיבַת צִיּוֹן הָיִינוּ
כְּחֹלְמִים: אָז יִמָּלֵא שְׂחוֹק פִּינוּ וּלְשׁוֹנֵנוּ רִנָּה אָז
יֹאמְרוּ בַגּוֹיִם הִגְדִּיל יְהוָה לַעֲשׂוֹת עִם־אֵלֶּה:
הִגְדִּיל יְהוָה לַעֲשׂוֹת עִמָּנוּ הָיִינוּ שְׂמֵחִים: שׁוּבָה
יְהוָה אֶת־שְׁבִיתֵנוּ כַּאֲפִיקִים בַּנֶּגֶב: הַזֹּרְעִים
בְּדִמְעָה בְּרִנָּה יִקְצֹרוּ: הָלוֹךְ יֵלֵךְ וּבָכֹה נֹשֵׂא
מֶשֶׁךְ־הַזָּרַע בֹּא־יָבֹא בְרִנָּה נֹשֵׂא אֲלֻמֹּתָיו:

תְּהִלִּים קכו : א–ו

*See H. M. Orlinsky, "Where Did Ezekiel Receive the Call to Prophesy?",*
Bulletin of the American Schools of Oriental Research, *122 (April,*
*1951), 34-36.*

He [God] said to me [Ezekiel], "O mortal,
I am sending you to the people of Israel, to that
rebellious nation that has rebelled against Me.
Both they and their fathers have defied Me to this
very day; ⁴and the sons too, the brazen of face
and the stubborn of heart. I am sending you to
them, and you shall say to them, 'This is what the
Lord God said.' ⁵But whether they will listen or
desist—for they are a rebellious House—let them
know that there is a prophet among them."

*Ezekiel 2.3-5*

וַיֹּאמֶר אֵלַי בֶּן־אָדָם שׁוֹלֵחַ אֲנִי אוֹתְךָ אֶל־בְּנֵי
יִשְׂרָאֵל אֶל־גּוֹיִם הַמּוֹרְדִים אֲשֶׁר מָרְדוּ־בִי הֵמָּה
וַאֲבוֹתָם פָּשְׁעוּ בִי עַד־עֶצֶם הַיּוֹם הַזֶּה: וְהַבָּנִים
קְשֵׁי פָנִים וְחִזְקֵי־לֵב אֲנִי שׁוֹלֵחַ אוֹתְךָ אֲלֵיהֶם
וְאָמַרְתָּ אֲלֵיהֶם כֹּה אָמַר אֲדֹנָי יְהוִה: וְהֵמָּה אִם־
יִשְׁמְעוּ וְאִם־יֶחְדָּלוּ כִּי בֵּית מְרִי הֵמָּה וְיָדְעוּ כִּי
נָבִיא הָיָה בְתוֹכָם:

יְחֶזְקֵאל ב : ג–ה

Thus said the Lord God: Clap your hands and
stamp your feet, and cry "Alas!" for all the vile
abominations of the House of Israel, who shall fall
by the sword, by famine, and by epidemic. ¹²Those
who are far away shall die of epidemic, those who
are near shall fall by the sword, and those who
survive and are protected (or besieged) shall die
of famine. Thus I will spend My fury against them.
¹³And you shall know that I am the Lord—when
their corpses lie among their fetishes around your
altars, on every high hill, on every mountain top,
under every green tree, and under every leafy oak,
wherever they offered pleasing odors to all their
fetishes. ¹⁴I will stretch out My hand against them
and lay their land waste and desolate—from the
wilderness as far as Diblah—in all their settlements. Then they shall know that I am the Lord.

*Ezekiel 6.11-14*

כֹּה־אָמַר אֲדֹנָי יְהוִה הַכֵּה בְכַפְּךָ וּרְקַע בְּרַגְלְךָ
וֶאֱמָר־אָח אֶל כָּל־תּוֹעֲבוֹת רָעוֹת בֵּית יִשְׂרָאֵל
אֲשֶׁר בַּחֶרֶב בָּרָעָב וּבַדֶּבֶר יִפֹּלוּ: הָרָחוֹק בַּדֶּבֶר
יָמוּת וְהַקָּרוֹב בַּחֶרֶב יִפּוֹל וְהַנִּשְׁאָר וְהַנָּצוּר בָּרָעָב
יָמוּת וְכִלֵּיתִי חֲמָתִי בָּם: וִידַעְתֶּם כִּי־אֲנִי יְהוָה
בִּהְיוֹת חַלְלֵיהֶם בְּתוֹךְ גִּלּוּלֵיהֶם סְבִיבוֹת
מִזְבְּחוֹתֵיהֶם אֶל כָּל־גִּבְעָה רָמָה בְּכֹל | רָאשֵׁי
הֶהָרִים וְתַחַת כָּל־עֵץ רַעֲנָן וְתַחַת כָּל־אֵלָה
עֲבֻתָּה מְקוֹם אֲשֶׁר נָתְנוּ־שָׁם רֵיחַ נִיחֹחַ לְכֹל
גִּלּוּלֵיהֶם: וְנָטִיתִי אֶת־יָדִי עֲלֵיהֶם וְנָתַתִּי אֶת־
הָאָרֶץ שְׁמָמָה וּמְשַׁמָּה מִמִּדְבַּר דִּבְלָתָה בְּכֹל
מוֹשְׁבוֹתֵיהֶם וְיָדְעוּ כִּי־אֲנִי יְהוָה:

יְחֶזְקֵאל ו : יא–יד

215

List of Assyrian (from early 9th cent.), Neo-Babylonian (Chaldean), and Persian Kings (after J. A. Brinkman, in A. Leo Oppenheim, *Ancient Mesopotamia*, Univ. of Chicago Press, 1964, pp. 335-352).

## ASSYRIA

| | |
|---|---|
| Ashurnaṣirpal II | 883-859 |
| Shalmaneser III | 858-824 |
| Shamshi-Adad V | 823-811 |
| Adad-nirari III | 810-783 |
| Shalmaneser IV | 782-773 |
| Ashur-dan III | 772-755 |
| Ashur-nirari V | 754-745 |
| Tiglath-Pileser III | 744-727 |
| Shalmaneser V | 726-722 |
| Sargon II | 721-705 |
| Sennacherib | 704-681 |
| Esarhaddon | 680-669 |
| Ashurbanipal | 668-627 |
| Several minor kings | 626-609 |

## NEO-BABYLONIAN (CHALDEAN) DYNASTY

| | |
|---|---|
| Nabopolassar | 625-605 |
| Nebuchadnezzar II | 604-562 |
| Evil-Merodach | 561-560 |
| Neriglissar | 559-556 |
| Labashi-Marduk | 556 |
| Nabonidus | 555-539 |

## PERSIAN (ACHAEMENID) KINGS

| | |
|---|---|
| Cyrus II | 559-530 |
| Cambyses II | 529-522 |
| Darius I | 521-486 |
| Xerxes I | 485-465 |
| Artaxerxes I | 464-424 |
| Darius II | 423-405 |
| Artaxerxes II | 404-359 |
| Artaxerxes III | 358-338 |

appurtenances of power would vanish like mist, once God's anger had run its course. Ezekiel would tolerate no momentary doubt of the inflexible justice of his God, nor would he accept the possibility that God would allow the innocent among the exiled to languish forever and without hope in the same durance with the wicked. With the same fiery faith Ezekiel preached that this punishment that made the bad good, made the good better, and assured, at least ultimately, deliverance for all who obeyed the Lord, observed His Sabbath, and kept themselves from heathen idols and heathen ways.

Ezekiel propounded his basic convictions in the vision of the Valley of Dry Bones (Ezekiel 37), one of the most electrifying passages of the entire Bible. Israel—in this vision—had ceased to be a living nation. Her people had lost faith in God and in themselves. To dramatize their plight, Ezekiel likened them to scattered heaps of bleached bones, lying in a valley. But the Lord, who had brought this terrible curse on His people, promised to bring the dead bones to life, and to restore a unified Israel to its own land under a descendant of King David, saying: "And I will make a covenant of friendship with them, and it shall be an everlasting covenant with them; and I will establish them and multiply them, and will set My sanctuary in their midst forever. . . . And the nations shall know that I the Lord sanctify Israel, when My sanctuary is in their midst forever" (Ezekiel 37; 26–28).

Ezekiel, the first to prophesy after the destruction of Jerusalem, was obsessed by the need to rebuild the Temple. As the abode of the Divine Presence, it was the center of Israelite religious life, the true setting for sacrifice and prayer, for in antiquity no less than nowadays, organized religion required a special place for the worship of the Deity.

The hand of the Lord came upon me. He took me out by the spirit of the Lord and set me down in the valley. It was full of bones. ²He led me all around them; there were very many of them all over the valley, and they were very dry. ³He said to me, "O mortal, can these bones live again?" I replied, "O Lord God, only You know." ⁴And He said to me "Prophesy over these bones and say to them: O dry bones, hear the word of the Lord! ⁵Thus said the Lord God to these bones: I am going to make breath enter you and you shall live again. ⁶I will lay sinews upon you, cover you with flesh, spread skin over you, and put breath into you; and you shall live again. And you shall know that I am the Lord." ⁷I prophesied as I had been commanded. As I was prophesying, suddenly there was a sound of rattling, and bones came together, bone to bone. ⁸I looked, and there were sinews on them, and flesh had grown, and skin spread over them; but there was no breath in them. ⁹Then He said to me, "Prophesy to the breath, prophesy, O mortal. Say to the breath: Thus said the Lord God: Come, O breath, from the four winds, and breathe into these slain, that they may live again." ¹⁰I prophesied as He commanded me; and the breath entered them and they came to life, and they stood up on their feet, an exceedingly great multitude. ¹¹And He said to me, "O mortal, these bones are the whole House of Israel. They say, 'Our bones are dried up and our hope is gone; we are doomed.' ¹²Therefore, prophesy and say to them: Thus said the Lord God: I am going to open your graves and lift you out of your graves, O My people, and bring you to the land of Israel."

*Ezekiel 37.1-12*

הָיְתָה עָלַי יַד־יְהֹוָה וַיּוֹצִאֵנִי בְרוּחַ יְהֹוָה וַיְנִיחֵנִי בְּתוֹךְ הַבִּקְעָה וְהִיא מְלֵאָה עֲצָמוֹת: וְהֶעֱבִירַנִי עֲלֵיהֶם סָבִיב | סָבִיב וְהִנֵּה רַבּוֹת מְאֹד עַל־פְּנֵי הַבִּקְעָה וְהִנֵּה יְבֵשׁוֹת מְאֹד: וַיֹּאמֶר אֵלַי בֶּן־אָדָם הֲתִחְיֶינָה הָעֲצָמוֹת הָאֵלֶּה וָאֹמַר אֲדֹנָי יְהֹוִה אַתָּה יָדָעְתָּ: וַיֹּאמֶר אֵלַי הִנָּבֵא עַל־הָעֲצָמוֹת הָאֵלֶּה וְאָמַרְתָּ אֲלֵיהֶם הָעֲצָמוֹת הַיְבֵשׁוֹת שִׁמְעוּ דְּבַר־יְהֹוָה: כֹּה אָמַר אֲדֹנָי יְהֹוִה לָעֲצָמוֹת הָאֵלֶּה הִנֵּה אֲנִי מֵבִיא בָכֶם רוּחַ וִחְיִיתֶם: וְנָתַתִּי עֲלֵיכֶם גִּדִים וְהַעֲלֵתִי עֲלֵיכֶם בָּשָׂר וְקָרַמְתִּי עֲלֵיכֶם עוֹר וְנָתַתִּי בָכֶם רוּחַ וִחְיִיתֶם וִידַעְתֶּם כִּי־אֲנִי יְהֹוָה: וְנִבֵּאתִי כַּאֲשֶׁר צֻוֵּיתִי וַיְהִי־קוֹל כְּהִנָּבְאִי וְהִנֵּה־רַעַשׁ וַתִּקְרְבוּ עֲצָמוֹת עֶצֶם אֶל־עַצְמוֹ: וְרָאִיתִי וְהִנֵּה־עֲלֵיהֶם גִּדִים וּבָשָׂר עָלָה וַיִּקְרַם עֲלֵיהֶם עוֹר מִלְמָעְלָה וְרוּחַ אֵין בָּהֶם: וַיֹּאמֶר אֵלַי הִנָּבֵא אֶל־הָרוּחַ הִנָּבֵא בֶן־אָדָם וְאָמַרְתָּ אֶל־הָרוּחַ כֹּה־אָמַר | אֲדֹנָי יְהֹוִה מֵאַרְבַּע רוּחוֹת בֹּאִי הָרוּחַ וּפְחִי בַּהֲרוּגִים הָאֵלֶּה וְיִחְיוּ: וְהִנַּבֵּאתִי כַּאֲשֶׁר צִוָּנִי וַתָּבוֹא בָהֶם הָרוּחַ וַיִּחְיוּ וַיַּעַמְדוּ עַל־רַגְלֵיהֶם חַיִל גָּדוֹל מְאֹד מְאֹד: וַיֹּאמֶר אֵלַי בֶּן־אָדָם הָעֲצָמוֹת הָאֵלֶּה כָּל־בֵּית יִשְׂרָאֵל הֵמָּה הִנֵּה אֹמְרִים יָבְשׁוּ עַצְמוֹתֵינוּ וְאָבְדָה תִקְוָתֵנוּ נִגְזַרְנוּ לָנוּ: לָכֵן הִנָּבֵא וְאָמַרְתָּ אֲלֵיהֶם כֹּה־אָמַר אֲדֹנָי יְהֹוִה הִנֵּה אֲנִי פֹתֵחַ אֶת־קִבְרוֹתֵיכֶם וְהַעֲלֵיתִי אֶתְכֶם מִקִּבְרוֹתֵיכֶם עַמִּי וְהֵבֵאתִי אֶתְכֶם אֶל־אַדְמַת יִשְׂרָאֵל:

יְחֶזְקֵאל לז : א–יב

---

And I will make a covenant of friendship with them, and it shall be an everlasting covenant with them; and I will establish them and multiply them, and will set My sanctuary in their midst forever. . . . ²⁸And the nations shall know that I the Lord sanctify Israel, when My sanctuary is in their midst forever.

*Ezekiel 37.26–28*

וְכָרַתִּי לָהֶם בְּרִית שָׁלוֹם בְּרִית עוֹלָם יִהְיֶה אוֹתָם וּנְתַתִּים וְהִרְבֵּיתִי אוֹתָם וְנָתַתִּי אֶת־מִקְדָּשִׁי בְּתוֹכָם לְעוֹלָם: ... וְיָדְעוּ הַגּוֹיִם כִּי אֲנִי יְהֹוָה מְקַדֵּשׁ אֶת־יִשְׂרָאֵל בִּהְיוֹת מִקְדָּשִׁי בְּתוֹכָם לְעוֹלָם:

יְחֶזְקֵאל לז : כו–כח

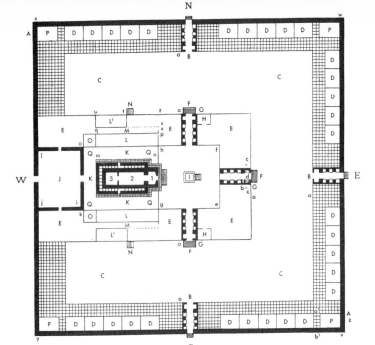

Plan of the Jerusalem Temple and Temple Precinct as envisioned by Ezekiel and understood by archaeologists and historians. The plan is based upon architectural features known elsewhere in the Bible and from excavations. These features belong to the general architecture of the whole Near East. The precinct is made up of two courts, an outer court surrounded by an outer wall with three multi-vestibuled gates, and an inner court surrounded by an inner wall with three multi-vestibuled gates. The Temple itself lay in the center of the inner court. Steps lead up to each court and to the Temple, suggesting that the Temple sanctuary stood well above the level of the surrounding streets.

Head of a Mede, part of a procession of tributary nations bringing gifts to their overlord, the king of Persia. This fragment of limestone relief comes from the Achemenid capital at Persepolis built by **Darius I** (521-486 B.C.E.) and his successors. About 9 inches high.

It was natural, therefore, that Ezekiel should also stress the preservation of a strict observance of the Temple ritual. In absolute accord with such exilic and postexilic prophets as the Second Isaiah, Haggai, Zechariah, and Malachi, not to mention his pre-exilic predecessors, Ezekiel warned that ritual laxity led to moral laxity. He and the other prophets of this later era were by no means men of coarser fiber; on the contrary, all of them believed—as firmly as their predecessors—that the efficacy of prayer and sacrifice depended on the worshipper's religious integrity. Their insistence on sacred forms and symbols stemmed not from a willingness to substitute such external tokens for the deeper religious truths but—on the contrary—from their experience that it is infinitely difficult for ordinary men to maintain active religious belief by faith alone.

## Babylonian Decline; The Second Isaiah

Ezekiel had never faltered in his convictions of deliverance even during the worst hours of the Exile, but he did not live to see his faith vindicated. Only a few decades after Ezekiel's career came to a close, however, the Babylonian empire began to show great cracks and fissures, and in shorter time than anyone would have believed possible, was on the brink of dissolution. The Persians and Medes had begun to take their place as major powers in the Mesopotamian region late in the seventh century. First the Medes helped the Babylonians crush Assyria and shared in the spoils. Then, about 545 B.C.E., Persia under Cyrus II (the Great) of the Achemenid dynasty absorbed Media, Lydia, and Ionian Greece in Asia Minor. Eventually the new power was to include territories extending all the way from the Indus to the Mediterranean, and from the Caucasus to the Indian Ocean, a dominion beside which the conquests of

When the just man rejects justice and commits iniquity, he shall die for it; [19]and when an unjust man rejects injustice and does what is right and just, he shall live because of this. [20]Yet you say: the way of the Lord is unfair! But I will judge you, O House of Israel, everyone by his deeds!

*Ezekiel 33.18-20*

בְּשׁוּב־צַדִּיק מִצִּדְקָתוֹ וְעָשָׂה עָוֶל וּמֵת בָּהֶם:
וּבְשׁוּב רָשָׁע מֵרִשְׁעָתוֹ וְעָשָׂה מִשְׁפָּט וּצְדָקָה עֲלֵיהֶם
הוּא יִחְיֶה: וַאֲמַרְתֶּם לֹא יִתָּכֵן דֶּרֶךְ אֲדֹנָי אִישׁ
כִּדְרָכָיו אֶשְׁפּוֹט אֶתְכֶם בֵּית יִשְׂרָאֵל:

יְחֶזְקֵאל לג: יח–כ

I will bring them to My holy mountain and cause them to rejoice in My House of prayer; their burnt offerings and their sacrifices shall be acceptable upon My altar, for My House shall be called a House of prayer for all peoples—[8]declares the Lord God, who gathers the dispersed of Israel . . .

*Isaiah 56.7-8*

וַהֲבִיאוֹתִים אֶל־הַר קָדְשִׁי וְשִׂמַּחְתִּים בְּבֵית
תְּפִלָּתִי עוֹלֹתֵיהֶם וְזִבְחֵיהֶם לְרָצוֹן עַל־מִזְבְּחִי
כִּי בֵיתִי בֵּית־תְּפִלָּה יִקָּרֵא לְכָל־הָעַמִּים: נְאֻם
אֲדֹנָי יְהוִה מְקַבֵּץ נִדְחֵי יִשְׂרָאֵל...

יְשַׁעְיָהוּ נו: ז–ח

In the second year of King Darius, on the first day of the sixth month, the word of the Lord came through the prophet Haggai to Zerubbabel son of Shealtiel, governor of Judah, and to Joshua son of Jehozadak, the high priest: [2]Thus said the Lord of Hosts, "This people has asserted that the time has not come, the time for the House of the Lord to be rebuilt." [3]The word of the Lord came through the prophet Haggai: [4]"Is it a time for you to live in your panelled houses, when this House lies in ruins?" [5]Therefore thus said the Lord of Hosts: Give thought to your way of life. [6]You have sown much but reaped little, you eat but not to satiety, you drink but are not filled, you clothe yourselves but cannot keep warm, and the earnings of him who hires himself out are for a bag of holes. [7]Thus said the Lord of Hosts: Give thought to your way of life. [8]Go up into the hills and fetch timber, and build the House, that I may take pleasure in it and be glorified, said the Lord. . . . [14]The Lord stirred up the spirit of Zerubbabel . . . and the spirit of Joshua . . . and the spirit of the rest of the people; and they came and set to work on the House of the Lord of Hosts, their God.

*Haggai 1.1-8, 14*

בִּשְׁנַת שְׁתַּיִם לְדָרְיָוֶשׁ הַמֶּלֶךְ בַּחֹדֶשׁ הַשִּׁשִּׁי בְּיוֹם
אֶחָד לַחֹדֶשׁ הָיָה דְבַר־יְהוָה בְּיַד־חַגַּי הַנָּבִיא
אֶל־זְרֻבָּבֶל בֶּן־שְׁאַלְתִּיאֵל פַּחַת יְהוּדָה וְאֶל־
יְהוֹשֻׁעַ בֶּן־יְהוֹצָדָק הַכֹּהֵן הַגָּדוֹל לֵאמֹר: כֹּה אָמַר
יְהוָה צְבָאוֹת לֵאמֹר הָעָם הַזֶּה אָמְרוּ לֹא עֶת־בֹּא
עֶת־בֵּית יְהוָה לְהִבָּנוֹת: וַיְהִי דְּבַר־יְהוָה בְּיַד־
חַגַּי הַנָּבִיא לֵאמֹר: הַעֵת לָכֶם אַתֶּם לָשֶׁבֶת בְּבָתֵּיכֶם
סְפוּנִים וְהַבַּיִת הַזֶּה חָרֵב: וְעַתָּה כֹּה אָמַר יְהוָה
צְבָאוֹת שִׂימוּ לְבַבְכֶם עַל־דַּרְכֵיכֶם: זְרַעְתֶּם
הַרְבֵּה וְהָבֵא מְעָט אָכוֹל וְאֵין־לְשָׂבְעָה שָׁתוֹ וְאֵין־
לְשָׁכְרָה לָבוֹשׁ וְאֵין־לְחֹם לוֹ וְהַמִּשְׂתַּכֵּר מִשְׂתַּכֵּר
אֶל־צְרוֹר נָקוּב: כֹּה אָמַר יְהוָה צְבָאוֹת שִׂימוּ
לְבַבְכֶם עַל־דַּרְכֵיכֶם: עֲלוּ הָהָר וַהֲבֵאתֶם עֵץ
וּבְנוּ הַבָּיִת וְאֶרְצֶה־בּוֹ וְאֶכָּבְדָה אָמַר יְהוָה:...
וַיָּעַר יְהוָה אֶת־רוּחַ זְרֻבָּבֶל בֶּן־שַׁלְתִּיאֵל פַּחַת
יְהוּדָה וְאֶת־רוּחַ יְהוֹשֻׁעַ בֶּן־יְהוֹצָדָק הַכֹּהֵן הַגָּדוֹל
וְאֶת־רוּחַ כֹּל שְׁאֵרִית הָעָם וַיָּבֹאוּ וַיַּעֲשׂוּ מְלָאכָה
בְּבֵית־יְהוָה צְבָאוֹת אֱלֹהֵיהֶם:

חַגַּי א: א–ח, יד

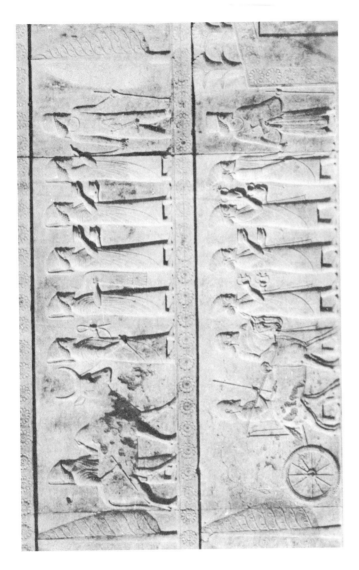

Out of the larger panorama showing representatives of some two dozen nations conquered by Xerxes I (485-465 B.C.E.), the upper of these two registers—from a stairway of the apadana (hall of pillars) at Persepolis—depicts six Babylonians (led by a Mede) and the lower four Syrians (led by a Persian) bringing their tribute. The Babylonians are bringing bowls, woven stuff, and an ox. The Syrians bear metal objects and vases with a team of horses and a chariot bringing up in the rear.

earlier Near Eastern empires pale into insignificance.

During this turbulent period, a great prophet arose to proclaim to his fellow Jews in Babylon that they were entering a new epoch. He is called nowadays the "Second" Isaiah, to distinguish him from the namesake who prophesied in Jerusalem some two hundred years earlier; the writings of this exilic prophet are found in Chapters 40–66 of the Book of Isaiah. They are easily differentiated from those of the First Isaiah by virtue of literary style, historical perspective, and theological emphasis.

Having followed political developments closely, the Second Isaiah realized that even greater events were in the making, and in the swift rise of Persia he sensed the promise of imminent deliverance for Israel. In poetic utterances rarely equaled for pathos and lyricism, he compared the Babylonian Exile with Israel's bondage in Egypt, and urged his conviction that even the Exodus would be surpassed by the new liberation and return, a triumph that would be consecrated in a renewed covenant between God and His people Israel. The one necessary condition, the unknown prophet of the Exile warned, was that the Judean exiles have complete faith in the ability and desire of the Lord to accomplish the restoration.

More than any other prophet since the days of Elijah, the Second Isaiah emphasized and reiterated the uniqueness and omnipotence of the God of Israel. He set himself the task of convincing his fellow Jews that the Babylonians and their gods were not victors over the Judeans and the Lord their God, but that, on the contrary, the heathen were no more than the rod of His anger and chastisement. God was the one ruler in the entire universe, and there was no one else beside Him:

And now, thus said the Lord,
Who created you, O Jacob,
Who formed you, O Israel:
Do not fear, for I will redeem you;
I have singled you out by name, you are Mine.
²When you pass through water,
I will be with you;
Through streams, they shall not overwhelm you.
When you walk through fire,
You shall not be scorched;
Through flame, it shall not burn you.
³For I the Lord am your God,
The Holy One of Israel, who brings you triumph.
I give Egypt as a ransom for you,
Ethiopia and Saba in exchange for you.
⁴Because you are precious to Me
And honored, and I love you,
I give men in exchange for you
And peoples in your stead.
⁵Do not fear, for I am with you:
I will bring your offspring from the East,
I will gather you out of the West;
⁶I will say to the North, "Give up!"
And to the South, "Do not hold back!"
Bring My sons from afar,
And My daughters from the ends of the earth—
⁷All who are called by My name,
Whom I have created for My glory,
Whom I have formed and made . . .
¹⁰You are My witnesses—
Declares the Lord—
My servant, whom I have chosen.
Therefore take thought, and believe in Me,
And understand that I am He:
Before Me no god was formed,
And after Me none shall exist.
¹¹I, I am the Lord,
Beside Me, none can grant triumph.
¹²I alone foretold and wrought the triumph;
I announced it, and no strange god was among you.
You are My witnesses to that—
Declares the Lord—
And I am your God.
¹³From of old I am He,
And none can deliver from My hand:
When I act, who can reverse it?

וְעַתָּה כֹּה־אָמַר יְהֹוָה בֹּרַאֲךָ יַעֲקֹב וְיֹצֶרְךָ
יִשְׂרָאֵל אַל־תִּירָא כִּי גְאַלְתִּיךָ קָרָאתִי בְשִׁמְךָ
לִי־אָתָּה: כִּי־תַעֲבֹר בַּמַּיִם אִתְּךָ אָנִי וּבַנְּהָרוֹת
לֹא יִשְׁטְפוּךָ כִּי־תֵלֵךְ בְּמוֹ־אֵשׁ לֹא תִכָּוֶה וְלֶהָבָה
לֹא תִבְעַר־בָּךְ: כִּי אֲנִי יְהֹוָה אֱלֹהֶיךָ קְדוֹשׁ יִשְׂרָאֵל
מוֹשִׁיעֶךָ נָתַתִּי כָפְרְךָ מִצְרַיִם כּוּשׁ וּסְבָא תַּחְתֶּיךָ:
מֵאֲשֶׁר יָקַרְתָּ בְעֵינַי נִכְבַּדְתָּ וַאֲנִי אֲהַבְתִּיךָ וְאֶתֵּן
אָדָם תַּחְתֶּיךָ וּלְאֻמִּים תַּחַת נַפְשֶׁךָ: אַל־תִּירָא
כִּי־אִתְּךָ אָנִי מִמִּזְרָח אָבִיא זַרְעֶךָ וּמִמַּעֲרָב
אֲקַבְּצֶךָּ: אֹמַר לַצָּפוֹן תֵּנִי וּלְתֵימָן אַל־תִּכְלָאִי
הָבִיאִי בָנַי מֵרָחוֹק וּבְנוֹתַי מִקְצֵה הָאָרֶץ: כֹּל
הַנִּקְרָא בִשְׁמִי וְלִכְבוֹדִי בְּרָאתִיו יְצַרְתִּיו אַף־
עֲשִׂיתִיו:... אַתֶּם עֵדַי נְאֻם־יְהֹוָה וְעַבְדִּי אֲשֶׁר
בָּחָרְתִּי לְמַעַן תֵּדְעוּ וְתַאֲמִינוּ לִי וְתָבִינוּ כִּי־אֲנִי
הוּא לְפָנַי לֹא־נוֹצַר אֵל וְאַחֲרַי לֹא־יִהְיֶה: אָנֹכִי
אָנֹכִי יְהֹוָה וְאֵין מִבַּלְעָדַי מוֹשִׁיעַ: אָנֹכִי הִגַּדְתִּי
וְהוֹשַׁעְתִּי וְהִשְׁמַעְתִּי וְאֵין בָּכֶם זָר וְאַתֶּם עֵדַי נְאֻם־
יְהֹוָה וַאֲנִי־אֵל: גַּם־מִיּוֹם אֲנִי הוּא וְאֵין מִיָּדִי מַצִּיל
אֶפְעַל וּמִי יְשִׁיבֶנָּה:

*Isaiah 43.1-13*     יְשַׁעְיָהוּ מג: א- יג

221

Inscribed brick found in 1850 at Warka (ancient Uruk, Biblical Erech), and now in the British Museum. The translation reads:
I am Cyrus, builder of Esagila and Ezida [two temples], son of Cambyses, the great king.

I am the Lord, that is My name:
I will not yield My glory to another
Nor My renown to idols [Isaiah 42:8].

This concept of a universal and omnipotent God was new, of course, only in emphasis. It stemmed in direct line from the teachings of Elijah and Amos, and had been eloquently expressed by the otherwise unknown "man of God" who said to King Ahab of Israel (ninth century), "Thus said the Lord: Because the Arameans have said, 'The Lord is a God of the mountains, but He is not a God of the valleys,' therefore I will deliver all this great multitude into your hands, and you shall know that I am the Lord" (I Kings 20:28). But as Ezekiel stressed the role of the lost Temple in the worship of the Lord and made its rebuilding a central object of faith, so the Second Isaiah emphasized the universal aspect of God, in his efforts to explain to his fellow Judeans their exile in the foreign land of a great empire which had destroyed the Temple of their God and carried them captive from His land.

The Second Isaiah, realizing that Babylonia was a mere shell of its former greatness, and that Persia was now the dominant power in the Near East, warned his listeners that they had little time to prepare themselves for the destruction of Babylon by God's "shepherd" and "anointed," Cyrus of Persia (Isaiah 44:28; 45:1), and for their liberation and return to Judah.

## Cyrus of Persia and the Edict of Liberation

About 540 B.C.E. Babylonia fell like a ripe fruit into the hands of Persia's king. In his first regnal year (about 538) Cyrus issued the famous Edict of Liberation; as the Bible worded it: "Thus said King Cyrus of Persia: All of the kingdoms of the earth has the

222

Ascend a lofty mountain,
O herald of joy to Zion;
Raise your voice with power,
O herald of joy to Jerusalem—
Raise it, do not fear,
Announce to the cities of Judah:
Behold your God!
¹⁰Behold, the Lord God comes in might,
His arm winning triumph for Him;
See, His reward is with Him,
His recompense before Him.
¹¹Like a shepherd He pastures His flock;
He gathers the lambs in His arms
And carries them in His bosom,
Gently He drives the mother sheep.
¹²Who measured the waters with the hollow of his
    hand,
Gauged the skies with a span,
Meted earth's dust with a measure,
And weighed the mountains with a scale
And the hills with a balance?
¹³Who has plumbed the spirit of the Lord,
What man could tell Him His plan?
¹⁴Whom did He consult, and who taught Him,
Guided Him in the way of right?
Who guided Him in knowledge
And showed Him the path of understanding?
¹⁵The nations are but a drop in a bucket,
Reckoned as dust on a balance;
The coastlands—He lifts them like motes . . .
¹⁷All nations are as naught in His sight;
He accounts them as less than nothing . . .
²⁷Why do you say, O Jacob,
Why declare, O Israel,
"My way is hid from the Lord,
My cause is ignored by my God?"
²⁸Do you not know?
Have you not heard?
The Lord is God from of old,
Creator of the boundaries of the earth.
He does not grow faint or weary,
His understanding cannot be fathomed.
²⁹He gives strength to the weary,
New vigor to the exhausted.

*Isaiah 40.9-29*

עַל הַר־גָּבֹהַּ עֲלִי־לָךְ מְבַשֶּׂרֶת צִיּוֹן הָרִימִי
בַכֹּחַ קוֹלֵךְ מְבַשֶּׂרֶת יְרוּשָׁלָם הָרִימִי אַל־תִּירָאִי
אִמְרִי לְעָרֵי יְהוּדָה הִנֵּה אֱלֹהֵיכֶם: הִנֵּה אֲדֹנָי יֱהוִֹה
בְּחָזָק יָבוֹא וּזְרֹעוֹ מֹשְׁלָה לוֹ הִנֵּה שְׂכָרוֹ אִתּוֹ
וּפְעֻלָּתוֹ לְפָנָיו: כְּרֹעֶה עֶדְרוֹ יִרְעֶה בִּזְרֹעוֹ יְקַבֵּץ
טְלָאִים וּבְחֵיקוֹ יִשָּׂא עָלוֹת יְנַהֵל: מִי־מָדַד בְּשָׁעֳלוֹ
מַיִם וְשָׁמַיִם בַּזֶּרֶת תִּכֵּן וְכָל בַּשָּׁלִשׁ עֲפַר הָאָרֶץ
וְשָׁקַל בַּפֶּלֶס הָרִים וּגְבָעוֹת בְּמֹאזְנָיִם: מִי־תִכֵּן
אֶת־רוּחַ יְהוָֹה וְאִישׁ עֲצָתוֹ יוֹדִיעֶנּוּ: אֶת־מִי נוֹעָץ
וַיְבִינֵהוּ וַיְלַמְּדֵהוּ בְּאֹרַח מִשְׁפָּט וַיְלַמְּדֵהוּ דַעַת
וְדֶרֶךְ תְּבוּנוֹת יוֹדִיעֶנּוּ: הֵן גּוֹיִם כְּמַר מִדְּלִי וּכְשַׁחַק
מֹאזְנַיִם נֶחְשָׁבוּ הֵן אִיִּים כַּדַּק יִטּוֹל:... כָּל־הַגּוֹיִם
כְּאַיִן נֶגְדּוֹ מֵאֶפֶס וָתֹהוּ נֶחְשְׁבוּ־לוֹ:... לָמָּה תֹאמַר
יַעֲקֹב וּתְדַבֵּר יִשְׂרָאֵל נִסְתְּרָה דַרְכִּי מֵיְהוָֹה וּמֵאֱלֹהַי
מִשְׁפָּטִי יַעֲבוֹר: הֲלוֹא יָדַעְתָּ אִם־לֹא שָׁמַעְתָּ אֱלֹהֵי
עוֹלָם | יְהוָֹה בּוֹרֵא קְצוֹת הָאָרֶץ לֹא יִיעַף וְלֹא
יִיגָע אֵין חֵקֶר לִתְבוּנָתוֹ: נֹתֵן לַיָּעֵף כֹּחַ וּלְאֵין אוֹנִים
עָצְמָה יַרְבֶּה:

יְשַׁעְיָהוּ מ׳: ט—כט

223

In the manner of Babylonian and Assyrian kings, this inscribed, barrel-shaped cylinder recounts the story of the conquest of the world and the establishment of Cyrus' kingship, divinely sanctioned by Marduk, chief god of Babylon. It describes how King Cyrus of Persia, king of the world, has come to possess the kingship of Babylonia and has rehabilitated desolate lands, cities, and temples. These possessions had been abandoned and misused by earlier inept rulers, especially the Babylonian King Nabonidus, who had not uttered the right prayers to his ancient god, Marduk, or worshiped him in the proper manner. Now, all the conquered subjects bring tribute to Cyrus from the Mediterranean coastal lands and the Upper Euphrates region.

The date of this composition is unknown. It was found at Babylon in 1879 and sent to the British Museum.

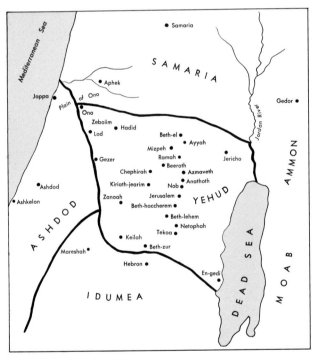

In the Persian period, Judah (Yehud) was one of the lands that constituted the fifth satrapy, Abar Nahara ("Beyond the Euphrates River"). Persia had become the largest empire that the ancient Near East had ever seen, what with Cambyses II (529-522 B.C.E.) conquering Egypt and Darius I, the Great (521-486 B.C.E.) reaching India. Judah was indeed a very tiny frog in a very large puddle.

Lord, the God of heaven, given me; and He has charged me to build Him a House in Jerusalem, which is in Judah. Whosoever there is among you of all His people—his God be with him—let him go up to Jerusalem" (Ezra 1:2–3; cf. II Chronicles 36:22–23). And he added:

Concerning the House of God at Jerusalem, let the House be built, the place where they offer sacrifices, and let its foundation be strongly laid. Its height shall be sixty cubits and its width sixty cubits, with three rows of great stones and a row of new timber; and let the expenses be paid out of the king's house. And also let the gold and silver vessels of the House of God, which Nebuchadnezzar took out of the Temple which is in Jerusalem and brought to Babylon, be restored and brought back to the Temple which is in Jerusalem, every one to its place. And you shall put them in the House of God [Ezra 6:3–5].

Sheshbazzar, apparently of the family of King Jehoiachin of Judah, was appointed governor of Judah. Taking with him the sacred vessels of the Temple, Sheshbazzar went to Jerusalem to take up his post, and prepared to lay the foundations for the new Temple.

## Developments in Judah

But the Judean homeland, devastated and impoverished by Babylonia, was in no condition to support a significant restoration. Many Judeans in Babylonia failed to take advantage of the new liberty to return to Judah. The majority, having adapted themselves well enough to their new home, lacked the necessary incentive to start all over again in a much poorer land. As for the many who had never been forced into exile, few evinced any enthusiasm for rebuilding the Temple and for recapturing a way of life long since abandoned. Nearly twenty years after Cyrus' edict, the prophet Haggai condemned the

Thus said King Cyrus of Persia: The Lord, the God of Heaven, has given me all the kingdoms of the earth. He has charged me to build Him a House at Jerusalem in Judah. ³To everyone of you among His people: May his God be with him. Let him go up to Jerusalem in Judah and (re)build the House of the Lord, the God of Israel—He is the God who is in Jerusalem.

*Ezra 1.2-3*

כֹּה אָמַר כֹּרֶשׁ מֶלֶךְ פָּרַס כֹּל מַמְלְכוֹת הָאָרֶץ
נָתַן לִי יְהֹוָה אֱלֹהֵי הַשָּׁמָיִם וְהוּא־פָקַד עָלַי לִבְנוֹת־
לוֹ בַיִת בִּירוּשָׁלַ͏ִם אֲשֶׁר בִּיהוּדָה: מִי־בָכֶם מִכָּל־
עַמּוֹ יְהִי אֱלֹהָיו עִמּוֹ וְיַעַל לִירוּשָׁלַ͏ִם אֲשֶׁר בִּיהוּדָה
וְיִבֶן אֶת־בֵּית יְהֹוָה אֱלֹהֵי יִשְׂרָאֵל הוּא הָאֱלֹהִים
אֲשֶׁר בִּירוּשָׁלָ͏ִם:

עֶזְרָא א: ב–ג

King Cyrus took out the vessels of the House of the Lord which Nebuchadnezzar had taken away from Jerusalem and placed in the temple of his god[s]—⁸King Cyrus of Persia had them taken out by Mithredath the treasurer, who counted them out to Sheshbazzar, prince [or leader] of Judah.

*Ezra 1.7-8*

וְהַמֶּלֶךְ כֹּרֶשׁ הוֹצִיא אֶת־כְּלֵי בֵית־יְהֹוָה אֲשֶׁר
הוֹצִיא נְבוּכַדְנֶצַּר מִירוּשָׁלַ͏ִם וַיִּתְּנֵם בְּבֵית אֱלֹהָיו:
וַיּוֹצִיאֵם כֹּרֶשׁ מֶלֶךְ פָּרַס עַל־יַד מִתְרְדָת הַגִּזְבָּר
וַיִּסְפְּרֵם לְשֵׁשְׁבַּצַּר הַנָּשִׂיא לִיהוּדָה:

עֶזְרָא א: ז–ח

The word of the Lord came to me: ²"O mortal, you dwell within the rebellious house, who have eyes to see but do not see, and ears to hear but do not hear; for they are a rebellious house. ³Therefore you, O mortal, prepare for yourself gear for exile, and go into exile by day before their eyes. Go into exile from your home to another place before their eyes; perhaps they will admit [lit. see] that they are a rebellious house. ⁴Carry out your gear as gear for exile by day before their very eyes; and you go out in the evening before their eyes, as on who goes out into exile. ⁵Before their eyes, break through the wall and carry out [the gear] through it. ⁶Before their eyes, carry it on your shoulder; take it out in the dark. Cover your face that you may not see the land, for I make you a warning sign [or portent] to the House of Israel." ⁷I did just as I was commanded: I took out my gear by day as gear for exile, and in the evening I broke through the wall by hand. In the darkness I carried out [the gear] on my shoulder, bearing it in their sight . . . ¹¹"Say: I am a warning sign for you: as I have done, so shall it be done to them. They shall go into exile, into capitivity."

*Ezekiel 12.1-11*

וַיְהִי דְבַר־יְהֹוָה אֵלַי לֵאמֹר: בֶּן־אָדָם בְּתוֹךְ
בֵּית־הַמֶּרִי אַתָּה יֹשֵׁב אֲשֶׁר עֵינַיִם לָהֶם לִרְאוֹת
וְלֹא רָאוּ אָזְנַיִם לָהֶם לִשְׁמֹעַ וְלֹא שָׁמֵעוּ כִּי בֵּית
מְרִי הֵם: וְאַתָּה בֶן־אָדָם עֲשֵׂה לְךָ כְּלֵי גוֹלָה וּגְלֵה
יוֹמָם לְעֵינֵיהֶם וְגָלִיתָ מִמְּקוֹמְךָ אֶל־מָקוֹם אַחֵר
לְעֵינֵיהֶם אוּלַי יִרְאוּ כִּי בֵּית מְרִי הֵמָּה: וְהוֹצֵאתָ
כֵלֶיךָ כִּכְלֵי גוֹלָה יוֹמָם לְעֵינֵיהֶם וְאַתָּה תֵּצֵא
בָעֶרֶב לְעֵינֵיהֶם כְּמוֹצָאֵי גוֹלָה: לְעֵינֵיהֶם חֲתָר־
לְךָ בַקִּיר וְהוֹצֵאתָ בּוֹ: לְעֵינֵיהֶם עַל־כָּתֵף תִּשָּׂא
בָּעֲלָטָה תוֹצִיא פָּנֶיךָ תְכַסֶּה וְלֹא תִרְאֶה אֶת־
הָאָרֶץ כִּי־מוֹפֵת נְתַתִּיךָ לְבֵית יִשְׂרָאֵל: וָאַעַשׂ
כֵּן כַּאֲשֶׁר צֻוֵּיתִי כֵּלַי הוֹצֵאתִי כִּכְלֵי גוֹלָה יוֹמָם
וּבָעֶרֶב חָתַרְתִּי־לִי בַקִּיר בְּיָד בָּעֲלָטָה הוֹצֵאתִי
עַל־כָּתֵף נָשָׂאתִי לְעֵינֵיהֶם:... אֱמֹר אֲנִי מוֹפֶתְכֶם
כַּאֲשֶׁר עָשִׂיתִי כֵּן יֵעָשֶׂה לָהֶם בַּגּוֹלָה בַשְּׁבִי יֵלֵכוּ:

יְחֶזְקֵאל יב: א–יא

Tomb of Cyrus the Great at his capital city, Pasargadae. The mausoleum is set above the level of the surrounding plain on several stepped courses. The structure is limestone, and the blocks are held together with clamps of iron. The base measures 47.7 x 42.4 feet.

To commemorate the re-establishment of royal authority in the Persian empire, Darius, the new king of Persia, had an enormous relief carved on the cliff above an important road leading from Mesopotamia to Iran (Persia). The rock-cliff is called Behistun (or Bisutun). Darius and a small retinue are pictured confronting opponents to his claim to the Persian throne. They come conquered before Darius, hands bound behind their backs. Above the relief, an account of the struggle was inscribed three times, each time in a different language: Babylonian (language of Mesopotamia-Babylonia), Elamite, and Old Persian.

Judeans for their inertia, saying bitterly, "Is this a time for you to dwell in your paneled houses, when this House lies in ruins?" (1:4). When drought and famine came upon the land, Haggai insisted that the hardships were a manifestation of God's displeasure at the people's failure to rebuild His Temple. The prophet Zechariah, too, castigated the people for their apathy.

The foreigners who had poured into Judah during the Exile saw the restoration of the Temple as a threat to their position and prosperity, and, accordingly, opposed it. Among those of mixed marriages, the attitudes ranged from complete indifference to a willingness to back the projects; but when some of this mixed population, chiefly the Samaritans, volunteered their assistance, their offer was rejected and they were denounced as idolators (Ezra 4:1–5, 24).

During this period, Zerubbabel, of the family of King Jehoiachin and the House of David, was the civil head of the community, and Joshua the high priest was recognized leader of the priestly group. Haggai and Zechariah had envisaged a restoration of Judah under a scion of the House of David, with a free priesthood in full charge of the Temple and religious matters.

It was, however, the representatives of the religious rather than the civil authority who finally came to power. Cambyses II, son and successor of Cyrus, committed suicide in 522 B.C.E., and for a brief interval the Persian empire faltered. During the confusion, several of the subject provinces revolted, creating the impression among some of the Judeans still at home—Haggai and Zechariah among them—that the end of the empire was at hand. Jumping at what they took to be a chance to restore Judah's independence at one blow, they named Zerubbabel God's

You look for much and instead there is little; and when you bring it indoors, I blow it away. Why? declares the Lord of Hosts. Because of My House, which lies in ruins while you run each to a house of his own. [10]That is why the heavens have withheld the dew against you and the earth has withheld its produce. [11]I have proclaimed a drought against the land and the hills, against the new corn, wine, and oil, against yield of the soil, against man and beast, and against all the yield of their labors [lit. palms].

*Haggai 1.9-11*

When the enemies of Judah and Benjamin heard that the returned exiles [lit. children of the exile] were building a Temple to the Lord, the God of Israel, [2]they approached Zerubbabel and the ancestral heads and said to them, "Let us build together with you; for we seek your God as you do, since it is to Him that we have been offering sacrifices ever since the days of King Esarhaddon of Assyria, who brought us here." [3]But Zerubbabel and Jeshua [=Joshua the high priest] and the rest of the ancestral heads of Israel replied to them, "You have nothing to do with us in building [lit. It is not for you and us to build] a House to our God; but we by ourselves will build to the Lord, the God of Israel, as King Cyrus, king of Persia, has charged us." [4]Then the people of the land caused the Judean people to lose heart [lit. weakened the hands] and frightened them off from building. [5]They hired [bribed?] counsellors [of the royal court] against them to frustrate their plans, throughout the reign of King Cyrus of Persia and until the reign of King Darius of Persia; . . . [24]Then the work on the House of God in Jerusalem ceased; and it remained interrupted until the second year of the reign of King Darius of Persia.

*Ezra 4.1-5,24*

The word of the Lord came to me [Zechariah [the prophet]: [9]The hands of Zerubbabel have laid the foundations of this House and his hands shall complete it; then you shall know that the Lord of Hosts sent me to you. [10]For whoever has despised the day of small beginnings [lit. things] shall rejoice on seeing the plumb line in the hands of Zerubbabel . . .

*Zechariah 4.8-10*

פְּנֹה אֶל־הַרְבֵּה וְהִנֵּה לִמְעָט וַהֲבֵאתֶם הַבַּיִת
וְנָפַחְתִּי בוֹ יַעַן מֶה נְאֻם יְהוָה צְבָאוֹת יַעַן בֵּיתִי
אֲשֶׁר־הוּא חָרֵב וְאַתֶּם רָצִים אִישׁ לְבֵיתוֹ: עַל־
כֵּן עֲלֵיכֶם כָּלְאוּ שָׁמַיִם מִטָּל וְהָאָרֶץ כָּלְאָה
יְבוּלָהּ: וָאֶקְרָא חֹרֶב עַל־הָאָרֶץ וְעַל־הֶהָרִים
וְעַל־הַדָּגָן וְעַל־הַתִּירוֹשׁ וְעַל־הַיִּצְהָר וְעַל אֲשֶׁר
תּוֹצִיא הָאֲדָמָה וְעַל־הָאָדָם וְעַל־הַבְּהֵמָה וְעַל
כָּל־יְגִיעַ כַּפָּיִם:

חַגַּי א: ט–יא

וַיִּשְׁמְעוּ צָרֵי יְהוּדָה וּבִנְיָמִן כִּי־בְנֵי הַגּוֹלָה
בּוֹנִים הֵיכָל לַיהוָה אֱלֹהֵי יִשְׂרָאֵל: וַיִּגְּשׁוּ אֶל־
זְרֻבָּבֶל וְאֶל־רָאשֵׁי הָאָבוֹת וַיֹּאמְרוּ לָהֶם נִבְנֶה
עִמָּכֶם כִּי כָכֶם נִדְרוֹשׁ לֵאלֹהֵיכֶם וְלוֹ אֲנַחְנוּ
זֹבְחִים מִימֵי אֵסַר חַדֹּן מֶלֶךְ אַשּׁוּר הַמַּעֲלֶה אֹתָנוּ
פֹּה: וַיֹּאמֶר לָהֶם זְרֻבָּבֶל וְיֵשׁוּעַ וּשְׁאָר רָאשֵׁי
הָאָבוֹת לְיִשְׂרָאֵל לֹא־לָכֶם וָלָנוּ לִבְנוֹת בַּיִת
לֵאלֹהֵינוּ כִּי אֲנַחְנוּ יַחַד נִבְנֶה לַיהוָה אֱלֹהֵי יִשְׂרָאֵל
כַּאֲשֶׁר צִוָּנוּ הַמֶּלֶךְ כּוֹרֶשׁ מֶלֶךְ־פָּרָס: וַיְהִי עַם
הָאָרֶץ מְרַפִּים יְדֵי עַם־יְהוּדָה וּמְבַהֲלִים אוֹתָם
לִבְנוֹת: וְסֹכְרִים עֲלֵיהֶם יוֹעֲצִים לְהָפֵר עֲצָתָם
כָּל־יְמֵי כּוֹרֶשׁ מֶלֶךְ פָּרָס וְעַד־מַלְכוּת דָּרְיָוֶשׁ
מֶלֶךְ פָּרָס: ...

עֶזְרָא ד: א–ה

וַיְהִי דְבַר־יְהוָה אֵלַי לֵאמֹר: יְדֵי זְרֻבָּבֶל יִסְּדוּ
הַבַּיִת הַזֶּה וְיָדָיו תְּבַצַּעְנָה וְיָדַעְתָּ כִּי־יְהוָה צְבָאוֹת
שְׁלָחַנִי אֲלֵיכֶם: כִּי מִי בַז לְיוֹם קְטַנּוֹת וְשָׂמְחוּ וְרָאוּ
אֶת־הָאֶבֶן הַבְּדִיל בְּיַד זְרֻבָּבֶל...

זְכַרְיָה ד: ח–י

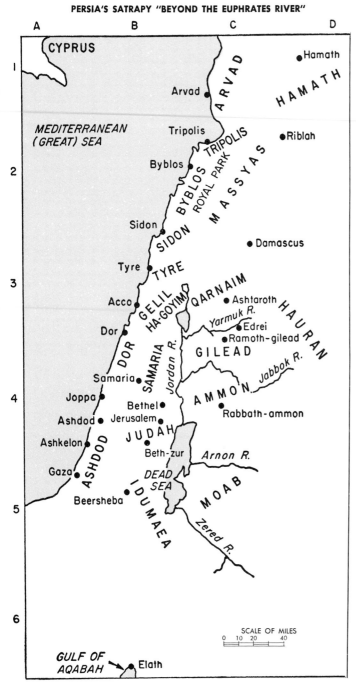

Judah was but a minor region and element in the Persian satrapy "Beyond (=West of) the Euphrates River," of which the most important subdivision was Phoenicia (Arvad, Byblos, Sidon, and Tyre).

chosen one, thus declaring independence of Persia (Haggai 2:20–23). The priestly group seems to have been more cautious. And their caution was rewarded when Darius I (522–486) crushed the widespread rebellion and re-established the imperial rule.

Just how Zerubbabel and his backers fared during this troubled interlude is not known, but the movement is never heard of again. Led by Haggai and Joshua, however, the Judeans persevered in their efforts to rebuild the Temple. The Persian government, in accordance with its general policy of supporting local priesthoods, ignored the objections of its own governor, Tattenai, and of the anti-Jewish section of the population, and granted the Jews permission to continue with the work. About 516 B.C.E. the second Temple was dedicated, just seventy years after the first had been destroyed. Judah now became a theocracy, under Persian rule, with Joshua the high priest at its head.

Little is known about the happenings in Judea during the earlier part of the fifth century. The Persian government continued its policy of granting its colonies, Judea included, a considerable degree of religious and cultural autonomy, keeping at the same time a firm hold on military, economic, and political affairs. The Jewish community in Judea grew in numbers and in prosperity only gradually, and while it seems to have taken good care of the Temple, it did not consider it politic to restore the walls of Jerusalem, destroyed by Nebuchadnezzar's army. At the same time, intermarriage between the Judeans and the gentiles continued, and their assimilation progressed.

## The Jewries of Egypt and Persia

Elsewhere in the Persian empire Jews were involved in two revealing incidents. It will be remembered that when Nebuchad-

228

The word of the Lord came a second time to Haggai, on the twenty-fourth day of the [ninth] month: 21Say to Zerubbabel, governor of Judah, "I am about to shake heaven and earth. 22I will overthrow the thrones of kings and destroy the mighty kingdoms of nations. I will overturn chariots and their riders, and horses and their riders shall go down, each by the sword of his fellow. 23In that day, declares the Lord of Hosts, I will take you, My servant Zerubbabel son of Shealtiel—declares the Lord—and designate you as a signet ring [i.e. as a scion of David; cf. Jer. 22.24]. For I have chosen you, declares the Lord of Hosts."

*Haggai 2.20-23*

Then Zerubbabel son of Shealtiel and Jeshua son of Jozadak set at once to building the House of God in Jerusalem; and the prophets of God were with them to help them. 3But at the same time, Tattenai governor of the province of Beyond-Euphrates, Shether-bozenai, and their associates came to them and said to them thus: "Who gave you authorization [lit. decree] to rebuild this House and to complete this structure?" . . . 5But the eye of their God was upon the elders of the Jews and they did not stop them, until the matter came before Darius . . .

*Ezra 5.2-5*

I also saw in those days the Jews who had married Ashdodite, Ammonite, and Moabite women. 24Half of their children spoke Ashdodite, and did not know enough [or how] to speak Judean, but each in the language of his people. 25I remonstrated with them and cursed [or reviled] them, and I hit some of them and tore their hair; and I made them swear by God, saying "You shall not give your daughters in marriage to their sons, or accept any of their daughters in marriage for your sons or for yourselves. 26Was it not in this manner (or for such women) that King Solomon of Israel sinned—who had no equal as king among the nations, and was loved by his God, and God made him king over all Israel? Even him did the alien wives lead to sin. 27Shall we then listen to you and commit this most wicked thing, breaking faith with our God by marrying alien women?"

*Nehemiah 13.23-27*

וַיְהִ֨י דְבַר־יְהוָ֤ה ׀ שֵׁנִית֙ אֶל־חַגַּ֔י בְּעֶשְׂרִ֧ים וְאַרְבָּעָ֛ה לַחֹ֖דֶשׁ לֵאמֹֽר׃ אֱמֹ֕ר אֶל־זְרֻבָּבֶ֥ל פַּֽחַת־יְהוּדָ֖ה לֵאמֹ֑ר אֲנִ֣י מַרְעִ֔ישׁ אֶת־הַשָּׁמַ֖יִם וְאֶת־הָאָֽרֶץ׃ וְהָֽפַכְתִּי֙ כִּסֵּ֣א מַמְלָכ֔וֹת וְהִ֨שְׁמַדְתִּ֔י חֹ֖זֶק מַמְלְכ֣וֹת הַגּוֹיִ֑ם וְהָפַכְתִּ֤י מֶרְכָּבָה֙ וְרֹ֣כְבֶ֔יהָ וְיָרְד֤וּ סוּסִים֙ וְרֹ֣כְבֵיהֶ֔ם אִ֖ישׁ בְּחֶ֥רֶב אָחִֽיו׃ בַּיּ֣וֹם הַה֣וּא נְאֻם־יְהוָ֣ה צְבָא֗וֹת אֶקָּחֲךָ֞ זְרֻבָּבֶ֤ל בֶּן־שְׁאַלְתִּיאֵל֙ עַבְדִּי֙ נְאֻם־יְהוָ֔ה וְשַׂמְתִּ֖יךָ כַּֽחוֹתָ֑ם כִּֽי־בְךָ֣ בָחַ֔רְתִּי נְאֻ֖ם יְהוָ֥ה צְבָאֽוֹת׃

חַגַּי ב: כ–כג

בֵּאדַ֡יִן קָ֠מוּ זְרֻבָּבֶ֤ל בַּר־שְׁאַלְתִּיאֵל֙ וְיֵשׁ֣וּעַ בַּר־יֽוֹצָדָ֔ק וְשָׁרִ֣יו לְמִבְנֵ֔א בֵּ֥ית אֱלָהָ֖א דִּ֣י בִירֽוּשְׁלֶ֑ם וְעִמְּה֛וֹן נְבִיאַיָּ֥א דִֽי־אֱלָהָ֖א מְסָעֲדִ֥ין לְהֽוֹן׃ בֵּהּ־זִמְנָ֞א אֲתָ֣ה עֲלֵיה֗וֹן תַּתְּנַי֙ פַּחַ֣ת עֲבַֽר־נַהֲרָ֔ה וּשְׁתַ֥ר בּוֹזְנַ֖י וּכְנָוָתְה֑וֹן וְכֵן֙ אָמְרִ֣ין לְהֹ֔ם מַן־שָׂ֨ם לְכֹ֜ם טְעֵ֗ם בַּיְתָ֤א דְנָה֙ לִבְּנֵ֔א וְאֻשַּׁרְנָ֥א דְנָ֖ה לְשַׁכְלָלָֽה׃ . . . וְעֵ֣ין אֱלָֽהֲהֹ֗ם הֲוָת֙ עַל־שָׂבֵ֣י יְהוּדָיֵ֔א וְלָֽא־בַטִּ֖לוּ הִמּ֑וֹ עַד־טַעְמָ֛א לְדָרְיָ֥וֶשׁ יְהָ֖ךְ . . .

עֶזְרָא ה: ב–ה

גַּ֣ם ׀ בַּיָּמִ֣ים הָהֵ֗ם רָאִ֤יתִי אֶת־הַיְּהוּדִים֙ הֹשִׁ֗יבוּ נָשִׁ֤ים אשדודיות עַמֳּנִיּ֣וֹת מֽוֹאֲבִיּֽוֹת׃ וּבְנֵיהֶ֗ם חֲצִי֙ מְדַבֵּ֣ר אַשְׁדּוֹדִ֔ית וְאֵינָ֥ם מַכִּירִ֖ים לְדַבֵּ֣ר יְהוּדִ֑ית וְכִלְשׁ֖וֹן עַ֥ם וָעָֽם׃ וָאָרִ֤יב עִמָּם֙ וָאֲקַֽלְלֵ֔ם וָאַכֶּ֥ה מֵהֶ֛ם אֲנָשִׁ֖ים וָֽאֶמְרְטֵ֑ם וָאַשְׁבִּיעֵ֣ם בֵּֽאלֹהִ֗ים אִם־תִּתְּנ֤וּ בְנֹֽתֵיכֶם֙ לִבְנֵיהֶ֔ם וְאִם־תִּשְׂאוּ֙ מִבְּנֹֽתֵיהֶ֔ם לִבְנֵיכֶ֖ם וְלָכֶֽם׃ הֲל֣וֹא עַל־אֵ֣לֶּה חָֽטָא־שְׁלֹמֹ֣ה מֶֽלֶךְ־יִשְׂרָאֵ֡ל וּבַגּוֹיִ֣ם הָֽרַבִּים֩ לֹֽא־הָיָ֨ה מֶ֜לֶךְ כָּמֹ֗הוּ וְאָה֤וּב לֵֽאלֹהָיו֙ הָיָ֔ה וַיִּתְּנֵ֣הוּ אֱלֹהִ֔ים מֶ֖לֶךְ עַל־כָּל־יִשְׂרָאֵ֑ל גַּם־אוֹת֣וֹ הֶחֱטִ֔יאוּ הַנָּשִׁ֖ים הַנָּכְרִיּֽוֹת׃ וְלָכֶ֣ם הֲנִשְׁמַ֗ע לַעֲשֹׂת֙ אֵ֣ת כָּל־הָרָעָ֤ה הַגְּדוֹלָה֙ הַזֹּ֔את לִמְעֹ֖ל בֵּֽאלֹהֵ֑ינוּ לְהֹשִׁ֖יב נָשִׁ֥ים נָכְרִיּֽוֹת׃

נְחֶמְיָה יג: כג–כו

229

Persepolis, the festival capital of the Persian kings from the time of Darius the Great (521-486 B.C.E.) on, and one of the most famous archaeological sites of modern times.

nezzar's forces were overrunning Judah, and again when the Judeans revolted—to their sorrow—against Gedaliah, some of the populace sought asylum in Egypt. About sixty years later (c. 525 B.C.E.) the Persians incorporated Egypt in their empire, whereupon some of the expatriate Jews there volunteered for military service with the conqueror, and were assigned to garrison duty.

The sudden reappearance of Jews in Egyptian history is recorded by the Elephantine Papyri, ancient documents of a Jewish military colony at the city of Elephantine, just below the first cataract of the Nile. Written in Aramaic—which was the "language of diplomacy and trade throughout Western Asia in the Persian period, and which was gradually replacing Hebrew as the everyday tongue of the Jewish people not only abroad, but also at home in Palestine" (J. Finegan, *Light from the Ancient Past* [Princeton, 1946], p. 201)—the Elephantine Papyri constitute a prime source for the reconstruction of Egyptian and Jewish history and throw important sidelight on the colonial history of Persia as well. They indicate, for example, that the imperial rule of the Persian government was generally liberal, at least in comparison with the naked despotism of her predecessors, Egypt, Babylon, and Assyria.

The Jewish colony was allowed its own temple where sacrifices were regularly offered up to God and around which the colony's activities revolved. The business contracts and other documents among the Papyri indicate that the Jews bought and sold land and houses, married and divorced, and, in general, lived a normal life. There is evidence that some Jews intermarried with the Egyptians and became more or less assimilated in the religious and social life of the country. The community as a whole, however, appears

230

# The Jewries of Egypt and Persia

The word that came to Jeremiah for all the Judeans who were living in the land of Egypt, who lived in Migdol, Tahpanhes, Noph [Memphis], and the region of Pathros: [2]Thus said the Lord of Hosts, the God of Israel, "You have seen all the disaster that I brought upon Jerusalem and all the cities of Judah . . . [3]because of the wicked acts which they committed to vex Me . . . [7]. . . Why then do you commit this wicked thing against yourselves, that will destroy in Judah every man and woman, every babe and suckling, leaving you no remnant—[8]by vexing Me with your idols [lit. the work of your hands], making offerings to alien [lit. other] gods in the land of Egypt where you have come to sojourn, so that you destroy yourselves and become a curse and a reproach among the nations of the earth? [9]Have you forgotten the wicked acts of your fathers and of the kings of Judah and their wives, and your own wicked acts and those of your wives . . . ? [10]To this day no one has shown remorse or fear: they have not followed My Teaching and My laws, which I set before you and your fathers. [11]Therefore," thus said the Lord of Hosts, the God of Israel, "I will set My face against you in hostility, to destroy all Judah. [12]I will take the remnant of Judah, who have decided [lit. set their faces] to go to Egypt to sojourn there, and they shall all come to an end; they shall fall in the land of Egypt, coming to an end by sword and famine—young and old [or low and high], they shall die by sword and famine, and become an execration and a horror, a curse and a reproach . . ."

*Jeremiah 44.1-12*

הַדָּבָר אֲשֶׁר הָיָה אֶל־יִרְמְיָהוּ אֶל כָּל־
הַיְּהוּדִים הַיֹּשְׁבִים בְּאֶרֶץ מִצְרָיִם הַיֹּשְׁבִים בְּמִגְדֹּל
וּבְתַחְפַּנְחֵס וּבְנֹף וּבְאֶרֶץ פַּתְרוֹס לֵאמֹר: כֹּה־
אָמַר יְהוָה צְבָאוֹת אֱלֹהֵי יִשְׂרָאֵל אַתֶּם רְאִיתֶם
אֵת כָּל־הָרָעָה אֲשֶׁר הֵבֵאתִי עַל־יְרוּשָׁלִַם וְעַל כָּל־
עָרֵי יְהוּדָה... מִפְּנֵי רָעָתָם אֲשֶׁר עָשׂוּ לְהַכְעִסֵנִי...
לָמָה אַתֶּם עֹשִׂים רָעָה גְדוֹלָה אֶל־נַפְשֹׁתֵכֶם
לְהַכְרִית לָכֶם אִישׁ־וְאִשָּׁה עוֹלֵל וְיוֹנֵק מִתּוֹךְ
יְהוּדָה לְבִלְתִּי הוֹתִיר לָכֶם שְׁאֵרִית: לְהַכְעִסֵנִי
בְּמַעֲשֵׂי יְדֵיכֶם לְקַטֵּר לֵאלֹהִים אֲחֵרִים בְּאֶרֶץ
מִצְרַיִם אֲשֶׁר־אַתֶּם בָּאִים לָגוּר שָׁם לְמַעַן הַכְרִית
לָכֶם וּלְמַעַן הֱיוֹתְכֶם לִקְלָלָה וּלְחֶרְפָּה בְּכֹל גּוֹיֵי
הָאָרֶץ: הַשְׁכַחְתֶּם אֶת־רָעוֹת אֲבוֹתֵיכֶם וְאֶת־
רָעוֹת | מַלְכֵי יְהוּדָה וְאֵת רָעוֹת נָשָׁיו וְאֵת רָעֹתֵיכֶם
וְאֵת רָעֹת נְשֵׁיכֶם... לֹא דֻכְּאוּ עַד הַיּוֹם הַזֶּה וְלֹא יָרְאוּ
וְלֹא־הָלְכוּ בְתוֹרָתִי וּבְחֻקֹּתַי אֲשֶׁר־נָתַתִּי לִפְנֵיכֶם
וְלִפְנֵי אֲבוֹתֵיכֶם: לָכֵן כֹּה־אָמַר יְהוָה צְבָאוֹת
אֱלֹהֵי יִשְׂרָאֵל הִנְנִי שָׂם פָּנַי בָּכֶם לְרָעָה וּלְהַכְרִית
אֶת־כָּל־יְהוּדָה: וְלָקַחְתִּי אֶת־שְׁאֵרִית יְהוּדָה
אֲשֶׁר־שָׂמוּ פְנֵיהֶם לָבוֹא אֶרֶץ־מִצְרַיִם לָגוּר שָׁם
וְתַמּוּ כֹל בְּאֶרֶץ מִצְרַיִם יִפֹּלוּ בַּחֶרֶב בָּרָעָב יִתַּמּוּ
מִקָּטֹן וְעַד־גָּדוֹל בַּחֶרֶב וּבָרָעָב יָמֻתוּ וְהָיוּ לְאָלָה
לְשַׁמָּה וְלִקְלָלָה וּלְחֶרְפָּה:

יִרְמְיָהוּ מד : א–יב

And so it was in the days of Artaxerxes that Bishlam, Mithredath, Tabeel, and the rest of their associates wrote to King Artaxerxes of Persia; the text of the document was written in Aramaic [i.e. the language or the script] and translated [? or interpreted?] in Aramaic.

*Ezra 4.7*

וּבִימֵי אַרְתַּחְשַׁשְׂתָּא כָּתַב בִּשְׁלָם מִתְרְדָת טָבְאֵל
וּשְׁאָר כְּנָוֹתָו עַל־אַרְתַּחְשַׁשְׂתְּא מֶלֶךְ פָּרָס וּכְתָב
הַנִּשְׁתְּוָן כָּתוּב אֲרָמִית וּמְתֻרְגָּם אֲרָמִית:

עֶזְרָא ד : ז

231

Letter in the form of a memorandum in which Bagoas and Shelemiah are said to have suggested that the Jewish sanctuary in Yeb (Elephantine) could be rebuilt if they petition the Persian satrap of Egypt and promise to sacrifice grain and incense on its altar. Bagoas is the governor of Judea, and Shelemiah, son of Sanballat, is governor of Samaria. The sanctuary was rebuilt. While undated, the message derives shortly after Nehemiah leaves Judea.

**Petition by Elephantine Jewry for Authority to Rebuild their Temple of Yaho (407 B.C.E.).**

> To our lord Bagoas, governor of Judah, your servants Yedoniah and his colleagues, the priests who are in the fortress of Elephantine. May the God of Heaven seek after the welfare of our lord exceedingly at all times and give you favor before King Darius [II] and the nobles . . . the priests of the god Khnub . . . conspired with Vidarang, who was commander-in-chief here . . . (and) he sent . . . this order: "The temple of the god Yaho in the fortress of Yeb is to be destroyed." . . . the Egyptians with the other troops . . . entered the temple and razed it to the ground . . . If it please our lord: Take thought of the temple to rebuild it . . . the meal-offering, incense, and burnt offering  will be offered in your name, and we shall pray for you  at all times . . . We have also set forth the whole matter in a letter in our name to Delaiah and Shelemiah, the sons of Sanballat the governor of Samaria. Also Arsames knew nothing of all this that was done to us. Dated the 20th day of Marheshwan year 17 of King Darius.

Interestingly, while no copy of the direct response—if any were ever made—to the above has has been found, a verbal reply was sent to the Persian governor, Arsames, and presumably also to the Jews of Elephantine. In the reply, permission was granted to rebuild the temple. The text of the memorandum reads:

> Memorandum of what Bagoas and Delaiah said to me: Let it be a memorandum to you in Egypt to say to Arsames concerning the house of offering of the God of Heaven which had been built in the fortress of Elephantine long ago, before Cambyses, which that scoundrel Vidaranag destroyed in the 14th year of King Darius—that it be rebuilt on the same site as it was before and that meal-offering and incense be offered upon that altar as formerly.

to have retained a distinct character. For one thing, it was organized along military lines, with Persians and Babylonians normally in command of the larger units. Then too, the Jews, unlike the native Egyptians, employed Aramaic as their official language. Finally the Jewish colonists, genuinely appreciative of the Persian colonial policy and their privileged position in the imperial organization, were the most loyal subjects that Persia had.

On several occasions the Egyptians revolted against their Persian conquerors. In one of these uprisings, during the reign of Darius II (about 410 B.C.E.), a mob incited by the local priests and merchants attacked and looted the Jewish temple in the first anti-Jewish pogrom on record. The motivation behind this directed outburst of violence—which the Persian authorities quickly suppressed and punished—appears to have been a combination of two related factors. First, the Egyptian upper classes sought to divert the social discontent among the general population against an alien religious group which could also be identified with Persian imperialism. Second, the Egyptian priests and merchants hoped to exploit the general social discontent to weaken and, if possible, to destroy their economic rivals in the Jewish community.

The Book of Esther describes a similar incident, this time at Susa (Shushan), at the eastern end of the Persian empire. A certain Haman, the highest official in the regime of King Ahasuerus—perhaps one of the Xerxes kings—persuaded his master to hand over to him for destruction and spoil the Jews of Susa and of the empire. Haman pointed out that the Jews were unassimilable, and that "their laws are different from those of every other people" (Esther 3:8). Indeed, Haman argued, it was "not in the king's interest to tolerate them," and for the privilege of stripping them—which would be a public service—he

But all the men who were aware that their wives were making offerings to alien gods, and all the women who were present [lit. standing]—a large crowd . . . replied to Jeremiah . . . : [16]"Concerning the message that you imparted to us in the name of the Lord—we will not listen to you. [17]Instead, we will fulfill everything that we have vowed: we will burn incense to the queen of heaven and pour libations to her, as we used to do, we and our fathers, our kings and our officials, in the towns of Judah and the streets of Jerusalem. We had plenty of food and fared well, and we experienced no harm. [18]But ever since we ceased burning incense and pouring libations to the queen of heaven, we have lacked everything; and we are consumed by sword and famine." [19][And the women said:] And when we burned incense and poured libations to the queen of heaven—was it without our husbands' knowledge [or approval, permission] that we made cakes for her bearing her image [?] and poured libations to her?

*Jeremiah 44.15-19*

Haman said to King Ahasuerus, "There is a certain people, utterly [lit. scattered and] dispersed among the other peoples in all the provinces of your empire, whose laws are different from those of any other people and who do not obey the laws of Your Majesty; and it is not in Your Majesty's interest to tolerate them. [9]If it please Your Majesty, let an edict be issued [lit. let it be written] for their destruction, and I will pay ten thousand talents of silver to the stewards for deposit in the royal treasury." [10]So the king removed his signet ring from his hand and gave it to Haman son of Hammedatha the Agagite, the foe of the Jews. [11]And the king said, "The money and the people are yours to do with as you see fit." [12]On the thirteenth day of the first month, the royal scribes were summoned and a decree was issued, as Haman directed, to the king's satraps, to the governors of every province, and to the officials of every people, to every province in its own script and to every people in its own language.

וַיַּעֲנוּ אֶת־יִרְמְיָהוּ כָּל־הָאֲנָשִׁים הַיֹּדְעִים כִּי־מְקַטְּרוֹת נְשֵׁיהֶם לֵאלֹהִים אֲחֵרִים וְכָל־הַנָּשִׁים הָעֹמְדוֹת קָהָל גָּדוֹל... הַדָּבָר אֲשֶׁר־דִּבַּרְתָּ אֵלֵינוּ בְּשֵׁם יְהוָה אֵינֶנּוּ שֹׁמְעִים אֵלֶיךָ: כִּי עָשֹׂה נַעֲשֶׂה אֶת־כָּל־הַדָּבָר ׀ אֲשֶׁר־יָצָא מִפִּינוּ לְקַטֵּר לִמְלֶכֶת הַשָּׁמַיִם וְהַסֵּיךְ־לָהּ נְסָכִים כַּאֲשֶׁר עָשִׂינוּ אֲנַחְנוּ וַאֲבֹתֵינוּ מְלָכֵינוּ וְשָׂרֵינוּ בְּעָרֵי יְהוּדָה וּבְחֻצוֹת יְרוּשָׁלִָם וַנִּשְׂבַּע־לֶחֶם וַנִּהְיֶה טוֹבִים וְרָעָה לֹא רָאִינוּ: וּמִן־אָז חָדַלְנוּ לְקַטֵּר לִמְלֶכֶת הַשָּׁמַיִם וְהַסֵּךְ־לָהּ נְסָכִים חָסַרְנוּ כֹל וּבַחֶרֶב וּבָרָעָב תָּמְנוּ: וְכִי־אֲנַחְנוּ מְקַטְּרִים לִמְלֶכֶת הַשָּׁמַיִם וּלְהַסֵּךְ לָהּ נְסָכִים הֲמִבַּלְעֲדֵי אֲנָשֵׁינוּ עָשִׂינוּ לָהּ כַּוָּנִים לְהַעֲצִבָה וְהַסֵּךְ לָהּ נְסָכִים:

יִרְמְיָהוּ מד : טו–יט

וַיֹּאמֶר הָמָן לַמֶּלֶךְ אֲחַשְׁוֵרוֹשׁ יֶשְׁנוֹ עַם־אֶחָד מְפֻזָּר וּמְפֹרָד בֵּין הָעַמִּים בְּכֹל מְדִינוֹת מַלְכוּתֶךָ וְדָתֵיהֶם שֹׁנוֹת מִכָּל־עָם וְאֶת־דָּתֵי הַמֶּלֶךְ אֵינָם עֹשִׂים וְלַמֶּלֶךְ אֵין־שֹׁוֶה לְהַנִּיחָם: אִם־עַל־הַמֶּלֶךְ טוֹב יִכָּתֵב לְאַבְּדָם וַעֲשֶׂרֶת אֲלָפִים כִּכַּר־כֶּסֶף אֶשְׁקוֹל עַל־יְדֵי עֹשֵׂי הַמְּלָאכָה לְהָבִיא אֶל־גִּנְזֵי הַמֶּלֶךְ: וַיָּסַר הַמֶּלֶךְ אֶת־טַבַּעְתּוֹ מֵעַל יָדוֹ וַיִּתְּנָהּ לְהָמָן בֶּן־הַמְּדָתָא הָאֲגָגִי צֹרֵר הַיְּהוּדִים: וַיֹּאמֶר הַמֶּלֶךְ לְהָמָן הַכֶּסֶף נָתוּן לָךְ וְהָעָם לַעֲשׂוֹת בּוֹ כַּטּוֹב בְּעֵינֶיךָ: וַיִּקָּרְאוּ סֹפְרֵי הַמֶּלֶךְ בַּחֹדֶשׁ הָרִאשׁוֹן בִּשְׁלוֹשָׁה עָשָׂר יוֹם בּוֹ וַיִּכָּתֵב כְּכָל־אֲשֶׁר־צִוָּה הָמָן אֶל אֲחַשְׁדַּרְפְּנֵי־הַמֶּלֶךְ וְאֶל־הַפַּחוֹת אֲשֶׁר ׀ עַל־מְדִינָה וּמְדִינָה וְאֶל־שָׂרֵי עַם וָעָם מְדִינָה וּמְדִינָה כִּכְתָבָהּ וְעַם וָעָם כִּלְשֹׁנוֹ

(continued)

Panel of glazed brick decoration from a wall of the Persian palace at Susa. The bricks of the background are covered with a green glaze. The guards stand in relief, and are glazed in many colors, such as black, yellow, blue, green, and brown. About 6 feet high.

General view of the mounds of Susa. This city was the central administrative capital and winter residence of the kings of Persia from Darius the Great (521-486 B.C.E.) to Artaxerxes II Memnon (404-359 B.C.E.).

offered to pay ten thousand talents of silver. In spite of the extraordinary offer Haman was thwarted by Ahasuerus' favorite, the Jewess Esther (Hadassah). Under the guidance of her wise cousin, Mordecai, she caused Haman to be hanged from his own gallows and his henchmen killed. But the Jews, in their turn, "did not lay hands on the spoil" of the Persians (Esther 3:11, 13; 9:15–16).

The Book of Esther, as so many critics have pointed out, is much too pat and wishfully contrived to be accepted as simple historical fact. Yet the account, however much idealized, follows closely, in essence, the objective chronicle of the Elephantine Papyri, and may therefore be considered as a reflection of fact. It seems more than likely that under the Achemenid regime expatriate Jews achieved positions of wealth and influence, not only in Egypt but throughout the Persian empire, and that this personal prosperity produced the usual inimical repercussions engendered by minority success—which would account for the story of Esther, or pogrom narrowly averted.

Among the Jews, the triumph of Esther came to be observed in the joyous feast of Purim, which recalls "the days on which the Jews had rest from their enemies, and the month which was turned for them from sorrow to gladness, and from mourning to festivity; they were to make them days of feasting and gladness, and of sending presents one to another, and gifts to the poor" (Esther 9:22). After the destruction of Judah and the Temple, and the subsequent exile, it was natural for a people to celebrate joyfully such a narrow and triumphant escape from great disaster.

## Ezra and Nehemiah

To return to Judah—or Judea, to keep its new status clear—the decisive turn toward

234

Orders were issued in the name of King Ahasuerus and sealed with the king's signet. [13]Written instructions were dispatched by couriers to all the king's provinces to destroy, massacre, and exterminate all the Jews, young and old, children and women, on a single day, on the thirteenth day of the twelfth month—that is, the month of Adar—and to plunder their possessions . . . [15]The couriers went out posthaste on the royal mission, and the decree was proclaimed in the fortress [or capital city] Shushan. The king and Haman sat down to feast [lit. drink], but the city of Shushan was stunned.

*Esther 3. 8 -15*

בְּשֵׁם הַמֶּלֶךְ אֲחַשְׁוֵרֹשׁ נִכְתָּב וְנֶחְתָּם בְּטַבַּעַת הַמֶּלֶךְ: וְנִשְׁלוֹחַ סְפָרִים בְּיַד הָרָצִים אֶל־כָּל־מְדִינוֹת הַמֶּלֶךְ לְהַשְׁמִיד לַהֲרֹג וּלְאַבֵּד אֶת־כָּל־הַיְּהוּדִים מִנַּעַר וְעַד־זָקֵן טַף וְנָשִׁים בְּיוֹם אֶחָד בִּשְׁלוֹשָׁה עָשָׂר לְחֹדֶשׁ שְׁנֵים־עָשָׂר הוּא־חֹדֶשׁ אֲדָר וּשְׁלָלָם לָבוֹז: . . . הָרָצִים יָצְאוּ דְחוּפִים בִּדְבַר הַמֶּלֶךְ וְהַדָּת נִתְּנָה בְּשׁוּשַׁן הַבִּירָה וְהַמֶּלֶךְ וְהָמָן יָשְׁבוּ לִשְׁתּוֹת וְהָעִיר שׁוּשַׁן נָבוֹכָה:

אֶסְתֵּר ג: ח–טו

---

The Jews of Shushan mustered again on the fourteenth day of Adar and slew three hundred men in Shushan; but they did not lay hands on the spoil. [16]The rest of the Jews, those in the king's provinces, also mustered and fought for their lives. They won respite [or gained relief] from their enemies, killing seventy-five thousand of their foes; but they did not lay hands on the spoil. [17]That was on the thirteenth day of the month of Adar; and they rested on the fourteenth day and made it a day of feasting and merrymaking. [18]The Jews in Shushan, however, mustered on both the thirteenth and fourteenth days, and so they rested on the fifteenth and made that a day of feasting and merrymaking. [19]That is why village Jews, who live in unwalled [or outlying] towns, observe the fourteenth day of Adar in merrymaking and feasting, and as a holiday, on which they send gifts to one another. [20]Mordecai recorded these events. And he sent dispatches to all the Jews throughout the provinces of King Ahasuerus, near and far, [21]enjoining them to observe the fourteenth and fifteenth days of Adar, every year, [22]as the days on which the Jews won respite from their foes and the month which had been transformed for them from one of grief to one of merrymaking, from mourning to a holiday. They were to observe them as days of feasting and merrymaking, and for sending gifts to one another and presents to the poor.

*Esther 9.15-22*

וַיִּקָּהֲלוּ הַיְּהוּדִיים אֲשֶׁר־בְּשׁוּשָׁן גַּם בְּיוֹם אַרְבָּעָה עָשָׂר לְחֹדֶשׁ אֲדָר וַיַּהַרְגוּ בְשׁוּשָׁן שְׁלֹשׁ מֵאוֹת אִישׁ וּבַבִּזָּה לֹא שָׁלְחוּ אֶת־יָדָם: וּשְׁאָר הַיְּהוּדִים אֲשֶׁר בִּמְדִינוֹת הַמֶּלֶךְ נִקְהֲלוּ | וְעָמֹד עַל־נַפְשָׁם וְנוֹחַ מֵאֹיְבֵיהֶם וְהָרוֹג בְּשֹׂנְאֵיהֶם חֲמִשָּׁה וְשִׁבְעִים אָלֶף וּבַבִּזָּה לֹא שָׁלְחוּ אֶת־יָדָם: בְּיוֹם־שְׁלוֹשָׁה עָשָׂר לְחֹדֶשׁ אֲדָר וְנוֹחַ בְּאַרְבָּעָה עָשָׂר בּוֹ וְעָשֹׂה אֹתוֹ יוֹם מִשְׁתֶּה וְשִׂמְחָה: וְהַיְּהוּדִיים אֲשֶׁר־בְּשׁוּשָׁן נִקְהֲלוּ בִּשְׁלוֹשָׁה עָשָׂר בּוֹ וּבְאַרְבָּעָה עָשָׂר בּוֹ וְנוֹחַ בַּחֲמִשָּׁה עָשָׂר בּוֹ וְעָשֹׂה אֹתוֹ יוֹם מִשְׁתֶּה וְשִׂמְחָה: עַל־כֵּן הַיְּהוּדִים הַפְּרָזִים הַיֹּשְׁבִים בְּעָרֵי הַפְּרָזוֹת עֹשִׂים אֵת יוֹם אַרְבָּעָה עָשָׂר לְחֹדֶשׁ אֲדָר שִׂמְחָה וּמִשְׁתֶּה וְיוֹם טוֹב וּמִשְׁלֹחַ מָנוֹת אִישׁ לְרֵעֵהוּ: וַיִּכְתֹּב מָרְדֳּכַי אֶת־הַדְּבָרִים הָאֵלֶּה וַיִּשְׁלַח סְפָרִים אֶל־כָּל־הַיְּהוּדִים אֲשֶׁר בְּכָל־מְדִינוֹת הַמֶּלֶךְ אֲחַשְׁוֵרוֹשׁ הַקְּרוֹבִים וְהָרְחוֹקִים: לְקַיֵּם עֲלֵיהֶם לִהְיוֹת עֹשִׂים אֵת יוֹם אַרְבָּעָה עָשָׂר לְחֹדֶשׁ אֲדָר וְאֵת יוֹם־חֲמִשָּׁה עָשָׂר בּוֹ בְּכָל־שָׁנָה וְשָׁנָה: כַּיָּמִים אֲשֶׁר־נָחוּ בָהֶם הַיְּהוּדִים מֵאֹיְבֵיהֶם וְהַחֹדֶשׁ אֲשֶׁר נֶהְפַּךְ לָהֶם מִיָּגוֹן לְשִׂמְחָה וּמֵאֵבֶל לְיוֹם טוֹב לַעֲשׂוֹת אוֹתָם יְמֵי מִשְׁתֶּה וְשִׂמְחָה וּמִשְׁלוֹחַ מָנוֹת אִישׁ לְרֵעֵהוּ וּמַתָּנוֹת לָאֶבְיוֹנִים:

אֶסְתֵּר ט: טו–כב

Remains of the wall of Jerusalem on the eastern slope of the Ophel mound. This wall was erected in the days of Nehemiah. The first building stage is visible in the foreground. Subsequent additions and rebuilding were made as needed, for example, the tower which dominates the center of the picture. Repairs were made by the Maccabeans, and the wall stood until the city was destroyed by Titus in 70 C.E.

Coin of the Persian Period (4th cent.) used in the province of Judea. On the obverse, a seated man (an official, or god, or king?) holds a bird (an eagle?). He is seated on a throne made of a wheel and a bird's wing. On the reverse is the head of a soldier wearing a war helmet of the type known from the war dress of the soldiers of the Greek city of Corinth. The inscription on the observe reads יהד (province of Judea). About 9/16 inches high.

national as well as religious revival came about in the time of Ezra the Scribe and Nehemiah. Just when Ezra lived is unknown —even whether he preceded, was contemporary with, or followed Nehemiah. But their combined influence on the history of Judea during the latter half of the fifth and the first decades of the fourth centuries is made abundantly clear in the Biblical text.

An important person in the Jewish community of Babylon and highly regarded by the Persian government, Ezra, "the priest and scribe of the Law of the God of Heaven," was authorized by King Artaxerxes to proceed to Jerusalem, and there, with the assistance of the king's officials, to reorganize the entire Jewish community in accordance with the Law of Moses (Ezra 7:12–26).

Ezra brought back with him to Judea the various compilations which recorded the early traditions of the patriarchal and Mosaic period. Chapter 8 of Nehemiah describes the dramatic scene in Jerusalem when the entire adult Jewish population gathered to hear Ezra read and explain to them the text of the Torah, the Law of Moses. Rabbi Jose of Palestine (second century C.E.) justly expressed the importance of Ezra, even in comparison with Moses, in the establishment of the Torah as the basis of Judaism, when he said, "Ezra was worthy of having the Law given through him to Israel, had not Moses preceded him." (Babylonian Talmud, Tractate Sanhedrin, folio 21b bottom.)

One of the important consequences of the official adoption of the Torah, in addition to the renewed observance of such holy days as the feasts of Tabernacles (Succoth) and Passover, was the decision of Ezra to order every Jew to divorce his gentile wife. This was a far-reaching decision, and not an easy one to carry out. Opposition to this move came from every walk of Jewish life, and it

This is a copy of the document that King Artaxerxes gave to Ezra the priest [and] interpreter [or scribe, scholar], who interpreted the words [or text] of God's commandments and laws to Israel: [12][From] Artaxerxes, king of kings, to Ezra the priest . . . [13]It has been decreed by me that every member of the Israelite people in my kingdom, or of their priests or Levites, who wishes [or volunteers] to go to Jerusalem, may go with you . . . [15]Also, you may convey the silver and gold that the king and his counsellors have freely offered to the God of Israel, whose abode is in Jerusalem, [16]together with all the freewill offerings of silver and gold that you acquire throughout the province of Babylon . . . [21]Further, I King Artaxerxes, issue this decree to all the treasurers of Beyond-Euphrates that whatever Ezra the priest, interpreter of the law of the God of Heaven, requests of you shall be done without delay . . . [25]As for you, Ezra, in accordance with the wisdom of your God which you possess, appoint magistrates and judges who are to judge all the people of Beyond-Euphrates . . . [26]And whoever will not obey the law of your God and the law of the king, let judgment be quickly executed upon him, be it death or banishment, confiscation of property, or imprisonment.

*Ezra 7.11-26*

All the people assembled as one man in the square . . . and requested Ezra the interpreter [or scribe] to bring the book of Moses' Teaching which the Lord enjoined on Israel. [2]Ezra the priest brought the Teaching before the assembly—every man and woman, all who understood what they heard . . . [3]He read it . . . from early morning to noon . . . the ears of all the people directed to the book of Teaching . . . [6] . . . Then all the people, with their hands upraised, answered, "Amen, Amen!"; and they bowed low to the ground in homage to God.

*Nehemiah 8.1-6*

R. Jose said, "Ezra was worthy of having the Torah given to Israel through him — had not Moses preceded him."

*Sanhedrin 21b (bottom)*

וְזֶה ׀ פַּרְשֶׁגֶן הַנִּשְׁתְּוָן אֲשֶׁר נָתַן הַמֶּלֶךְ
אַרְתַּחְשַׁסְתְּא לְעֶזְרָא הַכֹּהֵן הַסֹּפֵר סֹפֵר דִּבְרֵי
מִצְוֹת־יְהוָה וְחֻקָּיו עַל־יִשְׂרָאֵל: אַרְתַּחְשַׁסְתְּא
מֶלֶךְ מַלְכַיָּא לְעֶזְרָא כַהֲנָא... מִנִּי שִׂים טְעֵם דִּי
כָל־מִתְנַדַּב בְּמַלְכוּתִי מִן־עַמָּא יִשְׂרָאֵל וְכָהֲנוֹהִי
וְלֵוָיֵא לִמְהָךְ לִירוּשְׁלֶם עִמָּךְ יְהָךְ: ... וּלְהֵיבָלָה
כְּסַף וּדְהַב דִּי־מַלְכָּא וְיָעֲטוֹהִי הִתְנַדַּבוּ לֶאֱלָהּ
יִשְׂרָאֵל דִּי בִירוּשְׁלֶם מִשְׁכְּנֵהּ: וְכֹל כְּסַף וּדְהַב
דִּי תְהַשְׁכַּח בְּכֹל מְדִינַת בָּבֶל עִם הִתְנַדָּבוּת עַמָּא
וְכָהֲנַיָּא מִתְנַדְּבִין לְבֵית אֱלָהֲהֹם דִּי בִירוּשְׁלֶם: ...
וּמִנִּי אֲנָה אַרְתַּחְשַׁסְתְּא מַלְכָּא שִׂים טְעֵם לְכֹל
גִּזַּבְרַיָּא דִּי בַּעֲבַר נַהֲרָה דִּי כָל־דִּי יִשְׁאֲלֶנְכוֹן
עֶזְרָא כַהֲנָא סָפַר דָּתָא דִּי־אֱלָהּ שְׁמַיָּא אָסְפַּרְנָא
יִתְעֲבִד: ... וְאַנְתְּ עֶזְרָא כְּחָכְמַת אֱלָהָךְ דִּי־בִידָךְ
מֶנִּי שָׁפְטִין וְדַיָּנִין דִּי־לֶהֱוֹן דָּאיְנִין לְכָל־עַמָּא דִּי
בַּעֲבַר נַהֲרָה לְכָל־יָדְעֵי דָּתֵי אֱלָהָךְ וְדִי לָא יָדַע
תְּהוֹדְעוּן: וְכָל־דִּי־לָא לֶהֱוֵא עָבֵד דָּתָא דִּי־
אֱלָהָךְ וְדָתָא דִּי מַלְכָּא אָסְפַּרְנָא דִּינָה לֶהֱוֵא
מִתְעֲבֵד מִנֵּהּ הֵן לְמוֹת הֵן לִשְׁרֹשִׁי הֵן־לַעֲנָשׁ נִכְסִין
וְלֶאֱסוּרִין:

עֶזְרָא ז: יא–כו

וַיֵּאָסְפוּ כָל־הָעָם כְּאִישׁ אֶחָד אֶל־הָרְחוֹב...
וַיֹּאמְרוּ לְעֶזְרָא הַסֹּפֵר לְהָבִיא אֶת־סֵפֶר תּוֹרַת
מֹשֶׁה אֲשֶׁר־צִוָּה יְהוָה אֶת־יִשְׂרָאֵל: וַיָּבִיא עֶזְרָא
הַכֹּהֵן אֶת־הַתּוֹרָה לִפְנֵי הַקָּהָל מֵאִישׁ וְעַד־אִשָּׁה
וְכֹל מֵבִין לִשְׁמֹעַ... וַיִּקְרָא בוֹ... מִן־הָאוֹר עַד־
מַחֲצִית הַיּוֹם... וְאָזְנֵי כָל־הָעָם אֶל־סֵפֶר הַתּוֹרָה:
...וַיַּעֲנוּ כָל־הָעָם אָמֵן ׀ אָמֵן בְּמֹעַל יְדֵיהֶם וַיִּקְּדוּ
וַיִּשְׁתַּחֲווּ לַיהוָה אַפַּיִם אָרְצָה:

נְחֶמְיָה ח: א–ו

רַ׳ יוֹסֵי אוֹמֵר רָאוּי הָיָה עֶזְרָא שֶׁתִּנָּתֵן תּוֹרָה
עַל יָדוֹ לְיִשְׂרָאֵל אִילְמָלֵא קָדְמוֹ מֹשֶׁה.

סַנְהֶדְרִין כא:ב

237

Examples of the riches achieved in the Persian Empire because of efficient and regular tax collection and much accumulation of war booty.

A Fifth Century Persian drinking vessel (rhyton) of gold in the shape of a fierce-looking winged lion out of whose body the cup extends. Height about 6¼ inches, length about 9½ inches.

Gold armlets with inlays of blue-green paste to show the long hair of the lions' manes. Not all the inlay is preserved. These amulets were found in a grave at Susa, and are dated to the 4th century. Diam. about 8 inches.

238

found expression in the Book of Ruth. The author of this beautiful little novel expressed the opinion that no gentile who became a sincere convert to Judaism, such as Ruth the Moabitess, should be cast out or denied.

This attitude would not ordinarily have been rejected; but in this period intermarriage had become so extensive, and the consequences so detrimental to the Jews as God's people, that Ezra and his followers could no longer accept the results in silence. It should be noted, in this connection, too, that the author of Ruth did not favor Judean missionary activity among the gentiles. Biblical Israel was not evangelical, and genuine voluntary conversion to Judaism was at most condoned.

While maintaining the policy of continued loyalty to Persia, Ezra led a social and religious revival in Judea. At about this time some Jews began to rebuild the walls of Jerusalem. This prompted the governor of Samaria, under whose administration Judea lay, to notify King Artaxerxes that the Jews were planning to revolt. The king at once ordered the work stopped. Nehemiah, a loyal cup-bearer in the royal court and an ardent Zionist, hearing of the order, pleaded to be allowed to supervise the work himself, vowing that he would proceed in such a way that the imperial interest would not be jeopardized. "If it please the king," he begged, "and if your servant has found favor in your sight, send me to Judah, to the city of my fathers' sepulchres, that I may rebuild it" (Nehemiah 2:5).

Artaxerxes was persuaded, and Nehemiah went to Judea taking with him full credentials and authority. As would be expected, Nehemiah's extraordinary powers aroused bitter opposition in Judea. Sanballat, governor of Samaria and Nehemiah's superior, and Tobiah, governnor of Ammon, 'accused

But Ruth answered [Naomi], "Do not urge me to desert you, to turn back and leave you. For wherever you go, I'll go; wherever you lodge, I'll lodge; your people shall be my people, and your God my God. 17Where you die, I'll die, and there I will be buried . . ."

*Ruth 1.16-17*

וַתֹּאמֶר רוּת אַל־תִּפְגְּעִי־בִי לְעָזְבֵךְ לָשׁוּב מֵאַחֲרָיִךְ כִּי אֶל־אֲשֶׁר תֵּלְכִי אֵלֵךְ וּבַאֲשֶׁר תָּלִינִי אָלִין עַמֵּךְ עַמִּי וֵאלֹהַיִךְ אֱלֹהָי: בַּאֲשֶׁר תָּמוּתִי אָמוּת וְשָׁם אֶקָּבֵר...

רוּת א: טז–יז

. . . [Ruth] asked him, "Why are you so kind as to take notice of me, since I am a foreigner?" 11"Because I have been told," Boaz said in reply, "of all that you did for your mother-in-law after the death of your husband, how you left your father and mother and your native country . . . 12May the Lord reward your deeds. . . ."

*Ruth 2.10-12*

...וַתֹּאמֶר אֵלָיו מַדּוּעַ מָצָאתִי חֵן בְּעֵינֶיךָ לְהַכִּירֵנִי וְאָנֹכִי נָכְרִיָּה: וַיַּעַן בֹּעַז וַיֹּאמֶר לָהּ הֻגֵּד הֻגַּד לִי כֹּל אֲשֶׁר־עָשִׂית אֶת־חֲמוֹתֵךְ אַחֲרֵי מוֹת אִישֵׁךְ וַתַּעַזְבִי אָבִיךְ וְאִמֵּךְ וְאֶרֶץ מוֹלַדְתֵּךְ... יְשַׁלֵּם יְהוָה פָּעֳלֵךְ...

רוּת ב: י–יב

The women said to Naomi, "Blessed [or Praised] be the Lord who did not withhold a redeemer from you today! May his name be perpetuated in Israel! . . . 15For your daughter-in-law, who loves you and is better to you than seven sons, has borne him."

*Ruth 4.14-15*

וַתֹּאמַרְנָה הַנָּשִׁים אֶל־נָעֳמִי בָּרוּךְ יְהוָה אֲשֶׁר לֹא הִשְׁבִּית לָךְ גֹּאֵל הַיּוֹם וְיִקָּרֵא שְׁמוֹ בְּיִשְׂרָאֵל:... כִּי כַלָּתֵךְ אֲשֶׁר־אֲהֵבַתֶךְ יְלָדַתּוּ אֲשֶׁר־הִיא טוֹבָה לָךְ מִשִּׁבְעָה בָּנִים:

רוּת ד: יד–טו

(1 11. . . I was the king's cupbearer.) 2 1It was in the month of Nisan, the twentieth year of King Artaxerxes, when wine was before him, I took up the wine and gave it to the king. I had not shown sadness in his presence. 2But the king said to me, "Why do you look sad? You are not ill. It must be sadness of heart." I was overcome by fear [lit. I feared very much], 3and I said to the king, "May the king live forever. Why should I not look sad, since the city which contains my fathers' graves lies in ruins and its gates have been burnt down?" 4"What is it," the king asked, "that you would like?" I prayed to the God of Heaven, 5and I said . . . "If it please Your Majesty and if your servant enjoys your favor, I beg you to let me go to Judah, to the city of my fathers' graves, that I may rebuild it." 6The king asked me, his queen consort sitting at his side, "How long will your journey take, and when will you return?" The king gave his approval and let me go, after I set a time. 7I said further to the king, "If it please Your Majesty, let letters

...וַיְהִי | בְּחֹדֶשׁ נִיסָן שְׁנַת עֶשְׂרִים לְאַרְתַּחְשַׁסְתְּא הַמֶּלֶךְ יַיִן לְפָנָיו וָאֶשָּׂא אֶת־הַיַּיִן וָאֶתְּנָה לַמֶּלֶךְ וְלֹא־הָיִיתִי רַע לְפָנָיו: וַיֹּאמֶר לִי הַמֶּלֶךְ מַדּוּעַ | פָּנֶיךָ רָעִים וְאַתָּה אֵינְךָ חוֹלֶה אֵין זֶה כִּי־אִם רֹעַ לֵב וָאִירָא הַרְבֵּה מְאֹד: וָאֹמַר לַמֶּלֶךְ לְעוֹלָם יִחְיֶה מַדּוּעַ לֹא־יֵרְעוּ פָנַי אֲשֶׁר הָעִיר בֵּית־קִבְרוֹת אֲבֹתַי חֲרֵבָה וּשְׁעָרֶיהָ אֻכְּלוּ בָאֵשׁ: וַיֹּאמֶר לִי הַמֶּלֶךְ עַל־מַה־זֶּה אַתָּה מְבַקֵּשׁ וָאֶתְפַּלֵּל אֶל־אֱלֹהֵי הַשָּׁמָיִם: וָאֹמַר לַמֶּלֶךְ אִם־עַל־הַמֶּלֶךְ טוֹב וְאִם־יִיטַב עַבְדְּךָ לְפָנֶיךָ אֲשֶׁר תִּשְׁלָחֵנִי אֶל־יְהוּדָה אֶל־עִיר קִבְרוֹת אֲבֹתַי וְאֶבְנֶנָּה: וַיֹּאמֶר לִי הַמֶּלֶךְ וְהַשֵּׁגַל | יוֹשֶׁבֶת אֶצְלוֹ עַד־מָתַי יִהְיֶה מַהֲלָכְךָ וּמָתַי תָּשׁוּב וַיִּיטַב לִפְנֵי־הַמֶּלֶךְ וַיִּשְׁלָחֵנִי וָאֶתְּנָה לוֹ זְמָן: וָאוֹמַר לַמֶּלֶךְ אִם־עַל־הַמֶּלֶךְ

*(continued)*

Edge of a silver dish, reportedly from Tell el-Maskhutah (Succoth?) near Suez, and now in the Brooklyn Museum. This particular dish is interesting since it has preserved the Biblical name of Geshem. The inscription reads:

"Which Qainu, son of King Geshem of Qedar, brought as an offering to [the god?] Han-ilat."

Drawings of original official seals of the Persian province of Judah in the days of Ezra and Nehemiah (5th-4th cent. B.C.E.). The upper spells out Yehud (=Judah), and the lower Yerushalem (=Jerusalem).

240

Nehemiah of plotting a revolt against the king. Geshem the Arab, perhaps the governor of Dedan in Arabia, "whom it grieved greatly that someone had come to seek the welfare of the children of Israel" (Nehemiah 2:10), also took umbrage. Geshem became embroiled in the Judean situation because of his fear of a commercial revival to the north, which would have put him back in the same disadvantageous position that Arabia's Queen of Sheba had occupied in relation to Israel's King Solomon.

Nehemiah, however, was not deterred, nor did the Persian central government withdraw its support. The walls of Jerusalem, the Bible tells us, were restored in fifty-two days of heroic effort, as Nehemiah had boasted would happen in his prophetic defiance: "The God of Heaven will succeed for us; and we His servants, we will arise and we will build. And you will have no portion or right or memorial in Jerusalem" (2:20). The builders "did the work with one hand and held a weapon in the other," we are told in a passage (Nehemiah 4:11 ff.; 4:17 ff. in the English versions) that recalls the rebuilding of modern Israel.

As had so often happened before in Judea, improving fortune brought a corresponding increase of social inequity. Once again the upper-class Judeans enriched themselves at the expense of the poor. The moneylenders tightened their fists, the common folk began to lose their land and property, serfdom reappeared. "We are forcing our sons and daughters to become slaves," the people complained to Nehemiah, "Some of our daughters have been enslaved, and we cannot help it, for other men possess our fields and our vineyards" (Nehemiah 5:1 ff.).

The heavy tribute paid to Persia by Judea further aggravated the situation because the well-to-do industriously foisted onto the com-be given me for the governors of Beyond-Eu-phrates that they should assist me in my journey until I reach Judah . . . ¹¹I reached Jerusalem, and after three days there ¹²I rose during the night . . . ¹³and went out by the Valley Gate and inspected the walls of Jerusalem which had been torn down and whose gates had been burnt down . . . ¹⁷And I said [to the Jews] . . ., "Come, let us rebuild the walls of Jerusalem . . ." ¹⁸ . . . And they replied, "Let us get on with the rebuilding . . ." ¹⁹When Sanballat the Horonite, Tobiah the Ammonite slave, and Geshem the Arab heard of this, they jeered and derided us . . . ²⁰But I an-swered them saying, "The God of Heaven will Himself grant us success, and we His servants will get on with the rebuilding; but you will have no portion or claim or memorial in Jerusalem."

*Nehemiah 2.1-20*

טוֹב אִגְּרוֹת יִתְּנוּ־לִי עַל־פַּחֲווֹת עֵבֶר הַנָּהָר אֲשֶׁר יַעֲבִירוּנִי עַד אֲשֶׁר־אָבוֹא אֶל־יְהוּדָה . . . וָאָבוֹא אֶל־יְרוּשָׁלִַם וָאֱהִי־שָׁם יָמִים שְׁלֹשָׁה: וָאָקוּם ׀ לַיְלָה . . . וָאֵצְאָה בְשַׁעַר־הַגַּיְא . . . וָאֱהִי שֹׂבֵר בְּחוֹמֹת יְרוּשָׁלִַם אֲשֶׁר־הֵמְפֹרָצִים וּשְׁעָרֶיהָ אֻכְּלוּ בָאֵשׁ: . . . וָאוֹמַר אֲלֵהֶם . . . לְכוּ וְנִבְנֶה אֶת־חוֹמַת יְרוּשָׁלִַם . . . וַיִּשְׁמַע סַנְבַלַּט הַחֹרֹנִי וְטֹבִיָּה הָעֶבֶד הָעַמּוֹנִי וְגֶשֶׁם הָעַרְבִי וַיַּלְעִגוּ לָנוּ וַיִּבְזוּ עָלֵינוּ . . .: וָאָשִׁיב אוֹתָם דָּבָר וָאוֹמַר לָהֶם אֱלֹהֵי הַשָּׁמַיִם הוּא יַצְלִיחַ לָנוּ וַאֲנַחְנוּ עֲבָדָיו נָקוּם וּבָנִינוּ וְלָכֶם אֵין־חֵלֶק וּצְדָקָה וְזִכָּרוֹן בִּירוּשָׁלָםִ:

נְחֶמְיָה ב: א—כ

. . . some [lit. half] of my young men engaged in the work, while the others stood on guard with [lit. held] spears, shields, bows, and coats of mail . . . ¹¹ . . . Those who were carrying materials did their work with one hand while holding a weapon in the other. ¹²The workers [lit. builders] had each a dagger girded at his side while he worked, and the man who sounded the horn [to indicate danger] was at my side . . . ¹⁵Thus we labored at our task from daybreak until the stars came out . . . ¹⁷ . . . we did not take off our clothes . . .

*Nehemiah 4.10-17*

. . . חֲצִי נְעָרַי עֹשִׂים בַּמְּלָאכָה וְחֶצְיָם מַחֲזִיקִים וְהָרְמָחִים הַמָּגִנִּים וְהַקְּשָׁתוֹת וְהַשִּׁרְיֹנִים . . . וְהַנֹּשְׂאִים בַּסֶּבֶל עֹמְשִׂים בְּאַחַת יָדוֹ עֹשֶׂה בַמְּלָאכָה וְאַחַת מַחֲזֶקֶת הַשָּׁלַח: וְהַבּוֹנִים אִישׁ חַרְבּוֹ אֲסוּרִים עַל־מָתְנָיו וּבוֹנִים וְהַתּוֹקֵעַ בַּשּׁוֹפָר אֶצְלִי: . . . וַאֲנַחְנוּ עֹשִׂים בַּמְּלָאכָה . . . מֵעֲלוֹת הַשַּׁחַר עַד צֵאת הַכּוֹכָבִים: . . . אֵין־אֲנַחְנוּ פֹשְׁטִים בְּגָדֵינוּ . . .

נְחֶמְיָה ד: י—יז

A great outcry was raised by the people and their wives against their fellow Jews. ²Some of them said, "With our sons and daughters we are the majority; yet we must get grain so that we may eat and survive." ³Others said, "Our fields and vineyards and homes have been pawned to get grain in the famine." ⁴Still others said, "We bor-rowed money for the royal tax on our fields and vineyards. ⁵Our bodies [lit. flesh] are no different from those of our brothers, and our children from their children! Yet we have been forcing our sons and daughters into slavery . . ."

*Nehemiah 5.1-5*

וַתְּהִי צַעֲקַת הָעָם וּנְשֵׁיהֶם גְּדוֹלָה אֶל־אֲחֵיהֶם הַיְּהוּדִים: וְיֵשׁ אֲשֶׁר אֹמְרִים בָּנֵינוּ וּבְנֹתֵינוּ אֲנַחְנוּ רַבִּים וְנִקְחָה דָגָן וְנֹאכְלָה וְנִחְיֶה: וְיֵשׁ אֲשֶׁר אֹמְרִים שְׂדֹתֵינוּ וּכְרָמֵינוּ וּבָתֵּינוּ אֲנַחְנוּ עֹרְבִים וְנִקְחָה דָגָן בָּרָעָב: וְיֵשׁ אֲשֶׁר אֹמְרִים לָוִינוּ כֶסֶף לְמִדַּת הַמֶּלֶךְ שְׂדֹתֵינוּ וּכְרָמֵינוּ: וְעַתָּה כִּבְשַׂר אַחֵינוּ בְּשָׂרֵנוּ כִּבְנֵיהֶם בָּנֵינוּ וְהִנֵּה אֲנַחְנוּ כֹבְשִׁים אֶת־בָּנֵינוּ וְאֶת־בְּנֹתֵינוּ לַעֲבָדִים . . .

נְחֶמְיָה ה: א—ה

Tomb of Tobiah, identified by the Aramaic letters טוביה cut in the rock beside the opening of the tomb. The tomb is near the palace of Tobiah at Araq el-Amir ("Cliff of the Prince") in Trans-Jordan. The inscription has been dated anywhere from the 6th to the 2nd centuries B.C.E.

mon people as large a share as possible of this collective obligation. To correct the serious dislocation, Nehemiah attempted to force the rich to take an oath guaranteeing the return of mortgaged properties and goods held under pledge to their owners. This act of social justice, which may have been a political move to win mass support for the theocratic party, provoked the Persian overseers to recall Nehemiah to Shushan.

During his absence, religious conditions in Jerusalem deteriorated. Tobiah the Ammonite had set up living quarters in the court of the Temple. Many of the levitical and priestly workers had left the Temple because they were not being supported by its revenues. The Sabbath was being violated, by Jews as well as by local Phoenician merchants. Intermarriage between Jews and the gentile populations of Ashdod, Ammon, and Moab again increased, and the children were being raised in ignorance of their Jewish faith and of the Hebrew language.

When the zealot, Nehemiah, finally returned to Jerusalem, he wasted no time in throwing out Tobiah. He appointed honest treasurers, and restored the Temple staff to full complement. Breakers of the Sabbath laws were arrested and punished. And those who dared flout the ban on intermarriage were fined, cursed, and made to take an oath that never would they permit their issue to marry a gentile. Nehemiah ended his remarkable memoirs with the plea, "Remember me, O my God, for good."

## The Jewish Theocratic State

The historical legacy of Ezra and Nehemiah was the theocratic state of Judea. In graphic

I was enraged . . . [7]. . . and I remonstrated with the nobles and officials . . . [8]and I said to them, "As far as we have been able, we have bought back our fellow Jews who had been sold to other nations, and now you yourselves are selling your fellow [Jews] . . . [11]Give them back this very day their fields and vineyards and olive groves and houses, as well as a portion [? lit. a hundredth] of the money, new grain, wine, and oil that you exacted from them." [12]"We will give it back," they replied, "and seek nothing more from them . . ." I then summoned the priests and made them swear that this would be done.

*Nehemiah 5.6-12*

I was not in Jerusalem all this time, for in the thirty-second year of King Artaxerxes of Babylon I had gone to the king. Some time later I asked leave of the king, [7]and when I reached Jerusalem I learned of the wicked thing that Eliashib [the priest] had done for Tobiah, preparing for him a chamber in the court of the House of God. [8]I was greatly displeased, and I threw out from the chamber all the furnishings of Tobiah's quarters . . . [10]And I found out that the Levites had not been given their portions and had gone off each to his own field . . . [11]I remonstrated with the officials and said, "Why is the House of God deserted?" And I gathered them [the Levitical workers] and restored them to their stations . . . [15]In those same days I saw in Judah men treading wine presses on the sabbath, and bringing in heaps of grain loaded on asses, along with wine, grapes, figs, and all kinds of loads—bringing them to Jerusalem on the sabbath day . . . [16]The Phoenicians [lit. Tyrians] who lived there also brought fish and all kinds of goods and sold them on the sabbath . . . [21]But I warned them and said to them, ". . . if you do this again, I'll lay hands on you." And from then on, they did not come on the sabbath . . . [23]I also saw in those days the Jews who had married Ashdodite, Ammonite, and Moabite women . . . [25]I remonstrated with them and reviled [or cursed] them, and I beat them and tore their hair . . . [31]. . . Remember me, O my God, for good!

*Nehemiah 13.6-31*

וַיִּחַר לִי מְאֹד... וָאָרִיבָה אֶת־הַחֹרִים וְאֶת־הַסְּגָנִים... וָאֹמְרָה לָהֶם אֲנַחְנוּ קָנִינוּ אֶת־אַחֵינוּ הַיְּהוּדִים הַנִּמְכָּרִים לַגּוֹיִם כְּדֵי בָנוּ וְגַם־אַתֶּם תִּמְכְּרוּ אֶת־אֲחֵיכֶם... הָשִׁיבוּ נָא לָהֶם כְּהַיּוֹם שְׂדֹתֵיהֶם כַּרְמֵיהֶם זֵיתֵיהֶם וּבָתֵּיהֶם וּמְאַת הַכֶּסֶף וְהַדָּגָן הַתִּירוֹשׁ וְהַיִּצְהָר אֲשֶׁר אַתֶּם נֹשִׁים בָּהֶם: וַיֹּאמְרוּ נָשִׁיב וּמֵהֶם לֹא נְבַקֵּשׁ כֵּן נַעֲשֶׂה כַּאֲשֶׁר אַתָּה אוֹמֵר וָאֶקְרָא אֶת־הַכֹּהֲנִים וָאַשְׁבִּיעֵם לַעֲשׂוֹת כַּדָּבָר הַזֶּה:

נְחֶמְיָה ה: ו–יב

וּבְכָל־זֶה לֹא הָיִיתִי בִּירוּשָׁלִָם כִּי בִּשְׁנַת שְׁלֹשִׁים וּשְׁתַּיִם לְאַרְתַּחְשַׁסְתְּא מֶלֶךְ־בָּבֶל בָּאתִי אֶל־הַמֶּלֶךְ וּלְקֵץ יָמִים נִשְׁאַלְתִּי מִן־הַמֶּלֶךְ: וָאָבוֹא לִירוּשָׁלִָם וָאָבִינָה בָרָעָה אֲשֶׁר עָשָׂה אֶלְיָשִׁיב לְטוֹבִיָּה לַעֲשׂוֹת לוֹ נִשְׁכָּה בְּחַצְרֵי בֵּית הָאֱלֹהִים: וַיֵּרַע לִי מְאֹד וָאַשְׁלִיכָה אֶת־כָּל־כְּלֵי בֵית־טוֹבִיָּה הַחוּץ מִן־הַלִּשְׁכָּה:... וָאֵדְעָה כִּי־מְנָיוֹת הַלְוִיִּם לֹא נִתָּנָה וַיִּבְרְחוּ אִישׁ־לְשָׂדֵהוּ... וָאָרִיבָה אֶת־הַסְּגָנִים וָאֹמְרָה מַדּוּעַ נֶעֱזַב בֵּית־הָאֱלֹהִים וָאֶקְבְּצֵם וָאַעֲמִדֵם עַל־עָמְדָם:... בַּיָּמִים הָהֵמָּה רָאִיתִי בִיהוּדָה | דֹּרְכִים־גִּתּוֹת | בַּשַּׁבָּת וּמְבִיאִים הָעֲרֵמוֹת וְעֹמְסִים עַל־הַחֲמֹרִים וְאַף־יַיִן עֲנָבִים וּתְאֵנִים וְכָל־מַשָּׂא וּמְבִיאִים יְרוּשָׁלִַם בְּיוֹם הַשַּׁבָּת וָאָעִיד בְּיוֹם מִכְרָם צָיִד: וְהַצֹּרִים יָשְׁבוּ בָהּ מְבִיאִים דָּאג וְכָל־מֶכֶר וּמֹכְרִים בַּשַּׁבָּת... וָאָעִידָה בָהֶם וָאֹמְרָה אֲלֵהֶם... אִם־תִּשְׁנוּ יָד אֶשְׁלַח בָּכֶם מִן־הָעֵת הַהִיא לֹא בָאוּ בַּשַּׁבָּת:... גַּם | בַּיָּמִים הָהֵם רָאִיתִי אֶת־הַיְּהוּדִים הֹשִׁיבוּ נָשִׁים אַשְׁדֳּדִיּוֹת עַמֳּנִיּוֹת מוֹאֲבִיּוֹת:... וָאָרִיב עִמָּם וָאֲקַלְלֵם וָאַכֶּה מֵהֶם אֲנָשִׁים וָאֶמְרְטֵם... זָכְרָה־לִּי אֱלֹהַי לְטוֹבָה:

נְחֶמְיָה יג: ו–לא

243

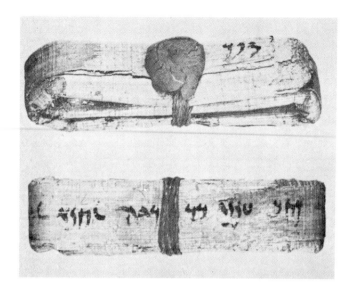

An unopened papyrus roll with seal and string (Elephantine), with the description of the contents: Document, concerning a residence which Anani bar Azariah the Servitor wrote to Yehoyishma his daughter.

form, it may be described as follows:

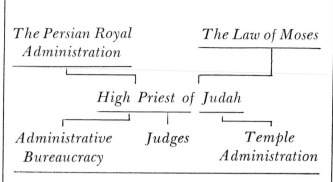

The urban and rural population, especially the peasantry, who supported the entire structure and accepted the Mosaic Law and priestly control, in the belief that their well-being was thus assured.

Plan of the Jewish District, Elephantine (Yeb).

The Jewish theocratic state was strong enough to withstand the various forces of opposition, both domestic and international, which beset her. Thus Sanballat of Samaria built a temple on Mount Gerizim for his son-in-law, Manasseh, grandson of Eliashib the high priest of Jerusalem. This Samaritan shrine and its adherents became in time a festering sore to the Jews of Judea.

The administrative and religious bureaucracies fought constantly for power. On one occasion (about 400 B.C.E.), Bagoas, the governor of Judea, threatened to dismiss Jonathan, the high priest, in favor of the latter's brother, Joshua. Jonathan murdered Joshua in the Temple, and Bagoas used this as a pretext to interfere with the Temple services and the priestly prerogatives.

A pattern of Judaism was being woven in Judea while the Persian empire at large was beginning to show signs of disintegration. The history of the Jewish people, shaped largely by the priests during the rest of the

The following are the priests and Levites who came back with Zerubbabel son of Shealtiel . . . [8]The Levites: Jeshua . . . [10]Jeshua begot Joiakim, Joiakim begot Eliashib, Eliashib begot Joiada, [11]Joiada begot Jonathan, and Jonathan begot Jaddua.

*Nehemiah 12.1-11*

וְאֵלֶּה הַכֹּהֲנִים וְהַלְוִיִּם אֲשֶׁר עָלוּ עִם־זְרֻבָּבֶל
בֶּן־שְׁאַלְתִּיאֵל . . . וְהַלְוִיִּם יֵשׁוּעַ . . . וְיֵשׁוּעַ הוֹלִיד
אֶת־יוֹיָקִים וְיוֹיָקִים הוֹלִיד אֶת־אֶלְיָשִׁיב וְאֶלְיָשִׁיב
הוֹלִיד אֶת־יוֹיָדָע: . . .

נְחֶמְיָה יב: א–יא

One of the sons of Joiada son of the high priest Eliashib was the son-in-law of Sanballat the Horonite; therefore I drove him out from my presence. [29]Remember them, O my God, for having defiled the priesthood, the covenant of the priesthood and the Levites.

*Nehemiah 13.28-29*

וּמִבְּנֵי יוֹיָדָע בֶּן־אֶלְיָשִׁיב הַכֹּהֵן הַגָּדוֹל חָתָן
לְסַנְבַלַּט הַחֹרֹנִי וָאַבְרִיחֵהוּ מֵעָלָי: זָכְרָה לָהֶם
אֱלֹהָי עַל גָּאֳלֵי הַכְּהֻנָּה וּבְרִית הַכְּהֻנָּה וְהַלְוִיִּם:

נְחֶמְיָה יג: כה–כט

## From Josephus, Antiquities of the Jews, *Book XI, Chapters VII and VIII*
### (translation by William Whiston)

#### CHAPTER VII.

*John slays his brother in the Temple—Sanballat.*
*B. C. 332.*

When Eliashib the high priest was dead, his son Judas succeeded in the high-priesthood. And when he was dead, his son John took that dignity; on whose account it was also that Bagoses, the general of another of Artaxerxes' army, polluted the temple, and imposed tributes on the Jews, that out of the public stock, before they offered the daily sacrifices, they should pay for every lamb fifty shekels. Now Jesus was the brother of John, and was a friend of Bagoses, who had promised to procure him the high-priesthood. In confidence of whose support, Jesus quarrelled with John in the temple, and so provoked his brother, that in his anger his brother slew him. Now it was a horrible thing for John, when he was high priest, to perpetrate so great a crime, and so much the more horrible, that there never was so cruel and impious a thing done, neither by the Greeks nor Barbarians. However, God did not neglect its punishment; but the people were on that very account enslaved, and the temple was polluted by the Persians. Now when Bagoses, the general of Artaxerxes' army,

knew that John, the high priest of the Jews, had slain his own brother Jesus in the temple, he came upon the Jews immediately, and began in anger to say to them, "Have you had the impudence to perpetrate a murder in your temple?" And as he was aiming to go into the temple, they forbade him so to do; but he said to them, "Am not I purer than he that was slain in the temple?" And when he had said these words, he went into the temple. Accordingly, Bagoses made use of this pretence, and punished the Jews seven years for the murder of Jesus.

Now when John had departed this life, his son Jaddua succeeded in the high-priesthood. He had a brother whose name was Manasseh. Now there was one Sanballat, who was sent by Darius, the last king [of Persia], into Samaria. He was a Cuthean by birth; of which stock were the Samaritans also. This man knew that the city Jerusalem was a famous city, and that their kings had given a great deal of trouble to the Assyrians, and the people of Coelesyria; so that he willingly gave his daughter, whose name was Nicaso, in marriage to Manasseh, as thinking this alliance by marriage would be a pledge and security that the nation of the Jews should continue their good will to him.

Persian period, was soon to enter a new stage, in the Hellenistic period, when the theocratic state was replaced by a commonwealth, and when the Torah constitution was reinterpreted by the liberal Pharisees in accordance with the new conditions. The Judaism which the Pharisees developed maintained a profound influence on all phases of Jewish life during the more than two thousand years which followed and is a potent factor in Judaism and in Israel today.

## CHAPTER VIII.

*Sanballat and Manasseh build a temple on Mount Gerizzim—Alexander the Great enters Jerusalem. B. C. 335-323.*

About this time it was that Philip, king of Macedon, was treacherously assaulted and slain at Aegea by Pausanias, the son of Cerastes, who was derived from the family of Orestae, and his son Alexander succeeded him in the kingdom; who, passing over the Hellespont, overcame the generals of Darius's army, in a battle fought at Granicum. So he marched over Lydia, and subdued Ionia, and overran Caria, and fell upon the places of Pamphylia, as has been related elsewhere.

But the elders of Jerusalem being very uneasy that the brother of Jaddua, the high priest, though married to a foreigner, should be a partner with him in the high-priesthood, quarrelled with him; for they esteemed this man's marriage a step to such as should be desirous of transgressing about the marriage of [strange] wives, and that this would be the beginning of a mutual society with foreigners, although the offence of some about marriages, and their having married wives that were not of their own country, had been an occasion of their former captivity, and of the miseries they then underwent; so they commanded Manasseh to divorce his wife, or not to approach the altar, the high priest himself joining with the people in their indignation against his brother, and driving him away from the altar. Whereupon Manasseh came to his father-in-law, Sanballat, and told him, that although he loved his daughter Nicaso, yet was he not willing to be deprived of his sacerdotal dignity on her account, which was the principal dignity in their nation, and always continued in the same family. And then Sanballat promised him not only to preserve to him the honour of his priesthood, but to procure for him the power and dignity of a high priest, and would make him governor of all the places he himself now ruled, if he would keep his daughter for his wife. He also told him further, that he would build him a temple like that at Jerusalem, upon Mount Gerizzim, which is the highest of all the mountains that are in Samaria; and he promised that he would do this with the approbation of Darius the king. Manasseh was elevated with these promises, and stayed with Sanballat, upon a supposition that he should gain a high-priesthood, as bestowed on him by Darius, for it happened Sanballat was then in years. But there was now a great disturbance among the people of Jerusalem, because many of those priests and Levites were entangled in such matches; for they all revolted to Manasseh, and Sanballat afforded them money, and divided among them land for tillage, and habitations also; and all this in order every way to gratify his son-in-law.

# Chapter VII

# THE HEBRAIC SPIRIT:
# THE PROPHETIC MOVEMENT AND SOCIAL JUSTICE

THE prophetic movement forms the climax of Biblical history. Not only was nothing comparable produced by any of the other Near Eastern civilizations of antiquity, but not even the heirs of the Hebraic tradition itself again equaled the power and eloquence of this great moral outburst. Moreover, its influence has followed the spread of, and dominated the development of, the three great world religions, Judaism, Christianity, and Islam, to such extent that for twenty centuries, over nearly half the land surface of the globe, the consciences of civilized men have spoken with the accents of the prophets. The atheistic socialists of the nineteenth century, who scorned all revealed religion, acknowledged the prophets as the first social reformers and the source of their own new doctrine. Even rationalist and skeptical schol-

ars of the period, who rejected nearly every part of the Bible as unhistorical, recognized the greatness of the prophets, the validity of their teaching, and the power of their eloquence.

## The Rise of the Prophetic Movement

The Hebrew word for "prophet" is *nabi,* but its original meaning is not known. It would seem that *nabi* in the Bible meant approximately "spokesman," as when the Lord told Moses, "Your brother Aaron shall be your spokesman" (Exodus 7:1; and compare the parallel statement in 4:16). That is how the Jews themselves translated *nabi* in the oldest Greek translation of the Pentateuch, the Septuagint, about 200 B.C.E.; and the Greek word which was there employed,

248

# The Rise of the Prophetic Movement

The Lord said to Moses, "See, I place you in the role of God to Pharaoh, with your brother Aaron as your spokesman. [lit. prophet]."

*Exodus 7.1*

וַיֹּאמֶר יְהֹוָה אֶל־מֹשֶׁה רְאֵה נְתַתִּיךָ אֱלֹהִים לְפַרְעֹה וְאַהֲרֹן אָחִיךָ יִהְיֶה נְבִיאֶךָ:

שְׁמוֹת ז : א

He shall speak for you to the people and thus serve as your spokesman, with you playing the role of God to him.

*Exodus 4.16*

וְדִבֶּר־הוּא לְךָ אֶל־הָעָם וְהָיָה הוּא יִהְיֶה־לְּךָ לְפֶה וְאַתָּה תִּהְיֶה־לּוֹ לֵאלֹהִים:

שְׁמוֹת ד : טז

Elkanah returned to his home in Ramah, and the lad (Samuel) became an attendant of the Lord under Eli the priest.

*I Samuel 2.11*

וַיֵּלֶךְ אֶלְקָנָה הָרָמָתָה עַל־בֵּיתוֹ וְהַנַּעַר הָיָה מְשָׁרֵת אֶת־יְהֹוָה אֶת־פְּנֵי עֵלִי הַכֹּהֵן:

שְׁמוּאֵל א׳, ב : יא

In the past in Israel, when a man went to inquire of God, he would say, "Come, let us go to the seer"; for the prophet of today was called seer in the past.

*I Samuel 9.9*

לְפָנִים בְּיִשְׂרָאֵל כֹּה־אָמַר הָאִישׁ בְּלֶכְתּוֹ לִדְרוֹשׁ אֱלֹהִים לְכוּ וְנֵלְכָה עַד־הָרֹאֶה כִּי לַנָּבִיא הַיּוֹם יִקָּרֵא לְפָנִים הָרֹאֶה:

שְׁמוּאֵל א׳ ט : ט

The word of the Lord came to the prophet Gad, David's seer, as follows.

*II Samuel 24.11*

...וּדְבַר־יְהֹוָה הָיָה אֶל־גָּד הַנָּבִיא חֹזֵה דָוִד לֵאמֹר:

שְׁמוּאֵל ב׳, כד : יא

249

*prophetes,* "declarer" or "interpreter," is the source of the English word "prophet." Indeed, it appears that the word "prophet" in English, at least until the time of Queen Elizabeth, meant simply "forthteller," or "preacher"; the meaning "foretelling," "predicting," is a later development. The prophet spoke for God, and interpreted His word and will to his fellow Israelites.

The prophetic movement in Israel developed in two distinct stages. In the earlier phase, the Biblical prophets were essentially no different from the priest-diviners common to the ancient Near East in general. In fact, the Bible itself states explicitly, in an editorial gloss at I Samuel 9:9, "Previously in Israel, when a person went to inquire of God, thus he said, 'Come, let us go to the seer'; for he who is now called a prophet was previously called a seer." Samuel the prophet was called a "seer" and "a man of God"; and he was no less a priest than his mentor, "Eli the priest" (I Samuel 2:11). And in II Samuel 24:11 we read that "the word of the Lord came to the prophet Gad, David's visionary [or, seer]."

Soothsayers, seers, miracle workers—that is, priests who divined by magic formula, who gave out oracular utterances, who professed expertness in transmitting the supernatural—were a definite social group in the ancient civilizations of the Near East. Ecstasy, frenzy, the examination of the liver and entrails of animals, the flight of birds, the interpretation of dreams, astrology, the casting of lots, divination by water—all these were the property and trademark of the priestly and related guilds from the Euphrates to the Nile. For the seers of antiquity were organized in guilds, which had set rules governing masters and apprentices, as surely as if they were stonemasons. These craftsmen in the supernatural worked both in groups and as individuals.

Cuneiform texts recently discovered at Mari, dating from the eighteenth century B.C.E., illustrate this earlier stage in Biblical prophecy. One describes how a deputation of priests advises the king to pay more attention to the gods that they represent, and to the sanctuary that they make it their business to tend. Another text, this one from Egypt and dating back to about 1100 B.C.E., illustrates how holy men resorted to states of frenzy in order to "divine." This text tells us that when the king of Byblos "was sacrificing to his gods, the god seized one of his great boys and made him frenzied. And he said to him, 'Bring up the god! Bring up the messenger who is carrying him! It is Amon who has sent him; he it is who made him come!'" (J. A. Wilson, in *Ancient Near Eastern Texts,* ed. J. B. Pritchard [Princeton, 1950], p. 26. Wilson notes, "The determinative (sign) of the word for [prophetically] possessed (or frenzied) shows a human figure in violent motion or epileptic convulsion.")

Divine seizures and frenzies are reported of Biblical prophecy in its formative stage, often in a context which suggests the existence of recognized soothsayer or seer groups specializing in the invocation of hysterical trances. For example, shortly after Saul was anointed king by Samuel, he ran into a "band of prophets coming down from the shrine, led by harp, tambourine, flute, and lyre . . . and the spirit of God rushed upon him, and he prophesied among them" (I Samuel 10:5–11). In fact, it seems probable that the early prophets were all to some degree professional soothsayers. Several, Nathan, Gad, and Iddo, for example, were attached to the royal court, just as the priests, the tax-collectors, the commander-in-chief of the army, and other royal functionaries. Others, like Samuel of Ramah and Ahijah of Shiloh, were attached to sanctuaries outside of Jerusalem; and in this early

[And Samuel said to Saul:] 5"Afterwards you will reach Gibeah of God, where the Philistine garrisons are stationed; and as you enter the town, you will encounter there a band of prophets coming down from the sanctuary, led by harp, tambourine, flute, and lyre, and they will be prophesying. 6The spirit of the Lord will rush upon you, and you shall prophesy with them; you shall become a new [lit. another] man . . ." 9 And when [Saul] turned around [lit. his shoulders] to walk away from Samuel, God gave him a new heart, and all those signs happened that day. 10When he reached that spot in Gibeah, he met a band of prophets coming toward him; the spirit of God rushed upon him, and he began to prophesy along with them. 11And when all who knew him previously saw him prophesying with the prophets, the people said to one another, "What has come over the son of Kish? Is Saul also among the prophets?"

*I Samuel 10.5-11*

[Elijah said to King Ahab of Israel:] 19Now order all Israel to join me at Mount Carmel, together with the 450 prophets of Baal and the 400 prophets of Asherah, who eat at Jezebel's table [i.e., are maintained by the Queen]. 20Ahab sent orders to all the Israelites and gathered the prophets at Mount Carmel. 21Elijah approached all the people and said, "How long will you keep hopping between two opinions? If the Lord is God, follow Him; and if Baal, follow him!" But the people answered him not a word. 22Then Elijah said to the people, "I am the only prophet of the Lord left, while the prophets of Baal number 450". . . . 36When it was time to present the meal offering, Elijah the prophet came forward and said, " . . . 37Answer me, O Lord, answer me, that this people may know that You, O Lord, are God. . . ." 38Then fire from the Lord descended and consumed the meal offering . . . 39When they saw this, all the people flung themselves on their faces and cried out, "The Lord alone is God! The Lord alone is God!"

*I Kings 18.19-39*

אַחַר כֵּן תָּבוֹא אֶל־גִּבְעַת הָאֱלֹהִים אֲשֶׁר־שָׁם
נְצִבֵי פְלִשְׁתִּים וִיהִי כְבֹאֲךָ שָׁם הָעִיר וּפָגַעְתָּ חֶבֶל
נְבִיאִים יֹרְדִים מֵהַבָּמָה וְלִפְנֵיהֶם נֵבֶל וְתֹף וְחָלִיל
וְכִנּוֹר וְהֵמָּה מִתְנַבְּאִים: וְצָלְחָה עָלֶיךָ רוּחַ יְהוָה
וְהִתְנַבִּיתָ עִמָּם וְנֶהְפַּכְתָּ לְאִישׁ אַחֵר:... וְהָיָה
כְהַפְנֹתוֹ שִׁכְמוֹ לָלֶכֶת מֵעִם שְׁמוּאֵל וַיַּהֲפָךְ־לוֹ
אֱלֹהִים לֵב אַחֵר וַיָּבֹאוּ כָּל־הָאֹתוֹת הָאֵלֶּה בַּיּוֹם
הַהוּא: וַיָּבֹאוּ שָׁם הַגִּבְעָתָה וְהִנֵּה חֶבֶל־נְבִיאִים
לִקְרָאתוֹ וַתִּצְלַח עָלָיו רוּחַ אֱלֹהִים וַיִּתְנַבֵּא
בְּתוֹכָם: וַיְהִי כָּל־יוֹדְעוֹ מֵאִתְּמוֹל שִׁלְשֹׁם וַיִּרְאוּ
וְהִנֵּה עִם־נְבִאִים נִבָּא וַיֹּאמֶר הָעָם אִישׁ אֶל־רֵעֵהוּ
מַה־זֶּה הָיָה לְבֶן־קִישׁ הֲגַם שָׁאוּל בַּנְּבִיאִים:

שְׁמוּאֵל א', י': ה–יא

וְעַתָּה שְׁלַח קְבֹץ אֵלַי אֶת־כָּל־יִשְׂרָאֵל אֶל־
הַר הַכַּרְמֶל וְאֶת־נְבִיאֵי הַבַּעַל אַרְבַּע מֵאוֹת
וַחֲמִשִּׁים וּנְבִיאֵי הָאֲשֵׁרָה אַרְבַּע מֵאוֹת אֹכְלֵי שֻׁלְחַן
אִיזָבֶל: וַיִּשְׁלַח אַחְאָב בְּכָל־בְּנֵי יִשְׂרָאֵל וַיִּקְבֹּץ
אֶת־הַנְּבִיאִים אֶל־הַר הַכַּרְמֶל: וַיִּגַּשׁ אֵלִיָּהוּ אֶל־
כָּל־הָעָם וַיֹּאמֶר עַד־מָתַי אַתֶּם פֹּסְחִים עַל־שְׁתֵּי
הַסְּעִפִּים אִם־יְהוָה הָאֱלֹהִים לְכוּ אַחֲרָיו וְאִם־
הַבַּעַל לְכוּ אַחֲרָיו וְלֹא־עָנוּ הָעָם אֹתוֹ דָּבָר:
וַיֹּאמֶר אֵלִיָּהוּ אֶל־הָעָם אֲנִי נוֹתַרְתִּי נָבִיא לַיהוָה
לְבַדִּי וּנְבִיאֵי הַבַּעַל אַרְבַּע־מֵאוֹת וַחֲמִשִּׁים אִישׁ:...
וַיְהִי | בַּעֲלוֹת הַמִּנְחָה וַיִּגַּשׁ אֵלִיָּהוּ הַנָּבִיא וַיֹּאמַר...
עֲנֵנִי יְהוָה עֲנֵנִי וְיֵדְעוּ הָעָם הַזֶּה כִּי־אַתָּה יְהוָה
הָאֱלֹהִים... וַתִּפֹּל אֵשׁ־יְהוָה וַתֹּאכַל אֶת־הָעֹלָה...
וַיַּרְא כָּל־הָעָם וַיִּפְּלוּ עַל־פְּנֵיהֶם וַיֹּאמְרוּ יְהוָה
הוּא הָאֱלֹהִים יְהוָה הוּא הָאֱלֹהִים:

מְלָכִים א', יח: יט–לט

*For a detailed discussion of the diviner as distinct from the literary prophet, see H. M. Orlinsky, "The Seer-Priest," cited on p. 19 above.*

stage, they frequently worked in groups. Samuel himself was head of such a "band of prophets" as Saul had met (I Samuel 19:20). When Jezebel murdered "the prophets of the Lord," one of her officials, Obadiah, saved the lives of one hundred of them (I Kings 18:4). In the days of Elijah and Elisha there is frequent mention of groups of prophets of the Lord, among them the groups located at Jericho and Bethel. (cf., e.g., I Kings 20:35 ff.; 22:6, 10; II Kings 2:3, 5; 4:1; 6:1.) On another occasion four hundred "prophets of the Lord" were summoned by Jehoshaphat of Judah and the king of Israel to interpret God's will in regard to an attack on Ramoth-gilead (I Kings 22:6). This incident recalls the 450 prophets of Baal and the 400 prophets of Asherah who contested with Elijah's God on Mount Carmel (I Kings 18).

Among the earlier priest-diviners, it was also characteristic to transmit the craft from generation to generation. Elijah trained Elisha and invested him as his successor (II Kings 2, a dramatic chapter), and before them, Jehu the prophet was the father of Hanani the seer (I Kings 16:1,7; II Chronicles 16:7–10). Likewise, nearly all performed miracles, as Moses did before Pharaoh to convince him that the God of the Hebrews was supreme. Samuel was a seer; and the prophets Elijah and Elisha freely worked miracles of various kinds.

## From Miracle to Rhapsody

In the eighth century, however, divination and miracle working were virtually eliminated from the prophetic tradition in Israel. Seers such as Samuel and miracle workers like Elijah and Elisha ceased to be the norm. The ecstatic element continued, but the prophets began to utilize and perfect another medium by which to convince their fellow Israelites of the truth of their teachings. To achieve this effect they began to rely more and more on the eloquence and logic of their literary compositions.

The development from the miracle-working to the rhapsodic stage of prophecy was not peaceful and evolutionary. The literary prophets were opposed to the diviner-prophet guilds, to the practice of prophecy as a craft, and to the idea that any person could be taught by the masters how to "prophesy."

There is no evidence that any of the later literary prophets functioned in groups or that they were heads or members of guilds or that they produced disciples. They were not representatives of any court or sanctuary, nor did they practice prophecy as a regular occupation or a way to earn a living. Instead, they felt themselves inspired directly by God, and only when God and the occasion demanded, as Amos insisted (in the eighth century): "For the Lord God does nothing without revealing His counsel to His servants the prophets. . . . The Lord God has spoken, who can help but prophesy!" (Amos 3:7–8). Thus when the chief priest at Bethel contemptuously dismissed Amos and told him to go back to his native Judah to make a living there from his craft, Amos was stung to protest, "I am not a [professional] prophet nor a member of a prophetic guild [literally, the son of a prophet]; but I am a herdsman, and a dresser of sycamore trees" (7:12 ff.). In time, the literary prophets came to scorn the priest-diviners—who were largely functionaries of local shrines or of the royal court—and they saw only themselves as the true spokesmen of God.

It should not be overlooked that several of the earlier "prophets" had produced important literary compositions. Thus we are told in I Chronicles 29:29: "The acts of King David, first and last, are written in the account of Samuel the seer, and the account of Nathan the prophet, and the account of Gad

As they were crossing, Elijah said to Elisha, "Ask, what shall I do for you before I am taken from you?" Elisha answered, "Let a double portion of your spirit descend upon me." [10]"You have asked a difficult thing," he answered. "If you see me being taken away from you, it shall be so for you; if you do not, it shall not be so." [11]They were walking along and talking, when suddenly a fiery chariot with fiery horses came between the two of them, and Elijah ascended in a whirlwind into heaven. [12]As Elisha saw this, he cried out, "O father, father! O chariotry of Israel and its horsemen!" And he saw him no more. . . . [14]Then he picked up Elijah's mantle, which had fallen from him, and struck the water . . . and it parted to either side, and Elisha crossed over. [15]When the prophets saw him . . . they said, "The spirit of Elijah has descended on Elisha." Then they came up to meet him, and prostrated themselves before him to the ground.

*II Kings 2.9-15*

וַיְהִי כְעָבְרָם וְאֵלִיָּהוּ אָמַר אֶל־אֱלִישָׁע שְׁאַל
מָה אֶעֱשֶׂה־לָּךְ בְּטֶרֶם אֶלָּקַח מֵעִמָּךְ וַיֹּאמֶר אֱלִישָׁע
וִיהִי־נָא פִּי־שְׁנַיִם בְּרוּחֲךָ אֵלָי: וַיֹּאמֶר הִקְשִׁיתָ
לִשְׁאוֹל אִם־תִּרְאֶה אֹתִי לֻקָּח מֵאִתָּךְ יְהִי־לְךָ כֵן
וְאִם־אַיִן לֹא יִהְיֶה: וַיְהִי הֵמָּה הֹלְכִים הָלוֹךְ וְדַבֵּר
וְהִנֵּה רֶכֶב־אֵשׁ וְסוּסֵי אֵשׁ וַיַּפְרִדוּ בֵּין שְׁנֵיהֶם וַיַּעַל
אֵלִיָּהוּ בַּסְעָרָה הַשָּׁמָיִם: וֶאֱלִישָׁע רֹאֶה וְהוּא מְצַעֵק
אָבִי אָבִי רֶכֶב יִשְׂרָאֵל וּפָרָשָׁיו וְלֹא רָאָהוּ עוֹד...
וַיִּקַּח אֶת־אַדֶּרֶת אֵלִיָּהוּ אֲשֶׁר נָפְלָה מֵעָלָיו וַיַּכֶּה
אֶת־הַמַּיִם... וַיֵּחָצוּ הֵנָּה וָהֵנָּה וַיַּעֲבֹר אֱלִישָׁע:
וַיִּרְאֻהוּ בְנֵי־הַנְּבִיאִים... וַיֹּאמְרוּ נָחָה רוּחַ אֵלִיָּהוּ
עַל־אֱלִישָׁע וַיָּבֹאוּ לִקְרָאתוֹ וַיִּשְׁתַּחֲווּ־לוֹ אָרְצָה:

מְלָכִים ב', ב: ט-טו

## From Miracle to Rhapsody

Indeed, the Lord God does nothing without having revealed His plan to His servants the prophets. [8]A lion has roared, / Who can but fear? / The Lord God has spoken, / Who can but prophesy?

*Amos 3.7-8*

כִּי לֹא יַעֲשֶׂה אֲדֹנָי יֱהֹוִה דָּבָר כִּי אִם־גָּלָה סוֹדוֹ
אֶל־עֲבָדָיו הַנְּבִיאִים: אַרְיֵה שָׁאָג מִי לֹא יִירָא אֲדֹנָי
יֱהֹוִה דִּבֶּר מִי לֹא יִנָּבֵא:

עָמוֹס ג: ז-ח

But Amos replied to Amaziah, "I am not a prophet nor a member of a prophetic guild. I am but a herdsman, and a dresser of sycamore trees."

*Amos 7.14*

וַיַּעַן עָמוֹס וַיֹּאמֶר אֶל־אֲמַצְיָה לֹא־נָבִיא
אָנֹכִי וְלֹא בֶן־נָבִיא אָנֹכִי כִּי־בוֹקֵר אָנֹכִי וּבוֹלֵס
שִׁקְמִים:

עָמוֹס ז: יד

The acts of King David, from first to last, are recorded in the account of Samuel the seer, in the account of Nathan the prophet, and in the account of Gad the visionary.

*I Chronicles 29.29*

וְדִבְרֵי דָוִיד הַמֶּלֶךְ הָרִאשֹׁנִים וְהָאַחֲרֹנִים הִנָּם
כְּתוּבִים עַל־דִּבְרֵי שְׁמוּאֵל הָרֹאֶה וְעַל־דִּבְרֵי
נָתָן הַנָּבִיא וְעַל־דִּבְרֵי גָּד הַחֹזֶה:

דִּבְרֵי הַיָּמִים א', כט: כט

The rest of the acts of King Solomon, from first to last, are recorded in the account of Nathan the prophet, in the account [lit. prophesy] of Ahijah the Shilonite, and in the account [lit., visions] of Iddo [lit. Jedo] the seer, concerning Jeroboam son of Nebat.

*II Chronicles 9.29*

וּשְׁאָר דִּבְרֵי שְׁלֹמֹה הָרִאשֹׁנִים וְהָאַחֲרוֹנִים הֲלֹא־
הֵם כְּתוּבִים עַל־דִּבְרֵי נָתָן הַנָּבִיא וְעַל־נְבוּאַת
אֲחִיָּה הַשִּׁילוֹנִי וּבַחֲזוֹת יֶעְדִּי הַחֹזֶה עַל־יָרָבְעָם בֶּן־
נְבָט:

דִּבְרֵי הַיָּמִים ב', ט: כט

253

the visionary." Similar accounts of Solomon's reign were written by the prophets Nathan and Ahijah, of Jeroboam's reign by Iddo the seer, and of Jehoshaphat's reign by Jehu the seer (II Chronicles 9:29; 20:34).

Nevertheless, the later prophets fully merit the characterization of "literary" or "rhapsodic," to distinguish them from their predecessors. This title, however, must not be allowed to obscure the important fact that this elevation of style reflects a lofty moral and religious experience, liberated from divination. It is this sublimated character which most fundamentally distinguishes the "literary" prophets from their precursors. Amos, Isaiah, Jeremiah, and the others, unlike Ahijah, Elijah, or Jehu, had a broad understanding of the historical situation in which they lived, and their formulations were strikingly eloquent. In the great poetic utterances of the literary prophets, the differences of degree unmistakably merge into a significant difference of kind.

All the later prophets—Amos, Hosea, Joel, Isaiah, Zechariah, the Second Isaiah, and so on—transmitted God's word directly to the people. Such "men of God," who were also "men of the hour," are unknown anywhere in the ancient world except in Israel. They were the products and the representatives of social strata, it is true, but quite unconnected with any vested religious group, archaic or otherwise.

## The Prophetic Concept of Social Justice: The Covenant and the Law

The prophets, the earlier as well as the later, took their stand on two fundamental ideas: first, that there was a covenant between God and His people Israel, and second, that this covenant bound the Israelites to a completely legal-moral relationship one to the other. It will be recalled that the patriarchs,

individually, had entered into the covenant with God so that they would worship Him only and that He would protect them. This personal covenant was broadened in the period of Moses, as a consequence of the Exodus from Egypt, so that the entire population of Israel became God's chosen people to recognize and serve Him as the only God in the world. This Covenant, it should be noted carefully, was voluntary on both sides. God elected Israel in His love and grace, and Israel freely undertook to carry out the will of God.

According to the prophets, God agreed, for His part, to reward His faithful people in the land of Israel with economic prosperity, good health, and peace from all enemies (Deuteronomy 7:12 ff.; and elsewhere). When Israel prospered, therefore, it could be assumed that her people had found favor in the sight of the Lord, and prophetic activity was consequently at a minimum. When, however, a difficulty arose or threatened to appear, it was a sure sign that Israel had transgressed against the Covenant and that God was punishing His people. It was in such times of crisis and distress that the prophets undertook to determine and expound the reasons for God's anger and the ways by which the Covenant could be restored.

Since it was not possible for God Himself to transgress the Covenant, the prophets necessarily sought the causes of conflict in the actions of the people. If the leaders or the common folk had worshipped other gods, as in the case of King Manasseh (II Kings 21), the prophets denounced those who practiced or tolerated this abomination. Far more often, however, Israelites broke the Covenant in their relations one with another, and it was such lapses that most frequently provoked the prophets' wrath.

The first obligation laid on the Israelites

And the rest of the acts of Jehoshaphat, from first to last, are recorded in the account of Jehu son of Hanani which is preserved in the annals of the kings of Israel.

*II Chronicles 20.34*

וְיֶ֫תֶר֮ דִּבְרֵ֣י יְהוֹשָׁפָט֒ הָרִאשֹׁנִ֖ים וְהָאַחֲרֹנִ֑ים הִנָּ֣ם כְּתוּבִ֗ים בְּדִבְרֵי֙ יֵה֣וּא בֶן־חֲנָ֔נִי אֲשֶׁ֥ר הֹעֲלָ֖ה עַל־סֵ֥פֶר מַלְכֵ֥י יִשְׂרָאֵֽל׃

דִּבְרֵי הַיָּמִים ב', כ: לד

## The Prophetic Concept of Social Justice: The Covenant and the Law

When the Lord your God brings you to the land that you are about to invade and occupy, and He dislodges many nations before you . . . ³You shall not intermarry with them: do not give your daughters to their sons or take their daughters for your sons. ⁴For they will turn your children away from Me to worship other gods, and the Lord's anger will blaze forth against you and He will promptly wipe you out. ⁵Instead, this what you shall do to them: you shall tear down their altars, smash their pillars, cut down their sacred posts, and consign their images to the fire.

⁶For you are a people consecrated to the Lord your God: of all the peoples on earth the Lord your God chose you to be His treasured people. ⁷It is not because you are the most numerous of peoples that the Lord set His heart on you and chose you—indeed, you are the smallest of peoples; ⁸but it was because the Lord loved you and kept the oath He made to your fathers that the Lord freed you with a mighty hand and rescued you from the house of bondage, from the power of Pharaoh king of Egypt.

⁹Know, therefore, that only the Lord your God is God, the steadfast God who keeps His gracious covenant to the thousandth generation of those who love Him and keep His commandments, ¹⁰but who instantly requites with destruction those who reject Him . . . ¹³He will love you and bless you and multiply you; He will bless the issue of your womb and the produce of your soil, your new grain and wine and oil, the calving of your herd and the lambing of your flock, in the land that He swore to your fathers to give you. ¹⁴You shall be blessed above all other peoples: there shall be no sterile male or female among you or among your livestock. ¹⁵The Lord will ward off from you all sickness; He will not bring upon you any of the dreadful diseases of Egypt, about which you know, but will inflict them upon all your enemies.

*Deuteronomy 7.1-15*

כִּ֤י יְבִיאֲךָ֙ יְהוָ֣ה אֱלֹהֶ֔יךָ אֶל־הָאָ֕רֶץ אֲשֶׁר־אַתָּ֥ה בָא־שָׁ֖מָּה לְרִשְׁתָּ֑הּ וְנָשַׁ֣ל גּוֹיִם־רַבִּ֣ים | מִפָּנֶ֒יךָ֒ . . . וְלֹ֥א תִתְחַתֵּ֖ן בָּ֑ם בִּתְּךָ֙ לֹא־תִתֵּ֣ן לִבְנ֔וֹ וּבִתּ֖וֹ לֹא־תִקַּ֥ח לִבְנֶֽךָ׃ כִּֽי־יָסִ֤יר אֶת־בִּנְךָ֙ מֵאַ֣חֲרַ֔י וְעָבְד֖וּ אֱלֹהִ֣ים אֲחֵרִ֑ים וְחָרָ֤ה אַף־יְהוָה֙ בָּכֶ֔ם וְהִשְׁמִֽידְךָ֖ מַהֵֽר׃ כִּֽי־אִם־כֹּ֤ה תַעֲשׂוּ֙ לָהֶ֔ם מִזְבְּחֹתֵיהֶ֣ם תִּתֹּ֔צוּ וּמַצֵּבֹתָ֖ם תְּשַׁבֵּ֑רוּ וַאֲשֵֽׁירֵהֶם֙ תְּגַדֵּע֔וּן וּפְסִילֵיהֶ֖ם תִּשְׂרְפ֥וּן בָּאֵֽשׁ׃ כִּ֣י עַ֤ם קָדוֹשׁ֙ אַתָּ֔ה לַיהוָ֖ה אֱלֹהֶ֑יךָ בְּךָ֞ בָּחַ֣ר | יְהוָ֣ה אֱלֹהֶ֗יךָ לִהְי֥וֹת לוֹ֙ לְעַ֣ם סְגֻלָּ֔ה מִכֹּל֙ הָֽעַמִּ֔ים אֲשֶׁ֖ר עַל־פְּנֵ֥י הָאֲדָמָֽה׃ לֹ֣א מֵֽרֻבְּכֶ֞ם מִכָּל־הָֽעַמִּ֗ים חָשַׁ֧ק יְהוָ֛ה בָּכֶ֖ם וַיִּבְחַ֣ר בָּכֶ֑ם כִּֽי־אַתֶּ֥ם הַמְעַ֖ט מִכָּל־הָעַמִּֽים׃ כִּי֩ מֵֽאַהֲבַ֨ת יְהוָ֜ה אֶתְכֶ֗ם וּמִשָּׁמְר֤וֹ אֶת־הַשְּׁבֻעָה֙ אֲשֶׁ֤ר נִשְׁבַּע֙ לַאֲבֹ֣תֵיכֶ֔ם הוֹצִ֧יא יְהוָ֛ה אֶתְכֶ֖ם בְּיָ֣ד חֲזָקָ֑ה וַֽיִּפְדְּךָ֙ מִבֵּ֣ית עֲבָדִ֔ים מִיַּ֖ד פַּרְעֹ֥ה מֶֽלֶךְ־מִצְרָֽיִם׃ וְיָ֣דַעְתָּ֔ כִּֽי־יְהוָ֥ה אֱלֹהֶ֖יךָ ה֣וּא הָֽאֱלֹהִ֑ים הָאֵל֙ הַֽנֶּאֱמָ֔ן שֹׁמֵ֧ר הַבְּרִ֣ית וְהַחֶ֗סֶד לְאֹהֲבָ֛יו וּלְשֹׁמְרֵ֥י מִצְוֹתָ֖יו לְאֶ֥לֶף דּֽוֹר׃ וּמְשַׁלֵּ֧ם לְשֹׂנְאָ֛יו אֶל־פָּנָ֖יו לְהַאֲבִיד֑וֹ . . . וַאֲהֵֽבְךָ֖ וּבֵרַכְךָ֣ וְהִרְבֶּ֑ךָ וּבֵרַ֣ךְ פְּרִֽי־בִטְנְךָ֣ וּפְרִֽי־אַדְמָתֶ֗ךָ דְּגָֽנְךָ֤ וְתִירֹֽשְׁךָ֙ וְיִצְהָרֶ֔ךָ שְׁגַר־אֲלָפֶ֖יךָ וְעַשְׁתְּרֹ֣ת צֹאנֶ֑ךָ עַ֚ל הָֽאֲדָמָ֔ה אֲשֶׁר־נִשְׁבַּ֥ע לַאֲבֹתֶ֖יךָ לָ֥תֶת לָֽךְ׃ בָּר֥וּךְ תִּֽהְיֶ֖ה מִכָּל־הָעַמִּ֑ים לֹא־יִהְיֶ֥ה בְךָ֛ עָקָ֥ר וַֽעֲקָרָ֖ה וּבִבְהֶמְתֶּֽךָ׃ וְהֵסִ֧יר יְהוָ֛ה מִמְּךָ֖ כָּל־חֹ֑לִי וְכָל־מַדְוֵי֩ מִצְרַ֨יִם הָרָעִ֜ים אֲשֶׁ֣ר יָדַ֗עְתָּ לֹ֤א יְשִׂימָם֙ בָּ֔ךְ וּנְתָנָ֖ם בְּכָל־שֹׂנְאֶֽיךָ׃

דְּבָרִים ז: א–טו

255

by the Covenant and the law was the worship of the Lord with prayer and sacrifice. The prophets deemed these formal aspects of worship both necessary and good, but they regarded them as valueless unless fraught with sincerity which found expression in daily conduct. Isaiah would not accept lip service as a substitute for active faith and an upright life. He warns on behalf of God in the majestic first chapter of his book (Isaiah 1:13–17):

> Bring no more futile offerings.
> Sacrifice is an abomination to Me . . .
> I cannot endure
> Iniquity and solemn assembly . . .
> When you hold up your hands,
> I will turn My eyes from you;
> Though you multiply prayer,
> I will not listen—
> Your hands are all covered with blood!
> Wash yourselves, cleanse yourselves,
> Put away your evil deeds from My sight.
> Learn to do good:
> Seek out justice,
> Relieve the oppressed,
> Take up the case for the orphan,
> Plead for the widow!

The prophets, from first to last, demanded with stubborn insistence that the people bring their practices to conform with their beliefs. The teachings of the Lord were not fulfilled unless put into daily use among fellow Israelites. Whne Saul disobeyed God's command to destroy all the flocks and herds of the Amalekites and instead offered up the choicest animals as a sacrifice, Samuel is reported to have rebuked him, saying:

> Has the Lord as great delight in burnt offerings and sacrifices
> As in obeying the command of the Lord?
> Behold, to obey is better than sacrifice,
> And to hearken than the fat of rams
>
> [I Samuel 15:22].

Jeremiah denounced mere lip service and empty ritual time and time again, and on one occasion proclaimed:

> **Thus said the Lord of Hosts, the God of Israel:** Add your burnt offerings to your sacrifices, and eat the flesh. For I did not speak to your fathers nor command them when I brought them out of the land of Egypt concerning burnt offerings and sacrifices. But this thing I commanded them, saying, "Obey My commandment, and I will be your God, and you shall be My people; follow only the path that I enjoin upon you, that it may go well with you [Jeremiah 7:21–23].

And Amos, well over a century before Jeremiah, had voiced the same conviction (5:21–24) in his famous exhortation which has been quoted ever since:

> But let justice well up as waters,
> And equity as a mighty stream.

Nowhere else but in ancient Israel has there been found such persistent and insistent emphasis on doing, on carrying out, not merely on believing in, the teachings of God's spokesmen. That is why Micah was able to put in so few words the essence of Biblical Judaism when he said:

> You have been told, O man, what is good
> And what the Lord requires of you:
> Only to do justice
> and to love loyally
> and to walk humbly with your God [Micah 6:8].

This basic principle, that the law had to be obeyed in spirit together with the letter, was summed up even more succinctly in Deuteronomy 16:20, in the three Hebrew words *Tsédek tsédek tirdof*, "Justice, justice shall you pursue." Worship of God by faith alone, or by deeds alone, was an unknown doctrine in the Bible; the letter was inseparable from the spirit, even as the act was inseparable from the faith. The insistence on this point may well have arisen from the fact that, difficult as it is to judge the depth and

Bring no more futile offerings.
Sacrifice is in abomination to Me . . .
I cannot endure
Iniquity and solemn assembly . . .
¹⁵When you hold up your hands,
I will turn My eyes from you;
Though you multiply prayer, I will not listen—
Your hands are all covered with blood!
¹⁶Wash yourselves, cleanse yourselves,
Put away your evid deeds from My sight.
Cease to do evil,
¹⁷Learn to do good:
Seek out justice,
Relieve the oppressed,
Take up the case for the orphan,
Plead for the widow¹

*Isaiah 1.13–17*

And Samuel said:
Has the Lord as great delight in burnt offerings
and sacrifices
As in obeying the command of the Lord?
Behold, to obey is better than sacrifice,
And to hearken than the fat of rams.

*I Samuel 15.22*

Thus said the Lord of Hosts, the God of Israel:
Add your burnt offerings to your sacrifices, and eat
the flesh.²² For I did not speak to your fathers nor
command them when I brought them out of the
land of Egypt concerning burnt offerings or sacri-
fices.²³ But this thing I commanded them, saying,
"Obey My commandment, and I will be your God,
and you shall be My people; follow only the path
that I enjoin upon you, that it may go well with
you.

*Jeremiah 7.21–23*

But let justice well up as waters,
And equity as a mighty stream.

*Amos 5.24*

You have been told, O man, what is good
And what the Lord requires of you:
Only to do justice
And to love loyally
And to walk humbly with your God.

*Micah 6.8*

Justice, justice shall you pursue.

*Deuteronomy 16.20*

לֹא תוֹסִיפוּ הָבִיא מִנְחַת־שָׁוְא קְטֹרֶת תּוֹעֵבָה
הִיא לִי חֹדֶשׁ וְשַׁבָּת קְרֹא מִקְרָא לֹא־אוּכַל אָוֶן
וַעֲצָרָה:... וּבְפָרִשְׂכֶם כַּפֵּיכֶם אַעְלִים עֵינַי מִכֶּם
גַּם כִּי־תַרְבּוּ תְפִלָּה אֵינֶנִּי שֹׁמֵעַ יְדֵיכֶם דָּמִים
מָלֵאוּ: רַחֲצוּ הִזַּכּוּ הָסִירוּ רֹעַ מַעַלְלֵיכֶם מִנֶּגֶד
עֵינָי חִדְלוּ הָרֵעַ: לִמְדוּ הֵיטֵב דִּרְשׁוּ מִשְׁפָּט אַשְּׁרוּ
חָמוֹץ שִׁפְטוּ יָתוֹם רִיבוּ אַלְמָנָה:

יְשַׁעְיָה א: יג–יז

וַיֹּאמֶר שְׁמוּאֵל הַחֵפֶץ לַיהוָה בְּעֹלוֹת וּזְבָחִים
כִּשְׁמֹעַ בְּקוֹל יְהוָה הִנֵּה שְׁמֹעַ מִזֶּבַח טוֹב לְהַקְשִׁיב
מֵחֵלֶב אֵילִים:

שְׁמוּאֵל א', טו: כב

כֹּה אָמַר יְהוָה צְבָאוֹת אֱלֹהֵי יִשְׂרָאֵל עֹלוֹתֵיכֶם
סְפוּ עַל־זִבְחֵיכֶם וְאִכְלוּ בָשָׂר: כִּי לֹא־דִבַּרְתִּי
אֶת־אֲבוֹתֵיכֶם וְלֹא צִוִּיתִים בְּיוֹם הוֹצִיא אוֹתָם
מֵאֶרֶץ מִצְרָיִם עַל־דִּבְרֵי עוֹלָה וָזָבַח: כִּי אִם־
אֶת־הַדָּבָר הַזֶּה צִוִּיתִי אוֹתָם לֵאמֹר שִׁמְעוּ בְקוֹלִי
וְהָיִיתִי לָכֶם לֵאלֹהִים וְאַתֶּם תִּהְיוּ־לִי לְעָם
וַהֲלַכְתֶּם בְּכָל־הַדֶּרֶךְ אֲשֶׁר אֲצַוֶּה אֶתְכֶם לְמַעַן
יִיטַב לָכֶם:

יִרְמְיָה ז: כא–כג

וְיִגַּל כַּמַּיִם מִשְׁפָּט וּצְדָקָה כְּנַחַל אֵיתָן:

עָמוֹס ה: כד

הִגִּיד לְךָ אָדָם מַה־טּוֹב וּמָה־יְהוָה דּוֹרֵשׁ מִמְּךָ
כִּי אִם־עֲשׂוֹת מִשְׁפָּט וְאַהֲבַת חֶסֶד וְהַצְנֵעַ לֶכֶת
עִם־אֱלֹהֶיךָ:

מִיכָה ו: ח

צֶדֶק צֶדֶק תִּרְדֹּף...

דְּבָרִים טז: כ

257

sincerity of purely religious devotion, the justice of a man's acts to his fellows was immediately and inescapably apparent in the small tribal society within which the people of Israel lived. When a merchant was discovered cheating a customer in weighing or measuring, his act was regarded not merely as a civil offense against a fellow Israelite, but—much worse—as a breach of the Covenant and an abomination of the Lord (Deuteronomy 25:13–16; Leviticus 19:35–37). This sense of equality, moreover, was so strong that a special warning had to be issued that care should be taken that a person not be favored in court merely because he was poor, any more than one be favored because of his wealth: "You shall judge your neighbor equitably" (Leviticus 19:15).

All the prophets considered all the Israelites to be equal before the Covenant and in the sight of God, be he king or priest, master or servant, rich or poor. It was this inherent equality which imposed on everyone the personal and inescapable obligation to hear, understand, and obey the divine law. To the prophets, therefore, every act of injustice on the part of one Israelite to another, or of one group against another, was an act of transgression against the Covenant and necessarily brought on appropriate punishment. The function of the prophets was to discern any such iniquities in whatever form, and to persuade the transgressors to repent of their sins and to return to God. This equality before the Covenant raised all Israelites to the common dignity of participating in the Covenant with God.

The injunction upon each Israelite to deal equitably with his fellows thereby became more than the defense of rights of property or persons; it became a defense of human dignity. Thus, if a man was to be lashed in punishment for a crime, then the maximum number of stripes was to be forty, "lest, if he

should be flogged further, to excess, your brother be degraded in your presence" (Deuteronomy 25:1–3). And if the law forbade the gleaning of the vineyard and commanded that "it shall go to the sojourner, the fatherless and the widow," it was expressly pointed out that God did so because He wanted the Israelites to remember that they too were once helpless slaves, in Egypt (24:21–22).

It has long been recognized that law played an extremely important part in the life of Israel, but even so, sufficient attention has not always been paid to the essential nature of Israel's laws. They established not only the code of conduct for all Israelites in dealing one with another—and especially the relations between members of the ruling classes and the less powerful—but through this code gave expression to the obligation for just and righteous behavior inherent in the Covenant. The prophets, more than any other group, emphasized the fact that the laws expressed God's will or, as one Psalmist said in praise of God and His Covenant: "Justice and equity are the foundation of Your throne, steadfast love and truth go before You" (Psalm 89:15).

Although the prophets are now usually recognized as the greatest source of inspiration for doctrines of social reform, they were nevertheless reformers within, rather than of, their social system. They supported the existing order and concentrated all their magnificent indignation on the need to infuse the observance of ritual and legal regulations with spiritual integrity and a deep sense of moral justice. It was this emphasis on the spirit of the law which at once provoked the prophets to their greatest denunciations and exhortations and at the same time brought them into conflict with the privileged members of their society. As has generally been the way of the rich and powerful, the privileged Israelites frequently succumbed to the

You shall not have in your pouch alternate weights, larger and smaller. [14]You shall not have in your house alternate measures, a larger and a smaller. [15]You must have completely honest weights and completely honest measures, if you are to endure long on the soil that the Lord your God is giving you. [16]For everyone who does those things, everyone who deals dishonestly, is abhorrent to the Lord your God.

*Deuteronomy 25.13-16*

You shall not falsify measures of length, weight, or capacity. [36]You shall have an honest balance, honest weights, an honest *ephah,* and an honest *hin.* I the Lord am your God who freed you from the land of Egypt. [37]You shall faithfully observe all My laws and all My rules: I am the Lord.

*Leviticus 19.35-37*

You shall not render an unfair decision: do not favor the poor or show deference to the rich; judge your kinsman fairly. [16]Do not deal basely with your countrymen. Do not profit by the blood of your fellow: I am the Lord.

[17]You shall not hate your kinsman in your heart. Reprove your kinsman, but incur no guilt because of him. [18]You shall not take vengeance or bear a grudge against your countrymen. Love your fellow as yourself: I am the Lord.

*Leviticus 19.15-18*

When there is a dispute between men and they go to law, and a decision is rendered declaring the one in the right and the other in the wrong—[2]if the guilty one is to be flogged, the magistrate shall have him lie down and be given lashes in his presence, by count, as his guilt warrants. [3]He may be given up to forty lashes, but not more, lest being flogged further, to excess, your brother be degraded before your eyes.

*Deuteronomy 25.1-3*

When you beat down the fruit of your olive trees, do not go over them again; that shall go to the stranger, the fatherless, and the widow. [21]When you gather the grapes of your vineyard, do not pick it over again; that shall go to the stranger, the fatherless, and the widow. [22]Always remember that you were a slave in the land of Egypt; therefore do I enjoin you to observe this commandment.

*Deuteronomy 24.20-22*

לֹא־יִהְיֶה לְךָ בְּכִיסְךָ אֶבֶן וָאָבֶן גְּדוֹלָה וּקְטַנָּה: לֹא־יִהְיֶה לְךָ בְּבֵיתְךָ אֵיפָה וְאֵיפָה גְּדוֹלָה וּקְטַנָּה: אֶבֶן שְׁלֵמָה וָצֶדֶק יִהְיֶה־לָּךְ אֵיפָה שְׁלֵמָה וָצֶדֶק יִהְיֶה־לָּךְ לְמַעַן יַאֲרִיכוּ יָמֶיךָ עַל הָאֲדָמָה אֲשֶׁר־יְהוָֹה אֱלֹהֶיךָ נֹתֵן לָךְ: כִּי תוֹעֲבַת יְהוָֹה אֱלֹהֶיךָ כָּל־עֹשֵׂה אֵלֶּה כֹּל עֹשֵׂה עָוֶל:

דְּבָרִים כה: יג–טז

לֹא־תַעֲשׂוּ עָוֶל בַּמִּשְׁפָּט בַּמִּדָּה בַּמִּשְׁקָל וּבַמְּשׂוּרָה: מֹאזְנֵי צֶדֶק אַבְנֵי־צֶדֶק אֵיפַת צֶדֶק וְהִין צֶדֶק יִהְיֶה לָכֶם אֲנִי יְהוָֹה אֱלֹהֵיכֶם אֲשֶׁר־הוֹצֵאתִי אֶתְכֶם מֵאֶרֶץ מִצְרָיִם: וּשְׁמַרְתֶּם אֶת־כָּל־חֻקֹּתַי וְאֶת־כָּל־מִשְׁפָּטַי וַעֲשִׂיתֶם אֹתָם אֲנִי יְהוָֹה:

וַיִּקְרָא יט: לה–לז

לֹא־תַעֲשׂוּ עָוֶל בַּמִּשְׁפָּט לֹא־תִשָּׂא פְנֵי־דָל וְלֹא תֶהְדַּר פְּנֵי גָדוֹל בְּצֶדֶק תִּשְׁפֹּט עֲמִיתֶךָ: לֹא־תֵלֵךְ רָכִיל בְּעַמֶּיךָ לֹא תַעֲמֹד עַל־דַּם רֵעֶךָ אֲנִי יְהוָֹה: לֹא־תִשְׂנָא אֶת־אָחִיךָ בִּלְבָבֶךָ הוֹכֵחַ תּוֹכִיחַ אֶת־עֲמִיתֶךָ וְלֹא־תִשָּׂא עָלָיו חֵטְא: לֹא־תִקֹּם וְלֹא־תִטֹּר אֶת־בְּנֵי עַמֶּךָ וְאָהַבְתָּ לְרֵעֲךָ כָּמוֹךָ אֲנִי יְהוָֹה:

וַיִּקְרָא יט: טו–יח

כִּי־יִהְיֶה רִיב בֵּין אֲנָשִׁים וְנִגְּשׁוּ אֶל־הַמִּשְׁפָּט וּשְׁפָטוּם וְהִצְדִּיקוּ אֶת־הַצַּדִּיק וְהִרְשִׁיעוּ אֶת־הָרָשָׁע: וְהָיָה אִם־בִּן הַכּוֹת הָרָשָׁע וְהִפִּילוֹ הַשֹּׁפֵט וְהִכָּהוּ לְפָנָיו כְּדֵי רִשְׁעָתוֹ בְּמִסְפָּר: אַרְבָּעִים יַכֶּנּוּ לֹא יֹסִיף פֶּן־יֹסִיף לְהַכֹּתוֹ עַל־אֵלֶּה מַכָּה רַבָּה וְנִקְלָה אָחִיךָ לְעֵינֶיךָ:

דְּבָרִים כה: א–ג

כִּי תַחְבֹּט זֵיתְךָ לֹא תְפַאֵר אַחֲרֶיךָ לַגֵּר לַיָּתוֹם וְלָאַלְמָנָה יִהְיֶה: כִּי תִבְצֹר כַּרְמְךָ לֹא תְעוֹלֵל אַחֲרֶיךָ לַגֵּר לַיָּתוֹם וְלָאַלְמָנָה יִהְיֶה: וְזָכַרְתָּ כִּי־עֶבֶד הָיִיתָ בְּאֶרֶץ מִצְרָיִם עַל־כֵּן אָנֹכִי מְצַוְּךָ לַעֲשׂוֹת אֶת־הַדָּבָר הַזֶּה:

temptation to use the law to their advantage; and while insisting most vehemently on the literal observance of ritual and legality, they often failed most significantly to live up to the highest standards implied in the Covenant. It was failings of this sort that provided the prophets with the texts for their most eloquent utterances.

Thus it was not social inequality but social injustice which they denounced, not the existence of rich and poor within the same society but the abuse of the poor by their richer brethren which they decried, not the creation of a new society but the infusion of the Israel they knew with a new spirit which they demanded. Their basic social philosophy rested on the conviction that if the people expressed their faith in God by obeying His commandments in their hearts as well as in their acts, the moral climate of Israel would be purified and the life of her society would be sound.

The alternative was clear. Transgression of justice and rejection of God's will were sure to be followed by swift and terrible punishment meted out by God Himself. Innumerable examples of this divine retribution are recorded in the Bible. Indeed, the frequency with which the prophetic warnings of doom were fulfilled revived, later on, the concept that prophets are foretellers, a concept which the rhapsodic prophets had abandoned. They were imputed to have the power to call down upon the hapless sinner the curse of heaven. To the prophets themselves, however, neither attribution was justified. Punishment was ordained by God, and the recognition that it would follow injustice was not a secret to be divined by a seer but rather the inescapable conclusion of the Covenant.

## The Fate of the Prophets and their Teachings

It was the fate of the prophets, however, that even within this limited context their teachings were not put into practice. The majestic simplicity and vigor of their language, together with their unswerving concentration on the basic elements of the Hebrew faith and moral code, make it all but impossible for their exhortations to be ignored. When, however, a prophet's denunciation of wrongdoing too strongly swayed the oppressed—if not the oppressors—the ruling classes frequently were forced to pay lip service to the prophetic message in order to maintain or strengthen their hold on the people. Thus the writings of Amos were accepted, to become part of Holy Writ, and used by the secular and priestly rulers to strengthen the institutions of law and public worship. Similarly, the so-called Reformation of Josiah, which Jeremiah first supported enthusiastically, provided one more occasion for the use of prophetic teachings in the special interests of the monarchy and the priesthood of Jerusalem. Vehemently, as the prophets demanded the substance of justice for the orphan and the widow, for the weak and the oppressed, the laws of the kingdom continued to punish ritual transgression more regularly and more severely than social injustice. The moral code into which the prophets made such magnificent attempts to breathe the spirit of living justice was one of the noblest and most demanding ever produced by man.

One of the outstanding characteristics of the prophets was the forthrightness and conviction with which they addressed themselves to those Israelites, without the least regard for their rank or power, who flouted or perverted the law. Through this uncompromising vehemence, the prophets continually risked and sometimes suffered abuse and even death at the hands of those they attacked. Indeed, believing that all Israelites

260

At the sound of the horsemen and bowmen
The whole city flees;
They enter the thickets, clamber among the rocks;
The whole city is deserted,
No inhabitant remains there.
<sup>30</sup>And you, who are doomed to ruin,
What do you accomplish by wearing scarlet,
By decking yourself in jewels of gold,
By enlarging your eyes with kohl?
You beautify yourself in vain:
Lovers despise you, they seek your life.
<sup>31</sup>I hear a voice of one in travail,
Anguish as of a woman bearing her first child,
The voice of Fair Zion
Panting, stretching out her hands:
"Alas for me!
I am faint before the murderers!"

*Jeremiah 4.29-31*

מִקּוֹל פָּרָשׁ וְרֹמֵה קֶשֶׁת בֹּרַחַת כָּל־הָעִיר בָּאוּ
בֶּעָבִים וּבַכֵּפִים עָלוּ כָּל־הָעִיר עֲזוּבָה וְאֵין־
יוֹשֵׁב בָּהֶן אִישׁ: וְאַתְּ שָׁדוּד מַה־תַּעֲשִׂי כִּי־תִלְבְּשִׁי
שָׁנִי כִּי־תַעְדִּי עֲדִי־זָהָב כִּי־תִקְרְעִי בַפּוּךְ עֵינַיִךְ
לַשָּׁוְא תִּתְיַפִּי מָאֲסוּ־בָךְ עֹגְבִים נַפְשֵׁךְ יְבַקֵּשׁוּ:
כִּי קוֹל כְּחוֹלָה שָׁמַעְתִּי צָרָה כְּמַבְכִּירָה קוֹל בַּת־
צִיּוֹן תִּתְיַפֵּחַ תְּפָרֵשׂ כַּפֶּיהָ אוֹי־נָא לִי כִּי־עָיְפָה
נַפְשִׁי לְהֹרְגִים:

יִרְמְיָה ד: כט–לא

## The Fate of the Prophets and Their Teachings

Hear this,
Heads of the House of Jacob,
Rulers of the House of Israel,
Who abhor justice
And pervert all equity,
<sup>10</sup>Who build Zion in bloodshed
And Jerusalem in iniquity.
<sup>11</sup>Her heads give verdicts for bribes,
Her priests give instruction for a price,
And her prophets divine for money.
Yet they rely on the Lord, thinking:
Since the Lord is among us,
No harm shall befall us.
<sup>12</sup>Assuredly,
Because of you Zion shall be a plowed field,
Jerusalem a heap of ruins,
And the Temple Mount a wooded height.

*Micah 3.9-12*

שִׁמְעוּ־נָא זֹאת רָאשֵׁי בֵּית יַעֲקֹב וּקְצִינֵי בֵּית
יִשְׂרָאֵל הַמְתַעֲבִים מִשְׁפָּט וְאֵת כָּל־הַיְשָׁרָה יְעַקֵּשׁוּ:
בֹּנֶה צִיּוֹן בְּדָמִים וִירוּשָׁלַם בְּעַוְלָה: רָאשֶׁיהָ
בְּשֹׁחַד יִשְׁפֹּטוּ וְכֹהֲנֶיהָ בִּמְחִיר יוֹרוּ וּנְבִיאֶיהָ בְּכֶסֶף
יִקְסֹמוּ וְעַל־יְהוָה יִשָּׁעֵנוּ לֵאמֹר הֲלוֹא יְהוָה
בְּקִרְבֵּנוּ לֹא־תָבוֹא עָלֵינוּ רָעָה: לָכֵן בִּגְלַלְכֶם
צִיּוֹן שָׂדֶה תֵחָרֵשׁ וִירוּשָׁלַם עִיִּין תִּהְיֶה וְהַר הַבַּיִת
לְבָמוֹת יָעַר:

מִיכָה ג: ט–יב

Equity and justice / Are the foundation of your
throne; / Steadfast love and truth / Go before You.

*Psalm 89.15*

צֶדֶק וּמִשְׁפָּט מְכוֹן כִּסְאֶךָ חֶסֶד וֶאֱמֶת יְקַדְּמוּ
פָנֶיךָ:

תְּהִלִּים פט: טו

261

were equal before the Covenant and in the sight of the Lord, the prophets could hardly have done otherwise than denounce the iniquities of the strong with the same freedom and vigor as those of the weak, and when they suffered it was for their fierce love of the inexorable justice of their God.

Nathan did not hesitate to denounce David the mighty king for his murderous action against Uriah the Hittite (II Samuel 12). Elijah had to flee for his life because of his vehement denunciations of Ahab and Jezebel. Micaiah was hit on the cheek and thrown into prison (I Kings 22:24–27). Amos the Judean risked limb and life when he audaciously invaded the royal sanctuary at Bethel, and he minced no words in telling the royal house and its supporters what lay in store for them as retribution for their rebellion against the Lord. Because he bitterly denounced the domestic and foreign policy of his government, Jeremiah's life was threatened, he was beaten, he was put in stocks, and he was thrown into a dungeon, so that he was constrained to cry out, "And I was like a docile lamb that is led to the slaughter" (Jeremiah 11:19). The Second Isaiah echoed these words when he described himself "as a lamb that is led to the slaughter, and as a sheep that is dumb before her shearers" (Isaiah 53:7). Ezekiel was told by God, "And you, son of man, be not afraid of them, neither be afraid of their words, though briers and thorns be with you and you dwell among scorpions" (Ezekiel 2:6). Uriah the prophet was killed by King Jehoiakim (Jeremiah 26:20–23), and the prophet Zechariah was stoned to death (II Chronicles 24:20–21).

Read in a later time and under wholly altered circumstances, the great denunciations appeared to carry meanings which would have been alien, if not repugnant, to the prophets themselves. The announcements of impending doom, which seldom waited long for fulfilment, suggested to later generations the power of foretelling not only swift retribution but, after that, the precise manner of divine intercession for the ultimate restoration of God's people in the land of Israel. Similarly, these sufferings were read as expiatory sacrifices meekly accepted by the prophets to atone for the iniquities of their people, and finally the prophetic insistence on the equality of all before the Covenant was interpreted as belief in a universality encompassing not merely the children of Israel but all men of all nations.

In the great prophecies of doom one of the most common and impressive themes is the warning to the Israelites that unless they hearkened to the word of the Lord they would suffer defeat and even conquest at the hands of their enemies. Thus in the reigns of Jehoiakim, Jehoiachin, and Zedekiah (about 608–586 B.C.E.), a powerful section of the Judean ruling class wanted to make a pact with Egypt and other countries against Babylonia. Jeremiah, however, openly and uncompromisingly condemned this move as contrary to the will of God and therefore a step toward certain disaster. Instead, he urged a policy of continued cooperation with Babylonia (Jeremiah 25–29; etc.). "Yet you have not listened to Me," Jeremiah said in the name of the Lord, "that you might provoke Me to anger with the work of your hands to your own harm. . . . This whole land shall become a ruin and a waste" (Jeremiah 25: 7 ff.).

The same pattern is evident over a century earlier, about 735 B.C.E., when Isaiah analyzed the efforts of King Pekah of Israel and King Rezin of Aram to force Judah into a coalition against the expanding Assyrian empire (Isaiah 7–8). The prophet advised Judah's government to avoid any such alliance, warning

Then Nathan said to David, "You are the man! Thus said the Lord, the God of Israel: I anointed you king over Israel and I delivered you from the hands of Saul. [8]I gave you possession of [lit. in your bosom] your master's household and your master's wives, and I gave you the House of Israel and Judah; and if that were not enough, I would give you more of the like. [9]Why then have you scorned the word of the Lord, committing wrong in His sight: you have put Uriah the Hittite to the sword and you have taken his wife for yourself . . . [10]Therefore the sword shall never depart from your House. . . ."

*II Samuel 12.7-10*

וַיֹּאמֶר נָתָן אֶל־דָּוִד אַתָּה הָאִישׁ כֹּה־אָמַר יְהוָה אֱלֹהֵי יִשְׂרָאֵל אָנֹכִי מְשַׁחְתִּיךָ לְמֶלֶךְ עַל־יִשְׂרָאֵל וְאָנֹכִי הִצַּלְתִּיךָ מִיַּד שָׁאוּל: וָאֶתְּנָה לְךָ אֶת־בֵּית אֲדֹנֶיךָ וְאֶת־נְשֵׁי אֲדֹנֶיךָ בְּחֵיקֶךָ וָאֶתְּנָה לְךָ אֶת־בֵּית יִשְׂרָאֵל וִיהוּדָה וְאִם־מְעָט וְאֹסִפָה לְּךָ כָּהֵנָּה וְכָהֵנָּה: מַדּוּעַ בָּזִיתָ | אֶת־דְּבַר יְהוָה לַעֲשׂוֹת הָרַע בְּעֵינַי אֵת אוּרִיָּה הַחִתִּי הִכִּיתָ בַחֶרֶב וְאֶת־אִשְׁתּוֹ לָקַחְתָּ לְּךָ לְאִשָּׁה... וְעַתָּה לֹא־תָסוּר חֶרֶב מִבֵּיתְךָ עַד־עוֹלָם...

שְׁמוּאֵל ב', יב : ז–י

And a spirit of God took possession of [lit., clothed] Zechariah son of Jehoiada the priest, and he stationed himself above the people and said to them, "Thus said God: Why do you transgress the commandments of the Lord, for you will not prosper: since you have forsaken the Lord, He has forsaken you." [21]But they plotted against him and, by order of the king, stoned him to death in the court of the House of the Lord.

*II Chronicles 24.20-21*

וְרוּחַ אֱלֹהִים לָבְשָׁה אֶת־זְכַרְיָה בֶּן־יְהוֹיָדָע הַכֹּהֵן וַיַּעֲמֹד מֵעַל לָעָם וַיֹּאמֶר לָהֶם כֹּה | אָמַר הָאֱלֹהִים לָמָה אַתֶּם עֹבְרִים אֶת־מִצְוֹת יְהוָה וְלֹא תַצְלִיחוּ כִּי־עֲזַבְתֶּם אֶת־יְהוָה וַיַּעֲזֹב אֶתְכֶם: וַיִּקְשְׁרוּ עָלָיו וַיִּרְגְּמֻהוּ אֶבֶן בְּמִצְוַת הַמֶּלֶךְ בַּחֲצַר בֵּית יְהוָה:

דִּבְרֵי הַיָּמִים ב', כד : כ–כא

There was also a man prophesying in the name of the Lord, Uriah son of Shemaiah from Kiriath-jearim, who prophesied against this city and against this land the same things as Jeremiah. [21]King Jehoiakim and all his warriors and all the officials heard about his speeches, and the king wanted to put him to death. Uriah heard of this and fled in fear, and came to Egypt. [22]But King Jehoiakim sent men to Egypt . . . [23]who took Uriah out of Egypt and brought him to King Jehoiakim. He had him put to the sword and his body thrown into the burial place of the common people.

*Jeremiah 26.20-23*

וְגַם־אִישׁ הָיָה מִתְנַבֵּא בְּשֵׁם יְהוָה אוּרִיָּהוּ בֶּן־שְׁמַעְיָהוּ מִקִּרְיַת הַיְּעָרִים וַיִּנָּבֵא עַל־הָעִיר הַזֹּאת וְעַל־הָאָרֶץ הַזֹּאת כְּכֹל דִּבְרֵי יִרְמְיָהוּ: וַיִּשְׁמַע הַמֶּלֶךְ יְהוֹיָקִים וְכָל־גִּבּוֹרָיו וְכָל־הַשָּׂרִים אֶת־דְּבָרָיו וַיְבַקֵּשׁ הַמֶּלֶךְ הֲמִיתוֹ וַיִּשְׁמַע אוּרִיָּהוּ וַיִּרָא וַיִּבְרַח וַיָּבֹא מִצְרָיִם: וַיִּשְׁלַח הַמֶּלֶךְ יְהוֹיָקִים אֲנָשִׁים מִצְרָיִם...וַיֹּצִיאוּ אֶת־אוּרִיָּהוּ מִמִּצְרַיִם וַיְבִאֻהוּ אֶל־הַמֶּלֶךְ יְהוֹיָקִים וַיַּכֵּהוּ בֶּחָרֶב וַיַּשְׁלֵךְ אֶת־נִבְלָתוֹ אֶל־קִבְרֵי בְּנֵי הָעָם:

יִרְמְיָה כו : כ–כג

that Israel and her Aramean ally would surely fall. "Behold," he said, "the young woman is with child and is about to give birth to a son; let her call him Immanuel. . . . And before the child knows to reject the bad and choose the good, the land whose two kings you dread shall be deserted" (Isaiah 7:14 ff.).

The historical context makes it clear that the prophets were, in fact, analyzing with extraordinary acumen the balance of forces in the world of the Levant, and urging their conclusions upon their fellow Israelites with the majestic eloquence of their tradition. Read in this light, the reference to the young woman and her child becomes nothing more than a dramatic measure of time, a warning that before the soon-to-be born child will be old enough to know the difference between good and evil, the Lord will bring devastation on Judah's enemies. A similar statement was made by Isaiah in this very connection about his own wife and child, whom he called symbolically Maher-shalal-hash-baz, literally "the spoil speeds, the prey hastens," the double name referring to the two kingdoms of Aram and Israel (Isaiah 8:1–4). Yet when passages of this sort were read in a later and wholly different set of conditions they laid the basis for the common belief that the prophets were foretellers and that their gift was based not merely on their power of analysis of an immediate situation, but that it derived rather from divine inspiration and implied distant and mystical promises.

After the destruction of the Jewish state in 70 C.E., the post-Biblical Jews accepted this concept of prediction as the most significant aspect of prophetic literature. The scrupulous analysis of long-past political and military situations no longer concerned the heirs of the Biblical tradition. The literary power of the prophets was such that their works were still read and increasingly searched for meanings relevant to a new age and a new situation. Warnings of defeat and destruction were no longer meaningful after the Dispersion, and the temptation to find hidden promises of restoration and final triumph was overpowering.

Not only did the Jews of the first and second century C.E. read in the prophets a prediction of the new exile and a second restoration, but the early Christians found in the same source predictions of the coming of Jesus and his messianic role. But just as the dubious quality of prediction was only retroactively associated with the prophetic writings, so too was the concept of messianism improperly projected back into the prophetic writings.

It is true that the prophets believed that God would restore His people Israel to their country under the rule of a descendant of the house of David. Anyone who was chosen by the Lord through His prophets to be ruler of His people was regarded as "His messiah," literally, "His anointed." Thus Saul was the "Lord's anointed" (I Samuel 24:7; and frequently), and so were David and Zedekiah (II Samuel 19:22; Lamentations 4:20). Even King Cyrus of Persia, whom the Second Isaiah recognized as God's agent to destroy Babylonia and restore Israel, is described as "His anointed" (Isaiah 45:1). In every case throughout the Biblical period, the "anointed" person was a human being. And when the physical restoration of Israel was contemplated, it was a scion of David who was to be the ruler, the anointed of the Lord. Thus it was Zerubbabel, of the House of David, who led the Restoration of Judah after the Babylonian Exile.

The idea of a superhuman anointed leader, indeed, the very use of the term "Messiah" (with capital "M"), who would be sent down by God at some distant time to intervene

"Behold," he said, "the young woman is with child and is about to give birth to a son; let her call him Immanuel. . . ."[16] And before the child learns to reject the bad and choose the good, the land whose two kings you dread shall be deserted.

*Isaiah 7.14–16*

הִנֵּה הָעַלְמָה הָרָה וְיֹלֶדֶת בֵּן וְקָרָאת שְׁמוֹ עִמָּנוּ אֵל:...כִּי בְּטֶרֶם יֵדַע הַנַּעַר מָאֹס בָּרָע וּבָחוֹר בַּטּוֹב תֵּעָזֵב הָאֲדָמָה אֲשֶׁר־אַתָּה קָץ מִפְּנֵי שְׁנֵי מְלָכֶיהָ:

יְשַׁעְיָה ז : יד-טז

The Lord said to me, "Take a large scroll and write on it in common script: For Maher-shalal Hash-baz" [or: Spoil hastens, Plunder speeds-- referring to Damascus and Samaria in v.4]. ²I got myself reliable witnesses, Uriah the priest and Zechariah son of Jeberechiah. ³I was intimate with the prophetess [i.e., Isaiah's wife] and she conceived and bore a son; and the Lord said to me, "Name him Maher-shalal Hash-baz. ⁴For before the boy learns to say 'Father' and 'Mother,' the wealth of Damascus and the spoil of Samaria shall be carried off for the king of Assyria."

*Isaiah 8.1-4*

וַיֹּאמֶר יְהוָה אֵלַי קַח־לְךָ גִּלָּיוֹן גָּדוֹל וּכְתֹב עָלָיו בְּחֶרֶט אֱנוֹשׁ לְמַהֵר שָׁלָל חָשׁ בַּז: וְאָעִידָה לִּי עֵדִים נֶאֱמָנִים אֵת אוּרִיָּה הַכֹּהֵן וְאֶת־זְכַרְיָהוּ בֶּן־יְבֶרֶכְיָהוּ: וָאֶקְרַב אֶל־הַנְּבִיאָה וַתַּהַר וַתֵּלֶד בֵּן וַיֹּאמֶר יְהוָה אֵלַי קְרָא שְׁמוֹ מַהֵר שָׁלָל חָשׁ בַּז: כִּי בְּטֶרֶם יֵדַע הַנַּעַר קְרֹא אָבִי וְאִמִּי יִשָּׂא אֶת־חֵיל דַּמֶּשֶׂק וְאֵת שְׁלַל שֹׁמְרוֹן לִפְנֵי מֶלֶךְ אַשּׁוּר:

יְשַׁעְיָה ח : א-ד

Samuel took the jug of oil and poured it on his [Saul's] head, and he kissed him and said to him, "The Lord has just anointed you ruler over His heritage."

*I Samuel 10.1*

וַיִּקַּח שְׁמוּאֵל אֶת־פַּךְ הַשֶּׁמֶן וַיִּצֹק עַל־רֹאשׁוֹ וַיִּשָּׁקֵהוּ וַיֹּאמֶר הֲלוֹא כִּי־מְשָׁחֲךָ יְהוָה עַל־נַחֲלָתוֹ לְנָגִיד:

שְׁמוּאֵל א׳, י : א

But he [David] said to his men, "The Lord forbid that I should do this to my lord [Saul], the Lord's anointed, that I should lift a hand against him: he is the Lord's anointed!"

*I Samuel 24.6*

וַיֹּאמֶר לַאֲנָשָׁיו חָלִילָה לִּי מֵיהוָה אִם־אֶעֱשֶׂה אֶת־הַדָּבָר הַזֶּה לַאדֹנִי לִמְשִׁיחַ יְהוָה לִשְׁלֹחַ יָדִי בּוֹ כִּי־מְשִׁיחַ יְהוָה הוּא:

שְׁמוּאֵל א׳, כד : ו

Abishai son of Zeruiah replied, "Shall not Shimei be put to death for this? He has cursed the Lord's anointed [David]!"

*II Samuel 19.22*

וַיַּעַן אֲבִישַׁי בֶּן־צְרוּיָה וַיֹּאמֶר הֲתַחַת זֹאת לֹא יוּמַת שִׁמְעִי כִּי קִלֵּל אֶת־מְשִׁיחַ יְהוָה:

שְׁמוּאֵל ב׳, יט : כב

The breath of our life, the Lord's anointed,
Was captured in their pits—
He in whose shade we had thought
To live among the nations.

*Lamentations 4.20*

רוּחַ אַפֵּינוּ מְשִׁיחַ יְהוָה נִלְכַּד בִּשְׁחִיתוֹתָם אֲשֶׁר אָמַרְנוּ בְּצִלּוֹ נִחְיֶה בַגּוֹיִם:

אֵיכָה ד : כ

265

directly in behalf of Israel against her oppressors, or in behalf of the righteous against the wicked, is a post-Biblical development in Jewish and Christian circles. Painfully aware that they were unable to cope with the might of Roman imperialism and casting about desperately for comfort and hope in this period of distress and despair, many Jews read back into the Biblical Books the idea and prediction of a superhuman Messiah who would bring deliverance to the Jews at the behest of God. To the Christians, this Messiah was the Christ, which in Greek means "the anointed."

Those who found in the great prophecies the promise of a Messiah tended also to find in the lives of the prophets, with their frequent sufferings, an anticipation of a later, primarily Christian, doctrine of atonement. It became widely assumed that the Second Isaiah, for example, accepted his undeserved suffering meekly and thereby succeeded in sparing his fellow Jews the punishment and doom which was their due for their transgressions against the law and the word of God. According to this doctrine the innocent prophets suffered for the iniquities committed by the people as a whole and served as a substitute for them. There is, however, no basis in the Bible for this principle. It is true that the wickedness of the people was followed by the appearance of the prophets, who as a consequence sometimes suffered abuse; but there is not to be found a single instance in the entire Hebrew Bible where the suffering of a prophet atoned for the sins of a group. Nothing could have been farther from the spirit of the prophetic teachings; that the just and faithful should suffer vicariously, that is, as a substitute, for the unjust and blasphemous, would have been the greatest injustice of all. The prophets insisted on

breathing human warmth and understanding into the law, but they never preached a doctrine which superseded the Covenant and which allowed the sacrifice—in any form—of the innocent in place of the guilty.

By the same canon of justice the prophets frequently found that Israel had suffered sufficient punishment for its sins. Repeated statements to this effect can be found in the Bible; the Second Isaiah himself, for example, far from harboring any notions of vicarious atonement, began his series of unsurpassed compositions to his fellow exiles with this tender consolation:

Comfort, oh comfort My people,
Says your God.
Speak tenderly to Jerusalem
And proclaim to her
That her term of service is completed,
That her iniquity is expiated;
For she has received at the hand of the Lord
Double for all her sins [Isaiah 40:1–2].

The concept of vicarious suffering and atonement, then, derives from and has meaning in post-Biblical times when the Jewish state was destroyed and many Jews exiled from the land by the Roman conqueror. It was then, according to one rabbinic interpretation, that the "servant of the Lord" in Isaiah 53—who is none other than the prophet himself—came to be identified with the people Israel and Israel came to be regarded as God's servant in suffering vicariously for the sins of the gentile world. Christianity, on the other hand, identified the "servant of the Lord" with Jesus. Consequently, the Second Isaiah came to be regarded as the "suffering" servant of the Lord. In reality, he was no more a "suffering" servant than Elijah, or Jeremiah, or Uriah, or Ezekiel. The common term "suffering servant" is wholly unjustified and misleading in this context.

Awake, awake, O Zion!
Clothe yourself in splendor,
Put on your robes of majesty,
Jerusalem, holy city!
For the uncircumsized and the unclean
Shall never enter you again.

*Isaiah 52.1*

עוּרִי עוּרִי לִבְשִׁי עֻזֵּךְ צִיּוֹן לִבְשִׁי בִּגְדֵי
תִפְאַרְתֵּךְ יְרוּשָׁלִַם עִיר הַקֹּדֶשׁ כִּי לֹא יוֹסִיף יָבֹא־
בָךְ עוֹד עָרֵל וְטָמֵא:

יְשַׁעְיָה נב: א

Comfort, oh comfort My people,
Says your God.
²Speak tenderly to Jerusalem
And proclaim to her
That her term of service is completed,
That her iniquity is expiated;
For she has received at the hand of the Lord
Double for all her sins.

*Isaiah 40.1–2*

נַחֲמוּ נַחֲמוּ עַמִּי יֹאמַר אֱלֹהֵיכֶם: דַּבְּרוּ עַל־
לֵב יְרוּשָׁלִַם וְקִרְאוּ אֵלֶיהָ כִּי מָלְאָה צְבָאָהּ
כִּי נִרְצָה עֲוֹנָהּ כִּי לָקְחָה מִיַּד יְהוָה כִּפְלַיִם
בְּכָל־חַטֹּאתֶיהָ:

יְשַׁעְיָה מ: א–ב

He [Second Isaiah] was maltreated, yet he was
   submissive,
He did not open his mouth;
Like a sheep being led to the slaughter,
Like a ewe, dumb before its shearers,
He did not open his mouth.

*Isaiah 53.7*

נִגַּשׂ וְהוּא נַעֲנֶה וְלֹא יִפְתַּח־פִּיו כַּשֶּׂה לַטֶּבַח
יוּבָל וּכְרָחֵל לִפְנֵי גֹזְזֶיהָ נֶאֱלָמָה וְלֹא יִפְתַּח פִּיו:

יְשַׁעְיָה נג: ז

And I [Jeremiah] was like a docile lamb that is
led to the slaughter . . .

*Jeremiah 11.19*

וַאֲנִי כְּכֶבֶשׂ אַלּוּף יוּבַל לִטְבוֹחַ...

יִרְמְיָה יא: יט

*The concept of vicarious suffering, etc., has been dealt with in detail in
H. M. Orlinsky,* The So-Called "Servant of the Lord" and "Suffering
Servant" in Second Isaiah *(= Supplements to Vetus Testamentum, Vol.
XIV, 1967, pp. 1-133). This concept was first applied to Isaiah 53 by
the author of the New Testament Book of Acts (8.1 ff.), and only then
read back into the days of Paul, and Jesus, and finally—with a leap of
over 600(!) years—Isaiah 53.*

Proclaim this among the nations:
  Prepare for [lit. Sanctify] war!
Rouse the warriors,
Let all the soldiers come forward and march.
¹⁰Beat your plowshares into swords
And your pruning hooks into spears.
Let the weakling say, "I am a warrior." . . .
¹²Let the nations rouse themselves,
Let them march to the Valley of Jehoshaphat
   [= "the Lord judges"];
For I will sit in judgment there
Over all the nations round about . . .

קִרְאוּ־זֹאת בַּגּוֹיִם קַדְּשׁוּ מִלְחָמָה הָעִירוּ
הַגִּבּוֹרִים יִגְּשׁוּ יַעֲלוּ כֹּל אַנְשֵׁי הַמִּלְחָמָה: כֹּתּוּ
אִתֵּיכֶם לַחֲרָבוֹת וּמַזְמְרֹתֵיכֶם לִרְמָחִים הַחַלָּשׁ
יֹאמַר גִּבּוֹר אָנִי: ... יֵעוֹרוּ וְיַעֲלוּ הַגּוֹיִם אֶל־עֵמֶק
יְהוֹשָׁפָט כִּי שָׁם אֵשֵׁב לִשְׁפֹּט אֶת־כָּל־הַגּוֹיִם

*(continued)*

## Nationalism and Universality in the Teachings of the Prophets

Another, and perhaps the most important of the concepts anachronistically read back into the tradition of the prophets was the idea that their teachings broadened out until they encompassed all humanity in a common brotherhood. One of the most frequently quoted, and erroneously interpreted, Bible texts is the well-known passage from Malachi: "Have we not all one father? Has not one God created us?" (2:10). But this verse has been wrenched violently out of its original context when it is made to refer to all mankind. Actually, it charges that the Judean priests of God "have corrupted the Covenant" of the Lord (verses 1–9), that all Israel "has profaned the holiness of the Lord" (verse 11), and that the Lord will punish the transgressors. Malachi's meaning is no different at this point than in the first chapter of his Book, where he proposes that the Lord will destroy Edom if they try to rebuild their land.

The prophetic tradition rests squarely on the idea of the Covenant between the Lord and His people Israel. The prophets were concerned directly and exclusively with this "chosen people," and they took notice of other peoples and nations only when the latter came into contact—invariably for bad rather than good—with Judah and Israel. "Hear this word that the Lord has spoken concerning you," Amos said. "You only, have I recognized of all the families of the earth" (3:1–2). The concept of equality between Israel and all other nations would have been incomprehensible to the prophets or their people. It was an idea which could develop only later and under wholly different circumstances and which, not surprisingly, was read back into the prophetic texts by both Jews and Christians when Rome forced the Jews into exile after 70 C.E. and they found themselves adrift in the vast reaches of the Empire.

The land of Israel which the prophets had known was geographically situated at the military crossroads of the ancient Near East. Its population was small and its possibilities of defense slight, with the result that it knew but few extended periods of peace or freedom from fear of Assyria, Aram, Egypt, and Babylonia. The greatest need and desire of Israel was for peace from her neighbors. Her people were not concerned with the international politics or the welfare of Egypt, Moab, or Phoenicia. Their one concern was to be left alone, and it was this overwhelming desire that Isaiah (2:4) and Micah (4:3) expressed in the famous lines:

> And [the Lord] shall judge between the nations,
> He shall render decision for many peoples.
> And they shall beat their swords into plough-
>    shares
> And their spears into pruning-hooks;
> Nation shall not lift up sword against nation,
> Neither shall they learn war any more.

(The prophet Joel [4:9–21; 3:9–21 in the English versions], in keeping with the prophetic tradition, put this passage to equally nationalistic use.)

Read wishfully, this majestic passage might be construed, as it so often has been, to imply a desire for the brotherhood of men and the universal peace on earth. In hard fact, the context excludes this sentimental interpretation. Isaiah and Micah rigidly predicate any such peace on the triumph of Israel. "Out of Zion shall go forth the law," they say, "and the word of the Lord from Jerusalem."

The Second Isaiah, whose outlook is generally regarded as the least exclusivist, consistently proclaimed his strongly national point of view. He assures his fellow exiles:

<sup>14</sup>Multitudes upon multitudes
In the Valley of Decision;
The day of the Lord is at hand
In the Valley of Decision.
<sup>15</sup>The sun and the moon have grown dark,
The stars have dimmed their glow.
<sup>16</sup>The Lord roars from Zion,
And makes His voice heard from Jerusalem;
And heaven and earth quake.
But the Lord is a refuge to His people,
A shelter to the children of Israel.
<sup>17</sup>Thus you shall know that I the Lord am your God,
Whose abode is in Zion, My holy mount.
Jerusalem shall be holy,
No aliens shall ever pass through it again.
<sup>18</sup>In that day . . .
<sup>19</sup>Egypt shall become a desolation
And Edom a desolate wilderness
For the violence done to the people of Judah,
Because of the innocent blood they shed in their land.
<sup>20</sup>But Judah shall be inhabited forever
And Jerusalem throughout the generations.
<sup>21</sup>I will avenge their blood
Which I have not yet avenged.
The Lord abides in Zion.

*Joel 4.9-21*

מִסָּבִיב:... הֲמוֹנִים הֲמוֹנִים בְּעֵמֶק הֶחָרוּץ כִּי
קָרוֹב יוֹם יְהוָֹה בְּעֵמֶק הֶחָרוּץ: שֶׁמֶשׁ וְיָרֵחַ קָדָרוּ
וְכֹכָבִים אָסְפוּ נָגְהָם: וַיהוָֹה מִצִּיּוֹן יִשְׁאָג וּמִירוּשָׁלַםִ
יִתֵּן קוֹלוֹ וְרָעֲשׁוּ שָׁמַיִם וָאָרֶץ וַיהוָֹה מַחֲסֶה לְעַמּוֹ
וּמָעוֹז לִבְנֵי יִשְׂרָאֵל: וִידַעְתֶּם כִּי אֲנִי יְהוָֹה אֱלֹהֵיכֶם
שֹׁכֵן בְּצִיּוֹן הַר־קָדְשִׁי וְהָיְתָה יְרוּשָׁלַםִ קֹדֶשׁ וְזָרִים
לֹא־יַעַבְרוּ־בָהּ עוֹד: וְהָיָה בַיּוֹם הַהוּא... מִצְרַיִם
לִשְׁמָמָה תִהְיֶה וֶאֱדוֹם לְמִדְבַּר שְׁמָמָה תִּהְיֶה מֵחֲמַס
בְּנֵי יְהוּדָה אֲשֶׁר־שָׁפְכוּ דָם־נָקִיא בְּאַרְצָם: וִיהוּדָה
לְעוֹלָם תֵּשֵׁב וִירוּשָׁלַםִ לְדוֹר וָדוֹר: וְנִקֵּיתִי דָּמָם
לֹא־נִקֵּיתִי וַיהוָֹה שֹׁכֵן בְּצִיּוֹן:

יוֹאֵל ד: ט–כא

## Nationalism and Universality in the Teachings of the Prophets

And now, O priests, this charge is for you:
<sup>2</sup>Unless you obey, and unless you lay it to heart, and do honor to My name, said the Lord of Hosts, I will send a curse on you and turn your blessings into curses . . . <sup>8</sup>But you have turned away from the [right] path; you have made many stumble by [your] instruction; you have corrupted the covenant of Levi, said the Lord of Hosts. <sup>9</sup>So I, in turn, make you despised and abased before all the people . . .

<sup>10</sup>Have we not all one father?
Has not one God created us?
Why then are we faithless to one another,
Profaning the covenant of our fathers?
<sup>11</sup>Judah has become faithless, and abomination has been committed in Israel and Jerusalem . . .

*Malachi 2.1-11*

וְעַתָּה אֲלֵיכֶם הַמִּצְוָה הַזֹּאת הַכֹּהֲנִים: אִם־לֹא
תִשְׁמְעוּ וְאִם־לֹא תָשִׂימוּ עַל־לֵב לָתֵת כָּבוֹד לִשְׁמִי
אָמַר יְהוָֹה צְבָאוֹת וְשִׁלַּחְתִּי בָכֶם אֶת־הַמְּאֵרָה
וְאָרוֹתִי אֶת־בִּרְכוֹתֵיכֶם... וְאַתֶּם סַרְתֶּם מִן־הַדֶּרֶךְ
הִכְשַׁלְתֶּם רַבִּים בַּתּוֹרָה שִׁחַתֶּם בְּרִית הַלֵּוִי אָמַר
יְהוָֹה צְבָאוֹת: וְגַם־אֲנִי נָתַתִּי אֶתְכֶם נִבְזִים וּשְׁפָלִים
לְכָל־הָעָם... הֲלוֹא אָב אֶחָד לְכֻלָּנוּ הֲלוֹא אֵל
אֶחָד בְּרָאָנוּ מַדּוּעַ נִבְגַּד אִישׁ בְּאָחִיו לְחַלֵּל בְּרִית
אֲבֹתֵינוּ: בָּגְדָה יְהוּדָה וְתוֹעֵבָה נֶעֶשְׂתָה בְיִשְׂרָאֵל
וּבִירוּשָׁלָםִ...

מַלְאָכִי ב: א–יא

Thus said the Lord God:
I will raise My hand to nations
And lift up My ensign to peoples;
And they shall bring your sons in their bosoms,
And your daughters shall be carried on their
    shoulders.
Kings shall be your attendants,
Their queens your nursing mothers.
Face to the ground they shall bow to you,
They shall lick the dust of your feet.
And you shall know that I am the Lord:
Those who trust in Me shall not be shamed
    [Isaiah 49:22–23].

In a germinal sense, in the sense that he was elementally responsive to the moods and emotions and sufferings of Israel, the Second Isaiah, as the other prophets, came to express many ideas that took on great meaning for later generations of Jews and Christians alike. Yet within his own historical setting these ideas applied only to his own people. "Awake, awake," he says:

Put on your garb of might, O Zion;
Put on your robes of splendor,
Jerusalem, holy city!
For none shall enter you again
Uncircumcised or unclean [Isaiah 52:1].

So speaks the prophet that his own people knew and understood, as they had known and understood Amos, Jeremiah, and the rest before him.

At the same time it would be misleading to leave the impression that the prophets' interest stopped short with their own people Israel and went no further. Tiny Israel, dwelling among other nations, was intimately and constantly affected by their actions, and the prophets' attention was repeatedly called to include them. Believing firmly that their God, the only God in existence, would ultimately deliver them from all threats from other nations, so that no more wars would come upon them, consciously aware that their teachings constituted the only code of laws and life by which man could live, the prophets expressed the conviction that all the peoples of the universe, after they had been through stress and strain at the hands of each other through the will of God, would come to realize that Israel and her religion and her God and His abode on Zion—that these constituted the only proper way of life in the entire world. The gentile peoples of the world would then come eagerly to the mountain of the Lord's House, to the House of the God of Jacob, in order that, in the words of Isaiah (2:3) and Micah (4:2):

He may teach us His ways
So that we may walk in His paths.
For instruction shall come from Zion
And the word of the Lord from Jerusalem.

To Israel, God was the God of Israel alone, that is, He was a national God. At the same time—and naturally so—He was also the God of the universe, the only God in existence in the whole wide world, the only God who ever existed or would ever exist. As God of the universe, He is the sole Creator of all heavenly bodies (sun, moon, stars), of all natural phenomena (lightning, thunder, rain, drought, earthquakes), of sky, earth, and waters, and all living beings, human and animal. All natural phenomena, all heavenly bodies, all living creatures, all peoples—all were subject to His direct supervision and will. So that as the national God of Israel and as the sole God and Master of the universe, He is not the God of any other nation; the God of Biblical Israel is a *national* and *universal* God, not an international God. With no nation or people other than Israel did God ever enter into a legally binding relationship, into a mutually exclusive contract. God was never—so far as the Biblical writers were concerned—the God of Moab, or of

270

In days to come, declares the Lord, I will make a new covenant with the House of Israel and the House of Judah. [32]It will not be like the covenant which I made with their ancestors when I took them by the hand to bring them out of the land of Egypt—a covenant which they have broken . . . [33]For this is the [new] covenant which I will make with the House of Israel . . . I will set My Teaching within them and record it on their hearts: I will be their God and they shall be My people. [34]No one will ever again have to teach his fellow, "Know (or Acknowledge) the Lord"; for all of them, young and old, shall know Me, declares the Lord. I will pardon their iniquity and remember their sin no more.

*Jeremiah 31.31-34*

הִנֵּה יָמִים בָּאִים נְאֻם־יְהֹוָה וְכָרַתִּי אֶת־בֵּית
יִשְׂרָאֵל וְאֶת־בֵּית יְהוּדָה בְּרִית חֲדָשָׁה: לֹא כַבְּרִית
אֲשֶׁר כָּרַתִּי אֶת־אֲבוֹתָם בְּיוֹם הֶחֱזִיקִי בְיָדָם
לְהוֹצִיאָם מֵאֶרֶץ מִצְרַיִם אֲשֶׁר־הֵמָּה הֵפֵרוּ אֶת־
בְּרִיתִי . . .: כִּי זֹאת הַבְּרִית אֲשֶׁר אֶכְרֹת אֶת־בֵּית
יִשְׂרָאֵל . . . נָתַתִּי אֶת־תּוֹרָתִי בְּקִרְבָּם וְעַל־לִבָּם
אֶכְתְּבֶנָּה וְהָיִיתִי לָהֶם לֵאלֹהִים וְהֵמָּה יִהְיוּ־לִי
לְעָם: וְלֹא יְלַמְּדוּ עוֹד אִישׁ אֶת־רֵעֵהוּ וְאִישׁ
אֶת־אָחִיו לֵאמֹר דְּעוּ אֶת־יְהֹוָה כִּי כוּלָּם יֵדְעוּ
אוֹתִי לְמִקְּטַנָּם וְעַד־גְּדוֹלָם נְאֻם־יְהֹוָה כִּי אֶסְלַח
לַעֲוֹנָם וּלְחַטָּאתָם לֹא אֶזְכָּר־עוֹד:

יִרְמְיָהוּ לא:לא–לד

Thus said the Lord,
Who made a road through the sea
And a path through mighty waters;
[17]Who led on chariots and horses,
The whole mighty host—
They sank down together, to rise no more,
They were extinguished, quenched like a wick.
[18]Do not recall what happened of old,
Or ponder what happened of yore.
[19]I am about to do something new,
In a moment it shall sprout up,
You will be sure to perceive it:
I will make a road through the wilderness
And rivers in the desert.

*Isaiah 43.16-21*

[20]The wild beasts shall honor Me,
Jackals and ostriches,
For I provide water in the wilderness,
Rivers in the desert,
To give drink to My chosen people,
[21]The people I formed for Myself,
That they might declare My glory.

כֹּה אָמַר יְהֹוָה הַנּוֹתֵן בַּיָּם דָּרֶךְ וּבְמַיִם עַזִּים
נְתִיבָה: הַמּוֹצִיא רֶכֶב־וָסוּס חַיִל וְעִזּוּז יַחְדָּו יִשְׁכְּבוּ
בַּל־יָקוּמוּ דָּעֲכוּ כַּפִּשְׁתָּה כָבוּ: אַל־תִּזְכְּרוּ רִאשֹׁנוֹת
וְקַדְמֹנִיּוֹת אַל־תִּתְבֹּנָנוּ: הִנְנִי עֹשֶׂה חֲדָשָׁה עַתָּה
תִצְמָח הֲלוֹא תֵדָעוּהָ אַף אָשִׂים בַּמִּדְבָּר דֶּרֶךְ
בִּישִׁמוֹן נְהָרוֹת: תְּכַבְּדֵנִי חַיַּת הַשָּׂדֶה תַּנִּים וּבְנוֹת
יַעֲנָה כִּי־נָתַתִּי בַמִּדְבָּר מַיִם נְהָרוֹת בִּישִׁימֹן
לְהַשְׁקוֹת עַמִּי בְחִירִי: עַם־זוּ יָצַרְתִּי לִי תְּהִלָּתִי
יְסַפֵּרוּ:

יְשַׁעְיָה מג:טז–כא

כֹּה־אָמַר אֲדֹנָי יֱהֹוִה הִנֵּה אֶשָּׂא אֶל־גּוֹיִם יָדִי
וְאֶל־עַמִּים אָרִים נִסִּי וְהֵבִיאוּ בָנַיִךְ בְּחֹצֶן וּבְנֹתַיִךְ
עַל־כָּתֵף תִּנָּשֶׂאנָה: וְהָיוּ מְלָכִים אֹמְנַיִךְ וְשָׂרוֹתֵיהֶם
מֵינִיקֹתַיִךְ אַפַּיִם אֶרֶץ יִשְׁתַּחֲווּ־לָךְ וַעֲפַר רַגְלַיִךְ
יְלַחֵכוּ וְיָדַעַתְּ כִּי־אֲנִי יְהֹוָה אֲשֶׁר לֹא־יֵבֹשׁוּ קֹוָי:

יְשַׁעְיָה מט: כב–כג

וְשָׁפַט בֵּין הַגּוֹיִם וְהוֹכִיחַ לְעַמִּים רַבִּים וְכִתְּתוּ
חַרְבוֹתָם לְאִתִּים וַחֲנִיתוֹתֵיהֶם לְמַזְמֵרוֹת לֹא־
יִשָּׂא גוֹי אֶל־גּוֹי חֶרֶב וְלֹא־יִלְמְדוּ עוֹד מִלְחָמָה:

יְשַׁעְיָה ב: ד; מִיכָה ד: ג

(See facing page for the English translation of Isaiah 49.22–23 and of Isaiah 2.4 and Micah 4.3.)

Ammon, or of Egypt, or of Canaan or Assyria or Babylonia or any other people; He was the God of Israel alone.

Just as Israel was to have no other God, just so was God to have no other people. However, as Master of the universe, God had a legal obligation to all non-Israelite peoples of the world, an obligation that at the same time embraced also all the living creatures of sky, earth, and waters, and all vegetation. After He destroyed the world that had become too wicked to merit preservation, God assured the survivors, Noah and his family, and all the animals with them, and their descendants forever, that never again would He bring destruction upon life on earth (Genesis 8:21–22):

Never again will I doom the earth because of man, since the devisings of man's mind are evil from his youth; nor will I ever again destroy every living being, as I have done.
So long as the earth endures,
Seedtime and harvest,
Cold and heat,
Summer and winter,
Day and night
Shall not cease.

But mankind, in turn, had to respect life, both human and animal life; wanton murder and the unwarranted shedding of blood would not be condoned. As put in Genesis 9:4–10:

You must not, however, eat flesh with its life-blood in it. But for your own life-blood I will require a reckoning: I will require it of every beast; of man, too, will I require a reckoning for human life, of every man for that of his fellow man!
Whoever sheds the blood of man,
By man shall his blood be shed;
For in His image
Did God make man . . .

And God said to Noah and his sons with him, "I now establish My covenant with you and your off-

spring to come, and with every living thing that is with you—birds, cattle, and every wild beast as well —all that have come out of the ark, every living thing on earth."

God further fixed the careers of all heavenly bodies, of the seasons, of the use of animals as food for man, and the like—what we generally subsume under the term "natural law." So that, while no nation other than Israel owes any allegiance to God, and while God has committed and restricted Himself exclusively to the interests of His chosen people Israel, He has the power, as the God of the universe, to interfere in the affairs of all peoples everywhere. He will not tolerate mass murder, unnatural conduct, excessive brutality—such action is contrary to God's ordered universe, to what was aptly called later by the Rabbis the Noahide Laws, laws which are obligatory upon all mankind, as distinguished from the laws that were binding upon Israelites only.

While it was the civilization of Israel which the prophets would advocate for the other nations, and while nothing of the gentile cultures was considered worthy of incorporation into the Israelite way of life, the monotheism of Israel and her prophetic spokesmen did lay the foundation for the later concept of internationalism. Gradually it came to be believed that all mankind, by adopting the principles of Israelite belief and practice— that is by accepting the obligations of the Covenant—might enjoy the fruits of God's bounty in the manner that God promised His own people Israel through His prophets. In this outlook, Biblical Israel and her prophets were unique in the Ancient Near East.

This is the point of Isaiah 19:18–25—considered by most scholars a late passage:

In that day there will be five cities in the land of Egypt which speak the language of Canaan [that

Hear this word that the Lord has spoken concerning you . . . ²You only have I recognized [or acknowledged, singled out] of all the families of the earth.

*Amos 3.1-2*

For the Lord God does nothing without revealing His counsel to His servants the prophets. . . .⁸ The Lord God has spoken, who can help but prophesy!

*Amos 3.7–8*

And you, mortal, do not fear them and do not fear their words, though they are thistles and thorns against you, and you live among scorpions . . .

*Ezekiel 2.6*

Never again will I doom the earth because of man, since the devisings of man's mind are evil from his youth; nor will I ever again destroy every living being, as I have done.

²²So long as the earth endures,
Seedtime and harvest,
Cold and heat,
Summer and winter,
Day and night
Shall not cease.

*Genesis 8.21–22*

You must not, however, eat flesh with its life-blood in it. ⁵But for your own life-blood I will require a reckoning: I will require it of every beast; of man, too, will I require a reckoning for human life, of every man for that of his fellow man!

⁶Whoever sheds the blood of man,
By man shall his blood be shed;
For in His image
Did God make man .

⁷Be fertile, then, and increase; abound on the earth and increase on it."

⁸And God said to Noah and to his sons with him, ⁹"I now establish My covenant with you and your offspring to come, ¹⁰and with every living thing that is with you—birds, cattle, and every wild beast as well—all that have come out of the ark, every living thing on earth.

*Genesis 9.4–10*

שִׁמְעוּ אֶת־הַדָּבָר הַזֶּה אֲשֶׁר דִּבֶּר יְהוָה עֲלֵיכֶם... רַק אֶתְכֶם יָדַעְתִּי מִכֹּל מִשְׁפְּחוֹת הָאֲדָמָה...

עָמוֹס ג: א–ב

כִּי לֹא יַעֲשֶׂה אֲדֹנָי יֱהוִֹה דָּבָר כִּי אִם־גָּלָה סוֹדוֹ אֶל־עֲבָדָיו הַנְּבִיאִים: . . . אֲדֹנָי אֱלֹהִים דִּבֶּר מִי לֹא יִנָּבֵא:

עָמוֹס ג:ז–ח

וְאַתָּה בֶן־אָדָם אַל־תִּירָא מֵהֶם וּמִדִּבְרֵיהֶם אַל־תִּירָא כִּי סָרָבִים וְסַלּוֹנִים אוֹתָךְ וְאֶל־עַקְרַבִּים אַתָּה יוֹשֵׁב...

יְחֶזְקֵאל ב: ו

...לֹא אֹסִף לְקַלֵּל עוֹד אֶת־הָאֲדָמָה בַּעֲבוּר הָאָדָם כִּי יֵצֶר לֵב הָאָדָם רַע מִנְּעֻרָיו וְלֹא־אֹסִף עוֹד לְהַכּוֹת אֶת־כָּל־חַי כַּאֲשֶׁר עָשִׂיתִי: עֹד כָּל־יְמֵי הָאָרֶץ זֶרַע וְקָצִיר | וְקֹר וָחֹם | וְקַיִץ וָחֹרֶף | וְיוֹם וָלַיְלָה | לֹא יִשְׁבֹּתוּ:

בְּרֵאשִׁית ח: כא–כב

אַךְ־בָּשָׂר בְּנַפְשׁוֹ דָמוֹ לֹא תֹאכֵלוּ: וְאַךְ אֶת־דִּמְכֶם לְנַפְשֹׁתֵיכֶם אֶדְרֹשׁ מִיַּד כָּל־חַיָּה אֶדְרְשֶׁנּוּ וּמִיַּד הָאָדָם מִיַּד אִישׁ אָחִיו אֶדְרֹשׁ אֶת־נֶפֶשׁ הָאָדָם: שֹׁפֵךְ דַּם הָאָדָם בָּאָדָם דָּמוֹ יִשָּׁפֵךְ כִּי בְּצֶלֶם אֱלֹהִים עָשָׂה אֶת־הָאָדָם: וְאַתֶּם פְּרוּ וּרְבוּ שִׁרְצוּ בָאָרֶץ וּרְבוּ־בָהּ: וַיֹּאמֶר אֱלֹהִים אֶל־נֹחַ וְאֶל־בָּנָיו אִתּוֹ לֵאמֹר: וַאֲנִי הִנְנִי מֵקִים אֶת־בְּרִיתִי אִתְּכֶם וְאֶת־זַרְעֲכֶם אַחֲרֵיכֶם: וְאֵת כָּל־נֶפֶשׁ הַחַיָּה אֲשֶׁר אִתְּכֶם בָּעוֹף בַּבְּהֵמָה וּבְכָל־חַיַּת הָאָרֶץ אִתְּכֶם מִכֹּל יֹצְאֵי הַתֵּבָה לְכֹל חַיַּת הָאָרֶץ:

בְּרֵאשִׁית ט: ד–י

273

is, Hebrew] and swear allegiance to the Lord of Hosts. . . . In that day there will be an altar to the Lord in the midst of the land of Egypt. . . . And the Lord will make Himself known to the Egyptians; and the Egyptians will acknowledge the Lord in that day and worship with sacrifice and burnt offerings, and they will make vows to the Lord. . . . In that day there will be a highway from Egypt to Assyria and the Assyrians will come into Egypt, and the Egyptians into Assyria. . . . In that day Israel will be the third with Egypt and Assyria, a blessing in the midst of the earth, whom the Lord of Hosts has blessed, saying, "Blessed be Egypt My people, and Assyria the work of My hands, and Israel My heritage."

When the Jewish descendants of the prophets, during the Hellenistic and especially the Roman periods, became more fully aware of living in a single great unified society that encompassed all of the known world, they drew upon and expanded the universalism of the prophets. The prophetic concept of the Covenant had aimed at making all men—of the Israelite society, to be sure—equal in their essential human dignity. This concept, in turn, led to one much broader in scope, of the universality and inevitability of individual moral responsibility toward all men, not merely neighbors and fellow Israelites. It is recorded (Babylonian Talmud, Shabbat 31a) that during the first century B.C.E. a heathen converted by Hillel, the great exponent of liberalizing Pharisaism in the days of Herod the Great, asked him for a brief exposition of Judaism. Hillel is said to have replied, "What is hateful to you, do not do to your felow man. This is the whole Law. The rest is mere commentary." Hillel recognized correctly the implication of the Biblical verse: "And you shall love your fellow as yourself: I am the Lord" (Leviticus 19:18). This precept was incorporated in Christianity and in the western tradition and transmitted from age to age with tremendous impact.

It is to the prophetic tradition more than any other source that western civilization owes its noblest concept of the legal and social obligations of the individual human being. Even if the prophets preached only to their fellow Israelites and saw justice only in the terms of their Covenant with their God, their ringing words have carried from age to age their belief that justice was for the weak as well as for the strong, that its fulfillment was as much a matter of the spirit as the letter of the law, that one could not serve God at the same time that he mistreated his fellow men, that to love God was to love justice, and that the love of justice placed within the conscience of each human being the ultimate inescapable obligation to denounce evil wherever he saw it, to defy a ruler who commanded him to break the Covenant, and to live in the law and the love of God no matter what the cost.

In that day there shall be five cities in the land of Egypt speaking the language of Canaan [that is, Hebrew] and swearing allegiance to the Lord of Hosts. . . . [19]In that day there shall be an altar to the Lord inside the land of Egypt. . . . [21]And the Lord will make Himself known to the Egyptians; and the Egyptians shall acknowledge the Lord in that day and worship with sacrifices and offerings, and they shall make vows to the Lord . . . [23]In that day there shall be a highway from Egypt to Assyria, and the Assyrians shall come into Egypt, and the Egyptians into Assyria . . . [24]In that day Israel shall be the third with Egypt and Assyria, a blessing in the midst of the earth, [25]whom the Lord of Hosts has blessed, saying, "Blessed be Egypt My people, and Assyria the work of My hands, and Israel My heritage."

*Isaiah 19.18–25*

בַּיּוֹם הַהוּא יִהְיוּ חָמֵשׁ עָרִים בְּאֶרֶץ מִצְרַיִם מְדַבְּרוֹת שְׂפַת כְּנַעַן וְנִשְׁבָּעוֹת לַיהוָה צְבָאוֹת . . . בַּיּוֹם הַהוּא יִהְיֶה מִזְבֵּחַ לַיהוָה בְּתוֹךְ אֶרֶץ מִצְרָיִם . . . וְנוֹדַע יְהוָה לְמִצְרַיִם וְיָדְעוּ מִצְרַיִם אֶת־יְהוָה בַּיּוֹם הַהוּא וְעָבְדוּ זֶבַח וּמִנְחָה וְנָדְרוּ־נֶדֶר לַיהוָה . . . בַּיּוֹם הַהוּא תִּהְיֶה מְסִלָּה מִמִּצְרַיִם אַשּׁוּרָה וּבָא אַשּׁוּר בְּמִצְרַיִם וּמִצְרַיִם בְּאַשּׁוּר וְעָבְדוּ מִצְרַיִם אֶת־אַשּׁוּר: בַּיּוֹם הַהוּא יִהְיֶה יִשְׂרָאֵל שְׁלִישִׁיָּה לְמִצְרַיִם וּלְאַשּׁוּר בְּרָכָה בְּקֶרֶב הָאָרֶץ: אֲשֶׁר בֵּרֲכוֹ יְהוָה צְבָאוֹת לֵאמֹר בָּרוּךְ עַמִּי מִצְרַיִם וּמַעֲשֵׂה יָדַי אַשּׁוּר וְנַחֲלָתִי יִשְׂרָאֵל:

יְשַׁעְיָה יט : יח–כה

"I regard this passage (Isaiah 19.18-25) . . . as evidence for the beginning of the development of internationalism as a flourishing factor in biblical Israel's outlook, and I should date this (passage) to the Seleucid-Ptolemaic period in Judean history (about 168 B.C.E.) It was then that an altar was actually erected to Israel's God on Egyptian soil, namely, the temple of Onias at Heliopolis. This historical setting is especially probable, if not indeed obligatory, if the preserved reading in verse 18, 'ir ha-héres—which is baffling as it stands . . . and is meaningless in the translations which reproduce it literally (traditional "City of Destruction." But why should a city that swears allegiance to God be designated "Destruction"?)—represents original 'ir ha-héres (with ḥeth in place of he), "City of the Sun"=Heliopolis. This reading is accepted by many scholars on independent grounds: a number of Hebrew manuscripts read 'ir ha-héres, as do the Targum (on which see, e.g., Rashi and David Qimhi) . . .

This is the period and region—the commercial routes and the Mediterranean shores of Asia and Egypt, the heart of the Jewish diaspora at the time—which marked the beginning of genuine and consistent international thinking in ancient Israel. It is not the forced Exile in Babylonia, consequent on the destruction of Judah and Zion, that brought about this outlook. Nor yet is it the antinationalistic reaction of a considerable portion of the nonpriestly segment of the Judean population, as

275

expressed by the authors of the books of Jonah and Ruth that brought about this outlook. *It was the presence of hundreds of thousands of Judeans in Egyptian and Syrian Mesopotamian territory (miṣráyim and 'ashur in the Hebrew text) earlier conquered by Alexander. In these lands, Jews lived a relatively free life, free to remain where they were and free to return to Judea whenever they wished and for as long as they desired. This would be the time and place for a new attitude—beyond the nationalistic-territorial-universalistic attitude of the prophets and of the pre-exilic period generally—according to which God could be worshiped anywhere, not just on Zion in Jerusalem in the holy land of Israel. An Egyptian (let alone a Judean) could remain in Egypt and be a full-fledged Jewish worshiper of Israel's God; and even an altar could be erected in Egypt for sacrifice to God.*

*Contrast this new, late post-exilic attitude with the late pre-exilic attitude, as exemplified by Deuteronomy 4.28 and Jeremiah 16.13. The former reads (Moses addressing his fellow Israelites):*

[25]*If . . . you act wickedly and make for yourselves a sculptured image in any likeness . . .* [27]*The Lord will scatter you among the peoples . . .*)
[28]*There you will serve man-made gods of wood and stone, that cannot see ar hear or eat or smell.*

*And Jer. 16.13 (Jeremiah addressing his fellow Judeans):*

([12]*You yourselves have acted more wickedly than your fathers . . .*)
[13]*So I will cast you out of this land to a land you have not known, you or your fathers, and there you will (have to) serve other (or: alien) gods (wa-'avadtem-sham 'eth-'elohim 'aherim) day and night, for I will show you no favor.*

*In pre-exilic times, one of the most severe punishments that God's chosen people could suffer for transgressing the covenant with God was not alone the devastation of their homeland and the destruction of the Temple but—and perhaps even more—exile from the holy land to an unclean land (cf. Amos 7.17) where they could not worship the Lord properly, that is, with sacrifice . . ."* (Quoted from pp. 223-225 of the chapter by H. M. Orlinsky on "Nationalism-Universalism and Internationalism in Ancient Israel," *in* Translating and Understanding the Old Testament: Essays in Honor of Herbert Gordon May, *ed. H. T. Frank-W. L. Reed, 1970.)*

---

The heathen then went to Hillel, who converted him and said to him, "What is hateful to you, do not do to your fellow man. This is the whole Law. The rest is mere commentary. Now go and study."

*Babylonian Talmud: Shabbat 31a (center)*

. . . And you shall love your fellow as yourself: I am the Lord.

*Leviticus 19.18*

... בָּא לִפְנֵי הִלֵּל, גַּיְּירֵיהּ. אָמַר לוֹ דַּעֲלָךְ סָנֵי לְחַבְרָךְ לָא תַּעֲבֵיד – זוֹ הִיא כָּל הַתּוֹרָה כּוּלָּהּ, וְאִידָךְ – פֵּירוּשָׁהּ הוּא, זִיל גְּמוֹר.

שַׁבָּת לא: א

... וְאָהַבְתָּ לְרֵעֲךָ כָּמוֹךָ אֲנִי יְהֹוָה:

וַיִּקְרָא יט: יח

# BIBLIOGRAPHIES

(see above "By Way of a Preface")

## Suggestions for Further Reading (from hardcover edition of *Ancient Israel*, 1960, pp. 174–184)

In understanding the development of western civilization the Bible is unquestionably the most important single text, and no heir to this tradition who has not read it can consider himself educated. Of the translations available in English the best are *The Revised Standard Version of the Old Testament* (New York, 1952), *The Old Testament—an American Translation*, rev. ed. by T.J. Meek (Chicago; several printings), and *The Holy Scriptures according to the Masoretic Text*, editor-in-chief M.L. Margolis (Jewish Publication Society, Philadelphia, 1917); a new translation of the last named (editor-in-chief H.M. Orlinsky) is now in progress. In spite of the tremendous contribution of the King James version not only to the literary style but also to the formation of character within the English-speaking tradition, this translation is unfortunately not sufficiently accurate to be useful in connection with Hebraic history. For those who would consult an introduction along critical lines there are G.B. Gray, *A Critical Introduction to the Old Testament* (London, 1919), R.H. Pfeiffer, *The Books of the Old Testament* (New york, 1957), G.W. Anderson, *A Critical Introduction to the Old Testament* (London, 1959), and N.K. Gottwald, *A Light to the Nations: Introduction to the Old Testament* (New York, 1959); a more conservative approach is followed in S.B. Freehof's *Preface to Scripture* (Cincinnati, 1950). [Several new translations are mentioned above, in "By Way of a Preface."]

Only in more recent times has the Hebrew Bible been treated as literature. Richard G. Moulton, *The Literary Study of the Bible*, rev. ed. (Boston, 1899), and the companion volume, *The Modern Reader's Bible* (New York, 1930), are worth reading. Any of J.A. Bewer, *The Literature of the Old Testament*, rev. ed. (New York, 1933), Mary E. Chase, *The Bible for the Common Reader* (New York, 1945), and A. Lods, *Histoire de la littérature hébraïque et juive*, etc. (Paris, 1950), will be rewarding to the reader—though they all leave much to be desired in their treatment of the historical background. A brief evaluation of "Hebrew Literature," including the Biblical, may be found in E. Silberschlag's chapter (pp. 175–212) in *The World through Literature* (New York, 1951). The Biblical literature is treated in broad perspective by H.M. and N.K. Chadwick, *The Growth of Literature* (2 vols., Cambridge, Eng., 1936), II, 629–777. The specifically Near Eastern background may be gauged in T.H. Gaster's retelling of some of *The Oldest Stories in the World* (New York, 1952).

The history of the Biblical period is subject to more frequent and serious change than any other, both because of the constant discovery of new texts and materials and the consequent reinterpretation of the older data. Whoever wishes to keep up with the latest discoveries and trends in the history of ancient Israel would do well to read regularly *The Biblical Archaeologist*, ed. G.E. Wright and others (American Schools of Oriental Research, New Haven, subscription $1.50 per year, for four issues). Ralph E. Turner's *The Great Cultural Traditions, the Foundations of Civilization* (2 vols., New York and London, 1941), serves as a useful introduction to the ancient world in general, though the specific sections on ancient Israel (pp. 329–359, 697–734) need drastic revision. Useful books on the beginnings of history are V. Gordon Childe's *Man Makes Himself* (Mentor Books, 1951), *New Light on the Most Ancient East*, 4th ed. (London, 1952), and *What Happened in History* (Pelican Books, 1954). A serviceable popular survey of the ancient Near East is S. Moscati, *Ancient Semitic Civilizations* (London, 1957). *Ancient Near Eastern Texts Relating to the Old Testament*, ed. J.B. Pritchard, 2d ed. (Princeton, 1955), and the companion volume, *The Ancient Near East in Pictures* (1954), constitute an excellent collection of documents which shed direct and indirect light on the Hebrew Bible; *The Ancient Near East: An Anthology of Texts and pictures* (1958) is a compendium of the two. [Add now: *The Supplementary Texts and Pictures Relating to the Old Testament*, 1969.] A useful work is *Documents from Old Testament Times*, ed. D. Winton Thomas (New York, 1958). *The Intellectual Adventure of Ancient Man*, ed. H. and H.A. Frankfort (Chicago, 1946), with chapters on Egypt (by J.A. Wilson), Mesopotamia (by T. Jacobsen), and the Hebrews (by W.A. Irwin), is an integrated attempt to explain the thinking of the ancient Near East; this volume (without the chapters on the Hebrews) appeared as *Before Philosophy* (Pelican Books, 1949).

The historical geography of Palestine has been very well treated by G.E. Wright and F.V. Filson in *The Westminster Historical Atlas to the Bible*, 2d ed. (Philadelphia, 1956); the text of this book constitutes also a fine sketch of Biblical Israel's history. Two detailed works on Israel's career are M. Noth, *The History of Israel* (New York, 1958) and J. Bright, *A History of Israel* (Philadelphia, 1959). A well-ordered and stimulating attempt to reconstruct the origin and development of Israel, her Law, her concept of God, her priesthood and prophets, may be found in T.J. Meek's *Hebrew Origins*, rev. ed. (New York, 1950). A compact sketch of "The Biblical Period," by W.F. Albright, constitutes Chap. I in *The Jews*, ed. L. Finkelstein (Philadelphia, 5710–1949); with which may be read profitably the same author's chapter on "The Old Testament World," in *The Interpreter's Bible*, Vol. I (New York and Nashville, 1952), pp. 233–271. Cyrus H. Gordon's *The World of the Old Testament* (Garden City, N.Y., 1958) and F. James's *Personalities of the Old Testament* (New York, 1958) are the best of their kind. [Add now KTAV reissue (1968) of R. Kittel, *Great Men and Movements in Israel*, with an acute Prolegomenon by T.H. Gaster.]

## Selected Bibliography for Teachers and Advanced Readers

In addition to *The Biblical Archaeologist*, the more advanced student should consult the *Bulletin of the American Schools of Oriental Research*, ed. W.F. Albright. The annual *Book List* published by the British Society for Old Testament Study (ed. H.H. Rowley, then by G.W. Anderson, and now by P.R. Ackroyd) and the virtually exhaustive bibliographic listing of books and articles in the Biblical and related fields in the journal *Biblica* are also useful tools for keeping abreast of the latest literature and developments.

When the revised *Cambridge Ancient History* appears, there will be available an up-to-date history of the entire ancient Near East; E. Meyer's *Geschichte des Altertums* likewise needs very considerable revision. A. Scharff and A. Moortgat, *Ägypten und Vorderasien im Altertum* (München, 1950), is the best available. H. Frankfort, *The Birth of Civilization in the Near East* (Anchor Books, 1950), is a penetrating study. A.J. Toynbee's *Study of History* (London, 1947) has rightly been rejected by specialists as having very little validity for the ancient Near East. J. Finegan's *Light from the Ancient Past*, 2d ed. (Princeton, 1959), is a reliable survey, archaeologically slanted, of the Fertile Crescent in antiquity; his companion volume, *The Archaeology of World Religions* (Princeton, 1952), deals with Zoroastrianism, Islam, and the Far East. O. Neugebauer, *The Exact Sciences in Antiquity*, 2d ed. (Princeton, 1957), is easily the best of its kind. So too is J.R. Forbes, *Studies in Ancient Technology*; six volumes have appeared to date (Leiden, 1956–1958). S.N. Kramer's *History Begins at Sumer* (Anchor Books, 1959), C.H. Gordon's *Ugaritic Literature* (Rome, 1949), T.H. Gaster's *Thespis: Ritual, Myth and Drama in the Ancient Near East* (New York, 1950)—all contribute useful background material for the Biblical literature. A. Heidel has written two works worth consulting, *The Babylonian Genesis, the Story of Creation*, rev. ed. (Chicago, 1951), and *The Gilgamesh Epic and Old Testament Parallels*, rev. ed. (Chicago, 1953). J.A. Wilson's *The Burden of Egypt* (Chicago, 1951; now *The Culture of Egypt* as a Phoenix Book, 1956), is a significant interpretation of ancient Egyptian culture. G. Steindorff and K.C. Seele, *When Egypt Ruled the East*, 2d ed. (Chicago, 1957); H. Frankfort, *Ancient Egyptian Religion* (New York, 1948); J. Cerný, *Ancient Egyptian Religion* (London, 1952)—all shed valuable light on the southwestern tip of the Fertile Crescent of old. O. R. Gurney's *The Hittites* (Pelican Books, 1952) is already the standard work on the subject.

The standard work on the historical geography of Palestine is F.M. Abel's *Géographie de la Palestine* (2 vols., Paris, 1933–1938). A recent useful work is Denis Baly, *The Geography of the Bible* (New York, 1957). A.J. Brawer's *Land of Israel* (in Hebrew; Tel Aviv, 5711–1951) is more broadly conceived. Two useful works are B. Maisler, *The Graphic Historical Atlas of Palestine, 2000–333* B.C. (English and Hebrew editions; Tel Aviv and Jerusalem, 1941), and H.G. May, C.C. McCown, and J.S. Kates, *The Remapping of the Bible World: Nelson's New Bible Maps* (New York, 1949). Recent works of note are L.H. Grollenberg's *Atlas of the Bible* (New York, 1956), and E.G. Kraeling's *Bible Atlas* (Chicago, 1956). M. Burrows, *What Mean These Stones?* (New Haven, 1941), C.C. McCown, *The Ladder of Progress in Palestine* (New York, 1943), W.F. Albright, *The Archaeology of Palestine* (Pelican Books, 1954), A. Parrot, *Discovering Buried Worlds* and *Studies in Biblical Archaeology*, nos. 1–8 (New York, 1955), J.B. Pritchard, *Archaeology and the Old Testament* (Princeton, 1958), and especially G.E. Wright, *Biblical Archaeology* (Philadelphia, 1957), constitute authoritative introductions to Biblical archaeology. E.L. Sukenik's chapter on the "History of Jewish Archaeology" in *The Jewish People, Past and Present*, I (New York, 1946), 48–77, is the best available. C.H. Gordon's *Adventures in the Nearest East* (Essential Books, 1957) is an interestingly written introduction to the rediscovery of the ancient Near East. E. Chiera's *They Wrote on Clay* (Chicago, 1938) is useful in this connection.

Among the older histories, T.H. Robinson and W.O.E. Oesterley, *A History of Israel* (2 vols., Oxford, 1932), has many good features, though it did not utilize adequately the archaeological materials available at the time. The same may be said of the two volumes by A. Lods, *Israel from Its Beginnings to the Middle of the Eighth Century* (New York, 1932), and *The Prophets and the Rise of Judaism* (New York, 1937). W.F. Albright's two works, *From the Stone Age to Christianity: Monotheism and the Historical Process* (Baltimore, 1940) and *Archaeology and the Religion of Israel* (Baltimore, 1942), although somewhat difficult, will prove rewarding reading to every student who wishes to probe into the character of Israel's history and religion. Albrecht Alt has added notably to our knowledge of the Biblical world; and such monographs as *Der Gott der Väter* (Stuttgart, 1929) and *Die Ursprünge des israelitischen Rechts* (Leipzig, 1934), have now been issued, together with several other studies, in three volumes as *Kleine Schriften zur Geschichte des Volkes Israel (1959).* [Five appeared in English in 1966 as *Essays on Old Testament History and Religion.*] Martin Noth's *Überlieferungsgeschichtliche Studien* (2 vols., Halle, 1943, 1948), and *Die Welt des Alten Testaments*, 2d ed. (Berlin, 1953) [now *The Old Testament World*, 1966] may be mentioned. A number of E. Dhorme's important articles have been brought together to form *Recueil Édouard Dhorme., Études bibliques et orientales* (Paris, 1951). R. de Vaux's writings are always worth reading, such as his series of articles on "Les Patriarches hébreux et les découvertes modernes" in *Revue biblique* (since 1946), and his long article on "Israel (Peuple d')" in *Supplement IV* (1947–1948), columns 729–777 of F. Vigouroux, *Dictionnaire de la Bible*; and now *Les institutions de l'Ancien Testament* (2 vols., Paris, 1958). J. Pedersen's *Israel, Its Life and Culture*, pts. I–IV (2 vols., Copenhagen, 1926 and 1940), and Max Weber's studies of *Ancient Judaism*, trans. and ed. by H.H. Gerth and D. Martindale (Glencoe, Ill., 1952), merit careful study.

The best Biblical encyclopedia is the Hebrew *Encyclopaedia Biblica* (Jerusalem, 1950); Vol. V covers the letter *samekh* of the Hebrew alphabet. The French *Dictionnaire de la Bible*, ed. F. Vigouroux (5 vols., Paris, 1895–1912), with numerous *Supplements*, ed. L. Pirot and A. Roberts, is very good. Soon to appear is the four-volume *Interpreter's Dictionary of the Bible. The Westminster Dictionary of the Bible*, 5th ed., by H.S. Gehman (Philadelphia, 1944), is the best of the one-volume reference works. A.E. Bailey's book on *Daily Life in Bible Times* (New York, 1943), M.S. and J.L. Miller's *Encyclopedia of Bible Life* (New York and London, 1944), and E. W. Heaton's *Everyday Life in Old Testament Times* (New York, 1956) are useful reference works for matters dealing with the everyday life of ancient Israel. [Add now *Everyday Life in Bible Times*, 1967; National Geographic Society.] For background, see G. Contenau, *Everyday Life in Babylon and Assyria* (London, 1954), and P. Montet, *Everyday Life in Egypt in the Days of Ramesses the Great* (about 1300–1100 B.C.; London, 1958). The Israel (formerly, Jewish Palestine) Exploration Society has issued an excellent Hebrew *Library of Palestinology*, ed. by S. Yeivin (9 vols., Jerusalem, 1937–1940).

Among the more detailed introductions to the Bible, S.R. Driver, *Introduction to the Literature of the Old Testament*, rev. ed. (New York, 1913; Meridian Books, 1956), Otto Eissfeldt, *The Old Testament: An Introduction* (New York, 1965), and R. H. Pfeiffer, *Introduction to the Old Testament* (New York and London, 1941), are outstanding. There is no single series of up-to-date adequate commentaries on the different Biblical books; the exegetical part of *The Interpreter's Bible* (12 vols., New York and Nashville, 1952–1957) will prove useful; Vols. I–VI constitute the Old Testament. *The Cambridge Bible for Schools and Colleges*, ed. A. F.

Kirkpatrick (Cambridge, Eng., 1895–1912), and *The Soncino Books of the Bible*, ed. A. Cohen (Hindhead, Eng., 1947), constitute two serviceable series of brief and popular commentaries on each book of the Old Testament. [Add now *The Century Bible: New Edition.*]

There are some excellent works on the history of the text and translations of the Hebrew Bible. The best among them are M.L. Margolis' little book on *The Story of Bible Translations* (Philadelphia, 1917), H.B. Swete's exhaustive *Introduction to the Old Testament in Greek*, rev. ed. by R.R. Ottley (Cambridge, England, 1914), and B. J. Roberts' clear and up-to-date *The Old Testament Text and Versions* (Cardiff, 1951). H.G. May has written an interesting account of *Our English Bible in the Making* (Philadelphia, 1952); two other works useful in this connection are *The Bible in Its Ancient and English Versions*, ed. H. Wheeler Robinson (Oxford, 1940), and I.M. Price, *The Ancestry of Our English Bible*, rev. by W.A. Irwin and A.P. Wikgren (New York, 1949). [Add now *Notes on The New Translation of The Torah*, ed. H.M. Orlinsky (Philadelphia, 5730-1969); F.F. Bruce, *The English Bible*, rev. ed. (New York, 1970).]

On the present state of Biblical research, the student may consult *The Study of the Bible Today and Tomorrow* (chapters by twenty-four different scholars), ed. H.R. Willoughby (Chicago, 1947), and *The Old Testament and Modern Study* (contributions by twelve scholars), ed. H.H. Rowley (Oxford, 1951). [Add now *The Bible in Modern Scholarship*, ed. J.P. Hyatt (Nashville, 1965).]

There is not yet available a standard work on the theology of the Old Testament; the most ambitious and detailed attempts at writing one are W. Eichrodt's *Theologie des Alten Testaments* (3 vols., Leipzig, 1933–1939) and Yehezkel Kaufmann's *History of the Israelite Religion*, etc. (in Hebrew; 8 vols., Tel Aviv, 1937). The various works on the subject, Christian and Jewish, tend too much to read into the text and thought of the Hebrew Bible the features of Christianity and Judaism which came into being long after the Biblical period terminated. There is likewise the methodologically and historically incorrect approach according to which the history and religion of the Israelites as expressed in the Hebrew Bible constitute but the preparation for the New Testament, Judaism being treated as but the preliminary phase of Christianity. G.E. Wright has rightfully protested against this view in his *Challenge of Israel's Faith* (Chicago, 1944); and in this connection see also J. Muilenburg, "The History of the Religion of Israel," pp. 292–348, and G.E. Wright, "The Faith of Israel," pp. 349–389, in Vol. I of *The Interpreter's Bible*, and N.H. Snaith, *The Distinctive Ideas of the Old Testament* (London, 1944). R.B.Y. Scott, *The Relevance of the Prophets* (New York, 1944), is worth reading. In the monograph series *Studies in Biblical Theology*, G.E. Wright's *The Old Testament against Its Environment* (Chicago, 1950) and *God Who Acts* (London, 1952) and W. Eichrodt's *Man in the Old Testament* (Chicago, 1951) are of especial interest. O.J. Baab, G.W. Anderson, and N.W. Porteous have contributed convenient surveys of recent studies in Biblical theology, the first mentioned in *The Study of the Bible Today and Tomorrow*, ed. H.R. Willoughby (Chicago, 1947), pp. 401–418, and the last two in the *Old Testament and Modern Study*, ed. H.H. Rowley (Oxford, 1951), pp. 283–310, 311–345. O.J. Baab also has written a sober account of *The Theology of the Old Testament* (New York, 1949), and L. Kohler's *Old Testament Theology* (Philadelphia, 1957) may be consulted. H.W. Smith's *Man and His Gods* (Boston, 1952) is worth careful reading. The post-Biblical *Legends of the Bible*, compiled by L. Ginzberg (Philadelphia, 1956), a shorter, one-volume version of *The Legends of the Jews* in 7 vols., makes for interesting and instructive reading.

The reader who wishes to pursue the history of the Jews in the period of the Second Jewish Commonwealth, and subsequently, may turn to S. Grayzel's popular *History of the Jews from the Babylonian Exile to the End of World War II* (Philadelphia, 5707–1947). M.L. Margolis and A. Marx, *A History of the Jewish People* (Philadelphia, 1927; Meridian Books, 1958), is a good reference book. A more up-to-date and detailed reference work is S.W. Baron, *A Social and Religious History of the Jews*, 2d ed., Vols. I and II, "Ancient Times" (Philadelphia, 5712–1952), covering the period from the patriarchs to the Talmud; several subsequent volumes continue the story down to our own times. *Great Ages and Ideas of the Jewish People*, ed. L.W. Schwarz (New York, 1956), covering the Biblical, Hellenistic, Talmudic, Judeo-Islamic, European, and Modern Ages, is worth careful study. *The Legacy of Israel*, ed. E.R. Bevan and C. Singer (Oxford, 1927), is easily the best of its kind. M. Lowenthal's unusually fascinating account of *The Jews of Germany, a Story of Sixteen Centuries* (Philadelphia, 1936), gives a very good idea of the career of the Jews in the Diaspora. G.F. Moore's three volumes on *Judaism in the First Centuries of the Christian Era* (Harvard, 1927–1930) and V. Tcherikover's *Hellenistic Civilization and the Jews* (Philadelphia, 1959) make thoughtful reading. An authoritative history of the Jews in the Hellenistic and Roman periods (the Second Jewish Commonwealth proper) is being prepared for publication by S. Zeitlin; see in the meantime his *Prolegomena to a History of the Second Jewish Commonwealth* (Philadelphia, 1933), *Who Crucified Jesus?* 2d ed. (New York, 1947), and numerous articles in the *Jewish Quarterly Review* (especially since 1930). [Add now S. Zeitlin, *The Rise and Fall of the Judaean State*, I (1962), II (1967), III (in preparation).] A convenient handbook for this period is R.H Pfeiffer, *History of New Testament Times, with an Introduction to the Apocrypha* (New York, 1949). The Dead Sea Scrolls, unfortunately, are post-Biblical in origin and are of negligible value in the reconstruction of Biblical Israel's career.

# BOOKS ON BIBLICAL HISTORY AND ARCHEOLOGY 1960–1966

[From *Jewish Book Annual*, 25 (5728-1967/68), 176–183.]

The past half-dozen years will hardly go down in history as memorable ones for the student of the Bible in general and of biblical history and archeology in particular. This is due only in part to the fact that little of revolutionary significance has been unearthed in and around the Holy Land in the period 1960–1966. The major reason for the continued "normalcy" is that while new data are constantly being brought to light and distributed among the conventional categories and concepts with which biblical scholars have long been wont to operate, a real breakthrough can be achieved only when all the data, both the new and the long familiar, will come under the scrutiny of trained historians and sociologists, when the *why*—not merely the *when* and *how*— of Biblical Israel's great events will be accounted for, when the significant changes in Israel's checkered and intriguing career will be explained, not merely described.

Thus in his "Foreword" to the volume on *Religion* (ed. P. Ramsey, 1965; see below, toward the end of this survey), in which I contributed the chapter on "Old Testament Studies," Prof. Richard Schlatter, general editor of the series as a whole, wrote:

> The Ford Humanities Project under the direction of the Council of the Humanities at Princeton University is looking at American humanistic scholarship of recent decades. We have commissioned about a dozen volumes by recognized scholars in each field . . . In the course of our discussions at Princeton about the volume having to do with scholarly work in the field of religion, we came upon a peculiar difficulty—peculiar that is to the field of religion scholarship. A number of American scholars maintain that religion is not a scholarly discipline like art history or musicology or classical studies because religion demands of its students creedal commitments incompatible with free scholarly inquiry . . . The present volume gets on with the task of describing and judging the work of American scholars who have studied various aspects of religion . . . the problems of definition of the field, of methodology, and of the relation of belief to scholarly objectivity are raised here again and again . . . Professor Orlinsky remarks that scholars too often "mix together scholarship and apologetics" and states that "until the student of biblical theology learns to deal with his data as critically as the student of ancient Greek, or Roman, or Assyrian, or Egyptian religion does, he can hardly expect his studies to achieve validity in scholarly circles."

What I wrote there about "biblical theology" is equally true of "biblical history and archeology." Biblical research, in spite of—in part, even because of—the volume of archeological and other extra-biblical data constantly coming to light, has in some areas already reached the point where it is transgressing the law of diminishing returns; the Hebrew-Yiddish expression for it is *ma'aleh gerah* ("brings up, or chews, the cud").

## The Field of Biblical History

In the field of biblical history, no major work has appeared since I noticed in my survey of "Recent Selected Books on Biblical History and Archeology" in volume 18 of *Jewish Book Annual* (5721–1960/61, pp. 38–43) John Bright's *A History of Israel* (1959) and Moshe Greenberg's abridgment in English (*Religion of Israel*, 1960) of Yehezkel Kaufmann's Hebrew work (*Toledot ha-Emunah ha-Yisraelit*, 8 vols., 1937–1965). [Add now C.W. Efroymson's English version of Kaufmann's chapters on *The Babylonian Captivity and Deutero-Isaiah*, New York, 1970.] Harry M. Orlinsky's *Ancient Israel* (2nd ed., 1960; reprinted 1965) has remained unopposed in the shorter, more popular form, though mention should be made of several very concise works covering an even longer period: M.A. Beek, *A Short History of Israel, from Abraham to Bar Cochba* (translated from Dutch by A.J. Pomerans; London, Hodder and Stoughton, 1963); F.F. Bruce, *Israel and the Nations: From the Exodus to the Fall of the Second Temple* (London, Paternoster Press, 1963); and E.L. Ehrlich's *A Concise History of Israel from the Earliest Times to the Destruction of the Temple in* A.D. *70* (translated from German by J. Barr; Harper Torchbook 128, 1965).

A number of rather bulky books have appeared in recent years that deal with our subject, and they generally contain enough archeological and other material to give them the appearance of being quite up to date. I have in mind such books as A. Biram, *The History of Israel in Biblical Times in the Framework of the History of the Ancient Near East*, 2 vols. (in Hebrew; Haifa, Reali School, 1964), Elmer W.K. Mould's *Essentials of Bible History*, 3rd ed., rev. by H. Neil Richardson and Robert F. Berkey (New York, Ronald Press, 1966), and Harry M. Buck's *People of the Lord: The History, Scriptures, and Faith of Ancient Israel* (New York, Macmillan, 1966). Unfortunately, as stated in the introductory statement above, they are not really aware of the significance and role of social forces in the fortunes of mankind. In this respect, none of the current works in the field approaches either A.T. Olmstead's *History of Palestine and Syria to the Macedonian Conquest* (1931; recently reprinted—unfortunately without any attempt at updating—by Baker Book House, Grand Rapids, 1965) or Robinson's vol. I in W.O.E. Oesterly-T.H. Robinson's two volumed *History of Israel* (Oxford, Clarendon Press, 1932), let alone Julius Wellhausen's brilliant work in his *Prolegomena zur Geschichte Israels* (6th ed., 1905) and *Israelitische und jüdische Geschichte* (4th ed., 1901)—with all the shortcomings brought on by the revolutionary discoveries of the past six decades. The methodology employed by Martin A. Cohen in his analysis of "The Role of the Shilonite Priesthood in the United Monarchy of Ancient Israel" (*Hebrew Union College Annual*, 36 [1965], 59–98) is well worth careful study and emulation.

On a happier note, the great *Cambridge Ancient History* of essentially pre-archeological days is being republished in completely revised form. Thus well over fifty fascicles have appeared to date, among them "The Cities of Babylonia," "Babylonia (*c.* 2120–1800 B.C.)," and "Hammurabi and the end of his Dynasty," all by C.J. Gadd; "Anatolia in the Old Assyrian Period" by Hildegard Lewy and "Anatolia *c.* 1600–1380 B.C." by O.R. Gurney; "The Struggle for the Domination of Syria (1400–1300 B.C.)," "Anatolia," and "The Hittites and Syria (1300–1200 B.C.)," all by A. Goetze; "Assyria and Babylonia": 1370–1300 B.C. by C.J. Gadd, and 1200–1000 B.C. by D.J. Wiseman; "The Armana Letters from Palestine" and "Syria, the Philistines, and Phoenicia" by W.F. Albright; several fascicles on "Egypt" in different periods, by W.C. Hayes; and "The Exodus and Wanderings" and "The Hebrew Kingdom" by O. Eissfeldt (1965).

In this connection may be mentioned *At the Dawn of Civilization: A Background of Biblical History*, ed. E.A. Speiser (Tel Aviv, Massadah, 1964; constituting vol. I of a projected multivolumed *World History of the Jewish People*); this fine study of Mesopotamia and Egypt before Israel became a sovereign people, consists of chapters by W.F. Albright, D. Ashbel, M. Avnimelech, F.S. Bodenheimer, S.N. Kramer, H. Polotsky, E.A. Speiser, J.A. Wilson, and M. Zohary.

## Books in Biblical Archeology

There has been no letup in the production of books in biblical archeology. Miss Kathleen M. Kenyon published a useful work on *Archaeology in the Holy Land* (London, E. Benn, 1960), and H.J. Franken and C.A. Franken-Battershill produced *A Primer of Old Testament Archaeology* (Leiden, Brill, 1963). G.E. Wright's fine *Biblical Archaeology* (1957) went into a revised edition (1962), after the first edition had appeared in drastically abridged form (and without the illustrations and figures) as (*An Introduction to*) Biblical Archaeology (London, Duckworth; Philadelphia, Westminster, 1960). J.B. Pritchard published a fascinating biography of *Gibeon—Where the Sun Stood Still* (Princeton University Press, 1962) and G.E. Wright did likewise for *Schechem: The Biography of a Biblical City* (New York, McGraw-Hill, 1965). The great dig at Hazor has been written up for the serious student by Y. Yadin, with the assistance chiefly of Y. Aharoni, R. Amiran, I. Dunayevsky, M. and T. Dothan, and J. Perrot: *Hazor*, vols. I, II, III–IV (Jerusalem, Hebrew University Magnes Press, 1958–1961).

The Seventeenth Archaeological Convention of the Israel Exploration Society has appeared as *The Beth Shean Valley* (in Hebrew; 5722–1962), the Eighteenth as *Elath* (in Hebrew; 5723–1963), and the Nineteenth as *Western Galilee and the Coast of Galilee* (5725–1965)—all on the high level of scholarship that characterizes the work of the Society. This level is maintained in *The Kingdoms of Israel and Judah* (in Hebrew; Jerusalem, 5722–1961; chapters by Y. Aharoni, H. Tadmor, B. Mazar, Y. Yadin, S. Yeivin, and A. Malamat, editor). Together with Mosad Bialik, the Society published what is now the standard work on *The Ancient Pottery of Eretz Yisrael from its Beginnings in the Neolit[h]ic Period to the End of the First Temple* (in Hebrew; Jerusalem, 5723–1963; the 358 photos and 101 plates were very effectively distributed by S.Y. Shweig), by Ruth Amiran, assisted by Pirhiya Beck and Uzza Zevulun. A very big boon for scholarship is on its way in the form of an Archaeological Dictionary that the Israel Exploration Society will publish in 1967. [Appeared in 1970.]

In my 1960 survey, I could mention only vol. I, *The Law* (Torah) of *Views of the Biblical World*, ed. M. Avi-Yonah and A. Malamat. Since then the remaining four volumes have appeared (with vol. V devoted to the New Testament), now under the title *The (Illustrated) World of the Bible* (New York, KTAV Publishing House); this set should be in every library and home. In 1962 M. Avi-Yonah and E.G. Kraeling put out a reduced, one-volume version titled *Our Living Bible* (New York, David McKay). In the same year there appeared two handsome volumes by G. Cornfeld: *Adam to Daniel* and *Daniel to Paul* (New York, Macmillan); and in 1964 the same editor's *Pictorial Biblical Encyclopaedia: A Visual Guide to the Old and New Testaments* (Macmillan). W. Keller's *The Bible as History* (1962; the title of the German was *Und die Bibel hat doch Recht*—whatever that can mean to a competent historian!) was too "journalistic" and gaudy for my taste. The companion volume, however, *The Bible as History in Pictures* (New York, Wm. Morrow & Co., 1964), is something else again; the three hundred or so pictures distributed among the first nine chapters (chapter ten, dealing with the period of Jesus and the Apostles—following a gap of about three centuries—is tasteless, probably commercially motivated) are interesting, clear, and informative. In this connection I might cite S. Yeivin's article "On the Use and Misuse of Archaeology in Interpreting the Bible," in *Proceedings of the American Academy for Jewish Research*, 34 (1966), 141–154.

E.F. Campbell, Jr. and D.N. Freedman have edited a very serviceable *Biblical Archaeologist Reader*, 2 vols. to date (Garden City, Doubleday Anchor, vol. I, 1961; vol. II, 1964), bringing together articles that had appeared previously in the *Biblical Archaeologist*. J.A. Thompson had published a nice introduction to *The Bible and Archaeology* (Exeter, Paternoster Press, 1962). A book that is more useful than its size (91 pp.) would indicate is R.D. Barnett's *Illustrations of Old Testament History* (London, British Museum, 1966). And this is as good a place as any to mention an important volume that I overlooked in my earlier survey, Beno Rothenberg's handsome and informative *Discoveries in Sinai* (in Hebrew; Tel-Aviv, Masada, 5718–1958; with chapters by Y. Aharoni, A. Hashimshoni, and B. Sapir).

Several of the important civilizations in antiquity that left their mark on Biblical Israel have received fine treatment in recent years. There is, e.g., S.N. Kramer's book on *The Sumerians; Their History, Culture, and Character* (University of Chicago Press, 1963); A. Leo Oppenheim's penetrating study of *Ancient Mesopotamia: Portrait of a Dead Civilization* (University of Chicago Press, 1964); H.W.F. Saggs, *The Greatness that was Babylon* (London, Sidgwick & Jackson, 1962) and *Everyday Life in Babylonia and Assyria* (New York, Putnams, 1965); K.M. Kenyon's *Amorites and Canaanites* (London, Oxford University Press, 1966; the Schweich Lectures of 1963); C.H. Gordon, *Before the Bible: The Common Background of Greek and Hebrew Civilizations* (New York, Harper & Row, 1962); E. Anati, *Palestine before the Hebrews* (London, Jonathan Cape, 1963); and N. Glueck's *Deities and Dolphins: The Story of the Nabataeans* (New York, Farrar, Straus, and Giroux, 1965). Two fascinating books on aspects of the modern rediscovery of the ancient Near East are Nora M. Kubie's *Road to Nineveh: The Adventures and Excavations of Sir A.H. Layard* (Garden City, Doubleday, 1964) and John A. Wilson's *Signs and Wonders upon Pharaoh* (University of Chicago Press, 1964). And there is now readily accessible, in Penguin Classics (L 100, 1960), *The Epic of Gilgamesh: An English Version with an Introduction*, by N.K. Sandars.

Among the books that deal with the geography of the Holy Land may be singled out Y. Aharoni, *The Land of Israel in Biblical Times: A Geographical History* (in Hebrew; Jerusalem, Mosad Bialik, 5723–1962), and the same author's *Carta's Atlas of the Bible* (in Hebrew; Jerusalem, Carta, 1964); there has just come to hand, in the same series, M. Avi-Yonah's *Carta's Atlas of the Period of the Second Temple, the Mishnah, and the Talmud* (assisted by S. Safrai; 1966). H.G. May (assisted by R.W. Hamilton and G.N.S. Hunt) edited the *Oxford Bible Atlas* (Oxford University Press, 1962); eight wall maps were reproduced from these to form *Abingdon Maps of Bible Lands* (1966). To his *Geography of the Bible* (1957), D. Baly has published a useful *Geographical Companion to the Bible* (New York, McGraw-Hill, 1963). Of direct interest, too, is M.A. Beek, *Atlas of Mesopotamia: A Survey of the History and Civilization of Mesopotamia from the Stone Age to the Fall of Babylon* (Edinburgh, Nelson & Sons, 1962).

The extremely sensitive use of archeological and literary materials has made possible the appearance of two standard works in a field not previously comprehended adequately; they are Y. Yadin's superb study of *The Art of Warfare in Biblical Lands*, 2 vols. (New York, McGraw-Hill, 1963) and the volume edited by J. Liver for Maarakhot (Israel Defence Forces Publishing House), *The Military History of the Land of Israel in Biblical Times* (in Hebrew; 1965; 32 studies by such scholars of quality as Y. Aharoni, A. Malamat, B. Mazar, Y. Yadin, and S. Yeivin, as well as the editor himself).

It is good to report that R.J. Forbes is proceeding apace with the publication of his standard *Studies in Ancient Technology*, including revision of some of the earlier volumes. In nine volumes (Leiden, Brill, 1957 ff.) he has dealt with such items as Bitumen and Petroleum; Irrigation and Drainage; Land Transport and Roadbuilding; Cosmetics and Perfumes; Food, Alcoholic Beverages; Paints; Fibres and Fabrics; Dyeing, Spinning, Sewing, Weaving; Leather; Sugar; Glass; Heating, Refrigeration; Geology; Mining and Quarrying; Metallurgy.

# Bible Reference Books

An excellent aid to the understanding of the Bible in matters archeological-historical is *The Interpreter's Dictionary of the Bible*, 4 vols. (New York-Nashville, Abingdon Press, 1962), an area that was under the charge of H.G. May. (In the area of theology-exposition, the *Dictionary* is far less successful; in many cases, it was specialists in the New Testament who wrote also on the Old Testament part of their subject, with most unfortunate results.) Mosad Bialik published in 1962 vol. IV of its famed *Encyclopedia Miqra'it* (covering the letter *kaf* in *kabed* through the letter *mem* in *meltaha*); incidentally, someone will be performing a very great service by making this biblical encyclopedia available in English, after the articles are updated and their theological aspects treated more fully and competently than they have been. [Vol. V, 1968, covers the letter *sámekh*]

G.E. Wright has edited a fine survey of *The Bible and the Ancient Near East: Essays in Honor of W.F. Albright* (Garden City, Doubleday, 1961; now an Anchor paperback, 1965), with chapters by J. Bright, G.E. Mendenhall, W.J. Moran, G.E. Wright, H.M. Orlinsky, F.M. Cross, Jr., D.N. Freedman, E.F. Campbell, Jr., Gus W. Van Beek, S.N. Kramer, T. Jacobsen, T.O. Lambdin, J.A. Wilson, and A. Goetze.

Several serious books deal with Israel's experiences in the light of the world about them; among those that deserve mention are S. Yeivin's *Studies in the History of Israel and its Land* (in Hebrew: Tel-Aviv-Jerusalem, Newman, 1960); J. Gray, *Archaeology and the Old Testament World* (Edinburgh, Nelson & Sons, 1962); the same author's *The Canaanites* (London, Thames & Hudson, 1964) and *The Legacy of Canaan: The Ras Shamra Texts and their Relevance to the Old Testament* (Leiden, Brill, 2nd rev. ed., 1965); and N.K. Gottwald, *All the Kingdoms of the Earth: Israelite Prophecy and International Relations in the Ancient Near East* (New York, Harper & Row, 1964). R. de Vaux's *Ancient Israel: Its Life and Institutions* (New York, McGraw-Hill, 1961; translated from the two-volume French work, *Les Institutions de l'Ancien Testament*, 1958–60) is an essentially descriptive treatment of aspects of the sociology of biblical Israel; an historical-analytical study, in the manner that specialists in sociology now employ, is an urgent desideratum.

In 1960 the American Council of Learned Societies published *Five Essays on the Bible* (originally read at the Council's 1960 Annual Meeting); of especial interest are "The Bible as Product of the Ancient World" by E.R. Goodenough, "Biblical Criticism and Its Effect on Modern Civilization" by M.S. Enslin, and "The Bible and Archaeology" by N. Glueck. In my essay "On Toynbee's Use of the Term *Syriac* for One of His Societies" (pp. 255–269 in the Abba Hillel Silver Jubilee volume, *In the Time of Harvest* [New York, Macmillan, 1963]), I have dealt *inter alia* with the self-confessed (as well as self-evident) ignorance and irrationality of A.J. Toynbee in matters biblical and Jewish.

At the invitation of Princeton University's Council of the Humanities (see introductory statement above), I contributed the chapter on "Old Testament Studies" to the volume *Religion*, ed. P. Ramsey (1965), pp. 51–109; in the series *Humanistic Scholarship in America: The Princeton Studies* (Englewood Cliffs, Prentice-Hall). A considerable body of data, covering approximately the middle third of our century (*cir.* 1930–1962), was there presented under the following fifteen headings: (1) Old Testament Studies Prior to about 1930 (pp. 53–54); (2) The Age of Archaeology (55–61); (3) Extrabiblical Research (62–65); (4) Negative Aspects of Archaeology (66–68); (5) The Decline of Biblical Philology; The Dead Sea Scrolls (68–73); (6) Bible Translations (73–76); (7) Biblical Theology (76–80); (8) Biblical History (80–86); (9) Social, Economic, and Legal Institutions (86–93); (10) Psychology–Psychoanalysis 93–95); (11) Chronology (95–97); (12) Commentaries, Introductions, and Textual Studies (97–103); (13) Paleography and Alphabet (103); (14) Septuagint Studies (104–106); and (15) Grammars, Lexicons, and Dictionaries (106–109).

As everyone knows, important analyses and advances in our knowledge of ancient Israel and the Near East may be found in scholarly journals no less than in books. That is why the interested student will always find worth consulting regularly such periodicals as *The Biblical Archaeologist, Bulletin of the American Schools of Oriental Research, Israel Exploration Journal, Yedi'ot* [now *Qadmoniyot*] of the Israel Exploration Society, the annual *Book List* of The (British) Society for Old Testament Study, the annual *Eretz-Israel* (now in its eighth year) of the Israel Exploration Society, *Hebrew Union College Annual*, the *Internationale Zeitschriftenschau für Bibelwissenschaft und Grenzgebiete* (*International Review of Biblical Studies*; vol. 12, 1965/66, has appeared), and the bibliographical sections of *Biblica* and *Zeitschrift für die alttestamentliche Wissenschaft*.

# ACKNOWLEDGMENTS

The numbers in bold type refer to the pertinent page in this book. The letters **a**, **b**, and **c** in bold type, indicate the relative position of the illustrative material from the top down.

## Photographs, charts, etc.

Aleppo Museum–**46**

American Schools of Oriental Research–**182b**

Archives Photographiques (Paris)–**100b**

Arthaud Mikaël Audrain–**196b**

Ashmolean Museum, Department of Antiquities–**36**

G. Bertin–**230**

British Museum–**14b**; **16a**; **38**; **40**; **108**; **124b**; **126**; **146b**; **154**; **158a**; **160**; **168c**; **172a**; **188**; **200a**; **214**; **222b**; **224**; **236b**

British School of Archaeology (Iraq)–**192**

Brooklyn Museum–**240**; **244**

Cairo Museum–**18a**; **32a**; **52b**; **64a**; **82a**

G. G. Cameron–**226b**

Cliché des Musées Nationaux (chiefly Louvre)–**14a**; **20**; **24**; **42**; **44**; **88a**; **100a**; **134**; **164**; **166**; **218b**; **234a**

*after* N. de G. Davies, *The Rock Tombs of el-Amarna*–**66**

Ewing Galloway–**90a**

E. Grant–G. E. Wright, *Ain Shems Excavations*–**98**

Harvard Semitic Museum–**22a**

Hittite Museum, Ankara–**120**

Israel Department of Antiquities and Museums–**10**; **12**; **88b**; **94**; **162c**; **168a, b**; **178**; **180a**; **190a**; **194a**; **200b**; **206b**

*Israel Exploration Journal*–**194a**

Israel Office of Information (New York, N.Y.)–**72b**; **76b, c**; **136b**

Istanbul, Museum of the Ancient Orient–**170** (original object now lost)

*after Jewish Encyclopedia,* vol. XI, p. 654–**60**

Kathleen M. Kenyon–**118**; **236a**

Z. Kluger–**26**

V. E. Krantz–**138**

A. H. Layard, *The Monuments of Nineveh* (London, 1849)–**172b**

*after* K. R. Lepsius, *Denkmäler aus Ägypten,* etc., vols. III and IV–**34**; **148**

Metropolitan Museum of Art–**22b**; **50**; **52a**; **54**; **238b**

Museo Civico, Torino–**174a**

National Aeronautics and Space Administration–**58**

National Museum, Amman–**242**

National Museum, Athens–**104c**

National Museum, Teheran–**228a**; **238a**

Edward T. Newell Collection–**184b**

Oriental Institute, University of Chicago–**78**; **92b**; **96b, c**; **104a**; **124a**; **140b**; **144a, b**; **150b**; **162a, b**; **208a**; **220**; **226a**; **234b**

Pacific School of Religion, Palestine Institute–**202**

Palestine Archaeological Museum–**158c**

Palestine Exploration Fund–**84**

James B. Pritchard–**86a, b**; **116a**; **144c**; **158b**

F. Thureau–Dangin, *Revue d'Assyriologie,* XXI (1924), 187–**146a**

Beno Rothenberg, *Tagliot Sinai* (Hebrew, 5718/1958), p. 64–**62**

Royal Air Force–American Schools of Oriental Research–**136a**

Smithsonian Institution, Museum of Natural History–**184a**

*after* E. Sollberger, *The Babylonian Legend of the Flood* (London, 1966), p. 36–**38**

Staatliche Museen zu Berlin–**32a**; **64b**; **114**; **150a**; **204**; **208b**; **210**; **212**

Tell Qasile Expedition (B. Mazar)–**106a**

E. Sellin, Tell Ta'annek (Wien, 1904)–**92**

University of London, Institute of Archaeology–**206a**

University of Tel-Aviv, Department of Archaeology–**132**; **194b**

University of Chicago Press—*When Egypt Ruled the East* by G. Steindorff and K. Seele (Copyright © 1957), p. 133, fig. 31–**48**; *idem,* p. 209, figs. 76a and 76b–**66**; *after* J. A. Brinkman, in A. Leo Oppenheim, *Ancient Mesopotamia* (Copyright © 1964), pp. 341, 347–**216**: quotation from *The Burden of Egypt,* by John A. Wilson, (Copyright © 1951), p. 292–**121**. Reprinted with permission.

University Museum, University of Pennsylvania–**104b**

*after* C. Watzinger, *Denkmäler Palästinas* (Leipzig, 1935), vol. II–**140a**

Trustees of the late Sir Henry S. Wellcome (Lachish Expedition)–**202b**

Westminster Press–from *The New Westminster Dictionary of the Bible,* © MCMLXX, The Westminster Press. Used by permission.–**60**; **218a**

*after* G. E. Wright–*Biblical Archaeology,* 2nd ed., fig. 145 (p. 202)–**240b**

*after* W. Wrezeszinski, *Atlas zur Altägyptischen Kulturgeschichte,* II–**56**

Yigael Yadin, Hazor Expedition (Hebrew University)–**88c**; **96a**; **142**

Yale University, Babylonian Collection–**16b**

Eva Avi-Yonah–**116b**

Zionist Archives and Library (New York, N.Y.)–**63a**; **72a**; **72c**

## Translations

*Ancient Near Eastern Texts Relating to the Old Testament,* ed., James B. Pritchard, *3rd edn.* with Supplement (copyright © *1969* by Princeton University Press): "Code of Hammurabi" (trans. T. J. Meek), 164a—**24**; "Babylonian and Assyrian Historical Texts" (trans. A. Leo Oppenheim), 265b—**36**; 564a—**200**; "Ugaritic Myths, Epics and Legends" (trans. H. L. Ginsberg), 133b-134a—**128**; 130b-131a—**130**; "Aramaic Letters" (trans. H. L. Ginsberg), 492a,b—**232**; "Palestinian Inscriptions" (trans. W. F. Albright), 320b—**164**; 321b—**190**. *after* J. A. Wilson, *Burden of Egypt* (Copyright © 1951 by University of Chicago Press), p. 227—**130**. *after* J. Mauchline, *Documents from Old Testament Times* (London, 1958), 201—**84**. *after* D. J. Wiseman, *Chronicles of the Chaldean Kings* (London, 1961), 59—**196**; 67f.—**198**.

*Every effort has been made to identify and credit the source of each photograph, illustration, map, chart, translation, quotation, etc., in this book. All corrections or supplementary data in the identification will be appreciated and acknowledged in subsequent editions. Acknowledgment credits by Sol Scharfstein.*

# INDEX OF BIBLICAL PASSAGES

The odd page numbers indicate both the Hebrew passages and their English translation. The even page numbers indicate, as a rule, a reference in the caption to illustrative material in the narrative text.

# GENERAL INDEX

**Authors; Biblical and Extra-Biblical Persons and Places; Subjects; and the like.**

Italicized numbers indicate a reference in a caption to an illustration or in a chart.

289